Medical Office Coding

Peg Austin
RHIA, CCS-P, CPC

Anne Mettler
MT(ASCP), CCS-P, CPC

PEARSON
Prentice Hall

Upper Saddle River, New Jersey 07458

Library of Congress Cataloging-in-Publication Data

Austin, Peg.
    Medical office coding / Peg Austin, Anne Mettler.
        p. ; cm.
    Includes index.
    ISBN 0-13-142532-3
1. Nosology—Code numbers.   2. Medicine—Code numbers.
    [DNLM: 1. Disease—classification—Problems and Exercises.   2. Forms and Records
Control—Problems and Exercises.   3. Medical Records—classification—Problems and Exercises.
4. Reimbursement Mechanisms—Problems and Exercises.]   I. Mettler, Anne.   II. Title.
    RB115.A94 2006
    616'.001'2—dc22

                                                                                        2004028222

Publisher: Julie Levin Alexander
Publisher's Assistant: Regina Bruno
Executive Editor: Joan Gill
Editorial Assistant: Bronwen Glowacki
Director of Manufacturing and Production: Bruce
    Johnson
Managing Editor for Production: Patrick Walsh
Production Editor: Karen Berry/Pine Tree
    Composition, Inc.
Manufacturing Manager: Ilene Sanford
Manufacturing Buyer: Pat Brown
Creative Director: Cheryl Asherman

Senior Design Coordinator: Christopher Weigand
Cover Designer: Amy Rosen
Director of Marketing/Marketing Manager: Karen
    Allman
Channel Marketing Manager: Rachele Strober
Marketing Coordinator: Michael Sirinides
Media Editor: John Jordon
Media Production Manager: Amy Peltier
Media Production Manager: Stephen Hartner
Composition: Pine Tree Composition, Inc.
Printer/Binder: Edwards Brothers, Inc.
Cover Printer: Phoenix Color Corporation

CPT five-digit codes, nomenclature, and other data are copyright 2005, American Medical Association. All Rights Reserved. No fee schedules, basic unit, relative values or related listings are included in CPT. *The AMA assumes no liability for the data contained herein.*

Credits and acknowledgments borrowed from other sources and reproduced, with permission, in this textbook appear on the appropriate page within text.

Pearson Education LTD.
Pearson Education Singapore, Pte. Ltd
Pearson Education, Canada, Ltd
Pearson Education–Japan
Pearson Education Australia PTY, Limited
Pearson Education North Asia Ltd
Pearson Educación de Mexico, S.A. de C.V.
Pearson Education Malaysia, Pte. Ltd
Pearson Education, Upper Saddle River, New Jersey

ISBN 0-13-142532-3

Contents

Preface

Welcome to the first edition of *Medical Office Coding.* This book was written to offer students a comprehensive textbook/workbook format that encompasses basic anatomy, terminology, ICD-9 coding, CPT coding, HCPCS coding, and real-life coding scenarios with operative reports. We have found, after years of teaching coding classes, medical terminology, and physician reimbursement, that students are eager to know not just "how to code," but why we code and what the diagnoses and procedures mean. Many times students will grasp one system easier than another—oftentimes it is the coding system that is presented first. By integrating the two coding systems, the student has a better grasp of how they work together. An introductory chapter to ICD-9 is presented, and this material is continued throughout each chapter of the book as it pertains to each body system. We have also found that in coding for physicians, the diagnosis codes are frequently given lower priority because reimbursement is driven by the procedural codes. This text is our answer to the multiple questions we have had over the years for more diagnosis coding, ICD-9 to CPT code linkage, and hands-on practice coding real operative reports.

This text can be concentrated into a single semester or used as a single textbook for a two-semester course if ICD-9 and CPT are required in separate semesters. A CD-ROM is available to supplement coding scenarios and case studies for ICD-9, and CPT will be available for advanced work in a two-semester program.

Highlights of *Medical Office Coding* include:

- Anatomy plates in Appendix A.
- Medical terminology and abbreviations specific to each organ system.
- Explanation of common disease processes for each chapter, followed by ICD-9 coding instructions and practice.
- Easy-to-understand table format of diagnoses and procedures.
- Linking exercises to demonstrate the importance of medical necessity for each procedure.
- Formula for Success—coding tips within each chapter to help with code assignment, interpretation, or reimbursement.
- Comprehensive exercises.
- Real-life case studies utilizing actual operative reports for each chapter.
- Photographs and illustrations of medical procedures and disease processes.

Since students learn by different degrees of seeing, hearing, and doing, we hope this format, along with your instructor's lectures, is a valuable tool in helping you learn medical office coding.

References:

AHA Coding Clinic Archives

AHIMA, 2003. *ICD-10-CM Preview.* Hazelwood and Venable: AHIMA

American Diabetes Association

American Cancer Society

American College of Obstetrics and Gynecology

American College of Orthopaedic Surgeons

American College of Rheumatology

American Lung Association

Brown, Faye, American Hospital Association, 2003

Coding and Principles of CPT® Coding, Second Edition

American Medical Association Reimbursement for Physician Services, 2002 Edition

CPT® Assistant Archives, American Medical Association

CPT® Changes, an Insider's View, American Medical Association 2003

CPT® Changes, an Insider's View, American Medical Association 2004

Coder's Desk Reference, St. Anthony/Medicode 2003

Diagnostic Coding Essentials, Ingenix, 2003

Hazelwood, Anita, MLS, RHIA, and Venable, Carol, MPH, RHIA. *ICD-9-CM Diagnostic Coding and Reimbursement for Physician Services,* 2002 and 2004

Lupus Foundation of America

Kuehn, Lynn, RHIA, CCS-P, FAHIMA, and LaVonne Wieland, RHIT. *2004 CPT/HCPCS Coding and Reimbursement for Physician Services*

Schraffenberger, Lou Ann, *Basic ICD-9-CM Coding*

CMS website, *www.cms.gov* and *www.cms.hhs.gov/medlearn*

Medline online medical encyclopedia: *www.nlm.nih.gov/medline plus encyclopedia.html.*

National Center for Health Statistics. Official coding guidelines for ICD-10 found at *www.cdc.gov/nchs/about/otheract/icd9/abticd10.htm.*

www.urologychannel.com

www.kidneyatlas.org   ISN Informatics Commission and NKF cyberNephrology

Acknowledgments

Special thanks to the following people and organizations who contributed to the book:

Deb Alickson
Jeffrey L. Bendt, MD
Black Hills Neurology and Sally Walter
Robert Burgess, MD
Amy Einspahr
Robert Ferrell, MD
Justin Green, PhD, MD
The Heart Doctors and Jim Gangelhoff
John Herlihy, MD
Lookout Memorial Hospital, Spearfish, SD
Barb Moen, CPC
Christal Pummel, RHIT
Radiology Associates LLC and Lori Nelson, CPC
Julie Raymond, MD
Daniel Rawson, MD
Michael Statz, MD
Harry C. Stearns III, MD
Lee Trotter, MD
Kenneth A. Vogele, MD
Greg Wittenberg, MD

An excerpt from 2003 ASA Crosswalk and Manual for Anesthesia Department Organization and Management, 2003–2004, from the American Society of Anesthesiologists. A copy of the full text can be obtained from the American Society of Anesthesiologists, 520 No. Northwest Highway, Park Ridge, IL 60068-2573.

Reviewers

Linda Arvigo, RHIA, CCS
Manager, Administrative Services
Meridian Resource Company
Naperville, Illinois

Jannie R. Billue-Adams, PhD, RN, MS-HSA, BSN
Assistant Professor
Clayton College & State University
Morrow, Georgia

Carolyn A. Edmonds, BA, LPN, CMA
Assistant Professor
Ivy Tech State College
Lafayette, Indiana

Cheri Goretti, MA, MT (ASCP), CMA
Associate Professor & Program Coordinator, Medical Assisting
Quinebaug Valley Community College
Danielson, Connecticut

Geri Kale-Smith, MS, CMA
Coordinator, Medical Office Administration Programs
William Rainey Harper College
Palatine, Illinois

Janette R. Kelly, MBA, RHIA, CCS
Chariperson, Health Information Management
Sinclair Community College
Dayton, Ohio

Jennifer Lame, MPH, BS, RHIT
Health Information Instructor
Idaho State University
Pocatello, Idaho

Valeria Truitt, MAEd
Program Co-ordinator, Medical Office Administration
Craven Community College
New Bern, North Carolina

Fred Valdes, MD
Medical Dept. Chairman
City College
Ft. Lauderdale, Florida

Walkthrough

■■■■ *OBJECTIVES*

1. Identify the basic anatomy of the respiratory system.
2. Recognize the link between the ICD-9-CM codes and the CPT® codes used in the Respiratory section.
3. Correctly apply ICD-9-CM codes to respiratory diagnoses.
4. Correctly apply CPT® codes to respiratory surgical procedures.

Each chapter opens with learning objectives to set the stage and provide students with a Learning Road map.

■■■■ *TERMINOLOGY AND ACRONYMS*

ARDS   Adult respiratory distress syndrome.

CTA   Clear to auscultation.

ET tube   Endotracheal tube.

LLL   Left lower lobe.

LUL   Left upper lobe.

Neb/Nebulizer   Medication administered by aerosol mist through a special machine.

PPD   Purified protein derivative, used for tuberculosis testing.

RAD   Reactive airway disease.

RDS   Respiratory distress syndrome.

RLL   Right lower lobe.

RUL   Right upper lobe.

SOB   Shortness of breath.

TB   Tuberculosis.

URI   Upper respiratory infection.

Terminology and acronyms are ideal prep tools, giving students the opportunity to review prior to the chapter.

ILLUSTRATIONS

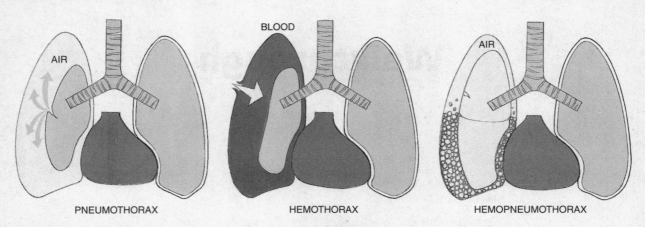

Figure 9–4 Examples of traumatic pneumothorax.

Illustrations bring the subject ALIVE with more illustrations and photos than most other books.

FORMULA FOR SUCCESS BOXES

Formula for Success

Remember to assign the fourth digit "8" for contiguous, or overlapping, sites of a primary neoplasm.

Formula for Success boxes provide useful tips and reminders from experienced coders. They help students avoid common mishaps.

EXAMPLES AND RATIONALE

Example A   A patient is unhappy with the appearance of her nose. Reshaping entails minor repairs, mostly involving the cartilage and nasal tip.

ICD-9-CM: V50.1
CPT®: 30400

Rationale:

When a procedure such as this is performed, it is important to represent the procedure and diagnosis accurately. Because it is the choice of the patient to improve her appearance, this is considered cosmetic. If the patient presented with an actual abnormality of the nose, the diagnosis should reflect an acquired deformity, ICD-9-CM code 738.0, or a congenital abnormality, code 748.1. In Example A, diagnosis code V50.1 would likely trigger a denial in payment since it is a cosmetic procedure. Manipulation or misrepresentation of diagnosis codes to obtain reimbursement from an insurer would result in a fraudulent claim.

Embedded examples are followed by rationales which provide students with insights and alert them to discussion points.

▰▰▰ EXERCISES

EXERCISE 9.6

Instructions: Give the correct CPT® codes for the following scenarios.

1. A patient is treated for chronic osteomyelitis of the ethmoid sinuses. The physician excises diseased tissue from the ethmoid sinuses through an incision between the nasal dorsum and the medial canthus. Dissection is continued and exposes the lateral ethmoid sinus. All diseased material is removed. _____

2. A patient has a history of headaches and acute sinusitis. He is treated with an endoscopic partial ethmoidectomy. _____

3. A patient with the complaint of excessive tearing is found to have an obstruction of the lacrimal duct. An endoscopic dacryocystorhinostomy was performed. Postoperative diagnosis is granuloma of the lacrimal passage. _____

Embedded Exercises increase retention by having students apply knowledge immediately.

Introduction to Coding

OBJECTIVES

1. Identify three primary coding systems used for physician reimbursement.
2. Define what is meant by "medical necessity."
3. Differentiate between fraud and abuse.
4. State the intent of a compliance plan.

TERMINOLOGY AND ACRONYMS

Abuse   Incidents that are inconsistent with good business practices and result in improper reimbursement.

Bundling   Individual procedures that are considered part of a larger operation and are grouped together, or "bundled." A cystoscopy is bundled into a transurethral resection of the prostate.

Capitation   A predetermined amount of reimbursement based "per capita" or per person. Commonly used by HMOs and certain federal programs.

CCI edits   Also known as NCCI, or National Correct Coding Initiative. Series of CPT® code sets in which one code is excluded from use because of its direct correlation to the other.

Clean claim   A complete, correct health insurance claim that passes through age, sex, diagnosis to procedure and other edits set up by third-party payers, Medicare and Medicaid.

CMS   A federal agency, the Center for Medicare and Medicaid Services, formerly HCFA (Health Care Financing Administration).

Clustering   Assigning codes to one or two middle levels of service codes exclusively, under the philosophy that some will be higher, some lower, and they will average out over an extended period. In reality, this overcharges some patients while undercharging others.

Compliance plan   A written statement by a healthcare entity, describing the ethical actions of that business. It must contain all of the steps required by the federal government.

Denial   Claim that is rejected by insurance companies, Medicare, or Medicaid after failing the edit system.

False Claims Act   Prohibits knowingly presenting a false or fraudulent claim to the federal government for payment or presenting false records or statements in order to get a claim paid.

Fraud   To purposely bill for services that were never given or to bill for a service that has a higher reimbursement than the service provided.

Fee for service   Basic reimbursement method based on individual physician charges.

HIPAA   Health Insurance Portability and Accountability Act.

LCD   (Local Coverage Determination) Determines Medicare coverage for individual Medicare carriers in the absence of a national policy.

Medical necessity   The reason why a service was provided, translated into an ICD-9 diagnosis code.

OIG   Office of Inspector General.

PPS   (Prospective Payment System) A reimbursement method designed to pay a fixed amount per hospitalization. It is based on the diagnosis, historical case-mix information, and geographic location.

Primary diagnosis   The principal diagnosis, or reason why a person seeks healthcare.

Qui Tam   A "whistleblower," or "relator," in reference to Qui Tam lawsuits.

Third-party payer   A nongovernmental insurance company. Also known as "private payer" or commercial insurance.

Unbundling   The practice of billing for multiple components of a service that must be included in a single fee. Example: Coding separately for a bowel resection and exploratory laparotomy, when both services are included as part of the code for bowel resection.

Upcoding   Billing for a more expensive service than the one that was actually performed.

INTRODUCTION

The art of medical coding is similar to the art of storytelling. Attention to detail and familiarity with anatomy, terminology, and disease processes enhance the coder's ability to retell in a numerical framework what happened during a patient encounter. This coded snapshot, or series of snapshots, provides information to insurance companies, healthcare providers, researchers, government agencies, and others who use the coded medical data. In the United States, our reimbursement systems are driven by coded data. In addition, private companies and state and federal agencies rely on coded data to help appropriate funding, determine trends in healthcare, and evaluate the quality of medical care.

HISTORY OF CODING

The need for standardized, statistical information has soared since the beginning of the Medicare program in 1965. As new systems for reimbursement were developed, a need for specialized information grew. Several types of coding methods evolved, in addition to one that was already in existence. The International Classification of Disease was developed and published by the World Health Organization approximately seventy-five years ago to classify diseases or diagnoses. This system is currently used throughout the world and has been through ten different modifications. The United States is now using the ICD-9-CM, or Ninth Clinical Modification of ICD, while many other countries have switched to ICD-10. Other coding systems used in conjunction with ICD-9-CM include CPT®-4 (Current Procedural Terminology, 4th Revision), which is a nomenclature for operations and diagnostic procedures, and HCPCS (Healthcare Common Procedural Coding System), used for the coding of medication, supplies, and other services not covered by CPT®. Additional medical coding systems exist in the United States and are used primarily in research, mental health, and pathology areas.

ICD-9-CM

Four organizations are currently responsible for the ongoing revision and updates to ICD-9-CM. Known as the Cooperating Parties, these organizations are The American Health Information Management Association, the National Center for Health Statistics, the

American Hospital Association, and the Center for Medicare and Medicaid Services. The basic ICD-9 system was adapted for use by hospitals, physicians, and insurance companies in the United States with the Clinical Modification in the late 1980s. The ICD-9 system was overhauled in 1993 to allow for better reporting and classifying of diseases. Implementation of ICD-10 in the United States is projected for 2006. Additional information on ICD-10 is provided at the end of this chapter. ICD-9 is revised annually, effective October 1 of each year.

Currently, the ICD-9-CM coding system drives the reimbursement process for acute care hospitals, nursing facilities, and rehabilitation hospitals. A prospective payment system (PPS) reimburses facilities based on the diagnosis of the patient, including any associated complications or co-morbid conditions.

CPT®-IV

CPT® (Current Procedural Terminology) was developed by the American Medical Association in 1966. This system is a nomenclature, or a "calling of names." All surgical operations and diagnostic procedures that can be performed by healthcare providers are given a standard "name," description, and corresponding code number. The CPT® coding system drives the reimbursement process for physician billing and outpatient hospital/ambulatory surgical billing. Diagnosis codes are equally important and must not be forgotten, however. All procedural codes must be submitted with one or more corresponding diagnosis codes to indicate medical necessity. Claims missing either the diagnosis code or the procedural code are denied by the payer. CPT® is revised annually, effective January 1 of each year.

HCPCS

Supplies, injections, and other services provided by individuals and hospitals are coded using a system known as HCPCS (Health Care Procedure Coding System), also known as Level II codes. The Health Care Financing Administration developed this system in 1983 for use on Medicare claims. In recent years, more third-party payers have increasingly accepted this system, and its use is not restricted to Medicare or Medicaid claims. Like the other coding systems, HCPCS is also revised on an annual basis, with changes effective January 1.

DOCUMENTATION AND MEDICAL NECESSITY

A patient's record is a medicolegal document, and information contained within it is expected to be timely and accurate. In addition, the medical record verifies that the claim submitted for reimbursement is indeed accurate. Services provided must be supported by documentation in the record, which is the responsibility of each caregiver. CMS states, "medical record documentation serves to facilitate high quality patient care . . . verifies and documents precisely what services were actually provided. The medical record may be used to validate: (a) The site of the service; (b) the appropriateness of the services provided; (c) the accuracy of the billing; and (d) the identity of the care giver (service provider)" (Centers for Medicare and Medicaid Services, *1997 Documentation Guidelines*, p. 1).

The diagnosis (ICD-9 code) must justify any diagnostic or therapeutic procedures (CPT® code) as well as any supplies or injectable medications (HCPCS code). When a medical encounter is coded correctly, there is a smooth transfer of coded data in exchange for reimbursement. This is called a **clean claim.** If there is insufficient documentation or an error in coding, the claim can be denied for lack of **medical necessity.** If documentation is not found within the record, then it is impossible to substantiate services or procedures that are done. "Not documented—not done" is a standard cliché within the healthcare industry.

Beginning in 1989, HCFA (Health Care Financing Administration) required physicians to use an ICD-9-CM diagnosis code on their claim forms for reimbursement purposes. Prior to this, only hospitals were required to report a diagnosis code, and physicians could be reimbursed for their services by submitting only a procedure code.

EXERCISE 1.1

Instructions: Define each reimbursement term:

1. Bundling _____

_____

_____

2. False claim _____

_____

_____

3. CCI edits _____

_____

_____

4. Medical necessity _____

_____

_____

5. Clean claim _____

_____

_____

FEDERAL REGULATIONS AND COMPLIANCE

Fraud and Abuse

Inappropriate reimbursement has soared over the past twenty-five years and has been partly responsible for the increased costs of healthcare. In an attempt to control fraud and abuse within the Medicare system, the Health Care Financing Administration developed numerous pieces of legislation in that time period that have been enacted into law. A distinction must be made here between fraud and abuse.

Abuse is defined as "Incidents or practices of providers, physicians, or suppliers which are inconsistent with accepted Medicare, business or financial practices, and which result in unnecessary cost to the program, improper reimbursement or reimbursement for services that fail to meet professionally recognized standards of care or are medically unnecessary" (Centers for Medicare and Medicaid Services, www.cms.gov/glossary). Examples of abuse include:

■ A lack of medical necessity documented in the patient's record.

■ Improper billing practices.

■ Excessive charges for supplies and/or services.

Fraud is defined as "Intentional deception or misrepresentations that the provider knows to be false, or does not believe to be true, and knows that the deception could result in some unauthorized benefit to himself/herself or to some other person" (Centers for Medicare and Medicaid Services, www.cms.gov/glossary). Examples of fraudulent claims include:

■ A claim for a service or supply that was never provided.

■ A claim indicating that the service was provided for some diagnosis code other than the true diagnosis code in order to obtain reimbursement for the service (which would not be covered if the true diagnosis code were submitted).

■ A claim indicating a higher level of service than was actually provided.

■ A claim for a service that the provider knows is not reasonable and necessary.

■ A claim for services provided by an unlicensed individual.

The National Correct Coding Initiative, or "**CCI edits**" as they are called, are a series of procedures (CPT® codes) that are **bundled** together. This prevents overpayment of surgical and diagnostic procedures. The edits are updated on a quarterly basis by **CMS.** Coders must stay vigilant to observe the CCI edits in their daily work. Ignoring these edits will at a minimum result in claim **denials** and possible penalties.

In addition to the National Correct Coding Initiative, the **False Claims Act** and Civil Monetary Penalties Law were brought to the forefront to help the Medicare and Medicaid programs recoup money lost due to inappropriate reimbursement, whether intentional or accidental. These laws, enforced by the **Office of Inspector General (OIG),** impose both criminal and civil penalties for submitting a false or fraudulent healthcare claim. The penalties include fines, imprisonment, and sanctions from the Medicare/Medicaid programs. Fines are assessed per line on a claim, up to $10,000 per line item. These commonly range from hundreds of thousands of dollars up into the millions.

Interestingly, the criminal statutes covering healthcare fraud extend beyond the obvious submission of fraudulent claims and include theft or embezzlement of federal funds, concealing facts, and obstruction of a criminal investigation.

Compliance Plans

Because of the growing awareness of problems within the healthcare industry, the Office of Inspector General began a campaign against healthcare fraud and abuse. In 1997, the Clinton administration launched "Operation Restore Trust" (ORT). Under this legislation, healthcare entities could self-report patterns of inappropriate overpayments and receive a reduced fine or penalty. Audits were also performed based on complaints by whistleblowers within the industry. The resultant "**Qui Tam,**" or whistleblower, lawsuits brought multimillion-dollar judgments against healthcare facilities.

Beginning in 1998, the OIG mandated that laboratories have a working **compliance plan** in place. Since that time, model compliance plans have emerged for hospitals, home health agencies, physician offices, and third-party billing entities, pharmacies, and rehab hospitals. Compliance plans are mandatory in all settings except physician offices. Although not required, a compliance plan is helpful for the physician office because it declares the intent to engage in ethical business practices and encourages open communication and education of employees, as well as an outline of disciplinary action when necessary. Practices that have a working compliance plan in place are less likely to engage in unlawful business practices. The purpose of a compliance plan is to ensure that the facility follows ethical business standards for reimbursement and that the business entity does what its plan outlines. All compliance plans must contain the same basic elements, although must be individually tailored to meet the specific requirements of each distinct healthcare entity. These are the elements that should be included:

- Establishing effective standards.
- Ensuring executive oversight.
- Delegating authority appropriately.
- Communicating and training staff effectively.
- Monitoring and reporting potential problems.
- Enforcing and disciplining appropriately.
- Responding with appropriate corrective action.

Facilities that are audited and found not to be in compliance with federal regulations are placed under a federally administered compliance plan, known as a Corporate Integrity Agreement, or CIA.

The area of coding and billing is a major part of a compliance plan for a physician practice. The OIG has spotlighted several areas of risk that are frequently targeted in audits and investigations. These areas include:

- Billing for items or services not rendered or not provided as claimed.
- Submitting claims for equipment, medical supplies, and services that are not reasonable and necessary.
- Double billing, resulting in duplicate payment.
- Billing for noncovered services as if covered.
- Knowing misuse of provider identification numbers, which results in improper billing.
- **Unbundling.**
- Failure to properly use coding modifiers.
- **Clustering.**
- **Upcoding.**

What Coders Can Do

Coders have become an invaluable asset to any medical practice. Although the ultimate responsibility for correct coding and claim submission lies with the provider, a well-rounded coder can relieve some of the frustrations for the physician by making sure that federal regulations are met, updates are disseminated, and the compliance plan is being followed as outlined. It is up to the coder to stay on top of the current coding changes and educate him- or herself.

The coder should also be very familiar with Medicare and Medicaid regulations. The CMS website should be visited frequently to check for transmittals, memos and **Local Coverage Determinations (LCDs)** for new information. Medicare bulletins should be read by the coding/billing staff and passed on to the physicians. Coders should print copies of the OIG work plan for the current and upcoming year, which informs providers far in advance where auditing funds will be directed. The federal government has made it very clear that medical providers cannot plead ignorance when it comes to federal healthcare regulations.

EXERCISE 1.2

Instructions: Mark each statement below in either the "Fraud" or "Abuse" category.

_____ 1. Billing excessive charges for supplies or services.

_____ 2. Misrepresentation of details on claims.

_____ 3. Knowingly submitting a claim that is false.

_____ 4. Submitting claims to Medicare instead of primary insurers.

_____ 5. Filing claims for services that are not medically necessary.

Look up the following websites and bookmark these for future reference:

CMS website: www.cms.gov

OIG website: www.oig.hhs.gov

Find the OIG Final Rule-Compliance Plan for Physician Practices (Federal Register/Vol. 65, No. 194/October 5, 2000) under Fraud Prevention and Detection, Compliance Guidance, 2000.

ICD-10

The current diagnosis coding system, ICD-9, is over twenty years old. Advances in medicine over the same time period have proven that ICD-9 is obsolete and cannot meet the present or future requirements of all the entities that use coded healthcare data in the United States. The World Health Organization adopted ICD-9 codes in 1979 as a worldwide system for collecting statistics on disease and injury. The classification continues to be revised on a yearly basis by the Cooperating Parties, an association of four health-related organizations. The Cooperating Parties is made up of the American Hospital Association (AHA), American Health Information Management Association (AHIMA), the Centers for Medicare and Medicaid Services (CMS), and the National Center for Health Statistics (NCHS). This group reviews the updates and develops official coding guidelines for the proper interpretation and application of the ICD-9 codes.

WHO published ICD-10 in 1992, but implementation has been delayed in the United States for a few more years. Currently, most of Europe, Australia, Canada, and South Africa are using ICD-10, or a modification of it. The fact that other countries are using a system different than the United States has led to frustrations in comparing statistics on an international level; however, it has allowed nosologists to examine different methods of implementation. Software vendors and the entire healthcare industry must make major changes in their systems, including training support staff and physicians before implementing ICD-10. The changes would be similar to those experienced with **HIPAA** and Y2K preparations.

Two ICD-10 systems are currently being developed in the United States. ICD-10-CM will replace Volumes 1 and 2 of ICD-9-CM, and ICD-10-PCS is being studied as a procedural coding system to replace Volume 3 of ICD-9-CM.

ICD-10-CM

The main advantages of ICD-10 include the capability of expanding to nearly twice as many codes as ICD-9 and increased specificity. This will result in precise information being produced and reported to those entities that rely on health statistics and clinical information. Other unique features of ICD-10 include:

- All codes are alphanumeric.
- Codes expand up to seven digits.
- Unique conditions are identified more precisely.
- Combination codes are available to reduce the number of codes needed to fully identify a condition.
- Laterality (right or left) is identified.
- V and E codes are integrated into the main text, unlike ICD-9.
- Intraoperative and postoperative complications are identified.
- Patient's trimester can be indicated.
- New codes are provided for alcohol level and blood type.
- Injuries are grouped by site, not type of injury.

One problem that is anticipated with ICD-10 five-digit codes is the possible confusion with HCPCS codes if computer software does not use or recognize the ICD-10 decimal point.

ICD-10 has twenty-one chapters. Coders may see some similarities to ICD-9 in the placement of the chapters as listed below:

1. Certain infectious and parasitic diseases (A00-B99)
2. Neoplasms (C00-D48)
3. Diseases of the blood and blood-forming organs and certain disorders involving the immune mechanism (D50-D89)
4. Endocrine, nutritional, and metabolic diseases (E00-E90)
5. Mental and behavioral disorders (F01-F99)
6. Diseases of the nervous system (G00-G99)
7. Diseases of the eye and adnexa (H00-H59)
8. Diseases of the ear and mastoid process (H60-H95)
9. Diseases of the circulatory system (I00-I99)
10. Diseases of the respiratory system (J00-J99)
11. Diseases of the digestive system (K00-K93)
12. Diseases of the skin and subcutaneous tissue (L00-L99)
13. Diseases of the musculoskeletal system and connective tissue (M00-M99)
14. Disease of the genitourinary system (N00-N99)
15. Pregnancy, childbirth, and the puerperium (O00-O99)
16. Certain conditions originating in the perinatal period (P00-P96)
17. Congenital malformations, deformations, and chromosomal abnormalities (Q00-Q99)
18. Symptoms, signs, and abnormal clinical and laboratory findings, not elsewhere classified (R00-R99)
19. Injury, poisoning, and certain other consequences of external causes (S00-T98)
20. External causes of morbidity (V01-Y98)
21. Factors influencing health status and contact with health services (Z00-Z99)

Once the final decision to implement ICD-10-CM has been made and published in the *Federal Register,* there will be a two-year implementation phase.

ICD-10-PCS

CMS has proposed the replacement of Volume 3 of ICD-9-CM with ICD-10-PCS (Procedural Coding System). ICD-10-PCS has seven-character alphanumeric codes. The first character identifies the "section," or the type of procedure. Characters 2 through 7 have standardized meanings within each section as described below:

Character 1—Section
Character 2—Body system
Character 3—Root operation
Character 4—Body part
Character 5—Approach
Character 6—Device
Character 7—Qualifier

What ICD-10 Means for Coders

The United States is already experiencing a shortage of qualified, credentialed coding personnel. In the next few years, coders will be in even greater demand due to the retirement of older coding professionals and the increased opportunities afforded by implementation of ICD-10. Coders will undoubtedly need to be very well versed in medical terminology, anatomy, and disease processes in order to be successful in ICD-10 coding. Coders with good communication skills can assist in training efforts for ICD-10, especially in helping physicians understand the need for greater specificity in documentation.

Coders who already have some experience with ICD-9 may find the transition to ICD-10 much easier than anticipated. A study of implementation in other countries has demonstrated a learning curve of approximately six months.

CHAPTER REVIEW

1. A Qui Tam lawsuit involves
   a. The False Claims Act
   b. Civil monetary penalties
   c. Relator action
   d. Operation Restore Trust

2. Compliance plans are mandatory for:
   a. Physician offices
   b. Rehabilitation hospitals
   c. Laboratories
   d. Acute care hospitals
   e. b, c, and d

3. Dr. A has not yet received his Medicare number, so he bills for his services under Dr. B's number, rather than slow down his accounts receivable. This is an example of:
   a. Abuse
   b. Fraudulent billing
   c. Negligence
   d. Double billing

4. Dr. Jones bumps up the level of service on his Medicare patients because he feels the fee schedule is too low for what his services are worth. This is an example of:
   a. Abuse
   b. Fraudulent billing
   c. Upcoding
   d. b and c

5. Dr. Smith's clinic discovers that all of the claims for a new satellite clinic have been billed with the wrong place of service. This has garnered them additional

reimbursement. The office staff first refunds the money, then refiles corrected claims with Medicare and Medicare secondaries. This is an example of:

   a. Abuse
   b. Erroneous billing
   c. Fraudulent billing
   d. Unlawful conduct

6. Medical record documentation must:
   a. Be timely and accurate
   b. Serve to substantiate services
   c. Identify the provider
   d. All of the above

7. Medical necessity is:
   a. Justification for what was done
   b. Analogous with CPT®
   c. A "clean claim"
   d. a and b

8. Coding for ICD-10 requires
   a. Previous ICD-9 experience
   b. Solid understanding of terminology
   c. Knowledge of anatomy and disease processes
   d. b and c

Introduction to ICD-9-CM Coding

■■ OBJECTIVES

1. Identify diagnostic codes as three-, four-, or five-digit codes.
2. Recognize supplementary classifications with V and E codes.
3. Interpret coding conventions.
4. Apply coding guidelines for correct code assignment.

■■ INTRODUCTION

The physician office typically uses three different coding systems to describe diagnoses, procedures/services, and supplies/injections. In this chapter, the student will be introduced to the basics of all three: ICD-9-CM diagnostic coding, CPT® procedural coding, and HCPCS supply coding. Students may wish to label the cover of their codebooks until they become familiar with the purpose of each book. ICD-9-CM is used for the diagnosis— why the patient came in. CPT® is for procedures—what was done for the patient. HCPCS is for supplies—what supplies were used or given to the patient. Details about specific diagnostic coding conventions will be presented in conjunction with the corresponding CPT® chapter in this text (i.e., ICD-9-CM Complications of Pregnancy, Childbirth, and Puerperium will be presented with CPT® Maternity Care and Delivery, and so on).

Coding of diagnoses, procedures, and other services must adhere to specific coding rules and regulations. The goal of coding is to be correct and consistent in code assignment. Such rules prevent individual interpretation and possible erroneous assignment. The student should also be aware that new codebooks should be purchased each year, in order to stay current with the most recent code updates.

■■ ICD-9-CM OVERVIEW

ICD-9-CM codes are used for the coding of diagnoses. Diagnosis coding is imperative to establish medical necessity, or the reason why a service was provided. Updates on ICD-9-CM become effective on October 1 of each year. The ICD-9-CM codebook is divided into three indices, or volumes that are published in one book. Volume I is the tabular index, containing a narrative description of each code. Volume II is the alphabetic index, in which each disease, condition, or circumstance is listed and/or cross-referenced in alphabetic fashion. The alphabetic index is usually placed at the front of the codebook, allowing for a practical method of code assignment. Volume III is the operative index, or index to procedures. Physicians use only Volumes I and II. Volume III is used exclusively by hospitals. Coding conventions (rules) and guidelines are located at the front of each codebook, regardless of publisher. Students should become familiar with these guidelines and refer to them often.

NAVIGATING ICD-9-CM

Coding Conventions

In the front of each ICD-9-CM codebook are explanations and instructions for all of the symbols, abbreviations, and rules that must be applied for accurate coding. ICD-9-CM conventions are listed below.

Abbreviations

- NEC—Not Elsewhere Classifiable. This abbreviation is commonly denoted by a fourth digit of "8." It means that a specific code for a particular diagnosis has not yet been created.

  Example: 011.8x Other specified pulmonary tuberculosis

- NOS—Not Otherwise Specified. This abbreviation is commonly denoted by a fourth digit of "9." It means that not enough information has been given to the coder to assign a more specific code.

  Example: 401 Essential hypertension. . . .
  401.9 Unspecified

Formula for Success

Do not assign NEC or NOS codes if information leading to a higher degree of specificity is documented in the medical record.

Symbols

}   Braces: Each brace encloses several terms found in the tabular index, which are modified by the statement to the right of the brace.

[ ]   Brackets: Contain explanatory phrases or terms. OR, they may enclose specific fifth digits that are valid only with the code above it. This symbol is also found in the tabular index.

( )   Parentheses: Enclose "nonessential modifiers," or descriptive words that do not affect code assignment. Parentheses are found in both the alphabetic and tabular indices.

:   Colons: Incomplete terms in the tabular index are followed by a colon and additional modifiers.

Italics   Italics identify codes that may not be used as primary diagnoses. It is also found on all exclusion notes.

The following instructional notes appear only in the tabular index:

Includes Found in a small white box appearing at the beginning of a chapter, sub-chapter category, subcategory, or subclassification. It further defines what conditions are included in that section.

Excludes Found in a small black box with italicized print. This instructs the coder that the condition being excluded is located elsewhere in ICD-9-CM. Specific cross-references may be given.

Formula for Success

Before assigning a code, any includes and excludes notes must be taken into consideration to determine the most appropriate and specific code.

Other Instructions

- Use Additional Code—This is a mandatory instruction to use a supplemental code if the information is available.
- Code First Underlying Disease—Codes that have this instruction appended may never be used as a primary diagnosis or alone.
- Code, if applicable, any causal condition first—If no causal condition is known, a code with this instruction may be sequenced as a primary diagnosis.
- Omit Code—No code should be assigned when this instruction is given.
- See also—Found in the alphabetic index; this is a mandatory instruction to cross reference another main term.

CODING GUIDELINES

Official Coding Guidelines for Coding and Reporting are also found in the introductory section of most codebooks. The Guidelines were developed by the Cooperating Parties to assist the coder in situations where there are no directions provided by the ICD-9-CM manual. Guidelines are divided into outpatient services, inpatient services, and long-term care. While the focus of this text is on physician professional service coding, the student should become familiar with other sets of coding guidelines. Some disease- or condition-specific instructions apply to both outpatients and inpatients and are found only in the inpatient guidelines.

Two main concepts distinguish outpatient guidelines from inpatient guidelines:

- The diagnosis may not be determined in a single outpatient visit and may require two or more encounters before a diagnosis can be confirmed.
- Diagnostic statements that include the words "rule out," "questionable," "suspected," "probable," and so on, are not coded in the outpatient setting. The coder is directed by the Outpatient Guidelines to assign codes for signs, symptoms, or abnormal test results when the physician has not established the diagnosis. The inpatient setting currently does allow these conditions to be coded as if they exist.

The following is a brief summary of the *Outpatient Coding Guidelines,* found in the front of the codebook.

Circumstances Other Than Disease or Injury

Patients may present for a medical encounter for other reasons besides illness or injury or for continuing care of a nonacute condition. A supplemental classification (V codes) contains codes that describe these different types of healthcare encounters, including vaccinations, screening tests, counseling and social circumstances, and other situations.

Sequencing/Code Specificity

The diagnosis or reason why a patient presents for healthcare should be reported as the primary diagnosis. Any other conditions that are addressed are coded as secondary diagnoses. ICD-9-CM codes contain between three and five digits. A few codes contain only three digits (called the "rubric") while most others subdivide to four and five digits, becoming increasingly more specific. Each diagnosis must be coded to the highest degree of specificity. Codes that are not expanded to the highest possible number of digits are not valid.

Formula for Success

The coder should remain cognizant of the fact that the provider may not sequence the diagnoses that he or she dictates the same as they are sequenced on a charge ticket for billing purposes. Provider education is extremely important to ensure that dictation and charge tickets match.

Chronic Disease

Chronic problems may be treated on an ongoing basis. These should be coded and reported as long as the patient continues to receive treatment for the condition.

> **Example:** A patient with diabetes mellitus, out of control, who presents for weekly visits for a period of time is coded as 250.02 at each visit.

Co-existing Conditions

All conditions that concurrently exist with the primary diagnosis should be coded if they are documented as being treated or if they are affecting the management of the patient. Conditions that no longer exist should not be coded.

> **Example:** Asthma, treated with nebulizer; 493.90
> Otitis media six weeks ago, resolved; not coded
> Acute tonsillitis, treated with antibiotics; 463

Ancillary Diagnostic and Therapeutic Services

When a patient presents for diagnostic or therapeutic services only, the primary diagnosis should be the reason responsible for the encounter. When a patient presents for therapeutic services only, the primary diagnosis should be the reason responsible for the encounter. An exception is made for chemotherapy, radiation therapy, or rehabilitation. In these cases, the V code for the visit should be listed first, and the disease or condition second.

> **Example:** Chemotherapy for adenocarcinoma of the prostate; V58.1, 185

Preoperative Evaluations

When a patient has a preoperative evaluation only, use a code from the V72.8 category as primary, with the reason for surgery as secondary.

Ambulatory Surgery

Code the reason why the surgery was performed. If the preoperative and postoperative diagnoses differ, the postoperative diagnosis is more definitive and should be used.

SEARCHING VOLUME II, THE ALPHABETIC INDEX

In order to use the ICD-9-CM codebook correctly, codes should be searched first in the alphabetic index and then cross referenced in the tabular listing. The coder should never code directly from the alphabetic listing alone, nor should the tabular index be referenced without checking the alphabetic listing first.

Formula for Success:

Beginning coders should search each word in a diagnostic statement until they are familiar with locating specific main terms.

Diagnoses should be broken down into main terms and searched in the alphabetic index. Laymen's terms are not commonly used, so the coder should be familiar with medical terminology. Choose the most obvious term in the diagnostic statement to search, such as signs, symptoms, or condition. Main terms can be broad, such as "disease" or "syndrome," or specific, as in "appendicitis." Main terms can be listed as nouns, adjectives, or eponyms (a person's name). Occasionally, conditions may be referenced under more than one main term.

EXERCISE 2.1

Instructions: Circle the correct answer for each statement.

1. Diagnostic statements that include the words "questionable," "rule out," or "suspected" should be coded on an outpatient record.   **True/False**

2. Chronic diseases should be coded only the first time the patient presents for treatment. **True/False**

3. Conditions that no longer exist should not be coded.   **True/False**

4. The primary diagnosis should always be the one that the physician sequences first without question.   **True/False**

5. If five digits are available to fully describe a condition, then submitting only four digits would create an invalid code.   **True/False**

6. Codes found in italics may not be used as primary diagnoses.   **True/False**

7. A preoperative diagnosis is preferable over a postoperative diagnosis when coding for ambulatory surgery.   **True/False**

8. Includes and Excludes notes should always be referenced in the tabular index before assigning a code.   **True/False**

9. Nonessential modifiers found in parentheses do not affect code assignment.   **True/False**

10. The term "Code first underlying disease" indicates the code may not be used as a primary diagnosis.   **True/False**

Volume II contains several tables: the Hypertension Table and Neoplasm Table are found in alphabetic order. The hypertension table consists of three columns that categorize types of hypertension by the severity of the disease; malignant, benign, and unspecified. The Neoplasm table is arranged alphabetically by anatomical site, with six columns describing the behavior of the neoplasm; primary, secondary, carcinoma *in situ*, benign, uncertain behavior, or unspecified. Neoplastic conditions such as leukemias and lymphomas are not found with the solid tumors in the neoplasm table. They are located in the alphabetic listing with other diseases and conditions.

Section II of Volume II contains the Table of Drugs and Chemicals. Each substance or chemical listed is assigned a code for poisoning. Five additional columns in table format identify corresponding E codes categorized by intent, such as accident, therapeutic use, suicide attempt, and assault or undetermined.

Section III of Volume II contains a separate alphabetic index to the External Cause of Injury (E code) section.

EXERCISE 2.2

Instructions: List the correct column heading for each of the following diagnosis codes using the Hypertension Table, Neoplasm Table, or Table of Drugs and Chemicals. Do not use the tabular index. The first answer is given as an example.

1.	Neoplasm, intestine, appendix.	211.3	Column Heading:	<u>Benign</u>
2.	Hypertension, postoperative.	997.91		_____
3.	Neoplasm, skin, ear.	173.2		_____
4.	Child ingestion of aspirin.	965.1		_____
5.	Pesticide dust inhalation.	E863.4		_____
6.	Hypertension due to ureteral calculus.	405.19		_____
7.	Attempted homicide with strychnine.	E962.1		_____

CROSS-REFERENCING VOLUME I, THE TABULAR INDEX

After selecting a code from the alphabetic index, the coder must cross-reference the tabular index, which is a full text description of the conditions, diseases, and circumstances listed in the alphabetic index. This index should *always* be cross-referenced for specific instructions or additional digits. The tabular index is broken down into three main sections: the tabular listing of disease and injury and two supplemental classifications.

Example from the Tabular Index:

*412 Old myocardial infarction

Healed myocardial infarction

Past myocardial infarction diagnosed on ECG (EKG) or other special investigation, but currently presenting no symptoms.

ICD-9-CM Appendices

Five appendices are listed at the end of Volume I:

- ■ Appendix A lists the morphology (behavior) of neoplasms. While primarily oncologists, pathologists, and tumor registries use the "M" codes listed here, they are helpful to coders in determining the behavior of a specific neoplasm.
- ■ Appendix B was deleted in 2005.
- ■ Appendix C is the Classification of Drugs by their American Hospital Formulary (AHFS) listing with a crosswalk to their corresponding ICD-9-CM diagnosis code.
- ■ Appendix D is a classification of industrial accidents according to Agency Type.
- ■ Appendix E is a listing of each three-digit category within ICD-9-CM.

EXERCISE 2.3

Instructions: Underline the main term for each diagnostic statement. Some may have more than one main term.

1. Granular pericarditis	8. Low back pain
2. Ankle sprain	9. Acute cholecystitis
3. Mental disorder	10. Migraine headache
4. Varicose vein	11. Paget's disease
5. Gastric ulcer	12. Klebsiella meningitis infection
6. Cellulitis, leg	13. Hodgkin's lymphosarcoma
7. Pelvic inflammatory disease	14. Incarcerated inguinal hernia

Some ICD-9-CM codes require the application of inpatient coding guidelines, even if they are assigned to outpatient or clinic records. Areas such as hypertension, neoplasms, obstetrics, poisoning, late effects, adverse effects, V codes, and E codes follow the same guidelines, regardless of outpatient/inpatient status. In this section, the student will build upon diagnostic coding concepts, from the simple to complex, regardless of the placement of that chapter in ICD-9-CM. Certain chapters of ICD-9 not covered here have been placed with their corresponding CPT® chapter elsewhere in this text for easier assimilation.

V and E Codes

The two supplemental classifications of ICD-9-CM consist of V codes (Factors Influencing Health Status and Contact with Health Services) and E codes (External Causes of Injury and Poisoning). These codes are alphanumeric in nature.

V codes are circumstances that fall into one of the following categories:

a. When a person encounters healthcare services for a specific purpose other than injury or disease; for example, wellness visits or immunizations.
b. When a patient with known health problems requires special treatment of that health problem, such as fracture care follow-up, chemotherapy, or radiation.
c. When a condition directs a patient's health status, yet is not a current illness or injury, such as a high risk pregnancy, postoperative status, or screening for neoplasms.

Examples of V codes:

1. A patient on Coumadin therapy who comes in monthly for lab work would be coded using V58.61 (long-term use of anticoagulant) in addition to the reason for anticoagulation.
2. A patient having a liposuction performed for cosmetic reasons is coded as V50.1.
3. Marriage counseling is coded as V61.10.

V codes may be searched in the alphabetic index under the following main terms:

Administration prophylactic
Admission for
Aftercare
Contraception, contraceptive
Fitting
Follow-up
Health
Healthy
Observation
Outcome
Problem
Procedure not carried out
Screening
Status
Supervision of

V codes are also used to describe the outcome of delivery on the mother's chart, as well as to classify the types of live-born infants. Coders may wish to highlight in their codebooks the notations under category V27 and V30–V39 to distinguish maternal codes from newborn codes.

Maternal code category V27 is broken down into subclassifications depending on the number of infants born and how many are live born. Categories V30–V39 intended for the newborn's chart are broken down by single, twin, and multiple births and how many of the mates are live or stillborn. A fourth-digit subclassification indicates the following:

■ 0—Born in hospital
■ 1—Born before admission to hospital
■ 2—Born outside hospital and not hospitalized

A fifth-digit subclassification is intended for use only with the fourth digit of 0–Born in hospital. These are:

■ 0—Delivered without mention of cesarean delivery
■ 1—Delivered by cesarean delivery

E codes provide data on how an incident happened, whether it was intentional or accidental, and the place of occurrence. They often correspond with diagnostic codes that describe the injury itself. E codes are assigned for accidents and injuries, poisonings and adverse effects of drugs, child/adult abuse, suicide, homicide, legal intervention, and acts of war. These codes are important for gathering statistics accumulated at the facility, state, and national levels. They are also important for insurance reasons, such as Worker's Compensation. *E codes may never be assigned as principal diagnosis or as a solo code.*

Tabular Example: E960.0 Unarmed fight or brawl
Beatings NOS
Brawl or fight with hands, fists, feet
Injured or killed in fight NOS
Excludes *homicidal;*
injury by weapons (E965.0-966, E969)
strangulation (E963)
submersion (E964)

Looking up terms in the alphabetic index for E codes is a little different than using the diagnostic alpha index. The coder must think less in terms of medical diagnoses and more in terms of a legal or forensic slant. Some key words to help locate proper E codes are listed below:

Accident
Accident occurring at
Assault
Burn
Collision
Fall
Injured
Misadventure
Shooting
Suicide
Terrorism

EXERCISE 2.4

Instructions: Assign the correct ICD-9-CM code for the following diagnostic statements.

V Codes:

1. Routine pap and pelvic exam _____

2. Admission for vaccinations—varicella and hepatitis B _____ _____

3. Aftercare, hip fracture _____

4. Refill of oral contraceptives _____

5. Penicillin allergy _____

6. Single live-born male, by C-section _____

7. Admission for chemotherapy _____

8. Surgery follow-up visit _____

9. Screening mammogram _____

10. Cancelled colonoscopy due to inadequate prep   _____

11. Negative pregnancy test   _____

12. Well baby check   _____

13. Personal history of breast cancer   _____

14. Observation following suspected rape, unsubstantiated ·   _____

15. Screening for diabetes and hypertension   _____ _____

E Codes:

1. Fall down stairs   _____

2. Burned by cigarette   _____

3. Bee sting   _____

4. Crushed fingers in car door   _____

5. Stepped on sharp scrap metal, cut foot   _____

6. Fingers avulsed from fireworks explosion   _____

7. Aspiration of peanut   _____

8. Allergic reaction to penicillin   _____

9. Fistfight—patient was kicked, punched, and bitten   _____ _____

10. Suicide attempt by carbon monoxide; car running in garage   _____

11. Fell off horse   _____

12. Rough landing on snowmobile; hurt back   _____

13. Vehicle rollover; passenger thrown out and injured   _____

14. Fall off small ski boat following collision with dock   _____

15. Accident in schoolyard   _____

Signs, Symptoms and Ill-Defined Conditions

This section is commonly used in physician offices, because a definitive diagnosis has not yet been established. When a diagnosis using the terms "rule out," "questionable," "suspected," or "probable" is used, the coder must code the reason why the patient came in. Signs, symptoms, or abnormal test findings should be coded to the highest degree of certainty.

> **Example:**   A patient presented to the physician's office with extreme fatigue, sore throat, and enlarged liver. The diagnosis was "Probable mononucleosis with suspected hepatitis" and blood tests were performed, along with a throat culture. The patient was advised test results would be available the next day.
>
> *Incorrect codes:* 075 and 573.x—infectious mononucleosis with hepatitis
> *Correct codes:* 780.79—Fatigue; 462—pharyngitis; 789.1—enlarged liver
> *Rationale:* Test results were not back. All that is currently known is symptomatology.

Symptoms such as headache, nausea and vomiting, fever, and palpitations are easy to find. Other more obscure signs and symptoms may be found by looking under these main terms in the alphabetic index:

Abnormal
Change
Decreased
Disturbance
Elevated
Findings, abnormal
Lack of
Pain

It is important, when ordering lab and x-ray tests, that a diagnosis be given to justify medical necessity. Diagnoses that contain the words "rule out," "suspected," "questionable," etc. should not be used. If a definitive diagnosis is not known at the time the test was ordered, a sign or symptom code should be assigned.

EXERCISE 2.5

Instructions: Find the correct ICD-9-CM code(s) for the following diagnostic statements:

1. Patient presents with cyanosis and shortness of breath. Further workup to be done.   _____

2. Thirty-five-year-old woman seen in clinic with pleuritic chest pain.   _____

3. Child complaining of diffuse, generalized abdominal pain.   _____

4. Urine test results show acetone and proteinuria.   _____

5. Patient with elevated blood pressure—recheck every week x 3.   _____

6. Abnormal mammogram result.   _____

7. Fifty-six-year-old male presents with nausea/vomiting, cause unknown.   _____

8. Seventy-five-year-old female with urge and stress incontinence.   _____

9. College student presents to student health with fainting spells.   _____

10. Two-month old infant with failure to thrive.   _____

Late Effect

A late effect is a condition that remains (residual effect) after the acute phase of an illness or injury. Two codes are needed to fully describe a late effect. The residual condition should be coded first, and the cause of the late effect is sequenced second. An example of a residual effect is a scar following a burn. The scar is sequenced first, and the late effect of a burn is sequenced second. One exception to the rule above is for coding late effects of cerebrovascular disease. Category 438 combines the neurological deficits of cerebrovascular disease with a late effect code. Late effects may occur at any time after the initial acute phase has passed. Certain late effects can manifest themselves almost immediately after the acute event, such as with a cerebrovascular accident. Other late effects, such as those due to polio, tuberculosis, or accidents may not become apparent for years.

A late effect code should never be assigned with a current injury. If a late effect is due to something other than illness, such as accident, medical misadventure, homicide attempt, or other external cause, then a late effect E code may be assigned as well. See the Alphabetic Index for External Cause of Injury under "Late Effect of."

Congenital Anomalies

A congenital anomaly is a birth defect—something a person is born with. This chapter of ICD-9-CM is fairly short and encompasses code categories 740–759. Main terms may be searched in the alphabetic index under "anomaly" or "deformity." When searching under "deformity," the coder will often be presented with a choice of a congenital deformity or an acquired deformity. The coder must remember, however, that not all deformities are congenital. An acquired deformity is something that happens later in life and therefore is not appropriate for coding congenital anomalies. An example of an acquired deformity is a deviated nasal septum due to nasal fracture following an assault.

EXERCISE 2.6

Instructions: Find the correct ICD-9-CM code for the following diagnostic statements. Do not assign E codes.

1. Aphasia secondary to stroke five weeks ago   _____

2. Burn contractures of right axilla and elbow, from house fire two years ago   _____

3. Congenital megacolon   _____

4. Brachial nerve damage, due to overuse injury six months ago   _____

5. Cleft palate, bilateral, complete   _____

6. Complete transposition of the great vessels   _____

7. Polycystic kidney disease, adult type   _____

8. Old poliomyelitis with deformities   _____

Mental Disorders

This section of ICD-9-CM contains codes for psychoses, neuroses, and other nonpsychotic disorders such as mental retardation, depression, and developmental problems. There are numerous Excludes notes throughout the mental disorders chapter, as well as fifth-digit assignments. Keep in mind that the healthcare provider will specify the severity of the diagnosis. It is not up to the coder to determine if the patient has mild, moderate, or severe disease or an acute exacerbation or remission for fifth-digit assignment. If this information is not documented in the record, then a fifth-digit assignment of "0," unspecified, should be assigned. Below are definitions of some terms to help understand the disease processes involved with mental disorders.

Dementia: A progressive impairment of abstract thinking, judgment, and memory, involving a long period of change. Personality changes are also common. Many different types of dementia are associated with organic causes, including kidney disease, alcoholism, and neurological conditions.

Delirium: A transient psychotic condition that develops with short or sudden onset. Patients exhibit confusion, delusions, and hallucinations.

Delusions: Strange or odd perceptions about one's environment.

Mood episodes: Most mood episodes require that symptoms be present for a specified period of time, days or weeks. A specified number of symptoms must be present for the patient to be diagnosed with a mood episode. For example: A major depressive episode requires that five or more of the following must be present more often than not for at least two weeks: Dysphoria, anhedonia, guilt feelings, insomnia, weight change, restlessness, daily fatigue, daily diminished concentration, and recurrent thoughts of death or suicidal ideation. Other episode types include manic and hypomanic.

Mood disorders: Require the presence of at least one and sometimes two mood episodes. Disorders can be recurrent, and each disorder has differing requirements for the time span in between episodes. Severity of the disease is specified with fifth-digit assignment.

Schizophrenia: Characterized by a group of psychoses in which the patient demonstrates distorted thinking, personality disturbance, delusions, hallucinations, catatonic states, and other symptoms. Many different types of schizophrenia exist; for example, paranoid, simple, schizoaffective, acute, chronic, latent, and residual. Fifth digits are assigned in category 295 to describe the attributes of the disease.

Substance Abuse

Category 303, Substance abuse, can include alcohol and all forms of drug abuse, to include prescription, over-the-counter (OTC), and illicit drugs. Correct coding of these conditions requires that the coder know whether the patient was dependent upon the drugs or merely abusing them without any type of physiological or chemical dependency involved, such as in recreational marijuana abuse.

Category 305, Dependence, implies that the patient cannot voluntarily stop using the substance and increasing tolerance is noted. ICD-9-CM also includes a note under code category 305: "Includes cases where a person, for whom no other diagnosis is possible, has come under medical care because of the maladaptive effect of a drug on which he is not dependent and that he has taken on his own initiative to the detriment of his health or social functioning." Abuse means that the patient is not dependent upon the substance, but it has reached a problematic stage.

Withdrawal can be reported for both alcohol and drugs. If this condition develops after admission, the principal diagnosis should be the withdrawal, and drug/alcohol abuse or dependence is sequenced as secondary. Any other mental conditions associated with either drug or alcohol withdrawal should be coded separately. In addition, any physical complications of alcohol dependence, such as hepatitis, esophageal varices, gastritis, etc., should be coded. Acute alcohol intoxication may be coded under either dependency or abuse, depending upon the documentation in the record. An excerpt from the alphabetic index is below:

> **Intoxication**
>> acid 276.2
>> acute
>>> alcoholic 305.0x
>>>> with alcoholism 303.0x

Fifth digits are assigned in categories 303, 304, and 305 based on the use of the substance:

- 0—Unspecified
- 1—Continuous
- 2—Episodic
- 3—In remission

The coder should not assign fifth digits of 1 through 3 unless there is specific documentation in the medical record describing the usage.

Formula for Success

Patients who are given drugs without their knowledge should be coded as a poisoning.

EXERCISE 2.7

Instructions: Find the correct ICD-9-CM code for the following diagnostic statements.

1. Alcoholism x 20 years with acute intoxication   _____
2. Anxiety disorder, generalized   _____
3. Manic depression   _____
4. Paranoid schizophrenia in remission   _____
5. Recreational marijuana use at parties   _____
6. Grief reaction due to death of spouse   _____
7. Attention deficit disorder, with hyperactivity   _____
8. Developmental dyslexia   _____
9. Acute alcohol intoxication, 14-year-old with first alcohol experience   _____
10. Oppositional defiant disorder   _____
11. Depressive senile dementia   _____
12. Obsessive-compulsive disorder   _____
13. Alcohol withdrawal syndrome with delirium tremens   _____
14. Huntington's chorea with dementia   _____ _____
15. Hysterical personality disorder   _____

Infections

The Infectious and Parasitic Disease chapter of ICD-9 is indexed according to organism. It includes all types of bacterial, viral, rickettsial, fungal, and parasitic diseases. Codes from this chapter are classified in several ways:

- Single codes—Codes for the organism
- Dual codes—Codes for the organism and condition separately
- Combination codes—Codes both organism and condition together in one code

When coding for infections, some main terms to look for in the alphabetic index include:

Infection
Infestation
HIV infection
Human immunodeficiency virus

Other conditions may include codes from the Infectious and Parasitic Disease chapter as well, such as cellulitis, food poisoning due to certain organisms, or complications of surgical procedures. Dual coding may be used with these conditions if the organism is known, or a combination code may be used.

Example 1   To code botulism, the coder should look under:

Poisoning

food

due to

bacillus

botulinus 005.1

Example 2   To code pneumonia due to specific types of infections, look under:

Pneumonia

due to

fungus NEC 117.9 *[484.7]*

Formula for Success

If the alphabetic index includes a secondary code in slanted brackets, this must be added as a secondary code.

HIV Infections

The physician's statement that a patient is HIV positive or has an HIV-related illness is sufficient to code with 042. If the patient is asymptomatic and *does not have any HIV symptoms* or conditions, then V08 should be used. Code 795.71, Nonspecific serologic evidence of HIV, is used when patients have inconclusive HIV test results. Once a patient has code 042 assigned for symptomatic HIV, it must be used on every subsequent admission. The patient cannot have V08 or 795.71 assigned again. Sequencing of codes depends on the reason the patient was seen. If it was for something other than HIV, then the patient will have another code as a primary diagnosis. If the patient comes in for an HIV-related condition, sequence the HIV first (042) and any other related condition as secondary.

If the patient comes in for HIV screening, use code V73.89, Screening for other specified viral disease. Code V69.8, Other problems related to lifestyle, may be used if the patient is in a high-risk group for HIV. When the patient returns for test results, use V65.44, HIV counseling, if the results are negative. If results are positive, and the patient is showing symptoms, use code 042.

Drug-Resistant Infections

Infections that are resistant to antibiotics have a specific V code assigned to them. ICD-9-CM indicates that this category is intended for use as an additional code for infectious conditions classified elsewhere to indicate the presence of drug resistant organisms. Category V09 is broken down into subclassifications for each type of medication.

Example   A common drug-resistant organism is Methicillin Resistant Staph Aureus, also known as MRSA. This is coded as V09.0, Infection with microorganisms resistant to penicillins.

Septicemia and Septic Shock

These two terms cause considerable confusion among coders. Septicemia is a systemic disease caused by the presence of pathogenic (disease-causing) microorganisms in the body. Symptoms are fever, malaise, hyperventilation, tachycardia, hypotension, and altered mental status. Death can ensue if this condition is not treated. Treatment usually consists of IV fluids and broad-spectrum antibiotics. Blood cultures are drawn from the patient before antibiotics are given. Category 038 is assigned for most cases of septicemia. Additional codes may be required for other manifestations. Septicemia can occur postoperatively or following other invasive procedures such as immunizations, transfusions, or injections. It may also occur in obstetrical patients. For these conditions look in the alphabetic index under "Complications" or "Pregnancy complicated by . . . septicemia." ICD-9 guidelines instruct that when general sepsis with septic shock is documented, code and sequence the septicemia first and the septic shock code second. If the type of bacteria is known, it should be identified. Category 038 also contains an instruction to use an additional code for systemic inflammatory response syndrome, or SIRS, from subcategory 995.9x.

Sepsis is a more generic term indicating the presence of microorganisms or their toxic waste in the blood. The term *urosepsis* is often used to mean bacteriuria or pyuria, rather than bacteria, in the blood. This term is often used incorrectly when a urinary tract infection has progressed into full-blown septicemia.

EXERCISE 2.8

Instructions: Find the ICD-9-CM code for the following diagnostic statements and sequence correctly for multiple codes. Note: Some answers may be outside the category 001–139 range.

1. Viral gastroenteritis _____
2. *H. pylori* gastritis _____
3. Salmonella food poisoning _____
4. Staph aureus septicemia _____
5. Asymptomatic HIV status _____
6. Pseudomonas urinary tract infection _____ _____
7. Pulmonary anthrax _____ _____
8. HIV with skin rash _____ _____
9. Klebsiella pneumonia _____
10. Plantar warts _____
11. Two-year-old with Respiratory Syncytial Virus _____
12. Nongonococcal urethritis, chlamydia _____
13. Athlete's foot _____
14. Scabies _____
15. Newborn with thrush _____

Injuries

Several conditions under this category will be presented in greater depth with the corresponding CPT® chapter. Burns are presented in the Integumentary chapter. Fractures, dislocations, and sprains will be visited again in the Musculoskeletal chapter.

When coding for multiple injuries, separate codes should be assigned for each individual injury. One exception to this guideline is when a combination code is available. Generic "multiple injury" codes are available, but their use is discouraged unless additional information is lacking in the chart. Multiple injuries should be sequenced with the most serious injury first, as determined by the physician. Superficial injuries are not coded when they are associated with a more severe injury of the same site; for example, a bruise of the ankle would not be coded with a fracture of the same ankle. If the injury involves nerves or blood vessels, then those injuries should be coded separately. Sequencing depends on which type of injury was more serious. Open wounds may be complicated by any delay in healing, delayed treatment, foreign body, or primary infection. A separate code may be assigned to indicate a complication.

Formula for Success

Fractures that happen spontaneously, or without trauma, are known as pathological fractures. Do not code these as traumatic fractures.

Finding injuries in the alphabetic index can be a challenge until the coder becomes familiar with terminology. A bruise in laymen's terms is known as a contusion. A cut is known as a laceration. Abrasions are indexed under injury, superficial. Look in the alphabetic index under the following main terms:

Contusion
Dislocation
Displacement
Fracture
Hematoma
Injury
Injury, blood vessel
Injury, nerve
Injury, superficial
Laceration
Sprain
Strain
Wound

Notice that the term "Strain" instructs the coder to *see also* Sprain by site. When presented with this instruction, the coder should always cross-reference the additional main term given. The main term Sprain includes a much larger selection of subterms.

EXERCISE 2.9

Instructions: Assign the correct ICD-9-CM code for the following diagnostic statements. Do not assign E codes.

1. Closed fracture head of radius, right side   _____

2. Laceration eyebrow, 2 cm with foreign body   _____

3. Avulsion, fingernail   _____

4. Contusion, liver   _____

5. Sprained ankle   _____

6. Closed head injury   _____

7. Infected mosquito bite, forearm   _____

8. Concussion with loss of consciousness of 3 to 5 minutes   _____

9. Bucket handle tear, medial meniscus   _____

10. Fracture C7 with spinal cord injury   _____

11. Crush injury to hand and finger with digital nerve injury.   _____ _____

12. Dog bite to lower leg   _____

Formula for Success

When coding actual medical encounters, remember to add an E code for the manner of injury!

Poisonings and Adverse Reactions

There is an important difference between a poisoning and an adverse reaction. A poisoning is a substance that is taken in error or deliberately, an overdose, or it may be the improper use of a medication, such as wrong dose, wrong route, or wrong substance. An adverse reaction, on the other hand, is a side effect to a medication that was properly prescribed and administered. Key words that indicate adverse reactions are "reaction" and "intoxication." Most drugs have therapeutic levels in the bloodstream. When the cumulative effect of a drug reaches a toxic level in the bloodstream, this is known as "intoxication" or toxicity.

Coding for poisonings and adverse reactions involves the use of E codes, which are needed to fully describe the circumstances surrounding the event. Sequencing of poisoning and adverse effect codes along with their corresponding E codes is particularly crucial. At least three codes are required to correctly code a poisoning, which are listed below:

1. Locate the substance in the Table of Drugs and Chemicals. Assign a diagnosis code from the "Poisoning" column of this table as the primary diagnosis.

2. Any other diagnoses that are manifestations or symptoms should be coded as secondary; i.e., nausea, vomiting, seizures, etc. Use as many diagnostic codes as necessary to describe the manifestation.

3. Last, assign an E code from one of the columns under External Cause. This will identify the poisoning as an accident, suicide attempt, assault, or undetermined. Do not use the column for Therapeutic Use when coding a poisoning.

Example: A toddler found an open bottle of cough syrup on the bedside table and drank it. He presented with palpitations and hypertension. This is coded as 975.4, Poisoning by antitussive; 785.1, Palpitations; 401.9 Hypertension; and E858.6, Accidental poisoning by agents primarily acting on the smooth and skeletal muscles and respiratory system.

At least two codes are required to correctly code an adverse effect:

1. Sequence the adverse effect first, which may be a symptom or a manifestation of the adverse effect.
2. Locate the substance in the Table of Drugs and Chemicals. Assign an E code from the "Therapeutic Use" column as a secondary diagnosis.

   Example: A young adult was given a prescription of erythromycin for an infection. Several days after starting the prescribed dosage, the patient developed nausea and vomiting after each dose. This is coded as 787.01, Nausea and vomiting; E930.3, Therapeutic use of erythromycin and other macrolides.

   Any codes taken from the Table of Drugs and Chemicals should be verified in the tabular listing before final assignment. Assign as many E codes as necessary to fully describe all substances involved.

EXERCISE 2.10

Part I

Instructions: Determine whether the statements below indicate a poisoning or an adverse reaction. Circle the correct category.

1. Three-year-old ate 10 children's vitamin tablets.   **Adverse reaction/Poisoning**
2. Seventy-six-year-old with an elevated prothrombin time, on Coumadin for valve replacement.   **Adverse reaction/Poisoning**
3. Overdose of narcotics in a suicidal gesture.   **Adverse reaction/Poisoning**
4. Rash and hives develop following second penicillin dose.   **Adverse reaction/Poisoning**
5. Patient develops shortness of breath and wheezing while using oven cleaner. **Adverse reaction/Poisoning**

Part II

Instructions: Determine the correct code—add E codes also.

1. Patient had acute nausea and vomiting following wild mushroom ingestion.   ____ ____
2. Severe hypokalemia on hydrochlorothiazide.   ____ ____
3. Heart palpitations from over-the-counter antihistamine.   ____ ____
4. Sixteen-month-old with lead poisoning; old paint on crib rails.   ____ ____
5. Esophageal burns and sequelae from drinking lye-based disinfectant.   ____ ____ ____

Neoplasms

In order for the coder to fully understand neoplasm coding, several terms must be clearly understood. The Neoplasm Table is a good place to start. As mentioned above, the Neoplasm Table is arranged by anatomical site. Six columns of possible codes that can be assigned are listed, depending upon the behavior of the neoplasm. The six columns are:

Primary, Secondary, Carcinoma *in situ*, Benign, Uncertain Behavior, and Unspecified. Examples of each are given below.

- *Primary:* The origin of a cancerous tumor. Carcinoma of the lung is a common primary site.
- *Secondary:* The site where a cancerous tumor spreads. Liver, bone, lymph nodes, brain, and lungs are common secondary sites.
- *Carcinoma* in situ: This is a Latin term for *place.* This tumor has not spread or invaded the mucosa surrounding it. Common *in situ* carcinomas are found in the cervix, breast, and skin.
- *Benign:* A tumor that is not cancerous. A lipoma is a benign fatty tumor and can be located almost anywhere in the skin.
- *Uncertain Behavior:* The pathologist cannot determine the behavior of the neoplasm—it may appear to have unusual characteristics that cannot be diagnosed as entirely malignant or entirely benign.
- *Unspecified:* Information regarding the behavior of the neoplasm is not documented. The term *brain tumor* does not specify the behavior of the neoplasm.

Formula for Success

A patient may have more than one primary neoplasm at a time. The original neoplasm may also recur in the same site.

Below are some additional definitions to help the coder understand neoplasm terminology:

- *Adjunct or adjuvant therapy:* Therapy that assists or enhances the primary treatment of surgery.
- *Behavior:* Determines how a neoplasm will grow and function.
- *Carcinoma:* A cancerous tumor that invades the tissues surrounding it and may spread to other organs.
- *Malignancy:* Cancer; a tumor with invasive growth.
- *Metastasis:* Spread of a cancerous neoplasm beyond the site of origin.
- *Morphology:* The behavior of a neoplasm at the cellular level.
- *Neoplasm:* A tumor. Depending upon the behavior of the tumor, a neoplasm can be classified into one of the types listed above.

Locating the Correct Neoplasm Code

The main term should be referenced in the alphabetic index for morphology before turning to the Neoplasm Table. This ensures the coder that the correct column in the Neoplasm Table is chosen.

Example from the alphabetic index: **Adenocarcinoma** (M8140/3—*see also* Neoplasm, by site, malignant

The number in parentheses (M8140/3) is the morphology code that is assigned to a particular type of neoplasm, based on the cell type and behavior. Tumor registries, oncologists, and pathologists use morphology codes on a daily basis. The coder is interested primarily in the number behind the slash—in this case 3—which indicates the behavior of the neoplasm. Neoplasm behavior is classified with the following digits:

- ■ 0—Benign
- ■ 1—Uncertain behavior, borderline malignancy
- ■ 2—Carcinoma *in situ*
- ■ 3—Malignant, primary site
- ■ 6—Malignant, secondary site

A full listing of morphology codes is located in Appendix A of the ICD-9-CM codebook. This is not used often, with the exceptions listed above; however, it is very useful to the coder when trying to determine the behavior of certain neoplasms.

Once the coder has determined the behavior of the neoplasm, look for a subterm in the alphabetic index indicating the site. If a specific site is not available, a cross-reference to the Table of Neoplasms will appear.

Example: **Adenocarcinoma** (M8140/3)—*see also*
        Neoplasm, by site, malignant
        Apocrine (M8401/3)
            Breast—*see* Neoplasm, breast, malignant

The coder should follow the cross-reference instructions and locate the anatomic site "breast" in the Neoplasm Table. If documented, a more specific site should be coded in any subterms listed below the anatomic site. Moving from left to right, the coder should assign a code from the correct column indicating the behavior of the neoplasm. Following this, the code should be checked in the tabular index.

When sequencing neoplasms, the coder must first determine what the patient is being seen for. This helps determine the sequencing of the neoplasm codes. The patient may be coming in for radiation or chemotherapy or may have a past history of cancer that is no longer present. Patients may also have surgery performed, with chemotherapy or radiation administered before leaving the hospital. In each case, the reason for admission will determine how the code is assigned.

Table 2.1 illustrates the special guidelines for neoplasm coding.

Secondary Neoplasms

Certain malignancies are always classified as secondary unless otherwise specified. Neoplasms of the bone, brain, meninges, spinal cord, lymph nodes, diaphragm, mediastinum, heart, liver, peritoneum, pleura, and retroperitoneum are considered secondary. Code 199.1 may be used for an unspecified site of either the primary or secondary neoplasm. Therefore, this code may be used in either the first or second position in a diagnostic statement where two codes are required.

Example: Metastatic carcinoma of the lymph nodes, <u>primary site</u> not specified.

        Codes: 199.1—Unknown primary neoplasm without specification of site
            196.9—Secondary site, lymph nodes

    Metastatic carcinoma of the breast, <u>secondary site</u> not specified.

        Codes: 174.9—Malignant neoplasm of the breast
            199.1—Unknown secondary neoplasm without specification of site

Confusion for the coder arises in the terminology used when describing metastatic sites. The term *"metastatic to"* implies that the site is secondary. For example, the diagnostic statement "Adenocarcinoma of the lung, metastatic to the brain," indicates that the brain is a metastatic site. When the statement is changed to read "metastatic adenocarcinoma from the lung," this indicates that the lung is the primary site.

Table 2–1 Guidelines for Neoplasm Coding

Reason for Admission	Coding Guideline
Treatment directed at primary neoplasm	Sequence malignancy as principal.
Chemotherapy or radiation therapy	Sequence chemotherapy (V58.1) or radiation therapy (V58.0) first, malignancy second.
Admitted for chemotherapy or radiation, but develops complications (nausea, vomiting)	Principal diagnosis is chemotherapy (V58.1) or radiation therapy (V58.0).
Surgical removal of malignancy with adjunct therapy or to determine extent of malignancy, or with a procedure and chemotherapy/radiation following	Sequence malignancy as principal.
Patient has only a history of neoplasm—no adjunct treatment currently and no remaining malignancy	Use appropriate code from V10 category to indicate the former site of the *primary* malignancy. Metastases to other sites may be coded.
Treatment directed at metastatic site only, with primary still present	Sequence the metastatic site as principal, even though the primary neoplasm is still present.
Primary or secondary site with associated signs and symptoms	Once the neoplasm has been diagnosed, do not use codes from Chapter 16 (symptoms, signs, and ill-defined conditions) as principal diagnosis, regardless of the number of admissions or encounters.
Complications:	
Anemia associated with malignancy	Sequence anemia as principal; malignancy second.
Anemia associated with chemo/radiation	Sequence anemia as principal, malignancy second.
Dehydration due to malignancy or therapy, and only the dehydration is treated	Dehydration as principal, malignancy second.
Treatment of complication of surgery for intestinal malignancy	Code complication as principal.

EXERCISE 2.11

Instructions: Find the correct ICD-9-CM code for the following diagnostic statements.

1. Bladder tumor   _____

2. Adenocarcinoma of the prostate   _____

3. Oat cell carcinoma of the lung, lower lobe   _____

4. Benign nevus, scalp   _____

5. Carcinoma of the breast, upper outer and lower outer quadrants   _____

6. Carcinoma *in situ,* cervix   _____

7. Ewing's sarcoma, femur   _____

8. Malignant melanoma of the external ear   _____

9. Acute lymphocytic leukemia   _____

10. Carcinomatosis, primary unknown   _____

11. Hodgkin's disease   _____

12. Acute lymphoma with metastasis to breast   _____ _____

13. Metastatic disease to bone, unknown primary   _____ _____

14. Endometrial neoplasm, pathology uncertain if malignant or benign   _____

15. Liver metastasis from lung   _____ _____

CHAPTER REVIEW

1. Identify the digit in Appendix A of ICD-9-CM that indicates a benign neoplasm.
   a. 0
   b. 1
   c. 2
   d. 3

2. The assignment of the principal ICD-9-CM diagnosis code depends upon:
   a. the reason the patient came in
   b. whatever the physician lists first as a diagnosis
   c. the condition that was ruled out
   d. what test results show

3. Identify the ICD-9-CM code(s) below.
   a. V27.0
   b. J1800
   c. 99212
   d. 530.81
   e. a and d

4. If a patient returns to his or her physician for treatment of chronic sinusitis, this should be coded and reported
   a. only once
   b. never as primary, if it is a chronic condition
   c. as many times as the patient receives treatment for it
   d. a and b

5. The ICD-9-CM instruction "Use additional code" should be taken into consideration
   a. if the coder feels like it
   b. as a mandatory instruction
   c. when documentation supports an additional code
   d. b and c

Critical Thinking Skills

A patient is diagnosed with a strange new infection of the skin, for which there is currently no specific code assigned in ICD-9-CM. After exhausting all other possibilities, the coder should assign a(n):

a. fifth digit of 9 in category 709
b. fifth digit of 8 in category 709
c. unlisted procedure
d. V code from the V02 category

Introduction to CPT® and HCPCS Coding

OBJECTIVES

1. Differentiate ICD-9, CPT®, and HCPCS codes and what each is used for.
2. Apply coding guidelines to CPT® surgical procedure codes.
3. Calculate basic medical dosages to correctly assign HCPCS "J" codes.
4. Recognize basic CPT® and HCPCS terminology.

INTRODUCTION

CPT® stands for "Current Procedural Terminology." It is a coding nomenclature developed by the American Medical Association in 1966. These codes become effective on January 1 of each year. CPT® was designed to report various surgical procedures and diagnostic tests for physician reimbursement. Use of any particular CPT® code is not restricted to any specialty; therefore, any provider who is licensed and working within the scope of his or her licensure may use the appropriate CPT® code to describe the services provided.

There are two levels of CPT®. Level I CPT® codes describe surgical procedures and diagnostic tests. Currently, the Center for Medicare and Medicaid Services (CMS), as well as third-party payers use CPT® codes, but often have conflicting interpretations of the codes that differ from the AMA. Level II codes are also known as HCPCS codes (Healthcare Procedural Coding System) and are coded from a separate codebook. HCPCS codes describe services not covered by CPT®, such as supplies, drugs, and nonphysician services. It is important to note that just because a code is listed in the CPT® or HCPCS book does not mean it will be paid on a claim. Not all insurance companies will allow payment for every code.

CPT®

Navigating CPT®

CPT® codes are characterized by five digits, ranging from 00100 to 99999. CPT® codes do not contain decimal points or alphabetic characters and thus are easy to identify. Until 1970, CPT® codes contained only four digits. The most frequently used codes are the Evaluation and Management codes, which are located within the 99000 category. Known as E/M codes, they are located in the front of the CPT® book out of sequence because of their frequent use. The remaining chapters of CPT® are broken down by body systems and include chapters for lab, radiology, and medicine. Following the E/M section are Anesthesia; Surgery, including Integumentary, Musculoskeletal, Respiratory and Mediastinum, Cardiovascular, Blood and Lymphatics, Digestive, Urinary, Male Genital, Female Genital and Obstetrics, Nervous System, and Eye/Ear; Radiology; Pathology and Laboratory; and Medicine.

EXERCISE 3.1

Instructions: Identify which codes are ICD-9 and which codes are CPT®.

1. 650	_____	6. E927	_____
2. 99211	_____	7. 82962	_____
3. 31500	_____	8. 011.90	_____
4. 00840	_____	9. V76.2	_____
5. 530.81	_____	10. 36000	_____

Similar to ICD-9-CM, the CPT® codebook also has several appendices that the coder must become familiar with. Category III codes, temporary codes for new technology, are found right before the Appendices. If a Category III code is available, it must be reported instead of a Category I unlisted code. The Appendices contain the following information:

- Appendix A contains a list of two-digit numerical modifiers. These can be added to a particular CPT® code to further describe extenuating circumstances or supply additional information about a procedure.
- Appendix B is a summary of additions, deletions, and revisions for the current year.
- Appendix C contains clinical examples for the Evaluation and Management codes. These are grouped by service type. Examples from various specialties are given for each code.
- Appendix D is a listing of all add-on codes.
- Appendix E lists all Modifier 51 exempt codes.

The coder should not code from the index alone. The main text must always be referenced to ensure code accuracy. The best way to assign a code is to find it in the index, cross-reference the specific code descriptor, and then read the codes above and below it to see if others nearby may describe the procedure better. Likewise, the coder should not code from the main text of CPT® without using the index.

The structure of CPT® follows a logical format, beginning with the Surgery section. Each section is broken down into precise groups:

Section
Subsection
Heading
Subheading
Codes

Headings, subheadings, and codes are consistently arranged from head to toe and from least invasive to most invasive. Subheadings in the Surgery section are also consistently arranged under each heading to include: Incision, Excision, Introduction, Removal of Foreign Body, Repair, Destruction, Endoscopy, and Other Procedures.

CPT® Guidelines

Punctuation and Symbols

In order to save space, CPT® has devised a method of using a semicolon in the description to avoid repetition. The portion of the descriptor *before* the semicolon is known as the *common* portion of the code, because that portion is common to all of the codes indented below it. After the semicolon is the *unique* portion of the code. The unique portion belongs only to one code and is not repeated.

Example:　11040 Debridement; skin, partial thickness

　　　　　　11041　　skin, full thickness (read as debridement, skin, full thickness)

　　　　　　11042　　skin, and subcutaneous tissue (read this as debridement, skin, and subcutaneous tissue)

Many CPT® books contain symbols on the bottom of each page to help guide in code selection.

- The symbol ⊘ before a code means that it is modifier 51 exempt. Modifier 51 is normally added to second and subsequent surgeries. The ⊘ symbol means that the code may be listed as a secondary code without use of the modifer.
- A + symbol before a code means that it is an add-on code, and therefore cannot be assigned as a stand-alone procedure. It *must* be listed secondary to another procedure. Add-on codes are also modifier 51 exempt due to this requirement.
- The triangle ▲ means that the description of the code has changed from the previous year. The triangle is located to the left of a CPT® code.
- The bullet ● indicates a new code for the current year.
- Arrows ▶ ◀ are used to enclose revised text.

Formula for Success

Check the legend on the bottom of the page in the CPT® code book; some books print the symbols for easy access.

CPT® Instructions

CPT® gives instructional notes at the beginning of each section. Additional instructions may also be found under subsections, headings, and subheadings that apply only to the codes in those areas. Other cross-references and instructions may be listed in parentheses located below a code or in the paragraphical instructions. In the index, the coder will find cross-references listed with the word "*See*" in italics.

Unlisted procedures are generic codes, which do not have a unique descriptor. These codes are located at the end of a subsection, heading, or subheading and typically end in "99." Search CPT® for more specific codes before assigning an unlisted procedure.

The coder is cautioned against assigning a code that is considered to be "close enough" in order to avoid an unlisted procedure code. Avoid the temptation of using "close enough" codes or risk potential accusations of fraud and abuse. Unlisted procedures typically slow down reimbursement because a manual review of the claim is required. Third-party payers require supporting documentation in the form of operative report and/or letter from the attending physician to justify the procedure and the reimbursement requested. Coders should check the listing of Category III codes at the back of the CPT® codebook to see if there is a temporary code for emerging technology that describes the procedure or service performed. If there is not a descriptor listed in the main text or in the Category III codes, the coder should use an unlisted code.

Example: A surgeon has created a new type of reconstructive surgery on the breast. It is not found in the Category III codes. The correct code to submit is 19499, Unlisted Procedure, breast.

EXERCISE 3.2

Part I

Instructions: Look up each of the following codes and identify the symbol that appears in front of each code. Describe the meaning of the symbol.

1. 49568
2. 93600

Part II: True/False

Instructions: Circle the correct answer to the statements below.

1. The use of CPT® codes is not restricted to a provider in any particular specialty. **True/False**
2. The unique portion of a CPT® code is the portion found before the semicolon. **True/False**
3. If the exact code cannot be found to match a procedure, the coder should pick the closest match. **True/False**
4. Unlisted code categories begin with "99." **True/False**

Formula for Success

Medicare will occasionally accept unlisted procedures. Check with individual carriers for specific instructions. Check Category III codes in the back of CPT® for new technology.

CPT® codes can often be found by referencing a number of terms in the index: anatomical site, eponym (person's name), name of the procedure, synonyms, or abbreviations.

Example: The abbreviation "FNA" in the index gives a cross-reference: *See* Fine Needle Aspiration.

EXERCISE 3.3

Instructions: Using the special instructions below, look up the following procedures in the CPT® index and give the correct code. Number 1 is given as an example.

Look under the procedure:

1. *Excision,* colon with anastomosis   44140
2. X-ray, clavicle   _____
3. Anesthesia for tubal ligation   _____
4. Fracture care, knee, open treatment   _____
5. Destruction, flat warts   _____
6. Endoscopy, colon with stent placement   _____
7. Exploration, gallbladder   _____
8. Incision, external hemorrhoids   _____
9. Injection, esophageal varices   _____

Look under the anatomic site:

10. Elbow implant removal   _____
11. Corneal biopsy   _____
12. Repair of fistula, anus   _____
13. Excision umbilicus   _____

Look under the eponym:

14. Keller procedure   _____
15. Kock pouch   _____
16. Proetz therapy   _____
17. Fowler-Stephens procedure   _____

Look under the abbreviation:

18. LDH   _____
19. LEEP procedure   _____
20. SMAS flap   _____

HCPCS

Coding Overview

In 1983, Medicare developed a new coding system to supplement CPT® Level I. It is currently known as HCPCS, which stands for Healthcare Common Procedural Coding System. It is also referred to as CPT®, National Level II. This system was established to describe non-physician services, durable medical equipment, supplies, and drugs that are not covered by CPT® Level I codes. Although the codes were originally developed for Medicare use, many codes are widely accepted by third-party payers.

Effective Dates

HCPCS codes become effective on January 1 of each year.

Overlap

Occasionally, there is an overlap between CPT® and HCPCS descriptors. In the event of identical narratives, the CPT® code should be used. If the HCPCS descriptor is more specific, then the Level II code should be used. Local Medicare carriers should also be consulted if there is duplication.

Coding Conventions

HCPCS uses the same coding conventions as CPT® Level I codes:

- The bullet ● indicates a new code for the current year.
- The triangle ▲ means that the description of the code has changed from the previous year.

HCPCS codes are alphanumeric in nature. They consist of one alphabetic character (A through V) and four numbers.

Example: A4550   Surgical tray
              J7030   Infusion, normal saline solution 1,000 cc

Appendices may differ somewhat depending upon the publisher.

HCPCS Modifiers

All publishers will append a listing of HCPCS modifiers, which are two-digit characters that are appended to HCPCS codes. Modifiers for HCPCS codes are recognizably different than those listed in CPT®.

Example: T4   Left foot, fourth toe
              HC   Adult program, geriatric

This is how the modifiers appear when they are attached to either CPT® codes or HCPCS codes:

Example:

Level I code with HCPCS modifier
26010-F1 Drainage of finger abscess, simple–left hand, second digit

Level II code and HCPCS modifier

S9443-TE Lactation classes, non-physician provider–LPN/LVN

Ambulance Modifiers

Ambulance codes and claims require a single-digit modifier to indicate the origin of the transport and a second single-digit modifier to indicate the destination. The claim for ambulance services is different than the physician's claim form. Ambulance services are found in codes A0021–A0999. The modifiers defining origin and destination are listed at the beginning of the A-code section.

Coding Instructions

To locate a HCPCS code, the coder must

- Identify services or procedures the patient received.
- Look up the appropriate term in the alphabetic index.
- Locate the code descriptor.
- Follow any cross-reference instructions.
- Check for any publisher-specific notes or color-coded references.
- Check appendices for coverage guidelines.
- Decide if modifiers should be applied.
- Assign the code.

HCPCS codes are arranged in the following categories:

A	Ambulance and transportation, surgical supplies, and miscellaneous
B	Enteral and parenteral therapy
C	Transitional pass-through and new technology
D	Dental procedures
E	Durable medical equipment
G	Temporary codes for procedures and professional services
H	Alcohol and drug abuse treatment services
J	Injectable drugs, inhalation medications, and chemotherapy drugs
K	Temporary codes for DME
L	Orthotic/prosthetic services
M	Medical services under the jurisdiction of the local carrier
P	Pathology and laboratory services
Q	Temporary codes for drugs, supplies, and services
R	Diagnostic radiology services
S	Temporary national codes—Non-Medicare
T	Medicaid services
V	Vision and hearing services

MODIFIERS AND REIMBURSEMENT

HCPCS and CPT modifiers should be appended to Medicare claims whenever applicable. In some cases, reimbursement may be denied or reduced due to lack of the appropriate modifier. For example, the QB modifier indicates that the service is being performed in a rural Health Professional Shortage Area (HPSA). Physicians who perform services within a HPSA are eligible for an additional 10 percent incentive payment on a quarterly basis. Reimbursement is lost when the QB modifier is not applied correctly. Other modifiers, such as the GA modifier, indicate that services may be the responsibility of the patient and may not be paid by Medicare.

EXERCISE 3.4

Part I

Instructions: Identify the modifiers listed below as CPT® or HCPCS modifiers. You may use the inside cover of your codebooks if your book has the modifiers listed there.

1. E4 _____   5. TC _____

2. G2 _____   6. 52 _____

3. 22 _____   7. 81 _____

4. T1 _____   8. QA _____

Part II

Instructions: A CPT® code is provided for each of the following Medicare scenarios. Find the correct modifier from the list at the bottom and assign it to the appropriate CPT® code. Key words/phrases are underlined.

1. Anesthesia for permanent transvenous pacemaker insertion, <u>services by CRNA</u>. 00530-_____

2. Repair laceration <u>left thumb</u>—2 cm, simple.   12001-_____

3. Level II established office visit, provided in a <u>Rural Health Professional Shortage Area</u>. 99212-_____

4. <u>State supplied</u> vaccine for MMR immunization.   90706-_____

5. Wet mount of vaginal secretions performed, <u>CLIA waived test</u>.   87210-_____

6. Thyroid test (TSH) performed at Medicare patient's request—<u>Not medically necessary</u>. Advance Beneficiary Notice signed.   84443-_____

7. <u>Court ordered</u> inpatient psychiatric treatment, initial interview.   90801-_____

8. Low level E/M service provided by a <u>Family Practice Resident MD without the presence of a teaching physician</u>.   99212-_____

Modifier Choices: **GE   SL   FA   QW   QZ   GA   H9   QB**

CALCULATING DOSAGE

HCPCS is most commonly used for coding injections in the medical office. Most drugs in HCPCS are indexed by their generic or chemical name. Some publishers include brand names in the index. Generic drugs are identified by lower case; brand name drugs are capitalized. When injections are coded, the dosage must be calculated to correctly match the amount given to the dose described by the HCPCS code.

Example: A patient is injected with 60 mg of Toradol.

HCPCS descriptor specifies, "Injection, ketorolac tromethamine (Toradol) per 15 mg."

Correct code: J1885 × 4

Rationale: Multiply 15 mg × 4 to equal 60 mg given to the patient.

When the code descriptor states "up to" a specified amount, anything less than that may be coded by assigning the code one time only.

Example: A patient is injected with 25 mg of Phenergan.

HCPCS descriptor specifies, "Injection promethazine HCL (Phenergan), up to 50 mg."

Correct code: J2550 × 1

Rationale: Code only once if less than the stated amount is given.

Calculating dosages is important for correct HCPCS coding. Often there is confusion between a liquid measurement and the strength of the medication. If there is ever a question regarding drugs or dosages, the coder should ask the provider for clarification. Some tips for calculating common dosages and liquid measurements are given below.

Liquid measurement   *Drug dosage*
1 ml (milliliter) = 1 cc (cubic centimeter)   1,000 mg (milligrams) = 1 gm (gram)
1,000 cc = 1 liter
1,000 ml = 1 liter

IV solutions listed in HCPCS are listed in either ccs or milliliters, so it is important that the coder realize that both measurements equal the same volume.

EXERCISE 3.5

Instructions: Locate HCPCS codes for the following scenarios. There may be more than one code in some cases.

1. Pelvic, breast exam, and pap smear on a 68-year-old woman   _____

2. Heparin lock flush   _____

3. Alcohol wipes, two boxes of 100 each   _____

4. Asthma education, private insurance   _____

5. Dental prophylaxis, child   _____

6. Metal forearm crutches, pair, complete   _____

7. Skin adhesive closure of laceration, Medicare patient   _____

8. Injection, DepoMedrol 40 mg.   _____

9. Thoracic rib belt   _____

10. Breast prosthesis, silicone   _____

11. Ten units of platelets   _____

12. Injection of epoitin alpha for chemotherapy patient; 80,000 units   _____

13. Injection of Epogen for dialysis patient.   _____

14. Smoking cessation gum, private insurance   _____

15. Medicaid Home Health Aide visit   _____

CHAPTER REVIEW

1. Identify the main term in CPT® index to find bladder catheterization.
   a. Insertion, catheter, bladder
   b. Bladder, catheterization
   c. Catheterization, bladder
   d. All of the above

2. Which of the following codes is modifier 51 exempt?
   a. 17004
   b. 62210
   c. 49410
   d. 37250

3. Find the codes below that accurately demonstrate sequencing of add-on codes:
   a. 69717, 69718
   b. 19000, 19001
   c. 17307, 17310
   d. 36248, 36215

4. Which of the following descriptors from code range 29806–29820 contains the common portion?
   a. Repair of SLAP lesion
   b. With removal of loose body or foreign body
   c. Synovectomy, partial
   d. Arthroscopy, shoulder, surgical; capsulorrhaphy

5. Using the inside cover of your CPT® book, identify the HCPCS modifier(s).
   a. 80
   b. P1
   c. E4
   d. 22
   e. b and c

Evaluation and Management Services

OBJECTIVES

1. Correctly assign Evaluation and Management codes.
2. Understand the basic requirements of the 1995 and 1997 Documentation Guidelines.
3. Describe how time is used as a controlling factor for Evaluation and Management coding.
4. Correctly assign modifiers to Evaluation and Management codes.

TERMINOLOGY AND ACRONYMS

Chief complaint   The reason for the healthcare encounter. This can be stated as a diagnosis, symptom, or problem.

Concurrent care   The provision of similar services to the same patient by more than one physician on the same day. For example: A family practitioner and cardiologist who both follow a patient in the hospital.

Counseling   A discussion with the patient and/or family concerning diagnostic test results and/or recommended studies; prognosis of the patient; treatment options; instructions for treatment and/or follow-up care. It also includes the importance of compliance with treatment options, patient/family education, and risk factor reduction.

Established patient   A patient who has received professional services at some time within the past three years from a physician or another physician of the same specialty who belongs to the same group practice.

Family history   A review of medical information that may impact the patient's current healthcare status. This includes the medical history; specific diseases and cause of death of parents, siblings, and children; and hereditary problems.

History of present illness   A chronological description of the development of the patient's illness. This includes the following elements in relation to the patient's problem: location, duration, quality, severity, timing, context, associated signs and symptoms, and modifying factors.

Nature of presenting problem   Relates to the chief complaint. Five levels of severity are defined:

> *Minimal:* A problem that may not require the presence of the physician, but service is provided under the physician's supervision.

Self-limited or minor: A problem that runs a definite and prescribed course, is transient in nature, and is not likely to permanently alter health status OR has a good prognosis with management/compliance.

Low severity: A problem where the risk of morbidity without treatment is low; there is little to no risk of mortality without treatment; full recovery without functional impairment is expected.

Moderate severity: A problem where the risk of morbidity without treatment is moderate, there is moderate risk of mortality without treatment; there is uncertain prognosis OR increased probability of prolonged functional impairment.

High severity: A problem where the risk of morbidity without treatment is high to extreme; there is a moderate to high risk of mortality without treatment OR high probability of severe, prolonged functional impairment.

New patient   A patient who has not received any professional services within the past three years from the physician or another physician of the same specialty who belongs to the same group practice.

Past history   A review of the patient's past medical and surgical history, to include allergies, current medications, illness, injury, diet, and immunization status appropriate to age.

Review of systems   An inventory of body systems used to define the problem, clarify diagnoses, identify needed testing, or document a baseline prior to management. CPT® has identified fourteen systems:

> Constitutional
> Eyes, Ears, Nose, Mouth, and Throat
> Cardiovascular
> Respiratory
> Gastrointestinal
> Genitourinary
> Musculoskeletal
> Integumentary
> Neurological
> Psychiatric
> Endocrine
> Hematologic/Lymphatic
> Allergic/Immunologic

Social history   An age-appropriate review of past and current activities to include employment and occupational history, marital status, sexual history, alcohol, drug and tobacco use, and other pertinent social factors.

◼◼◼ *INTRODUCTION*

This chapter will explain the use and selection of appropriate Evaluation and Management (E/M) codes. Additional information on choosing levels of service is presented at the end of this chapter. The student should follow along with the corresponding Evaluation and Management chapter in CPT®. Highlighting in the CPT® book is strongly encouraged.

Evaluation and Management codes were created to describe nonsurgical/procedural work that is performed by a medical provider. These codes encompass all settings–office, home, emergency room, hospital, and other sites of service. Evaluation and Management codes begin with code 99201. These codes are taken out of sequence and are located at the beginning of the CPT® book. Since E/M codes are commonly used by almost all specialties, their position in the front of CPT® codebooks allows easier access to the codes.

Within the last ten years, due to fraud and abuse regulations, much greater emphasis has been put on physician documentation within the record to substantiate the level of service that is billed. Documentation must support or justify the level of service that was billed. In 1994, HCFA (now known as CMS) required physician documentation to meet specific guidelines in order to bill a given level of service for Medicare or Medicaid. These guidelines are known as the 1995 Documentation Guidelines. Physicians were required to have certain elements of the history, physical examination, and medical decision making documented in the medical record.

The response of the medical community was less than enthusiastic. Physicians charged that they were not given "credit" for certain specialty-specific elements. The Guidelines were thus revised, and two years later, the 1997 Documentation Guidelines became effective. These were more definitive than the 1995 Guidelines, with expansion of the physical examination guidelines to twelve different specialty exams, as well as a multisystem examination. Once again, problems became apparent with the 1997 Guidelines. The additional requirements of the physical examination made it harder for the physician to achieve the same level of service that had been coded under the 1995 guidelines. The CMS final ruling was that physicians could use either the 1995 or 1997 Guidelines, whichever was to the physician's benefit. Currently, new guidelines are being developed with considerable discussion among physicians, the American Medical Association, and CMS. Several models have been tested but not approved as of this time.

ARRANGEMENT OF E/M CODES

Codes are arranged in categories by type of service—for example, Office or Other Outpatient, Hospital Observation, Hospital Inpatient, Consultations, Emergency Department, and so on. Many categories are further divided into subcategories that differentiate between new and established patients and initial or subsequent care. Subcategories are further divided into specific levels identified by a CPT® code and a description. Required documentation contents (key components) for each code are identified by bullets and are printed in bold type. The nature of the presenting problem is listed following the key components, along with the average time anticipated for that level of service.

Place of Service

The place where the Evaluation and Management service is rendered is important for correct code assignment, as well as for billing purposes. Billing staff must assign a mandatory two-digit place of service code on the insurance claim form for each CPT® code submitted. This informs the payer of the type of setting where the service was performed. Place of service codes are found in some versions of CPT® for reference purposes, as well as on the CMS website. Coding staff must ensure that the CPT® code assignment and place of service codes do not conflict and trigger a claim denial.

EXERCISE 4.1

Instructions: Determine what type of service was rendered for each of the following scenarios. Be as specific as possible regarding type of service. Levels of service are not required for this exercise.

Example: The family physician came to the Emergency Department after the patient had been seen by the ED physician. The correct E/M type of service is **<u>Established Office or Other Outpatient Services</u>**.

1. A patient was seen by a consultant while in observation status.   _____

2. A patient is referred to another physician on a permanent basis.
   State the type of service for the initial visit to the new physician.   _____

3. An inpatient is seen for the second time by a consultant for test
   results.   _____

4. A patient suffers a massive myocardial infarction in the Urgent
   Care Clinic and may not survive. Lifesaving measures are
   undertaken by the MD.   _____

5. A baby is born at home with the physician in attendance.   _____

6. A patient was seen at an assisted living facility by her attending
   MD.   _____

7. A physician performed a basic examination for life insurance,
   filled out required paperwork, and mailed it for the patient.   _____

8. A patient is seen in the Urgent Care Clinic for a sore throat.   _____

Time

E/M codes are no longer only time based, although time may be the controlling factor in special circumstances. Intraservice time is defined as *face-to-face time* for office and other outpatient visits and as *unit/floor time* for hospital and other inpatient visits. It is indicative of the amount of work involved with E/M services. Face-to-face time includes the total amount of work done before, during, and after the patient visit, such as reviewing test results, obtaining a history from the patient, performing an examination, planning for follow-up care, and communicating with other healthcare professionals. Unit/floor time includes the amount of time that the physician is present on the patient's hospital unit and at the bedside rendering services for that patient. It also includes the total amount of work done before, during, and after the visit for that patient.

Calculating Time

When greater than 50 percent of a visit is spend in **counseling** and/or coordination of care, then time becomes a controlling factor. The E/M code may be assigned based on the "average" time that is given within the individual code descriptor. Ideally, two times should be documented in the chart in order for a code to be assigned based on time. The total time spent face to face with the patient, as well as time spent counseling and/or coordinating care should be documented. If time is not documented, then the code cannot be assigned on this basis. Documentation should also substantiate counseling and coordination of care.

Example

Poor documentation:

A great deal of time was spent talking with the patient about his personal problems. Code assigned: 99214.

Good documentation:

PLAN: 25 minutes of a 30-minute visit was spent discussing the patient's problems with alcohol and drug abuse. He agreed to admit himself to Rehab tomorrow morning. Arrangements were made for admission, and the patient was given the name of the intake coordinator. The patient requested that I notify his employer in writing. A brief letter was dictated in the patient's presence and will be given to the patient before he leaves this afternoon. Code assigned: 99214.

Emergency Department codes do not have a time component. Time is difficult to determine in the Emergency Department when multiple patients may be cared for by the same provider. Patient acuity and the intensity of service must be considered for Emergency Department codes.

Some E/M Codes are assigned solely on time documented. Prolonged Services, Critical Care Services, Hospital Discharge Services, and Preventive Medicine Counseling are examples of time-based codes. If time is not documented, a time-based code cannot be assigned.

EXERCISE 4.2

Instructions: Determine the specific CPT® code BASED ON TIME, when time spent counseling/coordinating care is greater than 50 percent.

1. Documentation for an office consultation meets a 99241. However, the physician spent 20 minutes of a 30-minute visit counseling and coordinating care. _____

2. The physician documents a problem-focused exam and moderate complexity medical decision making on a subsequent care inpatient hospital visit. An interval history is not documented. The physician spent approximately 20 minutes of a 25-minute visit counseling the patient and his family and answering questions. _____

3. An attending physician made a home visit to a terminal patient. History and physical exam were problem focused; medical decision making was low complexity. The physician documented that 60 minutes of a 65-minute visit were spent counseling the patient and family, as well as coordinating with hospice nurses while she was there. _____

Formula for Success

Selecting E/M Services

Before selecting a code, determine the following:

- The category or type of service performed (Example: Emergency room visit, discharge services, etc.).
- Where the service is being provided.
- If the patient is new or established.
- If the service is initial or subsequent.

Levels of E/M Services

Three *key components* must be considered in controlling the level of service. They are History, Examination, and Medical Decision Making. Increased levels of acuity for each key component are assigned in a logical fashion to CPT® codes that are not based on time (i.e., documentation based). These three key components are set apart in bulleted format and bold type within the code descriptor.

Four additional components are known as *contributory components.* They are Counseling, Coordination of Care, **Nature of Presenting Problem,** and Time. When counseling and coordination of care dominate the visit, they become a controlling factor if time is documented.

The hierarchy of these components is dependent upon the documentation provided in the medical record. Tools are available to assist the physician as well as the coding staff in choosing the correct level of service.

Types of Service

Office or Other Outpatient Services

These codes were designed to describe services provided in either the physician office or another outpatient setting. According to CPT® guidelines, a patient is considered an outpatient until inpatient admission to a healthcare facility occurs. When assigning codes from this category, a distinction must be made between **new patient** and **established patient.** Table 4.1 shows several tips to help the coder distinguish if the patient is new or established.

In a large multispecialty group practice, a patient could potentially have more than one E/M visit on a given date. If the patient is seen by the same physician in more than one setting or place of service in a day, the highest level of service provided for that day should be assigned. For example, if the patient is seen in the clinic and then sent to the Emergency Room for treatment by the same physician, then only the Emergency Room visit would be coded for that day. If different physicians provided service in each setting, then each physician would submit codes for his or her service at the appropriate level.

Documentation: Office or Other Outpatient Services requires that all three key components must be met for new patients. Two out of three key components must be met for established patients.

Hospital Observation Services

This type of service is used for patients who have been admitted to "observation status" in a hospital. This means that the patient has not been admitted as an inpatient but is being observed for a period of time. The patient is not required to physically move to a designated observation area in order for these codes to be used. However, if a designated area *does* exist within the hospital and the patient is relocated there, then the observation codes must be utilized for that place of service.

The observation service codes are divided into Observation Discharge Service and Initial Observation Care. The discharge service code should not be used if the patient is admitted and discharged from observation on the same day. (See Observation or Inpatient Care Services [Including Admission and Discharge Services]) It is used when the patient is discharged from observation on a day subsequent to admission. The Initial Observation codes are used when the patient is admitted to observation status and remains at that status until discharged. When a patient is admitted by the same physician to inpatient status, the appropriate Initial Hospital Care code would be assigned. CPT® guidelines state that all E/M services on the same date provided in sites that are related to initiating "observation status"

Table 4–1   Patient Distinction

New Patient	Established Patient
• New to the practice.	• Has been seen by physician within the last three years.
• Has not been seen by regular physician for three years or longer.	• Seen by partner of regular physician.
• Referred by another physician to new doctor (**Not request for consult**).	• Seen by on-call physician, covering for regular physician.
• New to specialist in multispecialty group practice.	

should NOT be reported separately. In addition, the observation codes may not be used for postoperative recovery if the visit is part of the surgical package.

Documentation: Initial Observation Care requires that all three key components must be met. There are no documentation guidelines for Observation Care Discharge Services.

EXERCISE 4.3

Instructions: Combining the choices at the bottom of the exercise, determine the type of service(s) for the scenarios. More than one type of service may be needed.

1. The patient is seen by his regular family physician, Dr. A, and referred to the podiatrist for foot problems. Choose the type of service for each physician. _____

2. The patient is seen in the clinic as a new patient, and immediately admitted to observation at the hospital by the same physician. _____

3. Dr. A is on vacation, and has asked his friend across town, Dr. B, to see his patients while he is gone. Mrs. Jones visits Dr. B in his absence. _____

4. Mr. Brown moves back to his hometown after a four-year absence. He visits his old family physician for a checkup. _____

Established Patient/ New Patient/ Office Visit/ Other Outpatient Services/ Observation Services

Hospital Inpatient Services

These services are divided into Initial Hospital Care and Subsequent Hospital Care.

Initial Hospital Care.   The admitting physician makes no distinction between new and established patients. All services rendered by the admitting physician in different sites of service for that day are considered part of the initial hospital care. The documentation produced by this visit is known as a "History and Physical," or H&P. Similar to Observation Services, only three levels of service are available to code for Initial Hospital Care. Other physicians who see the patient the first day must use a different code to describe their services, such as Initial Inpatient Consultation.

Subsequent Hospital Care.   Subsequent Hospital Care services are also known as "follow-up days," "subsequent visits," "follow-up care," or "subsequent care days." There are three levels of Subsequent Hospital Care. One noticeable difference in these services is the term "interval history" located in the bolded key components. Documentation in the progress notes should include any changes in history since the last assessment by the physician. Depending upon the facility, the documentation of progress notes may be handwritten or transcribed. Care must be taken by the physician to avoid "block" coding—that is, the assignment of the same level of service throughout a hospitalization. A patient's status will change throughout the hospital stay, and documentation should reflect any improvement or complications. Code 99231 specifies that the patient is stable, recovering, or improving. Code 99232 states that the patient is responding inadequately to therapy or has developed a minor complication. Code 99233 states that the patient is unstable or has developed a significant complication or a significant new problem.

Documentation: Initial Inpatient Services requires that all three key components must be met. Subsequent Hospital Care services requires at least two out of three key components.

Formula for Success

Multiple physicians may be caring for a patient in the hospital. If services overlap and two or more physicians report the same primary diagnosis, there is a risk of one physician's services being denied by insurance. Each specialist should report only the diagnoses he or she is taking care of or addressing. When partners visit each other's patients in the course of a day for routine visits, only one E/M service is normally reported.

Observation or Inpatient Care Services (Including Admission and Discharge Services). Use these codes for physicians who admit and discharge a patient from either observation or from the hospital on the same date. Services for patients who are admitted and discharged on different dates must be reported separately. Use Initial Hospital or Initial Observation, Subsequent Hospital Care, and Discharge codes as appropriate for place of service.

Documentation: This code category requires that all three key components must be met.

Hospital Discharge Services

This is a time-based code used to report the discharge day management of the patient. It is utilized to report the total duration of time spent by the physician preparing the patient for discharge from the hospital and includes final examination, instructions for continuing care, preparation of records, prescriptions, and referral forms. Two codes are available—99238 is used for 30 minutes or less, and 99239 is for more than 30 minutes.

Consultations

One area of confusion among coders is the difference between a consultation and a referral. A consultation is a service that requires four things:

- A request for consultation
- The reason for the consultation
- Rendering of an opinion/treatment
- A formal report back to the originating physician

A consultant does not "keep" a patient, except to treat the particular problem that the patient was sent for. A referral is when a patient is sent to another physician on a permanent basis. Confusion arises because the originating physician in both cases may be called the "referring physician." It must be clear what type of services the receiving physician will be providing.

Place of service is very important in determining the correct consultation code to use. For example, an inpatient consultation code cannot be used in observation, because that is considered outpatient status. Conversely, an outpatient consultation code would not be appropriate for inpatient status. An insurance company would deny both examples because of wrong place of service.

Formula for Success

In order to bill a consultation, the billing staff needs to know the name of the physician who requested the consultation.

Office or Other Outpatient Consultation

These services can be provided in any type of outpatient setting. There is no distinction in CPT® made between new and established patient for these services. "Other Outpatient" may include the Emergency Room or Hospital Observation setting. Any follow-up consultations made in the outpatient setting would be coded using the Established Office Visit Codes, 99211–99215.

Initial Inpatient Consultations

These codes do not make a distinction between new or established patient. CPT® guidelines state that only one initial consultation should be reported per admission by any particular physician. Multiple physicians may perform consultations on a very sick patient, but they will each follow a problem that falls within the scope of their own specialty.

Follow-up Inpatient Consultations

The place of service for these codes must be inpatient hospital or inpatient nursing facility. These codes are used only for established patients, which means that an Initial Inpatient Consultation must have been previously performed. CPT® guidelines advise that these visits are to complete the initial consultation OR any subsequent visits requested by the attending physician.

Example: Dr. Smith signs off on his initial consultation after giving his opinion and recommendations to the attending physician for treatment. After several days, the patient becomes worse, and the attending requests Dr. Smith to come back and see the patient again. A Follow-up Inpatient Consultation code is used to describe his services.

Follow-up inpatient consultation codes may be used when only a few follow-up visits are necessary to wrap up the care of the initial consultation. Occasionally, the follow-up inpatient consultation codes are used inappropriately when the consultant assumes the care of a patient for the duration of the hospitalization.

Formula for Success

When the consultant uses the sentence, "Thank you for this consultation, I will follow the patient along with you" at the end of his or her report, it means he or she is assuming the care of the patient for that problem. After this point, the subsequent inpatient care codes should be used for visits provided by the consulting physician.

Confirmatory Consultations

These codes are used for second or third opinions. The consultant does not treat the patient, just renders an opinion. This category may also be used for self-referred patients. Since there is not a formal request or anyone to send a report to, the self-referred patients do not meet the criteria for a regular consultation code to be assigned. CPT® guidelines state that a 32 modifier should be used when a third party requests the consult, such as an insurance company or HMO.

Documentation: All initial consultations require all three key components to be met. Follow-up or subsequent consultations require at least two out of three key components. If time is documented, it may be used as a controlling factor. Be aware that some patients may refuse a physical exam once in the exam room. The physician should document that the physical exam was refused, and coding can be based on other contributory components.

EXERCISE 4.4

Instructions: Building on the concepts just learned, identify the type of service(s) provided in the scenarios below. Do not assign specific code numbers. Some scenarios will have more than one type of service.

1. Return visit for hospital inpatient. _____

2. A consultation performed by Dr. Jones in the Emergency Department. _____

3. History and Physical day 1, discharge visit on day 2 for hospital inpatient. _____

4. Patient admitted and discharged on the same day from observation. _____

5. Patient admitted to observation after being seen in Urgent Care. Both services were by the same MD. _____

6. Observation admission (day 1), follow-up visit (day 2), discharge services (day 3). _____

7. Surgical consultation performed in the office. _____

8. Second opinion requested in the hospital by insurance company prior to surgery. _____

9. Consultation on inpatient (day 1), second consultation after MRI results (day 2). _____

10. Consultation in office (first visit), physician assumed care of the patient, outpatient (second visit) _____

Emergency Department Services

An Emergency Department is an organized hospital-based facility for the provision of un-scheduled episodic services to patients who present for immediate medical attention. The facility must be open 24 hours a day, 7 days a week. A freestanding Urgent Care Clinic does not meet the definition of Emergency Department. Urgent Care services must be reported with Office or Other Outpatient Service codes.

CPT® does not make a distinction between new and established patients in the Emergency Department. Times have not been established for Emergency Department visits, due to the variable intensity of the visits and the difficulty in tracking the physician's face-to-face time with each patient.

Critical Care Services provided in the Emergency Department should be reported with Critical Care codes, 99291–99296.

Documentation: All three key components must be met for Emergency Department Services. However, the nature of presenting problem takes on a more significant role with these codes. The following code descriptors are changed slightly to accommodate the intensity of service in the Emergency Department:

- ■ 99281 Usually, the presenting problem(s) are self-limited or minor.
- ■ 99282 Usually, the presenting problem(s) are of low to moderate severity.
- ■ 99283 Usually, the presenting problem(s) are of moderate severity.
- ■ 99284 Usually, the presenting problem(s) are of high severity and require urgent evaluation by the physician but do not pose an immediate significant threat to life or physiologic function.
- ■ 99285 Usually, the presenting problem(s) are of high severity and pose an immediate significant threat to life or physiologic function.

In addition, HCFA 1997 Documentation Guidelines state that if the physician is unable to obtain a history from the patient or other source, the record should describe the patient's condition or other circumstance, which precludes obtaining a history. This guideline is particularly important to Emergency Services, where all three key components must be met.

Coding/billing issues may arise with Emergency Department visits if there is more than one physician involved in the care of the patient. If the ED physician and the patient's regular family physician both see the patient, then the ED physician will usually dictate/code the ED note, and the family physician will dictate/code for an office/other outpatient visit.

Occasionally, the ED physician will not see the patient at all. In that case, the family physician may use the ED codes, as long as the visit is emergent. If the visit is arranged at the convenience of either the physician or the patient, then it should be coded using Office or Other Outpatient Service codes, 99201–99215.

Consultants who are called to the ED will commonly use the Outpatient Consultation codes.

Pediatric Critical Care Patient Transport

These codes are time based and are used when a physician provides critical care during an interfacility transport. It includes face-to-face contact only. Physician directed two-way radio communication contact should be coded with 99288. Multiple services such as vascular access, ventilation management, routine monitoring, and computer-stored data are bundled into the Pediatric Critical Care Patient Transport codes. The CPT® book should be referenced for additional services not listed here. The patient must be critically ill or injured, with high probability of imminent or life-threatening deterioration of the patient's condition. Both the illness/injury and the treatment being provided must meet requirements for critical care.

Documentation: The provider should document time spent during the transport, as well as the intensity of service rendered. When the patient has been admitted to the receiving facility, the admitting physician will report the appropriate E/M service rendered.

Example: Critical care of 35 minutes provided in cross-town transfer of 1-year-old patient to waiting pediatrician. Code 99289 assigned.

Critical Care Services

These codes are time based and may be rendered anywhere the services are required on patients older than 24 months of age. Usually, the patient is in the Emergency Department or critical care unit. Like the Pediatric Critical Care Transport Services (see page 55), most of the requirements for Critical Care Services are the same. There must be a high probability of imminent or life-threatening deterioration in the patient's condition. Multiple services are bundled into the critical care service codes, including vascular access, chest x-rays, EKG, gastric intubation, temporary pacemakers, and ventilation management. Any procedures that are performed but are not listed as bundled procedures in this category may be separately coded and billed. Time spent on procedures that are separately reported should be "carved out" of the time reported for critical care services.

Example: Critical Care × 2 hours   99291-25x 1
                                               99292-25x 2
        Endotracheal intubation   31500

Rationale:
The endotracheal intubation is not bundled into the CPT® description of Critical Care. A modifier 25 is added to the primary code of 99291 because the Critical Care is a significant, separately identifiable E/M service provided on the same day as a procedure.

Below are additional tips for coding Critical Care Services:

■ Patients who are not critically ill but are occupying a bed in a critical care unit should be coded with other appropriate E/M codes.
■ Critical care and other E/M services may be provided on the same date by the same physician.
■ Documentation must support each service. Modifier 25 should be added to the other E/M service code.
■ Critical care may be reported on multiple days, as long as the patient's condition requires that level of care.
■ Critical care time does not have to be continuous—the attending physician or a physician of the same practice and specialty should report the total time spent per day.
■ Time spent must be recorded in the patient's medical record.
■ The physician must be immediately available to the patient, so activities off the unit/floor may not be counted as critical care.

Neonatal and Pediatric Critical Care Services

CPT® guidelines state that the definitions for critical care services are the same for adults, children, and neonates. These codes are categorized by age and weight of the patient, as well as initial and subsequent care. There are several major differences in these codes compared to the adult Critical Care Services. These include:

■ Pediatric and neonatal critical care are coded only once per day.
■ Care rendered also includes enteral and parenteral nutrition, respiratory and pharmacologic control of the circulatory system, as well as family counseling, case management services, and personal direct supervision of the healthcare team.
■ Bundled procedures include the same codes as listed for the hourly critical care services, and also includes umbilical venous/arterial catheters, endotracheal intubation, lumbar puncture, suprapubic bladder aspiration, bladder catheterization, and CPAP.

Intensive (Noncritical) Low Birth Weight Services.   These codes are subsequent care codes, used once per day. They are reported after the date of admission and are provided by a physician who is directing the continuing intensive care of a low birth weight or very low birth weight infant who is no longer critical. Codes are assigned based on the present body weight of the infant.

Nursing Facility Services

These services are provided at a nursing facility, which includes facilities formerly known as skilled nursing facilities (SNFs), intermediate care (ICFs), or long-term care facilities (LTCFs). These codes are also to be used to report services provided to a patient in a psychiatric residential treatment facility, which provides 24-hour staffed group living environment.

Three subcategories include Comprehensive Nursing Facility Assessments, Subsequent Nursing Facility Care, and Nursing Facility Discharge Services. Comprehensive assessments may be performed at any of the following places of service: hospital, observation unit, physician office, nursing facility, domiciliary, or patient's home. CPT® does not make a distinction between new or established patients for any subcategory. Nursing Facility Discharge Services are time-dependent and similar to hospital discharge management codes. They are based on 30 minutes or less or greater than 30 minutes of time. The place of service must be listed as nursing facility.

Guidelines for admission to the nursing facility are similar to other sites of service. All E/M services performed by the admitting physician on the same date of service are rolled into the initial nursing facility care. An exception to this guideline is a hospital discharge or observation discharge service that is performed on the same date of admission or re-admission to the nursing facility. These services may be reported separately.

Documentation: The logic assigned to the Comprehensive Nursing Facility key component scheme is somewhat different than we have seen in CPT®. All three key components must be met for these services. However, codes 99301 and 99302 require a detailed interval history, while 99303 requires a full comprehensive history. The three Subsequent Nursing Facility Care codes also require interval histories, but only two out of three key components are needed. Again, time may be utilized if appropriately documented.

Domiciliary, Rest Home (Boarding Home), or Custodial Care Services

These codes are used to report services provided by physicians who visit patients in one of the above listed facilities. These settings provide room, meals, and personal assistance on a long-term basis and do not employ nursing staff for a medical component. This category is divided into two sections: new and established patients. Times have not been determined for these codes.

Documentation: All three key components must be met for new patients; established patients must meet at least two out of three key components. An interval history must be included. Only three codes are available for each subcategory.

Home Services

Services provided in the patient's home (house calls) are reported with these codes. They are divided into new and established patients.

Documentation: All three key components must be met for new patients; established patients must meet at least two out of three key components. An interval history must be included. Five codes are available for each subcategory, and time may be used as a controlling factor, if documented appropriately.

Prolonged Services

This category is utilized when a physician provides services that are beyond the recommended time frames described in E/M codes. It is split into two different subcategories; With Direct (Face-to-Face) Patient Contact and Without Direct (Face-to-Face) Patient Contact. Face-to-Face codes are further subdivided into inpatient and outpatient place of service. All six codes in this category are add-on codes and are time based. The codes should only be used once per day, and discontinuous time may be added together, as long as it is appropriately documented. Prolonged services of less than 30 minutes total duration is not separately reported.

> **Example:** A new patient arrived at the Urgent Care Clinic with a profuse nosebleed. The bleeding point was identified in the anterior nasal cavity and was packed. The patient refused silver nitrate cautery and was observed for further bleeding for an additional 35 minutes. The patient's total time in the Urgent Care Clinic was 65 minutes. Documentation of the visit met E/M level 99203. Code 99354 assigned for additional 35 minutes of Prolonged Services.

Physician Standby Services

This subcategory consists of a single code, 99360, to be used for each full 30-minute segment of standby services. The service must be requested by another physician, without direct face-to-face patient contact. It may only be used if no other services are provided, and the physician is simply waiting. The physician may not be attending other patients or proctoring another physician. Services of less than 30 minutes are not reported. If the physician is on hospital-mandated call, codes 99026 or 99027 should be reported per hour, rather than standby services.

Case Management Services

These include two subcategories: Team Conferences and Telephone calls. Team conferences are time based, consisting of 30 minutes and 60 minutes. Telephone calls are designated as simple, intermediate or complex in nature. All telephone calls should be documented in the patient's medical record, however most payers do not allow separate reimbursement.

Care Plan Oversight Services

Care Plan Oversight involves one physician reporting the supervision of a home health, hospice, or nursing facility patient for a 30-day period of time. Codes are divided into 15–29 minutes, and 30 minutes or more. Services provided include physician development and/or revision of care plans, review of reports, diagnostic studies, communication, integration of new information into the medical treatment plan, and/or adjustment of medical therapy. Care must be taken to choose the correct place of service.

Preventive Medicine Services

Preventive medicine codes are used to describe age-appropriate preventive healthcare services including history, examination, counseling and anticipatory guidance, risk factor reduction, and ordering of immunizations and diagnostic tests. If abnormalities are discovered during the course of the visit, and the problem is significant enough to warrant additional work by the provider, it may be coded and billed in addition to the Preventive Medicine Service, as long as documentation supports the level coded. A modifier 25 should be added to the appropriate office visit code. Insignificant problems that do not require additional work should not be reported.

Preventive medicine codes are divided into New Patient and Established Patient. Within each subcategory, the codes are separated into seven age categories. CPT® guidelines state that the nature of these services does not equate to the comprehensive exam required in E/M codes 99201–99350.

Other services that may be provided at the time of the visit may be reported separately. These include immunizations, screening laboratory and radiology procedures, or other separately identifiable CPT® services.

Counseling, risk factor reduction, and anticipatory guidance visits should be reported with codes 99401–99412 if they are provided at a separate encounter distinct from the preventive medicine service.

Formula for Success

If an insurance plan allows preventive medicine/wellness visits, they will only cover one visit per year. Enlist the help of scheduling staff to make sure the patient has not had a preventive medicine visit in the previous 364 days. Children's coverage may allow multiple visits, depending on the age of the child.

ICD-9-CM Diagnosis

Diagnostic coding for preventive medicine services is extremely important. In ICD-9-CM, specific codes are assigned for wellness visits. These include:

V20.2	Routine infant or child health check
V25.4–V25.49	Routine exam in contraceptive management
V70.0	Routine general medical examination at a healthcare facility
V70.5	Health examination of defined subpopulations
V72.3x	Gynecological examination

V codes are especially important to remember for screening services as well. Screening services are those services that are performed without an established diagnosis. They may be done at the patient's request or as part of an age-specific screen. Screening codes must be carefully linked with the appropriate CPT® code. ICD-9-CM categories for screening codes are listed below:

V73–V75	Screening for infectious diseases
V76	Screening for malignant neoplasms
V77	Special screening for endocrine, nutritional, metabolic, and immunity disorders
V78	Special screening for disorders of blood and blood-forming organs
V79	Special screening for mental disorders and developmental handicaps
V80	Special screening for neurological, eye, and ear diseases
V81	Special screening for cardiovascular, respiratory, and genitourinary diseases
V82	Special screening for other conditions
V83	Genetic carrier status

EXERCISE 4.5

Instructions: List the appropriate diagnosis code next to the services ordered by the physician. Do not assign CPT® codes.

1. Screening for diabetes; accucheck performed   _____

2. Pap, pelvic, and breast exam done on Medicare-age patient   _____

3. Screening for hypothyroidism   _____

4. Well child check, 3-year-old established patient, and hematocrit   _____

5. Hemoccult for colon cancer screening   _____

6. Routine mammogram   _____

7. Lead screening, 15-month-old new patient   _____

8. Preventive medicine visit, established patient, age 40 with PPD placement   _____

9. Preventive medicine visit, new patient age 25 for cerumen impaction/removal   _____

10. Gynecological exam, age 65; office visit for hypertension   _____

HCPCS Codes and Preventive Medicine

Until recent years, Medicare has not paid for routine or screening services. Trends in healthcare have been moving toward a preventive model of healthcare, rather than a therapeutic one. Medicare has responded to this shift by gradually allowing reimbursement on some types of preventive services, using temporary HCPCS codes. The coder should be familiar with the local Medicare carrier policies, which delineate frequency of services, as well as covered ICD-9-CM diagnosis codes. Examples are listed below of a few Medicare allowed preventive services:

G0101	Cervical or vaginal cancer screening; pelvic and clinical breast examination
G0102	Prostate cancer screening; digital rectal examination
G0103	Prostate cancer screening; prostate specific antigen test (PSA), total
G0104	Colorectal cancer screening, flexible sigmoidoscopy
G0107	Colorectal cancer screening; fecal occult blood test, 1–3 simultaneous determinations

Medicare guidelines also state what elements need to be documented to support the use of these codes.

Identifying Preventive Medicine Services

These services cause considerable confusion for the physician as well as the coder at times. If the patient has other E/M services provided at the same time, the coder must be able to extract the preventive medicine services from the office visit and ensure that both services have adequate documentation.

Listed below are some services that suggest possible preventive medicine services:

Pelvic exam and pap smear	Mammography	Contraception
Developmental milestones	Water safety	Car seat use
Rectal exam	Screening for diabetes	STD screening
Breast exam	Screening for lipids	Immunizations
Hemoccult/colorectal cancer screening	PSA screening	Osteoporosis
Tobacco cessation/counseling	Drug/alcohol discussion	Diet/exercise
Skin cancer screening	Testicular cancer screening	Vision/hearing

Other clues may be found in the terminology of the physician. The coder should become familiar with the terms that the physician uses to describe his or her preventive medicine services, since terminology may vary across the United States. Terms such as wellness visit, annual exam, annual physical exam (APE), healthcare maintenance (HCM), preventive maintenance, well child check (WCC), and well baby check (WBC) all indicate preventive medicine services in different parts of the country.

Table 4.2 contains instructions on how to code for Pap, pelvic, and wellness exams either alone, or with an office visit.

EXERCISE 4.6

Instructions: Assign the correct CPT® and diagnosis codes for each scenario.

1. 45-year-old female returns for annual pap and pelvic. Patient also has a sore throat and fever. Physician prescribes antibiotics for strep throat and over-the-counter meds. Pap and pelvic are done. _____

2. 30-year-old commercial pilot presents for complete annual flight physical. It is his first visit to this physician. _____

3. A 4-year-old child presents to the pediatrician for a wellness exam and immunizations. The patient was noted to be ill with cough, fever, and malaise. Immunizations were held and the physician diagnosed pneumonia. The patient was sent home with antibiotics and nebulizer and instructed to return for follow-up visit in 2 weeks, with possible immunizations at that time. _____

4. A 75-year-old man had not seen a physician in twenty-five years. On his initial visit, the physician performed a complete physical exam and ordered screening labs for lipids and PSA. He also scheduled the patient for a screening sigmoidoscopy the following week and will recheck his blood pressure at that time. _____

5. Smoking, drug and alcohol abuse, and contraception were discussed with a healthy but at-risk teenager for approximately 35 minutes. _____

6. A woman grieving for her mother was counseled for approximately 20 minutes by her family physician. A two-week supply of sleeping pills was prescribed. _____

7. A 70-year-old Medicare patient schedules a pap, pelvic, and breast exam with her regular physician. _____

Table 4–2 Coding for Pap/Pelvic and Wellness Exams

Type of Visit	Reason for Visit as Scheduled in Computer	ICD-9 Code Linkage	CPT Code	Payment Responsibility
Wellness exam alone	Yearly exam/annual physical	V72.3x (w/pap) V70.0–V70.9 (w/o pap)	99381–99397	Patient
Wellness exam w/problems addressed as office visit	Annual or yearly + diagnosis (HTN, etc.)	Same as above plus dx code (401.9)	992xx–25 99285–99296	Medicare Patient
Screening pap and pelvic	Pap and pelvic only	V76.2/V76.49 Routine (q 2 yrs) V15.89 High risk (Annually)	G0101 & Q0091 G0101 & Q0091	Medicare Medicare
Office visit + screening pap	Medical problem + "oh, by the way, pap is due"	Code condition + V76.2	992xx–25 G0101 & Q0091	Ins/Medicare Medicare
Office visit for repap	Repeat pap (ex: abnormal pap)	Code condition: 795.0x	99211–99215 must meet doc. guidelines	Medicare/Ins (but no chg repap for insufficient specimen)

Please note: An office CPT code linked with a medical exam V-code will be denied (the two are incompatible). Likewise, a preventive medicine CPT code linked with a diagnosis code (ex: 401.9, 277.0, etc) will be denied for the same reason. These codes must be linked appropriately; i.e., no mix and match *regardless of payor.*

ASSIGNING LEVELS OF SERVICE

Now that you have mastered selecting the category of service along with the various sub-categories, it is time to learn about selecting the level of service. The level of service pertains to the different levels of History, Physical Examination, and Medical Decision Making within individual codes and the documentation that supports those levels. Contributory components of Counseling, Coordination of Care, Nature of Presenting Problem, and time play a part in this also. We have already discussed the use of time as a controling factor when counseling or coordination of care predominates the visit.

It is extremely important to recognize that CMS has published its recommended Documentation Guidelines, which are used by all Medicare/Medicaid carriers and by many private third-party insurers as well. Bookmark the following CMS site and review the 1995 and 1997 Documentation Guidelines: www.cms.gov/medlearn/emdoc.asp.

The categories listed below require all three key components to be documented. These categories specify new patients, and include some that do not distinguish between new or established:

- Office or Other Outpatient Services, New Patient
- Consultations
- Emergency Department Visits
- Observation Services
- Initial Hospital Care
- Observation or Inpatient Care Services (Including Admission and Discharge Services)
- Comprehensive Nursing Facility Assessments
- Domiciliary, Rest Home or Custodial Care Services, New Patient
- Home Services, New Patient

The following categories require that at least two out of three key components must be met:

- Office or Other Outpatient Services, Established Patient
- Subsequent Hospital Care
- Subsequent Nursing Facility Care, New or Established
- Domiciliary, Rest Home or Custodial Care Services, Established Patient
- Home Services, Established Patient

Step I: Documentation of History

There are four types of History, each building on the level below it. They are Problem Focused, Expanded Problem Focused, Detailed, and Comprehensive. Each type of history must include (to varying degrees) the following elements. Their acronyms and a short description are also listed:

- **Chief Complaint** (CC): What the patient came in for. All medical records should document this.
- **History of Present Illness** (HPI): Describes location, duration, quality, severity, timing, context, modifying factors, associated signs, and symptoms.
- **Review of Systems** (ROS): An inventory of body systems; may be a questionnaire of signs and symptoms.
- **Past, Family and/or Social History** (PFSH): A review of these areas and how they relate to the patient's problem. This is not required for services with only an interval history documented.

The Review of Systems consists of the following systems: Constitutional; Eyes; Ears, Nose, Mouth, and Throat; Cardiovascular, Respiratory, Gastrointestinal; Genitourinary; Musculoskeletal; Integumentary; Neurological; Psychiatric; Endocrine; Hematologic/ Lymphatic; Allergic/Immunologic. Review of Systems and the Past, Family and Social History may be delegated to another provider to document, such as the physician's nurse, or the patient may fill out a questionnaire-type of form that is made a permanent part of the medical record.

The table below illustrates how the levels of history build upon each other as they become increasingly complex. Each successive level requires more documentation by the provider.

Documentation of History

Type of History	HPI	Review of Systems	PFSH
Problem Focused	brief (1–3 elements)	N/A	N/A
Expanded Problem Focused	brief (1–3 elements)	problem pertinent (relates to HPI)	N/A
Detailed	extended (4 or more)	extended (2–9 systems)	pertinent (any one)
Comprehensive	extended (4 or more)	complete (10 or more systems)	complete

Step II: Documentation of Physical Examination

1995 Guidelines

Documentation of the physical exam varies considerably between the 1995 and the 1997 Documentation Guidelines. The 1995 Guidelines focus on body areas or systems.

Body Areas
- Head and face
- Neck
- Chest/breast/axillae
- Abdomen
- Genitalia/groin/buttocks
- Back
- Each extremity

Body Systems
- Constitutional
- Eyes
- Ears, nose, mouth, throat
- Cardiovascular
- Respiratory
- Psychiatric
- Gastrointestinal
- Genitourinary
- Blood/lymphatic/immune system

■ Skin
■ Neurological
■ Musculoskeletal

Four types of physical examinations and an explanation of each are listed below:

Problem Focused: A limited exam of affected body area or organ system.
Expanded Problem Focused: Limited exam of affected body area and other symptomatic or related organs.
Detailed: Extended exam of affected body areas/organ systems.
Comprehensive: A general multisystem examination or complete exam of a single organ system.

Except for the comprehensive examination, the 1995 Guidelines do not specify how many organ systems are required to meet each level of physical exam. Numerous auditing tools are available that attempt to quantify the amount of physical exam for consistency. Documentation Guidelines specify that a general multisystem examination should include findings in about eight or more of the twelve organ systems.

Documentation guidelines also state that specific abnormal and relevant negative findings of the examination should be documented. Notations of "abnormal" without elaboration is insufficient. In addition, any abnormal or unexpected finding of an unaffected or asymptomatic body area or organ system should be described. Normal findings may be documented with a brief statement indicating "negative" or "normal."

1997 Guidelines

In response to some of the "loopholes" created by the 1995 Guidelines, the 1997 physical examination guidelines focused on specific exams for single organ systems, as well as a general multisystem examination. Physicians need not be specialists in any particular area in order to use a single-organ system examination. The type of examination is based upon clinical judgment, the patient's history, and the nature of presenting problem.

The single organ system exams include:

■ Cardiovascular
■ Eyes
■ Ears, nose, mouth and throat
■ Genitourinary (female)
■ Genitourinary (male)
■ Hematologic/lymphatic/immunologic
■ Neurological
■ Psychiatric
■ Musculoskeletal
■ Respiratory
■ Skin

The physical examination levels are the same as the 1995 Guidelines, but the qualifications for meeting those levels are different in the 1997 Guidelines. Elements of the 1997 physical examination are characterized by "bullets." The levels for the general multisystem exam are listed below:

Problem Focused Examination: Should include performance and documentation of *one to five elements* identified by a bullet (●) in one or more organ systems or body areas.

Expanded Problem Focused Examination: Should include performance and documentation of *at least six elements* identified by a bullet (●) in one or more organ systems or body areas.

Detailed Examination: Should include *at least six organ systems or body areas.* For each system/area selected, performance and documentation of *at least two elements* identified by a bullet (●) is expected. Alternatively, a detailed examination may include performance and documentation of *at least twelve elements* identified by a bullet (●) in two or more organ systems or body areas.

Comprehensive Examination: Should include *at least nine organ systems or body areas.* For each system/area selected, *all elements* of the examination identified by a bullet (●) should be performed, unless specific directions limit the content of the examination. For each area/system, documentation of *at least two elements* identified by a bullet is expected.

Single Organ System Examinations.   Requirements for the documentation of single-organ systems exams are slightly different. For these exams, the bullets are located in boxes with either a shaded or unshaded border.

Problem Focused Examination: Should include performance and documentation of *one to five elements* identified by a bullet (●), whether in a box with a shaded or unshaded border.

Expanded Problem Focused Examination: Should include performance and documentation of *at least six elements* identified by a bullet (●), whether in a box with a shaded or unshaded border

Detailed Examination: Should include *at least six organ systems or body areas.* For each system/area selected, performance and documentation of *at least two elements* identified by a bullet (●), whether in a box with a shaded or unshaded border.

Comprehensive Examination: Should include performance of all elements identified by a bullet (●), whether in a shaded or unshaded box. Documentation of every element in each box with a shaded border and at least one element in each box with an unshaded border is expected.

Eye and Psychiatric Examinations: Should include the performance and documentation of at least nine elements identified by a bullet (●), whether in a box with a shaded or unshaded border.

Step III: Medical Decision Making

Medical decision making refers to the complexity of establishing a diagnosis and/or selecting a management option. Tables 4.3 and 4.4 were created by HCFA (now CMS) to assist in this process. The key component of medical decision making remains the same for both the 1995 and the 1997 Documentation Guidelines. In order to determine the level of medical decision making, three things must be measured:

1. The **number of possible diagnoses and/or the number of management options** that must be considered.

2. The **amount and/or complexity of data;** i.e., medical records, diagnostic tests, and/or other information that must be obtained, reviewed, and analyzed.

3. The **risk of significant complications, morbidity, and/or mortality,** as well as co-morbidities, associated with the patient's presenting problem(s), the diagnostic procedure(s), and/or the possible management options.

As noted in the full text of the Documentation Guidelines, the three elements listed above should be well described in the medical record to include any treatment, changes in therapy, referrals, test results, procedures performed or planned, and any comorbidities or

Table 4–3 Risk of Complications and/or Morbidity or Mortality

Level of Risk	Presenting Problem(s)	Diagnostic Procedure(s) Ordered	Management Options Selected
Minimal	• One self-limited or minor problem, e.g., cold, insect bite, timea corports	• Laboratory test requiring venipuncture • Chest X-rays • EKG/EEG • Urinalysis • Ultrasound, e.g. echo • KOH prep	• Rest • Gargles • Elastic bandages • Superficial dressings
Low	• Two or more self-limited or minor problems • One stable chronic illness; e.g., well-controlled hypertension of non-insulin dependent diabetes, cataract, BPH • Acute uncomplicated illness or injury; e.g., cystitis, allergic rhinitis, simple sprain	• Physiologic test not under stress; e.g., pulmonary function test • Noncardiovascular imaging studies with contrast; e.g., barium enema • Superficial needle biopsies • Clinical laboratory tests requiring arterial puncture • Skin biopsies	• Over-the-counter drugs • Minor surgery with no identified risks factors • Physical therapy • Occupational therapy • IV fluids without additive
Moderate	• One or more chronic illnesses with mild exacerbation, progression, or side effects of treatment • Two or more stable chronic conditions • Undiagnosed new problem with uncertain prognosis; e.g., lump in breast • Acute illness with systemic symptoms; e.g., pyelonephritis, pneumonitis, colitis • Acute complicated injury; e.g., head injury with brief loss of consciousness	• Physiologic test not under stress; e.g., cardiac stress tests, fetal contraction stress test • Diagnostic endoscopies with no identified risk factors • Deep needle or incisional biopsies • Cardiovascular imaging studies with contrast and no identified risk factors; e.g., arteriogram cardiac cath • Obtain fluid from body cavity; e.g., lumbar puncture, thoracentesis, culdocentesis	• Minor surgery with identified risk factors • Elective major surgery (open, percutaneous, or endoscopic) with no identified risks factors • Prescription drug management • Therapeutic nuclear medicine • IV fluids with additives • Closed treatment of fracture or dislocation with manipulation
High	• One or more chronic illnesses with severe exacerbation, progression, or side effects of treatment • Acute or chronic illnesses or injuries, that pose a threat to life or bodily function; e.g., multiple trauma, acute MI pulmonary embolus, severe respiratory distress, progressive-severer rheumatoid arthritis, psychiatric illness with potential threat to self or others, peritonitis, acute renal failure • An abrupt change in neurologic status, seizure, TIA, weakness, or sensory loss	• Cardiovascular imaging studies with contrast with identified risk factors • Cardiac electrophysiological tests • Diagnostic endoscopies with identified risk factors • Discography	• Elective major surgery (open, percutaneous, or endoscopic with identified risk factors) • Emergency major surgery (open, percutaneous, or endoscopic) • Parenteral controlled substances • Drug therapy requiring intensive monitoring for toxicity • Decision not to resuscitate or to descale care because of poor prognosis

Table 4–4   MDM Table

Number of Diagnoses or Management Options	Amount and/or Complexity of Data to Be Reviewed	Risk of Complications and/or Morbidity or Mortality	Type of Decision Making
Minimal	Minimal or none	Minimal	Straightforward
Limited	Limited	Low	Low Complexity
Multiple	Moderate	Moderate	Moderate Complexity
Extensive	Extensive	High	High Complexity

underlying diseases. To assist in choosing the level of risk (number 3 above), the Table of Risk (Table 4.3) was developed by CMS. Only the highest level of risk in any one category determines the overall risk.

Finally, in order to choose the correct level of medical decision making, each element (numbers 1–3) is considered in Table 4.4. Two out of three elements in the table must be either met or exceeded.

EXERCISE 4.7

Instructions: Choose the correct level and type of E/M service as described in the scenarios below.

1. A patient who is new in town receives treatment for an ear infection. The physician performed a problem focused history, problem focused exam, and medical decision making was straightforward.

2. An established patient returns to her physician for diabetic foot care. The physician performed a problem focused history, expanded problem focused exam, and medical decision making was of low complexity.

3. Dr. Brown, an internist, sent a patient to Dr. Smith, a cardiologist. In her office, Dr. Smith performed a comprehensive history, comprehensive exam, and medical decision making that was of moderate complexity. Dr. Smith sent the patient back to Dr. Brown for continuing care of her other medical problems.

4. Dr. Jones visited Mrs. Thomas on her third hospital day. He documented a problem focused interval history and reviewed her test results. Physical exam was deferred. Medical decision making was low.

5. A comatose patient was rushed to the Emergency Department via ambulance. History was not obtained due to the patient's condition, and family members were not in attendance. A comprehensive examination and high complexity medical decision making were documented in the record.

6. A patient was admitted to the nursing facility by his family physician. A detailed interval history was documented, along with a comprehensive examination and low complexity medical decision making.

CHAPTER REVIEW

1. New patients require _____ key components.

2. Medicare will allow reimbursement of certain screening services when these codes are used: _____

3. Bona fide Emergency Departments must be open:

   a. at least during daytime hours

   b. at least five days a week

   c. twenty-four hours a day, seven days a week

   d. from 6 AM to 11:30 PM daily

4. Critical care may be provided

   a. only in the ICU

   b. only in the CCU

   c. wherever it is necessary

   d. in the ER, ICU, and CCU

5. The term that identifies where a service is provided is _____.

6. A consultation request is the same thing as a referral.

   True/False

Case Studies

Instructions: For each dictated report, determine the following factors: type of service (consult, office visit, critical care, etc.) and the number of key components required. Score each key component from the documentation provided. Based on the documentation and time (if appropriate), determine the E/M code using the 1995 Documentation Guidelines.

1. **Family Medicine Office Visit**

   Subjective

   This 14-year-old female who is new to this practice presents today complaining of nasal congestion, sore throat, fatigue, some headache, and sinus pressure since approximately last night. She has been using over-the-counter cold remedies without relief. She said she had a hard time sleeping. No one else is sick at home.

   Objective

   Weight is 105 pounds. Temperature is 99.5. Ears—TMs are gray and mobile. Nose—mucous membranes are moist. Turbinates are pink. Oral cavity is free of lesions with no masses, ulcerations, or inflammation. Pharynx is mildly injected without exudate. Tonsils are not enlarged. Neck is supple without adenopathy. There is negative sinus tenderness.

   Assessment

   1. Sinus congestion
   2. Upper respiratory infection

   Plan

   Antihistamine/decongestant samples are given to the patient and she is to take one p.o. b.i.d. for the next five days. She can use non-aspirin pain relievers p.r.n. She is to increase her fluids and rest. She can use humidity in the home as well. She needs to return to the clinic in the next three to four days if her symptoms worsen or develop into something more treatable.

Type of Service:	_____
Level of History:	_____
Level of Exam:	_____
Level of Medical Decision Making:	_____
CPT® code:	_____

2. **Pulmonary Office Visit**

Subjective

The patient is in for follow-up of her COPD.

   The patient has been coughing quite a bit lately. Her breathing feels stable. She is still on her Combivent and her Flovent. She sees Dr. Smith for her osteoporosis, and he told her that she has another compression fracture, along with a cracked rib from the coughing.

   Review of Systems
   Cardiac: Denies any problems.
   Pulmonary: Breathing is stable.
   Musculoskeletal: She has more problems now with the compression fractures.

Objective

   Vitals: As above.
   Cardiac: No murmurs or gallops.
   Lungs: Reduced breath sounds bilaterally with no wheezes or rales. Prolonged expiratory phase.
   Abdomen: Soft; no tenderness of liver and spleen.
   Extremities: No edema.
   Pulse oximetry: Her O_2 saturation on room air is 94–95 percentage.

Impression

1. Moderate obstructive airway disease
2. Osteoporosis with multiple compression fractures

Plan

1. Continue the Combivent two puffs four times a day and the Flovent 110 two puffs twice a day.
2. Return to see me in six months.

   Type of Service: _____
   Level of History: _____
   Level of Exam: _____
   Level of Medical Decision Making: _____
   CPT® code: _____

3. **Emergency Department Visit**

Subjective

This 65-year-old female presents today complaining of what she thinks is a bladder infection. She said she had one approximately two years ago and recalls it being the same. She does have some dysuria and some burning. She has urgency and hesitancy. She did notice a little pink coloration to her urine last evening. She denies any vaginal discharge.

Past Medical History

She did have a hysterectomy in the year 2000. She also had her gallbladder out in 1999. She has been recently diagnosed with diabetes. Current medications are metformin and another medication that she could not recall. She is allergic to tetracycline and amoxicillin.

Review of Systems

She denies any fever or back pain. She does have a small amount of pressure noted to her bladder area. Her appetite has been good, and she is tolerating fluids well without nausea or vomiting.

Objective

Temperature is 97.3 degrees. Blood pressure is 130/80. Alert, oriented female in no acute distress. She is well nourished and well hydrated. HEENT—normocephalic. PERRL. Conjunctivae are clear; sclera are white. Ears—TMs are normal; canals are clear. Nose—mucous membranes are moist and turbinates are pink. Oral cavity is free of lesions with no ulcerations. Neck supple without adenopathy. Thyroid is not palpated. Heart—regular rate and rhythm S1, S2 and no murmur. Lungs are clear bilaterally. Abdomen is soft and nontender with positive bowel sounds to all four quadrants. There is no rebound or hepatosplenomegaly. There is no CVA tenderness. Extremities are without clubbing, cyanosis, or edema. Dip urine shows cloudy urine with a pH of 6, specific gravity of 1.015, leukocytes 2+, negative nitrites, 3+ protein, and 250 RBCs. There is no glucose in the urine.

Assessment

1. Urinary tract infection

Plan

Bactrim one double-strength tablet p.o. b.i.d. × 10 days, #20. Pyridium 200 mg once p.o. t.i.d. with food × 2 days, #6. She needs to increase her fluid intake and avoid caffeine. In two weeks she has an appointment with her primary care provider. I advised that they recheck her urine that time to ensure it is completely clear. She was advised if her symptoms do not improve over the next 2 to 3 days she needs to come back to the emergency room for follow-up.

Type of Service: _____

Level of History: _____

Level of Exam: _____

Level of Medical Decision Making: _____

CPT® code: _____

4. **Progress Note**

45 min.

S: Doing better. A little more alert when she awakens from sedation. Still heavily sedated and not responsive verbally. Cooperative.

O: Ventilator still on 30% O_2; tidal volume approximately equals in and out. Peak pressures 230!

Had a little regurgitation of tube feedings today. Output greater than intake. Weight 100.7. Atrial fib with heart rate in 70s-80s. BP 120-136/60. Monitor—short 5 beat run of Ashmans vs sustained V-tach. HEENT—symmetric. No JVD sitting. No adenopathy. Chest—still decreased breath sounds on right, OK on left. S1, S2 OK. Diastolic sound thought earlier to be an AJ blow—may instead be an S3. Abdomen soft, normal bowel sounds, nondistended, no masses. Trace edema, nontender. Neuro—sedated, nonfocal.

Labs: Suction on low yielding discolored gray-yellow mucus. ABG—PO_2 57, CO_2 61. O_2 sats monitor all in 90s with ET CO_2. High 50s to low 60s. BUN 41, K 3.3 increased to 4.1 after KCL replacement. Chloride 102 and Na 154. CXR—shows ETT OK with continued RLL pneumonia and effusion.

A: 1. Respiratory failure. ABGs, ET CO_2, PO and O_2 sat all acceptable. Airway pressures OK and no evidence of S4. Cuff leak still has a suspicion of post hypercapnea alkalosis. No spontaneous breaths. Will need continued ventilatory support.
2. Pneumonia. Slowly responding. Now getting more phlegm up.
3. Atrial fib; stable.
4. CHF—improved with decreasing JVD and weight.
5. Renal insufficiency and azotemia; better.
6. Increased Na persists.
7. Post hypercapneic alkalosis. Cl is normal. K was low. Now corrected. Need to fix this. Now with Cl OK, Na high and K normal, we can use Diamox to facilitate bicarb excretion to correct post hypercapneic alkalosis.

P: 1. Continue present ventilator settings until alkalosis corrected. Then will blow off more CO_2.
2. Diamox.
3. Probable D/C cardioversion next week if atrial fib persists.
4. Increase free water and KCL (IV changed to D5W with KCL).
5. Continue antibiotics and pulmonary toilet.
6. Increase calories now that we have Diamox.

Type of Service: _____

Level of History: _____

Level of Exam: _____

Level of Medical Decision Making: _____

CPT® code: _____

5. **Office Consult**

Chief Complaint

Referred by Dr. Smith for evaluation and management of recurrent right costal margin pain from about the mid-clavicular line to the midline. Recurred four to five weeks ago. Pain daily. Tends to vomit if she eats much, so she hasn't been eating well. Describes the pain as "just a continuous pain. Sometimes it doubles me up. It goes through to my back." She has had an extremely thorough evaluation for right upper quadrant pain in the past. I refer the interested reader to my exhaustive 11/4/03 evaluation. Her last study and treatment was ERCP with sphincterotomy 11/7/03. Recurrence of pain suggests that this procedure was a failure. While this is most likely due to the fact that pain is not related to sphincter of Oddi dysfunction, it is not entirely out of the question that sphincterotomy might have been inadequate or that she might have had scarring of the sphincterotomy site. 24-hour urine for quantitative porphyrins on 11/5/03 revealed trivial elevation of coproporphyrins. I have not seen her since 12/10/03.

She took a week off from work because of pain, and since then she has missed parts of some days because of pain. She does not know what pain pills she is taking, but she takes 3 to 4 per day of them and notes that if the pain is real bad, she is allowed to double up on her pills. She notes that when she vomits, pain is worse, and "it seems to be sharper."

For the past several weeks at least she has had dizziness. This is probably a vertigo because it bothers her when she lies flat in bed and also when she rolls over in bed. Her head has been hurting all of the time, "but it's not like a headache." Light bothers her at times. She has been on meclizine 25 mg pills two 4 x a day without much improvement.

Allergies

Probably none, but she carries a diagnosis of allergies to sulfa and Tylenol #3.

Medications

Meclizine 25 mg pills 2 q.i.d. and two medicines, the names of which she doesn't know.

Physical Exam

Chest clear. Heart unremarkable. Abdomen manifests a midline scar from about the mid-epigastrium down to the pubis. Extending across the lower RUQ is a horizontal scar that reaches to the midline and extending across both lowermost abdominal regions are scars that either reach or nearly reach the midline suprapubically. There appears to be a small hernia through the medial aspect of the horizontal RUQ scar. I cannot feel liver, spleen, or masses. There is mild to moderate tenderness in the right medial epigastrium. This is quite localized. I cannot feel a clear-cut defect. There is no tenderness along the rib margin in this region. There is still some tenderness in this area when rectus muscles are tensed by elevating the lower extremities off the bed with the patient in the supine position. However, this is less than when the abdomen is soft. I can create tenderness by pushing both downwards and upwards underneath the rib margin, and I think that this tenderness is coming from abdominal wall structures rather than from something within the abdomen.

Impression

1. Recurrent right medial epigastric pain of four to five weeks duration, etiology uncertain. This pain may well be of abdominal wall origin. She may have a trigger point in the right medial epigastic region. Another possibility is that she might have a small midline hernia, although I doubt that.
2. Small incisional hernia, medial lower RUQ.
3. Vertigo of a number of weeks duration, etiology uncertain. There is some associated headache.

Recommendations

CBC, sed rate, chemistry panel, amylase. Referral to anesthesiology for consideration of injection therapy directed at right medial epigastric region. They may call me if there are any concerns as to the exact area that I think her pain is coming from. Referral to neurologist. Will try to get her in to see Dr. A. Letter to Dr. Smith informing him of my recommendations.

Type of Service: _____

Level of History: _____

Level of Exam: _____

Level of Medical Decision Making: _____

CPT® code: _____

Anesthesia

OBJECTIVES

1. Correctly assign anesthesia codes according to AMA and ASA guidelines.
2. Identify situations in which anesthesia codes are not appropriate.
3. Calculate anesthesia fees correctly with a given formula.
4. Understand the difference between conscious sedation and Monitored Anesthesia Care.

TERMINOLOGY AND ACRONYMS

E-stim   Electrical stimulation.

ET tube   Endotracheal tube.

Endotracheal intubation   Insertion of an endotracheal tube between the vocal cords to establish an airway.

PCA   Patient Controlled Analgesia.

TENS   Transcutaneous Electrical Nerve Stimulator.

INTRODUCTION

The purpose of anesthesia is to provide pain relief to patients, whether for surgical procedures or for acute or chronic pain. Modern advances in pharmacology and technology have refined ancient techniques of acupuncture and herbal medicine to achieve an optimal balance of pain-free recovery with few side effects. Because of the emphasis on powerful drugs, anesthesia providers must be highly trained in pharmacology and human physiology. In addition, anesthesia providers who are responsible for all of the metabolic functions of the patient carefully monitor those receiving any type of anesthesia. Metabolic functions include ventilation of the patient, monitoring inhaled/exhaled gases, and administration of intravenous fluids, blood transfusions, and medications.

Anesthesiologists or Certified Registered Nurse Anesthetists (CRNAs) provide anesthesia. Either profession may administer anesthetics within the scope of its state regulations. Either the hospital or the anesthesiologist group employs many anesthetists in large hospitals. In rural settings or small hospitals, it is more common to see CRNAs working independently of an anesthesiologist. Anesthesiologists belong to the American Society of Anesthesiologists, which publishes two resource books used by anesthesia coders. *The Relative Value Guide* is a small condensed version of the anesthesia CPT®

codes containing anesthesia code descriptors, modifiers, and base units. *The Anesthesia Crosswalk* is a larger, full-scale version of the surgical CPT® codes with a crosswalk to the correct anesthesia CPT® and corresponding base units.

The ASA also publishes sample templates of anesthesia records to be used in the operating room. A sample is shown in Figure 5.1 for reference.

TYPES OF ANESTHESIA

In preparation for routine or scheduled surgery, patients are always queried about their anesthesia preference. The anesthesia provider takes this information into consideration along with the patient's age, physical condition, and previous responses to anesthesia, as well as the current illness. The anesthesia provider advises the patient, and together it is decided what type of anesthesia is best for the procedure and circumstances.

There are four primary types of anesthesia:

- Local
- General
- Regional (spinal and epidurals)
- Peripheral nerve blocks

Local Anesthesia

Local anesthesia consists of short acting "caine" type of anesthetics, such as nesacaine, xylocaine, and bupivicaine, which are injected into the skin or nerves of a small area to produce what is known as a *field block*. Local anesthetics are commonly used for outpatient procedures such as breast biopsies, hernia repairs, vasectomies, and skin grafting. The patient has little residual effects from the anesthetic and is quickly ambulating.

Formula for Success

CPT® surgery guidelines state that "local infiltration, metacarpal/metatarsal/digital block or topical anesthesia" is included in a surgical code and cannot be coded separately.

General Anesthesia

General anesthetics render a patient completely unconscious. Until the 1970s, general anesthesia most often meant only inhalation anesthesia. Modern anesthesia methods include a combination of gas, sedative/hypnotics, narcotics, tranquilizers, antiemetics, amnesics, and muscle relaxants. The patient is monitored very closely for any complications using heart monitor, temperature probe, pulse oximetry, and gas exchange monitoring equipment. The goal is to have a smooth induction, uncomplicated intraoperative course, and smooth emergence from anesthesia. Reversal agents are used at the end of surgery to help the patient quickly recover. These include drugs such as Narcan, which reverses the effects of narcotics, and neostigmine, which reverses muscle relaxants. The type of procedure determines the "depth" of anesthesia required. Patient recall, or memory of any part of the surgical procedure, is a constant concern for the anesthesia provider. There are

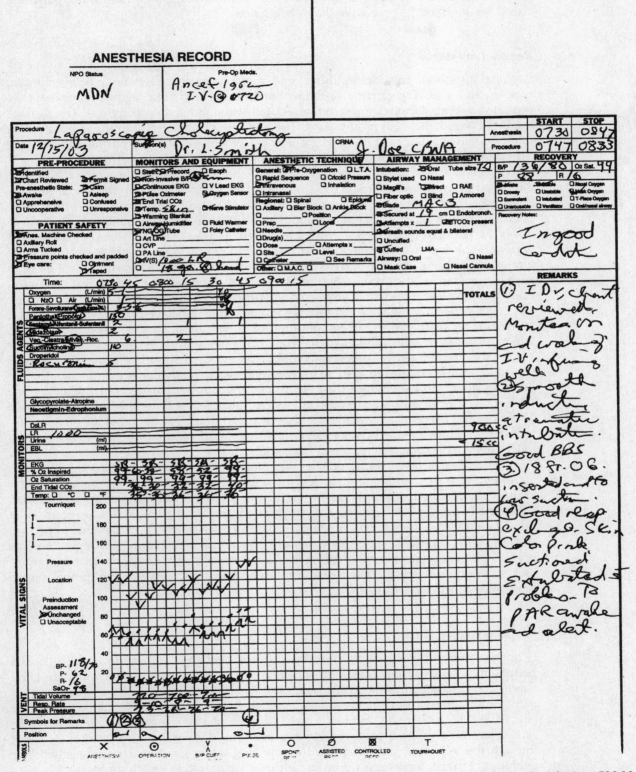

Figure 5–1 Anesthesia record. *Reprinted with permission of the American Society of Anesthesiologists, 520 N. Northwest Highway, Park Ridge, Illinois 60068-2573.*

multiple tests that are performed prior to the start of surgery to ensure the patient is "deep" enough for the procedure that is being done.

Regional Anesthesia

Regional anesthesia includes epidurals and spinals for procedures done below the diaphragm and also IV regionals for the extremities. Patients with regional anesthesia are typically awake, although most often sedated throughout the procedure. The "caine" family of anesthetics is typically used. The addition of narcotics into the regional anesthetic provides better postoperative pain management, while epinephrine added to the drug solution will help lengthen the effective time of short-acting anesthetics.

Epidural anesthesia is different from spinal anesthesia because of where the drug is deposited in the spinal column. The epidural space is separated from the spinal fluid by the dura, a heavy, tough covering protecting the spinal column. Drugs deposited in the epidural space reach the same nerve endings as spinal anesthetics, but larger volumes of drugs are required. A small test dose of anesthetic is always administered to the patient with epinephrine. A rapid rise in heart rate and blood pressure would indicate that the wrong area is being injected, such as directly into a blood vessel or into the spinal fluid. In such circumstances, the needle is withdrawn until the appropriate space is reached. Injection into the spinal fluid with a large epidural dose would kill a patient.

Spinal anesthetics are injected through a much smaller needle than epidurals, using a much smaller drug dose. One complication of spinal anesthetics is a spinal headache, which is caused by spinal fluid leaking from a hole in the dura. When a patient stands or sits for the first time after surgery, a combination of gravity and less spinal fluid causes traction on the brain, resulting in an excruciating headache that goes away when the patient lies down. To correct this, the hole in the dura can be "patched" by taking a small tube of blood from the patient's arm and re-injecting a few ccs into the same needle tract. This clots and prevents any further leakage of spinal fluid. Spinal and epidural anesthetics last for approximately the same amount of time; however, continuous infusions are no longer done with spinals due to complications.

Intravenous regional blocks, such as Bier blocks, are used on extremities. An IV with anesthetic is started in the arm or leg. An esmarch bandage is then wrapped tightly around the elevated extremity beginning at the fingers or toes and toward the heart. When the extremity has been fully exsanguinated, the distal part of the tourniquet is let down, and the IV is turned on, allowing the blood vessels below the tourniquet to perfuse the limb with anesthetic. Once the extremity is numb, the procedure can begin. Patients normally become uncomfortable from the inflated tourniquet after approximately 90 minutes, so this type of anesthesia is used on shorter procedures, such as carpal tunnel release or simple reduction of fractures.

Peripheral Nerve Blocks

Peripheral nerve blocks involve the injection of anesthetic alongside a nerve in the peripheral nervous system (meaning outside of the spinal column). Therefore, peripheral nerves can be blocked in the arms, legs, ribs, and facial areas. In order to achieve good pain control, at least three nerves must be blocked. Nerve stimulators are placed on the patient, and the anesthesia provider slowly advances the needle until the stimulator indicates placement is close to the desired nerve. The patient remains awake and alert through the following surgical procedure, making this a good choice of anesthetic for people at high risk for complications or for those with complex health problems.

Example: A patient with severe congestive heart failure is unable to tolerate general anesthetic for a fractured ankle. An ankle block is placed and the fracture is reduced.

EXERCISE 5.1

Instructions: Using the types of anesthesia listed in bold at the bottom of this exercise, determine what type of anesthesia is being administered.

1. A 22-year-old female in active labor is injected with Marcaine into the epidural space and set up for a continuous drip. _____

2. A patient with carpal tunnel syndrome is scheduled for a carpal tunnel release using a Bier block anesthetic. _____

3. Anesthetic is injected into the abdominal skin prior to skin grafting. _____

4. An axillary block is placed prior to reduction of a fractured elbow. _____

5. A patient requests to be awake for a hip replacement. Anesthetic is injected into the spinal fluid. _____

6. A 2-year-old child is scheduled for open-heart surgery. The anesthesia provider discusses inhalation anesthesia and the use of multiple drugs during the case. _____

Regional—epidural	**Regional—spinal**	**Regional—IV**
General	**Local**	**Nerve block**

PAIN MANAGEMENT

A fast growing subspecialty of anesthesia is pain management. Either chronic or acute postoperative pain can be addressed on both an outpatient and inpatient basis. Chronic pain is defined as pain that lasts a minimum of three to six months. Nerve blocks are coded from the 64400–64530 code range of CPT®. In order to code a nerve block correctly, the coder must know whether the nerve is a somatic or sympathetic nerve. If the coder cannot determine what type of nerve is being blocked, the provider should give clarification to assist with the coding process. Modifier 50 must be used if the nerve is blocked bilaterally. These codes are used to describe facet joint or facet nerve injections in the vertebral column, nerve blocks, and continuous epidurals. When coding for vertebral injections, the coder should be watchful for the level of injection, as these codes are differentiated by cervical/thoracic or lumbar/sacral levels. Add-on codes are available for additional levels.

Trigger point injections are also used for pain management. A trigger point is a painful area of irritated nerve endings. Trigger points can be caused by stress, trauma, overuse, underuse, or other problems and may lead to chronic pain in that area. Common locations of trigger points include the head, neck, shoulders, and back. Codes 20552 (one or two muscles) and 20553 (three or more muscles) are used for trigger point injections. The provider should document how many muscle groups are being injected. The CPT® descriptor for both of these codes specifies "single or multiple trigger point(s)" for each muscle, so more than one needle stick may be performed on a particular muscle. Drugs that are injected should also be coded separately using HCPCS codes.

Example: A patient with chronic right shoulder pain came in for trigger point injection. One cc of 1.5% Xylocaine was injected, along with 20 mg of Kenalog. Three injections were done in the right trapezius muscle.

Codes assigned:

ICD-9-CM diagnosis code: 719.41

CPT® procedure code: 20552

HCPCS supply code: J3301 × 2 for Kenalog. The local anesthetic is not coded.

Postoperative pain management is most often accomplished by the use of **PCA,** or Patient Controlled Analgesia. This allows the patient to administer his or her own pain medications on an "as needed" basis. Patients are able to mobilize faster when they can control their own pain medication, so this system saves time and money and adds to the recovery process. The PCA pump is loaded with a predetermined amount of medication with a lock-out rate calculated to prevent an overdose. Two services are provided with PCAs: the initial setup and daily management. The initial setup for a continuous infusion is coded with 62318 for cervical or thoracic epidurals or 62319 for lumbar/sacral epidurals. CPT® directs the coder to use E/M service codes for daily administration. Code 01996 should be used for daily *hospital* management of an epidural or subarchnoid catheter placed for the surgical procedure, but also used for postoperative pain management.

Acupuncture is assigned to codes 97780 and 97781, regardless of the number of needles inserted. Use 97780 for acupuncture without electrical stimulation and 97881 when electrical stimulation is applied to the needles.

Formula for Success

Insurance companies differ considerably in their recognition of pain management coding. Be sure to check with individual payers for their reporting requirements.

CODING ANESTHESIA SERVICES

Anesthesia services that are provided preoperatively and postoperatively are bundled into the global anesthesia code. This includes services such as preoperative and postoperative visits and the intraoperative portion. Anesthesia services include the usual preoperative and postoperative visits, anesthesia care during the procedure, administration of fluids and/or blood, and the usual monitoring services, such as EKG, temperature, blood pressure, oximetry, capnography, and mass spectrometry.

Coding begins with the anesthesia record. The anesthesia record is a source document for everything that occurred to the patient during the preoperative, intraoperative, and immediate postoperative period. The graphic portion of the anesthesia record allows vital signs to be reported in regular 5-minute increments. A standard method of graphing vital signs is used across the United States. Up and down arrows (▲▼) document blood pressure; circles are used for respiration; and dots or bullets are used for pulse rate. Anesthesia times that are documented on the anesthesia record are important for several reasons. They accurately reflect when medications and fluids are given, as well as when vital signs are recorded. The anesthesia provider documents the anesthetic start and stop times and also the surgeon's start and stop times. This is important for reimbursement, as well as for documentation purposes.

CPT® reports that unusual forms of monitoring, such as with Swan-Ganz catheters or central venous pressure lines, are not included in the anesthesia times. These large-bore lines are typically placed preoperatively for complicated surgical cases. Other separately billable services provided by anesthesia staff can include difficult IV starts, emergency intubation or resuscitation, pain management, and labor epidurals. Smaller services such as these are often missed for professional billing because they are not attached to a surgical procedure.

Correct anesthesia coding and billing is dependent upon correct ICD-9 diagnosis and surgical CPT® code assignment. *The Anesthesia Crosswalk* uses the surgeon's CPT® code and crosswalks it to the appropriate anesthesia code (see Figure 5.2). Both the surgeon and the anesthesia provider should use the same surgical CPT® code(s). Each anesthesia code is assigned a base unit value; therefore, an incorrect CPT® code may lead to inappropriate reimbursement.

EXERCISE 5.2

Instructions: Using the anesthesia record from Figure 5.1, find and record the following information below:

1. Anesthesia start and stop times _____

2. Name of the operative procedure _____

3. Surgery start and stop times _____

4. Anesthetic technique _____

Anesthesia Modifiers

Anesthesia coding and billing requires the use of modifiers and add-on codes to correctly identify who provided anesthesia services and the risk to the patient. There are three distinct types of modifiers used on anesthesia codes: physical status modifiers, CPT® modifiers, and HCPCS modifiers. Add-on codes known as "Qualifying Circumstances" supply extra information about the events surrounding the surgical procedure.

Physical Status Modifiers

These modifiers are appended to the anesthesia code to distinguish among the various levels of complexity of the anesthesia services provided. The letter "P" and a single digit distinguish the physical status anesthesia modifier from a HCPCS modifier. These modifiers are listed in the anesthesia guidelines in the CPT® book. The American Society of Anesthesiologists assigns additional reimbursement units to each modifier, which affects the calculation of anesthesia fees.

P1 A normal healthy patient—0 units

P2 A patient with mild systemic disease—0 units

P3 A patient with severe systemic disease—1 unit

P4 A patient with severe systemic disease that is a constant threat to life—2 units

P5 A moribund patient who is not expected to survive without the operation—3 units

P6 A declared brain-dead patient whose organs are being removed for donor purposes—0 units

Example: 00210-P3 Anesthesia for intracranial procedures, not otherwise specified. Patient is a 60-year-old male with a primary brain neoplasm, who also has severe congestive heart failure and brittle diabetes.

CPT-4 Proc Code	ASA RVG Code	Unit Value	Anesthesia Descriptor *Procedure Descriptor (CPT-4)*	47400–47570
47400	00790	7+TM	Anesthesia for intraperitoneal procedures in upper abdomen including laparoscopy; not otherwise specified. *Hepaticotomy or hepaticostomy with exploration, drainage, or removal of calculus*	
47420	00790	7+TM	Anesthesia for intraperitoneal procedures in upper abdomen including laparoscopy; not otherwise specified. *Choledochotomy or choledochostomy with exploration, drainage, or removal of calculus, with or without cholecystotomy; without transduodenal sphincterotomy or sphincteroplasty*	
47425	00790	7+TM	Anesthesia for intraperitoneal procedures in upper abdomen including laparoscopy; not otherwise specified. *Choledochotomy or choledochostomy with exploration, drainage, or removal of calculus, with or without cholecystotomy; with transduodenal sphincterotomy or sphincteroplasty*	
47460	00790	7+TM	Anesthesia for intraperitoneal procedures in upper abdomen including laparoscopy; not otherwise specified. *Transduodenal sphincterotomy or sphincteroplasty, with or without transduodenal extraction of calculus (separate procedure)*	
47480	00790	7+TM	Anesthesia for intraperitoneal procedures in upper abdomen including laparoscopy; not otherwise specified. *Cholecystotomy or cholecystostomy with exploration, drainage, or removal of calculus (separate procedure)*	
47490	00702	4+TM	Anesthesia for procedures on upper anterior abdominal wall; percutaneous liver biopsy. *Percutaneous cholecystostomy* Alternate(s): 00700	
47500	00702	4+TM	Anesthesia for procedures on upper anterior abdominal wall; percutaneous liver biopsy. *Injection procedure for percutaneous transhepatic cholangiography* Alternate(s): 00700	
47505	00700	4+TM	Anesthesia for procedures on upper anterior abdominal wall; not otherwise specified. *Injection procedure for cholangiography through an existing catheter (eg, percutaneous transhepatic or T-tube)*	
47510	00702	4+TM	Anesthesia for procedures on upper anterior abdominal wall; percutaneous liver biopsy. *Introduction of percutaneous transhepatic catheter for biliary drainage* Alternate(s): 00700	
47511	00702	4+TM	Anesthesia for procedures on upper anterior abdominal wall; percutaneous liver biopsy. *Introduction of percutaneous transhepatic stent for internal and external biliary drainage* Alternate(s): 00700	
47525	00700	4+TM	Anesthesia for procedures on upper anterior abdominal wall; not otherwise specified. *Change of percutaneous biliary drainage catheter*	
47530	00700	4+TM	Anesthesia for procedures on upper anterior abdominal wall; not otherwise specified. *Revision and/or reinsertion of transhepatic tube*	
47550			*** NOT A PRIMARY PROCEDURE CODE ***. *Biliary endoscopy, intraoperative (choledochoscopy) (List separately in addition to code for primary procedure)*	
47552	00700	4+TM	Anesthesia for procedures on upper anterior abdominal wall; not otherwise specified. *Biliary endoscopy, percutaneous via T-tube or other tract; diagnostic, with or without collection of specimen(s) by brushing and/or washing (separate procedure)*	
47553	00740	5+TM	Anesthesia for upper gastrointestinal endoscopic procedures, endoscope introduced proximal to duodenum. *Biliary endoscopy, percutaneous via T-tube or other tract; with biopsy, single or multiple*	
47554	00740	5+TM	Anesthesia for upper gastrointestinal endoscopic procedures, endoscope introduced proximal to duodenum. *Biliary endoscopy, percutaneous via T-tube or other tract; with removal of calculus/calculi*	
47555	00740	5+TM	Anesthesia for upper gastrointestinal endoscopic procedures, endoscope introduced proximal to duodenum. *Biliary endoscopy, percutaneous via T-tube or other tract; with dilation of biliary duct stricture(s) without stent*	
47556	00740	5+TM	Anesthesia for upper gastrointestinal endoscopic procedures, endoscope introduced proximal to duodenum. *Biliary endoscopy, percutaneous via T-tube or other tract; with dilation of biliary duct stricture(s) with stent*	
47560	00790	7+TM	Anesthesia for intraperitoneal procedures in upper abdomen including laparoscopy; not otherwise specified. *Laparoscopy, surgical; with guided transhepatic cholangiography, without biopsy*	
47561	00790	7+TM	Anesthesia for intraperitoneal procedures in upper abdomen including laparoscopy; not otherwise specified. *Laparoscopy, surgical; with guided transhepatic cholangiography with biopsy*	
47562	00790	7+TM	Anesthesia for intraperitoneal procedures in upper abdomen including laparoscopy; not otherwise specified. *Laparoscopy, surgical; cholecystectomy*	
47563	00790	7+TM	Anesthesia for intraperitoneal procedures in upper abdomen including laparoscopy; not otherwise specified. *Laparoscopy, surgical; cholecystectomy with cholangiography*	
47564	00790	7+TM	Anesthesia for intraperitoneal procedures in upper abdomen including laparoscopy; not otherwise specified. *Laparoscopy, surgical; cholecystectomy with exploration of common duct*	
47570	00790	7+TM	Anesthesia for intraperitoneal procedures in upper abdomen including laparoscopy; not otherwise specified. *Laparoscopy, surgical; cholecystoenterostomy*	

Figure 5–2   Anesthesia crosswalk. *Reprinted with permission of the American Society of Anesthesiologists, 520 N. Northwest Highway, Park Ridge, Illinois 60068-2573.*

Qualifying Circumstances. Add-on codes are available to describe extenuating circumstances and unusual risk factors for anesthesia services. These codes do not stand alone, but are reported in addition to the anesthesia code. Each carries the following instruction from CPT®: "List separately in addition to code for primary anesthesia procedure."

Formula for Success

Some payers, including Medicare, do not recognize qualifying circumstances, so it is best to check with the payer before reporting.

Similar to the physical status modifiers, additional reimbursement units are assigned to each Qualifying Circumstance code.

+99100   Anesthesia for patient of extreme age, under 1 year and over 70—1 unit
+99116   Anesthesia complicated by utilization of total body hypothermia—5 units
+99135   Anesthesia complicated by utilization of controlled hypotension—5 units
+99140   Anesthesia complicated by emergency conditions—2 units

Example: A patient was brought into the emergency department after falling off a roof and sustaining internal injuries along with fractures. He was taken directly to surgery, where a "crash induction" was performed due to a full stomach. Qualifying circumstance code 99140 would be appended for the additional services provided.

CPT® Modifiers

Some CPT® modifiers may be appropriate for use with anesthesia services, such as:

22   Unusual Procedural Services
23   Unusual Anesthesia
32   Mandated Services
51   Multiple Services
53   Discontinued Procedure
59   Distinct Procedural Service

These modifiers are added onto the anesthesia chapter CPT® code, not the qualifying circumstance codes.

HCPCS Modifiers

These modifiers are found in the HCPCS code book and identify who provided the service. The HCPCS modifier should always be sequenced first. The following modifiers are excerpts from the HCPCS codebook:

AA   Anesthesia service performed personally by anesthesiologist
AD   Medical supervision by a physician: more than four concurrent anesthesia procedures
G8   Monitored anesthesia care (MAC) for deep complex, complicated, or markedly invasive surgical procedure
G9   Monitored anesthesia care or patient who has history of severe cardiopulmonary condition

QB   Physician providing service in a rural HPSA

QK   Medical direction of two, three, or four concurrent anesthesia procedures involving qualified individuals

QS   Monitored anesthesia care service (MAC)

QU   Physician providing service in an urban HPSA

QX   Certified registered nurse anesthetist (CRNA) service, with medical direction by a physician

QY   Medical direction of one certified registered nurse anesthetist (CRNA) by an anesthesiologist

QZ   CRNA service: Without medical direction by a physician

It is important for the coder to recognize how the presence of these modifiers affects reimbursement.

EXERCISE 5.3

Instructions: Match the appropriate modifier or qualifying circumstance code to the description of the procedure. More than one modifier may apply. Do not assign anesthesia CPT® codes. Key terms are underlined.

1. <u>Brain dead</u> patient taken to surgery for organ harvesting, by <u>medically directed CRNA</u>   _____

2. <u>Healthy</u> 4-year-old scheduled for hernia repair   _____

3. <u>Healthy</u> 2-year-old brought in for dental restorations—<u>unable to cooperate in office</u>   _____

4. Patient with <u>mild lupus</u> scheduled for tubal ligation   _____

5. <u>Emergency</u> appendectomy performed by <u>CRNA working independently</u>   _____

6. <u>MAC</u> provided for patient undergoing EGD   _____

7. Anesthesia for hip replacement, <u>administered by anesthesiologist</u>   _____

8. Coronary artery bypass graft with saline slush for <u>cold</u> cardioplegia, by <u>solo CRNA</u>   _____

Conscious Sedation and Monitored Anesthesia Care

A distinction must be made between conscious sedation and MAC, which almost appear to be the same service. The surgeon administers conscious sedation. This is useful for procedures in which the patient must cooperate with the surgeon, such as during a colonoscopy. In order to use the conscious sedation codes, the physician must delegate one person exclusively to monitor and document the condition of the patient throughout the duration of the procedure, similar to anesthesia professionals. Codes 99141 and 99142 for conscious sedation are found in the medicine chapter of CPT® and typically are not used by anesthesia professionals.

Monitored Anesthesia Care (MAC) involves the services of an anesthesia professional to monitor a sedated patient. Under the Medicare Conditions of Participation, MAC services require documentation of the following:

■ A request for monitored anesthesia care by the attending physician.

■ Performance of a preanesthetic examination and evaluation.

■ Prescription of the anesthesia care required.

■ Personal participation in, or medical direction of, the entire plan of care.

■ Continuous physical presence of anesthesiologist or CRNA.

■ Presence or availability of the anesthesiologist for diagnosis or treatment of emergencies.

■ Usual noninvasive cardiocirculatory and respiratory monitoring.

■ Oxygen administration, when indicated.

■ Intravenous administration of sedatives, tranquilizers, and other pharmacologic therapy as may be required in the judgment of the anesthesiologist or CRNA.

CALCULATING ANESTHESIA REIMBURSEMENT

Anesthesia fees vary in each geographic region of the United States. The purpose of this section is to introduce the student to the basic method of calculating anesthesia reimbursement. Third-party payers and Medicare carriers should be checked prior to claim submission for individual billing requirements.

Calculation of anesthesia reimbursement is based on units of time. A unit may be as much as 15 minutes or as little as 10 minutes. Each increment of 15 minutes is assigned one unit. Most insurance companies and Medicare recognize a unit as 15 minutes. The dollar value, or conversion factor of a single unit, varies across the United States and from payer to payer. A unit can be worth as little as $16.00, or as much as $100.00. Time units, along with the number of base units assigned to each anesthesia code, are added together. Additional units are assigned to each modifier. Base units are arrived at by crosswalking the CPT® surgical code to the anesthesia code in the ASA crosswalk, or by using the RVU Guide. Thus, the basic formula for anesthesia reimbursement begins as:

Base + Time + Modifiers = Total Units

The total number of units is multiplied by the conversion factor to arrive at the anesthesia fee. The second half of the equation is:

Total Units × Conversion Factor = Anesthesia fee

Example: A 2-hour (120 minute or 8 time units) emergency laparoscopic surgery is performed on a 35-year-old woman for an ectopic tubal pregnancy. The involved fallopian tube was removed. She was a Physical Status P2 and had no other complications during surgery. The conversion factor is $50.00. The following codes were submitted following her procedure:

ICD-9-CM Diagnosis code: 633.10

CPT® Code: 59151

Anesthesia Code: 00840

Formula:

6 Base Units + 8 Time Units + 0 Physical Status Units + 2 Units for Qualifying
Circumstances (Emergency Condition) = 16 Total Units

16 × $50.00 = $800.00 Anesthesia fee

Individual payers should be queried as to how and where they want time reported on the claim form, and how they want multiple surgeries to be reported.

CHAPTER REVIEW

Instructions: Using the anesthesia record in Figure 5.1, along with the reprint of the ASA Crosswalk in Figure 5.2, and surgical operative note (below), determine the following:

Part I

a. Surgical CPT® code: _____
b. Anesthesia CPT® code: _____
c. Number of <u>base</u> units (Crosswalk):   _____
d. Total Anesthesia time: _____
e. Number of <u>Time</u> units (15 min increments):   _____
f. Physical Status modifier and units: _____
g. Qualifying Circumstance modifier and units: _____
h. CPT® modifier: _____
i. HCPCS modifier: _____

Anesthesia Preoperative Evaluation

The patient is a 45-year-old male with well-controlled diabetes mellitus. He does not smoke. No history of illicit drug use; no use of herbal medicines. No ephedrine use or family history of malignant hyperthermia. Weight is 175 lbs. No problems with teeth or jaw clicking. The patient does have a somewhat short neck.

Preoperative Diagnosis

Cholelithiasis with cholecystitis.

Postoperative Diagnosis

Cholelithiasis with cholecystitis.

Procedure

Laparoscopic cholecystectomy.

Anesthesia

General, by John Doe, CRNA. Not medically directed by anesthesiologist.

The patient was placed in the supine position on the OR table. General endotracheal anesthesia was administered. The abdomen was prepped and draped in sterile fashion. An umbilical incision was made. An open technique was used to insert a 10 mm trocar. Insufflation was then performed. The remaining three trocars were inserted in the right upper quadrant. The gallbladder was grasped and retracted cephalad. The cystic artery was identified, doubly clipped and divided. The gallbladder was retrieved using an Endo Catch bag. The right upper quadrant was irrigated and suctioned. There was good hemostasis. The trocars were removed and the insufflation was released. The incisions were all infiltrated with lidocaine and marcaine. The fascial incisions were closed with 0 Vicryl suture. The skin incisions were closed with 4-0 Vicryl subcuticular suture.

The patient tolerated the procedure well and was transported to the recovery room in stable condition.

Counts

All needle, sponge, and instrument counts were correct.

Part II

1. Using a conversion factor of $20.00, calculate the anesthesia fee for the above procedure:

Base _____ + Time _____ + Modifiers _____ =
Total Number of Units _____ × $20.00 = $_____.

2. Determine the correct ICD-9-CM diagnosis code for the procedure: _____

True/False Questions

1. The surgeon's diagnosis should be different from the diagnosis submitted by anesthesia.   **True/False**

2. CRNAs are required to report a HCPCS modifier.   **True/False**

3. A surgeon can use the conscious sedation codes if he or she sedates the patient but does not have anyone monitor vital signs.   **True/False**

Multiple Choice

Instructions: Choose the best answer for the scenario given.

1. Anesthesia codes are not reportable for
   a. Field blocks
   b. Digital blocks
   c. General anesthesia
   d. Spinal or epidural anesthesia

2. A patient came in to the pain clinic for trigger point injections of one muscle in her neck. The correct code(s) for this procedure is/are:
   a. 64413
   b. 64412
   c. 20550
   d. 20552

CHAPTER

6

Overview: The Surgery Section of CPT®

OBJECTIVES

1. Identify CPT® chapter arrangement.
2. Recognize the difference between diagnostic and therapeutic services.
3. State the basic concept of the Correct Coding Initiative.
4. Differentiate between bundling and unbundling.
5. Comprehend the concept of the surgical package, global periods, and associated modifiers.
6. Define unlisted and separate procedures.
7. Differentiate between add-on codes and Modifier 51 exempt codes.

TERMINOLOGY AND ACRONYMS

CPT® modifier   A two-digit numerical modifier added to the end of a CPT code that provides additional information about the procedure.

Global period   The time frame associated with a global package.

HCPCS modifier   Two-digit alpha or alphanumeric modifier added to the end of a CPT or HCPCS code. Originally intended only for Medicare.

Surgical package   The preoperative, intraoperative, and postoperative services that are included together for a predetermined fee.

SURGERY SECTION GUIDELINES

The surgery guidelines of CPT® are found on the colored pages following the Anesthesia chapter, just prior to the Integumentary System chapter. The surgery guidelines are used as a brief introduction to the Surgery section and give some basic commonalities of the Surgery section as a whole. The Surgery section of CPT® is the largest section and covers codes from 10000–69990.

■■■ *CHAPTER ARRANGEMENT*

The surgical chapters of CPT® are in order numerically as follows:

10000–19499	Integumentary System
20000–29999	Musculoskeletal System
30000–32999	Respiratory System
33010–39599	Cardiovascular System, Hemic/Lymphatic Systems; Mediastinum/Diaphragm
40000–49999	Digestive System
50000–53899	Urinary System
54000–55980	Male Genital System
56405–58999	Female Genital System
59000–59899	Maternity Care and Delivery
60000–60699	Endocrine System
61000–64999	Nervous System
65091–68899	Eye and Ocular Adnexa
69000–69990	Auditory System

■■■ *DIAGNOSTIC VERSUS THERAPEUTIC SERVICES*

A diagnostic procedure is one in which no curative or restorative procedures are undertaken. Examples of diagnostic procedures include endoscopies, arthroscopies, and injection procedures for x-rays, lab tests, and radiology procedures. These include only care that is related to the diagnostic procedure itself. Therapeutic surgical procedures include treatment, which is usually part of the global package for that procedure. Any type of treatment for complications or recurrences that require additional services are reported separately with the appropriate modifier.

■■■ *CORRECT CODING INITIATIVE AND BUNDLING/UNBUNDLING*

The Correct Coding Initiative is a database of CPT® codes with interdependent relationships. It is a method of edits formulated by the AMA and CMS to standardize the inherent parts of a procedure and to ensure uniform reporting of procedures across the United States. When a procedure has many smaller procedures included in the whole, these parts are considered to be bundled into the definitive procedure. To unbundle is to report each part of the whole separately. This should always be avoided. There are certain circumstances in which bundled procedures may be reported on the same date, with the use of modifiers. However, with a few exceptions, they are not reported in the same operative session.

■■■ *SURGICAL PACKAGE AND GLOBAL PERIODS*

According to the CPT® surgery guidelines, the **surgical package** includes the following:

1. Local anesthesia, metacarpal/metatarsal/digital blocks, or topical anesthesia.
2. After the decision for surgery has been made, one related Evaluation and Management service is allowed on the day of or day before surgery.

3. Postoperative, post-anesthesia recovery care, the dictation of the operative notes, talking with the family or other physicians.
4. The written orders for any subsequent testing.
5. Routine postoperative follow-up.

The typical or routine postoperative follow-up care is what divides procedures into "minor" or "major" surgeries. Although the number of postoperative days can depend on the third-party payer, the most common are 0, 10, and 90 days. This time period is referred to as the **global period.** Therefore, minor procedures are those with a global of 0 to 10 days, and major procedures have a 90-day global period. When counting global days, the coder must count 90 calendar days, not three months or business days.

UNLISTED PROCEDURES

When reviewing CPT® codes, the coder will find that, occasionally, there is not a code available that is accurate enough to adequately describe a procedure. For this reason, there are *unlisted codes* found at the end of many of the sections in the CPT® book. Because there is no descriptor available, office notes or operative reports are often requested by the insuror for claims adjudication purposes. Unlisted codes typically do not have fees assigned, so providers must compare the relative amount of work involved with other similar procedures in order to establish a fee.

SEPARATE PROCEDURES

The term *separate procedure* is closely tied to the subject of bundling and unbundling. Many smaller procedures will have the phrase *(separate procedure)* found after the code descriptor. This signifies that this code can only be used when it is the only procedure performed and not in conjunction with a larger, more comprehensive procedure. Separate procedures are generally included in more extensive procedures performed on the same area of the body. They are not usually bundled into procedures from another body area; however, bundling software or CCI edits should be followed before use.

ADD-ON CODES AND MODIFIER 51 EXEMPT CODES

Add-on codes are marked with a "+" sign. As the name implies, they are an addition to another code. These codes are used to build onto the main code, whether in additional numbers or additional difficulty due to a repeat procedure. These codes *never* stand alone and care should be taken to see that these codes are not reported by themselves. The Relative Value Units (RVUs), and therefore fees, are already calculated to take into account their subsequent nature.

In contrast, Modifier 51 exempt codes are signified by a "Ø" sign. Codes identified with this can be reported alone. When these procedures are performed in addition to other procedures, they are never assigned a Modifier 51. The RVUs are already calculated in consideration of Modifier 51 exempt codes (see Modifier 51 explanation below).

CPT® MODIFIERS

CPT® modifiers and **HCPCS modifiers** are an important part of medical coding. Just as the name implies, they modify the codes in different ways. They help the provider communicate the story of the service to the third-party payers, as well as identify who provided the service. Modifiers can dramatically change the meaning and the reimbursement of the codes submitted for payment.

We have previously discussed where to find the modifiers in the CPT® book, now we will discuss what they are and how to use them.

21 Prolonged Evaluation and Management Services

This modifier signifies that the highest code within a category of E/M codes was exceeded. A fee for this service may be higher than that usually charged for that level. Not all insurance companies will recognize or pay accordingly for this modifier, including Medicare. Expect the payer to request supporting documentation when submitting claims with modifier 21.

> **Example:** A physician performed a comprehensive history and physical upon admitting a patient. Approximately two hours was spent counseling the patient regarding newly diagnosed neoplasm.
>
> CPT®: 99223-21

22 Unusual Procedural Services

This modifier should be used to show that a procedure was, for some reason, more complicated than the average procedure of that type. Use of this modifier justifies a higher fee, usually 125 percent for Medicare. Expect a request for supporting documentation from the payer. Medicare, as well as other insurance companies, requires a separate letter addressing the difficulty encountered during the procedure.

> **Example:** Due to extensive abdominal adhesions, it was very difficult and time consuming to complete an appendectomy.
>
> ICD-9-CM: 540.9 and 568.0
> CPT®: 44950-22

23 Unusual Anesthesia

This modifier identifies the use of general anesthesia for a procedure generally requiring either local or no anesthesia. Append this modifier to the anesthesia code.

> **Example:** Due to the patient's mental retardation, a pelvic exam was performed under anesthesia.
>
> Physician: ICD-9-CM: V72.31 and 319 linked to surgical CPT® code 57410
> Anesthesia: ICD-9-CM: V72.31 and 319 linked to anesthesia CPT® code 00940-23

24 Unrelated Evaluation and Management Service by the Same Physician during a Postoperative Period

This modifier identifies an E/M service (office visit, consult, etc.) provided for a different condition than the original surgical procedure by the same physician. The time frame must be within the global period of the surgery. A medical necessity link is essential when using this modifier to further emphasize the difference in the services provided.

> **Example:** The patient had appendicitis, ICD-9-CM code 540.9, and subsequently underwent an appendectomy. A week postoperatively, the patient had trouble with a diabetic ulcer of the ankle and required an evaluation for this condition.
>
> ICD-9-CM: 250.8x, 707.13, linked with CPT®: 99213-24.

25 Significant, Separately Identifiable Evaluation and Management Service by the Same Physician on the Same Day of the Procedure or Other Service

It is not uncommon for several problems to be addressed when a patient is seen by a physician. When a minor procedure (0 to 10 day global) is performed along with an Evaluation and Management service of any category, and that service meets all of the criteria for that level of service, Modifier 25 is appended to the E/M code. Care should be taken with this modifier. Documentation of the E/M services must be above and beyond the procedure performed.

> **Example:**   An established patient is seen in the office for acute bronchitis, ICD-9-CM diagnosis code 466.0. While the patient is being evaluated, the patient states that he is having difficulty hearing. Upon examination, he is found to have bilateral cerumen impaction, ICD-9-CM diagnosis code 380.4.
>
> ICD-9-CM: 466.0 linked with CPT® 99213-25
> ICD-9-CM: 380.4 linked with CPT® 69210

26 Professional Component

Some procedural services incorporate the special talents of two physicians. When one physician is required to read and interpret results, but did not actually run, prepare, or use any of his or her facility's equipment for the test, the professional services are reported with Modifier 26. Modifier TC is used on the same CPT® code to report the technical component for services rendered by the facility.

> **Example:**   A two-view chest X-ray is taken at a family practice clinic. Due to some abnormal-appearing shadows on the film, the X-ray is sent to the radiologist for her expert opinion and written report.
>
> Family practice physician: CPT®: 71020-TC
> Radiologist: CPT®: 71020-26

32 Mandated Services

This modifier identifies any service that has been required by a payer. The payer can be governmental, legislative, regulatory, employer, or insurance.

> **Example:**   A patient applies for disability benefits. He is required to have a basic life and disability exam to complete his application.
>
> ICD-9-CM: V70.3, linked with CPT® 99450-32

47 Anesthesia by Surgeon

This modifier is added to a procedure code when the general anesthesia is performed and monitored by the surgeon. This is not used for local routine anesthesia.

> **Example:**   A pregnant patient in labor at 6 cm dilation was brought into the Emergency Room. The OB physician on call placed the epidural and went on to deliver the baby precipitously, vaginally, before the patient could be moved to the Labor and Delivery ward.
>
> ICD-9-CM: 661.31 and V27.0, linked with CPT® 59409-47

50 Bilateral Procedure

This modifier is used to signify that two identical procedures have been performed on bilateral body parts. Care should be taken to make sure that the code descriptor is not inherently bilateral. When using this modifier, the fee should equal 150 percent of the usual fee for the code unilaterally.

> **Example:** An adult patient has a bilateral open inguinal hernia repairs performed.
>
> ICD-9-CM: 550.92, linked with CPT® 49505-50

51 Multiple Procedures

Within an operative session, when more that one procedure is performed by the same provider, Modifier 51 is appended to all secondary procedures. Routinely, Modifier 51 procedures are reimbursed at half of the usual fee schedule. Care should be taken not to use this modifier with the Modifier 51 exempt or add-on codes. The coder should ensure that the highest priced procedure is sequenced as primary, so the necessary fee reduction is not applied inappropriately.

> **Example:** The gastroenterologist performed an esophagogastroduodenoscopy for gastroesophageal reflux and a colonoscopy to screen for colon cancer.
>
> ICD-9-CM: V76.51, linked with CPT® 45378
> ICD-9-CM: 530.81, linked with CPT® 43235-51

52 Reduced Services

Occasionally, a service is partially reduced or eliminated, but still meets the requirements of the completed service, such as a bilateral procedure performed on only one side.

> **Example:** Due to a mastectomy of the right breast for breast cancer five years ago, a patient returns yearly for a screening mammogram of the left breast.
>
> ICD-9-CM: V76.12 and V10.3, linked to CPT® 76092-52-LT. Note: Modifier-LT is a HCPC modifier signifying the left side.

53 Discontinued Procedure

This modifier is used when the physician elects to terminate a procedure due to extenuating circumstances or a situation that threatens the life of the patient. Surgery notes may be requested by the payer, and the reimbursement may be reduced.

> **Example:** A physician has begun a screening colonoscopy when suddenly the patient goes into cardiac arrest.
>
> ICD-9-CM: V76.51, 997.1, V64.1, linked to CPT® 45378-53

54 Surgical Care Only

When the global period of a procedure (pre-op, intra-op and post-op portion) is broken down and provided by more than one physician, the surgeon who provides only the intraoperative portion of the service uses this modifier to report the surgical procedure. This modifier changes the reimbursement to 80 percent instead of 100 percent of the Medicare allowable. Third-party payers typically reduce this fee as well.

Example: An ophthalmologist who practices in a metropolitan area travels to a rural hospital to perform a cataract extraction on a patient. The patient has elected to follow-up with her local physician instead of traveling to see the surgeon for her postoperative visits.

ICD-9-CM: 366.16, linked with CPT® 66984-54

55 Postoperative Management Only

This modifier signifies that the physician providing postoperative care is different than the surgeon who performed the procedure. Modifier 55 changes the reimbursement to 20 percent of the Medicare allowable. Third-party payers typically reduce this fee also.

Example: Using the same scenario as the one given for the Modifier 54 example: The local physician reports the same CPT® code as the surgeon, with a modifier 55 attached.

ICD-9-CM: 366.16, linked with CPT® 66984-55.

56 Preoperative Management Only

This modifier signifies that the preoperative evaluation is performed by a physician different than the physician performing the surgery.

Example: A rural physician evaluates a patient for cataract surgery to be performed by a visiting ophthalmologist.

ICD-9-CM: V72.83, linked with CPT® 66984-56

57 Decision for Surgery

This modifier is appended to any E/M code resulting in the decision for major surgery, i.e., procedures with a 90-day global period.

Example: A patient is seen in the Emergency Room by a consulting surgeon for lower right abdominal pain. The diagnosis is appendicitis and the decision is made to operate immediately.

ICD-9-CM: 789.03, linked with CPT® 99242-57

58 Staged or Related Procedure or Service by the Same Physician during the Postoperative Period

This modifier is used to signify that the procedure was planned or staged based on the findings of the original procedure. Occasionally, a staged procedure occurs because of the need for more extensive treatment or therapy based on the findings of the original procedure.

Example: A female patient has an excisional breast biopsy performed. The results from pathology are breast cancer of the lower outer quadrant. The decision for a complete mastectomy is made, and the patient returns to the operating room within the week.

ICD-9-CM: 174.5, linked with CPT® 19180-58

59 Distinct Procedural Service

Known as the "unbundling modifier," this is a very important modifier to understand. Misuse of the Modifier 59 can be labeled as fraud. This is important because it represents a distinct or independent service performed on the same day as a procedure normally considered bundled. Legitimate situations for Modifier 59 include different operative sessions or encounters, different site or organ system, separate incision or excision, and different lesion or injury. Because of the nature of this modifier, many editing systems used by insurance companies will flag or deny codes with this modifier and request notes for claims that look out of the ordinary.

> **Example:**   The physician took a biopsy of a skin lesion on the arm, which proved to be actinic keratosis. He also did a cryodestruction of a common wart on the finger.
>
> ICD-9-CM: 702.0, linked with CPT® 11100, and 078.10, linked with CPT® 17000-51-59
>
> Note the use of the modifier 51 as well, designating the multiple procedure.

62 Two Surgeons

This is also referred to as co-surgery. Modifier 62 is used when two surgeons are both working as the primary surgeon. When the surgery can only be described by one code and two surgeons are working together, neither as an assistant to the other, this modifier is used. Because of the additional work involved, typically the fee is raised to 125 percent and divided equally between the two surgeons.

> **Example:**   A general surgeon is asked to establish the approach for an orthopedic surgeon performing a lumbar arthrodesis by anterior approach.
>
> General surgeon: ICD-9-CM: 722.10, linked with CPT® 22558-62
> Orthopedic surgeon: ICD-9-CM: 722.10, linked with CPT® 22558-62

63 Procedure Performed on Infant Less Than 4 kg

Due to the increased risk and complexity involved when operating on neonates and infants in this weight range, this modifier was added in 2003. Be aware when using this modifier of the directives for the intended code. This modifier is to be used for codes 20000–69999, unless otherwise stated, and is not to be used for any Evaluation and Management, Anesthesia, Radiology, Pathology/Laboratory, or Medicine codes.

> **Example:**   A premature neonate of 3 kg is in need of a feeding tube placed endoscopically for failure to thrive.
>
> ICD-9-CM: 783.41, linked with CPT® 43246-63

66 Surgical Team

Append Modifier 66 to highly complex procedures that require the services of several physicians working together as a team. Sometimes this may include different specialties, specially trained personnel, and a variety of equipment. Each surgeon appends 66 to the procedures that he or she performs.

> **Example:**   Separation of conjoined twins involving neurosurgery, orthopedics, plastic surgery, and pediatric thoracic surgery specialties.

76 Repeat Procedure by Same Physician

When the need arises to repeat a procedure subsequent to an original service, Modifier 76 is appended to the code. This avoids appearances of a duplicate claim when the same physician performs the repeat service.

Example: A patient is admitted into observation for the evaluation of chest pain to rule out a myocardial infarction. EKGs were ordered twice within three hours for the physician to interpret.

ICD-9-CM diagnosis: 786.50, linked with CPT® 93010

ICD-9-CM diagnosis: 786.50, linked with CPT® 93010-76

77 Repeat Procedure by Another Physician

When the need arises to repeat a procedure subsequent to the original procedure, append Modifier 77 to the code submitted by the second physician.

Example: A dialysis patient comes in for a thrombectomy for his arteriovenous fistula graft in the morning. While still in the hospital, the graft clots again and the physician on call takes the patient to the operating room and performs the same procedure again.

Dr A: ICD-9-CM: 996.73, linked with CPT® 36831

Dr B: ICD-9-CM: 996.73, linked with CPT® 36831-77

78 Return to the Operating Room for a Related Procedure during the Postoperative Period

Occasionally, it is necessary to perform a procedure during the postoperative period of another procedure. When the subsequent procedure is related to the original procedure and performed by the same physician, add this modifier to the subsequent procedure.

Example: A dialysis patient with chronic renal failure is in need of a hemodialysis access. An indirect arteriovenous fistula with a nonautologous graft is performed. A week later, the graft has clotted and the patient is back in the hospital. An open revision and thrombectomy are performed by the same surgeon.

First Surgery: ICD-9-CM: 585, linked with CPT® 36825

Second Surgery: ICD-9-CM: 996.73, linked with CPT® 36832-78

79 Unrelated Procedure or Service by the Same Physician during the Postoperative Period

When a surgery is performed in the postoperative period of an unrelated procedure, modifier 79 is appended to the second procedure.

Example: A patient has a laparoscopic cholecystectomy performed for cholelithiasis. One month later he is readmitted for lower right abdominal pain. The subsequent surgery performed is an open appendectomy due to a ruptured appendix.

First Surgery: ICD-9-CM: 574.20, linked with CPT® 47562

Second Surgery: ICD-9-CM: 540.0, linked with CPT® 44960-79

80 Assistant Surgeon

An assistant at surgery uses this modifier to report his or her services. The assistant assigns the same CPT® code(s) as the surgeon and is reimbursed at a reduced fee. For Medicare, reimbursement is typically 16 percent of the allowable, and for other third-party payers it is approximately 20 to 25 percent.

Example: A laparoscopic cholecystectomy performed for cholelithiasis.

Surgeon: ICD-9-CM: 574.20, linked with CPT® 47562

Assistant: ICD-9-CM: 574.20, linked with CPT® 47562-80

81 Minimum Assistant Surgeon

Sometimes a second assistant at surgery is needed. Although not covered by many payers, minimum assistant surgeon services are reported with this modifier.

Example: Using the scenario from modifier 80, the minimum assistant would report as follows:

ICD-9-CM: 574.20 linked with CPT® 47562-81

82 Assistant Surgeon (When Qualified Resident Surgeon Not Available)

When a qualified resident surgeon is unavailable, this modifier is appended to the procedure code selected.

Example: Using the scenario listed above, this assistant would report codes:

ICD-9-CM: 574.20, linked with CPT® 47562-82

90 Reference (Outside) Laboratory

Use this modifier appended to the laboratory CPT® codes when laboratory tests are not actually performed by the reporting physician's office.

Example: The family practice physician orders a complete automated blood count and differential to monitor the patient's anemia. This is sent to a local reference lab to be performed. When the attending physician submits the lab charges to the insurance company, the codes assigned are:

ICD-9-CM: 285.9, linked with CPT® 85025-90

91 Repeat Clinical Diagnostic Laboratory Test

Under certain circumstances, repeat laboratory tests may be performed on the same day. These procedures are reported with this modifier appended to the usual CPT® code. Modifier 91 is not to be used for tests rerun for confirmation or testing problems with the equipment or specimen. In addition, this modifier may not be used with CPT® codes that describe a series of results, such as glucose tolerance testing.

Example: A patient is seen in the office of his family practice physician for his anemia. A complete automated blood count with a differential is performed. The patient is found to still be anemic. After having a transfusion of one unit packed red cells, his blood count is performed again.

ICD-9-CM: 285.9, linked with CPT® 85025

ICD-9-CM: 285.9, linked with CPT® 85025-91

99 Multiple Modifiers

When two or more modifiers are necessary to report all of the conditions of a procedure, this modifier may be used in the space available next to the CPT® code.

Example: Cataract surgery is performed on the left eye. The left eye procedure is performed within the global period of the right eye. The surgeon performs the intraoperative portion of the surgical services only.

> ICD-9-CM: 366.16, linked with CPT® 66984-LT, 79, and 55
>
> *Reported as:* ICD-9-CM diagnosis: 366.16, linked with 66984-99; with the modifiers LT, 79, 55 listed in box 19 of the CMS 1500.

EXERCISE 6.1

EVALUATION AND MANAGEMENT MATCHING

Instructions: Choose the correct modifier from the choices below each question.

1. Evaluation and Management Modifiers
   a. Significant, Separately Identifiable Evaluation and Management service by the Same Physician on the Same Day of the Procedure or other Service
   b. Prolonged Evaluation and Management Service
   c. Unrelated Evaluation and Management Service by the Same Physician During Postoperative Period
   d. Decision for Surgery
   > 57   25   24   21

2. Modifiers giving information about procedures:
   a. Multiple Procedures
   b. Surgical Care Only
   c. Bilateral Procedure
   d. Reduced Services
   e. Mandated Services
   f. Distinct Procedural Services
   g. Procedure Performed on Infants
   h. Preoperative Management Only
   i. Repeated Clinical Diagnostic Laboratory Test
   j. Unusual Procedural Service
   k. Discontinued Procedure
   l. Postoperative Management Only
   m. Unusual Anesthesia
   > 52   63   32   53   23   22   55
   > 50   56   51   91   54   59

3. Modifiers that describe procedures performed within a global of or subsequent to another procedure:
   a. Repeat Procedure by Same Physician
   b. Staged or Related Procedure or Service by the Same Physician during a Postoperative Period
   c. Return to the Operating Room for a Related Procedure during the Postoperative Period
   d. Repeat Procedure by Another Physician

    e. Unrelated Procedure or Service by the Same Physician

       79   **58**   **78**   **77**   **76**

4. Modifiers that identify who is performing a procedure:

    a. Assistant Surgeon

    b. Anesthesia by Surgeon

    c. Minimum Assistant Surgeon

    d. Two Surgeons/Co-Surgeons

    e. Assistant Surgeon (When a Qualified Resident Surgeon Is Unavailable)

    f. Professional Component

    g. Reference (Outside) Laboratory

    h. Surgical Team

       47   **80**   **62**   **82**   **26**   **66**   **90**   **81**

CHAPTER REVIEW

Instructions: Answer the questions below without referencing your text.

1. Local infiltration of anesthesia is included in the procedure; however, if a digital block is used, this can be billed separately.　**True or False**

2. A colonoscopy is an example of a <u>diagnostic</u> or <u>therapeutic</u> procedure.

3. Define bundling:

4. A separate procedure is performed at a different operative session on the same day as an extensive procedure. This can be reported in addition to the first procedure. **True or False**

5. The Surgery section is the largest section in CPT.　**True or False**

6. What two types of codes never have a Modifier 51 appended?

7. Which type of code can never stand alone?

8. Modifiers are used to identify who provided the service, why the service was billed, or to affect reimbursement.　**True or False**

The Integumentary System

OBJECTIVES

1. Assign correct diagnosis codes to skin conditions and diseases.
2. Identify the types of codes required to correctly code burns.
3. Recognize the conditions necessary for coding malignant or benign excisions.
4. State the individual measurements required for laceration repair, excisions, and skin grafting.

TERMINOLOGY AND ACRONYMS

Anasarca   Edema.

BCC   Basal cell carcinoma.

Bullous   Having the presence of blisters.

Bx   Biopsy.

I&D   Incision and drainage.

Keloid   Overgrowth of scar tissue.

SC   Subcutaneous.

SCC   Squamous cell carcinoma.

TBSA   Total body surface area.

INTRODUCTION

The integumentary system is the largest organ system in the body and is an interesting as well as challenging system to code. This chapter will give students the opportunity to code ICD-9 diagnoses in conjunction with CPT® procedures as experienced in an office setting.

DISEASE PROCESSES AND ICD-9 CODING OF THE SKIN AND SUBCUTANEOUS TISSUE

Skin manifests visible signs of disease processes at work in the body. Allergic reactions, infections, and other immune system disorders, such as lupus, are apparent to the physician's eye. Other conditions require microscopic examination of tissue in order to arrive at a diagnosis. See Anatomy Plate 1 of Appendix A for a diagram of the skin.

Correct ICD-9 diagnosis codes are important to establish medical necessity for the procedures that are performed on the skin. Body sites, as well as the cause of some reactions, must be known in order to code correctly. While many diagnosis codes will be located in the Diseases of the Skin and Subcutaneous Tissue chapter of ICD-9 (e.g., infections, dermatitis, psoriasis, pruritis, ulcers, and acne), some conditions are located in various other chapters of ICD-9. Primary malignant neoplasms of the skin are listed under category 173, while malignant melanomas are coded to category 172. Benign neoplasms are found in category 216. Burns are located in the Injury and Poisoning chapter of ICD-9, under categories 940–949. Surgical complications, such as skin graft failure, wound disruption, and nonhealing surgical wounds are also found in the Injury and Poisoning chapter.

Formula for Success

Tips for Coding Integumentary System Diagnoses

1. Be as specific as possible with diagnoses, including anatomic site of the lesion or condition.
2. The coder should wait until pathology reports are returned with malignant/benign diagnoses before coding lesions.

Medical terms involving the integumentary system are often confusing. A *furuncle* is also known in layman's terms as a boil; a severe boil with sinus tract formation is called a *carbuncle* (see Figure 7.1). These two conditions are coded to ICD-9 category 680, with fourth-digit assignment dependent upon anatomic site.

Cellulitis is an infection that spreads through the subcutaneous tissues. An *abscess* is a localized infection, with a cavity containing pus. Code these conditions to categories 681 and 682, with an additional code to identify the organism, if specified. Both cellulitis and abscess diagnosis codes include *lymphangitis,* or inflammation of the lymphatic vessels.

Dermatitis is an inflammation of the skin, with potential causes that include light exposure, ingested or externally applied medications, contact with plants, metals, detergents, chemicals, or infections. Category 691 describes *atopic dermatitis,* which is an allergic dermatitis. Category 692 includes *contact dermatitis* and conditions due to solar radiation. Fifth-digit subclassifications listed below 692.7x specify various degrees of sunburn, as well as other conditions due to overexposure to the sun. Excluded from category 692 are specific types of dermatitis, urticarial reactions, and allergy NOS. Be sure to read Includes and Excludes notes carefully. Category 694 describes bullous conditions.

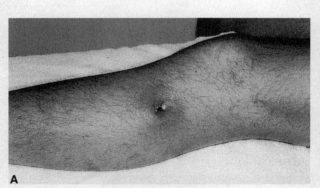
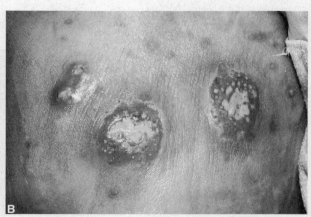

Figure 7–1 Examples of furuncle and carbuncles.

Category 695 classifies *erythematous* conditions in which the skin turns red, or lesions, which are red. *Discoid lupus erythematosis*, code 695.4, should not be confused with a more serious form of lupus known as *systemic lupus erythematosis*. The systemic form is classified under the musculoskeletal/connective tissue chapter of ICD-9 and is diagnosed with laboratory tests.

Psoriasis is a chronic skin condition distinguished by reddened patches of skin topped by silvery/white scales. Psoriasis and similar conditions are coded to category 696.

Category 697 describes specific lichen disorders of the skin. *Lichen* is an eruption of the skin. Thickening and hardening of the skin is called *lichenification*, which is different than a lichen disorder. Repeated chronic scratching, rubbing, or irritation of the skin will cause lichenification. Code this condition to 698.3.

Pruritic, or itchy, *skin conditions* are classified under category 698. Many skin conditions are already pruritic by their nature, so do not overcode when pruritis is a symptom of another condition, such as poison ivy or urticaria.

Categories 700–709 include other skin and subcutaneous (**SC**) tissue problems such as corns, **keloid** formation, ingrown nails, hair, sweat and sebaceous gland problems. Category 707 classifies skin ulcers. Use code 707.0x for *decubitus ulcers*, also known as bedsores or pressure ulcers. Code 707.1x describes ulcers of the lower limbs. Any causal conditions associated with the ulcer should be coded first, such as diabetes with skin ulcers, atherosclerosis of extremities with ulceration, postphlebitic syndrome with ulcer, and so on. See Figure 7.2 for a diagram of skin disorders.

EXERCISE 7.1

Instructions: Locating main terms in ICD-9 may be difficult when laymen's terminology is used. Using a medical dictionary if necessary, match the lay terms below to their corresponding key medical terms:

1. Athlete's foot   _____

2. Baldness   _____

3. Bedsore   _____

4. Boil   _____

5. Bruise   _____

6. Hives   _____

7. Mole   _____

8. Pustule   _____

9. Scar   _____

10. Wart   _____

11. Wen   _____

12. Skin tag   _____

Abscess	**Alopecia**	**Carbuncle**	**Cicatrix**	**Decubitus ulcer**
Ecchymosis	**Nevus**	**Pruritis**	**Tinea pedis**	**Urticaria**
Sebaceous cyst	**Verruca**	**Acrochordon**		

A macule is a discolored spot on the skin; freckle

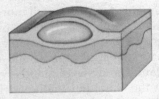

A wheal is a localized, evanescent elevation of the skin that is often accompanied by itching; urticaria

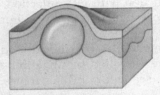

A papule is a solid, circumscribed, elevated area on the skin; pimple

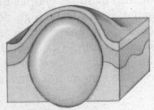

A nodule is a larger papule; acne vulgaris

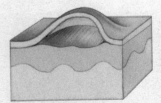

A vesicle is a small fluid filled sac; blister. A bulla is a large vesicle.

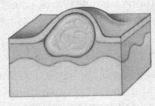

A pustule is a small, elevated, circumscribed lesion of the skin that is filled with pus; varicella (chickenpox)

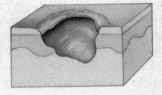

An erosion or ulcer is an eating or gnawing away of tissue; decubitus ulcer

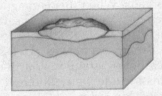

A crust is a dry, serous or seropurulent, brown, yellow, red, or green exudation that is seen in secondary lesions; eczema

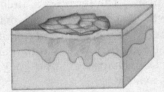

A scale is a thin, dry flake of cornified epithelial cells; psoriasis

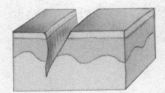

A fissure is a crack-like sore or slit that extends through the epidermis into the dermis; athlete's foot

Figure 7–2 Skin disorders.

Infections

Infections of the skin are located in the Infectious and Parasitic Disease chapter of ICD-9. Conditions such as warts, category 078; fungal infections, category 110 and 111; yeast infections, category 112; and parasites such as lice and scabies are found in category 132 and 133.

Neoplasms

Basal cell carcinoma (**BCC**) is a malignant neoplasm of the skin, most often found on the scalp and face. It is commonly removed with office-type surgical procedures. Another type of malignant neoplasm of the skin is *squamous cell carcinoma* (**SCC**). Both types of carcinomas are associated with sun-damaged skin. Squamous cell tumors are more common in the elderly and are also more prone to metastasize. *Malignant melanoma* is a tumor that arises from melanin-producing cells in the skin. This tumor is much more dangerous than basal or squamous cell carcinomas. ICD-9 divides the classification of malignant neoplasms of the skin into two categories: Category 172 describes malignant melanomas of various anatomic sites, except for the skin of the genital organs, and category 173 describes malignancies of the skin, sebaceous glands, and sweat glands with the exception of Kaposi's sarcoma, malignant melanoma of the skin, and malignancies of the skin of genital organs. Assign basal and squamous cell carcinomas to category 173 and malignant melanomas to category 172. *Kaposi's sarcoma* is a malignancy normally found on the lower extremities and is typically slow growing, eventually invading the lymphatics and internal organs. When this is diagnosed in conjunction with HIV infection, it becomes more aggressive. Assign Kaposi's sarcoma to category 176. Secondary malignant neoplasms of the skin are coded to 198.2.

Benign neoplasms are assigned to category 216. Be sure to read the various Excludes notes carefully. Fourth-digit codes are classified by anatomic site. Benign neoplasms include many different types of nevi (see Figure 7.3), or moles, as well as other types of skin lesions.

Code skin neoplasms of uncertain behavior to 238.2. Excluded from this code are neoplasms of the anus, genital organs, and vermilion border of the lips. Neoplams of unspecified nature are assigned to 239.2. This code also includes neoplasms of the bone and soft tissue. The term *mass,* unless otherwise stated, is not to be regarded as a neoplastic growth. Unspecified neoplasms of the skin include terminology such as "growth," "neoplasm," "new growth," and "tumor, not otherwise specified." Look at the term "mass" in the alphabetic index. Multiple anatomic sites are listed, but they are not classified to the neoplasm chapter. Instead, they are assigned to more generic disorders under a particular body system.

Figure 7–3   Example of nevus.

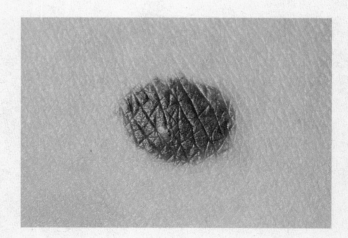

In the dermatology or primary care office, it is very important to make sure that the diagnosis to report the behavior of the neoplasm (benign or malignant) is coded after review of the pathology report. The behavior, or *morphology*, determines the appropriate CPT® procedural code assigned for the physician's services.

EXERCISE 7.2

Instructions: Locate the correct ICD-9-CM code for the diagnostic statements below.

1. Malignant melanoma of the pinna of the ear   _____

2. Metastatic skin lesion on shoulder, primary site unspecified   _____

3. Actinic keratoses, face   _____

4. Kaposi's sarcoma, dorsum of hand   _____

5. Benign pigmented nevus of scalp   _____

6. Subcutaneous lipoma, abdomen   _____

7. DSAP–disseminated superficial actinic porokeratosis   _____

8. Seborrheic keratosis   _____

9. Skin tag   _____

10. Hemangioma, skin of face   _____

Burns

Three categories of diagnosis codes describe a burn. These are:

1. Depth and site of burn: Category 940–947, 949
2. Total Body Surface Area (**TBSA**): Category 948
3. E code to determine external cause of injury

Burns are sequenced in order of their severity—the highest degree burn is sequenced first. If two types of burns occur in the same body area or overlap each other, only the most severe burn is coded. Separate codes should be assigned for each specific burn site. Do not use category 946, Burns of Multiple Specified sites, unless documentation is vague and does not specify location.

Patients who have healed burns may return for continued grafting or release of scar contractures for many years after the initial trauma. These are coded with the residual condition (i.e., contracture, etc.) reported as the primary diagnosis, with a late effect code from 906.5–906.9 as a secondary diagnosis. An optional late effect E code may also be reported.

Abrasion/friction burns, such as "rope burn," "rug burn," or "road rash" should be coded as superficial injury. These may be coded as open wounds if documented as a deep abrasion.

In order to code correctly from category 948 (burns classified according to extent of body surface involved), the size of the burn must be documented in the medical record. Burn size may be calculated several ways. One method is to use the Rule of Nines (see Figure 7.4) in which the adult head, extremities, and trunk are assigned either 9 or 18 percent.

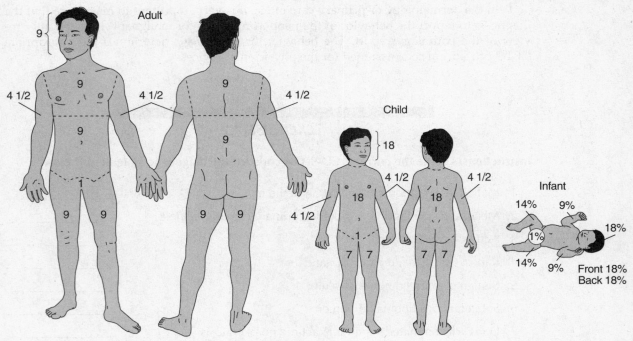

Figure 7–4   Adult and pediatric Rule of Nines.

A child's head and extremities differ in proportion compared to an adult, so the Rule of Nines on infants does not use multiples of 9. The second method of calculating burn size is to use the palmar surface of a patient's hand as a point of reference. The palm is considered to be 1 percent of a person's TBSA, so a burn of 6 percent would be the equivalent size of 6 "palms" of that patient.

Fourth- and Fifth-Digit ICD-9 Code Assignments

Fourth-digit assignments for categories 941–946 indicate the classification of the burn (i.e., first, second, or third degree). Fifth-digit assignments for the same categories indicate the specific site of the burn.

Fifth-digit assignment for category 948 indicates the percentage of TBSA with third-degree burn (see Figure 7.5).

Figure 7–5 Severe second- to third-degree burns.

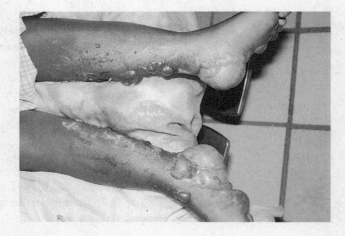

Other Trauma

Medical terms describing trauma to the skin can be confusing to the novice coder. You may wish to flag the following terms in your alphabetic index temporarily until familiar with these terms:

- Laceration—cuts. See "Wound, open" for larger listing
- Wound, open—cuts and open wounds
- Injury, superficial
- Abrasion—refers the coder to Injury, superficial
- Contusion (skin surface intact)

Formula for Success

Remember to sequence the most serious injury or burn first when multiple trauma is documented.

E Code Assignment

The manner of injury is important for statistical and reimbursement purposes. Look in the Index to External Causes under some of the following main terms to help locate the appropriate E code:

- Assault
- Bite
- Burn
- Collision
- Crush
- Cut
- Explosion
- Exposure
- Fall
- Injured by
- Radiation
- Scald
- Scratch
- Sting

EXERCISE 7.3

Instructions: Assign the ICD-9 diagnosis code for the diagnostic statements below. Assign E codes where appropriate.

1. Ingrown nail with onychomycosis.   _____

2. Polycystic ovarian syndrome and hirsutism.   _____

3. Laceration of forehead, with imbedded windshield glass. Patient was a passenger in a car that rolled.   _____

4. Laceration of right hand and forearm after punching plate glass window.   _____

5. Multiple contusions of head and back, shoulders, and arms following beating with a baseball bat by unknown persons.   _____

6. Suicide attempt by cutting wrist—simple transverse laceration noted.   _____

7. Second-degree sunburn.   _____

8. Abrasions to legs from tall weeds and grasses with allergic dermatitis.   _____

9. Frostbite, face, while playing outside.   _____

10. Infected mosquito bite, upper arm.   _____

11. Edema of the legs.   _____

Symptoms

In the physician office symptoms must be assigned on occasion for lack of definitive diagnoses. Category 782 codes are assigned for symptoms involving the skin and other integumentary tissues. These include numbness, burning and tingling, rashes, localized masses or lumps, edema, jaundice, cyanosis and other color changes, spontaneous bruising, and changes in skin texture.

V Codes

Code personal history of malignant melanoma of the skin to V10.82. Other malignant skin neoplasms are assigned to V10.83. Code V13.3 for personal history of diseases of skin and subcutaneous tissue. Allergies to medicines and other substances are often manifested by allergic dermatitis. Assign codes from categories V14 and V15 for personal history of allergies when they are listed as diagnoses or if required for statistical purposes.

In the physician office, patients are sometimes seen for cosmetic procedures, such as ear piercing. Category V50 is assigned to elective procedures, including plastic surgery.

Use code V58.77 for aftercare following surgery of the skin and subcutaneous tissue with other aftercare codes to fully identify the reason for the aftercare encounter.

EXERCISE 7.4

Instructions: Locate the correct ICD-9-CM code, including E codes if applicable

1. Sunburn, first degree   _____

2. Contact dermatitis, cause unknown   _____

3. Acute lymphangitis, site unspecified   _____

4. Erythema multiforme   _____

5. Cradle cap   _____

   6. Vibratory urticaria   _____

   7. Chronic neurogenic ulcer of heel   _____

   8. Acne vulgaris   _____

   9. Melanoma, ear   _____

  10. Neurotic itching with folliculitis   _____

  11. Second degree burn, foot, due to scalding water   _____

CPT® PROCEDURAL CODING

Multiple integumentary procedures may be performed on various parts of the body at the same encounter, often with the same diagnosis. In this section, the student will learn to code procedures, utilizing modifiers when necessary, and link them with the appropriate diagnosis code.

Using Modifiers with Integumentary System Codes

Appropriate use of modifiers is essential for proper reimbursement. Many codes also specify the number of procedures allowed in the code descriptor. If a code does not indicate a plural form or multiple procedures in the descriptor, then it should be listed as many times as appropriate. Modifier 51 should be appended to a secondary procedural code that is not an add-on code. Modifier 59 may also be applied to distinguish between several different procedures having the same CPT® and ICD-9 codes.

The modifiers listed below are the most common modifiers used for codes within the integumentary system. Additional modifiers may be used besides those listed here.

Modifier 25. This modifier should be appended to E/M services that are separately identifiable from any surgical procedures performed on the same day by the same physician.

Modifier 50. Bilateral procedures (such as bilateral mastectomies) may be coded in two ways, depending upon payer preferences. If the payer requires a one-line item, then append Modifier 50 to the CPT® code. If the payer requests a two-line item, list the CPT® code twice—once with modifier RT and again with modifier LT to identify right and left sides of the body.

Modifier 51. Correct use of the multiple procedure Modifier 51 is essential to integumentary system coding. This should be appended to any subsequent procedures *excluding* add-on codes and Modifier 51 exempt codes.

Modifier 52. This modifier should be used to indicate any *services* that are eliminated or partly reduced at the discretion of the physician. This modifier *should not* be used to reduce fees or to indicate a discount to the patient. Most payers expect the fee to be reduced on the claim form, but this is not required.

Modifier 58. Staged procedures, such as a breast reconstruction or skin grafting for burns that is performed over a period of time, will require use of Modifier 58. This modifier does not affect the reimbursement, but simply alerts the payer that the procedure was either planned, is more extensive than the original, or is done for therapeutic purposes following diagnostic procedures. Use Modifier 58 when the staged procedure is still within the global period of the first procedure.

Modifier 59. This modifier is commonly used in conjunction with Modifier 51 on the second line of a claim. It identifies a distinct procedural service, such as a different procedure, different organ, separate incision, excision or lesion. If this modifier is not used appropriately, multiple procedures could potentially be bundled together and

reimbursement lost. This modifier is especially helpful when coding multiple procedures that all have the same diagnosis code, as well as some that have the same diagnosis AND procedure code but are performed through different incisions.

Modifier 78. When a patient must return to the operating room within a global period
for a procedure related to the first procedure, Modifier 78 should be appended to the
CPT® code. (*Example:* Drainage of postoperative seroma following mastectomy.) Depending on the payer, this allows partial to full payment for services rendered. The
ICD-9 diagnosis code should also reflect the medical necessity of any return to the
operating room.

Modifier 79. This modifier is used with tissue transfers following Moh's procedures and
unrelated sites of surgery that are treated within the global period of a previous
surgery.

Formula for Success

Tips for Coding Integumentary System Procedures

Each procedure should have a matching diagnosis "link," even if the same diagnosis is
appropriate for multiple procedures. Use anatomical diagrams if possible to indicate
where procedures were performed.

Incision and Drainage

Incision and drainage (**I&D**) is done to rid the body of infection, fluid, or blood accumulated in abscesses, cysts, or hematomas within the skin layers, sweat glands, or along nail
edges. This involves the puncture and drainage or aspiration of the affected site. These
may be simple or complex, single or multiple in nature. Modifiers further describe the circumstances surrounding the procedure.

> **Example:**   A patient has a postoperative seroma two days following breast surgery.
>
>   ICD-9-CM: 998.13, Seroma complicating a procedure
>   CPT®: 10140-78, Incision and drainage of hematoma, seroma or fluid collection

EXERCISE 7.5

**Instructions: Using the words at the bottom of the exercise, match the correct term with
its definition or synonym.**

1. Chronic inflammatory disorder characterized by dilation of capillaries on the nose,
   cheeks, forehead, and chin _____

2. Hyperplastic mass of scar tissue _____

3. Fluid-filled blister on the skin, larger than 1 cm _____

4. Contagious disease characterized by pustules that burst and form a crust _____

5. Inflammation in the fold of tissue alongside a nail _____

6. Severe blistering of the skin _____

7. Warty, premalignant growths found on sun-exposed areas, particularly the face, neck, and arms _____

pemphigus	**rosacea**	**impetigo**	**bulla**
actinic	**keratoses**	**keloid**	**paronychia**

Excision–Debridement

Debridement is the removal of infection, unwanted tissue growth, or foreign bodies from the skin and subcutaneous tissues. Debridement may be performed with scalpels, forceps, or specialized brushes and rinsing tools.

Example: A patient is in the hospital with a painful, crusted eczema over 30 percent of her body due to contact with using solvents at work. She is taken to surgery where this is debrided.

ICD-9-CM: 692.2, Contact dermatitis and other eczema due to solvents, is linked to all three CPT® codes.

CPT®: 11000, Debridement of skin . . . up to 10% of body surface

CPT®: 11001, Each additional 10% of body surface, × 2

Example: A patient has experienced a necrotic skin flap two weeks post amputation of his lower leg. It is not infected. The necrotic area extends to the subcutaneous tissue only. This is debrided.

ICD-9-CM: 997.69, Other amputation stump complication

CPT®: 11042-78, Debridement of skin, partial thickness, skin and subcutaneous tissue

Paring or Cutting

These codes are used on corns and calluses and are reported by the number of individual lesions that are pared. Warts that are pared should not be coded using codes 11055–11057, according to CPT Assistant®.

Biopsy

Biopsies (**Bx**) are small pieces of tissue that are examined microscopically to diagnose diseases or conditions. Punch biopsies are commonly used on small lesions of the skin, usually measuring 0.5 cm or less. The punch biopsy instrument is a small, pencil-shaped tool that creates a circumferential incision around a lesion by gently twisting and pressing on the skin, like a cookie cutter. The lesion is then lifted up with a tweezers or forceps and snipped off at its base. A single suture is commonly used for closure. Biopsies are coded for a single lesion, with each additional lesion coded separately as an add-on. Needle biopsies are not coded using biopsy codes. They are assigned to codes within the specific anatomic area.

Do not confuse a biopsy with shaving. The difference between an excisional biopsy and a shave biopsy is the technique and whether sutures are used. A shave does not require sutures and is not a full-thickness excision.

Example: A patient had two small areas of thickened, itchy skin on her arm that had not responded to medication. The physician performed a punch biopsy of one area. A second area on the patient's temple appeared to be a squamous cell carcinoma, and this was punch biopsied as well. Both areas were closed with a single suture of 3-0

Vicryl. In addition, the patient had a small 0.2 cm benign-appearing nevus on her shoulder that was constantly irritated by her bra strap. This was shaved at the patient's request. Drysol was applied to the shave, and all areas were bandaged. The pathology report confirmed the nevus and squamous cell carcinoma, but showed only inflammatory reaction of the itchy area on the arm.

> CPT®: 11100, Punch biopsy #1, and ICD-9-CM: 698.9, Pruritic area
> CPT®: 11101, Punch biopsy #2, and ICD-9-CM: 173.3, Squamous cell carcinoma
> CPT®: 11300-51-59, Shave biopsy, and ICD-9-CM: 216.6, Nevus

Note that add-on code 11101 is Modifier 51 exempt, so Modifier 51 is added to only the third procedure.

EXERCISE 7.6

Instructions: Assign the correct CPT® codes to the following scenarios. Do not give E codes.

1. Incision of thigh to remove multiple superficial shotgun pellets. _____

2. Debridement of skin infection, 5 percent of body surface. _____

3. Biopsy of lip lesion with simple closure. Pathology report benign. _____

4. Paring of three calluses, right foot. _____

5. Incision and drainage, two axillary abscesses. _____

Skin Tags

Skin tags, or acrochordons, are found primarily on the face, neck, and trunk of patients over age 40. Depending on the size of the skin tag, it may be removed by a variety of methods including electrocautery, ligature, scissoring, or combinations of those methods. Anesthesia is elective, and is not coded separately if provided. Skin tag removals include *multiple* removals. Code 11200 involves 1 to 15 skin tags, any area, and code 11201 is added on for each additional group of 10 lesions.

Example: A patient who has 35 skin tags removed is coded as:

> ICD-9-CM: 701.9, linked to CPT® 11200, Removal of skin tags, any area, up to and including 15 lesions
> ICD-9-CM: 701.9, linked to CPT® 11201 × 2, Each additional ten lesions

Shaving of Epidermal or Dermal Lesions

Shaving is only a partial thickness excision that does not require suturing. Local anesthesia is applied and the wound may be chemically cauterized or electrocauterized to prevent bleeding. Codes are categorized first by site, then by the size of the lesion in each site category.

Formula for Success

It is important that the provider measure any lesion *prior* to removal. When skin is removed from the body, it will shrink. Chemical preservatives may cause even further shrinkage. Therefore, it is imperative that measurements be taken before removal and documented in the operative note. If the size is not documented, the coder must rely on the pathology report for measurements.

Excision of Lesions

The excision codes are divided into two sections—excision of benign lesions, and excision of malignant lesions. The CPT® code assignment is dependent upon the ICD-9-CM diagnosis code.

Benign lesions are defined as those that are composed of scar or fibrous tissue, cystic type structures, and inflammatory or congenital lesions. When they are removed, they are full thickness excisions. Local anesthesia and simple closure are included in these codes. If more than simple closure is required, then the coder should use the intermediate or complex closure codes to report the closure separately.

Similar to benign excisions, the excision of a malignant lesion involves local anesthesia, sharp removal, and simple closure. Closure that is intermediate or complex should be coded in addition to the excision.

Measuring of benign and malignant lesions was changed in 2003 to include the excised diameter of a lesion—that is, the lesion plus the margins. CPT® explains that

code selection is determined by measuring the greatest clinical diameter of the apparent lesion plus that margin required for complete excision (lesion diameter plus the most narrow margins required equals the excised diameter). The margins refer to the narrowest margin required to adequately excise the lesion, based on the physician's judgment. The measurement of lesion plus margin is made prior to excision. The excised diameter is the same whether the surgical defect is repaired in linear fashion, or reconstructed (e.g., with a skin graft).

The descriptors for all of the benign and malignant lesions were changed to reflect this new instruction.

Formula for Success

Excision of Lesion

The diagnosis must indicate a benign condition to link correctly with the procedure, excision of <u>benign</u> lesion. A code for a malignant lesion will trigger a denial of the claim. The diagnosis code for excision of a <u>malignant</u> lesion must indicate a malignancy, or the claim will be denied.

Example: A patient had a basal cell carcinoma 0.7 cm in excised diameter removed from his scalp.

> ICD-9-CM: 173.4, Other malignant lesion of scalp and skin of neck
>
> CPT®: 11621, Excision, malignant lesion, scalp, neck, hands, feet, genitalia, excised diameter 0.6 to 1.0 cm

Patients may return for a second procedure if the pathology report shows the malignancy extending to the edge of the tissue that was removed. This is called "excision of margins." The edges of the original surgical site are re-excised and sent to pathology to ensure margins that are free of malignancy.

The 2003 CPT® also gave new instructions for incomplete margins on frozen section. These instructions state, "When frozen section pathology shows the margins of excision were not adequate, an additional excision may be necessary for complete tumor removal. Use only one code to report the additional excision and re-excision(s) based on the final widest excised diameter required for complete tumor removal at the same operative session."

EXERCISE 7.7

Instructions: Assign the correct CPT® codes to the following scenarios.

1. Shave 0.2 cm benign nevus, chin; no closure needed.   _____

2. Removal 14 skin tags from waistline.   _____

3. Excision 0.7 cm benign nevus from scalp, simple closure.   _____

Insertions and Injections

The Introduction section of CPT® includes insertion and injection procedures.

Intralesional injections can be done for several different reasons—for example, scarring, hypertrophy of a scar, acne, or alopecia. Usually a steroid medication is injected into the lesion in an attempt to reduce swelling of tissue or stimulate hair growth. A single lesion or scar may require several injections. However, these codes specify the number of *lesions,* not the number of injections, so take care not to code multiple injections or needle sticks into the same lesion.

Subcutaneous injection of filling material is based on the amount of filling material per cc used. The filling material is commonly bovine collagen, which acts to restore a normal or cosmetically desired contour for skin or lip defects. Due to fears of mad cow disease in Europe, U.S. derived bovine collagen, as well as human autologous collagen are being increasingly used. Collagen is reported separately in addition to the procedure using a HCPCS supply code.

Tissue expanders described in this section of CPT® are utilized for several reasons. One is to stretch or expand the skin in preparation of permanent prosthesis insertion for other than breast. A second reason is to prepare an expanse of skin to be used for a flap or graft to cover a defect.

The insertion and removal of contraceptive capsules, such as Norplant®, are also covered in this section. Since these implants can remain in the patient for several years, the insertion, removal, and removal with reinsertion are all given separate codes. ICD-9-CM codes that correspond to these CPT® codes should be assigned as diagnoses.

Example: Link CPT® code 11975 with V25.5, Insertion of implantable subdermal contraceptive; CPT® code 11976 with V25.43, Implantable subdermal contraceptive; and CPT® code 11977 with V25.43 and V25.5.

Repairs

Repairs are grouped together by the type of wound repair and, within each type, the anatomic site and length of repair. Included in any type of wound repair would be an exploration to determine the depth and extent of injury. Codes outside of the integumentary system may be more appropriate if the wound requires enlargement or removal of foreign body or repair of internal structures (i.e., muscles, nerves, tendons, blood vessels).

Formula for Success

Tips for Wound Repairs

1. Measure the length *before* the repair is done.
2. For multiple repairs, add lengths together for wounds grouped in the same anatomic area and of the same classification (i.e., all simple lacerations of trunk and extremities are added together; all intermediate lacerations of trunk and extremities are added together and so on).
3. Do not add different wound classifications together, such as simple + complex.
4. Sequence the most complicated wound repair first. All secondary repairs will be listed with Modifier 51.
5. Debridement is bundled into the wound repair codes with the following exceptions:
   a. Requires prolonged cleansing of gross contamination.
   b. Large amount of dead or contaminated tissue is removed.
   c. Debridement carried out as a separate procedure without primary closure.
6. Report any blood vessel, tendon, or nerve repair under its respective systems (cardiovascular, musculoskeletal, or nervous systems).

Under the complex repair heading, add-on codes for each additional 5 cm or less is found under each anatomic grouping.

Example: A patient lost control of his motorcycle and had numerous dirty lacerations from sliding on pavement. The Urgent Care physician performed the following repairs: 3.0 cm simple repair on the chin with Water-Pik® removal of debris, 1.5 cm simple repair of hand, and 2.0 cm. simple repair of knee. ICD-9-CM codes are included to demonstrate code linkage for medical necessity.

1. ICD-9-CM: 873.54, Open wound of face, complicated, and E816.2, Motor vehicle traffic accident, due to loss of control, without collision on the highway

   CPT®: 12052, Intermediate repair of chin. This is the most extensive, so it is listed first. The simple repair is coded as an intermediate repair because it was heavily contaminated.
2. ICD-9-CM: 882.0, Open wound of hand except fingers alone, and 891.0, Open wound of knee, leg, except thigh and ankle

   CPT®: 12002-51, Simple repair of hand and knee added together. Extremities are listed in the same CPT® descriptor.

Skin Grafts

Skin grafts are listed in CPT® by size, location of the defect (recipient area), graft type and source. The two types of skin grafts are *split thickness* and *full thickness* (See Table 7.1).

Split grafts, or split thickness grafts, are made up of the epidermis and a small portion of the dermis. Using a dermatome, the donor site is harvested similar to a cheese cutter. This graft is then further prepared by using a mesher to create a lattice or mesh-like appearance, which allows the graft to stretch and cover more surface area. Certain types of wounds respond better to treatment with this type of graft. It is a temporary cover and allows greater oxygen exchange to the healing wound. These codes are listed by body site and by surface area measured in increments of 100 square centimeters or 1 percent body area.

Full thickness grafts differ from split thickness in that the full thickness is made up of the epidermis and all layers of the dermis. The code descriptor states that these codes include the direct closure of the donor site. Full thickness grafts are meant to be a permanent graft for the correction of a defect. Unlike the adjacent transfers, they are completely removed from their source and may originate from a distant part of the body. These codes are listed by body site; however, they are broken down further in comparison with the split thickness grafts. These are measured in increments of 20 square centimeters.

There are several different sources of skin grafts:

Autografts come from the patient's own body.

Allografts are made of human skin. These are not from the patient and typically come from cadaver sources. The prefix *allo* means same species. Codes for these grafts are 15350 for 100 sq cm or less and one add-on code 15351 for each additional 100 sq cm. These are temporary grafts also.

Bilaminate skin grafts are also referred to as an artificial substitute skin. These grafts are created from pigskin cells and are grown in a lab to form a dermal-like artificial skin. These codes are listed as 15342 for 25 sq cm and one add-on code of 15343 for each additional 25 sq cm.

Xenografts are thin meshed pigskin. These are typically used to aid in the healing of burns. Xenografts are temporary and are a type of biological dressing. Codes for these grafts are 15400 for 100 sq cm or less and 15401 for each additional 100 sq cm.

In order to restore a large defect, several grafts may be performed over a period of time. It is appropriate to use a Modifier 58 for these situations. This modifier is used for staged

Table 7–1   Types of Skin Graft

Type of Graft	Depth	Characteristics	Advantage
Split thickness	Epidermis and partial thickness of dermis	Creates scars of recipient and donor site. No blood supply is needed—tissue completely excised	Transplants well on sites that have a poor blood supply. Provides good coverage for temporary closures that are removed later. Good for large areas.
Full thickness	Epidermis and full thickness of dermis	Easily harvested from donor site. Thickness, "blush ability," and hair pattern should match recipient site.	Does best on areas with good blood supply. Less scar contracture than split thickness.

procedures and applies when a predetermined surgical plan is being followed for patient care.

EXERCISE 7.8

Instructions: Link the ICD-9-CM diagnosis code to the appropriate CPT® code.

a. 685.0	1. _____ 11620
b. 701.4	2. _____ 17340
c. 706.1	3. _____ 13160
d. 611.1	4. _____ 17250
e. 257.2	5. _____ 11772
f. 173.4	6. _____ 11980
g. 695.4	7. _____ 16000
h. 701.5	8. _____ 19140
i. 692.71	9. _____ 11900
j. 998.32	10. _____ 11100

Pressure Ulcers (Decubitus Ulcers)

Pressure or decubitus ulcers are also known as bedsores. These occur from the weight of a person's body pressing against a bony prominence, such as an elbow, hip, coccyx, or heel, which compresses blood vessels in the skin. Without movement, the lack of circulation causes tissue to decay. Decubitus ulcers can range from just a mild discoloration of the skin to an open, decaying wound extending down through muscle to the bone. The course of injury is similar to a burn wound, and these ulcers are also treated similarly to burns. Black, necrotic tissue known as eschar forms in chronic decubitus ulcers. See Figure 7.6.

Figure 7–6 Skin ulcer.

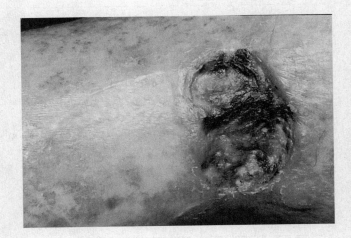

Burns

The burn codes in the Integumentary chapter of CPT® are to be used for the local treatment of the burned surface area of the skin. Burns can occur from multiple sources including solar, chemical, heat, and electrical. CPT® codes in this section are broken down by descriptions of procedures with or without anesthesia. These codes may also be used for dressing changes as well as debridement, so if a patient returns to the physician for multiple dressing changes over a period of time, these codes are more appropriate than E/M codes. The several types of burn classifications are shown in Table 7.2.

Example: A man poured lighter fluid on top of his charcoal grill in the backyard and it flared up, causing first-degree burns over his entire face, neck, arms, and hands. His eyes, mouth, and trachea were not burned. The clothing on his torso was not burned. He was brought to Urgent Care for treatment of multiple first-degree burns, calculated to be 22 percent TBSA. He was treated for the first-degree burns and released with instructions to force fluids. Additionally, he was asked to return to the Urgent Care if there was any change in the condition of his burns.

ICD-9-CM:	941.19, First-degree burn, multiple sites of face, head and neck
	943.19, First-degree burn, multiple sites of upper limb, except wrist and hand
	944.18, First-degree burn, multiple sites of wrist(s) and hand(s)
	948.20, 20–29 percent of body surface burn, with less than 10 percent third degree
	E895, Accident caused by controlled fire in private dwelling
CPT®:	16000, Initial treatment, first degree burn, when no more than local treatment is required

On Day 2, the right-hand burn appeared to have matured into second-degree burn; other burns had improved. The right hand was dressed with Silvadene and gauze.

ICD-9-CM:	944.28, Second-degree burn of multiple sites of wrist and hand
	943.19, First-degree burn, multiple sites of upper limb, except wrist and hand
	944.18, First degree burn, multiple sites of wrist(s) and hand(s)

Table 7–2   Types of Burns

Type of Burn	Sensation	Clinical Observations
First degree:		
Epidermis	Painful	Red, erythematous
Second degree:		
Moderate to deep dermis	Painful	Red, moist blisters, vesicles
Third degree:		
Through dermis into subcutaneous tissues, fat, and muscle. Full thickness skin loss.	Loss of sensation	White, brown, or black, dry leathery tissue (eschar). Burn "matures" over a period of 24–72 hours and percentage/depth may change.
Deep third degree or fourth degree:		
Necrosis of underlying tissues; extends down to bone	Loss of sensation	Charred tissue; may imply loss of an extremity.

948.20, 20–29 percent of body surface burn, with less than 10 percent third degree

CPT®: 16020, Dressing and/or debridement, initial or subsequent, without anesthesia, office or hospital, small

Rationale:

On the first visit, burns are sequenced in order of their severity. There was no third-degree burn at all, so 948.2 with a fifth digit of "0" is assigned for TBSA. The E code indicates this occurred in a private dwelling. On the second visit, the hand was the most severe burn documented, and treatment was directed toward that area, so it is sequenced as primary with code 944.28. TBSA did not change. An E code is not assigned for the subsequent visit, as the current injury is still being treated.

Formula for Success

Sunburns are not located in the alphabetic index under burns; they are cross-referenced to "sunburn." Friction burns likewise are cross-referenced to "Injury, superficial, by site."

Destruction

CPT® defines destruction as "the ablation of benign, premalignant, or malignant tissues by any method, with or without curettement, including local anesthesia, and not usually requiring closure." When a lesion is destroyed, there is not a surgical specimen to send to the lab. Since there is no pathology report, the diagnosis must therefore be based on the physician's clinical judgment (i.e., benign or malignant) or from a previous biopsy of the same area. The method of destruction can include laser, cautery, freezing, or chemical destruction.

Example: A port-wine birthmark, 4 square centimeters in size, is lasered off a patient's cheek.

ICD-9: 757.32, Vascular hamartomas

CPT®: 17106, Destruction of cutaneous vascular proliferative lesions, less than 10 sq cm

Destruction of flat warts, molluscum contagiosum, and milia are coded from this section. These conditions should not be confused with plantar warts or common warts. If plantar or common warts are destroyed, they should be coded using the 17000–17004 code range, along with diagnosis code 078.10, Viral warts, unspecified, or 078.19, Other specified viral warts.

Formula for Success

ICD-9-CM codes that link to procedures from the 17000–17250 code range must be benign in nature. Failure to link diagnosis to procedure properly will result in claim denial.

ICD-9-CM codes that link to procedures from the 17260–17286 code range must be coded from category 172, Malignant melanoma of skin, or 173, Other malignant neoplasm of skin. Failure to link diagnosis to procedure properly will result in claim denial.

Destruction of malignant lesions can be accomplished using the same methods as destruction of benign lesions. These codes differ dramatically from the benign lesions since they are coded by location and size, rather than the total number of lesions destroyed.

Example: Basal cell carcinoma, 0.3 cm in size on the nose, destroyed by laser.

Incorrect codes:

ICD-9-CM: 173.3, Other malignant neoplasm of skin and other and unspecified parts of face
CPT®: 17000, Destruction benign or premalignant lesions, first lesion

Correct codes:

ICD-9-CM: 173.3, Other malignant neoplasm of skin and other and unspecified parts of face
CPT®: 17280, Destruction malignant lesion, face, ears, eyelids, nose, lips, mucous membrane; lesion diameter 0.5 cm or less

Breast Procedures

Incision

Puncture aspiration of a cyst of the breast is performed with a needle and syringe. There are two aspirations codes: 19000 for the first cyst and 19001, an add-on code, for each additional cyst, whether in the same or opposite breast. Do not confuse puncture aspirations with a fine needle aspiration. If using a fine needle, the physician will usually state its use by name. See codes 10021–10022 for fine needle aspirations.

Example: Five breast cysts are aspirated, two from the right breast at the 2 o'clock and 5 o'clock positions and three from the left breast in the 12 o'clock, 3 o'clock, and 6 o'clock positions. Pathology showed fibrocystic breast disease in all specimens.

ICD-9-CM: 610.1, Diffuse cystic mastopathy—includes fibrocystic disease
CPT®: 19000, Puncture aspiration cyst of breast, and 19001, Each additional cyst × 4
Modifier 51 is not needed on the second procedure because it is an add-on code.

Excision

Breast biopsies can be done via several different methods. Among these methods are percutaneous, needle core without imaging, open, incisional, percutaneous needle core using imaging guidance, and percutaneous automated vacuum assisted or rotating biopsy device using imaging guidance. There are two sets of radiology codes in parentheses in this section that cross-reference the corresponding breast codes.

Use of the excision codes requires an understanding of how much tissue is removed and the sex of the patient. Code 19120, Excision of cyst, fibroadenoma or other benign or malignant tumor, male or female one or more lesions, is used once no matter how many lesions were removed, regardless of the patient's gender or the behavior of the tissue that is removed. Needle localization wires are extremely thin, almost hair-like wires that are injected into a mass or lesion to make it easily identified for removal. The placement of the wire is verified by various radiologic imaging methods prior to surgery.

Example: A breast lesion is excised using a preoperative needle localization wire. The lesion was in the lower outer quadrant of the right breast. The lesion returned with a diagnosis of breast cancer.

ICD-9-CM: 174.5, Malignant neoplasm of female breast, lower-outer quadrant

CPT®: 19125, Excision of lesion

CPT®: 19290-51, Needle localization wire

Mastectomies are removal of the male or female breast, and the codes for these procedures vary with the sex of the patient, as well as the extent of the procedure. Figure 7.7 shows carcinoma of the breast.

CPT® Formula for Success

1. Any percutaneous biopsy or partial excision will be bundled into a more extensive procedure on the same breast. It is important to use a 50 modifier if performed on both breasts. If a biopsy and subsequent excision are performed on the same day at different sessions, they may both be reported. Report the most extensive procedure as primary.
2. If a re-excision of margins is done for malignancy, assign the code for excision of malignant lesion on the second procedure.

ICD-9-CM Medical Necessity Formula for Success

1. "Sex" edits will throw out a claim in which the improper breast cancer code is used. ICD-9-CM code 174.x is used for female breast cancer, and 175.x is used for male breast cancer.
2. Note that category 174 has multiple fourth digits available to identify the specific area of the breast involved. If two or more areas overlap, use 174.8 to identify contiguous sites.
3. The male breast category only contains two fourth-digit subcategories.
4. Both categories *exclude* malignancies of the skin of the breast.
5. Use code 198.81 for a secondary, or metastatic, breast malignancy. See the Table of Neoplasms for other categories of breast neoplasms.

Figure 7–7 Carcinoma of the breast.

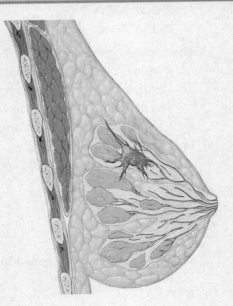

USING INTEGUMENTARY SYSTEM AND E/M CODES TOGETHER

Evaluation and Management codes are used in the dermatology office, but to a lesser extent than primary care, because more surgical procedures are performed in dermatology. A Modifier 25 should be appended to the E/M code to identify a significant, separately identifiable service. If documentation does not support an E/M code, it should not be assigned. A separate diagnosis for the E/M service is not required but is preferred.

> **Example:** An established patient comes into the dermatology office for destruction of three warts on her hand. At the same time, she asks the physician about treatment for her acne. The warts are treated with cryotherapy. The physician evaluates the acne and instructs the patient on skin care and treatments. A prescription is given to the patient. Office notes document the wart destruction, as well as the physical exam and medical decision making necessary to support a problem focused office visit.
>
> ICD-9-CM: 078.10, Viral warts, linked to CPT®: 17000, Destruction . . . first lesion
> ICD-9-CM: 078.10, Viral warts, linked to CPT®: 17003 × 2, Second through 14 lesions, each
> ICD-9-CM: 706.1, Other acne-NOS, linked to 99212-25, Established office visit, problem focused. Modifier 25 indicates separately identifiable E/M service, not related to procedure.

CHAPTER REVIEW

1. Identify the correct statement regarding the measurement of lesions for excision.
   a. Size is based on total surface area, length × width, in square centimeters.
   b. Wait to measure the lesion until after it has been excised.
   c. Size is based on the measurement of the greatest clinical diameter, in centimeters.
   d. Measure the size of the defect.

2. Assign ICD-9-CM codes for diabetic ulcer of the heel with gangrenous toes.
   a. 250.80, 707.14, 785.4
   b. 250.70, 785.4
   c. 250.00, 707.14, 785.4
   d. 250.80, 785.4

3. State why is it important to wait for the pathology report before coding an excision.
   a. Excision codes are divided into benign and malignant codes, based on the diagnosis.
   b. The size of the specimen is reported on the pathology report.
   c. The pathology reports if the margins are free, which affects the CPT® code.
   d. The physician's claim and the pathologist's claim need to be submitted together.

4. A child is brought back to the clinic with an itchy dermatitis due to ampicillin. Assign the correct ICD-9-CM codes.
   a. V14.0, E930.0
   b. 693.0, V14.0, E858.1
   c. 693.0, E930.0
   d. 693.0, E858.1

5. A simple closure can be coded in addition to an excision code.
   a. True
   b. False

6. A patient comes to the clinic for repacking of an axillary abscess that was drained previously. Cultures show a *Staphylococcus aureus* infection. Assign the correct ICD-9-CM code(s).

   a. 682.3, 041.00
   b. 682.8, 041.01. V58.3
   c. 682.3, 041.11, V58.3
   d. 682.9, 041.10

7. If several simple abscesses are drained, the correct code is 10061.

   a. True
   b. False

8. When coding a skin graft, the repair of the graft donor site is coded as a separate service.

   a. True
   b. False

9. The proper method to report the destruction of 17 benign lesions is:

   a. 17000×17
   b. $17000, 17003 \times 14, 17004$
   c. 17004
   d. $17000, 17003 \times 16$

10. The correct diagnosis and procedure codes for the destruction of a 2 cm common wart on the finger are:

    a. 078.19, 17110
    b. 078.10, 17272
    c. 078.19, 11422
    d. 078.10, 17000

11. Identify the code for a fine needle aspiration for a breast lesion without imaging.

    a. 19000
    b. 10021
    c. 19100
    d. 19102

12. The coder should independently determine the degree of burn based on documentation in the patient's record.

    a. True
    b. False

13. Burn diagnosis codes are sequenced by the following method:

    a. In order of total body surface area
    b. In order of severity
    c. By percent of third-degree burn
    d. Both A and B

Case Studies

1. **Case Study 7.1**

   Subjective

   The patient is seen today for new "rough" areas. The patient is found to have four scaly, erythematous patches involving both temples 2–3 mm in diameter.

Examination

The head, neck, and upper extremities were examined. He has a well-healed scar involving the left nasal ala with no evidence of recurrence of basal cell carcinoma.

Assessment and Plan

1. Actinic keratosis x 4, both temples. Four lesions were treated with cryotherapy.

     ICD-9-CM code: _____

     CPT® code: _____

The Musculoskeletal System

OBJECTIVES

1. Recognize various anatomical landmarks of the musculoskeletal system.
2. Understand common disease processes of the musculoskeletal system.
3. Correctly assign ICD-9-CM codes to musculoskeletal system diagnoses.
4. Correctly assign CPT® codes to procedural scenarios.

TERMINOLOGY AND ACRONYMS

CTS   Carpal tunnel syndrome.

Contusion   Superficial soft tissue injury or bruise.

Fx   Fracture.

Ganglion   Fluid-filled cystic structure located on joint capsules or tendon sheaths.

Interarticular   Located between two joints.

Intra-articular   Located within a joint.

OA   Osteoarthritis.

RA   Rheumatoid arthritis.

ROM   Range of motion.

SLE   Systemic lupus erythematosis.

Subluxation   Partial dislocation.

ANATOMY

The human skeleton is composed of approximately 206 bones of various sizes, shapes, and functions. Bones allow weight bearing and movement. Each bone is covered with a tough, thick protective layer of tissue called *periosteum*. The hard portion of the bone contains *osteoblasts*, cells that form new bone tissue, and *osteoclasts*, cells that dissolve bone. These two cell types work together to rebuild the skeletal system constantly.

Most bones are hollow and contain fatty tissue (yellow marrow) or blood-forming tissue (red marrow). The articulating ends (joints) of bones are covered with a gristly cushion called *cartilage*, which protects the bones from rubbing against each other. Fluid-filled sacs called *bursae* are located near joints and lubricate the joint spaces.

Table 8–1   Types of Muscle Tissue and Function

Type of Muscle	Action	Function
Cardiac	Involuntary	To make the heart beat. Only located in the heart; highly contractile.
Smooth	Involuntary	To provide transport of materials throughout the body involuntarily. Operates primarily by peristalsis; found in the viscera, esophagus, bowel, ureters, blood vessels, and glandular walls.
Striated	Voluntary	To move the eyes, face, and skeleton; also called "skeletal" muscle

Joint types can be distinguished from each other by the type of motion they allow:

- Ball and socket: Hips and shoulders
- Hinge: Knees, fingers, jaw
- Pivot: Elbow, wrists, vertebral column
- Fixed: Coccyx, skull

Bones also serve to protect vital organs such as the brain, heart, lungs, and major blood vessels.

See Plates 2 and 3 in Appendix A for anatomical charts of the musculoskeletal system.

Bones are connected to each other by *ligaments*, which are tough bands of fibrous connective tissue. *Tendons* attach muscles to bone. The human body contains approximately 650 muscles, which are layered on top of the skeletal framework and give shape to the body.

Three types of muscle tissue and their functions are listed in Table 8.1 and are shown in Figure 8.1.

A muscle arises from its *origin* on a bone and is connected to other bones by tendons at the tip of the muscle, called the *insertion.* The middle portion of a muscle is called the *belly.* Muscles can be attached to individual bones, or they may be layered upon other muscles and separated by slippery sheets of fascia, which allow the muscles to slide smoothly over each other.

Most skeletal muscles are arranged in pairs. Contraction of a muscle causes movement through flexion and extension. A muscle on one side shortens, or flexes, and an opposing muscle lengthens, or extend (see Figure 8.2).

Example: In order to *bend* the arm, the bicep muscle must flex while the tricep muscle extends. In order to *straighten* the arm, the tricep must flex while the bicep extends.

DISEASE PROCESSES AND ICD-9-CM CODING OF THE MUSCULOSKELETAL SYSTEM

Arthritis

Dozens of types of arthritis exist, with osteoarthritis (**OA**) being the most common. In osteoarthritis, cartilage cushioning the ends of joints is worn away and may be replaced with bone spurs or regular bone growth. Arthritis may be caused by age, normal wear and tear, overuse, or trauma. Weight-bearing joints such as hips and knees are most commonly affected. Treatments include physical therapy, rest, and anti-inflammatory medications, if appropriate. Extreme cases may require surgical intervention.

Rheumatoid arthritis, or "**RA**," as it is known, is an autoimmune disorder in which the joint lining destroys the joint surface and may invade tissues outside the joint capsule. Most commonly, rheumatoid arthritis attacks smaller joints of the hands and feet, but may involve larger joints.

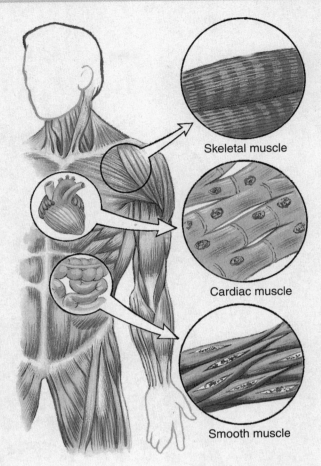

Figure 8–1   Types of muscle.

Surgery for any type of arthritis may include:

- Joint replacement
- Fusion
- Realignment of joints
- Removal of diseased joint tissue

ICD-9-CM diagnosis codes assigned to osteoarthritis are located in the 715 category. Fourth-digit subclassifications identify whether the condition is localized or generalized, primary or secondary. Fifth digits describe the anatomic location, such as forearm, pelvic region and thigh, lower leg, and so on. These fifth-digit subclassifications are cross-referenced to category 710 for further definition. Coders should flag this section of their tabular index until comfortable with the following fifth-digit definitions:

0 site unspecified
1 shoulder region
     Acromioclavicular joint(s)
     Clavicle
     Glenohumeral joint(s)
     Scapula
     Sternoclavicular joint(s)
2 upper arm
     Elbow joint

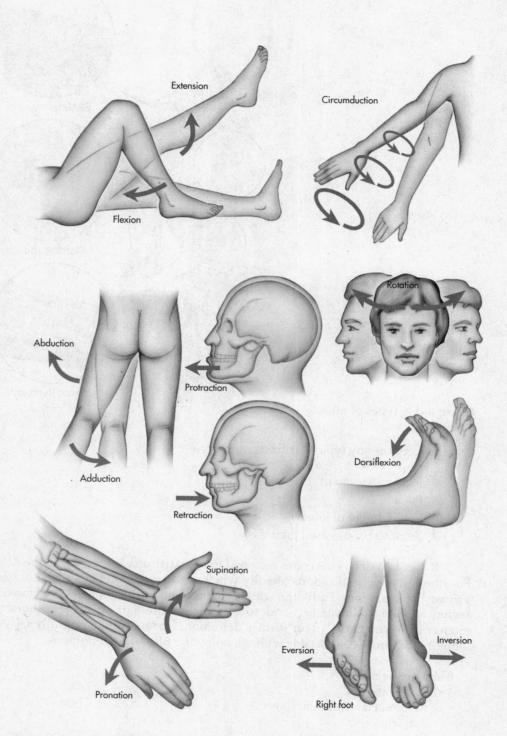

Figure 8–2   Types of body movements.

Humerus
3 forearm
Radius
Ulna
Wrist joint
4 hand
Carpus
Metacarpus
Phalanges (fingers)
5 pelvic region and thigh
Buttock
Femur
Hip (joint)
6 lower leg
Fibula   Patella
Knee joint   Tibia
7 ankle and foot
Ankle joint   Phalanges (foot)
Digits (toes)   Tarsus
Metatarsus   Other joints in foot
8 other specified sites
Head   Skull
Neck   Trunk
Ribs   Vertebral column
9 multiple sites

To avoid confusion in coding osteoarthritis of the spine, carefully read the Excludes note in category 715, which cross-references category 721 for arthritis of the spine. Arthritis of the spine falls under code ranges 720–724, which are *dorsopathies*, or diseases of the spine. Category 721 addresses osteoarthritis of the spine as *spondylosis*. This category describes only the bony portion of the spine. Conditions that affect the intervertebral disk material are coded to category 722 and will be discussed later in this text under the nervous system.

The conditions defined below all pertain to the spine (see also Figure 8.3). They sound similar, but are actually very different conditions. Most of them begin with injury or degenerative changes from osteoarthritis; however, in the case of ankylosing spondylitis, a genetic cause is suspected.

- Spinal stenosis: Narrowing of the spinal canal
- Spondylosis: Spinal osteoarthritis
- Spondylitis: Inflammation of the vertebrae
- Ankylosing spondylitis: Rheumatoid arthritis of the spine
- Spondylolisthesis: Slipping, or forward displacement of vertebral bones; usually L5 over S1

EXERCISE 8.1

Instructions: Using a medical dictionary if necessary, match the layman's term with the correct medical term.

1. Dowager's hump or buffalo hump _____

2. Knock-kneed _____

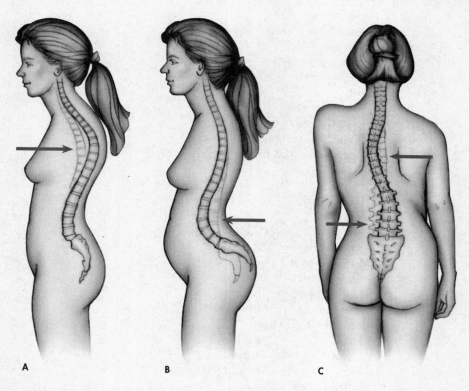

Figure 8–3   a) Kyphosis b) Lordosis c) Scoliosis

3. Swayback   _____

4. Hammertoe   _____

5. Flat foot   _____

6. Curved spine   _____

7. Broken bone   _____

Lordosis	**Fracture**	**Scoliosis**	**Pes planus**
Hallux malleus	**Kyphosis**	**Genu valgum**	

Bone and Joint Infections

Known as *osteomyelitis,* bone infections can become quite serious and require prompt diagnosis and treatment for the best outcome. Some low-grade bone infections may persist for years, causing extensive damage. Other infections may progress rapidly and are apparent within a day or so of onset. In either case, patients with bone infections risk amputations and loss of life if the infection is not treated aggressively. Infection can occur because of infectious diseases elsewhere in the body or because of a systemic disease. Risk factors for osteomyelitis include bedsores, retained metal fixation devices, diabetes, and a compromised immune system. Surgical treatment may include muscle flaps, bone grafting, and, as a last resort, amputation.

Joint infections are also called *septic arthritis.* A septic joint is serious and very difficult to manage. For this reason, joint replacement surgery often involves sealing the operating room door shut with tape to prevent any possible contamination of the new joint. No one may enter or leave until the procedure is complete. Risk factors for septic arthritis include immunosuppression, history of organ transplant, joint replacements, history of rheumatoid arthritis, systemic infection such as Lyme disease, TB, strep, gonorrhea, or staph.

EXERCISE 8.2

Instructions: Assign the correct ICD-9-CM code to the following diagnoses. Do not assign E codes.

1. Chondromalacia patella   _____
2. Inflammatory polyarthritis   _____
3. Painful knee   _____
4. Hemarthrosis due to sprain of radiohumeral joint   _____
5. Difficulty walking   _____
6. Wry neck   _____
7. Upper back pain   _____
8. Great toe bunion   _____
9. Painful spasms of trapezius muscle   _____
10. Aseptic necrosis head of femur   _____
11. Clubbing of fingers   _____
12. Ataxia   _____
13. Accessory fingers, both hands   _____
14. Congenital squashed nose   _____
15. Cervical rib   _____

Injuries

Sprains

A soft tissue injury to a joint and the surrounding tissue is known as a *sprain* or *strain*. The swelling from a sprain is due to ruptured or torn blood vessels bleeding into the surrounding tissue at the site of injury. *Edema* forms from intracellular fluid leakage and increases the swelling. *Ecchymosis*, or bruising, is due to continued bleeding into the injured area. Ankle sprains are the most common types of sprains and are graded on a scale of I to III in severity:

- Grade I: Mild pain and swelling; minor ligament tearing, but no instability
- Grade II: Moderate pain and swelling with bruising, moderate instability
- Grade III: Severe pain and bruising, unable to bear weight; complete rupture of ligaments

When ligament rupture is suspected, stress x-rays may be ordered. A technician will "stress," or twist the injured extremity while the x-ray is being taken, so the injured ligaments can be identified. Rest, ice, and anti-inflammatory medications are primary methods of treatment for sprains. A severe sprain can take up to six weeks to heal and in some cases may require reconstructive surgery on torn ligaments to improve range of motion (**ROM**).

A strain is assigned to the sprain codes in ICD-9-CM. The alphabetic index listing under sprains is much more comprehensive than the listing for strains. Instructions under "strain" tell the coder to *"see also"* Sprain, by site.

Dislocations

A *dislocation* is a joint that is forced out of its normal anatomic position. Most often, joints are dislocated by trauma, such as in contact sports or auto accidents, but dislocation may also occur with rheumatoid arthritis. The most commonly dislocated joint is the shoulder, followed by the elbow. The shoulder joint is the most mobile joint in the body and thus the most prone to injury. Dislocation can be forward, backward, or downward and can be partial or complete in nature. Often, dislocations cause a tear in the ligaments and tendons around the joint. A patient with multiple dislocations of the shoulder is said to have an *unstable shoulder.* Recurrent and/or severe dislocations may require surgery. Dislocations may also occur along with a fracture; these are known as *fracture dislocations.* Dislocations are coded to the 830–839 series and include the terms *displacement* and **subluxation.**

The ICD-9-CM includes the following terms as *closed* dislocation: simple, complete, partial, uncomplicated, and unspecified. *Open* dislocations include those specified as infected or compound, and dislocation, with foreign bodies. *Recurrent* dislocations are those listed as habitual, chronic, old, or recurrent. *Pathological dislocations* are located only under the alphabetic term "pathological." ICD-9-CM also refers the coder to code for a fracture if the patient has a documented fracture dislocation. Injuries of the same anatomical location are coded to the most severe injury. Congenital, pathological, and recurrent dislocations are excluded from this code range and are cross-referenced to other code categories. Pathological and recurrent dislocations are coded to the 718 category, while congenital dislocation is coded to the congenital anomaly chapter of ICD-9-CM, categories 754–755.

Fractures

A common layman's misinterpretation is that a fracture (**Fx**) is different from a broken bone. These two conditions are actually one and the same. Because most bones are so resilient, it takes a tremendous amount of pressure to break a bone. Fractures can happen in one of two ways: a traumatic injury, or a spontaneous (pathological) fracture in which brittle bone simply gives way.

ICD-9-CM classifies fractures as follows:

- Specific bone fractured
- Location of fracture on the bone
- Type of fracture

An *open fracture* indicates that bone fragments have broken the skin and there may be possible contamination of internal tissues. A closed fracture does not break the skin. Obvious deformity may not necessarily be present in either case.

The type of trauma to the bone further defines fractures. Common fractures and their definitions are listed below and shown in Figure 8.4.

- Avulsion: Tearing away a portion of bone; sometimes with skin and muscle; also known as a partial or incomplete amputation.
- Colles: Common fracture of the radial bone of the wrist; due to fall onto outstretched hand.
- Comminuted: Fracture in which the bone is shattered into pieces.

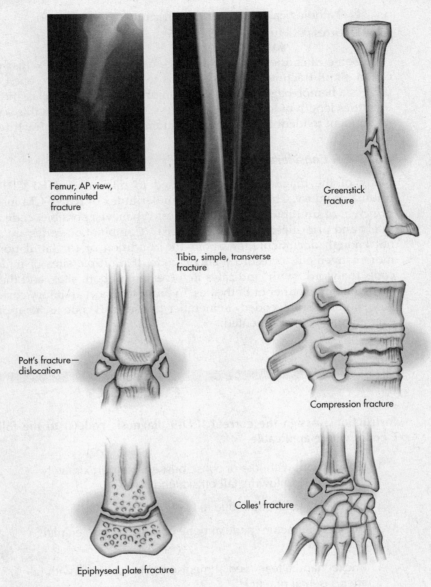

Femur, AP view, comminuted fracture

Tibia, simple, transverse fracture

Greenstick fracture

Pott's fracture—dislocation

Compression fracture

Epiphyseal plate fracture

Colles' fracture

Figure 8–4   Common fractures.

- Compound: An open fracture that protrudes through the skin.
- Compression: Vertebral fracture resulting from compression on the upper and lower parts of the vertebrae.
- Depressed: Fracture of the skull in which bone fragments are pushed down.
- Greenstick: Bending and partial fracture of the bone; not a complete fracture.
- Impacted: One end of the fractured bone is driven into the other.
- Oblique: Fractured ends are next to each other.
- Spiral: A twisting type of fracture often found in the tibia or femur.

Code range 800–829 describes fractures with the following exclusions:

- Malunion (733.81)
- Nonunion (733.82)

- Pathological or spontaneous fracture (733.10-733.19)
- Stress fractures (733.93-733.95)

Some categories within this range require their own exclusive fifth-digit subclassification. Skull fractures are classified as to whether they are open or closed and whether there is a hemorrhage or intracranial injury. Fifth-digit subclassification for codes 800–804 identifies length of loss of consciousness. Other fractures in this section require fifth-digit assignment to identify the specific anatomic location of the fracture.

ICD-9-CM Considerations for Trauma

Many of the diagnosis codes assigned to musculoskeletal CPT® procedures involve trauma or injury. Chapter 17 in the tabular index of ICD-9-CM instructs the coder on the principal of multiple coding of injuries. Whenever possible, code multiple injuries separately and prioritized in order of severity. Combination codes are available when there is not enough documentation about the condition or for tabulation purposes when it is more convenient to record a single code. If multiple sites of injury are specified in the code, the word "with" indicates involvement of both sites, and the word "and" indicates involvement of either or both sites. In order to report an injury correctly, the manner of injury should also be coded. Remember to use an E code as a supplementary code whenever an injury is documented.

EXERCISE 8.3

Instructions: Assign the correct ICD-9 diagnosis code(s) to the following diagnoses. Use E codes where applicable.

1. Concussion, with loss of consciousness of approximately 10 minutes, following fall off skateboard.

2. Sternoclavicular strain due to overexertion.

3. Accidental fracture parietal bone of skull, no intracranial injury noted.

4. Bucket handle tear, medial meniscus after collision with fall after baseball practice.

5. Blowout fracture left orbit following brawl.

6. Elbow dislocation after fall off monkey bars at school.

7. Fracture of pelvic rim after fall from horse.

8. Closed spiral fracture of femur shaft when struck by a motorcycle while jogging.

Lupus

Lupus is an autoimmune disorder that affects multiple areas of the body including skin, joints, kidneys, and blood. The cause of lupus is unknown, but the disorder may be triggered by certain prescription drug use, stress, and ultraviolet light. Researchers are currently studying possible genetic causes for the disorder. Approximately 85 percent of people who have lupus are women, with a higher incidence in non-Caucasian ethnic groups.

Three main types of lupus exist:

- Discoid: code 695.4, affects only the skin
- Systemic: code 710.0, affects multiple organ systems; known as "SLE," Systemic Lupus Erythematosus
- Drug-induced: Similar to systemic, but occurs after use of certain medications. Code adverse effect or poisoning, as appropriate.

The most common symptoms of lupus are aching and swelling of the joints, fever, and skin rash. Psychiatric conditions are also reported in a small percentage of patients. Corticosteroid treatment is commonly prescribed, and anti-malarial drugs are also known to be effective in controlling symptoms. Systemic lupus (**SLE**) is coded to 710.0 in ICD-9-CM. Discoid lupus of the skin is excluded from this category and is classified under the integumentary system. Other manifestations involving specific organs should be coded if present.

Scleroderma

As the name implies, scleroderma is a disease characterized by thickened, hardened skin. It is caused by excessive collagen production in the body. Two types of scleroderma exist:

- Localized: Affecting primarily the skin, manifested by oval patches or linear streaks of hardened tissue.
- Generalized: Manifests in the skin and over time gradually affects other organs; conversely may have sudden onset.

Scleroderma may involve the loss of hair and change in skin color, texture, and turgor. White lumps of calcium may appear under the skin. Patients with this disease can have arthritis, dry eyes and mouth, and problems with internal organs. The disease is controlled primarily with drugs. Systemic, or generalized, scleroderma is assigned to code category 710.1. Localized scleroderma is excluded from this category and should be coded to 701.0 in the integumentary system. Any manifestation that is identified should be coded in addition to 701.1.

EXERCISE 8.4

Part I

Instructions: Underline the main term in Part II for each diagnostic statement.

Part II

Instructions: Assign all pertinent diagnostic codes, including V and E codes where appropriate.

1. Rheumatoid arthritis _____

2. Acute osteomyelitis of the foot _____

3. Tear, rotator cuff, following repeated straining injury in baseball practice two days ago _____

4. Cast check, fractured tibia _____

5. Degenerative joint disease, knees _____

6. Uncomplicated dislocated ankle, following fall down stairs _____

7. Follow-up care for pathological fracture, lumbar vertebra   _____

8. Osgood-Schlatter disease of the knee   _____

9. Persistent pain hip, six weeks following joint replacement;
   x-rays ordered   _____

10. Systemic lupus erythematosis   _____

Neoplasms

Not all bone tumors are malignant. The suffix -*oma* implies tumor, while the prefix identifies the type of tumor or tissue of origin (i.e., *lymph*oma). Although primary bone tumors are not common, metastatic disease or spread of another tumor to the bones is very common. Bone lesions are found most commonly by x-ray, but may be studied further with CT, MRI and bone scans, needle and open biopsies.

Risk factors for bone cancer include:

- Rapid growth in children or young adults
- Other cancers treated with radiation
- History of Paget's disease

- Multiple exostoses (bone spurs)
- Multiple osteochondromas
- Multiple enchondromas (benign cartilage tumors)

Table 8.2 describes various types of primary bone tumors, where they are located, and how they are treated.

Metastatic bone cancer occurs when a malignant lesion sheds neoplastic cells into the bloodstream or lymphatic system, and the malignancy begins to grow in the bones. Bony metastasis occurs most often along the central axis of the body. The most commonly affected sites (in order of frequency) are:

- Spine
- Pelvis

Table 8–2   Types of Primary Bone Tumors

Type of Tumor	Treatment/Characteristics
Benign	Almost all benign tumors are cured by surgical intervention.
Giant cell—benign	Corticosteroid treatment; common in those with Italian ancestry or those with history of Paget's disease.
Osteoblastoma	Primitive bone tissue, commonly found on the spine of children.
Osteochondroma	Bony exostosis that occurs near the end of long bones.
Osteoma	Simple tumor composed of bone growing in an abnormal place.
Malignant	Radiation and/or surgery; systemic chemo or hormone therapy.
Chondrosarcoma	Develops most commonly in adults in cartilage of ribs, arms, legs, and pelvis.
Chordoma	Arises at the base of the skull and in vertebral column. Difficult to treat and may recur.
Ewing's sarcoma	Develops in the hollow part of long bones, usually striking children.
Fibrosarcoma	Connective tissue neoplasm that can spread to bone.
Giant cell tumor—malignant	Only a small portion of giant cell tumors is malignant. Affects long bones of young to middle-aged adults.
Osteosarcoma	Most common bone tumor; usually occurs in young males in bones of arms and legs.

- Hips
- Femur
- Skull
- Ribs
- Shoulders

A tumor is considered to be recurrent when the malignancy comes back after the patient has had a period of remission. Metastatic bone lesions are grouped into three different types of recurrence:

- Local: Near the same anatomical area/organ where the tumor started
- Regional: In lymph nodes near the original site
- Distant: Far from the site of origin, in different organs or tissues (also known as metastatic recurrence)

Treatment for bone tumors may be systemic, using chemotherapy, immunotherapy, or hormone treatments (testosterone/estrogen). Local therapy may also be performed, including radiation and/or surgery to excise the tumor or to apply an internal fixation device for support.

ICD-9-CM Considerations for Neoplasms

Documentation should support whether the tumor is primary or secondary, benign, or uncertain behavior. All of the secondary (metastatic) bone neoplasms are coded to 198.5, Secondary malignant neoplasm of the bone and bone marrow.

Patients who have a personal history of bone neoplasm should be coded with V10.81. If the patient is currently undergoing radiation or chemotherapy, use codes V58.0 or V58.1 along with a code to identify the site of the neoplasm. Aftercare following surgery for neoplasm is coded with V58.42.

EXERCISE 8.5

Instructions: Assign the correct ICD-9 neoplasm codes to the scenarios below.

1. Myelolipoma, gastrocnemius muscle   _____

2. Osteosarcoma, primary site, femur   _____

3. Metastasis to ribs, primary unknown   _____

4. Primary malignancy, soft tissue, shoulder with metastasis to scapula   _____

5. Malignant melanoma, metastatic to soft tissue of the anterior thigh   _____

V Codes

Important V codes to remember include V13.4, History of arthritis; V17.7, Family history of arthritis; and V13.5, History of other musculoskeletal system disorders. Use V82.1 for screening for rheumatoid arthritis. Other important V codes to consider include category V54, Other orthopedic aftercare. This category differentiates aftercare for healing traumatic fractures from aftercare for healing pathologic fractures. Use code V58.43 for aftercare following surgery for injury and trauma (excluding healing traumatic fractures), and code V58.78 for aftercare following surgery of the musculoskeletal system not elsewhere classified.

CPT® DEFINITIONS OF MUSCULOSKELETAL SYSTEM TERMS

Closed Treatment: No direct visual observation of fracture site by surgically opening the wound. Methods of treatment for closed fractures include:

- Without manipulation.
- With manipulation.
- With or without traction.

Open Treatment: Two methods include:

- Surgical opening with direct visualization of fracture site.
- Surgical opening without direct visualization, remote from fracture site, in order to insert fixation device.

ORIF: Open Reduction, Internal Fixation of fracture.

Percutaneous Skeletal Fixation: Fixation (pins) placed through the skin and across a fracture site with the aid of x-ray imaging.

Reduction of Fracture: Also known as "manipulation." Realignment of bone ends in their correct anatomical position; may be performed as an open procedure or closed.

CPT® CODING OF MUSCULOSKELETAL PROCEDURES

The Musculoskeletal chapter of CPT® is arranged anatomically from head to toe with only a few exceptions. Subheadings are arranged in a consistent, logical pattern, starting with incision, excision, introduction or removal, repair, revision and/or reconstruction, fracture/dislocation, and amputation. The exceptions to this arrangement include the following headings:

- General
- Spine
- Abdomen
- Application of casts and strapping
- Endoscopy/Arthroscopy

Familiarity with the arrangement of this chapter facilitates correct code assignment.

General

Incision

Codes 20000–20005 describe the incision of soft tissue abscesses. Abcesses in the musculoskeletal system are deeper than those described in the integumentary system. Documentation in the chart should differentiate between superficial and deep or complicated abscesses.

Wound Exploration

Four codes are available to describe exploration of penetrating wounds, depending upon the anatomical site of injury. Services include enlargement of the wound, surgical exploration, extensions of dissection, removal of foreign body, and ligation of minor blood vessels not requiring laparotomy or thoracotomy. If the service consists only of wound repair, without enlargement or extension of dissection, the coder is directed to the integumentary system and the repair codes located there. Any type of major repair to specific structures or blood vessels requires the use of codes specific to those areas, rather than the wound exploration codes.

Excision

This section involves primarily biopsy codes. Different approaches may include percutaneous needle or open (excisional biopsy) and may differentiate by depth (superficial vs. deep) or anatomic location (thoracic vs. lumbar).

Introduction or Removal

The term *aspiration* means to draw off fluid with a needle. The term *arthrocentesis* means to draw off fluid from a joint. In CPT®, the introduction of a needle into a joint may involve either aspiration or injection.

The code range for Introduction or Removal, 20500–20615, includes codes for injections of trigger points as well as joints and deeper structures in the musculoskeletal system. Coders should be watchful in this section for descriptors that differentiate simple vs. deep and diagnostic vs. therapeutic; those that mention specific diagnoses, such as carpal tunnel syndrome (**CTS**) or foreign body, or those that specify anatomic location—small, medium, or large joints. Codes 20550 and 20551 are used to report multiple injections of a single tendon sheath, tendon insertion, origin, ligament, or aponeurosis. Multiple injections to the same tendon sheath, ligament, origin, insertion, or aponeurosis are reported only once, and multiple injections to different sites are reported for each injection given. In contrast, codes 20552 and 20553 are used only for trigger point injections and are reported only once per session. The number of needle sticks is not a factor in code assignment for 20552–20553. Code 20612 is used for the aspiration and/or injection of a **ganglion** of any location.

Example:

Diagnosis: Trochanteric bursitis.

Procedure:

Joint injection, right hip. A sterile prep of the right greater trochanteric bursa is performed using Betadine. The skin is anesthetized with ethyl chloride spray. 40 mg of Depo-Medrol together with 4 cc of 1% plain lidocaine and 4 cc of 0.5% plain Marcaine are instilled into the right greater trochanteric bursa joint through the lateral portal without difficulty. A sterile bandage is applied. The patient tolerated the procedure well.

> ICD-9-CM: 726.5
>
> CPT®: 20610
>
> HCPCS: J1030, Depo-Medrol

Replantation

The term *replantation* is *not* synonymous with *amputation*. Replantation involves the re-attachment of a traumatically severed extremity. Each code in this section of CPT® requires "complete amputation" before the repair is performed. A partial (incomplete) amputation or avulsion is described by codes specific to the repair of the bones, nerves, tendons, and blood vessels with a Modifier 52 to indicate reduced services.

Grafts

Grafting procedures performed on the musculoskeletal system can be accomplished using various types of grafting materials. Cartilage, tendon, bone, and fascia can be used as grafts and coded separately when the graft is not described as part of the basic procedure. Codes in this section are all Modifier 51 exempt. If multiple surgeons are in-volved in a procedure, each reports his or her portion separately; therefore, a 62 modifier should not be reported with the bone graft codes.

Terminology for musculoskeletal grafting is the same as for the integumentary sys-tem; the only difference is in the materials used.

- **Allograft:** Tissue obtained from another human; usually obtained from a bone bank.
- **Autograft:** Tissue obtained from the patient in a fresh state.
- **Bone bank:** Source of sterilized cadaver bone; used for grafting in either large pieces or morselized (ground).
- **Homograft:** Human tissue graft.
- **Xenograft:** Graft from another species (bovine, porcine).

Other Procedures

This section includes a variety of miscellaneous procedures such as electrical stimulation/ultrasound to assist in bone healing, monitoring of interstitial fluid, and bone flaps with microvascular anastomosis.

EXERCISE 8.6

Instructions: Link the appropriate diagnosis to the procedures listed below.

1. 20220 _____
2. 22521 _____
3. 23210 _____
4. 20552 _____
5. 22850 _____
6. 24344 _____
7. 21386 _____
8. 28298 _____
9. 27130 _____
10. 21151 _____

a. Painful trapezius muscle
b. Mass, clavicle
c. Treacher-Collins syndrome
d. Blowout fracture, orbit
e. Fracture, lumbar vertebra
f. Aftercare for painful Harrington rod, spine
g. Malignant neoplasm, scapula
h. Tear, lateral collateral ligament, elbow
i. Osteoarthritis, hip
j. Bunion, great toe

Body Sections

In CPT®, each body section contains its own set of codes that refer to incision; excision; introduction or removal; and repair, revision, and/or reconstruction. Although the anatomical sites may differ, this text will address musculoskeletal procedures by method-ology. As in most sections of CPT®, the coder may notice that procedures are arranged under each subheading from the simplest to the most complex.

Formula for Success

Before assigning a musculoskeletal system code:

1. Double check the subheading for the correct anatomical site.
2. Make sure word endings match the operative report: *ectomy* is very different than -*otomy*.
3. Check to see if the code descriptor identifies procedures that are deep, complicated, each, single, multiple, or uses terms such as *and, or, with* or *without*.

Incision

Codes grouped under the incision subheading include many procedures with the suffix of -*otomy*, meaning "opening." Such procedures include incision (and drainage) of abscess or hematoma; incision into bone; incision and release of muscle, fascia, tendon, or scar tissue; exploration of joints with removal of foreign body; and decompression. The complexity of these procedures ranges from simple to difficult. Certain procedures, such as drainage of finger abscess, are split into two distinct codes. Code 26010 is a simple incision when the abscess is located in the cutaneous tissue. Code 26011 is a complicated incision used when the abscess is located in the deep subcutaneous tissue and a debridement with irrigation is performed. Coders should read carefully to ensure correct code assignment.

Example: 23930   Incision and drainage, upper arm or elbow area; deep abscess or hematoma

23931   bursa

Codes that use the terms "each" or "each digit" should be coded for as many times as the procedure is performed. Other codes specify the terms "single" or "multiple." The student should highlight these words when reading through each section of CPT®.

Excision

The terms *removal, resection,* and *excision* are very similar in meaning. The suffix -*ectomy* means to remove or excise. Biopsies and multiple types of excisions are located under this subheading. Also included are procedures that involve an incision (-*otomy*) along with an excision. Removal of tumors is often included in this section. The difficulty of the procedure is illustrated in terms such as "partial," "complete," and "radical."

Examples: 23105   Arthrotomy, glenohumeral joint, with synovectomy, with or without biopsy

23220   Radical resection of bone tumor, proximal humerus

Introduction or Removal: Specific Anatomic Sites

Joint injection procedures (arthrography) are listed under the "Introduction or Removal" subheading in their respective anatomic headings. Use these codes for the injection of dye prior to radiology procedures. In addition, this subheading is used to describe the removal of foreign bodies and joint implants. Throughout this entire chapter, the coder should vigilantly watch for terminology within the medical record or operative report that identifies the difficulty of the procedure, and is documented by the physician as described in the codes below.

Examples: 23330   Removal of foreign body, shoulder; subcutaneous

23331   deep (e.g., Neer hemiarthroplasty removal)

23332   complicated (e.g., total shoulder)

Repair, Revision, and/or Reconstruction

Procedures listed under this subheading include those with the following suffixes:

- plasty: Plastic repair
- orrhaphy: To suture
- tenodesis: Fixation of tendon
- pexy: To fix

Other terms encountered under this subheading include transfer, transplantation, tendon lengthening/shortening, repair and reinsertion, reconstruction, and realignment. Most notably, procedures performed on the hands and fingers are much more extensive than those performed on the feet or any other part of the body. The hand contains numerous small tendons, which control fine motor movements. These tendons are difficult to repair and often require a hand specialist. The area of the hand that is the most difficult to repair, called "zone 2" or "no man's land," is located between the upper palmar crease and the middle joints of all five fingers.

In order to code reconstruction/repair and revisions correctly, the coder must know exactly what and how many tendons are being operated on, whether a graft is involved, and whether the operating microscope is used. Use of the operating microscope is inherent in those codes with the term "microvascular" included in the descriptor and should not be coded separately.

Example: 26556 Transfer, free toe joint, with microvascular anastomosis
(Do not report code 69990 in addition to codes 26556)

Other types of procedures found in this section of CPT® include reconstruction of both acquired and congenital musculoskeletal deformities.

Bunion repairs are also listed under the subheading of Repair, Revision, and/or Reconstruction. These may be referred to by eponym; that is, by using the name of the surgeon who invented the procedure. Look in the index under the eponym or under the surgical term to find the correct type of bunion repair.

Example: 28292 Keller, McBride, or Mayo type procedure

Fracture Care vs. Application of Casts and Strapping

Although fracture care and casting/splinting/strapping comprise only a portion of the musculoskeletal chapter, there remains considerable confusion regarding the correct assignment of CPT® codes.

Fracture care codes are those codes listed under the anatomical headings in CPT®. In most cases, a 90-day global period is assigned. These codes are used when the physician provides initial fracture care as well as follow-up care for the full global period. These codes should not be used by a physician who is stabilizing a fracture by the application of a splint until the patient can be seen by an orthopedic specialist. Occasionally, Emergency Department physicians will reduce a fracture and send the patient elsewhere for follow-up. Modifiers 54 and 55 may be used by the ER physician and orthopedic specialist to split the global fee for fracture care. Billing with these modifiers must be carefully coordinated by both providers in order to prevent errors in modifier assignment. Occasionally, reimbursement of the entire global fee is paid to only one provider, so the coding/billing staff must be vigilant in monitoring payer response.

Fracture care codes may be assigned when:

- Care for the entire global period is provided, with first cast/splint or strap application included.
- Restorative treatment or procedure is rendered by second physician following initial cast/splint application.

Casting and strapping codes are located near the end of the Musculoskeletal chapter of CPT®. These codes should be used in the following circumstances:

- When casting/strapping or splinting is a replacement procedure during or after follow-up care.
- The initial casting/strapping or splinting service without a restorative treatment or procedure is provided.
- Casting/strapping or splinting is done to afford comfort to a patient.

Casting/strapping or splinting codes should *not* be used in the following circumstance:

- When the physician who applies the initial cast, strap, or splint assumes all of the subsequent fracture care.

Other things to contemplate when assigning these codes:

- Supply codes should be considered when applying casts, straps, or splints.
- Evaluation and Management services provided in addition to casting/splinting may be coded if the documentation supports and justifies the use of E/M codes.
- Cast removal codes should only be used when the physician removing the cast is different than the one who applied the first cast.

EXERCISE 8.7

Instructions: Assign the correct CPT® procedure codes for professional services to the following scenarios. Use modifiers where appropriate and <u>identify</u> billable supplies only for those procedures performed outside the hospital/facility setting. Do not assign diagnosis codes or HCPC codes.

1. Application of shoulder figure-of-eight strap for fractured clavicle by physician in free-standing Urgent Care Clinic.

   Procedure: _____   Supply: _____

2. Posterior short leg plaster half-splint applied by physician in the office for severe right ankle sprain.

   Procedure: _____   Supply: _____

3. Closed reduction, Colles fracture, in outpatient surgery; no manipulation required.

   Procedure: _____

4. Percutaneous pinning of base of first metacarpal bone and neck of second metacarpal bone, right hand, in ambulatory surgical center.

    Procedure: _____   _____

5. Open reduction, internal fixation fractured tibial shaft, as inpatient.

    Procedure: _____

Spine/Vertebral Column Surgery

Procedures in this section deal only with the bony portion of the spine. Operations on the spinal cord and intervertebral disk material are coded to the Nervous System chapter of CPT®.

Spinal procedures often include additional procedures, such as arthrodesis (fusion) of a joint, bone grafting, and instrumentation. Grafting and instrumentation codes are Modifier 51 exempt, since they are never performed as stand-alone procedures. Arthrodesis codes should be reported with a 51 when they are performed with another procedure, such as fracture care or laminectomy. When they are done as part of a spinal operation, they are designated as add-on codes and are Modifier 51 exempt.

Reimbursement Considerations

Depending on the surgical approach used, two surgeons may lend their specialized skills to a spinal procedure. When two surgeons work together as primary surgeons, a Modifier 62 is appended to the same CPT® code reported by each surgeon. This is known as the co-surgeon modifier. Each surgeon will dictate his or her own portion of the operative report, unlike assistant surgeons (Modifier 80), who do not dictate. Usually, a general surgeon establishes the approach and closes the surgical wound, while the second surgeon, an orthopedic or neurosurgeon, performs the definitive portion of the procedure.

Using Modifier 62 requires careful coordination of the billing to ensure that both surgeons are using the same correct CPT® code and diagnosis code. Reimbursement for this modifier is dependent upon payer preference. Some payers will allow 125 percent of the UCR (Usual, Customary and Reasonable) fee schedule in a geographic area and pay 62.5 percent to each surgeon; others will pay a flat rate to only one surgeon, who must split the payment with the second surgeon.

Table 8.3 displays the logic for assigning modifiers to different components of spinal surgery.

Surgical Approaches

Arthrodesis (fusion) is accomplished by one of two approaches:

- Posterior: Through the back with the patient lying prone.
- Anterior/anterolateral: Through the neck, chest, or abdomen with the patient lying supine.

Table 8–3   Assigning Modifiers for Special Surgery

Type of Surgery	Arthrodesis Codes	Instrumentation Codes	Bone Graft Codes
Osteotomy	Add -51	⊘51, ⊘62	⊘51, ⊘62
Fracture Dislocation	Add -51	⊘51, ⊘62	⊘51, ⊘62
Spinal Deformity	Add -51	⊘51, ⊘62	⊘51, ⊘62

The general surgeon provides the approach when the anterior/anterolateral approach is used. The muscles, blood vessels, and organs are moved out of the way to provide exposure of the spine for the orthopedic or neurosurgeon. While the approach is being established, a bone graft is often obtained by the second surgeon to use for the arthrodesis. Bone grafts are typically obtained from the iliac crest on the hip or from a rib.

Instrumentation

Internal fixation called *instrumentation* is affixed to the spinal column to maintain alignment of the spine while healing. The fixation device is screwed into the bone of the spine and occasionally requires hooks and wires to pull the spine into alignment. A common lay term to describe one type of instrumentation is a "rod." When a Harrington rod or any other instrumentation is used, the patient cannot twist or bend the spine at that point.

Two types of instrumentation are used to stabilize the spine:

- Segmental
- Nonsegmental

Each vertebrae of the spine is considered to be a segment. CPT® describes a segment as a single complete vertebral bone with associated articular processes and lamina. Thus, a fixation device that is attached to at least three points on the spine is considered to be a segmental instrumentation; that is, one attachment at each end of the construct, with at least one (possibly more) in between. A nonsegmental instrumentation is affixed only at each end of the construct, with nothing in between—similar to a suspension bridge.

These procedures are commonly performed for trauma or congenital malformations. Arthrodesis may also be performed at the same time. This creates a permanent fusion by grafting bone into the area where fusion is desired.

Amputation vs. Disarticulation

An *amputation* is a procedure that is performed to remove all or part of a limb. Amputations should not be confused with disarticulations, which are also grouped under the same subheading. A *disarticulation* is the removal of a limb through the joint. An amputation is the removal at a place on the limb other than a joint. Amputations and disarticulations involve creation of skin flaps to cover the bone or joint end and careful resection of blood vessels, nerves, and muscles.

Arthroscopy

Joint arthroscopy has made major advances within the last several years. While initially used only on knee joints, almost any joint in the body can now be "scoped." Advantages of joint arthroscopy include faster recovery, smaller incisions, and less blood loss than an open procedure. Arthroscopic procedures may be diagnostic or surgical in nature. A surgical scope *always* includes a diagnostic component, while a diagnostic scope may be performed without any additional surgical or therapeutic procedures.

Any scope procedure will involve more than one incision. Portal incisions are small, however, and allow passage of trocar sleeves through which various cutting and shaving instruments may be passed. Inflow and outflow cannulas for fluid irrigation, video camera, and suturing/cautery instruments may also pass through the trocar sleeves.

The arthroscopy codes in CPT® are arranged from the head to toe and include temporamandibular joint, shoulder, elbow, wrist, hip, knee, ankle, and metacarpophalangeal joints. The coder should carefully read the operative report and make sure that each individual procedure that is performed is listed separately.

The *meniscus* is a kidney-shaped piece of cartilage that cushions a synovial joint. The shoulder, elbow, hip, knee, and ankle are all synovial joints. Torn menisci are often repaired through arthroscopic surgery.

Meniscectomy procedures that are performed on the knee require careful reading of the code descriptors. Several codes contain the phrases "medial AND lateral" and "medial OR lateral," which significantly change the meaning of the code.

EXERCISE 8.8

Instructions: Assign the correct CPT® codes for the following (do not add modifiers).

1. Arthroscopic rotator cuff repair   _____

2. Arthroscopic anterior cruciate ligament repair   _____

3. Arthroscopic complete shoulder synovectomy, converted to open procedure   _____

4. Arthroscopy, knee, with medial and lateral menisectomy   _____

5. Diagnostic elbow arthroscopy, with synovial biopsy   _____

Modifiers

Both CPT® and HCPCS modifiers are appropriate for use with musculoskeletal system codes. CPT® modifiers that may be applied to some Evaluation and Management services include 24, Unrelated E/M service by the same physician during a postoperative period; 25, Significant, separately identifiable E/M service by the same physician on the same day of the procedure or other service; and 57, Decision for surgery. Some of the most common surgical modifiers used include 50 for bilateral procedure, 51 for multiple procedures, 52 for reduced services, 53 for discontinued procedure, 58 for staged or related procedure, 59 for distinct procedural service, and 62 for two surgeons.

HCPCS modifiers typically are used on Medicare patients to identify right (RT) and left (LT), fingers (FA–F9) and toes (TA–T9). Other payers may recognize these modifiers as well.

EXERCISE 8.9

Instructions: Choose the correct modifier for each scenario.

1. A 66-year-old trauma patient is admitted to the Emergency Department, and a fractured left femoral shaft is diagnosed. An orthopedic consultant arrives, evaluates the patient, and decides the best course of action is to perform an open reduction and internal fixation of the fracture. A consultation containing a comprehensive history, comprehensive physical exam, and medical decision making of moderate complexity is performed. The patient is admitted and taken to surgery. Once in the surgical suite, an open reduction with screws and plate fixation is accomplished.

Assign the correct modifier(s) to each CPT® code:

a. 99244 _____

b. 27507 _____

2. A 24-year-old patient had severe bilateral knee swelling following a fall from the roof of a house. The fall occurred 12 hours previously, and the patient landed on his hands and knees. The patient also suffered a grade III right ankle sprain and contusions of his hands. His regular family physician saw him in the clinic. X-rays demonstrated no fractures, but effusions of both knees. An expanded problem-focused history was obtained, and a detailed exam was performed. Medical decision making was of moderate complexity. Aspiration of the joint fluid of both knees was performed and the ankle sprain was splinted.

Assign the correct modifiers to each CPT® code:

a. 99214 _____

b. 20610 _____

c. 29540 _____ _____

CHAPTER REVIEW

1. Skeletal muscle is also called:
   a. cardiac muscle
   b. visceral muscle
   c. striated muscle
   d. smooth muscle

2. The meniscus is a piece of tissue that is:
   a. located in synovial joints
   b. similar to tendons and ligaments
   c. easily torn
   d. a and c

3. A 4-year-old child sustained a deep puncture wound to the thigh after tripping and falling on a sharp stick. Exploration with alligator forceps was performed to determine if any pieces of debris remained in the wound. No foreign bodies were found. Give the correct ICD-9 and CPT® codes for this scenario.
   a. 890.0, E885.9, 27372
   b. 890.0, E888.0, 20103
   c. 890.0, E885.9, 27301
   d. 890.1, E888.0, 27372

4. Stabilization rods affixed to L3, L4, and L5 are an example of:
   a. segmental instrumentation
   b. nonsegmental instrumentation
   c. arthrodesis
   d. external fixation

5. The most common type of bone malignancy is:
   a. Ewing's sarcoma
   b. osteosarcoma
   c. fibrosarcoma
   d. giant cell tumor

6. Casting and splinting codes should be used when:
   a. The physician is reducing the fracture and assumes all pre- and postoperative global care.
   b. The physician is reapplying a second cast.
   c. The physician applies a splint for supportive care and transfers to an orthopedic MD.
   d. b and c.

7. A sprain involving a complete tear of a ligament is a/an
   a. avulsion
   b. grade I
   c. dislocation
   d. grade III

8. A patient returns to her orthopedic physician for follow-up of a Colles fracture. Choose the correct ICD-9-CM code:
   a. V54.12
   b. V54.22
   c. V67.4
   d. V58.78

9. The term *microvascular anastomosis* implies:
   a. the excision of small vessels
   b. the suture repair of microscopic nerves
   c. the use of the operating microscope
   d. b and c

10. When bone, cartilage, tendon, or fascia lata grafts are obtained, they should be coded
    a. with a 51 modifier
    b. only if the graft is not included in the basic procedure
    c. only if an autograft is used
    d. only if an allograft is used

11. A patient with a previous C6-7 fusion is scheduled for thyroid surgery. The previous fusion affects the operative area and should be coded as:
    a. V13.5
    b. V45.4
    c. V15.5
    d. V58.75

Case Studies

Instructions: Assign the correct ICD-9-CM and CPT® codes for each scenario. Do not assign E codes.

Case Study 1

Preoperative Diagnosis:	Mass, left hand
Postoperative Diagnosis:	Benign giant cell tumor of the left hand
Operation:	Excision of 1.0 × 1.0 × 1.0 cm subcutaneous mass from hypothenar region

Details of Operation

The patient was taken to the operating room and placed supine on the operating table. A left Bier block was administered and achieved. The left upper extremity was prepped and draped free in standard fashion. Under satisfactory anesthesia and tourniquet control, a hockey-stick type incision was made with the longitudinal flap over the mass. The skin and subcutaneous tissues were divided sharply. Obvious bleeders were cauterized with needlepoint cautery. The flap was elevated over the mass. This was a 1.0 × 1.0 × 1.0 cm mass in the subcutaneous region. It did not appear to be attached to any deeper structures. It was bluntly dissected from the surrounding tissues and removed. It was sent to pathology for examination.

Hemostasis was obtained using needlepoint cautery. The skin flap was approximated with apical and horizontal mattress sutures of 4-0 nylon. Sterile dressings were applied. The tourniquet was deflated while pressure was applied to the wound. A quick check showed no evidence of obvious bleeding. Total tourniquet time was 24 minutes. The vascular status to the hand returned to normal promptly with no delay. There were no apparent complications and the patient tolerated the procedure well. She was transported to the recovery area in good condition.

Blood loss:	None
Complications:	None
Anesthesia:	Bier block
Specimen:	Mass

ICD-9-CM diagnosis code: _____

CPT® procedure code: _____

Case Study 2

Preoperative Diagnosis:	Fracture of the left femur shaft
Postoperative Diagnosis:	Fracture of the left femur shaft
Operation:	Closed reduction and then 1-½ hip spica cast application

Indications for Operation

This 2-year-old was being pushed in a swing and fell out, sustaining a spiral fracture of the midshaft of the left femur. This was somewhat displaced into varus. She was brought to the operating room for closed reduction and spica cast application under anesthesia.

Details of Operation

The patient was taken to the operating room. On her stretcher an IV was started and general anesthesia administered. She was then carefully placed on the hip spica frame. My assistant held her lower extremities in the appropriate position. I performed manipulative closed reduction of the femur and found a satisfactory position palpably. Felt padding was placed over the iliac crest, the sacral area, the left kneecap, and the left Achilles area and taped to the skin with paper tape. Ample cast padding was applied to a 1-½ left hip spica. A fiberglass hip spica was then applied. A dowel was placed between the thighs.

AP and lateral permanent x-rays were then taken, and there was an acceptable amount of slight anterior angulation with essentially no varus angulation on the AP view. The amount of shortening was approximately 1 cm, which was ideal.

There were no apparent complications, and the patient tolerated the procedure extremely well. She was transported to the recovery room in good condition.

Blood loss:	None
Complications:	None

ICD-9-CM diagnosis code: _____

CPT® procedure code: _____

Case Study 3

Preoperative Diagnosis:	Medial right knee pain with MRI evidence of tear of right medial and lateral meniscus
Postoperative Diagnosis:	Tear of medial meniscus, right knee
Operation:	Arthroscopy right knee and partial medial meniscectomy

Indications for Operation

This 40-year-old man had spontaneously arising pain in the medial aspect of his right knee for about three weeks prior to presenting. He could not recall any injury. An MRI showed an abnormality of both the medial and lateral meniscus involving the posterior horns. He did not seem to be having any lateral symptoms. He was brought to surgery for arthroscopy of his right knee.

Details of Operation

The patient was taken to the operating room and placed on the operating table supine. He was sat up for administration of spinal anesthesia, which was achieved, and then returned supine. The left leg was placed in a well-padded leg holder. A tourniquet was placed round the right proximal thigh and a leg holder below that. The right lower extremity was prepped and draped free in standard fashion. A stab wound was made superomedially and a drainage infusion trocar placed into the suprapatellar pouch. The joint was distended with saline. A stab wound was made lateral to the patellar tendon and a counter incision medial to the patellar tendon. The scope was initially introduced anterolaterally. The patellofemoral joint appeared normal. There were no significant plicae. The ACL was intact. There was slight hypertrophy of the ligamentum mucous, and this was debrided with the shaver. The medial compartment showed a tear of the posterior horn of the medial meniscus involving zones A, II, and III. This meniscus tear was rather fragmented. It was removed with a basket forceps and smoothed with an articular shaver. There were some fibrillations in the area of both the femur and the tibia that were shaved.

The lateral compartment appeared essentially normal. Probing the lateral meniscus indicated a weakness in zone F-111, but there was no actual tear in this area. It was therefore elected not to remove any of the lateral meniscus. The lateral compartment was otherwise pristine.

At this point, the joint was copiously irrigated with saline through the scope and all instruments were withdrawn. A solution containing 80 mg of Depo-Medrol, 4 cc 1% plain Lidocaine, and 4 cc of 0.25% Marcaine with 1:100,000 epinephrine was instilled into the joint through a separate needle puncture.

The stab wounds were approximated with simple 4-0 nylon suture. Sterile dressings followed by a Webrile/ACE bandage dressing were applied. The tourniquet was deflated after 41 minutes of tourniquet time. The vascular status of the foot returned to normal promptly with no delay. There were no apparent complications and the patient tolerated the procedure well. He was transported to the recovery room in good condition.

Anesthesia:	Spinal
EBL:	Zero
Complications	None

ICD-9-CM diagnosis code: _____

CPT® procedure code: _____

CHAPTER
9

The Respiratory System

OBJECTIVES

1. Identify the basic anatomy of the respiratory system.
2. Recognize the link between the ICD-9-CM codes and the CPT® codes used in the Respiratory section.
3. Correctly apply ICD-9-CM codes to respiratory diagnoses.
4. Correctly apply CPT® codes to respiratory surgical procedures.

TERMINOLOGY AND ACRONYMS

ARDS   Adult respiratory distress syndrome.

CTA   Clear to auscultation.

ET tube   Endotracheal tube.

LLL   Left lower lobe.

LUL   Left upper lobe.

Neb/Nebulizer   Medication administered by aerosol mist through a special machine.

PPD   Purified protein derivative, used for tuberculosis testing.

RAD   Reactive airway disease.

RDS   Respiratory distress syndrome.

RLL   Right lower lobe.

RUL   Right upper lobe.

SOB   Shortness of breath.

TB   Tuberculosis.

URI   Upper respiratory infection.

ANATOMY

The major function of the respiratory system is the exchange of gases. When air is inhaled, oxygen in the lungs replaces carbon dioxide in the blood. Carbon dioxide is then expelled from the body on exhalation.

Anatomically, the respiratory system is divided into two sections—the upper and lower respiratory systems. The upper respiratory system is made up of the nose, mouth, pharynx, and larynx. The function of the upper airway is to warm, humidify, and filter the air that is inhaled.

The lower respiratory system consists of the trachea, bronchi, bronchioles, and lungs. The bronchioles contain the alveoli, which are the chief elements of gas exchange in the lungs. Blockage of the lower airways can lead to respiratory distress and failure. The lower respiratory system also produces mucus, which acts to trap foreign particles. When a problem occurs with mucus production, atmospheric pollutants and irritants can enter and inflame the lungs, leading to pneumonia, bronchitis, or asthma.

The lungs are divided into lobes: three on the right and two on the left. Each lobe is further divided into lobules and segments. Lungs have a sponge-like appearance and contain clusters of air-filled sacs, called alveoli. Gas exchange takes place at the cellular level in the alveoli. Alterations in the gas exchange process or an airway obstruction can cause unoxygenated blood to be pumped through the body.

See Anatomy Plates 4 through 6 in Appendix A for an illustration of the respiratory system.

EXERCISE 9.1

Instructions: Using a medical dictionary if necessary, match the layman's term with the medical term.

1. Sore throat   _____

2. Cold   _____

3. Hay fever   _____

4. Consumption   _____

5. Black lung   _____

6. Grippe   _____

DISEASE PROCESSES AND ICD-9-CM CODING OF THE RESPIRATORY SYSTEM

The respiratory system is prone to many different diseases and conditions. A few of these are described below.

Sinusitis

Sinusitis is an infection of the nasal sinuses. It can be acute or chronic, viral, fungal, or bacterial in nature. Recurrent sinusitis is considered to be a chronic sinusitis, rather than acute. All sinuses may be involved with an infection (*pansinusitis*), or just a single sinus. Sinus infections are difficult to clear because the warm, moist atmosphere in the sinuses encourages growth of microorganisms.

Adult Respiratory Distress Syndrome (ARDS)

Adult Respiratory Distress Syndrome (**ARDS**) is a form of pulmonary edema. The buildup of fluids, or edema, can cause the lungs to stiffen. This reduces ventilation and reduces oxygenation of pulmonary capillary blood.

Asbestosis

Asbestosis is caused by prolonged exposure to airborne asbestos particles. This condition may occur fifteen to twenty years after a period of regular exposure to asbestos. The inhaled asbestos fibers become encased in sputum, or lung tissue, and cause an interstitial fibrosis.

Asthma

Asthma is a chronic reactive airway disorder. Asthma is caused by episodic airway obstruction resulting from bronchospasms, increased mucus secretions, and mucosal edema (see Figure 9.1). Asthma is divided into two ICD-9-CM subclassifications: Extrinsic asthma (493.0x), due to sensitivity to external allergens, usually beginning in childhood; and Intrinsic asthma (493.1x), which is a reaction to internal, nonallergenic factors. Intrinsic asthma has no external cause and usually occurs in adulthood after a severe respiratory tract infection. The following fifth-digit subclassifications specify the current status of the patient.

- 0 unspecified
- 1 with status asthmaticus
- 2 with (acute) exacerbation

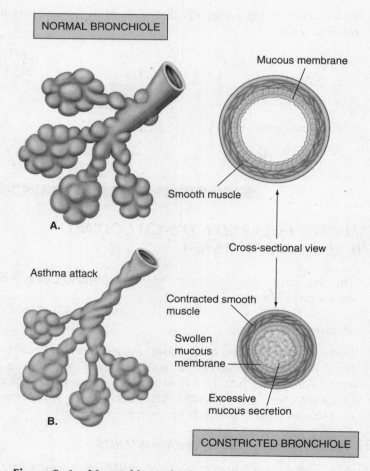

Figure 9–1   Normal bronchiole and constricted bronchiole during asthma attack.

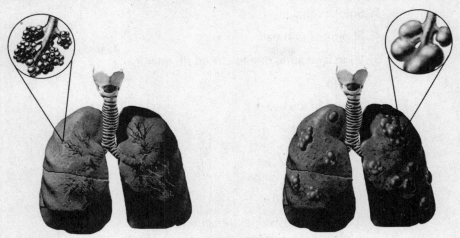

Figure 9–2 Normal lung (L) and emphasematous lung (R).

Status asthmaticus is a prolonged, severe, and life-threatening asthma attack that is unresponsive to the usual medical treatment. An acute exacerbation of asthma can range from a mild to severe flare that is responsive in varying degrees to medical treatment. If the type of asthma is not specified in the medical record, then Asthma Not Otherwise Specified (493.90) should be assigned. It is up to the physician to determine whether the patient is in status asthmaticus or having an acute exacerbation of asthma. The coder should not make this decision.

Chronic Obstructive Lung Disease (COLD)

Chronic Obstructive Lung Disease (COLD), also known as COPD, is a term that encompasses a host of related lung conditions. The most common conditions associated with COLD/COPD are asthma, chronic bronchitis, and emphysema (see Figure 9.2). Code assignment for these conditions depends on the acute or chronic nature of the disease and whether the patient is having an acute exacerbation. The coder should carefully read Include and Exclude notes in ICD-9-CM to ensure correct diagnosis code assignment. Assign code 496 to COPD, not otherwise specified.

Chronic bronchitis, code 491.x, is a form of COLD. Like many other diseases, there are specific criteria for diagnosing chronic bronchitis. The chronic productive cough with hypersecretion of mucus must last for at least three months of the year, for a minimum of two consecutive years. Fourth digits should be assigned to describe the acuity of the illness. Code 491.20 is assigned to chronic obstructive bronchitis without exacerbation, and 491.21 is assigned to COPD with an acute exacerbation. The term "COPD with exacerbation" is sufficient to assign 491.21 (see 3rd Quarter Coding Clinic, 2002). When this condition is present with asthma, it is assigned to category 493.

EXERCISE 9.2

Instructions: Assign the correct ICD-9 code for the diagnostic statements below. Do not assign E codes.

1. Insomnia with sleep apnea _____

2. Newborn respiratory distress syndrome _____

3. Smoke inhalation   _____

4. Shortness of breath   _____

5. Lung laceration due to closed rib fracture   _____

6. Cough   _____

7. Peanut in trachea   _____

8. Bronchiolitis   _____

9. Farmer's lung   _____

10. Influenza-like illness   _____

11. Stenosis of larynx   _____

12. Tracheal stenosis due to tracheostomy   _____

Cor Pulmonale

Cor pulmonale is a dilated, hypertrophic condition of the right ventricle of the heart caused by a disease affecting the structure or function of the lungs. The acute stage is coded 415.0, and the chronic or Not Otherwise Specified (NOS) form is assigned 416.9. Cor pulmonale is the end stage of various chronic disorders of the lungs and is not connected to congenital heart disease.

Emphysema

Emphysema, 491.2x and 492.x, is another form of COPD and involves the permanent enlargement of the alveolar walls. The obstruction in this disease is caused by tissue changes, not mucus production. The lungs lose their elasticity and thereby limit the airflow. Emphysema is caused primarily from cigarette smoking.

Pneumonia

Codes 480–486 describe different types of *pneumonia* (see Figure 9.3). Respiratory specialists classify pneumonia by location, type, or infectious origin. Pneumonias are acute lung infections that normally have a good prognosis unless the patient has a compromised immune system. In ICD-9-CM, pneumonias are classified by the infectious component. When the organism is not identified, the location (broncho or lobar pneumonia) refers the coder to codes 481 or 485.

Pneumothorax

Pneumothorax is more commonly known as a collapsed lung. It is caused by air in the pleural cavity. As air accumulates between the visceral and parietal pleura, the lung continues to collapse. A pneumothorax may be traumatic, caused by a closed or open chest wound, or spontaneous. A spontaneous pneumothorax is further subdivided as primary, caused by the rupture of a subpleural bleb (or blister) at the surface of the lung, or secondary, which is related to a specific disease. In penetrating injuries, such as stab wounds or gunshot wounds, there may be an accumulation of blood in the pleural cavity as well. This is known as a *hemothorax*. Treatment involves the use of chest tubes to equalize the pressure on the inside and the outside of the chest cavity. Code category 512 describes different types of postoperative and spontaneous pneumothorax, and category 860 describes traumatic pneumothorax (see Figure 9.4).

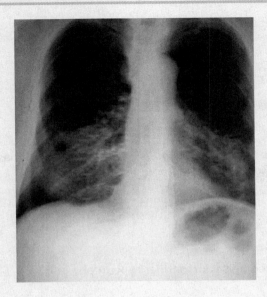

Figure 9–3 Chest x-ray demonstrating lobar pneumonia.

Pulmonary Edema

Various forms of pulmonary edema are described with codes 428.x, 506.x, 508.x, 514, and 518.4. *Pulmonary edema* is the accumulation of fluid in the extravascular space of the lung and is a common complication of cardiac disorders. These disorders include left-sided heart failure caused by arteriosclerotic, cardiomyopathic, hypertensive, or valvular heart disease.

Tuberculosis

Tuberculosis (**TB**) is an infectious disease that affects primarily the lungs, but may also affect other organ systems as well. Pulmonary tuberculosis is characterized in the early stages by night sweats, fever, coughing, and malaise. The disease can lie dormant in a person who has been infected, only to become active years later. Advanced stages of tuberculosis can lead to massive tissue destruction and respiratory failure. ICD-9-CM categories 011–018 are devoted to the many different types of tuberculosis. Fifth-digit

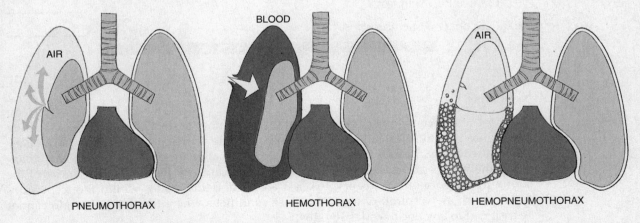

Figure 9–4 Examples of traumatic pneumothorax.

subclassification for these categories is assigned based on bacterial or histological confirmation of the disease.

EXERCISE 9.3

Instructions: Assign the correct ICD-9-CM diagnosis code for the conditions listed below. Not all codes will be from the Respiratory chapter of ICD-9-CM.

1. Acute pharyngitis   _____

2. Screening for tuberculosis   _____

3. Streptococcal pharyngitis   _____

4. Chronic tonsillitis and adenoiditis with tonsillar hypertrophy   _____

5. Chronic bronchitis   _____

6. Chronic obstructive bronchitis with acute exacerbation   _____

7. Spontaneous pneumothorax   _____

8. Aspiration pneumonia after choking on food   _____

9. Deviated nasal septum following traumatic injury   _____

10. Adult respiratory distress syndrome   _____

11. Allergic rhinitis due to pollen   _____

12. Upper respiratory infection   _____

13. Pseudomonas pneumonia   _____

14. Tuberculosis of lung   _____

15. Candida pneumonia   _____

16. Asthmatic bronchitis, chronic   _____

17. Chronic obstructive pulmonary disease (COPD)   _____

18. Radiation pneumonitis   _____

19. Positive PPD skin test   _____

20. Pulmonary cystic fibrosis   _____

Neoplasms

The most common malignant neoplasm of the respiratory system is carcinoma of the lung (see Figure 9.5), most often caused by smoking. Code primary malignancies to category 162 for the trachea, bronchus, and lung and 163 for malignancies of the pleura. Malignancies of the sinuses and nasal cavities are assigned to category 160, and malignancies of the larynx to category 161. Category 165 is used for ill-defined sites within the respiratory system, such as "respiratory tract," or those conditions where the point of origin cannot be assigned to any one of codes 160–164.

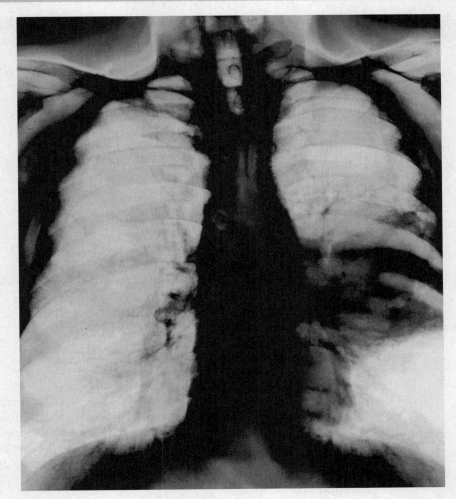

Figure 9–5   Carcinoma of the lung.

Formula for Success

Remember to assign the fourth digit "8" for contiguous, or overlapping, sites of a primary neoplasm.

Secondary or metastatic spread of malignancies is assigned to 197.0–197.3.

Benign conditions are assigned to category 212 and include the nasal cavities, larynx, trachea, bronchus, lung, pleura, other specified sites, and unspecified sites, such as "respiratory tract NOS." Benign respiratory tumors make up only a small portion of the neoplastic conditions diagnosed and include adenomas, lipomas, leiomyomas, fibromas, endometriomas, and other types of benign tissue.

EXERCISE 9.4

Instructions: Assign the correct ICD-9-CM diagnosis codes for the following neoplasms:

1. Metastatic lung carcinoma   _____

2. Primary neoplasm, right upper lobe of lung   _____

3. Carcinoma, ethmoid sinus, with mets to mediastinal nodes   _____   _____

4. Benign tumor of larynx   _____   _____

5. Oat cell carcinoma of the LUL of lung with metastasis to brain   _____   _____

6. Acute radiation pneumonitis secondary to radiation therapy   _____   _____

7. Admission for radiation therapy for bone metastasis   _____   _____

8. Primary carcinoma of the maxillary sinus   _____

CPT® CODING OF RESPIRATORY PROCEDURES

Nose

Incision

Codes 30000–30020 describe the drainage of abscess or hematoma, nasal or nasal septum. These codes refer to the collection of blood or purulent fluid in the nasal mucosa and allow for drainage and decompression of fluid by a simple incision. The nasal cavity may be packed to assist drainage, or a latex drain may be placed in the nasal cavity. For lateral rhinotomy, the coder is referred to more specific codes such as 30118 and 30320.

Excision

Code 30100 describes an intranasal biopsy of the mucosa to be sent to a pathologist for analysis. Polyps found in nasal passageways can obstruct breathing and sinus drainage. Key words to remember in the descriptors of codes 30110 and 30115 are *simple* and *extensive*. Simple nasal polyp excision generally takes place in the office, whereas an extensive excision normally takes place in a hospital or outpatient facility setting. The polyps are removed by wire snares, scalpel, or biting forceps.

Example: During a routine exam, a patient is found to have a suspicious-looking intranasal lesion. A biopsy is taken and the specimen is found to be a malignant neoplasm of the nasal cavity.

   ICD-9-CM: 160.0
   CPT®: 30100

The surgeon decides from the pathology results to excise the remaining lesion through an external approach, ensuring that he has the entire lesion.

   ICD-9-CM: 160.0
   CPT®: 30118-58

Rationale:

Modifier 58 is used on the second procedure because it is decided upon and planned based on the results of the pathology from the first procedure (biopsy). Code 30118 is the external approach to an intranasal lesion. The diagnosis code remains 160.0, because it is still the same lesion as reported in the biopsy.

Tips for Coding Nasal Excisions

1. Bilateral codes have been deleted. To report, use Modifier 50 on the code for procedures that are performed bilaterally.
2. Reduction of the turbinates is reported as 30140-52.

Soft tissue lesions can be excised or destroyed as described by codes 30117 for an internal approach or 30118 for an external approach. Techniques such as cryosurgery, chemical application, or laser surgery are used. *Rhinophyma* is a condition of the nose that includes coarse, thickened, ruddy-appearing skin. It is surgically treated by excision or planing of the skin of the nose described in code 30120. This procedure is accomplished with the use of scalpels, dermabrasion, and lasers. Skin grafting is separately reportable.

Excision of a dermoid cyst of the nasal skin is described with code 30124. Code 30125 describes a complex cyst under bone or cartilage. These cysts may be removed through either skin or intranasal incisions.

Codes 30130 and 30140 are both inherently unilateral and can be performed by any method. The physician removes all or part of the turbinates either through a mucosal or submucosal incision.

Example: A patient has been seen repeatedly for maxillary sinusitis. Despite multiple treatments, no change is recognized in the patient's condition. A decision is made to excise the turbinates.

ICD-9-CM: 473.0

CPT®: 30130

Codes 30150 and 30160 describe a rhinectomy or resection of the nose. The descriptor specifying partial or total removal is determined by the extent of trauma or tumor.

Introduction

Three codes are found in this section. The injection of steroids or other pharmacological agent to treat allergic hypertrophy (diagnosis code 478.1), is reported with CPT® code 30200. Code 30210 describes the displacement of mucopurulent secretions with a saline solution for the treatment of ethmoid and sphenoid sinusitis (diagnosis codes 473.2, 473.3 for chronic, or 461.2, 461.3 for acute). Treatment for an opening in the nasal septum is described in code 30220. The opening is closed with an alloplastic button.

Example: After years of recreational cocaine abuse, a patient has developed a hole in the nasal septum. Following drug rehabilitation and successful remission of the abuse, the patient wishes to have the defect corrected. The surgeon corrects the deformity with a nasal septal button.

ICD-9-CM: 305.63

CPT®: 30220

Rationale:

Since the patient's cocaine use is not described as dependent, a nondependent cocaine abuse code is used. A fifth digit of 3 is assigned for remission.

Removal of Foreign Body

Three levels of procedural codes describe removal of foreign body. These include:

- Simple office removal, 30300
- Removal of foreign body requiring general anesthesia, 30310
- Foreign body removal requiring more extensive removal, 30320

The last code involves a full thickness incision that is made from the nostril and can continue all the way to the eyebrow if needed. This removal includes a multilayer closure.

Repair

Primary rhinoplasty, described in codes 30400 and 30410, involves reshaping of the external nose. Code 30410 also involves the bony pyramid. Code 30420 is more extensive and involves the septum. It is important for diagnosis coding to understand the full extent and the reason for the repair to ensure accuracy. Rhinoplasties described in codes 30430–30460 are performed for secondary or minor revisions.

Formula for Success

Tips for Coding Nasal Repairs

1. Exercise caution in assigning diagnosis codes for nasal repair. Some repairs are cosmetic; others are extensive repairs of congenital abnormalities.
2. For the use of tissue grafts, the coder is referred to 20900–20926 and 21210.

Example A   A patient is unhappy with the appearance of her nose. Reshaping entails minor repairs, mostly involving the cartilage and nasal tip.

ICD-9-CM: V50.1

CPT®: 30400

Rationale:

When a procedure such as this is performed, it is important to represent the procedure and diagnosis accurately. Because it is the choice of the patient to improve her appearance, this is considered cosmetic. If the patient presented with an actual abnormality of the nose, the diagnosis should reflect an acquired deformity, ICD-9-CM code 738.0, or a congenital abnormality, code 748.1. In Example A, diagnosis code V50.1 would likely trigger a denial in payment since it is a cosmetic procedure. Manipulation or misrepresentation of diagnosis codes to obtain reimbursement from an insurer would result in a fraudulent claim.

Example B   A child presents with several respiratory abnormalities. Upon examination, it was found that the patient had a deviated septum, caused by fracture during birth. It was decided to perform a rhinoplasty with major septal repair.

ICD-9-CM: 470, 905.0, and 786.09

CPT®: 30420

Rhinoplasties described by codes 30460, 30462, and 30465 are for congenital cleft lip and/or palate. Grafting is not included in 30465 and may be reported separately using codes 20900–20926 and 21210 from the musculoskeletal system. Unlike other codes in this section, code 30465 is considered bilateral.

The congenital abnormality of an absent opening between the nasal cavity and the pharynx can be repaired as described by codes 30540, for intranasal approach and 30545, for transpalatine approach. The coder is directed not to use the modifier 63 with either codes 30540 or 30545. Modifier 63 identifies a procedure performed on an infant.

Example: A young patient presents with a congenitally absent opening between the nasal cavity and the pharynx. The surgeon performs a reconstruction to form a new opening through the palate.

ICD-9-CM: 748.0

CPT®: 30545

A fistula is an abnormal opening between two cavities. An oral to maxillary fistula repair is coded 30580. An oronasal fistula repair is coded with 30600. Repair of a diseased nasal septum is described by code 30620 and does not include the graft. Code 30630 describes repairs of septal perforations using separately reportable grafts.

Destruction

Two codes in this section describe the cautery and ablation processes to reduce inflammation or excessive mucosa. These codes are bilateral and are performed by any method. Code 30801 describes superficial and 30802 describes intramural procedures.

Other Procedures

Codes 30901–30915 are used to describe the control of nasal hemorrhage. *Epistaxis* is the medical term for a nosebleed. Codes in this section are considered unilateral and are arranged from simple control to cautery or ligation of the vessels.

EXERCISE 9.5

Instructions: Link the diagnostic statement to the corresponding CPT® procedure. Put the correct number in front of the CPT® procedure.

1. Posterior nasal hemorrhage	_____ 30300
2. Dermoid cyst, subcutaneous skin of nose	_____ 30465
3. Nasal cavity polyp	_____ 30120
4. Peanut in nasal cavity	_____ 30000
5. Congenital stenosis of nasal vestibule	_____ 30905
6. Rhinophyma	_____ 30124
7. Abscess, nasal mucosa	_____ 30110

Accessory Sinuses

Incision

The majority of the codes in this section describe openings made in the sinuses to allow for drainage or for another procedure. Each code in this section is specific to a particular sinus. The first procedures listed refer to lavage, which is a method of irrigation to reduce inflammation and remove purulent discharge from the infected sinuses. Figure 9.6 illustrates the nose, nasal cavity, and pharynx.

Codes 31020 and 31030 are differentiated by the approach. The intranasal approach is a surgically created opening from the nasal cavity into the maxillary sinus. The Caldwell-Luc approach is an intraoral approach into the maxillary sinuses. This is an extensive procedure and is usually performed as a last resort after more conservative methods have failed.

Formula for Success

1. Sinus section codes are unilateral in nature.
2. Report procedures performed on the left and right sides bilaterally with Modifier 50.

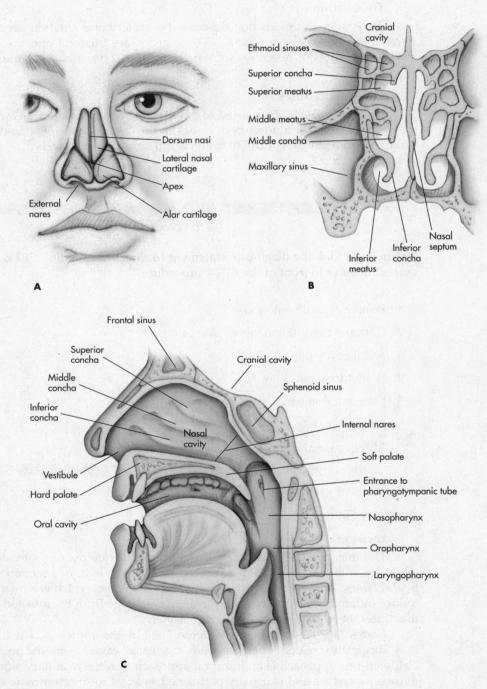

Figure 9–6   Example of nose, nasal cavity, and pharynx.

Example: A patient has severe headaches due to recurrent maxillary sinusitis. The surgeon performs a bilateral maxillary antrotomy by intranasal approach to relieve pressure.

ICD-9-CM: 473.0, 784.0

CPT®: 31020-50

The sinusotomy codes include procedures for the sphenoid and frontal sinuses specifically and a general code for three or more paranasal sinuses. The sphenoid sinuses are found deep in the skull; therefore, the most common approach is intraoral. An operating microscope is used to remove the sinus contents. For the frontal sinuses, a small incision just below the medial eyebrow is made. Codes 31080–31085 describe a technique in which the sinus cavity is obliterated with fat from the abdomen or buttocks. The types of incisions include a brow incision, which utilizes an approach just above the eyebrows, or a coronal incision, which involves an incision along the hairline. Codes 31084 and 31085 make use of a frontal bone flap. Both of these procedures include the removal of mucosa, which is replaced with a material to prevent regrowth. When no obliteration is done, the contents of the sinus are removed with curettes and burs.

Excision

The excision codes describe the removal of diseased tissue from either the ethmoid or maxillary sinuses. The approach for ethmoidectomies is either intranasal, which involves an incision made inside the nose, or extranasal. An extranasal approach involves an incision between the nasal dorsum and the medial canthus of the eye. Code choices for maxillectomy include those performed with or without orbital exenteration. Exenteration means that all of the orbital contents are removed, including the eye and all of the soft tissue of the orbit.

Endoscopy

Sinus endoscopy codes are inherently unilateral and include a sinusotomy and diagnostic endoscopy. Exploration of the following areas is not separately reportable, as inspection of these areas is considered routine:

- Nasal cavity
- Middle and superior meatus
- Turbinates
- Spheno-ethmoid recess

Formula for Success

Tips for Coding Sinus Endoscopies

1. A diagnostic endoscopy is used to describe a procedure that has no surgical component. This means that no biopsies are taken, and no polyps are removed.
2. Once a more invasive procedure is performed while the endoscopy is taking place, it is converted into a surgical endoscopy code to better describe the procedure performed.
3. Pay close attention to which sinus is being scoped. The endoscopy codes are very specific about which sinus is being examined.

Codes 31231–31235 are diagnostic nasal and sinus endoscopy codes. These codes are for endoscopic evaluation and do not have a surgical component. Endoscopic procedures can be performed for a wide variety of diagnoses including neoplasms, polyps, sinusitis, rhinitis, cellulitis, edema or cysts, congenital abnormalities, fractures, and foreign bodies.

Codes 31237–31240 are surgical nasal/sinus endoscopy codes. These codes include biopsies, and control of bleeding, or epistaxis. Electrocautery or lasers may be utilized for this method. *Dacryocystorhinostomy* is the treatment of a lacrimal obstruction. This procedure is used to allow for lacrimal drainage from the lower eyelid into the nose. Procedures in this code range are performed for varices or hemorrhage complicating procedure, dacryops, 375.11; epiphora, an abnormal development of tears due to a stricture of lacrimal passages, 375.2x; dacrocystitis, 375.30; obstruction or stenosis of the nasolacrimal duct, 375.55 and 375.56; or granuloma of the lacrimal passages, 375.81.

Resection of concha bullosa is treatment for the distention of the turbinate bone caused by an intranasal cyst; the code is 478.1.

Codes 31254 and 31255 describe partial or total ethmoidectomy. Blockage or disease of the ethmoid sinus may also block the maxillary sinus drainage. Ethmoidectomy includes the removal of polyps. Medical necessity links for this type of procedure may include:

- Malignant neoplasms of the nasal cavities and ethmoidal sinus, 160.0 and 160.3
- Acute sinusitis and ethmoidal sinusitis, 461.2, 461.8, and 461.9
- Deviated septum, 470
- Sinus polyps, 471.8
- Chronic sinusitis, 473.X
- Other diseases of the nasal cavity and sinuses, 478.1.

A maxillary antrostomy is the creation of an opening for drainage of the maxillary sinus. Antrostomies are performed for:

- Malignant neoplasms of the maxillary sinus, 160.2 and 197.3
- Benign neoplasms, 212.0
- Acute maxillary and other sinusitis, 461.0, 461.8 and 461.9;
- Chronic maxillary and other sinusitis, 473.0, 473.8, and 473.9
- Sinus polyps, 471.8
- Congenital anomalies, 748.1
- Closed and open maxillary fractures, 802.4, 802.5
- Closed and open orbital fractures, 802.6 and 802.7
- Inflammatory reaction due to unspecified device, 996.60

A sphenoidotomy is an opening created in the sphenoid sinus. It is performed for drainage purposes, and removal of tissue can be performed during the procedure, as well. The middle turbinate may be fractured or partially removed for access. Sphenoidotomy is performed for malignancies, acute and chronic sinusitis, sinus polyps, congenital anomalies, and late effects of skull fractures.

Leaking cerebrospinal fluid due to trauma can also be repaired endoscopically either through the ethmoid or sphenoid region. Facial, nasal, and orbital fractures are the primary causes of leaking CSF fluid.

The final codes in the endoscopy section deal with surgical access to decompress the orbit. The inferior orbital wall is also the roof of the maxillary sinus. Removal of the orbital bone allows the expansion of orbital contents into the maxillary sinus while still preserving the orbital periosteum. The medial, or sidewall, of the orbit is also the lateral wall of the ethmoid sinus. The removal of bone in this area allows the orbital contents to expand into the ethmoid region. The optic nerve is accessed through the optic foramen also known as the orbital apex. The orbital apex is approached through the sphenoid sinus. Bone is removed from the lateral portion of the sinus to allow decompression of the optic nerve. These procedures are performed primarily for injuries, such as fractures of the orbital floor and facial fractures, optic nerve injury, and injuries of the head, face, and neck.

As with all injuries, the coder should remember to use the appropriate E code to describe the cause of injury.

EXERCISE 9.6

Instructions: Give the correct CPT® codes for the following scenarios.

1. A patient is treated for chronic osteomyelitis of the ethmoid sinuses. The physician excises diseased tissue from the ethmoid sinuses through an incision between the nasal dorsum and the medial canthus. Dissection is continued and exposes the lateral ethmoid sinus. All diseased material is removed. _____

2. A patient has a history of headaches and acute sinusitis. He is treated with an endoscopic partial ethmoidectomy. _____

3. A patient with the complaint of excessive tearing is found to have an obstruction of the lacrimal duct. An endoscopic dacryocystorhinostomy was performed. Postoperative diagnosis is granuloma of the lacrimal passage. _____

Larynx

Excision

Laryngotomy code 31300 describes removal of a tumor or laryngocele. A laryngocele is an air-filled dilation of the laryngeal ventricle. The cordectomy term in this code refers to the excision of all or part of the vocal cord.

Formula for Success

Tips for Coding Excision Codes for the Larynx

1. Watch for the terminology laryngotomy versus laryngectomy. Remember that -otomy means to incise while -ectomy means to surgically remove.
2. Use caution when code descriptors specify "with" or "without" radical neck dissection.
3. Be aware of the approach and whether the laryngectomy is total or subtotal.

The main purpose for any of the layngectomy procedures is to remove a neoplasm in the immediate area of the larynx. This can include primary or secondary malignancies or a neoplasm of uncertain behavior. The laryngectomy codes describe "with" or "without" extensive dissection, including the removal of the sternocleidomastoid muscle, submandibular salivary gland, the internal jugular vein, and lymph nodes. Subtotal supraglottic laryngectomies performed without the radical neck dissection include an approach through the thyroid cartilage. When a radical neck dissection is done, a horizontal neck incision is made. The difference in the partial laryngectomies codes is in the type of incision made.

Pharyngolaryngectomy is the removal of the larynx and pharynx. Both codes 31390 and 31395 include a radical neck dissection and are differentiated by "with" or "without" reconstruction. Reconstruction for this procedure can include a myocutaneous flap using the pectoris major muscle. The arytenoid process referred to in code 31400 is cartilage that is tacked against the thyroid ala. The arytenoid cartilage is just above the cricoid cartilage and the vocal cord.

Introduction

Two introduction codes are found in the larynx section. Code 31500 is an emergency endotracheal intubation and is Modifier 51 exempt. Code 31502 is used for changing an endotracheal tube (see Figure 9.7).

Formula for Success

Tips for Coding Endotracheal Tubes

1. Always make sure to check the list of procedures bundled into critical care—some of these procedures may include code 31500.
2. There are many reasons for endotracheal intubation. Be sure to justify the use of the emergency intubation code with the appropriate ICD-9-CM diagnosis code.

Endoscopy

Laryngoscopy is performed by either an indirect or direct method. The indirect method involves the use of mirrors to visualize the larynx; the direct method is performed using either a rigid or flexible scope.

Indirect laryngoscopy codes range from 31505 to 31513. Code 31505 is the base code for this section and is diagnostic in nature. The surgical codes describe biopsies, removal of foreign body, removal of lesion, and vocal cord injection. Injection of vocal cords by indirect laryngoscopy utilizes substances such as Teflon, glycerin, or gelfoam to either temporarily or permanently cause a hardening of the cords. It also helps them retain their shape and improve voice quality. A wide variety of diagnosis codes can be linked to these procedures including:

- Malignancies, 161.X primary and 197.3 secondary
- Benign neoplasms, 212.0 and 212.1
- Acute laryngotracheitis, 464.21; acute epiglottitis, 464.31
- Acute laryngopharyngitis, 465.0
- Chronic laryngitis, 476.0 and 476.1
- Paralysis of the vocal cords, 478.3x
- Other diseases of the larynx, 478.7x
- Congenital anomalies, 748.x
- Symptoms of the head and neck, 784.x
- Dysphasia, 787.2
- Foreign bodies, 933.0 and 933.1

The direct laryngoscopy codes begin with an aspiration code. The removal of excess saliva or other semi-solid foreign material can be done using an aspirator passed through the laryngoscope. Diagnostic laryngoscopy codes in this section include: 31520, newborn; 31525, except newborn; and 31526, with operating microscope. Because code 31520 is specified for the newborn, modifier 63 should not be added to this code. Do not use the operating microscope code 69990 with code 31526 because code 31526 includes the operating microscope in its descriptor. The medical necessity links for these codes are very similar to that of the indirect laryngoscopy codes.

It is important to note that codes 31531, 31541, 31561, and 31571 add the use of the operating microscope to the common portion of these procedures. For example, code 31530 describes a direct laryngoscopic removal of a foreign body. Code 31531 utilizes the same descriptor *plus* the use of the operating microscope. When the description includes operating microscope, do not assign code 69990 in addition to the procedure code.

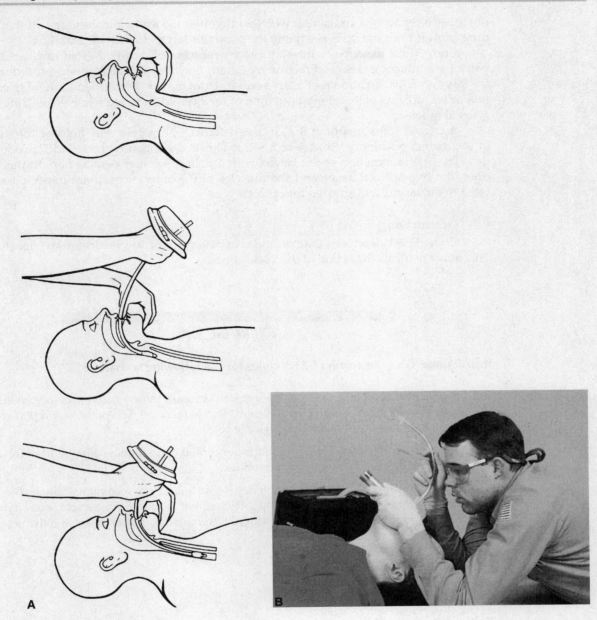

Figure 9–7   Intubation.

Codes 31575–31578 describe procedures using a flexible fiberoptic laryngoscope. The coder is directed not to use these codes with 92612–92617 from the medicine chapter of CPT® because those codes include a separate laryngoscopy. The last code in this section, 31579, utilizes either a flexible or rigid fiberoptic scope and stroboscopy. The stroboscope is used to visualize vocal cord function by responding to the frequency of vibrating vocal cords.

Repair

The repair codes 31580 and 31582 describe treatment by excision of a laryngeal web, which is a congenital malformation of the larynx. In code 31580, the web is between the vocal cords. A second-stage procedure is performed after the site has healed. Code 31582 describes a repair of a congenital web that involves the arytenoid cartilage. In this procedure, a graft from the rib is sewn into the posterior larynx to provide stability.

Code 31584 describes wire stent placement to stabilize the thyroid cartilage and repair of any mucosal defects. Fracture treatment may also utilize a closed procedure with the laryngoscope. Treatment of a laryngeal fracture may be performed without manipulation or by utilizing external manipulation of the thyroid cartilage while visualizing the laryngeal mucosa.

A cricoid split, or split in the laryngeal cartilage, is repaired by holding the cartilage in the correct position with wire or a stent. This is described by code 31587. Code 31590 describes the innervation of the larynx with a neuromuscular pedicle flap. In this procedure, the hypoglossal nerve and the muscles of the anterior neck are dissected and rotated to the larynx and sutured into place.

Destruction

Code 31595 describes the resection, or severing, of the recurrent laryngeal nerve. This nerve controls the action of the vocal cords.

EXERCISE 9.7

Instructions: Give the correct CPT® codes for the following scenarios:

1. A patient is seen for a mass in the neck. It is found to originate in the arytenoid cartilage. The entire mass along with the cartilage is resected. The pathology report shows a malignant neoplasm of the aryepiglottic fold. _____

2. A direct laryngoscopy for aspiration is performed on a patient suffering from inhalation pneumonitis due to aspiration of vomitus. _____

3. A patient is brought into the Emergency Room with acute respiratory failure. The physician performs a direct laryngoscopy. The patient is found to have chronic laryngotracheitis and requires dilation. The patient is admitted for observation and the procedure is repeated the next day.

   ■ Day 1: _____

   ■ Day 2: _____

Critical Thinking Skills:

Determine whether modifiers are needed on #3. Why or why not?

Trachea and Bronchi

Incision

Incisions in the trachea are made for exposure or to create an artificial opening for breathing. Several codes describe various types of tracheostomies. Tracheostomies may be planned or performed on an emergency basis. Planned tracheostomies are differentiated based on the age of the patient. Since many critical newborns or premature infants require tracheostomies, children under 2 years of age are assigned to code 31601. Code 31600 is designated as a separate procedure, as it may be performed as part of a more extensive procedure.

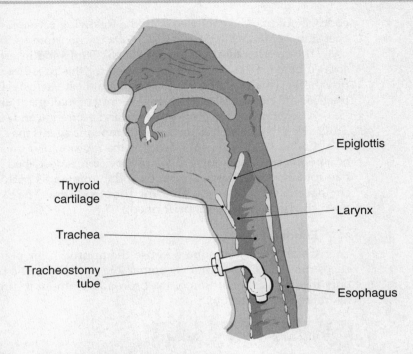

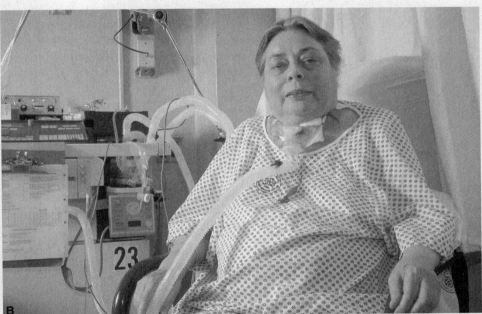

Figure 9–8   Example of tracheostomy.

Code 31603 describes a transtracheal tracheostomy. This is the most common type of tracheostomy (see Figure 9.8). A cricothyroid approach is described by code 31604. The incision is located higher, or more cephalad, on the trachea than the transtracheal approach. Code 31610 describes skin flaps used to create a permanent stoma. Diagnoses for the tracheostomy codes include malignancies, respiratory failure, congenital anomalies, respiratory problems of the newborn, respiratory arrest, and injuries of the trachea and larynx.

The opening, or stoma, of an existing tracheostomy may need to be revised after a period of time. This can be performed as a simple or complex procedure. These incision codes should not be confused with the following revision codes: surgical closure of a tracheostomy (31820–31825) or revision of a tracheostomy scar (31830).

The creation of a tracheoesophageal fistula and insertion of speech prosthesis is described by code 31611. Other terms used for this prosthesis are voice box or Blom-Singer prosthesis. This procedure is performed almost exclusively for anomalies of the larynx, trachea, and bronchus or a personal history of malignant neoplasm of the larynx.

A percutaneous tracheal puncture and aspiration and/or injection is described by code 31612. Secretions can be aspirated or therapeutic agents may be injected via this method.

Codes 31613 and 31614 describe the revision of a tracheal stoma due either to a scar or a poorly healing wound. A simple revision is described in 31613, and a revision with a flap rotation is performed in 31614. A flap rotation is performed by incising the skin in a circular manner while still allowing for blood flow. The skin is then rotated to cover the open area, and a closure is performed.

Endoscopy

Code 31615 is unique because the approach, or point of entry, is an existing tracheostomy. This procedure is comparable to a diagnostic bronchoscopy since it contains only the diagnostic portion of the procedure without a surgical component. Figure 9.9 illustrates a bronchoscopy.

Formula for Success

Tips for Coding Bronchoscopy

1. Code the appropriate individual endoscopy for each anatomic site examined.
2. A surgical bronchoscopy always includes the diagnostic bronchoscopy when performed in the same operative session by the same physician.
3. For fluoroscopic guidance, the coder is directed to codes 71040 and 71060.

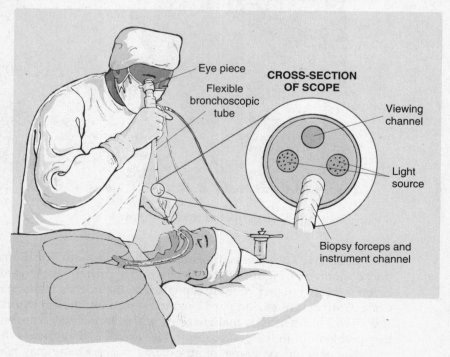

Figure 9–9   Bronchoscopy using flexible fiberoptic bronchoscope.

Diagnostic bronchoscopy includes cell washing using either a rigid or flexible bronchoscope. The scope is passed through the nasal or oral cavity down the larynx to the bronchus of the lungs. Samples for analysis are collected by brushing, washing, or biopsy.

Retrieval of a foreign body may be performed through a scope with the use of a snare, basket, or forceps. Common ICD-9-CM codes may include: foreign body in the main bronchus, 934.1; in other specified parts of trachea, bronchus, and lung, 934.8; and in the respiratory tree, unspecified, 934.9.

Aspiration of fluid or abscess is performed with a needle passed through the scope to collect initial or subsequent aspirates. These procedures may be performed for all different types of pneumonia, bronchitis, chronic airway obstruction, or COPD and emphysema.

Code 31656 describes the use of contrast material to visualize a segment of the lung. In this procedure, the physician may use fluoroscopy to guide placement of the tip of the bronchoscope. The physician then inserts a needle or catheter through the scope to inject the contrast material. The coder is directed to the radiology codes 71040 or 71060 to be used for fluoroscopic guidance. Visualization done with this procedure also helps locate neoplasms.

Introduction

Code 31700 describes a passageway established via needle. Since it is often used as an approach for other surgeries, this code is designated as a separate procedure.

Codes 31708–31715 describe laryngography or bronchography, which are performed after the patient has inhaled a radiopaque gas. Code 31710 describes the placement of an oral or nasal catheter into the larynx, with the injection of contrast material. Use code 31715 for an injection into the trachea just below the voice box. The coder is directed to use 70373, 71040, and 71060 for the corresponding radiology codes. These procedures may be used to visualize malignant and benign neoplasms of the glottis, larynx, bronchus, and lung.

Code 31717 describes a tracheal catheterization with brush biopsy. The surgeon catheterizes the trachea by passing a needle through the cricoid cartilage or trachea. A catheter is inserted over the needle, and a brush is placed through the catheter to obtain a specimen. This procedure is performed to help diagnose malignancies of the lung and bronchus, pneumonia, asbestosis, alveolar and parietoalveolar pneumonopathy, and other diseases of the lung.

Catheter aspirations are described by 31720 and 31725. These are done to collect specimens to identify the type of bacteria causing the pneumonia or bronchitis, alveolar and parietoalveolar pneumonopathy, and other diseases of the lung.

The last code in this section, 31730, explains the transtracheal introduction of a needle wire dilator or in-dwelling tube for oxygen therapy. A needle is placed through the cricoid membrane of the trachea and a tube is inserted over the needle to maintain the opening.

Repair

The suffix *plasty* means to surgically repair. This section of CPT® contains several repair codes. The tracheoplasty codes, 31750–31760, differ in their approach—via cervical, intrathoracic, or a fistulization done in stages. A device such as a speech prosthesis may be inserted as part of the surgical repair.

Code 31766 describes a reconstruction of the carina, which is the junction of the trachea and bronchi. Access is obtained through a midline sternotomy or a lateral thoracotomy. Bronchoplasties are described in codes 31770, graft repair, or 31775, excision stenosis and anastomosis.

Excision of tracheal stenosis is described in codes 31780, for a cervical approach, and 31781, utilizing a cervicothoracic approach. Stenosis is an abnormal narrowing or stricture and can be caused by a congenital abnormality, neoplasm, or late effects of an injury.

Excision codes 31785–31786 are specifically for tumor or carcinomas removed either by cervical or thoracic approach. Due to the description of these codes, the only diagnoses allowed are for a benign or malignant neoplasm or history of neoplasm.

When a tracheostomy is no longer needed, codes 31820 or 31825 should be used to describe the closure. Code 31830 describes the scar revision. Diagnosis codes such as V44.0, Tracheostomy status; V55.0, Attention to tracheostomy, or V51, Aftercare, are suitable for these procedures.

EXERCISE 9.8

Instructions: Give the correct CPT® codes for the following scenarios:

1. A newborn suffering from respiratory distress syndrome requires a tracheostomy. _____

2. During a barroom brawl, the patient was struck in the throat and was found to have a fractured larynx upon bronchoscopic examination. This was treated by a closed method using the bronchoscope to place a stent. _____

3. A patient is brought into the Emergency Room with acute respiratory distress. An emergency transtracheal tracheostomy is performed. _____

4. A patient's respiration is obstructed due to an overgrowth of scar tissue at the tracheal stoma site. A complex revision of the tracheostoma is performed. _____

Lungs and Pleura

Incision

Thoracentesis, code 32000, is the removal of fluid from the chest cavity by puncturing through a space between the ribs to gain access into the pleural cavity (see Figure 9.10). This code is Modifier 51 exempt, which means that the corresponding surgical fee is not reduced and may be reported with other procedures without appending Modifier 51. Code 32002 describes a tube that is left in the chest for drainage. A water seal may be attached to prevent air from being drawn into the chest cavity.

Chemical pleurodesis, code 32005, is performed to prevent recurrent pneumothorax. A plastic catheter is inserted into the chest cavity, and fluid is introduced to cause adhesion, or scarring of the lung surface to the inside of the chest cavity.

A thoracostomy is also known as a chest tube. Code 32020, tube thoracostomy, is also Modifier 51 exempt. In this procedure, a tube is inserted through the tissue between the ribs. A syringe may be attached to the catheter for drainage, or it may be connected to a water seal system to prevent air from entering the chest cavity. Chest tubes are inserted to equalize the pressure between the lung and the outside of the body, allowing the collapsed lung to re-expand.

Thoracostomy with rib resection or open flap drainage for empyema is reported with 32035 or 32036. Empyema is an accumulation of purulent fluid in the respiratory cavity. A rib resection involves the removal of a small portion of rib to allow a release of fluid from the cavity. Another method, described by 32036, makes use of a flap made from the skin and subcutaneous tissues to ensure that the drainage wound stays open.

Thoracotomies are procedures that involve opening the chest cavity and spreading the ribs apart. The procedure may be a limited one, such as described by code 32095, or it may be a major thoracotomy, described by codes 32100–32160. The codes listed under major thoracotomy are performed for specific diagnostic conditions, such as traumatic

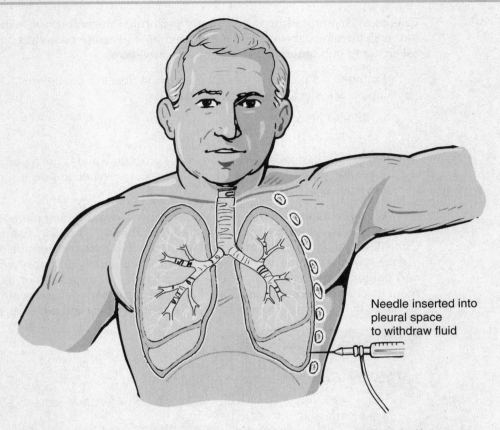

Figure 9–10   Example of thoracentesis performed to treat pleural effusion.

hemorrhage, cysts, or foreign body. Code 32160 describes a thoracotomy with cardiac massage. In this procedure, the chest is opened and the heart is manually squeezed to mimic cardiac contractions, thereby pumping the blood through the body. The heart also may be countershocked to produce spontaneous heartbeats. This procedure is used to treat cardiac arrest, ICD-9-CM code 427.5, when it occurs with an open chest wound.

Code 32141 describes the removal of a lung bullae, which is similar to a large blister containing serum or blood, by blunt dissection. This procedure is very dependent upon the diagnosis, therefore the corresponding diagnosis code is 492.0, emphysematous bleb, or bullae.

Repeated pneumothorax is a common condition among young men and in older patients with a history of chronic lung disease. Treatment involves the deliberate production of adhesions between the surface of the lung and the inside surface of the chest cavity as described by code 32215. This is created by the injection of a chemical solution through a catheter inserted between the ribs into the pleural cavity. Diagnosis codes for pneumothorax are 512.0, spontaneous; 512.1, iatrogenic; and 512.8, other pneumothorax.

Decortication is the act of removing the constricting membrane or layer of tissue from the surface of the lung. This enables the lung to expand more fully. Code 32220 describes a total decortication, and code 32225 is used to report a partial decortication. Both of these are designated as separate procedures.

Excision

The first code in this section, 32310, describes a parietal pleurectomy. In this procedure, the surgeon removes the membranous tissue lining the inside surface of the chest cavity, also known as the parietal pleura. A chest tube may be inserted and left in for drainage. This procedure is commonly performed in conjunction with a more extensive surgery; therefore, this code is designated as a separate procedure, and care should be taken not to unbundle it from larger procedures.

> **Example:**   A patient is seen for pleurisy. To treat this condition, the surgeon performs a pleurectomy and inserts a chest tube.
>
> ICD-9-CM: 511.0
> CPT®: 32310

Note: The chest tube is included in this procedure and is not reported separately. Both procedures are considered separate procedures. When this occurs, code for the more extensive procedure.

Biopsies of the pleura may be performed via two different methods. Code 32400 describes a biopsy collected percutaneously, or through the skin using a biopsy needle. Code 32402, in contrast, is an open biopsy involving an incision. Be cautious of the approach when assigning these biopsy codes. Occasionally, a biopsy with frozen sections and pathological evaluation will be done. Based on the results of the frozen section, a more extensive procedure may be performed during the same operative session. In this scenario, the biopsy is bundled into the larger procedure and not reported separately.

Formula for Success

Tips for Coding Biopsies

1. Frequently, visualization can be improved by imaging devices. These codes are listed under the procedure descriptors.
2. Fine needle aspirations/biopsies are different from percutaneous needle biopsies. Consider the methodology used. Fine needle aspiration codes are listed directly under the percutaneous biopsy codes in the integumentary system—10021 or 10022.

> **Example:**   Percutaneous biopsies of the pleura and lung are performed. Both were positive for malignancies. The pleural fluid was found to have a malignancy secondary to the lung carcinoma identified in the lower lobe of the right side.
>
> ICD-9-CM: 162.5 and 197.2
> CPT®: 32405-RT and 32400-RT-51

The first diagnosis code is linked to the first procedure, and the second diagnosis code is linked to the second procedure. Observe how the diagnosis codes are linked to the biopsy codes specific to the biopsy area. Note also that the lung cancer is the primary malignancy and the malignancy of the pleura is the secondary based on the information given. The sites of the biopsies are specifically named in the descriptors; since they are taken from different anatomical parts, they are not bundled.

A *pneumonectomy* is the excision of a lung. The pneumonectomy codes 32440–32500 describe the various types of lung resections, including lobectomy, segmentectomy, and wedge resections. Each refers to a different amount of lung tissue that is removed. A lung may be removed for a number of different reasons; however, malignancy is the most common. The pneumonectomy described by 32442 includes the removal of a segment of the trachea as well. The extrapleural pneumonectomy is described by 32445. In this procedure, the entire lining of the chest is stripped away.

The lobectomy codes begin with 32480. The codes in this section are described as the partial removal of lung, other than total pneumonectomy. Code 32480 is a single lobectomy, 32482 describes two lobes. A bilobectomy is the removal of two of the three lobes on the right side. When the only two lobes on the left are removed, this is considered a pneumonectomy, or removal of the entire left lung. The bilobectomy is not to be used when one right lobe and one left lobe are removed. In code 32484, the term used is a segmentectomy. This refers to the further division of the lung into bronchopulmonary segments. Figure 9.11 illustrates some lung resections.

Code 32486 is used when a portion of the lung is removed and the bronchial tube is repaired. After the removal of the diseased portion of the lung, the healthy part of the bronchial tube of the remaining lobe is sutured to the main bronchial tube. These procedures are performed most commonly for upper lobectomies.

Code 32488 describes a lobectomy on the remaining portion of the previously resected lung. Although no lung tissue remains on the operated side, the removal is not considered a total pneumonectomy, since only a partial lung was removed at the time of the second procedure.

> **Example:** In June, a patient is treated for lung carcinoma of the left lower lobe. A single lobectomy is performed. The pathology reports states that the margins are clear.
>
> ICD-9-CM: 162.5
> CPT®: 32480-LT
>
> In August, the same patient is treated for lung carcinoma of the left upper remaining lobe. Once again a single lobectomy is performed.
>
> ICD-9-CM: 162.3
> CPT®: 32488-78-LT
>
> Note that on the second surgery the Modifier 78 is used. The second surgery is within the 90 day global of the June procedure. Because the lung cancer is a recurrence, the second procedure is related to the first surgery.

Code 32491 specifies the diagnosis of emphysema. The ICD-9-CM codes for emphysematous bleb, 492.0, or other emphysema, 492.8, may be used. In the disease state of emphysema, there is an enlargement of the air space of the lungs and an accumulation of air in the tissues. This procedure involves the excision of a portion of lung so it may further expand.

A wedge resection is described by code 32500 and may be either single or multiple. As the descriptor implies, a wedge-shaped piece of lung is removed. The cut portions of

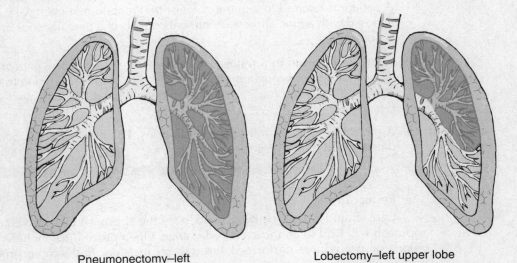

Pneumonectomy—left   Lobectomy—left upper lobe

Figure 9–11 Pneumonectomy versus lobectomy of the left lung.

the lung tissue remaining are repaired. This procedure is performed for either the growth of a neoplasm, abscess or bleb, or the repair of an injury.

Code 32501 is an add-on code. When a repair of a portion of the bronchus is performed at the time of a lobectomy or segmentectomy, this code is listed along with the primary code without modifiers. Further description of this code states that a portion of the bronchus to the preserved lung is removed and requires plastic closure. Resection of the proximal end of the bronchus does not justify use of this code.

Formula for Success

Add-on Codes

- Do not use add-on codes alone.
- Add-on codes are all Modifier 51 exempt.
- Do not reduce the surgical fee for add-on codes.

The lung resection codes begin with code 32520. These codes describe removal of part of one lung as well as a portion of the chest wall. Code 32522 explains reconstruction of the chest wall performed without prosthesis. Code 32525 adds the prosthesis to fill in the chest wall and add stability.

Code 32540 describes very specific treatment of empyema. Empyema is the accumulation of purulent fluid in the respiratory cavity. This collection may be surrounded by a membrane and described as an abscess. The surgeon removes the empyema abscess entirely, including the membrane of the abscess. Medical necessity linkage may include empyema with fistula, 510.0, or empyema without fistula, 510.9. Further identification of the organism can be coded additionally if information is available.

EXERCISE 9.9

Instructions: Give the correct CPT® codes for the following scenarios:

1. A patient is referred to a pulmonologist for an abnormal chest X-ray. The patient is diagnosed with a lung abscess. Treatment consists of a percutaneous drainage of the lung abscess. _____

2. A patient involved in a rollover motor vehicle accident. The patient was the driver of the vehicle. He is brought into the Emergency Room and is found to have a lung laceration and a chest contusion without an open wound. The damaged segment of lung is removed. _____

3. A patient is suffering from pleural effusions. Pneumocentesis is performed to relieve pressure and obtain a specimen for analysis. _____

Endoscopy

Care should always be taken to identify the approach for a procedure, as the wrong approach will lead to an incorrect code range. Open procedures include incisions and excisions or procedures performed through an incision. Endoscopic procedures are performed through a fiberoptic or rigid scope. The descriptions in this section are very similar to those of the open procedures.

Formula for Success

Tips for Coding Thoracoscopies

1. Confirm the approach as being through a scope.
2. Surgical thoracoscopies include the diagnostic thoracoscopy.
3. Code for each appropriate endoscopy for each anatomical site.
4. If a thoracoscopy is performed for a diagnostic purpose, but is used to complete a surgical procedure, the definitive surgical thoracoscopy code is used instead of the diagnostic code.

In order to perform a thoracoscopy, a pneumothorax is surgically created first. This is not reported separately. Thorough examination of the thoracic cavity can only be done when the pneumothorax is completed. This allows space for instrumentation and viewing. When a thoracoscopy is further enhanced with a video, the term *VATS*, or Video Assisted Thoracic Surgery, may be used as well. This allows the physician to see images from multiple viewers on a monitor.

Codes 32601–32606 are described as diagnostic. Diagnostic scopes describe an examination and biopsy only. These codes are divided into the following anatomical areas:

- Lung and pleural space
- Pericardial sac
- Mediastinal sac

Each area is subdivided into codes that specify "without biopsy" and "with biopsy."

Surgical thoracoscopy codes begin with 32650. It is common to perform several procedures during the same thoracoscopy. The major procedure should be listed first followed by secondary procedures reported with Modifier 51. These scopes are not considered bundled with one another, but Medicare may require a Modifier 59, signifying a different site, for payment. Occasionally, a procedure is attempted thoracoscopically but cannot be completed due to extenuating circumstances and is aborted. If the procedure is completed using the open technique, both procedures may be reported with a Modifier 52 or 53 on the thoracoscopic procedure. However, some insurance companies and Medicare will pay for only the completed open procedure. It may be more appropriate to use the open procedure code with Modifier 22 appended, if the documentation justifies its use.

Example: A patient with biopsy-confirmed lower left lobe lung carcinoma is scheduled for a thoracoscopic wedge resection. During the procedure, extensive pleural effusion is encountered and the procedure is converted to an open wedge resection.

ICD-9-CM: V64.4, linked to CPT®: 32657-53 AND

ICD-9-CM: 162.5, linked to CPT®: 32500

OR

ICD-9-CM: 162.5, linked to CPT®: 32500-22

Check with the payer before submitting codes.

Pleurodesis can be performed thorascopically by inserting the scope between two ribs. This procedure is performed mainly as treatment for pneumothorax.

Partial and total pulmonary decortication can be performed with the use of the scope. Just as with the open decortication, this procedure is commonly done for malignancies of the pleura, emphysematous bleb, and emphysema with fistula.

Removal of a foreign body is done with the help of a second or third trocar (see Figure 9.12) to retrieve the foreign body while the first trocar encases the scope for

Figure 9–12 Trocar.

visualization. A foreign body of the lung can be common with an injury, aspiration into the trachea, bronchus, or lung or foreign body left accidentally during a procedure.

Several codes in this section with corresponding thoracotomy codes are excision of bullae, wedge resection, and lobectomy. If the coder is not clear about the approach, the physician should be consulted to clarify and possibly amend the record prior to coding and billing.

Other codes in this section deal with the pericardial sac, which is the membrane covering the heart. Code 32658 describes a removal of foreign body or clot. This procedure is usually performed as a result of an injury, late effect of injury, or a complication due to a cardiac device.

> **Example:**   A patient recently went to a large cardiac specialty hospital to have a coronary artery bypass performed. The patient experienced severe postoperative chest pain and cardiac irritability. The thoracic surgeon performed a thoracoscopy and encountered a blood clot in the pericardial sac.
>
> Codes submitted for the second surgery:
>
>   ICD-9-CM: 996.72
>   CPT®: 32658-78

Pericardial procedures such as the creation of a pericardial window can be made via thoracoscopy. The pericardial sac is viewed using a video camera. Using instruments introduced through a second trocar, the physician creates an opening, allowing drainage of the pericardial sac. The removal of the pericardial sac and the excision of a cyst, tumor, or mass can also be performed thoracoscopically. Diagnoses commonly linked to these procedures include neoplasms of the heart, different types of pericarditis, and congenital anomalies of the heart.

The mediastinum is the space between the lungs that contains the heart, thoracic blood vessels including the aorta and pulmonary arteries, esophagus, bronchial tubes, and a large number of lymph nodes. A mediastinal cyst, tumor, or mass may be excised through a scope. One trocar is passed in between the ribs and into the mediastinal space for viewing through the endoscope. Additional trocars are used to remove the mass while the endoscope acts as a guide. Corresponding diagnoses include malignant neoplasms of the mediastinum, benign lesions, and swelling or mass in the chest. Procedures performed on the mediastinum via thoracoscopy should not be confused with mediastinoscopy. A mediastinoscopy is described by code 39400 and is listed under the Cardiovascular chapter of CPT®. The difference between these lies in the approach:

■ Thoracoscopy of the mediastinal space, approach is through the chest wall

■ Mediastinoscopy, approach is cut under the sternal notch at the base of the throat

Repair

A lung hernia is a protrusion of tissue through the chest wall. Repair is done through an incision through the skin and inside lining of the chest cavity. The defect is then repaired by suturing tissue or a rotational flap over the area. This condition is most often congenital, with a diagnosis code of 748.69, Other congenital anomaly of the lung. ICD-9 code 518.89 is assigned for acquired conditions of the lung.

Code 32810 describes the secondary closure of the chest wall following a period of six to eight weeks after drainage of empyema.

Example: A patient is hospitalized and diagnosed with empyema. To treat the patient, a thoracostomy with open flap drainage is performed. The patient is discharged and is treated with repeated antibiotic irrigation of the empyema space. After undergoing this treatment for six weeks, he then has a closure of the drainage flap.

First surgery: ICD-9 diagnosis 510.9, linked with CPT® procedure 32036

Second surgery: ICD-9 diagnosis 510.9, linked with CPT® procedure 32810-58

Rationale:

A 90-day global period is recognized for code 32036. Since it is known at the time of the original procedure that the flap will be closed, Modifier 58 is appended to the second surgical code to describe a staged or related procedure in a postoperative period. The diagnosis remains the same until treatment of the empyema is completed.

A bronchial fistula is an abnormal passage, usually occurring after surgery, between the remaining end of a bronchial tube and surrounding tissue or pleura. Code 32815 describes repair of the fistula by reamputation of the bronchial tube, treating it with silver nitrate, then suturing. Silver nitrate is a cauterizing chemical that is also used on granulation tissue to prevent further overgrowth of tissue.

Example: A patient had a left upper lobectomy for carcinoma of the lung. Two weeks later, the patient experienced chest pain and, upon examination by the surgeon, is found to have a postoperative bronchial fistula. The surgeon reopened the wound and closed the fistula.

First surgery: ICD-9 diagnosis 162.3, linked with CPT® procedure 32480

Second surgery: ICD-9 diagnosis 998.6, linked with CPT® procedure 32815-78

Rationale:

Modifier 78 is used because the second surgery is in a global period of the lobectomy, and the complication is directly related to the original surgery. A surgical complication code is used to describe the need for the second procedure.

EXERCISE 9.10

Instructions: Give the correct CPT® codes for the following scenarios:

1. While working at a height of 30 feet, a man falls from a steel girder and sustains a small traumatic tear of the pulmonary artery. An immediate emergency thoracoscopy is performed to repair the pulmonary artery. _____

2. A patient with acute pericarditis is brought to the surgical suite for a pericardial window. A thorascopic pericardial window is created for drainage of the excess pericardial fluid. _____

Lung Transplantation

The codes in this section of CPT® apply only to lung transplantation. Code 32850 describes the removal of one or both of the lungs from a donor who has been declared brain dead. Before the removal of the organs, functioning of the heart, lungs, and circulatory system of the donor are maintained artificially. During the surgical procedure to remove the lungs, anesthesia is provided for ethical reasons. The patient is placed on a cardiopulmonary bypass machine to continue the circulation of blood to the organs until they are completely removed. The lungs are transported to the recipient patient under refrigeration.

The remaining codes in the lung transplant section deal with the recipient. Code 32851 describes transplantation without cardiopulmonary bypass, in which the patient's circulation and oxygenation is maintained by the patient's own heart and remaining lung. Code 32852 describes transplantation with cardiopulmonary bypass, in which the circulation is accomplished by a cardiopulmonary bypass machine. Code 32853 should be used if both lungs are being transplanted, "without cardiopulmonary bypass," or 32854 "with cardiopulmonary bypass."

Surgical Collapse Therapy; Thoracoplasty

Thoracoplasty means repair of the chest. Code 32900 describes the resection of rib, which is the removal of a portion of a single rib. This code is performed for surgical collapse of the thoracic cavity. For the resection of a rib and chest wall for the purpose of tumor removal, see code 19260 in the Integumentary chapter of CPT®. A partial excision of a rib is described by codes 21600, 21615, and 21616. Thoracoplasty is often performed for malignancy of the rib, sternum, and clavicle; multiple myeloma; chronic osteomyelitis; bone cysts; and acquired deformity of chest and ribs.

Two types of thoracoplasty codes are found in CPT®. Code 32905, Schede type or extrapleural, describes the removal of a portion of the chest wall to treat chronic thoracic empyema. Code 32906 describes the resection of a bronchopleural fistula. A bronchopleural fistula is an abnormal passageway between the remaining end of the bronchial tube and lung tissue that occurs as a result of surgery. Corresponding diagnoses for these procedures may include:

- Empyema with fistula and without fistula
- Spontaneous pneumothorax
- Acquired deformity of the chest and rib
- Open fracture of the sternum
- Complicated open wound of the chest wall

Code 32940 describes pneumonolysis, which is the lysis, or cutting, of adhesions that form between the surface tissues of the lung, periosteal, and the chest wall. The operative area is then packed to prevent the development of scar tissue. This is referred to as the extraperiosteal method. The equivalent procedure performed via open approach is described by code 32124. Common diagnoses linked with pneumonolysis include late effects of tuberculosis, emphysema, empyema without fistula, pleurisy without mention of effusion, and postinflammatory pulmonary fibrosis.

Procedure code 32960 describes the therapeutic intrapleural injection of air. This is accomplished by using a needle attached to a syringe to puncture into the pleural cavity between the ribs. The physician injects air into the chest cavity and thereby partially collapses the lung. A tube may be attached for repeated treatments. Do not confuse this code with the procedures to correct a pneumothorax. This procedure is used to treat pleurisy with effusion, bacterial cause other than tuberculosis, iatrogenic pneumothorax, lung abscess, and hemoptysis.

Other Procedures

Code 32997 describes an interesting procedure: a total lung lavage, or washing (unilateral). This procedure is different than the minor rinsing via bronchoscope. The coder is directed to code 31624 for bronchoscopic lavage. In a total lung lavage, the lung is completely degassed and small amounts of saline are instilled at the same time to prevent air pockets. Once the lung is filled to capacity, it is drained by gravity or suction. This procedure may need to be repeated several times. This code specifically states that it is unilateral. When performed on both lungs, one at a time, Modifier 50 is appended to 32997. This procedure is used to treat Legionnaire's disease; bacterial pneumonia; unspecified pneumonias; pneumonitis; empyema; lung abscess; traumatic pneumo and hemothorax; lung laceration; multiple injury to intrathoracic organs, with and without open wounds; and posttraumatic wound infection.

EXERCISE 9.11

Instructions: Give the correct CPT® codes for the following scenarios. Include the appropriate modifier(s).

1. A patient is seen for chronic maxillary sinusitis. Her physician performs a lavage by cannulation of both maxillary sinuses. _____

2. Mrs. Jones had a mass on her chest x-ray. Her surgeon performed a bronchoscopy with biopsy and washings of the left lung. _____

THE MULTIPLE SCOPE RULE

Medicare has developed a method to reimburse physicians for multiple endoscopic procedures performed during the same session. Normally, when more than one procedure is performed on the same day, the primary procedure is paid at 100 percent, and for the second and subsequent procedures, a Modifier 51 is appended to each code, with the fee reduced by 50 percent. When more than one endoscopic procedure is performed, the primary procedure sequenced is the procedure with the highest Relative Value Unit (RVU), or fee. The fees for the second and subsequent endoscopic procedures are calculated by subtracting out the fee for the diagnostic portion, or base code. This gives the physician payment for the additional procedures while not paying for more than one approach.

Example: 31622 is the base or diagnostic code for the bronchoscopy family. The family includes codes from 31622 to 31645. Keeping in mind the base code of 31622 with a fee of $150.00, a physician who performed a 31628 and a 31629 calculates his fees as follows:

- 31628: $250.00 (100% fee schedule)—highest priced procedure is listed first
- 31629-51: $200.00 (100% fee schedule) minus base code fee of $150.00 for code 31622: $50.00 for second procedure

Formula for Success

Multiple Scopes

1. Remember that the base code does not have to be performed but is used in the calculation of fees
2. Always list the highest priced procedure first.
3. Use a Modifier 51 for the secondary procedure.
4. Some carriers may require a Modifier 59 in addition to 51.

▬▬ CHAPTER REVIEW ▬▬

1. List three functions of the upper respiratory system.

2. Name the gas that is exhaled from the lungs.

3. Describe the chief function of the lower respiratory system.

4. State the number of lobes on the right lung vs. the left lung.

5. State the classification of lung disorder for asthma.

6. Give the layman's, or common, term for a pneumothorax.

7. Codes from the section on the nose are unilateral unless otherwise specified.   **T or F**

8. A surgical endoscopy includes the diagnostic portion.   **T or F**

9. Describe how the indirect laryngoscopy method differs from the direct method.

10. Name the components included in a diagnostic bronchoscopy.

11. List two major categories of tracheostomy codes.

12. List the two approaches similar in wording that coders should be watchful for in the section for Lungs and Pleura.

13. Name the different types of pneumonectomies.

Case Studies

Case Study 9.1

Preoperative and Postoperative Diagnosis
Complex, loculated, left parapneumonic effusion/empyema.

Procedure Performed
1. Left video-assisted thoracoscopy with pleural biopsy.
2. Left thoracotomy with complete pulmonary decortication and drainage of empyema.

Anesthesia
General endotracheal.

Estimated Blood Loss
Approximately 250 cc.

Indications for Procedure
The patient is a 20-year-old male with a left-sided pneumonia who has developed parapneumonic empyema, loculated effusion, requiring drainage, and decortication.

Summary of Procedure
Informed consent for the procedure was obtained. The patient was taken to the operating room and placed on the operating table in a supine position. General endotracheal anesthesia was established. The patient was then repositioned in the right lateral decubitus position and prepped and draped in sterile fashion.

An initial attempt at thoracoscopy was made by placing a thoracoscopic port in the level of the anterior latissimus line at the level of the sixth interspace. The thoracoscope was introduced, and a dense pleural mass of adhesions and loculated fluid collections was noted. A second thoracoscopic port was placed in the same line at the level of the fourth interspace. Thorascopic instruments were introduced, and an attempt at pneumolysis and drainage of fluid was accomplished. A representative sample of fluid was aspirated and submitted to the laboratory for culture and sensitivity. A generous pleural biopsy of the inflamed pleura was then accomplished with blunt and sharp dissection.

Due to dense inflammation, the procedure was converted to a left thoracotomy. The latissimus dorsi was separated from the fascia and retracted. The serratus anterior and intercostals musculature was taken down along the superior border of the fifth rib. The rib was then transected.

Through blunt and sharp dissection, the dense pleural adhesions were lysed. A thick, inflammatory peel overlying the upper and lower lobes of the lung was noted. This was decorticated using blunt and sharp dissection.

Following the decortication, the chest was irrigated and suctioned. A test inflation of the lung revealed significant expansion of the upper and lower lobes of the lung. No additional pleural peel or loculated fluid collection was noted.

Two straight chest tubes were placed. These were secured to the skin by sutures. The intercostals musculature and serratus musculature were reapproximated. The latissimus was reapproximated to its investing fascia. The chest tubes were connected to the pleur-evac suction. Sponge, needle, and blade counts were correct. The patient was moved to the post anesthesia care unit in good condition.

ICD-9-CM Diagnosis Code(s): _____
CPT® Procedure Code(s): _____

Case Study 9.2

Preoperative and Postoperative Diagnosis
Renal cell carcinoma with bilateral pulmonary metastases.

Procedure
Left apical segmentectomy.

Anesthesia

General endotracheal.

Blood Loss

Minimal.

Indications for Procedure

The patient is a 41-year-old female with a history of renal cell carcinoma with bilateral pulmonary metastases requiring surgical excision.

Summary of Procedure

Informed consent for the procedure was obtained. The patient was taken to the operating room and placed on the operating table in the supine position. General endotracheal anesthesia was established. The patient was then repositioned into a right lateral decubitus position, prepped and draped in sterile fashion. The hemi thorax was entered through the vertical muscle-sparing thoracotomy extending from the level of the fourth intercostals space to the eighth intercostals space. Through blunt and sharp dissection, the subcutaneous tissues were divided to the level of the latissimus dorsi, which was separated from the fascia and retracted.

The serratus anterior musculature was then sharply incised along the superior border of the fifth rib. The left lung was deflated and the intercostals musculature was sharply incised. The fifth rib was transected and rib-spreading retractors were placed.

Following a thorough exploratory thoracotomy, the mass of interest was identified in the apical segment of the left upper lobe. The metastatic lesion was isolated. It became rapidly obvious that simple wedge resection would not obtain adequate surgical margins. Therefore, an apical segmentectomy was initiated. The apical vein was dissected and ligated. The apical segmental, as well as the posterior segmental arterial branches were dissected, tied, and clipped. The pulmonary parenchyma was dissected free. The apical segmental bronchus was felt coursing within the parenchyma but was not individually dissected and stapled. The stapler was fired and a generous segmental resection was accomplished.

Evaluation of the margins suggested that additional pulmonary parenchyma should be taken. Additional parenchymal dissection off the pulmonary arterial trunk was accomplished and a second surgical resection wedge was accomplished.

The wound was irrigated copiously with sterile water. Inflation of the left lung demonstrated good inflation of the remaining segments as well as the lower lobe. The irrigation was suctioned free and a chest tube was placed. The ribs and musculature were reapproximated and sutured. The subcutaneous tissues were reapproximated and sutured. Dressing was applied. Sponge, needle, and blade counts were correct. The patient was returned to the post anesthesia care unit in good condition.

ICD-9-CM Diagnosis Code(s): _____

CPT® Procedure Code(s): _____

Case Study 9.3

Preoperative Diagnosis

Suspected foreign body aspiration.

Postoperative Diagnosis

Normal bronchoscopy.

Anesthesia

General.

Summary of Procedure

The patient was brought into the operating room and placed in the supine position on the operating table. General anesthesia was induced. Using the MAC laryngoscope, the patient's supraglottic area was examined. There was no abnormality or evidence of a foreign body. Vocal chords were visualized, and a 3.0 bronchoscope was inserted past the true vocal chords into the trachea. The patient was then ventilated through the bronchoscope and the bronchoscope was passed through the right lung bronchial. There was no foreign body noted. She did have some thin secretions, which were suctioned. The bronchoscope was then brought back to the carina and passed into the left bronchus. Again, no foreign bodies were visualized. The bronchoscope was then removed. There was no damage to the tracheal walls or the true vocal chords. The patient tolerated the procedure well and was transferred to the recovery room in stable condition.

    ICD-9-CM Diagnosis Code(s): _____

    CPT® Procedure Code(s): _____

Case Study 9.4

Preoperative Diagnosis

Chronic sinusitis.

Postoperative Diagnosis

Chronic sinusitis.

Procedure Performed

Bilateral endoscopic maxillary ethmoidectomy, bilateral endoscopic total ethmoidectomy.

Anesthesia

General endotracheal.

Summary of Procedure

The patient was brought into the operating room and placed supine on the operating table. General anesthesia was induced. Endotracheal intubation was performed. Lidocaine 2% with 1:100,000 parts epinephrine was injected into the lateral nasal wall and anterior septum bilaterally. Four percent cocaine-soaked pledgets were placed under the middle turbinate bilaterally. The patient was prepped and draped.

    The left side of the nose was addressed first. An uncinectomy was first performed with a sickle knife and straight-ahead forceps. The oscillator was then used to penetrate the ethmoid bulla and open the anterior ethmoid sinus. The patient had thickened polypoid mucosa within the sinus cavities. The basal lamina was then identified, penetrated, and the posterior ethmoid cells were widely opened. The natural os of the maxillary sinus was identified and opened.

    The right side of the nasal cavity was addressed in a similar fashion. Again, an uncinectomy was first performed. The anterior ethmoid cells were then widely opened using the oscillator. The basal lamina was then penetrated and the posterior ethmoid cells were widely opened. The natural os of the maxillary sinus was identified and opened. She had thickened polypoid mucosa throughout the sinus cavities.

    Bactroban and Aclovate ointment were placed under the middle turbinate bilaterally followed by gelfilm. The patient tolerated the procedure well and was transferred to the recovery room in stable condition.

    ICD-9-CM Diagnosis Code(s): _____

    CPT® Procedure Code(s): _____

Case Study 9.5

Preoperative Diagnosis

Right pansinusitis with nasal polyposis.

Postoperative Diagnosis

Right pansinusitis with nasal polyposis.

Procedure

Nasal polypectomy, right endoscopic maxillary antrostomy with tissue removal, and right endoscopic total ethmoidectomy.

Anesthesia

General endotracheal.

Summary of Procedure

The patient was brought into the operating room and placed in the supine position on the operating table. General anesthesia was induced. Endotracheal intubation was performed. Lidocaine 2% with 1:100,000 parts epinephrine was injected into the visible nasal polyps and 4% cocaine-soaked pledgets were placed in the nasal cavity on the right. The patient was prepped and draped.

Using an oscillator, the visible nasal polyps were removed, including the polyp extending down into the nasopharynx. A biopsy of the polypoid tissue was sent for pathology. An uncinectomy was first performed using a sickle knife. Using the oscillator, the anterior ethmoid cells were then widely opened. She had polypoid tissue within the sinuses themselves and had purulence emanating from the opposite side of the basal lamina, which was then widely opened. The natural os of the maxillary sinus was then widened and she had polypoid tissue within the sinus itself. The 30-degree scope was then used along with an angled oscillating blade, and the maxillary sinus tissue was removed. Aclovate with Bactroban ointment was placed under the middle turbinate bilaterally followed by gelfilm. The patient tolerated the procedure well and was transferred to the recovery room in stable condition.

ICD-9-CM Diagnosis Code(s): _____

CPT® Procedure Code(s): _____

Case Study 9.6

Operative Procedures

A. Emergency Intubation

This patient has Guillain-Barré. I was called to see her emergently because of dropping saturations. She has coarse rhonchi throughout both lung fields, as though she is filling up with airway secretions that she cannot clear. With her encephalopathy, she is not able to protect her airway, and she is not able to cough. Considering all these problems, she needs to be intubated emergently.

She was given a total of 5 mg Versed IV for sedation. No paralytics. She was intubated using a straight #2 blade. She was intubated without difficulty using an 8-0 ET tube. After getting it in, I quickly did a bronchoscopy to make sure that it was in good position. She has thick secretions completely occluding her airways. After confirming that I was in the airway, the bronchoscope was withdrawn, she was bagged, and put on a ventilator. On the ventilator, she had difficulty maintaining her volumes. At that point, we continued bagging her while I performed a formal bronchoscopy.

B. Emergency Bronchoscopy

Preoperative Diagnosis

Retained secretions with respiratory failure.

Postoperative Diagnosis

Retained secretions with respiratory failure.

After intubating this patient, I performed a formal bronchoscopy. Her airways are absolutely loaded throughout all the way up into the trachea with very thick tenacious, tan, purulent-looking secretions. I spent a great deal of time aggressively clearing the secretions. After clearing the secretions from the trachea and the left mainstem and the right mainstem bronchus, I was able to concentrate on the various lobes. She did have significant mucus plugs coming up from both the left lower lobe and the right lower lobe. Sterile saline was instilled to clear these thick mucus plugs.

After getting all the secretions cleared, I was able to have good visualization. The trachea now looks clear. The ET tube is in good position. The main carina itself looks sharp and normal.

The bronchoscope was passed down the left mainstem bronchus into the left upper lobe, left lingual lobe, and left lower lobe. No endobronchial masses or lesions were seen. She still had some minimal mucus plugs coming up from the left lower lobe after clearing the majority of her secretions.

The scope was withdrawn to the main carina, passed down the right mainstem bronchus into the right upper lobe, right middle lobe, and right lower lobe. No endobronchial masses or lesions were seen. She still has some thick mucus plugs coming up from the right lower lobe.

Washings that were obtained from her airways have been collected and sent for routine cultures.

ICD-9-CM Diagnosis Code(s): _____

CPT® Procedure Code(s): _____

Cardiovascular System

▮▮ *OBJECTIVES*

1. Gain an understanding of the basic anatomy and function of the cardiovascular system.
2. Correctly apply diagnosis codes to the cardiovascular system.
3. Identify the correct modifiers for cardiovascular system procedures.
4. Assign CPT® codes to cardiovascular system procedures.

▮▮▮ *TERMINOLOGY AND ACRONYMS*

ASHD Arteriosclerotic heart disease.

Bifurcation Division of blood vessel into two branches.

CABG Coronary artery bypass graft.

CAD Coronary artery disease.

CHF Congestive heart failure.

Endovascular Within a blood vessel.

MI Myocardial infarction.

Trifurcation Division of blood vessel into three branches.

▮▮▮ *ANATOMY*

The heart, arteries, veins, and lymphatics make up the cardiovascular system. The primary function of the cardiovascular system is to transport oxygen and nutrients to the cells and remove metabolic waste. The beating of the heart causes the circulation of blood from the right ventricle of the heart into the lungs and then through the pulmonary artery. After the blood is oxygenated in the lungs, it returns to the left atrium of the heart through the pulmonary vein. From there it passes to the left ventricle and is pumped through the aorta and out to the rest of the body through the arteries. At the most peripheral location, the blood passes through the capillaries, the smallest of the blood vessels, where the oxygen is delivered to the cells. From there the blood is picked up by the veins and travels back to the heart by way of the superior and inferior vena cava and back to the right atrium where it begins the cycle again.

Normal blood flow is in one direction across the valves. The valves respond to the pressure of the blood flow. When the pressure increases, the valves open. Conversely, when the pressure drops, the valves close, preventing backflow. If a valve is diseased, it allows blood to regurgitate or flow backward across the valve cusps. Regurgitation causes the heart to pump even harder to move the blood.

See the cardiac anatomy, Plates 7, 8, and 9 in Appendix A.

DISEASE PROCESSES AND ICD-9-CM DIAGNOSTIC CODING OF THE CARDIOVASCULAR SYSTEM

Aneurysm

Aneurysm, 441.x and 442.x, is an abnormal widening or out-pouching of an artery usually due to a weakness or thinning of the vessel wall at that location. The aneurysm may be relatively asymptomatic until it becomes large enough to rupture. Symptoms of severe pain and shock follow the rupture. The treatment of a ruptured aneurysm only has a 50 percent success rate. A pseudoaneurysm or false aneurysm is usually due to trauma, which ruptures the vessel. Blood from the tissues forms a clot, which can pulsate, making it appear to be a true aneurysm.

Cardiac Tamponade

Cardiac tamponade, 423.9, is caused by an increase in the intrapericardial pressure due to an accumulation of blood or fluid in the pericardial sac. If untreated, this can cause cardiogenic shock and death.

Coronary Artery Disease

Coronary artery disease, 414.0x (**CAD**), is most commonly caused by atherosclerosis, which is the accumulation of fat, fibrin, and calcium deposits on the inside of the vessels that causes a narrowing, thus reducing the volume of blood that can flow through the vessels.

Angina

Category 413 describes different types of angina. Angina is caused by coronary artery disease. The symptoms of angina include burning, squeezing, or crushing tightness of the chest radiating down the left arm, neck, jaw, and shoulder blade. Stable angina is relieved by rest or nitrates. If this condition persists, it is called unstable angina or unpredictable angina. Angina can progress into a myocardial infarction (**MI**).

EXERCISE 10.1

Instructions: Draw a line to connect the diagnosis on the left to the procedure on the right that best matches medical necessity.

1. Chest pain, 786.50	Arterial blood draw, 36600
2. Cardiac arrest, 427.5	EKG, 93000
3. Atrial fibrillation, 472.31	Cardiopulmonary resuscitation, 92950
4. Hypoxia, 799.0	Blood transfusion, 36430
5. Bleeding esophageal varices, 456.0	Elective cardioversion, 92960

Dilated Congestive Cardiomyopathy

Dilated congestive cardiomyopathy, 425.4, results from extensive damage to the myocardial muscle fibers. Prognosis is poor because this condition usually goes undetected until it reaches an advanced stage. The exact cause is unknown. Dilated cardiomyopathy can lead to intractable heart failure, arrhythmias, and emboli. Sudden death is caused by ventricular arrhythmias. Dilation of the chambers occurs due to increased volumes and pressures of blood. Blood pooling or slowed blood flow can occur, forming clots, which may lead to emboli.

Heart Failure

Heart failure, 428.x, occurs when the myocardium cannot pump well enough to meet the metabolic needs of the body. Right-sided heart failure occurs because of ineffective right ventricular contractions. Left-sided heart failure occurs because of poor left ventricular contractions. Forward-heart failure is due to inadequate blood delivery to the arterial system, usually caused by hypertension or aortic stenosis. Backward-heart failure happens when the left ventricle fails to empty, causing an accumulation of fluid in the left side of the heart. This is associated with myocardial infarction and cardiomyopathy.

Hypertension

Hypertension (see hypertensive table in ICD-9-CM for codes) is an intermittent or sustained elevation of diastolic or systolic blood pressure. *Systole* is the name for contraction and *diastole* is the name for relaxation. Therefore, when blood pressure is measured, the upper number is the measurement of systole, the pressure at contraction, and the lower number is the measurement of diastole, the pressure at relaxation.

ICD-9-CM Coding Guidelines classify hypertension in three categories: malignant, benign, and unspecified.

Essential hypertension, or hypertension not otherwise specified, is assigned to category 401, with the fourth digit indicating malignant, benign, or unspecified. Guidelines instruct not to use the malignant or benign fourth digits unless the medical record specifies this designation.

Hypertension with heart disease may be assigned to a combination code from category 402 when a causal relationship is stated or implied. Documentation may state, ". . . due to hypertension," or "hypertensive." Assign an additional code from category 428 if the patient has heart failure. If there is no causal relationship stated, these conditions are coded separately.

Example #1:   Hypertensive cardiomyopathy, code to 402.90

Example #2:   **1.** Congestive heart failure, code to 428.0
                   2. Hypertension, code to 401.9

Hypertension with renal disease assumes a cause-and-effect relationship when conditions from categories 585–587 are present. Assign these conditions to category 403.

Hypertensive heart and renal disease, category 404, may be assumed when the patient has hypertensive heart disease and hypertensive renal disease specified. If heart failure is present, assign an additional code from category 428.

Formula for Success

Since some of these concepts are hard to remember, mark the following reminders in your tabular index next to the codes listed below:

402–Don't assume
403–Assume cause and effect
404–Assume cause and effect

Use category 405 to classify *secondary hypertension*. Two codes will be needed to fully describe the condition: one for the underlying cause, and another for the hypertension.

Code 796.2 is assigned to *transient hypertension, elevated blood pressure*, and *white coat hypertension*.

Hypertension found in pregnant women should be classified to category 642. This category identifies *pre-existing hypertension* and varying degrees of *eclampsia* and *pre-eclampsia* that threaten the well-being of the pregnancy.

EXERCISE 10.2

Instructions: Assign the correct ICD-9-CM code to the diagnoses below:

1. Accelerated renal hypertension   _____

2. Benign essential hypertension   _____

3. Hypertension with heart disease   _____

4. Hypertension with renal disease   _____

5. Hypertensive cardiorenal disease with heart failure   _____

6. Codes from the hypertensive table in the alphabetic index may be
   assigned directly from the table without referencing the tabular index.   **True/False**

Hypertrophic Cardiomyopathy

Hypertrophic cardiomyopathy, *425.1* or *425.4*, is a primary disease of the cardiac muscle. This condition is characterized by left ventricular hypertrophy and cellular hypertrophy of the upper ventricular septum. These changes result in an obstruction of blood outflow.

Myocardial Infarction

Myocardial infarction, *410.x*, is the result of reduced blood flow through one of the coronary arteries. When the myocardial muscle, the muscle that makes up the heart itself, is denied a sufficient amount of blood, ischemia, injury, and necrosis result. Codes in this category are assigned by the anatomic location of the infarction. Use the following fifth digits to identify the episode of care:

- 0, Episode of care unspecified: Use when the source document does not contain enough information for the assignment of fifth digit 1 or 2.
- 1, Initial episode of care: Use to designate the first episode of care (regardless of facility site) for a newly diagnosed myocardial infarction. The fifth digit 1 is

assigned regardless of the number of times a patient may be transferred during the initial episode of care.

■ 2, Subsequent episode of care: Use to designate an episode of care following the initial episode when the patient is admitted for further observation, evaluation, or treatment for a myocardial infarction that has received initial treatment but is still less than 8 weeks old.

Use code 412 to identify an old or healed myocardial infarction that is currently asymptomatic.

EXERCISE 10.3

Instructions: Assign the correct ICD-9-CM code to the diagnoses below:

1. MI in 2001   _____

2. Rupture, anterolateral wall of myocardium today   _____

3. Status post coronary occlusion with MI 3 weeks ago   _____

4. Acute coronary insufficiency   _____

5. Impending myocardial infarction   _____

Pericarditis

Pericarditis, *423.1, 423.9, 420.9x,* is an inflammation of the fibrinous sac surrounding the heart. This can occur in both an acute and chronic form. The most common cause of pericarditis is infection, which can be bacterial, fungal, or viral in nature.

Rheumatic Heart Disease

Rheumatic heart disease, *397.1, 397.9, 398.9x,* is the result of untreated childhood rheumatic fever. Rheumatic fever develops after a Group A Streptococci infection. As a long-term effect, the mitral and aortic valves are often destroyed. This, in turn, leads to severe heart inflammation, pericardial effusion, and heart failure.

V Codes

The cardiovascular system is well represented with numerous V codes to report postprocedural status, family history, screening, aftercare and other encounters. Look in the alphabetic index under admission for, aftercare, history of, status post, long-term (current) drug use, and screening.

EXERCISE 10.4

Instructions: Assign the correct ICD-9-CM code for the diagnostic statements below:

1. Patient in for Coumadin labs   _____

2. Status post CABG in 1982   _____

3. Pacemaker status   _____

4. Pacemaker reprogramming   _____

5. Two-week checkup following valve replacement surgery   _____

6. Screening for hypertension   _____

7. Status post PTCA   _____

8. Status post heart transplant   _____

9. History of thrombophlebitis   _____

10. History of MIs in the family   _____

CPT® CODING FOR THE CARDIOVASCULAR SYSTEM

Not all subheadings in the cardiovascular system of CPT® are covered in this chapter. Only basic- to intermediate-level information is explained in this text. For more advanced work and additional coding exercises, please review the attached CD-ROM. Diagnostic tests on the cardiovascular system are discussed in Chapter 21, Medicine.

The cardiovascular system in CPT® is split into two main headings:

- Heart and pericardium
- Arteries and veins

Coding the cardiovascular system seems daunting until a few simple rules are remembered. First of all, take note of which anatomical portion of the cardiovascular system is being coded. Code assignments are easier if the coder can mentally separate the procedures on the heart from those on the arteries and veins outside of the heart. Some of the terminology and procedures are very similar between the two areas, which confuses many beginning coders.

Heart and Pericardium

Pericardium

Codes 33010–33050 describe procedures on the pericardium. The pericardium is the membrane that surrounds the heart. Fluid within the pericardium enables the heart to beat freely. *Pericardiocentesis* is the draining of excess fluid from the pericardial space. To perform this procedure, a long needle is placed below the sternum and into the pericardial space. After the fluid has been aspirated, a guide wire may be passed through the needle and a drainage catheter is placed. The procedures in this section include:

- Initial pericardiocentesis.
- Subsequent pericardiocentesis procedures.
- *Pericardiostomy:* The opening into the pericardium is maintained with a catheter and a sterile bag is attached for drainage.
- *Pericardiotomy:* An incision made into the pericardium to remove a clot or foreign body. Pericardiocentesis procedures are incidental to this procedure, unless performed at a different time, and should not be reported separately.
- Pericardial window or opening: Another method of drainage. The procedure can be performed by an open method or thoracoscopically. Use code 32603 when performed thoracoscopically. The surgical approach is important in order to code correctly.
- *Pericardectomy:* Removal of the pericardium.

These procedures are performed for pericarditis, late effects of internal injury to the chest, and complications of cardiac devices, implants, or grafts.

The excision of a pericardial cyst or tumor is performed utilizing the cardiopulmonary bypass device. When this procedure is performed thorascopically, use code 32661.

Pacemaker or Pacing Cardioverter–Defibrillator

Pacemakers aid the heart in maintaining normal sinus rhythm and are inserted for treatment of bradycardia. Diagnoses that are linked with the pacemaker procedure codes include heart blocks and conduction disorders, category 426, and rhythm disorders, code 427.x. When adjustments, revisions, or replacements are done, generally they are done for mechanical complications, codes 996.61 or 996.09, or complications due to infection, code 996.72.

The pacemaker is made up of a pulse generator (battery) and electrodes (leads). The pulse generator is placed subcutaneously either in a subclavicular site or underneath the abdominal muscles just below the rib cage. The electrodes are inserted either through a vein by transvenous method or placed by thoracotomy on the surface of the heart, the epicardial method.

Formula for Success

Before coding for pacemakers, ask yourself the following questions:

1. Is the pacemaker temporary or permanent?
2. Is it a single or dual chamber?
3. Will this involve the pulse generator, electrodes, or both?

Pacemakers are either single- or dual-chamber systems. Both contain a pulse generator. The single-chamber pacemaker inserts an electrode in either the atrium, or more commonly, in the ventricle of the heart. A dual-chamber pacemaker has one electrode inserted in the right ventricle and one in the right atrium. It uses a generator, which can pace both the atrium and ventricle. Occasionally, an additional electrode may be required to achieve pacing of the left ventricle. Transvenous electrode placement is reported in addition to the other pacemaker codes using 33224 or 33225.

The cardioverter–defibrillators treat ventricular tachycardia or ventricular fibrillation using a combination of antitachycardia pacing, low-energy cardioversion, or defibrillating shocks. A pacing cardioverter–defibrillator also includes a pulse generator and electrodes; however, it may require multiple leads even if only one chamber is being paced. A pacing cardioverter–defibrillator may be single or dual chamber.

The difference between the temporary and the permanent pacemaker is that the temporary pacemaker generator is not implanted in the body. Temporary pacemakers are used for patients with syncope due to a slow, drug-induced heart rate, or for cardiac emergencies, such as myocardial infarctions, category 410, and mechanical complications of cardiac devices, implants, and grafts, code 996.0x. Temporary pacemakers are described by two codes for single chamber and dual chamber.

Different parts of the pacemaker can be replaced of removed when necessary. Coders need to carefully read operative reports to identify the exact procedure and determine which components are being replaced or removed. Codes within this subheading of CPT® include:

- 33200–33208, Insertion of permanent pacemaker
- 33210–33211, Insertion of temporary pacemaker
- 33245–33246, Insertion of pacing cardioverter–defibrillator
- 33249, Insertion of electrode leads and insertion of pulse generator

- 33212–33213, 33240, Insertion of pulse generator only
- 33216–33217, Insertion of transvenous electrodes
- 33224–33225, Insertion of pacing electrodes
- 33245, Insertion of epicardial electrodes
- 33214, 33218, 33220, Maintenance of pacemaker systems
- 33215, 33222, 33223, 33226, Repositioning and revision of implanted devices
- 33233–33238, 33241–33244, Removal pulse generator or leads

Formula for Success

Coding Tips for Pacemakers and Pacing Cardioverter–Defibrillators

1. Most procedures include repositioning and adjustment within the first fourteen days of placement. Repositioning and revision codes are not reported separately in these cases.
2. When the "battery" of a pacemaker or cardioverter–defibrillator is changed, it is actually the pulse generator containing electronics and a battery.
3. The removal of pulse generator and insertion of a new pulse generator are both reported when a pulse generator is changed.

EXERCISE 10.5

Instructions: Assign the correct CPT® codes.

1. A patient is seen in the Emergency Room for chest trauma caused by a kick from a bull. After a chest X-ray is performed, a clot the size of a nickel is identified in the pericardium. A pericardiotomy is performed and the clot is removed. _____

2. A patient is seen in the office for a first-degree atrioventricular heart block. It is decided that the patient needs to have a pacemaker. The patient receives a dual-chamber pacemaker with transvenous placement of the electrodes. _____

3. A patient is in need of an additional electrode placement in the left ventricle, removal of a pacing generator, and insertion of a pacing generator due to a mechanical complication. _____

Patient-Activated Event Recorder

Surgically implanted event recorders enable the physician to monitor a patient's heart rhythm for more than a year. Because some conditions are intermittent, they can be hard to capture or demonstrate during a simple office visit. The procedures in this section include:

- *Implantation* of the cardiac event recorder into the subcutaneous tissue in the pectoral or mammary area. This implantation is very similar to that of a pacemaker pulse generator without the leads. When symptoms occur, the patient uses a handheld device to record the event.

■ *Removal* of the event recorder. Analysis and reprogramming are reported using code 93727 from the Medicine chapter of CPT®.

These procedures are commonly performed for conduction disorders, cardiac dysrhythmias, congenital heart block, syncope, dizziness, tachycardia, palpitations, or mechanical complications.

Example: A patient is seen in the physician's office for reported dizziness. He states it is recurrent and without apparent cause such as heat, fatigue, etc. He describes racing of the heart before onset of the dizziness. Lab tests are run, a chest X-ray is taken, and an EKG is performed, but the cause remains unknown. The physician orders an event recorder to be placed at the hospital. The event recorder is to stay in place for six months or until the cause of the dizziness is determined. The problem is diagnosed as palpitations, cause unknown.

First procedure: CPT® 33282 for placement with diagnosis of dizziness, 780.2.

Second procedure: CPT® 33284 for removal of the monitor six months later with a diagnosis of palpitations, 785.0.

Cardiac Valves

When coding for cardiac valve procedures, determine which valve is being operated on. CPT® divides the valve codes into each anatomic site: aortic, mitral, tricuspid, and pulmonary. Many procedures under each anatomic site are similar to each other—valvotomy, replacement, and repair—so the coder must read carefully to ensure the correct anatomic site is chosen. The coder must also know if the procedure is being performed open or closed heart, with or without a bypass.

Formula for Success

Coding Cardiac Valve Procedures

1. Use add-on code 33530 in addition to the main procedure if a re-operation takes place more than one month after the original procedure.
2. Do not to use the Modifier 63 with codes 33400–33403, 33470, or 33472.

Aortic Valve

The aortic valve is the three-leafed valve between the left ventricle and ascending aorta. This valve regulates the flow of oxygenated blood from the heart, through the aorta, to the rest of the body. When it becomes *stenotic,* or narrowed, there is a backflow of blood into the heart instead of the blood flow continuing out to the rest of the body. Stenosis of the aortic valve is most commonly seen in men over age 50. Another common aortic valve disorder is *insufficiency,* which is a malfunction of the valve itself. Also known as *regurgitation* or *incompetence,* this condition also causes a backflow of blood into the right ventricle of the heart. Valve disorders cause heart murmurs. Codes 33400–33496 describe surgical treatment of rheumatic diseases of the aortic valve, aortic valve disorders, congenital problems, complications due to prosthetic valves, or infection. See Figure 10.1 for a diagram of the heart valves.

Mitral Valve

The mitral valve is located between the left atrium and the left ventricle of the heart. Mitral valve stenosis is more common in women than in men and often follows rheumatic fever. When the mitral valve becomes stenotic (see Figure 10.2), it causes congestion in the veins and fluid from the blood is retained in the tissues, causing edema. Poor circulation also causes *cyanosis,* a dark blue condition of the skin or mucous membranes due to an in-

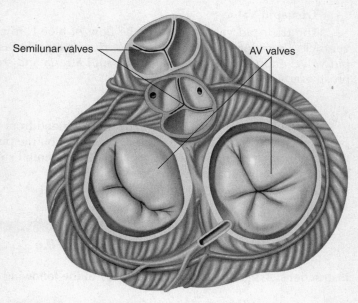

Figure 10–1   Cross-Section of heart valves.

adequate amount of oxygen reaching the tissues. *Mitral valve insufficiency* is the term used when the valve is too large and cannot close completely. This causes a backflow of blood into the left atrium, which leads to an increase in blood pressure in the vessels from the lungs, resulting in lung congestion. Procedures on the mitral valve are performed for diseases and disorders of the mitral and aortic valves, congenital stenosis, and insufficiency.

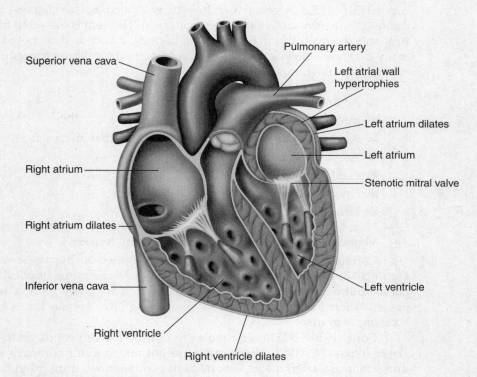

Figure 10–2   Mitral stenosis.

Tricuspid Valve

The tricuspid valve regulates the flow of blood from the right atrium to the right ventricle. Procedures on this valve are performed for diseases and disorders of the tricuspid valve, endocarditis, congenital tricuspid atresia and stenosis, complications of valve prosthesis, and other infections.

Pulmonary Valve

The pulmonary valve controls the flow of blood from the right ventricle through the pulmonary artery and into the lungs. Procedures on the pulmonary valve are performed for pulmonary valve disorders, endocarditis, congenital stenosis of the pulmonary valve and complications of heart valve prosthesis.

EXERCISE 10.6

Instructions: Assign the correct CPT® code to the following scenarios:

1. A patient with a diagnosis of rheumatic aortic stenosis is treated with transventricular dilation. The patient had this same surgery six months previously. _____

2. Due to endocarditis, a patient requires a valvotomy of the mitral and pulmonary valves. The closed method is performed on both valves and the pulmonary valve is accessed through the pulmonary artery. _____

Endoscopy

The only code in this section, 33508, is an add-on code intended for use only with codes 33510–33523. A vascular endoscopy is a video-assisted harvest of a portion of a vein through an incision above the saphenous vein. The vein is dissected from surrounding tissues and removed through a cannula. Because this code does not stand alone, there are many diagnoses that can be linked according to the primary procedure performed. Some examples of diagnoses include:

- Acute myocardial infarction
- Intermediate coronary syndrome
- Acute coronary occlusion without myocardial infarction
- Angina pectoris
- Coronary atherosclerosis
- Aneurysm and dissection of the heart
- Heart failure

Venous Grafting Only for Coronary Artery Bypass

Coronary artery bypass surgery is performed to bypass an occluded vessel (see Figure 10.3) that feeds the heart muscle itself. As the name implies, the occlusion is bypassed but not cleared. The codes in this section are based on how many vessels are bypassed. There is a separate code for one through five venous grafts and another code for six or more grafts.

Codes 33510–33516 are used to report the use of venous grafts for use in coronary artery bypass (**CABG**). These codes are not intended for coronary artery bypass procedures that use arterial and venous graft combinations during the same procedure. Procurement of the saphenous vein is included in these codes. Occasionally, an upper

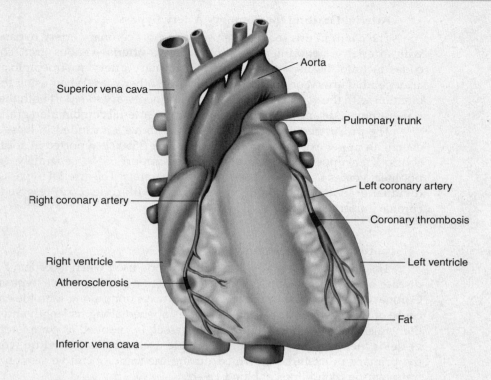

Figure 10–3 Blockage of coronary arteries.

extremity vein is used instead of the saphenous vein; therefore, the code for its procurement is reported separately with 35500. If the femoropopliteal vein graft is used, report 35572 for the procurement. When an assistant surgeon performs the graft procurement, report the bypass grafting code with the Modifier 80; do not report this as a co-surgery with the Modifier 62 for both surgeons.

Combined Arterial–Venous Grafting for Coronary Bypass

Codes 33518–33530 are used in combination with the arterial grafting codes performed during the same operative session for coronary artery bypass grafting (CABG). These codes are Modifier 51 exempt and are never reported alone. When using these codes, include the arterial–venous grafting code and the appropriate arterial graft code together. The procurement of the saphenous vein graft is included in these codes; however, if an upper extremity *vein* is used, this may be reported separately with code 35500. If an upper extremity *artery* is used, report this separately with code 35600. The use of the femoropopliteal vein for grafting, code 35572, would be reported in addition to the bypass procedure code. If an assistant surgeon is performing the graft procurement, report the bypass code with a Modifier 80. Do not report this as a co-surgery with the Modifier 62 on the bypass code for both surgeons.

Combined arterial–venous grafting codes are listed in the order of how many venous grafts and arterial grafts are performed. They are listed individually from one to five venous grafts (codes 33517–33522) and six or more venous grafts (code 33523.) This section also includes an add-on code for the re-operation of a coronary bypass or valve procedure more than one month after the original procedure. Because these procedures become increasingly more difficult when a patient requires more bypasses or valve repair, this code gives the physician "extra credit" for the additional difficulty. As with all add-on codes, this code must be reported with a primary procedure and never alone. The RVUs and fee have been adjusted so that the Modifier 51 and any associated fee reduction are not needed.

Arterial Grafting for Coronary Artery Bypass

The codes in this section are used to report coronary artery bypass grafting (CABG) with arterial grafts, either alone or with the arterial–venous graft combination. These codes include the use of the internal mammary artery, gastroepiploic artery, epigastric artery, radial artery, or arterial conduits from other sites. When using these codes in combination with the venous grafting codes, it is necessary to report both the appropriate arterial grafting code and the appropriate venous–arterial combination grafting code together.

The procurement of the arteries listed above is included in these procedures; however, if an upper extremity artery is used, code 35600 is reported in addition to the bypass codes. If an upper extremity vein is used, report 35500 separately, and if the femoro-popliteal vein is used, report code 35572 separately. The arterial bypass codes describe individual grafts for one through three grafts, with code 33536 reserved for four or more coronary arterial grafts.

Coronary Endarterectomy

The code in this section is an add-on code used when a coronary artery is so full of disease or occlusion along its entire length that a good site for a bypass cannot be found. Coronary artery bypass grafts are almost always done along with the endarterectomy. Because of the extent of disease, the artery is opened along its length and the plaque within the vessel, along with the lining of the vessel, is removed as completely as possible. The vessel is then repaired. The diagnosis code used for this procedure would correspond to the primary procedure performed during the same operative session. Figure 10.4 illustrates various conditions of blood vessels.

EXERCISE 10.7

Instructions: Assign the correct CPT® codes for the following scenarios:

1. A patient with cardiac chest pain is evaluated and found to have an aneurysm of a coronary artery and coronary atherosclerosis. A bypass of three coronary arteries with saphenous venous grafts is performed. _____

2. A patient who has been diagnosed with an acute myocardial infarction of the antero-lateral wall has a coronary artery bypass procedure performed with four venous and one arterial grafts. _____

Thoracic Aortic Aneurysm

Codes 33860–33877 describe repairs of thoracic aortic aneurysms. An aneurysm is an abnormal widening or out-pouching of an artery. Because the aorta is such a large muscular artery, if a rupture were to occur, a massive internal hemorrhage would result. The repair of a thoracic aortic aneurysm with a graft is performed by opening the aneurysm and grafting with felt strips sewn over the resulting hole. This can also be performed with coronary reconstruction or aortic root replacement using a composite prosthesis with coronary reconstruction. Another method of repair is to use an aortic graft and suture the great arteries to it. The last two procedures in this section use a graft to repair the descending, or thoracoabdominal, aortic aneurysm with a graft. Read operative notes to determine if cardiopulmonary bypass was performed, as codes differentiate with or without bypass.

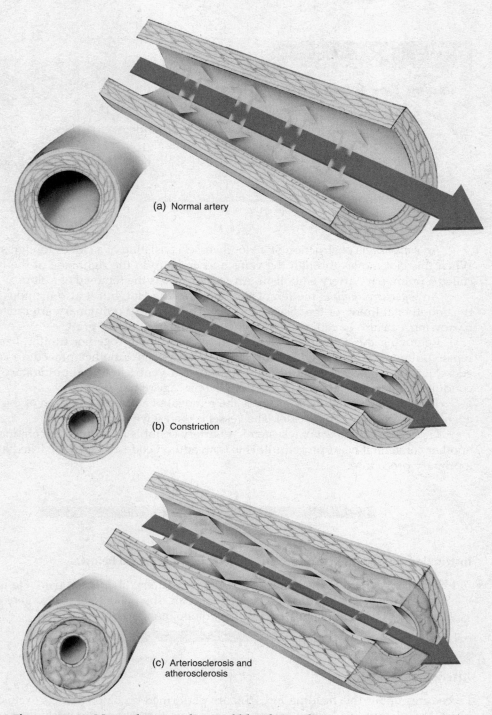

(a) Normal artery

(b) Constriction

(c) Arteriosclerosis and
    atherosclerosis

Figure 10–4 Normal versus diseased blood vessels.

Pulmonary Artery

Procedures performed on the pulmonary artery are commonly done for pulmonary embolism and infarction, trauma, stenosis, and congenital anomalies.

Formula for Success

Coding Tips for Pulmonary Artery Repairs

1. Do not use the Modifier 63 with codes 33918, 33919, or 33922.
2. Use 33608 to code the repair of other complex cardiac anomalies by construction or replacement of right or left ventricle to pulmonary artery.
3. The add-on code 33924 is to be used only with the list of codes immediately following the code descriptor.

An *embolism* is obstruction of a blood vessel consisting of a clot or foreign substance. When this clot moves through the veins and ends up in the right side of the heart, it is called a pulmonary artery embolism. An *embolectomy* is the removal of a clot.

An e*ndarterectomy* is the removal of any existing clot, but it also includes stripping the endothelial lining of the diseased artery. The repair of pulmonary artery stenosis, or narrowing, can also be repaired by reconstruction with patch or graft.

Removing the anomalous arteries and sewing them together (unifocalization) can repair pulmonary atresia with ventricular septal defect. Another procedure commonly constructs or replaces a conduit from right or left ventricle to the pulmonary artery. A conduit is a surgically created channel for the passage of blood.

Transection of pulmonary artery is the removal of a diseased portion of the vessel by a lengthwise cut across the vessel. The vessel is then sewn back together.

Ligation and takedown of a systemic-to-artery shunt is performed in conjunction with another congenital heart procedure. This is an add-on code and must be listed along with a primary procedure.

EXERCISE 10.8

Instructions: Assign the correct CPT® code(s) in the scenario below.

1. A patient is seen in the emergency room for extreme abdominal pain. He is found to have a dissecting thoracoabdominal aneurysm. The patient goes to surgery and has a grafting of the descending aorta with cardiopulmonary bypass. _____

Arteries and Veins

Procedures under this heading in CPT® are performed on blood vessels exclusive of the heart. Included in this section are aneurysm repair, thromboendarterectomy, angioplasty, bypass graft, exploration and revision, vascular injection procedures, transvenous access, hemodialysis access, and ligation. The student must remain vigilant to the type of blood vessel being operated on—many subheadings differentiate between arteries and veins in their codes.

Formula for Success

Coding Tips for Arteries and Veins

1. Primary vascular procedures include establishing inflow and outflow required for a procedure.
2. The arteriogram performed by the surgeon is included.
3. When a sympathectomy is performed, this is included in the aortic procedures.

Embolectomy/Thrombectomy

Codes 34001–34490 are site-specific and differentiated by arterial or venous anatomy. Arterial procedures include an incision over the site of the clot. Embolectomy or thrombectomy is performed by inserting a balloon catheter beyond the clot inflating it and withdrawing the balloon. This is performed for occlusion and stenosis, transient cerebral ischemia, and atherosclerosis. Notice in the venous subheading beginning with code 34401, the term "embolectomy" has been removed from the descriptor.

EXERCISE 10.9

Instructions: Assign the correct CPT® code(s) for the scenarios below:

1. A patient has crush injury to the left arm when a car door is shut on it. As a complication to this injury, the patient has formed a thrombosis in the radial artery. The treatment for this patient is a thrombectomy by incision of the radial artery. _____

2. A patient sustains a closed fracture of the tibia when he falls from a ladder and drops six feet to the ground. A complication of the fracture is a thrombophlebitis of the femoral vein. The treatment for this patient is a direct thrombectomy by leg incision. _____

Endovascular Repair of Abdominal Aortic Aneurysm

Codes 34800–34834 describe the placement of an endovascular graft for the repair of an abdominal aortic aneurysm. This is a relatively new procedure and is considered much safer than treatment of a ruptured abdominal aneurysm. The prosthetic graft is placed within a small carrier. Under fluoroscopic guidance, the carrier is placed into an artery, usually the femoral artery, and advanced to its proper location. When the graft is deployed, it springs open. A balloon may be inflated to help fully expand the device. The graft is long enough to overlap normal tissue at the ends and is held in place by hooks, springs, or stents.

Formula for Success

Coding Tips for Endovascular Aneurysm Repair

1. Do not report a balloon angioplasty and/or stent deployment separately when it is performed before or after endograft deployment and within the same treatment zone.
2. The introduction of guidewires and catheters should be reported separately (codes 36200, 36245–36248, and 36140)
3. Extensive repair or replacement of an artery should be reported separately.
4. The fluoroscopic guidance used for these procedures should be reported separately using code 75952 or 75953.
5. Interventional procedures performed in addition to aneurysm repair should be reported separately.

The codes in this section are meant to be component codes and are combined with separate codes for primary repair, surgical exposure of the femoral artery, and the radiologic supervision and interpretation codes. Because each aneurysm and patient is different, this component coding allows the most accurate way of reporting all of the steps taken. The medical necessity link for the codes in this section includes:

- Atherosclerosis of the aorta and renal artery
- Dissecting aortic aneurysm, abdominal
- Abdominal aneurysm without rupture
- Aneurysm of the renal and iliac arteries
- Embolism and thrombosis of abdominal aorta
- Acute and chronic insufficiency of intestine
- Vascular disorders of kidney
- Congenital anomalies of circulatory system
- Injury to blood vessels
- Late effect of injury to blood vessel
- Vascular complications

Formula for Success

Watch for bilateral procedures, which require Modifier 50, or staged procedures, which require Modifier 58.

Different types of prostheses can be deployed depending upon the location of the aneurysm. These are listed below to assist in code selection:

- *Aortic tube prosthesis* spans only the aorta. The description calls the placement of the device infrarenal, because it is deployed just below the renal arteries.
- *Bifurcated prosthesis* device extends into the iliac vessels. This is needed when the aneurysm is larger and continues into the iliac arteries or when it is low enough not to have another point to attach the prosthesis. This device has two separate components or modules that are inserted individually into the site. The attachment of these two pieces is referred to as docking.
- *Unibody bifurcated prosthesis* uses a one-piece prosthesis, which is two-legged and extends from the aorta into both iliac vessels, but does not require modular docking components.
- *Uniliac or unifemoral* is a one-legged prosthesis.
- When an occlusion device is used when making the repair, the add-on code 34808 is used. This device is placed distally to the aneurysm by separately reportable fluoroscopy. A directive under the descriptor lists the codes to report with add-on codes.
- *Open exposure* of the artery for the delivery of the prosthetic device is a dissection performed to expose and make the femoral or iliac artery more accessible. Repair codes 34800–34804 do not include the exposure of the artery and are, therefore, reported in addition to the aneurysm repair codes.

Direct Repair of Aneurysm or Excision (Partial or Total) and Graft Insertion for Aneurysm, Pseudoaneurysm, Ruptured Aneurysm, and Associated Occlusive Disease

Use codes 35001–35162 for direct repair of aneurysm. These are listed in CPT® by their anatomic location.

Formula for Success

Coding Tips for Direct Repair of Aneurysm

1. Preparation of the artery for anastomosis and endarterectomy are included.
2. Direct repairs because of occlusive disease only should use codes 35201–35286.
3. The codes in this section are listed by site and are further differentiated by incision site and whether the aneurysm is ruptured.
4. Angiography performed to locate the aneurysm should be reported separately using code 35400.
5. Angiography used to establish the inflow and outflow is included.
6. Graft harvesting is not reported separately.

The direct repair is performed by making an incision in the skin above the site of the aneurysm or pseudoaneurysm, and then the defect is either repaired or removed. The diagnoses that can be linked to the procedures in this section include:

- Steal syndrome
- Atherosclerosis
- Aortic aneurysm and dissection
- Peripheral vascular disease
- Embolism and thrombosis
- Stricture of artery
- Rupture of artery
- Congenital vessel anomaly
- Blood vessel injury
- Late effect of injury to blood vessel
- Complications due to vascular device, implant, and graft

EXERCISE 10.10

Instructions: Assign the correct CPT® code(s) to the scenarios below

1. A patient has been diagnosed with an abdominal aortic aneurysm and has elected to have it repaired before it ruptures. The endovascular repair is performed on the aneurysm with an aorto-aortic tube with unilateral open iliac exposure and fluoroscopic guidance. _____

2. A patient has been admitted for an elective abdominal aortic aneurysm repair; however, overnight he develops extreme abdominal pain. With the assistance of diagnostic

imaging, it is determined that the aneurysm has ruptured, and the patient is rushed to the operating room for emergency surgery. _____

3. A patient is seen in the Emergency Room for leg and groin pain. It is determined from diagnostic imaging that the patient has a pseudoaneurysm of the common femoral artery. The patient states that he has had this pain for a period of time with increasing intensity and wishes to have it repaired. He is taken to the operating room and the pseudoaneurysm is repaired. _____

Repair Arteriovenous Fistula

A *fistula* is an abnormal tube-like passage between two body cavities; therefore, an arteriovenous fistula is an opening between an artery and vein. Surgeons repair this by isolating and dissecting the vessels, then closing the walls of the artery and vein by sutures. The codes in this section describe procedures that repair congenital, acquired, and traumatic arteriovenous fistulas. The codes are then listed by body site; head and neck, thorax and abdomen, and extremities.

Repair Blood Vessel Other Than for Fistula, with or without Patch Angioplasty

Codes 35201–35286 are divided into three different methods and then further subdivided by body site. The methods are:

- *Direct:* An incision is made in the skin over the site of the injury and is repaired by sutures or with a patch graft sutured over the defect.
- *Venous graft:* An incision is made over the site of injury; however, for this method, a vein graft is harvested from another part of the body and is sutured end-to-end to the vessel, replacing the excised portion.
- *Graft other than vein:* An incision is made over the site of injury and a synthetic graft is used to repair the injury site.

Thromboendarterectomy

Codes 35301–35390 describe an open removal of an occlusion, which is made up of a clot, thrombus (see Figure 10.5), and plaque. An incision is made in the skin over the site of the occlusion and the vessel is isolated, dissected, and incised. A blunt tool is used to remove the plaque and the vessel lining. To prevent further separation of the arterial wall layers, the artery wall may be sutured. These codes are reported with or without the use of a patch graft and are divided into anatomic sites. Use the add-on code 35390 with code 35301 for a reoperation of a carotid thromboendarterectomy when it has been over one month from the original surgery. Diagnoses commonly linked with these procedures include occlusion and stenosis, cerebrovascular disease, atherosclerosis, peripheral angiopathy, peripheral vascular disease, arterial embolism, thrombosis, and stricture.

Transluminal Angioplasty

A transluminal angioplasty is the enlargement of a narrowed blood vessel lumen by the use of a catheter. The angioplasty can be performed through an open technique or percutaneously through the skin. Both open and percutaneous techniques are divided by anatomic site.

Angioplasty performed by the open method involves an incision made in the skin overlying the affected site. The physician creates an opening into the vessel. A catheter is placed into this opening and threaded into the vessel. Once the balloon tip reaches the narrowed portion of the vessel, the balloon is inflated and the blood vessel is stretched to allow a normal flow of blood. This method sometimes requires several inflations of the balloon, although the code is used only once. The balloon is then deflated and the catheter is removed from the vessel.

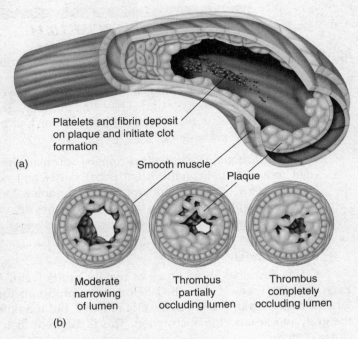

(a)

Platelets and fibrin deposit on plaque and initiate clot formation

Smooth muscle

Plaque

Moderate narrowing of lumen

Thrombus partially occluding lumen

Thrombus completely occluding lumen

(b)

Figure 10–5   Thrombus formation.

Use codes 35470–35476 for angioplasty performed through a skin puncture overlying the artery. Except for the approach, the method of treatment and conditions for which the procedure is performed is the same as for the open method.

Formula for Success

CPT® instructs to use Modifier 51 or 52 if the transluminal angioplasty is done as part of another operation. Use radiology codes 75962–76968 and 75978 for the physician reporting radiology supervision and interpretation of catheter placement.

Transluminal Atherectomy

The difference between an atherectomy and angioplasty is in the cutting of plaque, rather than stretching the vessel. The approach for an atherectomy is essentially the same as for an angioplasty. Atherectomy catheters contain a cutting device instead of a balloon. This device cuts and suctions the fatty tissue and/or plaque blocking the vessel. As with the open angioplasty, open atherectomy involves a cutdown technique to locate and insert the catheter into the vessel.

The percutaneous method is essentially the same as that described in the percutaneous angioplasty, using a cutting device. Both open and percutaneous codes are listed by site.

Formula for Success

CPT® instructs to use Modifier 51 or 52 if the transluminal atherectomy is done as part of another operation. Use radiology codes 75992–75996 for the physician reporting radiology supervision and interpretation of catheter placement.

EXERCISE 10.11

Instructions: Assign the correct CPT® codes for the scenarios below.

1. A patient is seen in the Emergency Room for a deep wound of the forearm. The patient was attacked by a mugger and is bleeding profusely. The patient is rushed to the operating room and is found to have a severed brachial artery. The brachial artery is repaired using a venous graft. _____

2. A type II diabetic patient with peripheral vascular disease is found to have a swollen right foot with pain, nonexistent pedal pulse, and skin with a bluish color. He is brought to the operating room for a femoral-popliteal transluminal angioplasty. Due to swelling and poor vascularity, the patient requires an open method. _____

Bypass Grafts

CPT® describes three types of bypass grafts: vein, *In-situ*, and Other Than Vein. Each of these types is described below. It is important for the coder to remember that when a bypass graft is placed, the clot remains, but the flow of blood is diverted through the graft and around the obstruction. This is different than a repair procedure, when the clot is removed.

Vein. The first code in this section, 35500, is an add-on code describing the procurement of an upper extremity vein for lower extremity or coronary artery bypass grafting. The descriptors in the coronary artery bypass section make reference to this code because the procurement of the saphenous vein is normally included in the coronary artery bypass procedure. However, if the graft segment is obtained from an upper extremity, code 35500 is reported in addition to the coronary bypass code. The list of codes that this add-on code can be reported with is listed under the descriptor for 35500.

The last code in this section, 35572, is an add-on code describing the procurement of the femoropopliteal vein for vascular reconstruction procedures. Under the code descriptor is a list of codes that this add-on code may be used with.

The venous bypass graft codes are listed by site with the direction of the flow of blood shown by the order in which the vessels are listed.

> **Example:** Code 35506, Carotid-subclavian graft, describes graft placement so that the flow of blood around the blockage goes from the carotid to the subclavian vein.

***In-Situ* Vein.** *In-situ* vein bypass grafts are another method of bypassing an occlusion. In certain conditions such as diabetes mellitus, 250.xx, and peripheral vascular disease, 443.9, blood flow to the lower extremities is compromised. When occlusions occur, the loss of all or part of a lower extremity can result. As was mentioned in an earlier section, arteries carry blood away from the heart through muscular vessel walls. Veins carry the blood back to the heart, but do not have muscular walls; instead they have valves that prevent backflow. Throughout the body, where there is an artery, there is a complimentary vein. In the legs, the femoral artery and its branches supply the leg with a blood supply. The saphenous vein is the largest leg vein to carry blood back toward the heart. The *in-situ* bypass graft is unique because it stays in its original position in the leg, next to the femoral artery and its branches. When an occlusion is bypassed, the vein and artery above and below the occlusion are exposed and incised. Because the vein has valves that prevent backflow, these valves are destroyed with a special kind of catheter, and the vein is sutured to the two incisions in the artery either by an end-to-end or end-to-side anastomosis or connection of the two vessels. When this is completed, the blood flows down the artery, is diverted into the vein bypassing the previous occlusion, and delivers blood to the peripheral sites of the extremity. The codes in this section are site specific with the vessel where the bypass graft begins being named first and the receiving end of the bypass graft named second.

> **Example:** In code 35583, the femoral-popliteal *in-situ* bypass, the bypass begins in the femoral artery, is diverted around the occlusion through the venous graft, and is attached to the popliteal arterial branch on the opposite side of the occlusion. From there the blood flow continues down the leg.

Other Than Vein. The procedures described in this section are another method of bypassing an occlusion.

The first code in this section, 35600, is a Modifier 51 exempt code for the harvesting of an upper extremity artery for coronary artery bypass. The harvesting of graft artery is included in the coronary artery bypass procedure, except when an upper extremity artery is used. This code is reported along with the coronary artery bypass code(s).

Formula for Success

Coding Tips for Bypass Grafting, Other Than Vein

1. The codes in this section describe the bypass grafting with a synthetic material.
2. The codes in this section are listed according to the bypass site, with the direction of the flow of blood shown by the order in which the vessels are listed.
3. The diagnoses linked to these procedures are essentially the same as those listed for the venous bypass grafts previously listed.

The use of synthetic graft material in these procedures is what differentiates them from the bypass codes of previous sections. When coding bypass procedures, it is always important to understand the site of the bypass and what type of graft is being used.

Composite Grafts

This section is made up of three add-on codes:

- 35681, Bypass graft composite, prosthetic, and vein for one graft
- 35682, Harvest and anastomosis of two vein segments for arterial bypass grafting
- 35683, Harvest and anastomosis of two or more vein segments for arterial bypass grafting

Report these add-on codes with 35556, 35566, 35571, and 35583–35587 when appropriate.

Exploration/Revision

Exploration or revision is commonly performed for a postoperative hemorrhage, thrombosis, infection, or other complication. Codes for exploration not followed by surgery are used when the inspection is complete, no perforation or injury is found, and the surgeon simply repairs the incision site. These codes are listed by vessel, beginning with 35701 through 35761. When a problem is identified, it is corrected and this is included in the exploration code, using 35800–35860. These codes are listed according to body area instead of specific vessel. This group of codes also includes excision of infected graft, codes 35901–35907, and several types of thrombectomy, including those with revision of bypass grafts.

Example: An exploration of the neck is done due to suspected postoperative hemorrhage. Upon inspection, a vessel is identified as leaking and is repaired by simple suture. The code reported is 35800-78 with a diagnosis of 998.11.

Vascular Injection Procedures

Catheters can be inserted into almost any blood vessel in the vascular anatomy. When catheters are used for diagnostic or therapeutic purposes, codes in the Cardiovascular chapter of CPT® are used to describe the surgical component. Radiologists typically report the imaging portion of the study, which may be done by the same physician who also performs the surgical portion. Blood vessels can be thought of like a tree—with branches that get progressively smaller and smaller coming off a trunk. Each branch, or **bifurcation,** off the main trunk is considered to be a vascular family. Each family contains additional branches, known as *orders*.

The main trunk of the systemic arteries is the aorta. The aorta is comprised of the ascending aorta, descending aorta, and the arch. There are two types of catheter placement procedures, nonselective and selective.

- *Nonselective* is when a catheter is placed directly in an artery and either not advanced further or placed only into the aorta. Think of a nonselective catheterization like shining a flashlight into a dark room. A nonselective procedure often tells the radiologist where to go next.
- *Selective* catheter placement indicates that the catheter has been deliberately guided into an arterial position other than the aorta or the artery where the catheter entered.

Venous Procedures.   The venous section of the vascular procedures is very broad and includes a wide variety of codes describing venipuncture, needle or catheter for diagnostic study, or intravenous therapy performed percutaneously.

Formula for Success

Coding Tips for Coding Venous Injection Procedures

1. Venipuncture and percutaneous catheter codes are age specific.
2. Use of the Modifier 63, Procedures on infants, is variable.
3. Codes for venous catheters, ports, and implantable infusion pumps are based on the location of the insertion and technique, not the brand name of the device.

Venipuncture and the collection of venous blood are different methods of obtaining blood specimens for diagnostic studies. These codes are age-specific. Some codes use one year and other codes use three years as a cutoff point. Venipuncture codes for patients under 3 years of age are broken down to:

- 36400, Femoral or jugular vein, necessitating physician's skill; not for routine venipuncture
- 36405, Scalp
- 36406, Other vein

Code 36415 is typically referred to as the "routine venipuncture code." Code 36416, Collection of capillary blood, is also referred to as a finger or heel stick. The remaining venipuncture codes are performed by a "cutdown" technique. The physician performs this technique by making an incision in the skin directly over the vessel and frees the vessel from the surrounding tissue to facilitate the collection of a blood sample. This procedure is performed on patients who are difficult to obtain a blood specimen from by the routine methods. Use code 36410 for non-routine venipunctures requiring a physician's skill on patients over 3 years of age.

Arterial Procedures.   Percutaneous puncture of the radial, brachial, or femoral artery for the withdrawal of blood for diagnosis is most commonly used for an arterial sample for blood gas analysis; however, many other diagnostic tests may be run. Use code 36600 for arterial punctures.

Arterial catheterization, code 36620, is used for sampling, transfusion, or prolonged infusion therapy and can be performed by either the percutaneous or cutdown methods. These procedures can be performed on any major artery of the arm. To review, the percutaneous method is a puncture through the skin into the vessel, and cutdown is an incision over the vessel followed by simple dissection of the vessel and puncture. In newborns, the umbilical artery can be used for catheterization for medication infusion or specimen collection.

Hemodialysis Access, Intravascular, Cannulation for Extracorporeal Circulation, or Shunt Insertion.   Patients with chronic renal failure or end-stage renal failure (ESRD), ICD-9-CM code 585, typically receive dialysis three times per week, although a cycle is developed based on the individual patient. Because of the frequency and the anatomic difference from patient to patient, there are many different ways of creating a dependable access for hemodialysis. Because this section is specifically for hemodialysis access, the diagnoses linked to these codes must indicate a problem with the renal system.

Arteriovenous anastomosis, codes 36819–36821, is a connection is created between an artery and a vein used for hemodialysis. Because this needs to heal or mature, an external cannula may be inserted for interim dialysis. The most common method is the side-to-side anastomosis of any site. This is referred to as the Cimino method and is performed beginning at the lowest or most distal portion of the arm. When this area eventually becomes nonfunctional, the surgeon must move upward on the arm in another operative session, creating new sections of anastomosis. This method creates one large vessel for hemodialysis access.

Other codes in this section include thrombectomy, open or percutaneous, and revisions with or without thrombectomy.

EXERCISE 10.12

Instructions: Assign the correct CPT® codes to the following scenarios.

1. An infant requires the placement of a central venous catheter for antibiotics to treat pneumococcal meningitis. The surgeon performs a tunneled method for the placement of the catheter. _____

2. A patient is brought into the Emergency Room suffering from acute exacerbation of chronic obstructive pulmonary disease. The physician on duty obtains an arterial blood sample for blood gas analysis. _____

3. A patient with the diagnosis of end-stage renal failure is in need of a permanent access for dialysis. The patient has surgery to form a Cimino left wrist arteriovenous fistula end-to-side. _____

4. A patient with an arteriovenous fistula graft for dialysis develops a clot. The patient is surgically treated with an open thrombectomy without revision. _____

CHAPTER REVIEW

1. A pacemaker is made up of all of the following except:
    a. battery
    b. pulse generator
    c. electrodes
    d. recording device

2. When the battery of a pacemaker is changed, it is actually the pulse generator that is changed.   **T or F**

3. There is a 90-day global period with the insertion of pacemakers and cardioverter–defibrillators. Any adjustments or repositioning is included in the 90-day global period.   **T or F**

4. When reporting bypass grafting, which of the following code combinations cannot be reported together?
    a. 33534 and 33572
    b. 33511 and 33572
    c. 33512 and 33534
    d. 33519 and 33535

5. When coding for endovascular repair of abdominal aortic aneurysm, all of the following can be reported separately except:
    a. angioplasty of the aneurysm
    b. fluoroscopic guidance
    c. arterial embolization
    d. intravascular ultrasound

6. The direct repair of an aneurysm includes an endarterectomy.   **T or F**

7. All of the following can be reported separately when performed for venous bypass grafting except:
    a. construction of an autogenous composite graft
    b. procurement of the saphenous vein graft
    c. procurement of an upper extremity vein graft
    d. procurement of the femoral-popliteal vein graft

8. An *in-situ* vein bypass is unique because the vein used to bypass the occlusion remains in its original position.   **T or F**

9. Select the correct code(s) for reporting an initial third order selective thoracic catheterization:
    a. 36246
    b. 36245, 36246, and 36247
    c. 36217
    d. 36215, 36216, and 36217

10. Identify the difference between a selective and nonselective catheterization: When a catheter is placed right into the area of interest, it is referred to as selective. When a catheter is placed in a vessel and the bifurcations make the course of the catheter, it is referred to as nonselective.   **T or F**

11. The "routine" venipuncture code is:
    a. 36420

      b. 36400

      c. 36410

      d. 36415

12. The code for the collection of blood for arterial blood gases is:

      a. 36620

      b. 36415

      c. 36600

      d. 36625

13. A "Cimino" arteriovenous anastomosis is a side-to-side anastomosis of the radial artery and cephalic vein of the arm.   **T or F**

14. When a patient has varicose veins "stripped," the correct code would be:

      a. 37618

      b. 37730

      c. 35556

      d. 35226

15. Match the modifiers with the definitions:

      a. Unusual Procedural Service _____

      b. Bilateral Procedure _____

      c. Return to the Operating Room for a Related Procedure During a Postoperative Period _____

      d. Staged Procedure _____

      e. Unrelated Procedure or Service by the Same Physician During a Postoperative Period _____

      f. Multiple Procedures _____

      g. Distinct Procedural Services _____

    51   **58**   **78**   **22**   **50**   **79**   **59**

16. Match the term and definitions:

      a. A procedure code that is meant to be used alone and is usually bundled into a more extensive procedure from the same body area. _____

      b. A procedure that cannot stand alone and is not subject to modifier 51 or a reduction in fee _____

      c. A procedure that is used when no other code within the same section accurately describes a procedure. _____

      d. A Modifier 51 is not appended to this code even when performed with another procedure and the fee is not reduced. _____

    Add-on   **Modifier 51 Exempt**   **Separate procedure**   **Unlisted Procedure**

Case Studies

Case Study 10.1

Preoperative Diagnosis

Bradyarrhythmia.

Postoperative Diagnosis

Bradyarrhythmia.

Procedure Performed

Insertion of a dual chamber pulse generator and atrial and ventricular permanent transvenous endocardial electrodes.

Anesthesia

Local with standby.

Summary

With the patient in a supine position, the left infraclavicular area was prepped and draped in a sterile fashion. Following infiltration of 1% plain xylocaine, percutaneous entry was made into the subclavian vein without difficulty, and a guidewire was inserted and confirmed to be in the venous system by fluoroscopy. Further infiltration of 1% plain xylocaine was carried out and a transverse incision was made through the guidewire insertion site. A subcutaneous prepectoral pocket was then created using blunt dissection with hemostasis by electrocautery. A #11 introducer was passed over the retained guidewire into the superior vena cava and the ventricular electrode was inserted. The introducer was then removed but the guidewire was left in place, following which another 11 introducer was then passed over the retained guidewire into the superior vena cava. The atrial electrode was then placed through the introducer into the superior vena cava, and both the introducer and the guidewire were then removed. Using fluoroscopic guidance, the ventricular electrode was maneuvered in the apex of the right ventricle. Quite a bit of maneuvering was required in order to find a satisfactory visual position and a satisfactory sensing and pacing position, but ultimately a good position was found with the ventricular lead volts to capture being 0.5 with resistance of 560 ohms and the R-wave reading ranged form 7 to 11 mV. The ventricular lead was then secured to the fascia using 2-0 black silk and Silastic collar. The arterial lead was then deployed into the right atrial appendage. After several positioning maneuvers, satisfactory visual position was achieved. Testing ultimately did reveal volts to capture of 0.6, with 460 ohms resistance and a P-wave reading of 2.0. The atrial lead was then secured to the fascia using black silk and the Silastic collar. The pulse generator was then attached to the electrodes and placed in the prepectoral pocket with the inscription facing anteriorly. The wound was then closed in layers of 3-0 and 5-0 Vicryl. A sterile dressing was applied and the patient was taken to the recovery area in satisfactory condition, having tolerated the procedure well with no complications. The pacemaker inserted was a model 9999, DDR, by Pacermaker Co. and the ventricular electrode was a 1234T 58 cm lead by Pacermaker Co. The atrial electrode was 5678T 52 cm lead by Pacermaker Co.

ICD-9-CM code(s):   _____

CPT® code(s):   _____

Case Study 10.2

Preoperative Diagnosis

End of service pacemaker pulse generator.

Postoperative Diagnosis

End of service pacemaker pulse generator.

Anesthesia

Local with standby.

Procedure Performed

Replacement of pacemaker pulse generator.

Summary

With the patient under satisfactory sedation in the supine position, the left infraclavicular area was prepped and draped as a sterile field following infiltration of 1% plain xylocaine through the old scar at the pacemaker pulse generator pocket. Incision was created down through the subcutaneous tissue to the generator, and, using very careful sharp dissection, the capsule of the generator pocket was incised and the generator was carefully extruded. The electrodes were quite well scarred in behind the generator. With external pacing in place, the electrodes were disconnected from the old pulse generator. Lead testing revealed impedance of 250 ohms in the atrial lead and 330 ohms in the ventricular lead. The ventricular threshold was 0.5 volts. The leads were felt to be satisfactory; therefore, a new pulse generator was connected to the electrodes appropriately. The new generator was an Identity DR model 1234 by Pacermaker. The serial number is 567899. Base rate of 70 beats per minute had been preprogrammed. With the electrodes securely connected to the generator, the generator was returned to the pocket with inscriptions facing anteriorly and electrodes posterior to the generator. The pocket was then reclosed with interrupted 3-0 Vicryl in the subcutaneous tissue, and the skin was closed with subcuticular 5-0 Vicryl. Sterile dressing was applied. Due to slight oozing at the skin edge, a bulky compression dressing using Microfoam tape was applied over the Tegaderm and 4X4 dressing. The patient was pacing satisfactorily in the DDD mode upon leaving the operative area.

ICD-9-CM code(s): _____

CPT® code(s): _____

Case Study 10.3

Preoperative Diagnosis

Symptomatic high-grade left carotid artery stenosis.

Postoperative Diagnosis

Symptomatic high-grade left carotid artery stenosis.

Procedure Performed

Left carotid endarterectomy.

Summary

The patient was prepped and draped in the usual sterile manner in the supine position with the neck extended and turned toward the right.

An oblique incision was made in the skin crease 1½ fingerbreadths below the angle of the jaw. The carotid bifurcation was dissected. Venous branches were clipped and/or ligated with clips and 2-0 silk ties with good hemostasis. The vagus nerve was preserved.

Some of the ansa nerves were sacrificed. Good exposure was obtained. The patient was fully heparinized. Supplement of 2500 units of heparin was given. After four minutes, the artery was extremely calcified circumferentially. This was more prevalent anteriorly. A second Fogarty hydragrip clamp was placed 1 cm proximal to the original clamp to get a good transition of the plaque dissection on the common carotid artery at least 1 cm proximal to the bifurcation. The distal endarterectomy point feathered nicely. This was secured with four separate 7-0 Prolene horizontal mattress tacking sutures. Fine forceps were used for dissection of minimal debris. This area was extremely calcified with ulcerative-type plaque and loose debris. It was copiously irrigated with pressured heparinized saline irrigation and subsequently with Dextran solution. The arteriotomy was closed with a running 6-0 Prolene from distal to proximal. Prior to completing the closure, the vessels were all flushed and reflushed, especially after the common carotid artery was opened. The common carotid artery was flushed on two occasions, more than usual, to clear any loose debris from the circumferential plaque of the common carotid artery. Before releasing to the external carotid circulation, the internal carotid artery was clamped with a DeBakey forceps at its origin and flow was established first from the common carotid artery to the external carotid artery for approximately 30 to 45 seconds and then released to the internal carotid artery. The arteriotomy closure was very hemostatic.

Protamine was given appropriately for reversal. Fibular Surgicel was used for hemostasis of the arteriotomy closure. We used 3-0 Vicryl for sternocleidomastoid deep fascia closure with three interrupted sutures and then the platysmal layer was also closed with interrupted 3-0 Vicryl inverted sutures. The skin was closed with a running 4-0 Prolene.

There were no EEG changes throughout, and no shunting was required. The patient tolerated all of this very well. Some intermittent hypertension was controlled by anesthetic agents. He was extubated and moving both right upper and lower extremity at the time of this dictation. The heparin drip was discontinued at the time of arterial closure. Dextran 22 cc/hr was continued perioperatively.

Estimated Blood Loss

Around 150 cc.

ICD-9-CM code(s): _____

CPT® code(s): _____

Hemic and Lymphatic Systems, Mediastinum and Diaphragm, and Endocrine System

▬▬ *OBJECTIVES*

1. Correctly assign diagnostic codes to blood, lymphatic, and endocrine conditions.
2. Recognize neoplastic conditions and different types of anemias.
3. Identify various complications of diabetes.
4. Differentiate between diabetes and dysmetabolic syndrome.
5. Correctly assign CPT® codes to surgical procedures.

▬▬ *TERMINOLOGY AND ACRONYMS*

Coagulopathy   Disease or defect in coagulation.

DM   Diabetes mellitus.

Fibrin   The basic constituent of a blood clot.

FBS   Fasting blood sugar.

Erythrocyte   Red blood cell.

Guiac test   Test for occult, or "hidden," blood in feces or stomach aspirate.

HD   Hodgkin's disease.

Hemolytic   Causing disintegration of red blood cells.

HGB   Hemoglobin, the oxygen-binding protein found in red blood cells; also gives a red color.

Hypochromia   Iron deficiency.

IDDM   Insulin-dependent diabetes mellitus.

Lymphoblast   Immature lymphocyte, a type of white blood cell.

Macrocytic   Larger than average cells with a high level of hemoglobin.

Megaloblast   A large, embryonic red blood cell found in patients with pernicious anemia or folic acid deficiency.

Microcytic   Iron deficient.

Myeloblast   The early stage of a granulocyte; can differentiate into other types of white blood cells.

NIDDM   Non-insulin-dependent diabetes mellitus.

NHL   Non-Hodgkin's lymphoma.

Normocyte   A red blood cell of normal size.

PKU   Phenylketonuria, nerve and brain cell damage due to deficient amino acid production.

Plasma   The clear, uncoagulated portion of blood and lymph.

Platelet   A type of blood cell.

PRBC   Packed red blood cells; a type of blood transfusion.

RBC   Red blood cell.

Thalassemia   A congenital hemolytic anemia.

Thrombin   An enzyme in the blood; creates clots by changing fibrinogen into fibrin.

Thrombocytopenia   Deficiency of circulating platelets in the blood.

TSH   Thyroid-stimulating hormone.

WBC   White blood cells.

DISEASE PROCESSES AND ICD-9-CM CODING OF THE HEMIC AND LYMPHATIC SYSTEMS

The hemic and lymphatic systems are made up of the body's two main fluids that circulate through separate vessel systems. Blood is circulated through arteries, capillaries, and veins. The fluid of the lymph system does not circulate, but is moved in one direction away from its source through larger lymph vessels, which eventually drain into veins in the circulatory system. The valves within the lymph vessels allow the movement of the fluid in only one direction.

The hemic and lymphatic systems are made up of the following organs and structures:

- *Blood* is a colloidal fluid (liquid; serum or plasma and solid; cells) and is responsible for transport of gases and chemical substances and protecting the body from infection.

- *Lymphatic fluid* is a clear fluid containing white blood cells and a few red blood cells. It is absorbed by lymphatic vessels, ducts, and lymph nodes, which move lymph from the tissue to the blood, proteins, and fluid. It protects the body with the immune responses and acts as a pathway for the absorption of fats from the small intestines into the bloodstream.

- The *spleen* is the major site of destruction of the red blood cells (**RBC**). It serves as a reservoir for blood and acts as a filter, removing microorganisms from the blood.

- *Bone marrow* produces blood constituents, including all types of white blood cells (**WBC**), red blood cells, and **platelets.** See Figure 11.1 for a cross-section of lymphatic structures.

See Anatomy Plate 10, the lymphatic system, in Appendix A.

Anemias

Anemia is a generic term describing an abnormally low red blood cell count. Different types of anemias are classified in ICD-9-CM according to abnormalities in the shape, size, and hemoglobin (**HGB**) content of the red blood cells. A normal hemoglobin level is approximately 12.0 to 14.0 gm/dL in females and 14.0 to 16.0 gm/dL in males.

Patients with iron deficiency anemia suffer from fatigue, headache, palpitations, and shortness of breath. In most cases, increasing iron in the diet or using iron supplements is

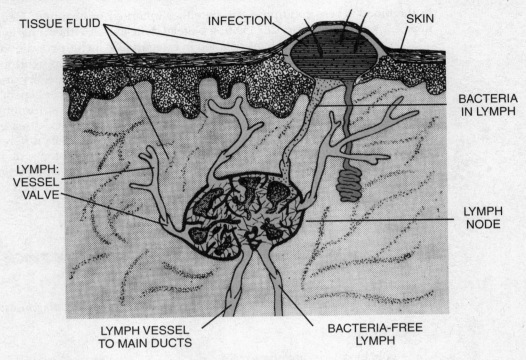

TISSUE FLUID   INFECTION   SKIN

BACTERIA
IN LYMPH

LYMPH:
VESSEL
VALVE

LYMPH
NODE

LYMPH VESSEL
TO MAIN DUCTS

BACTERIA-FREE
LYMPH

Figure 11–1   Lymph nodes and vessels in the skin.

sufficient to increase the hemoglobin levels. Severe cases may require blood transfusion. Iron deficiency anemias are assigned to category 280. Use code 280.0 for iron deficiency anemia due to chronic blood loss, 280.8 for other specified types of iron deficiency anemia, and 280.9 for unspecified iron deficiency anemia. Other types of deficiency anemias are coded to category 281. This includes vitamin deficiency anemias such as pernicious anemia, folate deficiency, protein deficiency, and other types.

Hemolytic anemias occur when the bone marrow cannot compensate for the premature destruction of red blood cells. Hemolytic anemias can be inherited or acquired. Hereditary hemolytic anemias include sickle-cell anemia, **thalassemias,** and anemias due to enzyme deficiency, protein abnormalities, and other problems with red blood synthesis. Hereditary types of anemia are coded to category 282 in ICD-9-CM. The acquired types can be due to autoimmune disorders, medications, and infection. Code acquired hemolytic anemias to category 283.

Aplastic anemias occur when the bone marrow stops producing some or all of the blood components. Patients do not have enough white blood cells to stop infections or enough platelets to stop bleeding. Treatment consists of blood transfusions and medications, and in severe cases, bone marrow transplant. Code aplastic anemias to category 284.

Patients with acute blood loss are assigned to ICD-9-CM code 285.1. Excluded from this subcategory is anemia due to chronic blood loss, which is cross-referenced to 280.0. Anemia of chronic illness is different from anemia of chronic blood loss. Patients who are undergoing treatment for end-stage renal disease or cancer often have anemia. Code anemia in end-stage renal disease with 285.21 and anemia in neoplastic disease with 285.22. Anemia due to other chronic illness is assigned to 285.29.

Anemia NOS is assigned to 285.9. This includes conditions that are not due to blood loss and may include terminology such as "normocytic, normochromic anemia." This means that the cells are of normal size, shape, and color, but are decreased in number.

Categories 286 and 287 describe coagulation defects and *purpura*, in which spontaneous subcutaneous bleeding causes purple spots on the skin. Disorders such as hemophilia and similar coagulation defects are due to deficiencies of different clotting factors in the blood. These conditions can be either inherited or acquired. Hemorrhagic conditions assigned to category 287 include platelet deficiencies, either inherited or acquired.

White blood cell problems detailed in category 288 include conditions marked by too few or too many of the various types of white blood cells, such as neutrophils, leukocytes, and eosinophils. Leukemia is specifically excluded from this category and is classified in the neoplasm chapter of ICD-9-CM. These conditions can be either genetic or acquired.

Category 289 classifies other diseases of the blood and blood-forming organs and includes conditions such as chronic lymphadenitis, polycythemia, diseases of the spleen, and hypercoaguable states. Codes 289.1, 289.2, and 289.3 describe different types of lymphadenitis, an inflammation of the lymph nodes. The symptoms of mesenteric lymphadenitis mimic those of appendicitis. Assign code 289.4 to *hypersplenism*, which is an overactive state of the spleen. This results in enlargement of the spleen with **thrombocytopenia**, anemia, or neutropenia.

EXERCISE 11.1

Instructions: Assign the correct ICD-9-CM code to the following diagnoses:

1. Sickle cell trait _____
2. Acute blood loss anemia _____
3. Pernicious anemia _____
4. Hereditary methemoglobinemia _____
5. Allergic eosinophilia _____
6. Family history of anemia _____
7. Primary thrombocytopenia _____
8. Screening for iron deficiency anemia _____
9. Inherited hemophilia _____
10. Aplastic anemia _____
11. Bone marrow donor exam _____
12. Anemia due to metastatic lung disease _____
13. Secondary polycythemia _____
14. Exercise induced hemoglobinuria _____
15. Chronic lymphadenitis _____

Neoplasms

Malignancies of the blood and lymphatic systems are classified under categories 200–208. Specific malignancies include lymphosarcomas, Hodgkin's disease (**HD**), multiple myeloma, and various types of leukemias.

Hodgkin's disease is a solid tumor of the lymphatic system. It often originates in the supraclavicular lymph nodes. Untreated, it may spread to the spleen and other organs. Prognosis is dependent upon staging of the tumor; when caught early, it has at least a 70 percent cure rate.

Myeloma, also known as multiple myeloma, is a malignancy of the plasma cells found in bone marrow. The abnormal cells proliferate and crowd out normal bone marrow, causing bone pain and osteolytic lesions on the bones. Common sites of these lesions are found in the vertebrae, ribs, and skull. Treatment includes chemotherapy with stem cell transplantation. Code myeloma to category 203.

Leukemias are divided into two main categories—myelogenous or lymphocytic. These are further subdivided into acute or chronic types. Lymphocytic leukemias are assigned to category 204 in ICD-9-CM. Other terms for lymphocytic types of leukemia include lymphatic, lymphoid, lymphoblastic, and lymphogenous, all referring to the increased number of **lymphoblasts** in the spleen, lymph nodes, and bone marrow. Myelocytic leukemias are assigned to category 205 and are commonly called myelocytic, myeloblastic, myelogenous, or granulocytic leukemia. These terms all refer to the large number of granulocytes in the blood.

Benign neoplasms of the hemic and lymphatic systems include hemangiomas, which are coded to 228.0x, with the fifth digit assigned for specific sites, and lymphangioma, 228.1. Other benign neoplasms of the lymph nodes are assigned to 229.0. Neoplasms of uncertain behavior include mast cell tumors, myelodysplastic syndrome, plasma cell tumors, and polycythemia vera. These are assigned to codes 238.4–238.7.

Formula for Success

Categories 200–202 require fifth-digit assignment to indicate lymph node involvement. Categories 203–208 require fifth-digit assignment to identify disease remission.

The lymphatics are common sites of metastatic spread of other types of malignancies in the body. Use category 196 codes to specify secondary malignancy sites. Excluded from this category are any neoplasms that are recognized as being primary lymphatic neoplasms in codes 200.0–202.9, including Hodgkin's disease, lymphoscarcoma, and reticulosarcoma. Fourth-digit subclassification in category 196 identifies specific sites of lymph node involvement.

Code metastatic disease of the bone and bone marrow to code 198.5.

EXERCISE 11.2

Instructions: Assign the correct ICD-9-CM code to the following diagnoses.

1. Lymphomatous tumor of the axilla _____

2. Chronic histiocytic leukemia _____

3. Hodgkin's lymphoma, inguinal lymph nodes _____

4. History of myeloid leukemia _____

5. Metastatic disease to supraclavicular nodes _____

6. Acute lymphocytic leukemia, in remission _____

7. Polycythemia vera _____

8. Multiple myeloma _____

9. Graft vs. Host disease   _____

10. Symptomatic hemophilia A carrier   _____

Injuries to the Spleen

When coding for traumatic injuries to the spleen (or any other internal organ), it is important for the coder to determine if there is an open wound associated with the injury. Look for closed or blunt trauma in the alphabetic index under "Injury, internal" and find the specific anatomic site. Penetrating or open wounds are located under "Wound, open." The main term "Rupture" lists many different types of rupture (traumatic, spontaneous, with open wound, etc.) and also contains a cross-reference to "Injury, internal" by site.

DISEASE PROCESSES AND ICD-9-CM CODING OF THE ENDOCRINE SYSTEM

The endocrine system is composed of ductless glands that excrete hormones directly into the bloodstream. Endocrine glands include the thyroid, pancreas, parathyroid, hypothalamus, pituitary, thymus, adrenal glands, ovaries, and testicles (see Figure 11.2). Hormones excreted by these glands direct metabolic activities in the body. Diseases and disorders of the endocrine glands vary from mild to life threatening. Contrasting with the endocrine glands are exocrine glands, which require ducts for secretion. Examples of exocrine glands are the prostate and salivary glands.

See Anatomy Plates 11 and 12, endocrine anatomy and endocrine glands, in Appendix A.

Thyroid Disorders

The thyroid gland controls the metabolic rate of the entire body by controlling oxygen and calorie consumption on a cellular level. Hyper- and hypothyroidism are caused by a disruption in the normal balance of thyroxine, a hormone produced by the thyroid gland.

A goiter is an enlarged thyroid gland. Goiters are rare in the United States and usually result from a lack of iodine in the diet. The only known function of iodine is in the synthesis of thyroid hormones. When **TSH** levels are low, the thyroid gland attempts to produce more thyroid hormone by growing larger and eventually becoming nodular. ICD-9-CM classifies three types of nodular thyroid:

- Diffuse
- Uninodular
- Multinodular

Sometimes nodules begin secreting thyroid hormones independent of the TSH level in the blood. A toxic multinodular goiter can result from the oversecretion of thyroid hormone. A thyrotoxic crisis or "storm" can occur from a toxic goiter, with a sudden increase in hormone activity. Progressive symptoms of nausea and diarrhea with an increase in basal metabolic rate will eventually lead to coma and death if the condition is not treated promptly.

Code simple goiters to category 240 and nontoxic nodular goiters to category 241. Thyrotoxicosis is assigned to category 242 with fifth digits assigned as follows:

- 0, without mention of thyrotoxic crisis or storm
- 1, with mention of thyrotoxic crisis or storm

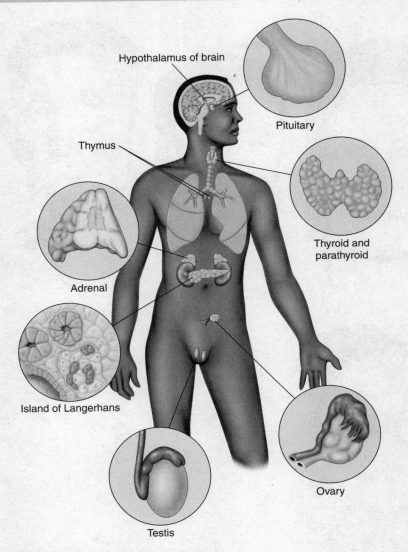

Hypothalamus of brain

Pituitary

Thymus

Thyroid and parathyroid

Adrenal

Island of Langerhans

Ovary

Testis

Figure 11–2   Endocrine glands.

Example: Graves' disease is also known as a toxic diffuse goiter, code 242.0x. The most obvious characteristic of Graves' disease is exophthalmos (see Figure 11.3), or bulging of the eyes.

Hypothyroidism is caused by a deficiency of circulating thyroid hormone. Treatment is provided by oral replacement. This prevents dry skin, hair loss, and slowed mentality and metabolism found in untreated hypothyroidism. A severe form of hypothyroidism is known as myxedema.

Hypothyroidism can be congenital or acquired later in life. Code congenital hypothyroidism or cretinism to code 243. Babies with untreated congenital hypothyroidism become mentally retarded. Acquired hypothyroidism is assigned to category 244.

Category 245 classifies different types of thyroiditis. Use code 245.9 for unspecified thyroiditis.

Diabetes Mellitus

Diabetes mellitus, or **DM,** is a chronic systemic disease caused by a disorder in carbohydrate and insulin metabolism. It is characterized by glucosuria, elevated blood sugar, excessive urination, and thirst. Diabetes can be insulin dependent (**IDDM**) or non-insulin

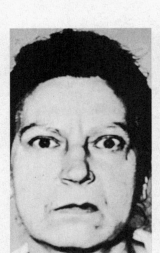 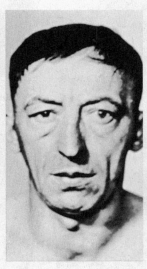  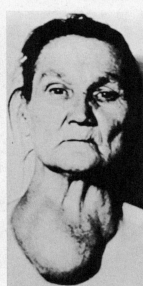

A

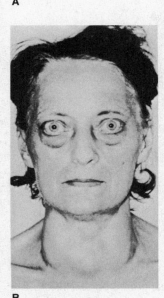

B

Figure 11–3 a) Different stages of goiters. b) Graves' disease.

dependent (**NIDDM**). Insulin-dependent diabetes mellitus is most common in children and teenagers and is also known as juvenile-onset diabetes mellitus. This has a rapid onset and is best controlled with insulin injections. Adult onset, or NIDDM, is found primarily in adults and is of slow onset. Due to increasing problems with obesity in the American public, however, NIDDM is now being diagnosed in children and teenagers. This form of diabetes can also be diet controlled.

Category 250 of ICD-9-CM classifies diabetes mellitus and complications associated with it. Excluded from this category are gestational diabetes, hyperglycemia, neonatal diabetes mellitus, and nonclinical diabetes.

Always use one of the following fifth-digit subclassifications with category 250:

0, Type II [non-insulin-dependent type] [NIDDM type] [adult-onset type] or unspecified type, not stated as uncontrolled. Fifth-digit 0 is for use for type II, adult-onset diabetic patients, even if the patient requires insulin.

1, Type I [insulin-dependent type] [IDDM] [juvenile type], not stated as uncontrolled.

2, Type II [non-insulin-dependent type] [NIDDM type] [adult-onset type] or unspecified type, uncontrolled. Fifth-digit 2 is for use for type II, adult-onset diabetic patients, even if the patient requires insulin.

3, Type I [insulin dependent type] [IDDM] [juvenile type], uncontrolled.

Formula for Success

Patients with non-insulin-dependent diabetes mellitus may require insulin injections occasionally as a supplement to oral medications. Do not assign Type I fifth digits of 1 and 3 to these patients.

Code 250.0x is only assigned when the patient does not have a documented complication of his or her diabetes. When complications are present, the fourth digit identifies the complication, and an additional code is assigned to identify the manifestation. Manifestations are italicized in the alphabetic index of ICD-9-CM to remind coders that they should not be assigned as a primary diagnosis. The diabetes code should always be sequenced first.

Example:
1. Diabetic retinopathy, 250.50 and 362.01
2. Diabetic gangrene, 250.70 and 785.4
3. Foot ulcer, left heel, due to DM, now out of control, 250.72 and 707.14

Despite diabetes being a systemic disease, do not assume that all other medical conditions are related to the diabetes. Some health problems will develop regardless of the diabetic condition. When a patient has multiple complications due to diabetes, more than one code from category 250 may be assigned to fully describe the condition.

Example:
Correct code assignment:
1. Type II diabetes, uncontrolled, 250.02
2. Senile cataract, left eye, 366.10
3. Carpal tunnel syndrome, 354.0

Incorrect code assignment:
1. Type II diabetes, uncontrolled, 250.52 and 250.62
2. Senile cataract, left eye, 366.41
3. Carpal tunnel syndrome, 354.0

Rationale:
Since a direct relationship to the diabetes is not specifically stated, codes should not be assigned as a complication of diabetes. Only the physician may establish the relationship, not the coder.

Diabetes insipidus is not the same condition as diabetes mellitus. The term *insipidus* means "tasteless," in reference to the dilute urine resulting from excessive thirst. This is in contrast to diabetes mellitus, in which sugar is excreted in the urine. Code diabetes insipidus to code 253.5.

Gestational diabetes is a condition that arises only during pregnancy, then subsides after delivery. Women who have gestational diabetes are prone to developing Type II diabetes later in life. Additional information is presented on this topic in Chapter 15 of this text.

Subcategory 790.2 classifies abnormal glucose levels. Diabetes mellitus, dysmetabolic syndrome X, gestational diabetes, glycosuria, and hypoglycemia are excluded from this category. Assign elevated or impaired <u>fasting</u> glucose tests to code 790.21. An abnormal or elevated <u>oral</u> glucose tolerance test is assigned to code 790.22. Other abnormal glucose tests including those not otherwise specified, nonfasting glucose, random glucose, or prediabetes are assigned to 790.29.

Cardiovascular dysmetabolic syndrome, also known as *CDS, Syndrome X, insulin resistance syndrome, metabolic syndrome,* or *cardiac dysmetabolic syndrome,* is a newly coined term for a metabolic condition that is a precursor to diabetes. In order to be diagnosed with CDS, a patient must have two or more of the following critical elements: dyslipidemia, insulin resistance, obesity, or hypertension, also known by the acronym DROP. The number of patients with this syndrome has grown over the last ten years to near epidemic levels. Approximately 47 million people in the United States have this condition, and about 33 percent of them will eventually develop diabetes mellitus. Many people will die of complications of dysmetabolic syndrome before they even develop diabetes. The risk of heart attack and stroke is greatly increased with each additional critical element that the patient exhibits. Major contributors to this problem are obesity, overeating, and lack of physical exercise. The American Association of Clinical Endocrinologists has identified a list of major criteria that indicate dysmetabolic syndrome:

- Insulin resistance (denoted by hyperinsulinemia relative to glucose levels) or
- Acanthosis Nigricans
- Central obesity (waist circumference > 102 cm for men and >88 cm for women)
- Dyslipidemia (HDL cholesterol <45 mg/dl for women, HDL cholesterol <35 mg/dl for men, or triglycerides >150 mg/dl)
- Hypertension
- Impaired fasting glucose or Type 2 diabetes
- Hyperuricemia

This condition strikes all ages and is becoming increasingly more prevalent among children. Code 277.7 is assigned to dysmetabolic syndrome. Use an additional code for any associated manifestation such as cardiovascular disease (414.00–414.06) and obesity (278.00–278.01)

EXERCISE 11.3

Instructions: Assign the correct ICD-9-CM code to the following diagnoses:

1. Adenomatous goiter   _____

2. Diabetic glomerulosclerosis   _____

3. Hashimoto's thyroiditis   _____

4. Morbid obesity   _____

5. Hypoglycemia   _____

6. Hypokalemia   _____

7. Cushing's disease   _____

  8. Gout   _____

  9. Severe fluid retention   _____

10. Hyperlipidemia   _____

11. Hypoglycemic coma   _____

12. Hyperparathyroidism   _____

13. Diabetic ketoacidosis coma   _____

14. Type I diabetes mellitus   _____

15. Diabetic hypoglycemia, DM out of control   _____

Lipid Disorders

Inherited disorders are often caused by the absence of certain enzymes or other proteins that affect metabolism at the cellular level. Secondary hyperlipidemias have multiple risk factors, which include the following:

- Disease risk factors: Diabetes mellitus, hypothyroidism, some types of renal failure and Cushing's disease. Smoking also puts these patients at greater risk of heart disease.
- Dietary risk factors: High fat diet, cholesterol intake greater than 300 mg per day, alcohol use, and obesity.
- Drugs: Birth control pills and other hormones, beta blockers, and diuretics.

Code lipid disorders to category 272, taking care to assign the fourth-digit subcategory. Use code 272.4 for hyperlipidemia, not otherwise specified, and 272.9 for unspecified disorders of lipoid metabolism. Excluded from category 272 is localized cerebral lipidoses (330.1).

Dehydration

Assign code 276.5 to dehydration. When a patient presents for treatment and has other conditions that may cause dehydration, such as vomiting/diarrhea due to gastroenteritis, the physician must determine which condition is the reason for the visit. If the treatment is directed at the dehydration, then this should be sequenced first. If treatment is directed at the gastroenteritis, then dehydration should be sequenced as a secondary diagnosis. Physician documentation is very important for proper code assignment and sequencing.

Obesity

ICD-9-CM classifies two types of obesity under category 278. Simple or nutritional obesity is coded to 278.00. Morbid or severe obesity is coded to 278.01. Definitions of morbid obesity vary. The ICD-9-CM interprets morbid obesity as someone who is 125 percent or more over their ideal body weight. Morbid obesity is considered to be a life-threatening condition due to overload on the circulatory, metabolic, and skeletal systems.

EXERCISE 11.4

Instructions: Assign ICD-9-CM codes to the following diagnoses:

1. Pituitary adenoma   _____

2. Benign islet cell tumor of pancreas   _____

3. Adrenal gland carcinoma with metastasis _____

4. Admission for chemotherapy for ovarian carcinoma _____

5. Thyroid adenocarcinoma _____

6. Stab wound, neck, with open wound to thyroid _____

7. Cancer of the thymus, with heart and mediastinal involvement _____

8. Screening for PKU _____

9. Pancreatic carcinoma with mets to mediastinal lymph nodes _____

10. Screening cholesterol level _____

11. Pancreas transplant _____

12. Insulin pump status _____

Note: ICD-9-CM does not contain a corresponding chapter to CPT® with diagnoses for the mediastinum and diaphragm. Therefore, no distinction for ICD-9-CM diagnoses pertaining to the mediastinum or diaphragm is made in this chapter.

CPT® CODING OF THE HEMIC AND LYMPHATIC SYSTEMS

Spleen

CPT® contains only a few codes directly related to the spleen. Three splenectomy procedures include:

- 38100, Total splenectomy, a separate code that cannot be reported in addition to a more extensive procedure in the same body area.
- 38101, Partial splenectomy, also a separate procedure.
- 38102, Total splenectomy, used in conjunction with a primary procedure as an add-on code.

Use codes 38115 for repair of a ruptured spleen and 38120 for a laparoscopic splenectomy.

General

Use code 38220 for a bone marrow aspiration, or 38221 for a biopsy performed using a needle or trocar.

Lymph Nodes and Lymphatic Channels

Radical Lymphadenectomy (Radical Resection of Lymph Nodes)

Codes 38700–38780 describe procedures that dissect the lymph nodes from the surrounding tissue and vessels so they can be examined by frozen section pathology to detect an early stage of metastasis. Because cancer cells can easily travel in the lymph fluid to other parts of the body, physicians monitor the spread of cancer through lymph node procedures such as those listed in this section. The codes in this section are listed by body area, and in some cases, by the extent of the procedure—for example, superficial versus complete. Codes 38746 and 38747 are add-on codes that report lymphadenectomies to thoracic and abdominal procedures. Inguinofemoral and pelvic lymphadenectomy codes are not inherently bilateral, and the Modifier 50 should be used if procedures on both the right and left sides are performed.

Introduction

The procedures described by codes 38790–38794 are used to visualize the lymph nodes. Injection for lymphangiography is performed with a vital blue dye into the subcutaneous tissues for outlining the skin lymphatics, identification of lymph nodes and lymph vessels. With the use of X-rays, the radiological supervision and interpretation can be performed and reported separately using codes 75801–75807. The injection for sentinel node identification uses the nuclear medicine code 78195 for supervision and interpretation. The cannulization of the thoracic duct includes the placement of a cannula or catheter for the injection of medication.

EXERCISE 11.5

Instructions: Assign the correct CPT® code(s) for the following scenario.

1. A patient with a history of breast cancer is seen for an axillary lump. The patient is surgically treated with an open excision of the deep axillary lymph nodes. The pathology report confirms malignancy of the axillary lymph node secondary to the breast cancer. _____

CPT® CODING OF THE MEDIASTINUM AND DIAPHRAGM

The mediastinum is the area between the lungs and includes the heart, pericardium, bases of great vessels, trachea, bronchi, esophagus, thymus, thoracic lymph nodes, thoracic duct, and phrenic and vagus nerves.

Procedures performed in this area include incisions for exploration, drainage, removal of foreign body, biopsy, excision, and endoscopy. Do not confuse mediastinoscopy, code 39400, with a thoracoscopy of the mediastinal space, code 32605. The approach for a mediastinoscopy is through a small incision at the base of the neck at the sternal notch. A thoracoscopy is carried out through an incision between the ribs.

Procedures performed on the diaphragm include repairs of hiatal hernias and diaphragmatic hernias and resection of the diaphragm. Read code descriptors carefully. Some codes specify neonatal repair versus other than neonatal repair or acute versus chronic. These procedures may be performed through a transthoracic or thoracoabdominal approach.

EXERCISE 11.6

Instructions: Assign the correct CPT® codes to the following scenarios:

1. A newborn is diagnosed with a diaphragmatic hernia. The infant is surgically treated. _____

2. An adult is surgically treated for an esophageal hiatal hernia with a thoracoabdominal approach. _____

CPT® CODING OF THE ENDOCRINE SYSTEM

Thyroid Gland

Incision

There is only one code in this section: Incision and drainage of a thyroglossal duct cyst, 759.2. This cyst is also referred to as a thyrolingual cyst and is found in the neck between the thyroid and the back of the tongue. The excision of a thyroglossal duct cyst can be found in the excision section, codes 60280 and 60281.

Excision

The procedures described in this section begin with the least invasive techniques: aspiration of cyst, percutaneous needle biopsy, and excision of thyroid cyst. The thyroid is made up of two lobes. The lobectomy procedures are as follows:

Partial thyroid lobectomy:

- Unilateral, with or without isthmusectomy
- Contralateral subtotal lobectomy, with isthmusectomy

Total thyroid lobectomy:

- Unilateral, with or without isthmusectomy
- Contralateral subtotal lobectomy, with isthmusectomy

Thyroidectomy:

- Total or complete
- Total or subtotal for malignancy with limited dissection
- Total or subtotal for malignancy with radical neck dissection
- Removal of all remaining thyroid tissue following partial thyroidectomy
- Including substernal thyroid by sternal split or transthoracic approach
- Including substernal thyroid by cervical approach

The diagnostic link for these procedures includes:

- Malignant neoplasm of the thyroid
- Secondary malignant neoplasm of specified sites
- Malignant neoplasm of lymphoid and histiocytic tissue
- Benign neoplasm of the thyroid
- Carcinoma *in-situ* of other and unspecified sites
- Neoplasms of uncertain behavior endocrine and nervous system
- Neoplasms of unspecified nature by specified sites
- Goiter, simple and unspecified
- Thyrotoxicosis with or without goiter
- Thyroiditis
- Thyroid disorders, other
- Congenital anomalies, other and unspecified
- Endocrine and metabolic disturbances specific to fetus and newborn

EXERCISE 11.7

Instructions: Assign the correct CPT® codes to the following scenario.

1. A patient is seen for a routine physical. During the physical, the physician notices a lump on the thyroid. The patient is scheduled for surgery, and a percutaneous core

needle biopsy of the thyroid lump is performed. The results indicate a malignant neoplasm of the thyroid. The patient is treated surgically with a total thyroidectomy with limited neck dissection. Code both procedures. _____   _____

Parathyroid, Thymus, Adrenal Glands, and Carotid Body

The parathyroid glands are two pairs of small bodies located on the dorsal surface of the thyroid gland. The parathyroid is responsible for the secretion of parathormone, which maintains a normal level of serum calcium. The *parathyroidectomy* procedures include:

- Exploration
- Re-exploration
- Mediastinal exploration by sternal split or transthoracic approach

The add-on code in this section is for a parathyroid autotransplantation. Because the parathyroid is needed to regulate serum calcium, half of one gland is transplanted to the muscle of the sternocleidomastoid or the upper arm after removal of all four parathyroid glands.

The diagnostic link for these procedures includes:

- Malignant neoplasm of endocrine glands and related structures
- Secondary malignant neoplasm of other specified sites
- Benign neoplasm of the endocrine glands and other related structures
- Carcinoma *in-situ* of other and unspecified sites
- Neoplasm of uncertain behavior of the endocrine and nervous system
- Neoplasms of unspecified nature by specified sites
- Parathyroid gland disorders

The thymus is located in the mediastinum between the lungs and is responsible for the production of antibodies important for the body's immune system. *Thymectomies* can be done as either partial or total and are listed by approach:

- Transcervical approach
- Sternal split or transthoracic approach without radical mediastinal dissection
- Sternal split or transthoracic approach with radical mediastinal dissection

The diagnostic link for these procedures includes:

- Malignant neoplasm of the thymus, heart, and mediastinum
- Secondary neoplasm of other specified sites
- Benign neoplasm of the respiratory and intrathoracic organs
- Neoplasm of uncertain behavior of the digestive and respiratory systems
- Neoplasm of unspecified nature by specified sites
- Thymus gland diseases
- Myasthenia, myoneural disorders

The adrenal glands are located on top of each kidney and secrete the hormones glucocorticoids, mineralcorticoids, and androgens. *Adrenalectomies* can be performed either partially or completely. Exploration of the adrenal gland can be performed with or without biopsies, transabdominal, lumbar, or dorsal and can include the excision of adjacent retroperitoneal tumor if present. This procedure can also be performed laparoscopically. The diagnostic link for these procedures includes:

- Tuberculosis of other organs
- Malignant neoplasm of connective and other soft tissue
- Malignant neoplasm of other endocrine glands and related structures
- Secondary malignant neoplasm of other specified sites
- Carcinoma *in-situ* of other and unspecified sites
- Neoplasm of uncertain behavior endocrine and nervous systems
- Neoplasms of unspecified nature by specified sites
- Pancreas disorders
- Adrenal gland disorders

Carotid body excision can be performed with or without the excision of the carotid artery. The diagnostic link for these procedures includes:

- Malignant neoplasm of other endocrine gland and related structures
- Benign neoplasm of the endocrine glands and other related structures
- Carcinoma *in-situ* of other and unspecified sites
- Neoplasm of uncertain behavior of the endocrine and nervous systems
- Neoplasms of unspecified nature by specified sites

EXERCISE 11.8

Instructions: Assign the correct CPT® codes to the following scenarios.

1. A clinic patient is found to have hypocalcemia. Through further laboratory studies, the patient is diagnosed with hypoparathyroidism. The patient is surgically treated with a parathyroidectomy and parathyroid autotransplantation. _____

2. A patient is diagnosed with hypertrophy of the thymus. The patient is surgically treated with a total thymectomy. _____

3. A patient with a diagnosis of malignant neoplasm of the adrenal gland is surgically treated with a complete adrenalectomy by transabdominal approach. _____

4. What CPT® code would be used if the patient in question 3 had a laparoscopic adrenalectomy? _____

5. A carotid body excision is performed on a patient with a diagnosis of paraganglioma. _____

CHAPTER REVIEW

1. Leukemias are classified with solid tumors in ICD-9-CM.   **True/False**

2. The relationship between diabetes and other medical conditions may be assumed by the coder.   **True/False**

3. Endocrine glands secrete hormones directly into the bloodstream.   **True/False**

4. A patient with biopsy proven thyroid carcinoma has a thyroidectomy with dissection of two lymph nodes. Choose the correct ICD-9-CM and CPT® codes.

    a. 164.0, 60240

    b. 193, 60252

    c. 234.8, 60260

    d. 193, 60240-22

5. A patient is brought to surgery for repair of a lacerated spleen with extension into the parenchyma following a rollover car accident. A partial splenectomy is performed. Choose the correct ICD-9-CM and CPT® codes.

    a. 865.14, E816.9, 38120

    b. 865.12, E816.9, 38101

    c. 865.04, E816.9, 38115

    d. 865.03, E816.9, 38115

6. A patient undergoing treatment for breast carcinoma on the right side is brought back to the OR for identification of a sentinal node. The surgeon performed an injection procedure, and three superficial nodes were excised from the axilla. These tested positive for metastasis. Choose the correct ICD-9-CM and CPT® codes. Do not code for radiology services.

    a. 196.3, 174.9, 38792, 38500

    b. 174.9, 196.1, 38500

    c. 199.1, 196.3, 38792

    d. 196.3, 38792, 38500 x 3

7. A patient with Type II diabetes, out of control, presents to the ER by ambulance in a hypoglycemic coma. The patient also has nephropathy associated with his diabetes. A comprehensive history, detailed physical exam, and moderate medical decision-making are documented in his record. Choose the correct ICD-9-CM codes and Evaluation and Management level.

    a. 250.32, 583.81, 99285, 99291

    b. 250.42, 583.81, 99285

    c. 250.32, 250.42, 583.81, 99284

    d. 250.32, 250.42, 99284

8. A 13-year-old is brought to the ER with severe nausea and vomiting. It is unclear if the patient has gastroenteritis or food poisoning. The patient appears clinically dehydrated and cannot keep fluids down. An IV of Lactated Ringer's is started, and she is given an injection of Reglan. She is discharged after the IV is finished and is able to tolerate sips of water. An expanded problem-focused history, detailed exam, and moderate complexity medical decision making is documented. Choose the correct ICD-9-CM codes and Evaluation and Management Level.

    a. 558.9, 99283

    b. 558.9, 005.9, 99284

    c. 276.5, 787.01, 99283

    d. 787.01, 276.5, 99284

9. A patient with multiple myeloma is admitted for a bone marrow biopsy by trocar to check the progression of his disease. Assign the correct ICD-9-CM and CPT® codes for this. _____ _____

10. A 55-year-old male is brought to the OR with a mediastinal mass suspected of being sarcoidosis. A mediastinoscopy with biopsy is performed and pathology

confirms the diagnosis. Assign the correct ICD-9-CM and CPT® codes for this. _____ _____

11. When a total splenectomy is performed at the same operative session as another procedure, the correct CPT® code is:
   a. 38100
   b. 38101
   c. 38102
   d. 38120

12. The CPT® code used for obtaining a bone marrow sample for pathological analysis is:
   a. 38220
   b. 38240
   c. 38241
   d. 38230

13. The correct CPT® code for a deep axillary lymph node biopsy is:
   a. 38740
   b. 38745
   c. 38525
   d. 38500

14. The correct code set for a repair of a diaphragmatic hernia with thoracoabdominal approach is:
   a. 553.3, 39520
   b. 756.6, 39503
   c. 552.3, 39531
   d. 553.3, 39530

Case Studies

Case Study 11.1

Preoperative Diagnosis
Lymphadenopathy, left neck.

Postoperative Diagnosis
Lymphadenopathy, left neck.

Procedure Performed
Excision of enlarged lymph node, left neck.

Anesthesia
General.

Summary
The patient was placed in the supine position on the OR table. General anesthesia was administered. The left neck was prepped and draped in a sterile fashion. An incision was made over the palpable abnormality, which was just posterior to the external jugular vein. The incision was carried down through the platysma. An enlarged lymph node was then elevated into the field and the connective tissue was transected using cautery. A small vein in the region was clipped. The lymph node was sent for pathology. Hemostasis was achieved. The skin was closed in two layers with 4-0 Vicryl suture. Steri-Strips were applied. The patient tolerated the procedure well.

ICD-9-CM code(s): _____

CPT® code(s): _____

Case Study 11.2

Preoperative Diagnosis

Papillary carcinoma of the thyroid.

Postoperative Diagnosis

Papillary carcinoma of the thyroid.

Anesthesia

General endotracheal.

Procedure Performed

Total thyroidectomy.

Description of Operation

With the patient under satisfactory general anesthesia in a supine position with head and neck extended, the neck was prepared anteriorly and draped as a sterile field. A collar-type incision was made just above the sternal notch and carried down sharply through the subcutaneous tissue and through the platysma. A superior flap was created by mobilizing the skin, subcutaneous tissue, and platysma cephalad off the strap muscles. Strap muscles were incised in the midline. There was a large venous structure just to the right of the midline, which required suturing. That was done with 6-0 Prolene. The strap muscles were separated down to the thyroid and the left lobe of the thyroid was addressed. Using careful blunt and sharp dissection with hemostasis by hemoclips and by electrocautery where appropriate, the superior pole of the left lobe of the thyroid was taken down. The superior pole vessels were doubly clipped with hemoclips and divided. The dissection was carried out away from the overlying musculature; some of the muscle fibers were left in place where the tumor contacted the muscle even though there was no evidence of direct in-growth. The tumor could be mobilized away from the surrounding tissue, and the left lower lobe of the thyroid was carefully dissected off the trachea.

Care was taken to avoid injury to the recurrent laryngeal nerve, and the nerve was identified and protected during the course of dissection. Ultimately, the specimen was free and was submitted for pathologic examination. The specimen was calcified and the pathologist indicated difficulty in getting a very good frozen section because of the calcification. However, there were papillary elements evident consistent with a papillary carcinoma. Accordingly, in view of the clinical situation and the needle biopsy previously showing findings consistent with a papillary carcinoma, the decision was made to continue with total thyroidectomy and remove the isthmus and the right lobe of the thyroid. Once again, using blunt and sharp dissection with hemostasis by electrocautery and hemoclips, the right lobe of the thyroid was very carefully mobilized.

Once again the recurrent laryngeal nerve was identified and protected throughout the dissection. Ultimately, the thyroid was free and was removed from the field. Hemostasis was then checked and secured as needed with hemoclips and electrocautery. With the wound dry, the strap muscles were approximated in the midline using interrupted sutures. The platysma and subcutaneous tissue were closed with interrupted sutures. The skin was closed with subcuticular sutures. Sterile dressing was applied. The patient was taken to the recovery area in satisfactory condition having tolerated the procedure well with no complications.

ICD-9-CM code(s): _____

CPT® code(s): _____

The Digestive System

OBJECTIVES

1. Identify the different parts of digestive anatomy.
2. Differentiate between open, laparoscopic, and endoscopic procedures.
3. Recognize digestive diseases and disorders for diagnostic coding.
4. Apply correct ICD-9-CM and CPT® codes to scenarios and case studies.

TERMINOLOGY AND ACRONYMS

Ablation   Destruction of a lesion.

Anastomosis   Suturing of two tubular structures together, such as intestines or blood vessels.

BE   Barium enema.

EGD   Esophagogastroduodenoscopy.

GERD   Gastroesophageal reflux disease.

GI   Gastrointestinal.

IBD   Irritable bowel disease.

I&D   Incision and drainage.

LFT   Liver function test.

UPPP   Uvulopharyngealpalatoplasty.

UGI   Upper gastrointestinal.

LLQ   Left lower quadrant.

LUQ   Left upper quadrant.

RLQ   Right lower quadrant.

RUQ   Right upper quadrant.

ANATOMY

The digestive system begins with the mouth and ends with the anus. It is a single continuous tube covered with involuntary (smooth) muscle, blood vessels, and nerves. Several one-way valves and sphincters control the movement of food through this tube. Food is chewed into small pieces in the mouth and mixed with saliva, which moistens the food and allows it easier passage down the esophagus and into the stomach. Digestion actually begins in the mouth, where enzymes such as ptyalin initiate the breakdown of starches. After a bolus of food is swallowed, involuntary muscle contractions called *peristalsis* carry the food through the esophageal sphincter and into the stomach. Digestive juices are secreted in the stomach and include hydrogen chloride, gastric enzymes, and intrinsic factor, which aids in the absorption of Vitamin B12. The stomach churns the food mixture, now called *chyme,* into a thick liquid that can be passed into the intestines where additional enzymes are secreted. This is also where the absorption of nutrients begins. The gastric outlet, or cardiac sphincter, relaxes every few minutes, allowing a small amount of chyme to squirt into the upper portion of the small intestine, or duodenum.

Three accessory organs of digestion are involved in the process and begin secreting enzymes into the small intestine: the gallbladder, liver, and pancreas. The gallbladder is a small pouch-like organ located on the undersurface/posterior side of the left lobe of the liver. Bile secreted by the liver is collected in this pouch and stored until a meal is eaten. Bile is instrumental in the breakdown of fats. A fatty meal stimulates more production of bile and may cause severe pain, or biliary colic, in people who have an obstruction in the common duct leading to the intestine or stones within the gallbladder itself. The liver is a "multitask" organ. It assists with the breakdown of food by releasing enzymes into bile and filters waste products from the blood. The pancreas plays a dual role in digestion. Part of the pancreas secretes digestive enzymes and part secretes insulin, which regulates carbohydrate metabolism. Digestive enzymes are secreted into the pancreatic duct and squirted into the duodenum. Like the bile duct, blockage of the pancreatic duct can cause severe pain and digestive problems.

Absorption of chyme takes place throughout the small intestine, which can measure up to 25 to 30 feet in length. There are three sections of the small intestine: the duodenum, jejunum, and ileum.

One-way valves at the cardiac sphincter of the stomach prevent backflow of chyme into the stomach. The esophageal sphincter may be forced open by the vomiting reflex, when the body needs to rid itself of all gastric contents. Occasionally, after prolonged vomiting and "dry heaves," small amounts of yellow-green bile may be forced into the stomach and vomited.

The small intestine empties into the large intestine, which has the primary function of absorption of water. The large intestine is approximately 3 feet long and begins in the lower right quadrant (**RLQ**) of the abdomen. The ileocecal valve controls movement of digestive byproducts into the large intestine. The small intestine joins the first segment of large intestine at the cecum, just above the appendix. The function of the appendix is not completely known at this time, but it is thought to have played a more important role in primitive man. The cecum is also called the ascending colon and makes a 90-degree turn at the hepatic flexure. At this point, it becomes the transverse colon and lays across the abdomen from right to left. In the upper left quadrant (**LUQ**), the colon makes another 90-degree turn at the splenic flexure and becomes the descending or sigmoid colon. At the termination of the sigmoid, the rectum or rectal pouch collects the digestive byproducts. These are expelled from the body via the anus. Papillae are located throughout intestinal walls to increase surface area for absorption of fluid and nutrients.

See the gastrointestinal system on Anatomy Plate 13 in Appendix A.

DISEASE PROCESSES AND ICD-9-CM CODING OF THE DIGESTIVE SYSTEM

Diverticula, Diverticulosis, and Diverticulitis

A diverticulum is an abnormal pouch in the side walls of a tubular structure. Diverticula are common in the digestive system, and less so in the urinary system. They may be congenital or acquired. ICD-9-CM categorizes congenital diverticula in Chapter 14. The

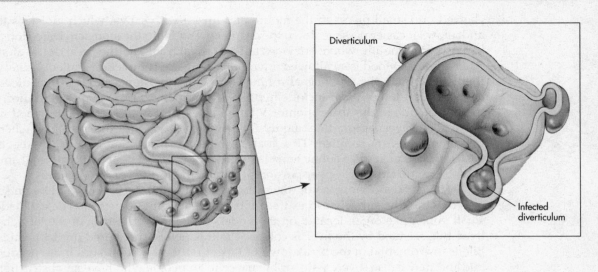

Figure 12–1   Diverticulitis.

condition of having diverticuli is called diverticulosis. In the digestive system, these occur as a herniation through a weakness in the intestinal wall and are often asymptomatic. When infection within the diverticula occurs, it is called diverticulitis and may be treated with antibiotics or surgery in severe cases (see Figure 12.1). Several common sites of diverticula are listed below:

- Ileum: Congenital diverticulum, called Meckels diverticulum.
- Intestinal: Most commonly found in the colon.
- Pharyngoesophageal region: Commonly called Zencker's diverticulum.

Ulcers

An ulcer is the erosion of a mucous membrane. In the gastrointestinal system, ulcers may be due to an infectious organism such as *H. pylori,* or they may be due to stress, diet, alcohol, or other problems. They can occur throughout the digestive tract, beginning in the mouth. Treatment depends on location, diameter, depth, and cause.

Depending upon the depth of the ulcer, there may be associated hemorrhage and/or perforation. Perforations are acute and require surgical intervention to prevent contamination of the abdominal cavity. Hemorrhages are also acute and may be treated surgically via endoscope or open procedure. Acute hemorrhages should not be confused with chronic **GI** bleeding, in which blood loss is due to a slow bleed.

Inflammation

The mucosa of the digestive tract is subject to inflammation from the mouth through the intestines. Causes for inflammation may include reflux of gastric acid, allergies, alcohol, autoimmune conditions, or dietary problems. Gastroenteritis is a generic term given for an inflammation of the stomach and intestines characterized by nausea and vomiting. Code 558.9 is assigned for acute gastroenteritis. It is a self-limiting inflammation and, if unresolved, may indicate another condition masked by the symptoms of gastroenteritis.

Irritable bowel disease, or **IBD,** is a broad term used to categorize two types of bowel disorders. Ulcerative colitis and Crohn's disease are both marked by inflammation, pain, and bloody diarrhea. The difference between these conditions lies primarily in the location and depth of inflammation. Ulcerative colitis is a shallow inflammation that occurs mainly in the large intestine. Crohn's disease is found deep within the mucosa and, unlike ulcerative colitis, skips sections of healthy tissue. Both conditions are treated with medications and avoidance of triggers such as alcohol, smoking, and certain foods. Surgery is indicated in severe cases, with 25 to 40 percent of ulcerative colitis patients requiring surgery.

Crohn's disease is classified by site of inflammation in ICD-9-CM under category 555. This condition is known by several names, including regional enteritis and granulomatous enteritis.

Ulcerative colitis is also classified according to site of inflammation in category 556. The generic term Irritable Bowel Syndrome is coded to 564.1.

Infection

Infection is not the same thing as inflammation: An infection implies exposure to a disease-causing microorganism, and inflammation is the body's response to an injury or irritation. Digestive infections are contracted from ingested foods or infectious sources. They may be self-limited, short-term infections, such as a food poisoning, or long-term, chronic infections such as an untreated *H. pylori*. Candida and monilia infections are common in the mouths of infants, immunosuppressed adults, and patients who are undergoing antibiotic therapy. Candida and monilia are yeast infections, which require warmth and moisture to reproduce. Digestive tract infections are coded under the Infectious and Parasitic Disease chapter of ICD-9-CM. Most gastrointestinal infections are listed under the following three-digit code categories:

- Salmonella   003
- Shigella   004
- Bacterial food poisoning   005
- Amebic dysentery/colitis/liver abscess   006
- Protozoal infections   007
- *E. coli*/other organisms   008

Systemic infections such as tuberculosis and syphilis are found in multiple-organ systems besides the gastrointestinal tract. Code these to the specific infection and site of occurrence.

Helminthiases are parasitic worms and flukes that are commonly ingested from tainted water sources or raw foods. Look for parasites in the alphabetic index under "Infestation, parasite."

Viral Hepatitis

The liver is prone to multiple disorders and diseases, which have a cascading effect on almost every organ system within the body. One of the most common disease states of the liver is hepatitis.

The alphabetic index of ICD-9-CM lists approximately 100 different references to hepatitis, some of which are categorized together. Viral hepatitis is coded to the 070 category of the Infectious and Parasitic Disease chapter, with fourth digits for the different types of hepatitis, with or without coma present. Categories 070.2 and 070.3 have an additional fifth-digit subclassification available, specific to hepatitis delta.

Although the risk factors and symptoms are similar for the different types of viral hepatitis, each is identified as a distinct disease entity.

Alcoholic Liver Disease

Approximately 50 percent of heavy alcohol users have a condition known as "fatty liver." This may progress into alcoholic hepatitis, in which more liver cells die as a result of continued heavy alcohol ingestion. The last stage of alcoholic liver disease is cirrhosis, with irreversible liver damage. In this stage, too many liver cells have died, and the liver cannot detoxify the body. Wastes and toxins build up in the body, and gradually organ systems begin to shut down. These three conditions are detailed in category 571 as:

571.0 Alcoholic fatty liver
571.1 Acute alcoholic hepatitis
   Acute alcoholic liver disease
571.2 Alcoholic cirrhosis of liver
   Florid cirrhosis
   Laennec's cirrhosis (alcoholic)
571.3 Alcoholic liver damage, unspecified

The remainder of category 571 deals with chronic hepatitis and specifically excludes viral hepatitis.

Cholelithiasis and Cholecystitis

Cholelithiasis are stones in the gallbladder. Typically, stones are asymptomatic until a stone blocks the common bile duct, causing cramping, right upper-quadrant (**RUQ**) pain, nausea, jaundice, and fever. If the stone is large enough that it will not pass, bacteria may flourish in the gallbladder and cause cholangitis. Stones that block the lowermost portion of the common bile duct can also block secretions from the pancreas and cause pancreatitis. Both of these conditions are serious and require prompt medical treatment. Tests to determine the presence of stones or blockage includes ERCP (Endoscopic Retrograde Cholangiopancreatography) or imaging studies such as cholecystogram, ultrasound, CT scan, abdominal x-ray, and radionuclide scan. ESWL (electroshockwave lithotripsy) effectively breaks up small stones without acute disease. The most common treatment of cholelithiasis is laparoscopic surgery. Figure 12.2 shows the pancreas and other digestive organs.

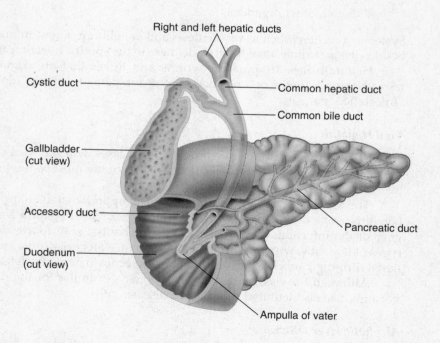

Figure 12–2   Gallbladder and pancreatic drainage system.

Cholelithiasis is coded to category 574 in ICD-9-CM. Fourth digits are assigned based on the location of the stone, with various combinations of acute, chronic, acute *and* chronic, and unspecified cholecystitis present. Fifth-digit subclassification is assigned as follows:

- 0 without mention of obstruction
- 1 with obstruction

Cholecsystitis is an inflammation of the gallbladder. It can be either acute, chronic, or acute superimposed on a chronic condition. Symptoms of cholecystitis include nausea, belching, and indigestion. Cholecystitis is more common in women, especially after age 40. Weight reduction and avoidance of fatty foods help control symptoms. Diagnosis and treatment are similar to that of cholelithiasis.

Category 575 in ICD-9-CM describes "Other disorders of gallbladder," which include acute cholecsytitis (575.0), unspecified cholecystitis (575.10), chronic cholecystitis (575.11), acute and chronic cholecystitis (575.12), obstruction of gallbladder (575.2), as well as other conditions. Categories 575.0, 575.1, and 575.2 exclude the use of these codes when calculi are present. Notes should be read carefully for specific exclusions.

Hernias

A hernia is a weakness in the wall of the abdomen that causes a bubble-like protrusion of tissue through the defect (see Figure 12.3). Hernias may be acquired or congenital in nature. Those that can be pushed back into the abdominal cavity are known as reducible hernias. A nonreducible hernia will not ease back into the abdomen. Occasionally, a loop of intestine may bulge out of the abdominal wall and become obstructed or strangulated, requiring urgent surgical repair.

The type of surgical repair can also make a difference on the rate of recurrence of hernias. With tension-type repairs, where the tissues are pulled together over the defect, hernias will commonly recur within five years. Newer techniques involving the use of mesh and tension-free repair have reduced the rate of recurrent hernias. Tissue grows through the mesh and thereby strengthens the defect in the abdominal wall. Mesh can be used on any type of hernia when indicated, although for reimbursement purposes, the CPT® code for mesh is only assigned with ventral/incision type of hernias.

Different types of hernias and their locations are listed below:

- Inguinal — Groin
- Hiatal (diaphragmatic) — Junction of esophagus and stomach
- Incisional (ventral) — Commonly in straight line from sternum to pubic bone
- Umbilical — Umbilicus
- Femoral — Junction of thigh and groin area

Hernias are assigned to categories 550–553 in ICD-9-CM. Check the Includes and Excludes notes carefully. Documentation should state whether the hernia is unilateral or bilateral, if it is recurrent, and whether it is obstructed and/or gangrenous. Category 550 also lists the following fifth-digit subclassifications:

- 0, Unilateral or unspecified (not specified as recurrent)
- 1, Unilateral or unspecified, recurrent
- 2, Bilateral (not specified as recurrent)
- 3, Bilateral, recurrent

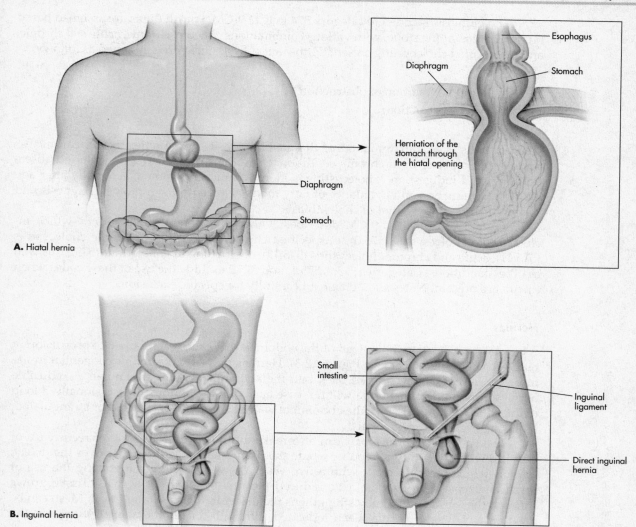

A. Hiatal hernia

B. Inguinal hernia

Figure 12–3   Examples of hiatal and inguinal hernias.

EXERCISE 12.1

Instructions: Assign the correct ICD-9-CM code to each of the following diagnoses

1. Postoperative dumping syndrome

2. Radiation enteritis

3. Recurrent inguinal hernia with gangrene

4. Acute gastric ulcer with hemorrhage and perforation

5. Salmonella gastroenteritis due to food poisoning

6. Chronic hepatitis C with hepatic coma

7. Acute and chronic cholecystitis with cholelithiasis

8. Infection by sheep liver fluke   _____

9. Pancreatic pseudocysts   _____

10. Acute alcoholic hepatitis   _____

Neoplasms

Primary malignant neoplasms of the digestive system are broken into two classifications in ICD-9-CM. Malignant neoplasms of the lip, oral cavity, and pharynx are coded to 140–149. Malignant neoplasms of the digestive organs and peritoneum are coded to 150–159. The last group includes the accessory organs of digestion, as well as other and ill-defined sites and the spleen. Benign neoplasms of the lip, oral cavity, and pharynx are coded to category 210, and benign neoplasms of the other parts of the digestive system to category 211. Numerous types of neoplasms affect the digestive system, so only the most common are discussed below.

Esophagus

Leiomyoma (fibroids) are the most common type of benign esophageal neoplasm. Most are asymptomatic and are located in the lower third of the esophagus. Men have twice the rate of occurrence as women. Polyps are the second most common type of benign neoplasm, but these are found most often in the upper esophagus. Again, polyps are twice as prevalent in men as in women. Open surgical treatment is recommended rather than endoscopic removal.

Dysphagia, foreign body sensation, and weight loss are symptoms of esophageal carcinoma. Squamous cell carcinoma used to be the most common type of esophageal malignancy in the United States, attributed to alcohol, tobacco, aspirin, and NSAID use. In the last twenty years, however, adenocarcinoma has replaced squamous cell carcinoma as the most common type. Current studies point to a link with chronic reflux (Barrett's esophagus, ICD-9-CM code 530.85) and the rise of adenocarcinoma. Males outnumber females 3:1 in rates of esophageal malignancy.

Stomach

In the last twenty years the United States has also seen a rise in the rate of gastric carcinoma in the areas of the cardia and gastroesophageal junction. Cure rates for early stage malignancies are greater than 50 percent. Most cases involve advanced metastatic disease, however, and five-year survival rates are low.

Colon

Adenomatous polyps are a precancerous type of neoplasm that is most common in the colon. These polyps are slow growing and should be removed before they gradually become malignant. People with a family history of colon cancer and anyone over age 50 should be routinely screened for colon cancer via colonoscopy. Diets high in fiber, fruits, and vegetables are beneficial in preventing colon cancer. A screening test called a "stool guiac," or "hemoccult," is a test for occult (hidden) blood performed on a fecal sample. A positive test can indicate a colon polyp or tumor.

Signs of colon cancer include bleeding, change in bowel habits, and abdominal pain. Surgery is the treatment of choice for malignancies. When a piece of intestine is removed, the ends can be joined together as an **anastomosis**, or brought out of the skin to form an ostomy. Chemotherapy following surgery reduces the risk of recurrent tumors. Radiation is not normally used unless there is a specific site of metastasis.

EXERCISE 12.2

Instructions: Assign the correct ICD-9-CM codes to the following diagnostic statements

1. Colon carcinoma at hepatic flexure and transverse colon   _____

2. Metastatic disease to the liver   _____

3. Benign rectal polyps   _____

4. Carcinoma *in-situ* of the salivary gland   _____

5. Tumor, ampulla of Vater, behavior undetermined   _____

V Codes

The physician office coder will find numerous opportunities to assign V codes for the gastrointestinal system. Assign codes from category V01–V06, Persons with potential health hazards related to communicable diseases, for patients who have had contact with or exposure to communicable diseases, or are carriers or suspected carriers of infectious diseases. Codes that are excluded from this series are V18.8, Family history of infectious and parasitic diseases, and V12.0, Personal history of infectious and parasitic diseases.

- ■ V01   Contact with or exposure to communicable diseases
- ■ V01.0   Cholera
- ■ V02   Carrier or suspected carrier of infectious diseases
- ■ V02.0   Cholera
- ■ V02.1   Typhoid
- ■ V02.3   Amebiasis
- ■ V02.3   Other gastrointestinal pathogens
- ■ V02.6x Viral hepatitis

Category V02.6 should be examined carefully before assigning a fifth digit for the specific type of hepatitis.

The following categories are set aside for prophylactic vaccinations:

- ■ V03, Need for prophylactic vaccination and inoculation against bacterial diseases
- ■ V04, Need for prophylactic vaccination and inoculation against certain viral diseases
- ■ V05, Need for other prophylactic vaccinations and inoculation against certain viral diseases

Vaccinations are assigned from the Medicine chapter of CPT®, which is discussed in Chapter 21 of this textbook. Details on procedural coding will appear in that chapter.

Codes V10–V19 are specified for persons with potential health hazards related to personal and family history. Codes exclusive to the gastrointestinal system include categories

- ■ V10.0, Personal history of malignant neoplasm of the gastrointestinal tract
- ■ V12.7, Personal history of diseases of digestive system
- ■ V16.0, Family history of malignant neoplasm of the gastrointestinal tract

The status of artificial openings is coded to category V44. These codes should not be used if the artificial opening requires attention or management. The code indicates only that the patient has a stoma and is for informational purposes only.

Categories V50–V59 should be assigned to indicate the reason for care in a patient who may have been previously treated for a condition no longer present, for a residual state, or to prevent recurrence of a disease. Assign codes from category V55, Attention to artificial openings, if the patient has a stoma that requires removal, readjustment, replacement, or cleansing of the appliance or catheter or passage of dilators to stretch the opening.

Assign code V58.75, Aftercare following surgery of the teeth, oral cavity, and digestive system, in conjunction with other aftercare codes to fully identify the reason for the aftercare encounter.

Categories V74–V75 identify special screening examinations for infectious diseases and include bacteria, viral, and parasitic infections.

When screening for malignant gastrointestinal neoplasm, assign the following codes as a medical necessity link to the test performed:

- V76.41 Rectum
- V76.50 Intestine, unspecified
- V76.51 Colon
- V76.52 Small intestine

EXERCISE 12.3

Instructions: Assign the correct ICD-9-CM Diagnosis code(s) and E codes where applicable to the following scenarios.

1. Accidental needle stick to hospital employee following injection given to hepatitis patient. _____

2. Family history of colon cancer, in for screening sigmoidoscopy. _____

3. Change of PEG tube button on gastrostomy feeding tube. _____

CPT® CODING OF THE DIGESTIVE SYSTEM

This chapter discusses surgical procedures performed on the digestive system. Other diagnostic tests and nonsurgical therapeutic procedures are coded in the Medicine chapter of CPT®. Please see the attached CD-ROM for advanced coding practice scenarios.

Lips

Excision and Repair

Excisional procedures involving the lips are performed on what is known as the *vermilion,* or pink-colored portion of the lips. The junction between skin and vermilion is known as the vermilion border. Coders must be watchful of the areas of excision or repair in order to assign the correct code. Code procedures done on the skin around the lips to the integumentary system and procedures on the vermilion portion of the lips to the digestive system.

Codes 40700–40761 describe the plastic repair of cleft lip/nasal deformity. These codes are separated into unilateral and bilateral procedures; therefore, Modifier 50 cannot be used. Other terms used in the code descriptors are *primary, secondary,* and *stage.* Primary is the first repair. The term *stage* is used to describe how many times the surgery has been performed. Revision needed after healing is referred to as a two-stage procedure. Care must be taken when matching ICD-9-CM to CPT® codes for medical necessity purposes. ICD-9-CM category 749 for cleft lip and/or palate specifies unilateral and bilateral conditions. Make sure that a bilateral procedure is not reported for a unilateral condition. Figure 12.4 illustrates the oral cavity.

Vestibule of Mouth

The vestibule is the portion of the oral cavity outside the dentoalveolar structures that includes the mucosal and submucosal tissue of the lips and cheeks.

Incision

Incisional procedures are divided into simple and complicated types. Multiple incision and drainage of different sites are reported with Modifiers 51 and 59 with code 40801 to indicate that the same procedure is being performed on a different site or on a different lesion. Use code 40805 when a larger incision is required to remove a foreign body or if the wound needs suture closure.

Excision, Destruction

Codes 40808–40820 describe biopsy, excision, destruction of lesion or scar, and repair of the vestibule. Look for documentation describing the excisional repair as simple, complex, or complex with excision of underlying muscle.

Repairs

Repairs of the vestibule are done to close lacerations or as plastic repairs for neoplasms, trauma, and congenital anomalies. Coders should watch for the length of repair and the location of vestibuloplasty—anterior, posterior, unilateral or bilateral.

EXERCISE 12.4

Instructions: Assign the correct CPT ® codes to the following scenarios.

1. A patient is seen in the urgent care facility after being struck in the mouth with a baseball. His lip is split through the full thickness of the lip and slightly into the skin surrounding the lip. The physician performs a complex, plastic procedure on the vermilion of the lip. _____

2. Using the same scenario as question 1, for a laceration that does not include the vermilion of the lip, a CPT® code from the Integumentary section should be used. **True or False**

3. A physician repairs a complete bilateral cleft lip in two stages. The first procedure is performed in June and the second procedure, which re-opens the defect and closure, is performed a month later after the tissue has had a chance to heal. Assign the code for both procedures. _____

4. A patient is seen for a lesion on the inside of the cheek. The physician performs an excision with complex repair of the mucosa of the cheek. The pathology report shows a malignancy of the cheek mucosa. _____

Tongue and Floor of Mouth

Incision

Codes 41000–41018 are divided into intraoral and extraoral sections and are listed according to site. The intraoral method uses an incision from inside the mouth, and the extraoral method uses an incision from the face either along the jawline or under the

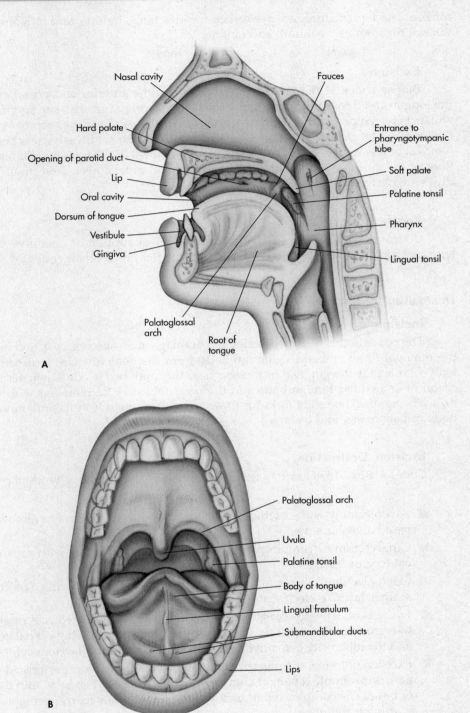

Figure 12–4   Structures of the oral cavity.

tongue. These procedures are performed for infections, trauma, and inflammatory conditions of the floor of the mouth and tongue.

Excision

Biopsy codes 41100–41108 are performed on the anterior and posterior portions of the tongue and floor of the mouth. Excisions of the tongue are also site specific and differentiate between procedures with or without a closure. A *glossectomy* removes all or part of the tongue. The glossectomy codes are listed with increasing invasiveness beginning with removal of less than one-half of the tongue, to removal of the tongue with resection of the floor of the mouth, with mandibular resection, and radical neck dissection. These procedures are performed for neoplasms.

Repair

Codes 41250–41252 are used for trauma and disruption of operative wounds. The length of repair and the location of the laceration determine repair codes.

Dentoalveolar Structures

Incision

The codes in this section describe the drainage of an abscess, cyst, and hematoma, or the removal of an embedded foreign body from the dentoalveolar structures. The dentoalveolar area is the gingival or mucosa near the tooth bed. Code 41806 describes the incision of embedded foreign bodies in the bone that may be removed with the use of a drill. The medical necessity links for these procedures include cysts, inflammatory conditions and abscesses, and trauma.

Excision, Destruction

Codes 41820–41850 listed in this section include the following types of procedures:

- Alveolectomy with curettage of osteitis or sequestrectomy: For removal of diseased alveolar bone.
- Gingivectomy: Trimming of an overgrowth of the gingival with a scalpel, electrocautery, or laser.
- Operculectomy: Removal of a small piece of gingival overlying a tooth with a scalpel, laser, or electrocautery.
- Excision of dentoalveolar tuberosities, either fibrous or osseous: A *tuberosity* is an overgrowth of the hard palate in the dentoalveolar area. The soft palate is incised and the tuberosity is removed with the use of drills and files to recontour the area.
- Excision of lesion or tumor of the dentoalveolar structures performed without repair, with simple repair, or complex repair. The lesion can be within the mucosa or bone. The complex repair includes the use of tissue rearrangement and tissue grafting techniques.
- Excision of hyperplastic alveolar mucosa, overgrowth of the tissue surrounding the teeth, for each quadrant or subsection of the mouth.
- Destruction of dentoalveolar lesion is performed without excision and may be performed with the use of electrocautery, cryotherapy, or chemical injection.

Excision and destruction procedures are performed for neoplasms, dentofacial anomalies, and diseases of the gingival, jaw, and oral tissues.

EXERCISE 12.5

Instructions: Assign the correct CPT® codes to the following scenarios.

1. A patient is seen for an abscess of the intraoral submandibular area. The physician performs an incision and drainage of the abscess. _____

2. A patient with a history of chewing tobacco is seen for a lump on the tip of the tongue that appeared about two months previously. The physician performs a biopsy. The pathology report confirms a malignancy. _____

3. A patient is seen for a flap of tissue in the back of the mouth that is left after the last molars have grown in. The flap becomes irritated and sore, and the patient complains of discomfort. The physician performs a destruction of the tissue overlaying the molar. _____

Palate and Uvula

Excision, Destruction

Codes 42100–42160 include biopsy and excision of lesion of the palate or uvula. Watch for documentation in the operative note indicating the type of closure. Some procedures are performed without a closure or may require simple, or flap, closure. Resection of the palate removes the lesion and any adjacent tissue where the lesion may have spread. Resection includes an intermediate or complex closure, tissue transfers and grafting. Code 42140 describes *uvulectomy*, a full thickness incision/excision of the uvula. Code 42145 describes a palatopharyngoplasty, which is the excision of excessive tissues of the uvula, soft palate, and pharynx. This procedure is also known by the acronym **UPPP**.

Formula for Success

Check with individual payers for reimbursement guidelines on UPPP procedures.

Repair

Procedures in this section of CPT® include

- Repair of laceration of the palate
- Palatoplasty

Laceration repairs are divided by the length of repair—up to 2 cm, over 2 cm, and complex. These codes are commonly linked to diagnoses in category 873 of ICD-9-CM for open wounds of the palate. Palatoplasty procedures are used for the repair of cleft palate. This is a congenital condition where the palate has not fused. Varying degrees of severity require different types of repair codes, ranging from a simple closure of the soft tissue of the alveolar ridge to major revisions that sometimes involve multiple surgeries. Some of these codes may be used in conjunction with cleft lip procedures from 40700–40761. Be sure to assign the most specific ICD-9-CM code from category 749 for the patient's condition.

Other remaining procedures in this section of CPT® are performed for neoplasms, congenital anomalies, sleep disturbances, chronic sinusitis, and diseases of the upper respiratory tract, jaw, and oral soft tissues.

EXERCISE 12.6

Instructions: Assign the correct CPT® codes to the following scenarios.

1. A patient is evaluated for insomnia and sleep apnea. He is found to have extra tissue in the back of the throat in the area of the uvula. As surgical treatment for this condition, the physician removes excessive uvular tissue and repairs the area. _____

2. A patient is seen for complete unilateral cleft palate. The surgical treatment of palato-plasty is performed. _____

Salivary Gland and Ducts

Incision

Three pairs of salivary glands are located in the head and neck. These glands are:

- Parotid: Located in the cheek in front of the ear.
- Submaxillary: Located in the soft tissue under the tongue.
- Sublingual: Located in the soft tissue under the tongue.

Use parotid incision codes 42300 for simple incision and 42305 for complicated incision and drainage. Code 42310 specifies an intraoral incision and drainage of abscess. Code 42320 requires an extraoral incision to drain the submaxillary gland. Codes 42330–42340 describe a *sialolithotomy*, or removal of a stone in the salivary gland. Look for documentation of the type of gland, intraoral or extraoral technique, and the complexity involved.

Excision

Codes 42400–42450 describe biopsy, *marsupialization*, or excision of the salivary glands. Marsupialization is the removal of the roof of a cyst. The code assignment for excision of the parotid gland is dependent upon the extent of surgery. Read the descriptors under codes 42410–42426 carefully to determine the depth of dissection. Procedures in this section are performed for neoplasms, hypertrophy of salivary glands, stones or calculi, abscess, and mucocele of the salivary glands.

Repair

The plastic repair of a salivary duct, or *sialodochoplasty*, is described by codes 42500–42505. These are listed as primary/simple or secondary/complex procedures. Use codes 42507–42510 for diversion procedures. When performing a bilateral parotid duct diversion, the normal anatomic path of the duct is moved to bypass a blockage. Code assignment is dependent upon the excision/ligation of one or both of the submandibular glands. Diagnostic links to these procedures commonly include salivary gland disorders and trauma.

EXERCISE 12.7

Instructions: Assign the correct CPT® codes to the following scenario.

1. A patient is seen for a lump under the tongue and is diagnosed with a stone of the salivary duct. The stone is removed by simple excision. _____

Pharynx, Adenoids, and Tonsils

Incision

Peritonsillar abscesses, code 42700, are incised with an angled forceps or hemostat and left open to drain. The incision and drainage of a retropharyngeal or parapharyngeal abscess may be performed by either an intraoral or external approach, described by codes 42720–42725. The external approach is performed through an incision under the jaw, with blunt dissection used to isolate the abscess.

Excision, Destruction

The *oropharynx* is located between the anterior edge of the soft palate and the top of the epiglottis. The *hypopharynx* is located from the upper edge of the epiglottis to the juncture of the larynx and esophagus, or the *nasopharynx*, in the back of the throat. The excision and destruction section contains a variety of codes addressing this area, including biopsy, excision, foreign body removal, T&A, and resection.

Codes 42810–42815 describe the excision of a *branchial cleft cyst*, which is an embryological remnant that resembles gills. This is located under the sternocleidomastoid muscle in the neck and is confined to skin and subcutaneous tissues. It can also have a fistula, which extends beneath the subcutaneous tissue and into the pharynx. The diagnostic link for this procedure includes congenital branchial cleft cyst or fistula; preauricular sinus, 744.4x, and specified congenital anomaly of face and neck, 744.89.

The tonsils can be surgically removed or destroyed by electrocautery, laser, or cryogenic methods to perform a *tonsillectomy*. Adenoids are located in the nasopharynx and are commonly removed at the same time as the tonsils. The adenoids are removed using a mirror or *nasopharyngoscope*, which is a flexible endoscope used for visualization, and an adenotome or curette to excise. Tonsils and adenoids can grow back, so the terminology in CPT® indicates primary or secondary procedures to identify the operative episode. The procedure codes for tonsillectomy and adenoidectomy are further divided into under age 12 and age 12 and over. The procedure codes are shown in Table 12.1.

Formula for Success

Watch patient age carefully when assigning T&A codes. Age edits will cause claim denials if the wrong code is assigned for the patient's age.

Repair

Wounds of the pharynx may be repaired using an intraoral, mouth, or transhyoid approach, depending on the type of wound. Code 42900 should be linked to a diagnosis code for open wound of the pharynx, category 874 in ICD-9-CM.

Pharyngoplasty, code 42950, is a repair of the pharynx, which can include reconstruction techniques such as skin grafts, tongue flaps, regional cutaneous flaps, and microvascular free-tissue transfers. *Pharyngoesophageal* repair, code 42953, is performed through a horizontal neck incision to correct a tear at the pharyngeal–esophageal junction.

Table 12–1 Procedure Codes for T&As

Procedure	Under 12 Years of Age	Over 12 Years of Age
Tonsillectomy and adenoidectomy	42820	42821
Tonsillectomy primary or secondary	42825	42826
Adenoidectomy, primary	42830	42831
Adenoidectomy, secondary	42835	42836

Other Procedures

A *pharyngostomy*, code 42955, is an opening into the pharynx for long-term feeding. CPT® has assigned six codes for the control of postoperative hemorrhages following tonsillectomy or adenoidectomy. Use codes 42960–42961 for posttonsillectomy hemorrhage, and codes 42970–42972 for postadenoidectomy hemorrhage. Each group is divided by the type of intervention—simple, complicated, or requiring surgical intervention. Treatment can include clot evacuation and pressure applied by sponges, electrocautery, or the application of vasoconstrictive solutions. In cases of profuse bleeding, emergency ligation of the external carotid artery may be performed. Hemorrhages may occur up to two weeks after the initial procedure.

Formula for Success

Modifier 78 will need to be assigned for patients who are returning to the operating room within the global period by the same surgeon.

EXERCISE 12.8

Instructions: Assign the correct CPT® codes to the following scenarios.

1. A patient is seen for a peritonsillar abscess in the physician's office. The physician performs a simple incision and drainage of the abscess. _____

2. A 10-year-old patient is surgically treated for chronic pharyngitis with a tonsillectomy. _____

3. A 30-year-old patient is treated for chronic maxillary sinusitis and chronic tonsillitis with a tonsillectomy and adenoidectomy. Three days later, the patient begins vomiting blood and blood clots. She is seen in the Emergency Room for an acute hemorrhage of the operative wounds of the tonsils and subsequently rushed to surgery for control of the hemorrhage. _____

Esophagus

Incision

Esophagotomy with removal of foreign body is performed by either a cervical or thoracic approach. The cervical approach is performed through an incision in the lateral neck. The thoracic approach is performed through an incision and dissection of the left posterior chest wall. Use code 43020 for a cervical approach and code 43045 for a thoracic approach.

Excision

Excisions of the esophagus are performed for neoplasms, ulcers and trauma. When using codes from this section, watch for key words to help determine the extent of surgery, such as; cervical approach, thoracic, or abdominal approach; with or without thoracotomy; microvascular anastomosis; total or partial. Highlight key words in CPT® to help differentiate some of these codes from each other.

EXERCISE 12.9

Instructions: Assign the correct CPT® codes to the following scenarios.

1. The surgical excision of an esophageal lesion is performed by the cervical approach on a patient. The pathology report confirms carcinoma *in-situ* of the esophagus. _____

2. A patient is brought into the Emergency Room after being assaulted and stabbed repeatedly in the chest. He is rushed to the operating suite for surgical treatment and exploration of the wounds. It is decided that due to the extensive damage to the esophagus, a near-total esophagectomy would be performed. A thoracotomy is performed for drainage and a cervical esophagogastrostomy is performed to replace the esophagus. _____

Repair

Esophageal repairs are distinguished by the approach and extent of repair. Highlight the approaches for codes 43300–43425 in your CPT® book where they are specified. These include terminology such as cervical, thoracic, transthoracic, abdominal, and transabdominal. Watch for terminology within the descriptor that references specific diagnoses, such as varices, wound or injury, perforation, and fistula.

Manipulation

Manipulation codes 43450–43460 describe different types of esophageal dilation. Several techniques for dilation include the use of a bougie, a long, flexible instrument to measure the degree of narrowing of a tubular structure; a sound, a cylindrical, curved instrument used to dilate a canal; or dilators, instruments used to enlarge a passageway.

EXERCISE 12.10

Instructions: Assign the correct CPT® codes to the following scenarios.

1. A patient presents with achalasia. It has been decided that he will undergo surgical treatment with a Heller-type procedure with an abdominal approach. _____

2. A 10-year-old boy is brought into the Emergency Room after being shot with a BB gun in the chest. Through imaging studies he is found to have a perforated esophagus with no other damage to internal organs. The repair is performed through a transthoracic approach and the injury is repaired with suturing. _____

3. A patient in the office is presenting with dysphagia and is found to have stenosis of the esophagus. The physician performs a dilation of the esophagus over a guide wire. _____

Stomach

Incision

Gastrotomy procedures, codes 43500–43520, are performed through a midline incision into the stomach for the purpose of exploration. The codes are listed by the different types of procedures performed such as foreign body removal, suture of a bleeding ulcer, suture repair of an esophagogastric laceration, and esophageal dilation with insertion of permanent intraluminal tube. Pyloromyotomy, code 43520, is an incision of the pyloric muscle to release tension.

Excision

Codes 43600–43641 describe stomach biopsies, excision of ulcers, tumors, partial or total removal of the stomach, and reconstruction. Codes 43610 and 43611 differentiate between benign and malignant tumors, so it is important to read descriptors carefully to avoid inappropriate ICD-9-CM diagnosis code assignment. Gastrectomy procedures, codes 43620–43634, are differentiated by the extent of stomach removal—total or partial. Each technique determines where the anastomosis will be made to reconnect the esophagus or stomach to the intestines.

Introduction

Gastrostomy tubes are used for feeding patients who have congenital anomalies, cerebral palsy, nutritional problems, malignant neoplasms, or are otherwise unable to feed themselves long term. The tubes can be inserted endoscopically or percutaneously. Code 43750 refers to the percutaneous placement of a gastrostomy tube. Code 43760 is used for the change of a gastrostomy tube. Code 43761 describes repositioning of the gastric feeding tube through the duodenum for enteric nutrition. Use this code when repositioning a gastric feeding tube that has been previously placed. The diagnostic link for this procedure is attention to other artificial opening of digestive tract, V55.4.

Formula for Success

Tips for Coding Percutaneous Gastrostomy Tubes

1. When reporting an endoscopically placed percutaneous gastrostomy tube (PEG tube), use code 43246, not 43750.
2. Do not report code 43752 with critical care or neonatal intensive care.
3. Use the appropriate Evaluation and Management code to report the removal of a gastrostomy tube.

EXERCISE 12.11

Instructions: Assign the correct CPT® codes to the following scenarios.

1. A patient is diagnosed with a tumor of the stomach. An excision is performed and the pathology report confirms that the growth is benign. _____

2. A patient diagnosed with carcinoma of the fundus of the stomach is surgically treated with a total gastrectomy with a Roux-en-Y reconstruction. _____

3. A patient suffering from protein malnutrition has a percutaneous gastrostomy tube placed. _____

Other Procedures

Codes 43800–43846 describe gastric bypass and revisions, gastric banding, and other procedures for obesity. Other codes in this section describe gastrostomy creation and closure procedures. A gastrostomy is an opening made into the stomach. This is done to construct an outlet for temporary or permanent gastrostomy. Watch for age edits when assigning code 43831: This code is used to report a neonatal gastrostomy for feeding.

EXERCISE 12.12

Instructions: Assign the correct CPT® codes to the following scenarios.

1. A patient is brought into the Emergency room after the vehicle he was driving went out of control and the patient was thrown through the front windshield of the car. The patient was diagnosed with a closed intracranial injury. A surgeon has been called to place a temporary gastrostomy tube for feeding. This is performed using an open procedure. _____

2. A morbidly obese patient is seeking a permanent weight management option and has decided to undergo a Roux-en-Y gastric bypass. _____

Intestines (Except Rectum)

Surgical procedures on the intestines are described by a variety of codes, including some rather unique ones. Similar types of procedures that are commonly performed on other areas of the body are also performed on the intestines, including foreign body removal, excision of lesions, suture repair, and resection. Some unique codes in the digestive system include 44050 and 44060, reduction of volvulus or intussusceptions of the intestine. This condition is best described as a kind of telescoping collapse of the bowel. Codes 44132–44136 describe the procurement of donor intestines and transplant procedures.

Enterostomy procedures including revisions are assigned to codes 44300–44346. An enterostomy is the creation of an opening from the intestines to the skin to allow passage of waste. It can be temporary or permanent, and either type can require revision. Codes are assigned based on the part of the intestine that is brought up—cecostomy, ileostomy, or colostomy (see Figure 12.5). These are commonly performed for neoplasms, trauma, or for bowel rest following certain intestinal conditions.

Repair codes 44602–44680 include descriptions of suture repairs with or without colostomy creation. Use codes 44620–44626 for closure of colostomies.

Formula for Success

Watch for scheduled/planned or staged procedures on the gastrointestinal system. Use Modifier 58 for staged procedures, such as colostomy closures, if performed within the global period of the first surgery.

EXERCISE 12.13

Instructions: Assign the correct CPT® codes to the following scenarios.

1. A newborn is suffering from an intestinal obstruction and is in need of emergency surgery. The physician performs a surgical reduction of the intussusception. _____

2. A patient with diverticulitis of the small intestine is surgically treated with an enteroenterostomy and anastomosis of the intestine. _____

3. A partial colectomy with removal of the terminal ileum and creation of an ileocolostomy is performed on a patient with chronic ulcerative proctosigmoiditis. _____

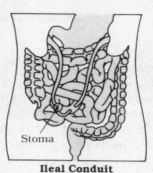
Ileal Conduit

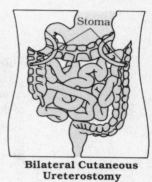
Bilateral Cutaneous Ureterostomy

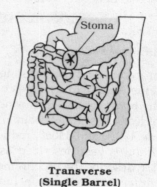
Transverse (Single Barrel)

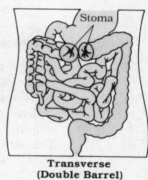
Transverse (Double Barrel)

Figure 12–5 Types and placements of ostomies.

Enterostomy–External Fistulization of Intestines

The codes in this section describe a connection of a segment of intestine to an opening in the abdominal wall, creating fistula to the outside of the body. All of the codes in this section are labeled as separate procedures, which means that they are bundled into or are considered an integral part of a more extensive procedure in the same body area. Use codes 44300–44346 when they are performed as stand-alone procedures or when they are distinct from other procedures performed the same day.

Repair

Procedures in this section of CPT® are performed for perforated ulcers, diverticuli, trauma, obstruction, closure of enterostomy, or fistula. Watch for terminology that identifies single or multiple perforations, with or without colostomy, or other terms indicating more extensive procedures.

EXERCISE 12.14

Instructions: Assign the correct CPT® codes to the following scenarios.

1. A patient who has been surgically treated for colon cancer the previous month has a colostomy in place. He has developed a hernia around the colostomy opening. The surgeon performs a revision of the colostomy, which includes a repair of the hernia. _____

2. A patient with multiple perforations due to diverticulosis of the colon requires surgical intervention for a hemorrhage. Due to the extent of the diverticulosis, a colostomy is also placed during the same operative session. _____

3. The closure of an enterostomy is performed on a patient with a history of rectal cancer. The patient is completely healed from the major abdominal surgery of the previous month and the enterostomy is no longer needed. _____

4. A patient with a fistula between the small intestine and the bladder requires surgical intervention. A closure of the fistula is performed. _____

Meckel's Diverticulum and the Mesentery

Meckel's diverticulum is a remnant of early fetal development and is a pouch found on the ileum 50 cm from the ileocecal junction. Treatment for this is excision of Meckel's diverticulum or omphalomesenteric duct, code 44800. The excision of lesion of mesentery is the removal of a growth on the double layer of peritoneal tissue that encloses most of the abdominal organs and attaches them to the abdominal wall. The mesentery provides the abdominal organs with blood vessels and nerves.

Suturing of the mesentery, code 44850, is considered a separate procedure and should not be reported with a more definitive procedure from the same body area.

Procedures on Meckel's diverticulum and the mesentery are performed for neoplasms, peritonitis, adhesions, ulcers, and trauma.

Appendix

Incision

The appendix is a small, fingerlike protrusion near the end of the cecum. Its function is not completely known, but it is felt to be a vestigal organ that no longer functions in humans. Incision and drainage **(I&D)** of an appendiceal abscess may be performed with either an open or percutaneous method. When a percutaneous I&D is performed, it may be necessary to utilize radiology methods to visualize (see code 75989 if needed). Either method may require that a drain be left in place. The diagnostic link for these procedures includes acute appendicitis with peritoneal abscess, 540.1, and other appendicitis, 542.

Excision

The open appendectomy procedures are divided into three codes:

- 44950, Appendectomy. When an incidental appendectomy is performed at the same time as another major abdominal procedure, CPT® guidelines state code 44950 with the Modifier 52 should be used.
- 44955, Add-on appendectomy, which is used when performed for an indicated purpose in the same session as another major abdominal procedure.
- 44960, Ruptured appendix with abscess or generalized peritonitis.

Formula for Success

Assign diagnosis codes for appendicitis carefully. Appendicitis is coded to categories 540–543. These categories include acute appendicitis with generalized peritonitis, with or without mention of peritonitis or abscess, chronic appendicitis, and other diseases of the appendix. Incidental appendectomy procedures are often bundled into larger procedures by payers. Check with insurers for reimbursement guidelines.

Rectum

Incision

The incision and drainage procedures for this section include transrectal drainage of pelvic abscess, submucosal abscess of the rectum, and deep abscess. A transrectal drainage means that the incision is made from inside the dilated rectum. Deep abscesses can be quite dangerous with the potential to develop into fistulas.

Excision

The biopsy of the anorectal wall is performed with an anal approach. Almost a dozen types of proctectomy procedures exist in CPT®. These procedures can include either partial or complete excision of the rectum. Read descriptors carefully to determine the extent of the procedure. The codes become increasingly more complex and invasive and are performed in most cases for malignancies or congenital problems.

EXERCISE 12.15

Instructions: Assign the correct CPT® codes to the following scenarios.

1. A patient comes into the Emergency Room with lower right abdominal pain. Through laboratory testing and examination it is determined that the patient has acute appendicitis. The patient is rushed to the operating room and an open appendectomy is performed. _____

2. A surgeon performs an incision and drainage of a submucosal rectal abscess. _____

3. A patient with biopsy-proven carcinoma of the rectum has a complete proctectomy by abdominoperineal approach, including a colostomy. _____

4. A surgeon performs a partial proctectomy and anastomosis with a transacral approach as surgical treatment for carcinoma *in-situ* of the colon. _____

5. A patient with megacolon is surgically treated with a complete proctectomy using the Swenson procedure. _____

6. A surgeon performs an excision of rectal prolapse and anastomosis using a perineal approach. _____

Destruction

The destruction of a rectal tumor can be performed using electrodessication, electrosurgery, laser ablation, laser resection, or cryotherapy and is performed using a transanal approach. Keep in mind that the destruction of a tumor indicates that there will not be any tissue removed for a pathology specimen because the tissue is destroyed.

Repair

Repairs of the rectum are performed for stenosis, prolapse, exploration and repair of injury, and closure of fistulas with or without colostomy. Take care when assigning codes 45540–45550 for different approaches. Code 45560, repair of *rectocele*, is listed as a separate procedure. Rectocele repair corrects a herniation of the rectum into the vagina. This is commonly performed as part of a posterior colporrhaphy. When the two procedures are done together, use only code 57250 as instructed by CPT®.

Manipulation

The procedures in this section are all labeled as separate procedures. Any of these procedures that are performed in conjunction with a more extensive procedure in the same body area will be bundled and not reported separately. These procedures also require anesthesia. Codes 45905 and 45910 specify that dilations are done under anesthesia other than local. This means that either general or regional anesthesia is required.

Anus

Procedures on the anus include incision, excision, introduction, endoscopic procedures, repair, destruction, and suture. These procedures are performed for fistulas, hemorrhoids, lesions, incontinence, and congenital malformations. Coders should exercise caution when assigning codes for hemorrhoids. These codes are located in four different subheadings including excision, introduction, destruction, and suture. Check documentation carefully to determine the method of treatment for hemorrhoids. Documentation should specify whether the hemorrhoid was internal, external, or both. This information is important for both diagnostic as well as procedural code assignment.

Destruction of anal lesions are classified as simple or extensive. Each method of destruction—chemical, electrodessication, cryosurgery, laser, and surgical excision—has an individual code.

Procedure codes for cryosurgery of rectal tumor are divided into a benign and malignant code. Because these codes are specifically divided according to malignancy, the diagnostic link must correspond accordingly.

Other Digestive Procedures

The digestive system also contains several distinct organs—liver, pancreas, and gallbladder. Common procedures that are assigned to the liver include percutaneous needle biopsy of liver, code 47000, and open liver biopsy, 47001.

The gallbladder can be removed through a scope or through an open incision into the abdomen. Code open cholecystectomy with 47600 and 47605 if imaging studies are performed of the biliary system. Cholecystectomy done through a scope is coded to 47562–47564.

Formula for Success

Make a notation in your CPT® book next to code 47001 as a reminder that this is an open procedure, not performed through a scope.

An exploratory laparotomy, code 49000, is reported as a separate procedure when abdominal exploration is needed. This may include biopsies, if necessary. An exploratory laparotomy is often listed as a surgical approach, and as a bundled procedure it should not be coded when performed with other, more definitive procedures.

Hernia Repair

Hernias can be repaired through an open approach or through a scope. Codes 49491–49611 are performed as open procedures. Below are coding tips for open hernia procedures. Italic is added for emphasis:

1. Hernia codes are listed according to type: inguinal, lumbar, femoral, incisional/ventral, epigastric, umbilical, spigelian, and omphalocele.
2. Inguinal, femoral, and incisional/ventral hernias can be initial or recurrent.

3. Inguinal, femoral, incisional/ventral, epigastric, and umbilical hernias can be reducible and incarcerated/strangulated.

4. Inguinal and umbilical hernias are categorized by age.

5. Use of a mesh or prostheses is included in the hernia repair and is not separately coded except for incisional/ventral hernias.

6. Use add-on code 49568 to report the mesh used with incisional/ventral hernias.

7. Excision/repair of strangulated organs or structures is reported in addition to the appropriate strangulated hernia repair code.

8. Modifier 63 is not used with codes 49491–49496, 49600, 49606, 49610, or 49611.

9. For the repair of inguinal hernias on preterm infants, the preconception age is equal to the gestational age at birth plus infant age in weeks on the surgery date.

The medical necessity link for the hernia procedures is important because of the specificity of both the CPT® and ICD-9-CM codes.

- **Inguinal** hernia, 550.xx
- **Femoral** hernia with gangrene, 551.2x
  –with obstruction, 552.0x
  –without obstruction or gangrene, 553.0x
- **Umbilical** hernia with gangrene, 551.1
  –with obstruction, 552.1
  –without obstruction or gangrene, 553.1
- **Ventral** hernia with gangrene, 551.2x
  –with obstruction, 552.2x
  –without obstruction or gangrene, 553.2x

Endoscopy

The endoscopy codes are placed under each specific anatomic area of the digestive system in CPT®. They are listed with a separate subheading under esophagus and stomach, small bowel and stomal, rectal, and anus headings. Endoscopy coding is truly an art and can be somewhat complex. Therefore, only an introduction to endoscopy coding is outlined below.

Endoscopies are scope procedures that are performed with a lighted instrument to examine internal organs or body cavities. Scopes can be flexible or rigid in nature and allow for the passage of different types of instruments to treat abnormalities encountered. Some of the same techniques are used whether the scope is an upper endoscopy—through the mouth—or a lower endoscopy—through the anus. These techniques include biopsy, injection, ligation, removal of foreign body, hot biopsy, snare technique, insertion of stent, balloon dilation, insertion of guidewire, control of bleeding, and **ablation.**

Endoscopy codes are grouped by *family.* Most "families" are headed by a diagnostic scope, or a *base code* that is listed as a separate procedure. It may be helpful to highlight these in your CPT® book. Indented below the diagnostic scope there may be a number of therapeutic scopes.

Basic rules apply for all types of scopes. Below are some general coding tips for gastrointestinal endoscopy procedures:

1. Code the appropriate endoscopy for each anatomic site examined.

2. Surgical endoscopy always includes the diagnostic endoscopy.

3. Multiple lesions treated by the same method are only reported once.

4. Multiple lesions each treated by different methods are reported by multiple codes using the Modifiers 51 and 59 for subsequent procedures.

Formula for Success

Look in the CPT® index under "endoscopy." Mark this section of your index with a flag or sticker for easy reference when coding.

CPT® gives the following definitions and instructions for lower endoscopy:

- *Proctosigmoidoscopy* is the examination of the rectum and sigmoid colon.
- *Sigmoidoscopy* is the examination of the entire rectum and sigmoid colon and may include examination of a portion of the descending colon.
- *Colonoscopy* is the examination of the entire colon, from the rectum to the cecum, and may include the examination of the terminal ileum.
- For an incomplete colonoscopy, with full preparation for a colonoscopy, use a colonoscopy code with the Modifier 52 and provide documentation.

Some of the techniques used for endoscopy include:

- Removal of a foreign body: Suctioned, grasped with forceps, or by placing a balloon beyond the foreign body, inflating it, and pulling the balloon and the foreign body out.
- Removal of tumor(s), polyp(s) or other lesion(s) procedures are separated based on method. These methods include:
  –Hot forceps or bipolar cautery that electocoagulates and severs the lesion at the same time.
  –Snare loop placed around the base of the lesion severing and electrocoagulating at the same time.
- Stent placement: Performed with a guide wire, often after a dilation technique performed on the esophagus.
- Control of bleeding: By any method, which can include laser, electrocoagulation, rubber band ligation, and injection with sclerosants, ethanol, or adrenaline.
- Ablation of tumor(s), polyp(s) or other lesion(s), which are not removable by hot forceps, bipolar cautery, or snare technique.

Codes 43260–43272 describe *endoscopic retrograde cholangiopancreatography (ERCP)* procedures. In these procedures, an endoscope is passed through the patient's oropharynx, esophagus, and stomach and into the small intestine. A smaller subscope is threaded up the sphincter of Oddi and into the ducts that drain the pancreas and the gallbladder. The diagnostic scope in this section of CPT® is code 43260, which includes the collection of specimens by brushing or washing. The collection of biopsies, placement of stents, foreign body removal, dilation of ducts, and ablation of tumors are performed in a similar manner to that of the **EGDs**.

EXERCISE 12.16

Instructions: Assign the correct CPT® codes to the following scenarios.

1. An ERCP (endoscopic retrograde cholangiopancreatography) with sphincterotomy is performed on a patient with a blockage of pancreatic duct. _____

2. A patient with chronic pancreatitis has an ERCP with lithotripsy destruction of a calculus from the pancreatic duct. _____

3. A gastroenterologist performs a small intestinal endoscopy including the ileum to control an acute duodenal ulcer hemorrhage. During the endoscopy, the collection of specimens is performed by brushing technique. _____

4. A gastroenterologist performs a diagnostic flexible sigmoidoscopy for colon cancer screening on a patient with a family history of colon cancer. _____

5. A gastroenterologist performs a flexible sigmoidoscopy on a patient and encounters an area of congenital stenosis of the rectum. The physician is able to dilate the section with balloon. _____

6. A patient is prepared and sedated for a flexible colonoscopy. During the procedure, the physician is unable to complete the procedure due to incomplete bowel prep. The physician does identify areas of diverticulosis of the colon, but no biopsies are taken. _____

7. A patient is seen with the complaint of blood in the stool. The physician performs a colonoscopy the next day after the proper preparation of the patient. During the colonoscopy, bleeding diverticula of the colon are identified and the bleeding is stopped using bipolar cautery. _____

8. An internal medicine physician performs an anoscopy including balloon dilation for rectal stenosis and removal of several lesions by snare technique. _____

Laparoscopy

A laparoscopy is an endoscopic viewing of the abdominal cavity for diagnostic or therapeutic procedures. Several small incisions are made with the insertion of *trocars*, or sleeves, to hold various instruments. The abdomen is insufflated with carbon dioxide to create a working area that allows more freedom of movement and better visibility for the surgeon.

Laparoscopic procedures are all located within the digestive system chapter of CPT®. These codes are separately located under each anatomic heading, similar to the endoscopy codes. Many of the procedures described in each laparoscopy section are almost identical to the corresponding descriptions in the open excision section. Under many laparoscopic code descriptors is a cross reference to the open procedure of the same name. Because the descriptions and names of the procedures are so close, understanding the surgical approach is crucial. Any time the approach is not clear in the operative report, the surgeon should be consulted and appropriate corrections to the operative documentation should be made. The diagnostic links for medical necessity are the same as those for open procedures.

Formula for Success

The Cardinal Rule for Laparoscopy
A surgical laparoscopy always includes a diagnostic laparoscopy.

In order to correctly assign laparoscopy codes, the coder must know what organs are being diagnosed or treated through the scope. Use code 49320 to report a diagnostic scope. Only brushings and washings may be performed with a diagnostic scope. This code is also listed as a separate procedure and cannot be used when a more definitive procedure is performed.

The Multiple Scope Rule

Coders who routinely assign endoscopic codes must understand Medicare's rule for reporting multiple scopes. This reporting requirement is specific to Medicare and requires a good understanding of how endoscopic codes are assigned and sequenced. The multiple scope rule is explained in detail in the Medicare billing manual.

EXERCISE 12.17

Instructions: Assign the correct CPT® code for the following scenarios.

1. A patient with an ovarian cyst is surgically treated with a laparoscopic aspiration. _____

2. An adult patient is surgically treated for bilateral inguinal hernias laparoscopically. _____

3. A patient with bleeding diverticulosis of the colon is surgically treated with a partial colectomy with anastomosis performed laparoscopically. _____

4. A patient comes into the Emergency Room with lower right abdominal pain. Through laboratory testing and examination it is determined that the patient has acute appendicitis. The patient is rushed to the operating room and a laparoscopic appendectomy is performed. _____

Modifiers

Operative procedures on the digestive system are often performed in multiples, requiring the use of Modifier 51. Unless the student is given relative value amounts, fee schedules, or access to computer software, it is difficult for a beginning coder to know which procedure to sequence first. Use Modifier 52 to describe procedures that are reduced or cannot be completed as planned. Modifier 78 is used for a return to the operating room for a related procedure during the postoperative period.

CHAPTER REVIEW

1. When choosing a code for the repair of the lip, either a code from the integumentary or digestive system may be used.   **T or F**

2. Identify the most extensive procedure below:
   a. Biopsy
   b. Resection
   c. Excision with primary closure
   d. Excision with local flap closure

3. Adenoids are always removed with tonsils.   **T or F**

4. Give the correct code for a tonsillectomy on a 12-year-old patient:
   a. 42820
   b. 42821

   c. 42825
   d. 42826

5. The acronym EGD stands for:
    a. Esophagoscopy
    b. Esophagectomy
    c. Endoscopic Retrograde Cholangiopancreatography
    d. Esophagogastroduodenoscopy

6. A suture repair of a gastric ulcer is referred to as:
    a. Pyloroplasty
    b. Gastroduodenostomy
    c. Gastrorrhaphy
    d. Gastrostomy

7. Code 44015 is meant to be used when the placement of a feeding tube is the only
    procedure performed.   **T or F**

8. Give the correct code for a total laparoscopic colectomy with ileostomy.
    a. 44210
    b. 44211
    c. 44150
    d. 44205

9. Which modifier is used when a patient is fully prepped for a colonoscopy but the
    procedure is incomplete?
    a. 51
    b. 59
    c. 52
    d. 53

10. A proctosigmoidoscopy is the endoscopic examination of the rectum and sigmoid
    colon?   **T or F**

11. The code for the excision of an external thrombosed hemorrhoid is:
    a. 46255
    b. 46260
    c. 46250
    d. 46063

12. The code for a percutaneous liver biopsy is:
    a. 47000
    b. 47001
    c. 47011
    d. 47100

13. The code for a Roux-en-Y cholecytoenterostomy is:
    a. 43846
    b. 47740
    c. 47785
    d. 48540

14. When coding for an inguinal hernia repair, all of the following is needed except:
    a. Age
    b. Recurrent

   c. Incarcerated

   d. Mesh

15. When coding for a ventral hernia repair, all of the following is needed except:

   a. Age

   b. Recurrent

   c. Incarcerated

   d. Mesh

16. Match the modifiers to the correct definitions:

   a. Multiple procedures _____

   b. Reduced services _____

   c. Assistant surgeon _____

   d. Return to the operating room for a related procedure during a postoperative period

   _____

   e. Staged procedure _____

   f. Distinct procedural services _____

   g. Return to the operating room for an unrelated procedure during a postoperative period _____

   h. Discontinued procedure _____

   79   58   51   59   52   78   53   80

Case Studies

Case Study 12.1

Diagnosis

Esophagogastroduodenoscopy with cold biopsies.

Anesthesia

Fentanyl 200 mcg and Versed 7 mg.

Summary

Esophagus: Abnormal. Gastroesophageal junction was located at 38 cm. A single tiny 2 to 3 mm dart of erosive esophagitis was noted. No other esophagitis. No varices. Stomach: A 2 cm long hiatus hernia. No other abnormalities. The cardia and fundus normal as viewed during retroflexion. The pylorus was normal. Duodenum: Normal end of the mid third portion. No erosions, ulcers, or angiodysplasias seen in either the duodenum or the stomach. *Hypopharynx:* The left true vocal cord has a whitish plaque-like area on its posterior half. The significance of this is unclear.

Impression

1. No explanation for possible melena.
2. Very, very mild erosive esophagitis (LA classification grade A).
3. A 2-cm long hiatus hernia.
4. A slightly raised plaque-like abnormality posterior half of left vocal cord, etiology and significance uncertain.
5. Otherwise, normal esophagus, stomach, and proximal duodenum.

   ICD-9-CM code(s): _____

   CPT® code(s): _____

Case Study 12.2

Preoperative Diagnosis

Lymphadenopathy.

Postoperative Diagnosis

1. Diffuse large cell B-cell lymphoma
2. Moderate steatosis and moderate active steatohepatitis

Procedure Performed

1. Laparoscopy with biopsy of mesenteric lymph node.
2. Percutaneous liver biopsy.

Anesthesia

General.

Summary

The patient was placed in the supine position on the OR table. General anesthesia was administered. The abdomen was prepped and draped in a sterile fashion. An incision was made into the umbilicus and entrance into the abdomen was gained. The abdomen was insufflated and laparoscopy was performed. Two additional trocars were placed in the left lateral abdomen for manipulation of the omentum. Some omental adhesions were taken down to the anterior abdominal wall. The intestines were then swept superiorly and laterally to the right. We were then able to identify the large lymphadenopathy at the root of the mesentery. The capsule of the node was scored using cautery. We then used a large spoon to obtain tissue. Frozen section showed lymphoma. Additional tissue had been taken and was sent for permanent section. The patient's liver appeared slightly cirrhotic. We therefore performed percutaneous liver biopsies as well. Two biopsies were taken using a Tru-Cut needle. There was good hemostasis. All trocars were removed and the CO_2 was released. The incisions were infiltrated using lidocaine and marcaine. The umbilical incision was closed with 0 Vicryl suture. The skin incisions were closed with 4-0 Vicryl subcuticular suture. Steri-Strips and sterile dressings were applied.

Estimated Blood Loss

Minimal.

   ICD-9-CM code(s): _____

   CPT® code(s): _____

Case Study 12.3

Preoperative Diagnosis

Cholelithiasis with cholecystitis.

Postoperative Diagnosis

Cholelithiasis with cholecystitis.

Procedure

Laparoscopic cholecystectomy.

Anesthesia

General.

Summary

The patient was placed in the supine position on the OR table. General endotracheal anesthesia was administered. The abdomen was prepped and draped in sterile fashion. An umbilical incision was made. An open technique was used to insert a 10 mm trocar. Insufflation was then performed. The remaining three trocars were inserted in the right upper quadrant. The gallbladder was grasped and retracted cephalad. The cystic artery was identified, doubly clipped, and divided. The gallbladder was retrieved using an Endo Catch bag. The right upper quadrant was irrigated and suctioned. There was good hemostasis. The trocars were removed and the insufflation was released. The incisions were all infiltrated with lidocaine and marcaine. The fascial incisions were closed with 0 Vicryl suture. The skin incisions were closed with 4-0 Vicryl subcuticular suture. The patient tolerated the procedure well and was transported to the recovery room in stable condition.

Counts

All needle, sponge, and instrument counts were correct.

ICD-9-CM code(s): _____

CPT® code(s): _____

The Urinary System

■ OBJECTIVES

1. Identify the basic anatomy of the urinary system.
2. Recognize various disease entities and neoplasms affecting the kidneys, ureter, bladder, and urethra.
3. Correctly assign ICD-9-CM diagnosis codes to conditions and diseases specific to the urinary system.
4. Correctly assign CPT® codes to urodynamic services and surgical procedures.

■ TERMINOLOGY AND ACRONYMS

Anastomosis   Suturing of two tubular structures together.

ATN   Acute tubular necrosis.

Azotemia   Excessive amount of urea/nitrogen in the blood.

BPH   Benign prostatic hypertrophy.

BUN   Blood urea nitrogen.

Calculus   Stone, often occupies cavities in the body where it forms from minerals.

Calyx   A subdivision at the outermost portion of the kidney.

DRE   Digital rectal exam.

ESRD   End-stage renal disease.

ESWL   Extra corporeal shock wave lithotripsy.

Glomerulonephritis (GN)   Type of kidney disease caused by a change in the filtering structure of the kidney.

IVP   Intravenous pyelogram.

KUB   Kidney, ureters, and bladder.

Lysis   To cut.

Medulla   The innermost portion of the kidney, containing the collecting ducts and loops of Henle.

Nocturia   Urination at night.

Oliguria   Scanty urine production.

Proteinuria   Protein in the urine.

Pyelonephritis Inflammation of the kidney, focusing on the renal pelvis as a site of infection.

TURP Transurethral resection of the prostate.

UA Urinalysis.

Uremia Toxicity from waste substances normally filtered by the kidney, which continue to circulate in the blood.

UTI Urinary tract infection.

ANATOMY

The urinary system consists primarily of two organs—the kidney and the bladder—and the tubes that connect them to each other and to the outside of the body. Each bean-shaped kidney is located in the flank area, lateral to the spinal column, and is protected by the lower ribs. A thick covering of fat provides further protection. The kidney functions as a sophisticated filtration system, cleansing the bloodstream as it passes through the kidneys, and then passing the waste product, urine, on to the bladder for storage and then excretion. Kidneys also regulate electrolytes, fluid absorption, and blood pressure and assist in the formation of red blood cells. When the kidneys fail and cannot properly cleanse the blood of waste products, the filtration process is artificially substituted by dialysis.

A cross-section of the kidney demonstrates an outermost layer of tissue called the cortex. Inside the cortex is a deeper layer called the **medulla.** The medulla contains fan-shaped structures called the renal pyramids, which extend outward to the cortex. The renal pyramids drain urine into larger channels called the renal **calyx,** which open into a larger drainage chamber, the renal pelvis. The nephron is the functional structure of the kidney, where capillary blood crosses cell membranes and the exchange/regulation of electrolytes, ions, water, and metabolites take place. Self-contained within each nephron are one Bowman's capsule, glomerulus, and tubules, which collect and concentrate urine. There are approximately one million nephrons in each kidney.

See the urinary system and a coronal section of a kidney on Anatomy Plates 14 and 15 in Appendix A.

Other components of the urinary system include the ureters and urethra, which are muscular tubes designed to transport urine. Ureters are approximately 16–18 cm long and drain urine from the renal pelvis into the bladder by peristaltic waves in the muscular layer. The bladder is located deep in the pelvis and is protected by the pelvic bone. The bladder is a muscular sac with an average capacity of 350–650 cc that can hold as much as 1200 cc of urine. The only portion of the bladder that does not stretch is the trigone, which is a triangular shaped area of tissue created by the ureteral orifices on the backside of the bladder and the urethral sphincter at the bottom of the bladder. The top portion of the bladder is referred to as the "dome." The urethra is much shorter than the ureter. In males, it is approximately 6 to 8 inches long, while in females it is only 2 to 3 inches long.

DISEASE PROCESSES AND ICD-9-CM CODING OF THE URINARY SYSTEM

Hypertension and Kidneys

Renovascular hypertension is the term used to describe hypertension affecting the kidneys. A narrowing of the renal arteries, usually secondary to atherosclerosis, causes this. Many patients report no symptoms, while others note nausea and vomiting, chest pain, headaches, fatigue, confusion, congestive heart failure, and vision changes. Renal hypertension is difficult to control and should be an indicator in patients who require multiple hypertensive medications to manage their blood pressure. Treatment with medications can have variable results, and patients require frequent monitoring and adjustment of their antihypertensive medications. Surgical treatment with stenting or balloon angioplasty to open up the renal arteries has good overall results for patients who are surgical candidates.

Renal hypertension is assigned to category 403 in ICD-9-CM. Any condition classifiable to rubrics 585, 586, or 587, in addition to conditions classifiable to 401, should be assigned to category 403. A cause-and-effect relationship between hypertension and renal failure is implied. The physician is not required to explicitly state the relationship between the two.

Acute renal failure, renal disease stated as not due to hypertension, and renovascular hypertension are excluded from this category. Fourth digits are assigned based on documentation of malignant or benign types of hypertension. Unspecified hypertension is assigned the fourth digit of 9. In addition, fifth-digit subclassifications indicate the presence or absence of renal failure in addition to the diagnosis of hypertensive renal disease.

Example: Severe renal sclerosis with benign hypertension

Incorrect ICD-9-CM code assignment: 587, Renal sclerosis, and 401.1, Benign essential hypertension.

Correct ICD-9-CM code assignment: 403.10, hypertensive renal disease, benign, without mention of renal failure.

When a patient has both hypertensive heart disease and hypertensive renal disease, a combination code from rubric 404 should be assigned. This includes any condition classifiable to both categories 402 and 403. The type of heart failure should be described by use of an additional code from category 428. Fourth digits are assigned based on documentation specifying malignant, benign, or unspecified types of hypertensive disease. Fifth-digit subclassifications are expanded to include the following:

- 0, Without mention of heart failure or renal failure
- 1, With heart failure
- 2, With renal failure
- 3, With heart failure and renal failure

Example:

1. Hypertensive heart disease
2. Chronic renal failure

Incorrect ICD-9-CM code assignment: 402.90, Hypertensive heart disease unspecified, without heart failure, and 585, Chronic renal failure.

Correct ICD-9-CM code assignment: 404.92, Hypertensive heart and renal disease, unspecified, with renal failure.

Renovascular hypertension is excluded from category 403 but is cross-referenced in the Excludes note to category 405, with a fifth digit of 1. Category 405 describes hypertensive conditions that are secondary to, or due to, other conditions. Renovascular hypertension is due to stenosis, stricture, atherosclerosis, scarring, or other obstruction of the renal arteries, which causes an increase in blood pressure. Fifth-digit subclassifications in this category are demonstrated below:

- 1, Renovascular
- 9, Other

Example:

Hypertension secondary to renal artery atherosclerosis, 405.91 (Secondary hypertension, unspecified renovascular)

Malignant hypertension due to pheochromocytoma, 405.09 (Secondary hypertension, malignant, other)

Diabetes and Chronic Renal Failure

Diabetes is the primary cause of chronic kidney failure in the United States. Diabetes can damage capillaries throughout the body. Hypertension and arteriosclerosis can then develop secondary to diabetes. For diabetics, high blood pressure may predict the development of kidney failure in the future, so it is important that hypertension is controlled. Another important factor in the development of kidney disease is how long a person has had diabetes. The longer a person has had diabetes, the greater the risk of developing chronic kidney failure. Some indications of diabetic kidney disease include:

- Nausea and vomiting
- **Nocturia**
- **Proteinuria**
- Hypertension
- Peripheral edema
- Rise in BUN and creatinine levels
- Pruritis
- Decreased need for anti-diabetic medications

Controlling blood sugar and blood pressure and decreasing protein intake may help control the progression of chronic kidney failure into end-stage renal disease (**ESRD**).

Category 250, Diabetes mellitus, contains fourth digits that are assigned to various complications of diabetes. Use code 250.4x to describe diabetes with renal manifestations. The physician must indicate a cause-and-effect relationship between the diabetes and kidney disease before this code can be assigned. Diagnoses with statements such as "renal failure with diabetes" or "nephrosis and diabetes" are not sufficient to establish cause and effect. Documentation should be researched for terminology that indicates "due to," "from," "secondary to," or "caused by." Fifth-digit subclassifications are assigned based on the type of diabetes as follows:

0, Type II [non-insulin-dependent type] [NIDDM type] [adult-onset type] or unspecified type, not stated as uncontrolled

Fifth digit 0 is for use for type II, adult-onset diabetic patients, even if the patient requires insulin.

1, Type I [insulin-dependent type] [IDDM] [juvenile type], not stated as uncontrolled

2, Type II [non-insulin-dependent type] [NIDDM type] [adult-onset type] or unspecified type, uncontrolled

Fifth digit 2 is for use for Type II, adult-onset diabetic patients, even if the patient requires insulin.

3, Type I [insulin-dependent type] [IDDM] [juvenile type], uncontrolled

Additional codes should be assigned to identify any manifestations of kidney disease to fully describe the condition of the patient.

Example 1 Chronic renal failure due to diabetes

Incorrect codes: 585, chronic renal failure; and 250.00, diabetes mellitus without mention of complication, unspecified type.

Correct codes: 250.40, Diabetes with renal manifestations, and 585, chronic renal failure.

Example 2   Diabetic nephropathy, currently uncontrolled

Incorrect codes: 250.02, Diabetes mellitus without mention of complication, uncontrolled, and 583.81, Nephritis and nephropathy, not specified as acute or chronic, in diseases classified elsewhere.

Correct codes: 250.42, Diabetes mellitus with renal manifestations, uncontrolled, and 583.9, Nephropathy, not otherwise specified.

Acute and Chronic Renal Failure

Renal failure may be caused by a sudden interruption in the functioning of the kidney. Three classifications of acute renal failure identify different causes of acute renal failure:

- Prerenal: Can occur from burns, dehydration, hemorrhage, cardiac problems, obstruction, and conditions causing severe vasoconstriction.
- Intrarenal or Intrinsic: Caused by damage to the nephrons from toxins, acute kidney infections, lupus, sickle cell disease, and obstetrical complications. The vast majority of acute renal failure is due to acute tubular necrosis. Mortality is often greater than 50 percent, most often due to complications from infections following the acute phase.
- Postrenal: Caused by a bilateral obstruction of the urine flow, such as prostate hyperplasia.

Acute renal failure is assigned to category 584. Excluded from this rubric is acute renal failure following labor and delivery (669.3), posttraumatic renal failure (958.5), or that complicating abortion (634–638 with .3, 639.3,), ectopic or molar pregnancy (639.3). Fourth digits describe cell death in various parts of the kidney. Acute tubular necrosis (584.5) describes the destruction of the tubules in the kidney, while renal cortical necrosis (584.6) and renal papillitis (584.7) describe destruction in the outermost layer of the kidney and in the pyramid regions, respectively. Acute renal failure that does not specify location or lesion within the kidney is assigned 584.9, acute renal failure, unspecified.

Chronic renal failure is usually of insidious onset, meaning that it is gradual and progressive. Kidney function can be decreased to 10 percent in some cases before symptoms are recognized. The symptoms are the same as those found with chronic renal failure due to diabetes. A strict low-protein diet and blood pressure control is key to slowing the progression of chronic renal failure.

Example 1   A dialysis patient was admitted to the hospital with anemia due to end-stage renal disease. The attending physician dictated a history and physical, which documented a comprehensive history and examination, and moderate complexity medical decision making.

ICD-9-CM diagnosis codes: 285.21, Anemia in end-stage renal disease; V45.1, renal dialysis status.

CPT® code: 99222, Initial hospital care.

Example 2   A burn patient experiences acute renal failure with tubular necrosis from insufficient fluid resuscitation in the first eight hours following a second degree burn to the front of both legs, upper and lower. A grease fire caused the burn. A renal specialist is called for a consult. He performs a comprehensive history and exam, with high-level medical decision making. The patient is transferred to a burn center later that day. Codes assigned by the renal specialist:

ICD-9-CM diagnosis code: 584.5, Acute tubular necrosis; 945.29, second degree burn, multiple sites of lower limbs; 948.10, eighteen percent total body surface area; E894, Ignition of highly flammable material.

CPT® code: 99255, Initial inpatient consultation.

EXERCISE 13.1

Instructions: Correctly assign the V codes to the following diagnoses. Some may require more than one V code.

1. History of bladder cancer three years ago with currently functioning ureterostomy   _____

2. History of renal calculi   _____

3. Status postrenal transplant   _____

4. Replacement of Foley catheter   _____

5. History of testicular carcinoma ten years ago   _____

6. Removal of suprapubic cystostomy catheter   _____

7. Status post right nephrectomy due to ESRD   _____

8. History of prostate carcinoma, in for surgical follow-up   _____

9. Donation of kidney to recipient with ESRD   _____

10. Family history of polycystic kidney disease   _____

Neoplasms

Neoplasms of the urinary system are becoming increasingly common. Bladder cancer is currently the sixth most common type of cancer. Smoking seems to be a factor in both bladder and kidney malignancies, with family history and polycystic kidney disease also playing a role in a predisposition for kidney cancer. Chemical exposure may also be a risk factor for bladder cancer. Most urinary neoplasms are initially diagnosed because of hematuria, dysuria, or a dull ache in the back or pelvis. Urinalysis **(UA)** shows red blood cells, and further workup to determine the cause of bleeding may include cystoscopy, CT/MRI scan, ultrasound, and intravenous pyelogram. See Figure 13.1 for an example of a bladder malignancy.

Malignant neoplasms that have extended beyond the margins of the original site are prone to metastasis in lymph nodes and bone. When coding for surgical procedures, the operative report should be searched for documentation of any lymph node dissection or biopsies.

Malignant neoplasms of the bladder, kidney, ureter, and urethra are classified to codes 188 and 189 in ICD-9-CM. Benign neoplasms are coded to category 223, and carcinoma *in-situ* is coded to 233. Use category 236 for neoplasms of uncertain behavior.

In addition to malignancies, the urinary system is also prone to cysts, benign neoplasms, and dysplastic conditions that may eventually become malignant.

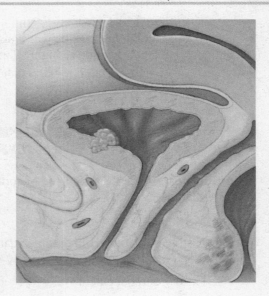

Figure 13–1 Neoplasm with invasion into the muscle wall of the bladder.

EXERCISE 13.2

Instructions: Correctly assign the diagnosis codes to the following neoplasm exercise. Some may involve more than one code.

1. Renal cell carcinoma, with metastasis to retroperitoneal nodes   _____

2. Adenocarcinoma of urinary bladder, trigone   _____

3. Metastatic disease to kidney, unknown primary   _____

4. Metastatic disease of the bone, from transitional cell carcinoma of the bladder   _____

5. Benign mesonephroma   _____

6. Papilloma of urinary bladder   _____

CPT® CODING OF URINARY PROCEDURES

Kidney

Incision

Access to the kidneys is gained through several different types of surgical approach. One method is percutaneous, which involves an incision through the flank, with the patient lying on his or her side. An open approach can be either through the flank or through the abdomen and involves a larger incision than a percutaneous stab incision. A laparoscopic approach requires the use of a laparoscope inserted into the abdominal cavity, while an endoscopic approach is gained through the urethra, bladder, and ureter into the kidney. The important thing to remember is whether the approach is open, percutaneous, or through a scope.

Many of the procedures done on the kidney itself include the removal of various types of calculi, or stones. Large stones that cannot be crushed by lithotripsy, or staghorn calculi that are deeply embedded into the renal pelvis, must be removed surgically. See Figure 13.2 for an example of renal calculi.

Key terms in this section of CPT® include the endings *-ostomy* and *-otomy*. A nephrostomy is the creation of an opening in the kidney (such as with a tube) for drainage. A nephrotomy is simply an incision. A distinction should also be made between the root terms *nephro* and *pyelo*. A pyelotomy is an incision into the renal pelvis; a nephrotomy is an incision into the main part of the kidney. Although both terms refer to the kidney, the exact location is fine-tuned by these terms.

Codes 50080 and 50081 involve multiple procedures on the kidney including incision, possible dilation, endoscopy, lithotripsy, stenting, or basket extraction for removal of stones. The size of the calculi should be documented in the operative or pathology report in order to assign the correct code.

Example: A patient with a small staghorn calculus is scheduled for a percutaneous nephrostolithotomy. At the time of surgery, a 1.8 cm stone is retrieved via basket extraction.

ICD-9-CM diagnosis: 592.0, Staghorn calculus

CPT® code: 50080, Percutaneous nephrostolithotomy or pyelostolithotomy, with or without dilation, endoscopy, lithotripsy, stenting, or basket extraction, up to 2 cm.

Excision

Excision codes in CPT® define biopsy by percutaneous approach or open surgical approach. The removal of kidney cysts is also included in this section. A specific instruction refers the coder to the laparoscopic procedures on the kidney if a laparoscopic approach is used for either nephrectomy or ablation of lesions. Nephrectomy is the excision of the entire kidney or partial kidney. This may be performed with partial or total ureterectomy and may include a portion of the bladder cuff. Surgical dictation should be closely reviewed to determine the extent of the procedure.

Example 1 An open renal biopsy is performed to determine the morphology of a mass lesion seen on IVP.

ICD-9-CM diagnosis: 593.9, Kidney lesion

CPT® code: 50205, Renal biopsy, by surgical exposure of kidney

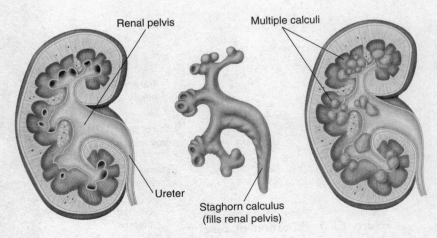

Figure 13–2 Types of renal calculi.

Example 2   Using the same scenario as above, but with nephrectomy performed following frozen section pathology.

CPT® code: 50220, Nephrectomy, including partial ureterectomy, any open approach including rib resection.

Transplantation

Kidney transplants involve donor nephrectomy and recipient transplantation. Two terms are commonly used to describe the types of transplantation:

- *Allo*transplantation: A transplant obtained from another human donor.
- *Auto*transplantation: A reimplantation of one's own kidney.

Allotransplantation may involve a living donor or a cadaver donor. Operative reports for the nephrectomy portion will specify whether the donor is living, and if a cadaver, whether it is a unilateral or bilateral nephrectomy.

Regardless of the type of donor, the existing kidney must be detached from the ureter and associated blood vessels in order for the transplant to be sutured into place. Code 50340 describes a recipient nephrectomy. This specific code has been designated as a "separate procedure," thus, it may be performed independent of the transplant procedure. When a recipient nephrectomy and transplant are done concurrently, use code 50365. Figure 13.3 identifies the location of a transplanted kidney.

Introduction

This section of CPT® describes the introduction of tubes, catheters, or needles into the renal pelvis or kidney, as well as dilators, injection procedures, and change of ostomy tubes. Cross-references are made throughout to various radiological supervision and interpretation codes that allow x-ray visualization of these procedures as they are being performed.

Formula for Success

A Different Approach

Check to see if surgical procedures are done percutaneously, via open approach, or through an endoscope.

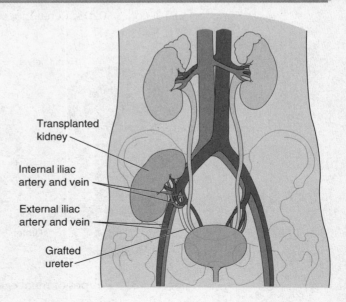

Transplanted kidney

Internal iliac artery and vein

External iliac artery and vein

Grafted ureter

Figure 13–3   Location of renal allotransplant.

Repair

Suturing and repairs of the kidney are defined by the suffixes *-orrhaphy* and *-plasty*. This subheading in CPT® may include simple or complex repairs of the kidney, suturing of lacerated kidney, and closure of fistula. Once again, the approach is important for several codes: 50525 specifies an abdominal approach for closure of fistula and 50526 identifies a thoracic approach.

Laparoscopy and Endoscopy

Renal procedures performed through a scope are divided into two types—laparoscopic (abdominal approach) and endoscopic.

Laparoscopic procedures involve ablation of kidney lesions; partial, radical nephrectomy with partial or total ureterectomy; donor nephrectomy; and pyeloplasty. New codes in the laparoscopic section include those for a laparoscopic ablation of renal mass, 50542, and laparoscopic partial nephrectomy, 50543.

Endoscopic procedures are less invasive than laparoscopy and include biopsy; dilation; irrigation; fulguration (cautery) of lesions; and removal of tumor, foreign body, or **calculus;** and insertion of stents or radioactive substances. The key to correctly coding endoscopic procedures is to know whether the scope was passed through an existing nephrostomy or pyelostomy opening or a newly created opening.

Example:

1. A renal biopsy was performed through an existing nephrotomy, 50555.
2. The right kidney was examined endoscopically through an incision in the flank; a stent was placed following dilation of proximal ureteral stricture, 50575.

Other Procedures

Code 50590 describes lithotripsy (see Figure 13.4), which describes breaking kidney stones by shockwave treatment.

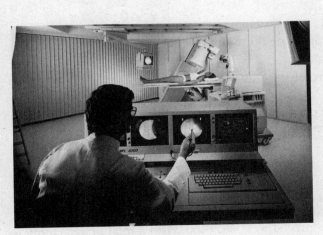

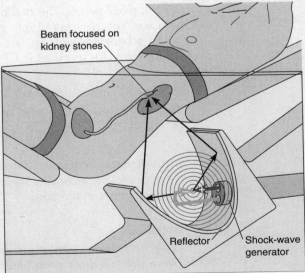

Beam focused on kidney stones

Reflector

Shock-wave generator

Figure 13–4   Extracorporeal shock wave lithotripsy used to break kidney stones.

EXERCISE 13.3

Instructions: Look up each ICD-9-CM code given at the bottom and link the correct diagnosis to the appropriate procedure in the space provided.

1. Voiding cystometrogram to evaluate urine leakage _____
2. Simple bladder repair due to rupture from car accident _____
3. Cystourethroscopy with removal of ureteral calculus _____
4. Dilation of female urethra, subsequent, for stricture _____
5. Renal biopsy, percutaneous to evaluate renal insufficiency _____
6. Pelvic exenteration, complete, for prostatic malignancy _____
7. Nephrotomy with removal of staghorn calculus from renal pelvis _____
8. Laparoscopy with ablation of renal cyst _____
9. Excision of urethral diverticuli, 56-year-old male _____
10. Transurethral resection of prostate, for BPH without obstruction _____

ICD-9-CM Codes:	593.2	867.0	185	599.2	788.37
	867.0	592.0	600.00	592.1	598.9

Ureter

Incision

Ureterotomies are commonly performed to insert stents and remove stones, both via open procedure. Stents are thin, flexible tubes that are inserted inside the ureters and hold them open for drainage. They are useful when a patient has had multiple renal calculi. They allow small stones to pass and prevent obstruction of the ureter from swelling. Typically, the stent has a "pigtail," or curl on each end. One end is curled in the bladder, the other in the renal pelvis. The curling of the stent should prevent it from migrating without the use of sutures to hold it in place. Assignment of ureterolithotomy codes is dependent upon where the incision is made in the ureter. The following anatomic areas for ureterolithotomy are specified in CPT®:

- 50610   Ureterolithotomy; upper one-third of ureter
- 50620   middle one-third of ureter
- 50630   lower one-third of ureter

Multiple cross-reference instructions are given to the coder in this section for other types of approaches, including laparoscopic approach, stone basket extractions via cystotomy, or endoscopic extraction.

Excision

Only two codes currently exist in this subheading for excision of the ureter. Use 50650 for a ureterectomy with bladder cuff when that is the only procedure that is performed. It is designated as a separate procedure. Use 50660 when a total ureterectomy is performed with a combination of abdominal, vaginal, and/or perineal approach.

Introduction

Introduction procedures include injection of contrast material through ureterostomy or indwelling ureteral catheter or for visualization of ileal conduit and change of ostomy tube. Any radiological supervision and interpretation is coded separately with 74425; if imaging guidance is performed while changing a ureterostomy tube, 75984 should be used.

Repair

Most of the codes found under this subheading refer to various methods of **lysis** with **anastomosis** to the renal pelvis, the opposite ureter, bladder, or intestine. When anastomosis is used in conjunction with the suffix "ostomy," such as with ureteroneocystostomy or ureterocalycostomy, this means that the ureter is being sutured into another organ for drainage. Commonly, this is used to reroute the drainage of urine due to neoplasm or severe ureteral damage. The development of a ureteral conduit means that an artificial bladder has been created out of intestine that opens to the skin through a stoma. Transplantation of the ureter directly to the skin is described by code 50860.

Example: A patient with radiographic evidence of ovarian vein syndrome was taken to the OR for ureterolysis.

ICD-9-CM diagnosis: 593.4, Other ureteric obstruction

CPT® code: 50722, Ureterolysis for ovarian vein syndrome

Other codes in this section include ureterorrhaphy, or suture of the ureter, which is designated as a separate procedure. Takedown of ostomy, deligation of ureter, and closure of fistulas (spontaneously occurring communication between organs) are also described.

Laparoscopy and Endoscopy

Only a few codes currently exist under the laparoscopic subheading. CPT® instructions under laparoscopy advise the coder to report a diagnostic laparoscope separately using code 49320. Surgical laparoscopic codes on the ureters include the removal of ureteral stones by incision with code 50945, and creation of a new ureteral opening into the bladder, with or without stent placement, with codes 50947 and 50948.

Ureteral endoscopy can be performed through a pre-existing stoma or a new opening of the ureter to the skin. Similar to renal endoscopy through a stoma, multiple procedures can be performed through the artificial opening such as catheterization, biopsy, fulguration, insertion of radioactive substance, and removal of foreign body or calculus. Codes 50951–50961 describe those procedures performed through an established ureterostomy. Use codes 50970–50980 for procedures performed through an incision (ureterotomy). These codes follow the same pattern as those in the 50951–50961 range—catheterization, biopsy, fulguration, insertion of radioactive substance, and removal of foreign body or calculus. The difference between the two families of codes involves an established ureterostomy for 50951–50961, and a newly created ostomy for 50970–50980.

Example:

1. Ureteral endoscopy with biopsy through ureterostomy tube, 50955.
2. Ureteral endoscopy and biopsy, using guidewires to dilate ureterotomy tract, 50974.

Bladder

Incision

A surgical opening into the bladder is called cystotomy. Several codes in this section of CPT® describe cystotomies that are performed to remove a calculus, insert a ureteral catheter, or drain the bladder.

Excision

Surgical excisions in the bladder vary from simple excisions of cyst to complete bladder removal with associated abdominoperineal resection of rectum and colon. Like most sections of CPT®, codes are arranged in order of least to most invasive. Since a complete bladder removal is often part of larger surgical procedures, code 51570 is listed as a separate procedure. This code should only be used when the complete bladder removal is performed independent of other urinary or intestinal procedures. Operative reports should be read closely to determine the extent of the surgical procedures, including any minor procedures performed at the same time.

Example: Bladder cancer, primary; with complete pelvic exenteration and abdominoperineal resection and pelvic lymphadenectomy.

ICD-9-CM diagnosis: 188.9, Primary malignant neoplasm of the bladder

CPT® procedure: 51597, Pelvic exenteration, complete, for vesical, prostatic or urethral malignancy . . . with or without hysterectomy and/or abdominoperineal resection of rectum and colon and colostomy, or any combination thereof.

Introduction

Injections of contrast material for various radiographic procedures are described by codes 51600–51605. Use code 51700 for irrigation of the bladder with sterile solutions to flush out blood clots. Three new codes were introduced in 2003 to describe the insertion of catheters when performed independent of a larger procedure. These codes are:

- 51701, Insertion of non-indwelling bladder catheter (e.g., straight catheterization for residual urine)
- 51702, Insertion of temporary indwelling bladder catheter; simple (e.g., Foley)
- 51703, Insertion of temporary indwelling bladder catheter; complicated (e.g., altered anatomy, fractured catheter/balloon)

Other codes within this section include change of cystostomy tube, simple or complicated. Use code 51715 for injection of implant material into the urethra and/or bladder neck to prevent incontinence. Occasionally, anticarcinogenic materials are instilled through a catheter into the bladder.

Urodynamics

Urodynamics is the study of urine storage and voiding capacity. By performing various tests and services on the bladder and bladder outlet, both urinary and neurological conditions can be precisely determined for appropriate treatment. All of the codes in this section of CPT® involve a test or measurement of bladder filling, storage, or emptying. CPT® directs coders to use a Modifier 51 when multiple tests are done from this section of the urinary chapter. Use a Modifier 26 to identify the professional component of these services when the physician interprets the results or operates the equipment.

Example: Voiding cystourethrogram, 51795, and ultrasonic measurement of post-void residual urine, 51798-51.

Repair

Bladder repairs are performed for four primary reasons:

- To correct problems with incontinence due to prolapse or other diseases.
- To suture wounds of the bladder.
- To close fistulas/abnormal openings between the bladder and other organs.
- To correct bladder defects caused by neoplasms or congenital anomalies.

Age, childbearing, neoplasm, chronic infection, or problems with the nerves and/or muscles of the bladder and bladder outlet may cause incontinence. Urethropexy and vesicle neck suspensions are performed to prevent bladder prolapse and reposition the urethra in a normal anatomic position. Suspensions of the bladder and urethra are performed by placing heavy sutures through fascia and/or attaching sutures passed through the urinary tissues to the back of the pubic bone in a sling-like fashion.

A Burch procedure is also known as an anterior vesicourethropexy. Many of the procedures in the urinary chapter of CPT® are known by eponyms, or people's names, often the name of the surgeon who created the procedure. Check the CPT® index for the eponym, if mentioned in the operative report.

Abnormal openings may sometimes develop between the bladder and other organs in the pelvis. Table 13.1 describes various types of fistulas, the organs involved, and codes that describe the condition, as well as the corrective procedure. Fistulas that involve the intestines are repaired using codes from the Digestive chapter of CPT®.

Laparoscopy, Endoscopy, and Transurethral Procedures

Procedures for urinary incontinence are currently the only two procedures that are performed laparoscopically on the urinary system. Code 51990 describes a urethral suspension and code 51992 describes a sling procedure.

Endoscopic procedures are those that are performed through the natural orifice and include cystoscopy, urethroscopy, and cystourethroscopy. Code 52000 (cystoscopy) is listed as a separate procedure. Since cystoscopy is a common approach to many transurethral procedures, code 52000 should be used only when a diagnostic cystourethroscopy is performed alone.

Transurethral procedures are those that are performed using a scope and include biopsy, resection of tumors, dilation, and insertion/removal of stent, calibration, dilation, and crushing of stones. Codes 52224–52240 require documentation of the size of the bladder tumor or lesions. Coders should also be watchful for terminology that specifies spinal vs. local anesthesia, male vs. female procedures, and simple vs. complicated procedures.

Temporary stents that are inserted and removed during a cystourethroscopic procedure should not be reported separately. However, if a self-retaining, in-dwelling stent is inserted at the time of a diagnostic or therapeutic intervention, this should be reported using 52332-51 as a subsequent procedure.

A procedure that is performed in retrograde fashion on the urinary system is one that is performed in the opposite direction of urine flow. Normal urine flow is antegrade, so when a retrograde procedure is performed, it is done against the flow of urine. Code 52334 is a cystourethroscopy with insertion of ureteral guidewire through the kidney to establish a percutaneous nephrostomy, retrograde. This means that a guide wire is inserted through the urethra, bladder, through the ureters, and then advanced through the kidney and out through a small stab wound or incision in the skin. The tract created by the guidewire is gradually dilated and a nephrostomy tube is sutured into place.

Access to the prostate gland in males is commonly approached through the urethra. CPT® separates transurethral procedures in the urinary chapter from other approaches described in Chapter 14. The prostate gland is a donut-shaped gland, with the urethra

Table 13–1 Types of Fistula, Location, and Codes

Type of Fistula	Location	ICD-9-CM Diagnosis Code	CPT® Procedure Code
Vesicovaginal	Bladder to vagina	619.0	51900/57320–57330
Vesicouterine	Bladder to uterus	619.0	51920–51925
Vesicoenteric	Bladder to intestine	596.1	44660–44661
Rectovesical	Bladder to rectum	596.1	45800–45805

passing through the center of the gland. Enlargement of the gland through hypertrophy, tumor, or other condition causes frequency, dribbling, urinary retention, gradual slowing of the urinary stream, and eventual obstruction of the bladder. A cystoscope is inserted through the urethra and obstructive or excess tissue is removed through laser ablation, vaporization, cutting, or fulguration. Other minor procedures are often performed at the same time and may include urethral calibration and dilation, meatotomy, vasectomy, cystourethroscopy, and internal urethrotomy. Code descriptors should be read carefully to determine if minor procedures are bundled into the primary procedure.

Example: Benign prostatic hypertrophy with obstruction, with transurethral resection of the prostate, urethral calibration/dilation and internal urethrotomy

ICD-9-CM diagnosis code: 600.01, benign prostatic hypertrophy with urinary obstruction

Incorrect CPT® procedure: 53000, Urethrotomy; 52601, Transurethral resection of prostate; 53600, Dilation of urethral stricture by passage of sound or urethral dilator, male; initial.

Correct CPT® procedure: 52601, Transurethral resection of prostate, including control of postoperative bleeding, complete (vasectomy, meatotomy, cystourethroscopy, urethral calibration and/or dilation and internal urethrotomy are included).

Occasionally, prostate tissue will grow back and cause obstruction in the future, or a flap of prostate tissue left at the time of the original surgery may fall into the urethra and cause obstruction. Second operations for these conditions are assigned specific codes in CPT®, which stipulate the passage of time following the first procedure.

Example:

52620 Transurethral resection; of residual obstructive tissue after 90 days postoperative

52630   of regrowth of obstructive tissue longer than one year postoperative

Table 13.2 illustrates various transurethral acronyms, their meaning and associated procedural codes:

Table 13–2   Transurethral Acronyms, Meanings, and Codes

Acronym	Translation	Description	CPT® Code
TURP	Transurethral resection of prostate	Resection of obstructive tissue using a resectoscope	52500, 52606–52640
TUIP	Transurethral incision of prostate	Widens the urethra with small cuts in the bladder neck	52450
TUVP (minimally invasive)	Transurethral electro-evaporation of the prostate	Evaporation with simultaneous coagulation of blood vessels	52647–52648
TUMT (minimally invasive)	Transurethral microwave therapy	Office based, no anesthesia, using microwave with cooling system	53850
TUNA (minimally invasive)	Transurethral radio-frequency needle ablation	Can be done in the office; needle inserted into prostate heats/shrinks tissue	53852

Urethra

Incision

Codes 53000–53085 describe urethrotomy or urethrostomy; meatotomy, which is the incisional enlargement of the urethral opening; and drainage of abscesses. Codes 53020 and 53025 are meatotomies differentiated by the age of the patient. Use 53025 for meatotomy on an infant and 53020 for a patient other than an infant.

Excision

Codes 53200–53275 describe biopsy of the urethra, excision of the urethra, diverticula, polyps, caruncle, or associated glands. Codes 53230 and 53235 differentiate between excisions of urethral diverticula performed on females vs. males. These two procedures are designated as separate procedures, and thus are bundled into many larger procedures of the same area.

Repair

Plastic repair of the urethra (urethroplasty) is commonly performed as a staged procedure following removal of neoplasms, following trauma, or for correcting congenital anomalies. Included in this section of CPT® are procedures used to treat incontinence. These include insertion of inflatable bladder neck sphincters and various types of sling procedures for male incontinence.

Manipulation

Codes 53600–53665 involve dilation of the urethra. This section should be read carefully before choosing a code. The unique portion of each code determines whether the procedure is performed on a male or female, if it is an initial or subsequent procedure, or if general or spinal anesthesia is used. Many of these codes are easily performed in the physician office.

Modifiers

The most commonly used modifiers and examples are listed below.

Evaluation and Management Modifiers

Modifiers common to the urinary system include 25, which should be appended to any Evaluation and Management code when E/M services are provided at the same time as a minor urinary procedure. If the decision for surgery involves a major procedure the same day, Modifier 57 should be used on the E/M code.

Examples:

1. An established patient came into the office with complaints of slowing urinary stream. An expanded problem-focused history, problem-focused exam, and low complexity medical decision making was dictated. In addition, the urologist performed a subsequent urethral dilation on this female patient.

   Codes submitted:

   ICD-9-CM diagnosis code: 788.62
   CPT® codes: 99213-25 and 53660

2. An 8-year-old female patient was brought into the emergency room after sustaining a urethral tear following a fall onto the bar of a boy's bicycle. After a detailed consult in the emergency room, the urologist decided to repair the injury as soon as an operating room became available.

Codes submitted:
   ICD-9-CM codes: 867.0 and E826.1
   CPT® codes: 99243-57 and 53502

Common Surgical Modifiers

Modifier 22 should be appended to any procedure that requires significant additional time and effort.

Example: Raz procedure performed with extensive adhesions complicating the repair, which added an additional 45 minutes to the procedure.

   CPT® code: 51845-22

Use Modifier 50 with unilateral procedures that are performed bilaterally, unless the code specifies the procedure is done on a paired organ.

Example: Insertion of bilateral indwelling ureteral stents.

   CPT® code: 52332-50

Modifier 51 should be used on secondary procedures that are not bundled into a primary surgery.

Example: Diagnostic cystourethroscopy with biopsy of ureter and insertion of ureteral stent, right side.

   CPT® codes: 52354 and 52332-51

Use Modifier 58 to report staged procedures that are not already designated as staged procedures in the code descriptor. The guidelines for Modifier 58 state: "The physician may need to indicate that the performance of a procedure or service during the postoperative period was (a) planned prospectively at the time of the original procedure (staged); (b) more extensive than the original procedure; or (c) for therapy following a diagnostic surgical procedure. This circumstance may be reported by adding the modifier '58' to the staged or related procedure . . ."

Examples:

1. Removal of urethral stent one week following urethrorrhaphy.
   CPT® code: 52310-58

2. Complete cystectomy for neoplasm with bilateral pelvic lymphadenectomy one week following bladder biopsy via cystoscope.
   CPT® code: 51575-58

3. Instillation of chemotherapy into bladder for recurrent neoplasm, two days following cystostomy.
   CPT® code: 51720-58

EXERCISE 13.4

Instructions: Assign the correct CPT® code(s) for the scenarios along with the appropriate modifier, if required. Some scenarios may involve more than one CPT® code. Modifiers may include those not listed in this chapter.

1. Cystourethroscopy with urethral dilation of stricture. Procedure discontinued due to patient discomfort. _____

2. Established office visit; problem-focused history and problem-focused physical exam with low medical decision making. Change of cystostomy tube was performed at the same time. _____

3. Cystourethroscopy with bilateral ureteral meatotomy. _____

4. Bilateral ureteroneocystostomy with anastomosis of single ureter to bladder. _____

5. Hospital consult with comprehensive history, comprehensive physical exam, and high medical decision making with decision to perform surgery for kidney neoplasm. _____

CHAPTER REVIEW

Instructions: Find the correct ICD-9-CM and/or CPT® codes for each scenario. Do not supply codes for ancillary services, such as lab and x-ray.

1. A patient comes into the ER complaining of severe right-sided flank pain and hematuria. Urinalysis reveals 5–10 WBCs and packed RBCs. The pain started suddenly at 4:30 P.M. Until that point, the patient felt fine. IVP is ordered and demonstrates a calculus at the ureteropelvic junction. The patient is taken to surgery for removal of the calculi and placement of a ureteral stent.

    a. 592.0
    b. 599.0, 592.0
    c. 592.0, 789.00
    d. 599.0, 592.0, 789.00

2. A patient visits his physician for nausea, vomiting, and flu-like symptoms. The patient has an ileostoma due to history of bladder cancer some years ago. Diagnosis of gastroenteritis is made. Circle the diagnosis codes correctly sequenced.

    a. 787.01, 558.9
    b. 558.9, V44.2
    c. 787.01, 558.9, V10.51, V44.2
    d. 558.9, V10.51, V44.2

3. A patient with a left ureteral stent experiences increased pain on that side with hematuria. Cystoscopy indicates migration of the distal stent out of the bladder and into the ureter. Considerable time was spent trying to grasp the end of the stent. The stent was finally replaced and sutured with one 4-0 Prolene stitch distally to hold it into position.

    a. 996.39, 50961, 52332-22
    b. 996.76, 52332
    c. 996.65, 50961, 52332
    d. 996.39, 52332-22

4. An 81-year-old patient is admitted to the hospital with what initially appears to be a pathologic fracture of the hip. X-rays reveal a metastatic lesion in the greater trochanter. A workup is done to search for the primary site. CT of the pelvis reveals a small mass in the bladder. Cystoscopy with biopsy results shows a transitional cell carcinoma of the bladder.

    a. 188.9, 198.5, 52234
    b. 198.5, 188.9, 52204
    c. 198.5, 733.14, 52234
    d. 733.14, 198.5, 188.9, 52204

5. A patient is admitted to outpatient surgery for percutaneous drainage of a perirenal abscess.
   a. 590.2, 50541
   b. 592.0, 50541
   c. 567.2, 50130
   d. 590.2, 50021

6. A patient with cauda equina syndrome with neurogenic bladder comes to the ER with symptoms of acute urinary tract infection. He has an indwelling Foley catheter that is suspected of being the cause of the UTI. Urinalysis shows acute UTI. Urine cultures are taken and the patient is started on antibiotics. An expanded problem-focused history, expanded problem- focused physical exam, and moderate level medical decision making was performed.
   a. 344.61, 599.0, 99282
   b. 596.54, 344.61, 599.0, 99283
   c. 596.4, 599.0, 99282
   d. 599.0, 99283

7. Urethral stricture following TURP.
   a. 598.1
   b. 598.8
   c. 598.2
   d. 598.9

8. Polycystic disease of the kidney, congenital.
   a. 593.2
   b. 753.1
   c. 591
   d. 592.0

9. A patient is three weeks into radiation therapy treatment and is now being admitted for severe radiation cystitis.
   a. 595.82, E926.5
   b. 595.4, E926.3
   c. 595.0, E926.5
   d. 595.2, E926.3

10. A 92-year-old patient is brought to the ER with decreased mentation, fever, and confusion. Cath UA demonstrates Pseudomonas urinary tract infection. Blood is drawn for cultures to rule out septicemia.
    a. 038.43, 780.6
    b. 599.0, 038.43, 780.99
    c. 041.7, 599.0, 780.6
    d. 599.0, 041.7, 780.99

11. Functions of the bladder include:
    a. absorption of excess water
    b. filtration of urine
    c. urine storage and excretion
    d. transport of urine from the kidney

12. The term *urosepsis* should be used to indicate septicemia.
    a. True
    b. False

13. Hypertension has a direct effect on poorly functioning kidneys.
    a. True
    b. False

Case Studies

Case Study 13.1

Preoperative Diagnosis:	Severe endometriosis.
Postoperative Diagnosis:	Same.
Procedure:	Removal of bilateral Double-J pigtail stents.
Anesthesia:	General.
Blood Loss:	Minimal.

Indications

This 38-year-old female is brought back to the operating room three days after a total abdominal hysterectomy for severe, Grade IV endometriosis involving the entire pelvis. At the time, I was called into the operating room midway through the hysterectomy to assist Dr. Smith in locating the ureters. Double-J pigtail stents were placed bilaterally to define the anatomy. The patient is returned to the OR today for removal of the stents.

Procedure

The patient was prepped and draped and placed in the dorsolithotomy position. Her Foley catheter was removed; urine was noted to be light red in color. A #22 French cystoscope was inserted into the bladder, and several 1 cm blood clots were removed. Stents were seen curled bilaterally. The right stent was grasped and easily removed, followed by the left stent. There was no frank bleeding, and the bladder was draining slightly pink-tinged urine at the end of the procedure.

The patient was taken to the recovery room in good condition.

ICD-9-CM code(s): _____

CPT® code(s): _____

Case Study 13.2

Name of Operation:	Right nephrostomy tube placement.
Indication:	Infected nephrostomy catheter. Tube maintenance.

Discussion

The patient is an 83-year-old female with an existing right nephrostomy catheter. This has been in place for approximately three months and now she returns for routine maintenance.

Consent for the procedure was obtained from the patient. The area of the existing catheter was prepped and draped in the usual fashion. Lidocaine was used for local anesthesia. The guidewire was advanced through the existing catheter. It was then removed. A new #10 French nephrostomy catheter was placed with the pigtailed formed in the renal pelvis and locking closed. The catheter was attached to an external drainage device. The patient tolerated the procedure well. The catheter was secured to the skin surface with suture.

ICD-9-CM code(s): _____

CPT® code(s): _____

Case Study 13.3

Preoperative Diagnosis:	Perineal abscess.
Preoperative Diagnosis:	Prostatic abscess with perineal fistula.

Procedure: Complicated incision and drainage of prostatic abscess and urethroplasty.

Anesthesia: Spinal.

Description of Procedure

The patient was placed in the supine lithotomy position after spinal anesthetic had been administered. The perineum was prepped and draped in a sterile fashion. An incision was made in the perineum and carried down through the levators into the perineal space. The urethra could be palpated, and there was a hole in the posterior prostatic urethra. We stayed posterior to the urethra and found the abscessed cavity. This was dissected bluntly. Inside the abscessed cavity we were able to feel the Foley catheter. Cystoscopy was then performed. There was pus coming from the urethra. Cystoscopy revealed the bladder to be unremarkable, but there was a large prostatic abscess cavity in the posterior portion of the prostate undermining the bladder. The area was thoroughly cleaned and tissues were closed in two layers with 2-0 chromic sutures. Care was taken not to wall off and close the abscess cavity. There was good, clear blue flow of indigo carmine through both ureters. The bladder was intact. A new #16-French silastic catheter was inserted using a mandarin catheter guide. No further urine drained out of the perineal wound. The skin was left open to drain. The patient tolerated the procedure well and was taken to the recovery room in stable condition.

ICD-9-CM code(s): _____

CPT® code(s): _____

Case Study 13.4

Preoperative Diagnosis: Meatal stenosis.
Postoperative Diagnosis: Meatal stenosis.
Operation: Urethral meatotomy.

Operative Description

After the patient was identified and placed on the operating table, mask anesthesia was administered and achieved. He was placed in the lithotomy position. He was prepped and draped in the routine sterile fashion after instilling jelly into his urethra. A clamp was placed in the 6 o'clock position on the very stenotic meatus. This was placed at about 4 mm at the 6 o'clock position and left in place for three to five minutes. This was removed and the crushed tissue was then cut with straight scissors. The patient then had antibiotic ointment applied. Anesthesia was reversed and he was taken to the recovery room in good condition.

ICD-9-CM code(s): _____

CPT® code(s): _____

Case Study 13.5

Preoperative Diagnosis: Bladder outlet obstruction.
Postoperative Diagnosis: Bladder outlet obstruction.
Operation: TURP.

Operative Description

After the patient was identified and placed on the operating room table, spinal anesthesia was administered. After achieving adequate level, he was placed in the low dorsal lithotomy position and prepped and draped in routine sterile fashion. After instilling a copious amount of lubricating jelly into the urethra, the cystoscope using a #24 French resectoscopic sheath with Optiray 30 degree lenses was placed. The bladder was trabeculated and unremarkable. There was a large median lobe. Resection was done at the level of the bladder neck and taken to, but not distal to, the verumontanum. All obstructing pieces of prostate were resected. The chips were removed from the bladder using the Ellik evacuator. Electrocautery was used to obtain hemostasis. The scope was removed. The #22 French Foley with continuous bladder irrigation was begun. He was taken to the Recovery Room in good condition.

ICD-9-CM code(s): _____

CPT® code(s): _____

The Male Reproductive System

OBJECTIVES

1. Identify common disease processes and disorders of the male reproductive system.
2. Correctly assign ICD-9-CM codes to male reproductive system diagnoses.
3. Correctly assign CPT® codes to procedural scenarios.
4. Differentiate between open, closed, endoscopic, and laparoscopic approaches to surgical procedures.

TERMINOLOGY AND ACRONYMS

BPH   Benign prostatic hypertrophy.

Condyloma acuminatum   Moist, cauliflower-like clusters of warts on the external genitalia.

HPV   Human papillomavirus.

Hypogonadism   Underdevelopment of the testicles.

Hypospadias   An abnormal opening of the urethra on the underside of the penis.

Leukoplakia   Irregular white patches found on mucous membranes; may become cancerous.

NGU   Nongonococcal urethritis.

Orchiectomy   Removal of the testicle through an incision in the scrotum.

PIN   Prostatic intraepithelial neoplasia.

Priapism   Painful, prolonged erection.

TCA   Trichloracetic acid.

Torsion   Twisting of an organ, such as the testicle or ovary.

ANATOMY

The male reproductive system includes the penis, prostate, and testicles. Spermatogenesis begins inside the testicles within the seminiferous tubules. Immature spermatozoa pass into the epididymis, which is coiled along the outside wall of each testis, then pass into the vas deferens. The vas deferens joins the seminal vesicles to become the ejaculatory duct, which enters the urethra. The prostate, seminal vesicles, and bulbourethral glands secrete hormones, mucous, and sugars to nourish and maintain proper pH for sperm survival.

DISEASE PROCESSES AND ICD-9-CM CODING OF THE MALE REPRODUCTIVE SYSTEM

See Plate 16 in Appendix A for an illustration of the male reproductive system.

Prostatic Hyperplasia

Benign prostatic hypertrophy is an overgrowth of prostatic tissue, common in men over 50. Symptoms include frequency, dribbling, urgency, and incomplete emptying of the bladder. Enlargement of the prostate gland (see Figure 14.1) is measured on a scale of 1–4. Code **BPH** as 600.0x. Fifth-digit assignment identifies whether the benign condition is accompanied by bladder neck obstruction. Use codes for urinary incontinence, 788.30–788.39, when these conditions are documented. Other conditions assigned to category 600 include nodular prostate, 600.1x; benign localized hyperplasia of prostate, 600.2x; cyst of prostate, 600.3; and hyperplasia of prostate, unspecified, 600.9x. The presence or absence of urinary obstruction is crucial to fifth-digit code assignment in this category.

Prostate Inflammation and Other Disorders

Prostatitis and prostatic abscesses are coded to category 601. If an infectious organism is identified as the source of the infection, it should be coded as a secondary code. Other disorders of the prostate are classified in category 602. These include atrophy (shrinking), calculus, congestion, hemorrhage, and dysplasia. Dysplasia of the prostate is a premalignant condition noted on biopsy. Pathology reports, which identify **PIN** I or PIN II, should be coded as 602.3. PIN III is also known as carcinoma *in-situ* of the prostate and is coded to 233.4.

Hydrocele

A *hydrocele* is a painless collection of fluid above the testicle. This can be drained with a needle, but has a tendency to recur. Code hydroceles using code 603 and congenital hydroceles to 778.6. Documentation should be reviewed carefully to determine if the hydrocele is congenital, as this condition is excluded from category 603.

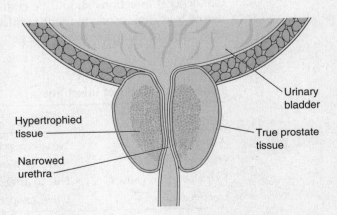

Figure 14–1 Enlargement of the prostate gland.

Orchitis and Epididymitis

Orchitis and *epididymitis* are infections of the testicle and epididymis respectively. Causes of these conditions range from sexual transmission to other infectious disease, such as mumps and tuberculosis. Documentation should be carefully screened to determine if the cause of the infection has been identified. If a specific organism is mentioned, such as *E. coli* or *Staphylococcus,* the organism should be identified in addition to the 604-category code. Fifth-digit subclassification for code 604.9 indicates whether an abscess is present. Subclassification 604.91 instructs the coder to code first any underlying infectious disease such as diphtheria, filariasis, or syphilis and also excludes orchitis due to gonococcus, mumps, tuberculosis, and tuberculous epididymitis.

> **Example:**   A patient is brought into the ER with mumps orchitis.
>
> Incorrect ICD-9-CM code: 604.91, Orchitis and epididymitis in diseases classified elsewhere, and 072.0, Mumps orchitis.
> Correct ICD-9-CM code: 072.0, Mumps orchitis.

Phimosis and Redundant Foreskin

Phimosis is rare among circumcised males. It occurs when the penile foreskin becomes adherent to the glans of the penis, due to infection or congenital origin. This is most common in older uncircumcised men as well as infants and young children. Use code 605 to describe this condition.

Male Infertility

Multiple causes have been identified for male infertility. Fertility rates for Caucasian males have been dropping in the last century worldwide. Category 606 is assigned to all types of male infertility. Table 14.1 demonstrates the types of infertility and specific codes assigned to each. Figure 14.2 shows the basic structure of spermatozoa.

Disorders of the Penis

Category 607 in ICD-9-CM includes various skin disorders and infections of the penis, including **leukoplakia,** boils, ulcers, abscesses, **priapism,** edema, and vascular disorders.

Other Disorders of the Male Genital Organs

Category 608 includes **torsion** of the testicle, atrophy, seminal abscess, and spermatocele. Gonococcal infections should be coded to 098.14–098.34. Code 608.4 directs the coder to use an additional code to identify infectious organisms causing boils or abscesses, if identified. Figure 14.3 shows the male genital organs.

Table 14–1   Types of Infertility

Type of Infertility	Meaning	Code
Azoospermia	No sperm present	606.0
Oligospermia	Reduced number of sperm	606.1
Extra testicular causes	Due to drugs, trauma, infection, chromosome anomaly	606.8
Unspecified	Other unspecified causes	606.9

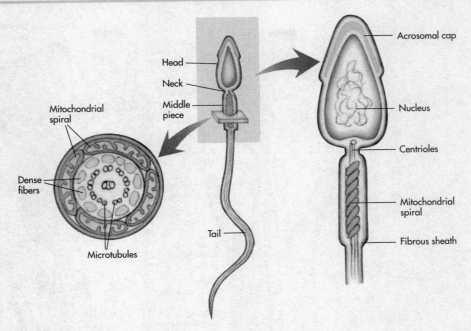

Figure 14–2 Structure of spermatozoa.

Neoplasms

Testicular cancer occurs in approximately 1 percent of American males. The rate of this cancer is thought to be increasing in industrialized countries, along with other reproductive problems such as **hypogonadism** and decreased fertility rates. Worldwide, the lowest rates of testicular cancer are in Africa and Asia. Causes of testicular cancer may be multifactorial, including embryonic, chemical exposure, and a possible weak link to vasectomy. Primary malignancies are coded to category 186. Code carcinoma *in-situ* of the testis to 233.6. Benign neoplasms of the testes are coded to 222.0.

Penile cancer is a relatively rare neoplasm that affects older men, characterized by an ulcer or colored growth on the head of the penis, under the foreskin. Occasionally, it is found on the shaft of the penis. Lymphadenopathy often manifests itself in the groin if the disease has metastasized, or spread. Diagnosis is obtained by biopsy or fine needle aspiration and imaging studies. Treatment includes *penectomy*, an excision of the penis or partial penectomy, along with removal of sentinal nodes, if metastasis is present. Prevention of penile cancer includes limiting the number of sexual partners, not smoking, and delaying the onset of sexual activity. Risk factors such as infection with **HPV** (Human Papilloma Virus) and vasectomy are poorly understood at this point. Code primary malignancies of the penis to category 187 and carcinoma *in-situ* to 233.5.

Benign conditions of the penis, such as cysts and skin neoplasms should be coded to 222.1.

EXERCISE 14.1

Instructions: Assign the correct ICD-9-CM diagnosis code to the following neoplasm scenarios.

1. Metastatic bone lesion, pelvic rim, with history of testicular cancer, remote past.

   _____   _____   _____

2. Primary penile cancer, without spread to lymph nodes. _____

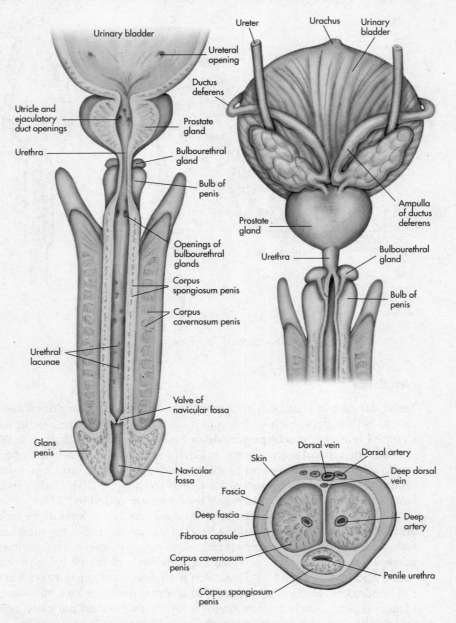

Figure 14–3   Structures of the bladder, prostate gland, and penis.

3. Seminoma, with metastasis to lungs. _____ _____

4. Benign tumor of the epididymis. _____

5. Tumor, skin of scrotum: cell type undetermined. _____

Sexually Transmitted Diseases and Other Infections

Greater than 50 percent of the sexually transmitted diseases in the United States are due to chlamydia infection. This infection may be confused with gonorrhea, since both infections have the same symptoms of pain, burning on urination, and discharge. Women may be asymptomatic, while men experience symptoms rather quickly after infection.

Chlamydia is treated with azithromycin and doxycycline. Code chlamydia infections of the urethra to 099.41. Other sexually transmitted sites are assigned to category 099.

Gonorrhea is most common in people under age 30 and in urban areas more than rural areas. Patients who remain asymptomatic and untreated are at risk for developing complications of skin, joint, and reproductive problems. Category 098 is assigned to gonorrhea. The infections are differentiated by anatomic location. Infections of the upper genitourinary tract are further divided into acute vs. chronic stages. ICD-9-CM instructs that any condition classifiable to 098.1, which is stated as having a duration of two months or more, is considered to be chronic.

The human papilloma virus causes genital warts, as well as other types of cutaneous lesions. Genital warts are sexually transmitted. There is no known cure for HPV; a person who has the virus will always be a carrier of it, even when visible warts are gone. Code these conditions to 079.4 for human papillomavirus, and 078.11 for **condyloma acuminatum.** Use code 078.19 for genital warts, not otherwise specified. Treatment for genital warts depends on the size and severity of the lesion. Conservative treatment consists of topical application of caustic ointments or creams that contain trichloracetic acid (**TCA**) or podophyllin resin. Surgical treatment includes excision, laser, or cryotherapy.

The herpes virus causes an outbreak of blisters or lesions on the external genitalia within several days to two weeks after exposure. Similar to HPV, there is no known cure for herpes, but outbreaks can be controlled with antiviral medications. Genital herpes is also called herpes simplex 2, venereal herpes, or herpes progenitalis. Code unspecified genital herpes to 054.10 and herpetic infection of the penis to 054.13. Other specified types of venereal herpes are coded to 054.19.

EXERCISE 14.2

Instructions: Assign the correct ICD-9-CM code to the infections specified below.

1. Balanoposthitis _____

2. Candidal infection of the scrotum _____

3. Nongonococcal urethritis with chlamydia infection _____ _____

4. "Jock itch" _____

5. Acute gonococcal prostatitis _____

6. Trichomonas urethritis _____

7. Penile herpetic lesions _____

8. Exposure to chlamydia _____

9. Pubic lice _____

10. Abscess of vas deferens _____

11. Postoperative wound infection following vasectomy _____

Complications and Trauma Involving the Male Reproductive System

Surgical complications involving the male reproductive system are assigned to categories 996–999 in ICD-9-CM. Codes commonly encountered for surgical complications include:

■ Mechanical complication of urinary continence device, 996.39
■ Infection and inflammatory reaction due to indwelling catheter, 996.64

- ■ Fibrosis of genitourinary implant, 996.76
- ■ Hematoma complicating vasectomy, 998.12

Traumatic injuries to the male reproductive system are found in the alphabetic index under the main terms crush, burn, amputation, injury, laceration, wound, etc. Be sure to assign E codes describing the surgical misadventure or manner of injury.

EXERCISE 14.3

Instructions: Assign the correct ICD-9-CM diagnosis code(s) and E code to the following scenarios.

1. Injury to testicles following altercation _____ _____

2. Crush injury to scrotum and hip, caught in excavating machinery _____ _____ _____

3. Accidental shotgun wound with multiple pellets in penis, scrotum, and testes _____ _____ _____

4. Contusion of penis after fall off playground equipment _____ _____

V Codes

Common V codes used with the male reproductive system include:

- ■ Personal history of malignant neoplasm of the genital organs, V10.4x
- ■ Family history of malignant neoplasm of the genital organs, V16.4x
- ■ Personal history of other genital system and obstetric disorders, V13.29
- ■ Family history of other genitourinary diseases, V18.7
- ■ Postvasectomy sperm count, V25.8
- ■ Vasoplasty after previous sterilization, V26.0
- ■ Sperm count for fertility testing, V26.21
- ■ Aftercare following vasectomy reversal, V26.22
- ■ Vasectomy status, V26.52
- ■ Acquired absence of genital organs, V45.77
- ■ Other genital problems, V47.5
- ■ Aftercare following surgery of the genitourinary system, V58.76
- ■ Screening for venereal disease, V74.5
- ■ Screening for malignant neoplasms: prostate, V76.44 and testis, V76.45

Depending on documentation, other V codes to be considered include those for counseling on sexually transmitted disease, surgical aftercare, convalescence and palliative care, and high-risk sexual behavior.

EXERCISE 14.4

Instructions: Assign the correct V code to the following diagnostic statements.

1. Personal history of testicular cancer   _____

2. History of hypospadius   _____

3. Admission for vasectomy   _____

4. Sperm count following reversal of vasectomy   _____

5. Vasectomy ten years ago   _____

6. Problems with sexual function   _____

7. Problems with genitals, not specified by provider   _____

8. Routine circumcision   _____

9. Aftercare following surgery to GU system   _____

10. Counseling on STDs   _____

11. Teenager with >5 sexual partners   _____

12. PSA screening   _____

CPT® CODING FOR THE MALE REPRODUCTIVE SYSTEM

Penis

Incision

Only a few codes exist in this section of CPT®. The incision of penis, codes 54000 and 54001, include of the slitting of prepuce, more commonly called the foreskin, for two types of patients—newborn and other than newborn. Slitting the foreskin allows the foreskin to retract over the head of the penis. CPT® also reminds coders not to assign Modifier 63 (Procedures performed on infants less than 4 kg) in conjunction with code 54000.

Use code 54015 for incision and drainage of a deep penile abscess if the incision is deeper than subcutaneous tissue. When the drainage of penile abscess is superficial and involves the skin and subcutaneous tissue, assign codes 10060–10160.

The diagnostic link for these procedures includes conditions such as redundant prepuce and phimosis, disorders of the penis, other specified anomalies of genital organs, and complications due to other specified surgical procedures.

Destruction

The destruction of lesions of the penis can be performed by many different methods. The codes in this section are divided into simple and extensive destruction. Simple methods include electrodessication, cryosurgery, laser surgery, and surgical excision. Use the extensive code when the procedure is time consuming, larger in size, more lesions are involved, or if several different methods are employed.

These procedures may be performed for the following conditions:

- Herpetic infection of penis
- Other diseases due to viruses and chlamydia
- Genital syphilis
- Malignant neoplasm of the penis
- Secondary malignant neoplasm of the genital organs
- Benign neoplasm of the penis
- Carcinoma *in-situ* of the penis
- Neoplasms of unspecified nature of the genitourinary organs
- Disorders of the skin and subcutaneous tissue including dyschromia and vitiligo

Excision

The excision procedure codes begin with biopsy and increase in invasiveness through code 54135. These procedures include biopsies; excision of plaque; simple, with graft up to 5 cm in length and greater than 5 cm in length; removal of foreign body; and varying degrees of amputation, including lymphadenectomy. These procedures are performed for conditions and diseases such as

- Viruses and chlamydia
- Congenital syphilis
- Genital syphilis
- Gonococcal infections
- Neoplasms of the penis and genital organs
- Disorders of the penis

Another procedure included in this section is circumcision. Circumcision is the removal of the foreskin of the penis. Table 14.2 demonstrates the various types of circumcision by age of patient and the codes that are assigned to each.

The lysis or excision of penile postcircumcision adhesions, repair of incomplete circumcision, and frenulotomy of the penis are the remaining procedures described in this section. The *frenulum* of the penis is the membrane that attaches the foreskin to the glans and shaft of the penis, and thus, a *frenulotomy* is an incisional release of this membrane. Diagnostic codes linked to these procedures include surgical complications and phimosis.

Introduction

The procedures in this section describe the treatment or study of specific conditions of the penis. *Peyronie's disease*, ICD-9-CM code 607.85, is a toughening of the spongy body of the penis, which causes a painful curvature. The treatment for this condition consists of injection of medication into the fibrous tissue or incision in the dorsum of the penis followed by injection directly into the abnormal fibrous tissue.

Irrigation of corpora cavernosa for priapism involves the aspiration of blood from the spongy tissue of the penis and replacing it with 20 to 30 ml of saline or medication. Erectile dysfunction can be evaluated by injecting the *corpora cavernosa*—the spongy tissue of the penis—with contrast and observing the blood flow under diagnostic imaging, with and without a constricting band around the penis. When studying the dynamic cavernosometry, the injection of vasoactive drugs is used to evaluate leakage between diastolic and systolic pressure of the penis. The injection of the corpora cavernosa with pharmacologic drugs is used to produce an erection. A penile plethysmography is performed to

Table 14–2   Types of Circumcision by Age

Method	Age of Patient	Diagnosis Examples	CPT® Code
Clamp	Newborn	Routine circumcision, V50.2	54150
Clamp	Other than newborn	Routine circumcision, V50.2; Phimosis, 605; Disorders of penis, 607.x	54152
Surgical excision other than clamp, device, or dorsal slit	Newborn	Routine circumcision, V50.2	54160
Surgical excision other than clamp, device, or dorsal slit	Other than newborn	Routine circumcision, V50.2; Phimosis, 605; Disorders of penis, 607.x	54161

measure the volume of an organ and the amount of blood passing through it in order to determine the volume of blood needed to attain and maintain an erection. The nocturnal penile tumescence and/or rigidity test monitors the nighttime erection during sleep and is performed either in a sleep center or in the patient's home.

Examples of diagnostic links for these procedures include:

- Disorders of the pituitary gland and hypothalamus
- Testicular dysfunction
- Specific disorders of sleep
- Disorders of the penis
- Other general symptoms
- Personal history of malignant neoplasm of other specified male genital organs
- Problems with sexual function
- Other specified examinations

Repair

An abnormal curvature of the penis, or *chordee*, can be surgically corrected. A **hypospadias** is a urethral opening that is in an abnormal location, such as on the bottom or side of the penis. Almost two dozen codes exist in CPT® that describe various types of repairs for a chordee/hypospadias, depending upon the degree of repair that is required. These procedures can include several stages, meatal advancement, local skin flaps, skin grafts, and the correction of complications such as fistula, stricture, and diverticula.

Diagnoses that support these procedures include:

- Hypospadias
- Urethral stricture
- Urinary tract infection
- Phimosis
- Disorders of the penis
- Congenital chordee

Code 54360 describes surgical treatment specifically to correct the angulation of the penis. This is accomplished by using a series of excisions of tissue on the side of the penis. This procedure is performed primarily for

- Acute gonococcal infection of the lower genitourinary tract
- Disorders of the penis
- Penile anomalies

Codes 54380–54390 describe the surgical repair of *epispadias*, which is the congenital absence of the upper wall of the urethra. This procedure can be for epispadias alone or with incontinence or exostrophy of the bladder. The repair is performed using the reapproximation of tissue and skin grafts. Epispadias and congenital urinary system anomalies are the most common diagnoses associated with these procedures.

Codes 54400–54417 describe the insertion, repair, and removal of different types of penile prostheses. A penile prosthesis consists of a noninflatable semi-rigid or multicomponent prosthesis. A multicomponent prosthesis contains a reservoir, pump, and two inflatable cylinders. The diagnostic link for these procedures includes:

- Psychosexual dysfunctions
- Disorders of the penis

■ Disorders of the male genital organs
■ Late effects of injuries to the nervous system
■ Surgical complications
■ Personal history of malignant neoplasm of the male genital organ

Codes 54420–54435 describe the treatment of priapism by use of a shunt to divert blood from the penis to the femoral vein or an adjacent region.

Code 54440 describes the surgical treatment for an injury to the penis. This repair can include skin grafts, tissue grafts, urethral repair, extensive debridement, microsurgical repairs, or various combinations of methods. This procedure is performed specifically for trauma, including open wounds to the genital organs, traumatic amputation, and crush injury.

Manipulation

Congenital phimosis and adherent prepuce are corrected by manipulation of the foreskin, lysis of adhesions, and stretching, which allows the foreskin to retract. This is accomplished with the use of a clamp. Use code 54450 for this procedure.

EXERCISE 14.5

Instructions: Assign the correct CPT® codes to the scenarios below.

1. A patient is seen in the office and is treated for condyloma acuminatum with cryosurgery. _____

2. A pediatrician performs a circumcision on a newborn in the office using the clamp method. _____

3. A patient with a history of erectile dysfunction has a nocturnal penile tumescence test and is found to have testicular feminization. _____

4. A patient with hypospadias has a one-stage perineal surgical repair with chordee correction and urethroplasty using an island flap. _____

5. Following scenario 4, one month later, the patient develops a urethral diverticulum, requiring surgical repair. _____

Testis

Excision

Excisional procedures for the testis in CPT® begin with needle or incisional biopsies. Codes become increasingly more invasive as they describe excision of lesions and continue through the **orchiectomy** codes. The orchiectomy procedures are divided into simple, partial, and radical excisions. Radical orchiectomies are performed for tumors, using either an inguinal approach or abdominal exploration. Diagnoses associated with these procedures include infectious diseases, neoplasms, orchitis and epididymitis, anomalies of the genital organs, open wounds and injuries, and prophylactic organ removal.

Codes 54550 and 54560 describe the exploration for undescended testis, either inguinal/scrotal or abdominal. This is performed by an incision in the lower pelvic or inguinal area. Once the testis is located, several surgical options are available and may include several stages.

Repair

Repairs are performed on the testis to treat torsion of the testis or spermatic cord by either reduction or fixation, which anchors the testis to the inside wall of the scrotum.

Orchiopexy is the surgical fixation of an undescended testicle into the scrotum. This is performed using an inguinal approach and includes a hernia repair when performed or with an abdominal approach. Orchiopexies are commonly performed for neoplasms, congenital anomalies, and history of testicular malignancy.

Testicular prostheses are inserted for cosmetic reasons due to the acquired absence of genital organs described in ICD-9-CM code V45.77. Use code 54660 for insertion of prosthesis as a separate procedure.

An injury to the testis can occur as a result to blunt or penetrating injury. Code 54670 describes the repair of testicular injury or removal of devitalized tissue by sharp dissection. A drain can also be placed to prevent the accumulation of fluid and blood in the scrotum.

Transplantation of a testis under the skin of the thigh is done to preserve function and viability of the testis due to massive injury or surgical loss of the scrotal skin. This procedure is performed for neoplasms of the penis and other male genital organs, open wounds, traumatic amputation of the penis, crush injuries, and burns.

EXERCISE 14.6

Instructions: Assign the correct CPT® codes for the scenarios listed below.

1. A patient finds a suspicious lump on the right testicle and is scheduled for surgery. The surgeon performs an incisional biopsy and the specimen is sent to pathology for a frozen section analysis. Malignancy of the testicle is confirmed and the surgeon continues the surgery with and orchiectomy through the scrotal incision and insertion of prosthesis. _____

2. A patient is brought into the Emergency Room after slipping and falling trying to board his yacht. The patient's foot slipped on the boat ladder and he straddled the dock as he fell, sustaining a crush injury to the testis. He required repair but the testis were intact and an orchiectomy was not required. _____

Laparoscopy

Procedures on the testes can be performed laparoscopically. Typically, a laparoscopic procedure is better tolerated and requires less recovery time than an open procedure. Smaller instruments are also less traumatic to the tissues.

Formula for Success

1. A surgical laparoscopy always includes the diagnostic laparoscopy.
2. Use code 49320 to report a diagnostic laparoscopy as a separate procedure.

The codes in this section describe orchiectomy, the removal of a one or both testicles through a laparoscope, and orchiopexy for the fixation of undescended intra-abdominal testicle(s).

Epididymis

Incision

I&D of the epididymis, testis, and/or scrotal space are performed through a small incision into the skin of the scrotum. This is performed to drain abscesses or hematomas. Use code 54700 to report this service.

Excision

The excision procedures for the epididymis begin with the least invasive—needle biopsy—and become increasingly more complex. Documentation should be carefully read to determine whether the procedure was done with or without biopsy, with or without epididymectomy, and unilaterally or bilaterally.

Repair

The repair procedures consist of an epididymovasostomy, anastomosis of epididymis to the vas deferens. This procedure can be performed either unilaterally or bilaterally. When the bilateral repair is performed, a Modifier 50 should not be used. This procedure is the surgical treatment for an obstruction of the flow of spermatozoa from the epididymis to vas deferens.

Diagnostic linkage for all procedures performed on the epididymis includes conditions such as tuberculosis of the epididymis, diphtheria and syphilis involving the epididymis, acute gonococcal epididymo-orchitis, filarial infection, neoplasms of the epididymis, orchitis and epididymitis, and congenital anomalies of the genital organs.

Tunica Vaginalis

Incision

This section consists of the puncture aspiration of a hydrocele in the tunica vaginalis or along the spermatic cord. The aspiration can include the injection of medication if performed. Use code 55000 when a puncture aspiration is done.

Excision

The excision of a hydrocele, or fluid-filled sac, can be performed either unilaterally or bilaterally. When performed with a hernia repair, the excision of hydrocele is bundled into the larger procedure. Use age-appropriate codes 49495–49501 when a hernia repair is also performed.

Repair

A "bottle-type" tunica vaginalis hydrocele repair is performed by removing the abnormal fluid-filled sac in the scrotum or in the inguinal canal. This procedure is performed for acquired and congenital hydroceles and chylocele.

Scrotum

Incision

Codes 55100–55120 describe incision of the scrotum for the drainage of an abscess or exploration or removal of a foreign body. Code 55100 is very similar to code 54700, I&D of the epididymis, testis, and/or scrotal space. Documentation should be carefully read to distinguish the anatomical structures.

Excision

Resection of the scrotum is performed to remove excessive or diseased scrotal skin. The extent of the procedure can vary due to the disease process. If skin is needed to replace the defect, grafts and flaps may be used from the thigh and are separately reportable.

Repair

Scrotoplasty is the surgical repair of defects and developmental defects. It can be simple or complicated based on the reconstruction if skin, mesh, or pedicle grafts are used.

Diagnostic links for these procedures include neoplasm of the scrotum or genital organs; testicular dysfunction; scrotal varices; orchitis and epididymitis; other disorders of the male genital organs and disorders of skin and subcutaneous tissue, soft tissue; superficial injury to the trunk; congenital anomalies of the genital organs; open wound of genital organs, including traumatic amputation; crush injury of the trunk, external genitalia; and surgical complications.

Vas Deferens

Many of the codes in this small section of CPT® describe procedures that are performed either unilaterally or bilaterally. The coder should note that Modifier 50 should not be appended to procedures that have this option. In addition, some procedures on the vas deferens inherently require the use of the operating microscope, thus code 69990 for the operating microscope should not be assigned.

Incision

An incisional vasotomy can be performed for obtaining a sample of semen or to check patency testing of the tubes.

Excision

Vasectomy can be performed either unilaterally or bilaterally and includes postoperative semen examination. The effectiveness of sterilization is based upon the absence of sperm in the postoperative semen. Use diagnosis code V25.2, Admission for interruption of vas deferens, for this procedure.

Introduction

Vasotomy for vasograms, seminal vesiculograms, or epididymograms is performed to study the patency of spermatozoa-collecting system.

Repair

Vasovasostomy or vasovasorrhaphy is performed as a surgical treatment for blockage of the vas deferens. Semen sampling and studies are done after the injection of dye to determine the exact location of the obstruction. Use code 69990 in addition to the procedure code to report the use of the operating microscope.

Suture

The percutaneous ligation of the vas deferens is a vasectomy without an incision into the skin. A puncture is made with an instrument that ligates and clips each cut end of the vas at the same time.

Spermatic Cord

Excision

Two common conditions are treated by excisional procedures: a hydrocele (fluid-filled sac) and varicocele (abnormal dilation of spermatic cord veins). The excision of a varicocele can be performed by an incision in the pubic area, using an abdominal approach, or with a hernia repair. The coder should take care to distinguish between hydroceles that are congenital, 778.8, and other types found in category 603.

Laparoscopy

The ligation of spermatic veins can be performed laparoscopically to repair conditions such as spermatic cord varicocele, code 456.4.

Formula for Success

1. A surgical laparoscopy always includes the diagnostic laparoscopy.
2. Use code 48320 to report a diagnostic laparoscopy.

Seminal Vesicles

Incision

Vesiculotomy, code 55600, describes an incision or puncture of one of the seminal vesicles that produces fluid mixed with semen produced in the testis. When the procedure requires extensive dissection, use the complicated procedure code, 55605. These codes are unilateral and the Modifier 50 should be appended if a bilateral procedure is performed.

Excision

Vesiculectomy is the removal of one of the seminal vesicles by any approach. The Mullerian duct cyst is a remnant of a prenatal development of the seminal vesicle and may be excised through an incision in the lower abdomen. Bilateral procedures should have Modifier 50 appended to the surgical code. These procedures are performed for malignant neoplasms, seminal vesiculitis, and congenital anomalies.

EXERCISE 14.7

Instructions: Assign the correct CPT® codes for the scenarios below.

1. A couple that has tried to conceive for several years consulted an infertility specialist. The male patient had a low to nonexistent sperm count. Further testing determined that the patient had an atresia of the epididymis. He elected to undergo a microsurgical re-anastomosis of the epididymis to the vas deferens to correct his infertility. _____

2. A patient is seen in the physician's office for an infected hydrocele of the tunica vaginalis. The physician performs a puncture aspiration and injection of antibiotics. _____

3. A patient is seen for a lesion on the scrotum. The lesion is suspicious-looking and the decision is made to perform a surgical resection of the lesion. The pathology report confirms a benign lesion of the skin of the scrotum. _____

4. A male patient is seen in the physician's office requesting to be sterilized. The physician counsels the patient on the permanency of the procedure and provides the patient with written information on the procedure. The physician performs a bilateral vasectomy on the patient the following week. _____

5. A surgeon performs an open recurrent inguinal hernia repair on a 30-year-old male and finds a lipoma of the spermatic cord, which he removes at the same operative session. _____

6. A patient receives surgical treatment for a Mullerian duct cyst. _____

Prostate

Incision

Code 55700 describes prostatic biopsy performed by needle or punch method and includes a single biopsy or multiple biopsies obtained at the same time. An incisional biopsy is coded with 55705. Both techniques can be performed by any approach. Prostatotomy is the method used for the external drainage of a prostatic abscess either simple or complicated. There are two usual approaches: a puncture through the perineum or the advancement of a needle into the rectum.

Excision

Prostatectomies can be performed by a number of different methods and vary in the degree of tissue removed. The prostatectomy procedure codes describe the following methods.

Prostatectomy, perineal. This method is performed through an incision in the perineum. The opening of the urethra is enlarged (meatotomy) and the diameter of the penile urethra is enlarged (internal urethrotomy). The prostate is removed through the perineum with the help of a tractor instrument placed in the urethra. The procedure can be subtotal or radical and can include lymph node biopsy and lymphadenectomy in addition to the basic procedure.

Prostatectomy, suprapubic or retropubic. This method is performed through an incision in the lower abdomen just above the pubic area. This procedure code includes the meatotomy and internal urethrotomy. Through the abdominal incision, the prostate is dissected and removed. The procedure is subtotal.

Prostatectomy, retropubic, radical. This method is performed through an incision in the lower abdomen, and the entire prostate gland, seminal vesicles, and portions of the vas deferens are removed by blunt dissection. This procedure can be performed with a lymph node biopsy or pelvic lymphadenectomy in addition to the basic procedure.

Table 14.3 describes the types of prostatectomies and different formats.

The transperineal placement of needles or catheters into the prostate for interstitial radioelement application is a form of *brachytherapy*. Brachytherapy is the application of radioactive isotope capsules for internal radiation treatments. The capsules are placed with ultrasound or fluoroscopic guidance. Radiology codes 77776–77778 or 76965 are reported separately in addition to the procedure.

Code 55860 describes exposure of the prostate by any approach for the insertion of radioactive substance, performed through an abdominal incision. A needle is placed into the prostate tumor, and radioactive seeds are placed. This procedure can be performed with a lymph node biopsy or lymphadenectomy in addition to the basic procedure.

Table 14–3   Types of Prostatectomies by Format

Type of Prostatectomy	Surgical Approach	Lymph Node Removal	CPT® Code
Subtotal	Perineal	No	55801
	Suprapubic	No	55821
Radical	Perineal	No	55810
	Perineal	Yes	55812, 55815
	Retropubic	No	55840
	Retropubic	Yes	55842, 55845

The diagnostic link for these procedures includes neoplasms of the

- Rectum, rectosigmoid junction, and anus
- Retroperitoneum and peritoneum
- Connective tissue of the pelvis
- Connective tissue and other soft tissue
- Prostate
- Male genital organs

Non-neoplastic conditions may include anal fissures and fistula, abscess of anal and rectal regions, disorders of the intestine and bladder, hyperplasia, inflammation and other diseases of the prostate, male infertility, and other conditions affecting the male reproductive system.

Laparoscopy

A laparoscopic prostatectomy accomplished using the retropubic method cannot be performed on a patient with prior open prostate surgery. This approach is indicated for only a few diagnoses, compared to the open prostatectomy method. Reasons for undergoing a laparoscopic prostatectomy include only neoplasms of the prostate—malignant, benign, *in-situ*, uncertain behavior—and neoplasms of unspecified nature of other genitourinary organs.

Formula for Success

1. A surgical laparoscopy always includes the diagnostic laparoscopy.
2. Use code 48320 to report a diagnostic laparoscopy.

Other Procedures

Electroejaculation, described by code 55870, is the use of an electrovibratory device to stimulate ejaculation for artificial insemination. The diagnostic link for this procedure includes psychosexual dysfunction, other paralytic syndromes, and impotence of organic origin.

Code 55873 describes cryosurgical ablation of the prostate that is performed using a cryoprobe. With the use of ultrasonic guidance, the probe is inserted into the rectum, and needles are placed through the perineum and into the prostate. Dilators are inserted over the needle guidewires, which are removed, and a cryoprobe is inserted. The prostate is completely frozen and destroyed by this method. Use diagnosis code 185, Prostate cancer, with this procedure.

Intersex Surgery

Two codes in this section describe a series of staged procedures where the male/female genitalia are reversed. In the male-to-female procedure, 55970, the male genitals are removed and female external genitals are formed. In the female-to-male procedure, code 55980, a penis and scrotum are formed from pedicle flap and free grafts. Use diagnosis codes from category 302, Sexual disorders; category 752, Congenital genital organ anomalies; and category 758, Chromosomal anomalies to link with these procedures.

Modifiers

Evaluation and Management Modifiers

Modifiers common to the male reproductive system include 25, which should be appended to any Evaluation and Management code when E/M services are provided at the same time as a minor procedure. If the decision for surgery involves a major procedure the same day, Modifier 57 should be used on the E/M code.

Common Surgical Modifiers

■ Modifier 50, for bilateral procedures. Use this modifier when bilateral procedures are performed on a paired organ.

Example: A bilateral, simple orchiectomy is done prophylactically for a patient with primary prostatic carcinoma.

ICD-9-CM Diagnosis: Prostate cancer, 185
CPT® Procedure: Simple orchiectomy, with or without testicular prosthesis, 54520-50

■ Modifier 58, Staged or related procedure or service by the same physician during the postoperative period.

Example: A radical perineal prostatectomy performed two days following a punch biopsy of the prostate, which revealed malignancy.

ICD-9-CM Diagnosis: Prostate cancer, 185
CPT® Procedure: Radical perineal prostatectomy, 55810-58

■■■ *CHAPTER REVIEW* ■■■

Instructions: Assign the correct ICD-9-CM and CPT® codes for the scenarios below.

1. A circumcision by excision on a 60-year-old man for recurrent cellulitis of the foreskin.
   a. 607.2, 54152
   b. 682.9, 54160
   c. 682.9, 54161
   d. 607.2, 54161

2. A patient has a laparoscopic orchiectomy for testicular cancer performed. Pathology confirms the malignancy.
   a. 185, 54690
   b. 186.9, 54690
   c. 186.9, 54530
   d. 186.0, 54692

3. The excision of a hydrocele is bundled into an inguinal hernia repair for an adult male.   **T or F**

4. The code for a routine vasectomy is located in the section for the vas deferens.   **T or F**

5. A patient is scheduled for a subtotal suprapubic prostatectomy. Assign the correct CPT® code.
   a. 55810
   b. 55840
   c. 55821
   d. 55831

Case Study

Case Study 14.1

Preoperative Diagnosis:	Symptomatic left varicocele.
Postoperative Diagnosis:	Symptomatic left varicocele.
Operation:	Left inguinal varicocelectomy.

Operative Description

After the patient was identified, he was placed on the operating table. General endotracheal anesthesia was administered, and he was then placed in the supine position, shaved, prepped, and draped in the routine sterile fashion. We made a small skin incision approximately 2.5 cm in length halfway between the anterior leg supine and the pubic tubercle. This was taken down sharply through the Scarpa's fascia until the fascia external bleed was identified. This was incised about 3 cm in length. The cord was dissected free using blunt dissection and DeBakey's until the offending veins were visualized. There were three large veins. These were isolated from other vascular structures, taking care not to injure the arteries or the veins. These three offending veins were then tied off and sectioned out. Then 3-0 silk was used to tie these off. The cord remained in anatomic position at the end of the procedure. The fascia was closed using interrupted 2-0 Vicryl. This was followed by 3-0 Chromic on the Scarpa's followed by staples. A compressive dressing was applied before closing the skin. Marcaine 5 cc. 0.5% without epinephrine was injected into the field block of the anterior iliac spine. After placing a compressive dressing, anesthesia was reversed. The patient was extubated and taken to the recovery room in good condition.

ICD-9-CM Diagnosis code: _____

CPT® Procedure code: _____

The Female Reproductive System

▮ OBJECTIVES

1. Understand common disease processes of the female reproductive system.
2. Correctly assign ICD-9-CM codes to female reproductive system diagnoses.
3. Correctly assign CPT® codes to procedural scenarios.
4. Recognize diagnosis and procedural codes assigned by gender.

▮ TERMINOLOGY AND ACRONYMS

BUS Bartholin's, urethral, and Skene's glands.

Curettage Therapeutic or diagnostic scraping of the uterine cavity with instruments.

DUB Dysfunctional uterine bleeding.

Dysmenorrhea Painful menstruation.

ECC Endocervical curettage.

Endometriosis Aberrant growth of uterine lining outside the uterus.

HRT Hormone replacement therapy.

IUD Intrauterine device.

LEEP Loop electrosurgical excision procedure.

Menometrorrhagia Abnormal or heavy menstruation.

Menorrhagia Excessive menstruation.

Menses/menstruation Monthly discharge of bloody fluid from the uterus.

Metrorrhagia Bleeding unrelated to the menstrual cycle.

Mittleschmerz Ovulation pain.

PID Pelvic inflammatory disease.

PMS Premenstrual syndrome.

ANATOMY

The female reproductive system includes the following organs:

- Internal
  - Uterus
  - Ovary
  - Fallopian tubes
  - Vagina
- External
  - Vulva: Labia majora and labia minora
  - Clitoris
  - Vestibule: Urethral meatus, Bartholin's, and Skene's glands
  - Vaginal orifice

See Anatomy Plate 17 in Appendix A for anatomical charts of the female reproductive system.

The ovaries lie on either side of the uterus, deep within the pelvic cavity. The *fallopian tubes* arise out of the *fundus,* or top of the uterus, in an area called the *adnexa.* Fallopian tubes extend from either side of the uterus toward the ovaries, and finger-like protrusions called *fimbria* overlie the top of each ovary. The ovary produces one or more eggs, known as *ovum* or *ova,* in a regular monthly cycle known as the menstrual cycle. When an ovum is released by the ovary into the pelvic cavity, the fimbriated ends of the fallopian tubes help to sweep the egg into the opening of the tube, where it travels toward the innermost area, or *body,* of the uterus. If fertilization takes place, the ovum implants itself in the thickened lining of the uterus. When fertilization does not occur, the lining of the uterus is sloughed off during **menstruation,** and the cycle starts over again.

The uterus is a thick-walled, muscular organ that stretches to accommodate a full-term fetus and contracts to push the fetus out. The distal-most portion of the uterus is called the *cervix,* which dilates to allow the passage of the fetus during childbirth.

The cervix contains cells that are sampled to microscopically screen for cervical or endometrial cancer. Other conditions—such as *Nabothian cysts,* cervicitis, and *HPV (human papilloma virus)*—can be seen on colposcopic exam of the cervix.

The vagina is also known in layman's terms as the *birth canal.* This also stretches large enough to allow for passage of an infant.

The vestibule contains the Bartholin gland, urethra, and Skene's gland, together known by the acronym, **BUS.** Both the Bartholin and Skene's glands are responsible for lubrication of the vagina. Skene's glands are located just inside the urethral meatus, and the Bartholin's glands are located on either side of the vaginal opening, or *introitus.*

DISEASE PROCESSES AND ICD-9-CM CODING OF THE FEMALE REPRODUCTIVE SYSTEM

Inflammatory Disease of the Pelvic Organs

Categories 614–616 in ICD-9-CM classify inflammatory conditions of the internal female reproductive system. Both acute and chronic conditions are addressed. Specific instructions at the beginning of this section tell the coder to use an additional code to identify any responsible organism, such as *Staphylococcus* or *Streptococcus.* Excluded from these codes are any conditions that are associated with pregnancy, abortion, childbirth, or postpartum state. Codes for excluded conditions are cross-referenced to categories 630–676.9. Each individual code should also be checked for excludes notes specific to that code.

Salpingitis and *oophoritis* are infections of the fallopian tubes and ovaries. ICD-9-CM makes the distinction between the acute condition, 614.0; chronic condition, 614.1; and also salpingitis and oophoritis that is not specified as acute, subacute, or chronic, 614.2. Subacute conditions should be coded as acute. Excluded from code 614.2 are those infections that are caused by tuberculosis or gonococcus.

Pelvic inflammatory disease (**PID**) is a nonspecific, generalized infection assigned to 614.9. This condition may be caused by an unidentified sexually transmitted disease. It is treated with antibiotics and pelvic rest. Patients who have had PID multiple times, or inappropriately treated PID, are at higher risk of infertility, as well as spontaneous abortions.

Endometritis is an infection of the uterus, which is more common following delivery. Category 615 excludes endometritis following delivery or complicating pregnancy. Also excluded is hyperplastic endometritis, which is cross-referenced to code 621.3x. Category 615 distinguishes between acute and chronic conditions, and also unspecified types of endometritis. Endometritis should not be confused with **endometriosis,** a condition in which endometrial tissue grows abnormally outside the uterine cavity.

Vaginitis can have several causes. *Monilial* or *candidal infections*, also known as yeast infections, present with a thick, cheesy, malodorous vaginal discharge. Yeast infections should be coded to 112.1. These infections commonly occur as a side effect of antibiotic treatment, which eliminates the normal bacterial flora of the vagina and allows yeast to proliferate. Bacterial infections also produce a malodorous discharge and may be due to specific bacteria, such as staph or *E. coli.* Organisms that are identified should be coded in addition to code 616.10. Excluded from this category is noninfective leukorrhea and postmenopausal or atrophic vaginitis, which are cross referenced to 623.5 and 627.3, respectively.

> **Example:** Staph vaginitis.
>
> ICD-9-CM diagnosis codes: 616.10, Vaginitis and vulvovaginitis, unspecified, and 041.1, Staphylococcus infection.

Code 616.11, Vaginitis and vulvovaginitis in diseases classified elsewhere, includes infections caused by other diseases. The underlying disease should be coded first, with the vaginitis coded as a secondary diagnosis.

Endometriosis

Endometriosis, as previously described, is aberrant tissue normally found in the lining of the uterus that has implanted on various organs. The exact cause of endometriosis is unknown, but it does tend to run in families and may be due in part to immune system dysfunction and exposure to toxins. Category 617 classifies endometriosis by site. The coder should read documentation carefully because more than one site of implantation is common.

> **Example:** Endometriosis implants found on the bladder and intestine during laparoscopy.
>
> ICD-9-CM diagnosis codes: 617.8 and 617.5.

Genital Prolapse

Genital prolapse is common in women who have borne children, who are obese, or who suffer from severe muscle strain. Prolapse is caused by a weakening of the pelvic muscles, which allows the uterus and/or vaginal walls to prolapse into the vagina. Category 618 instructs the coder to use an additional code for urinary incontinence as an additional code. This may not be present in all cases, but is expected with many types of genital prolapse. The type of prolapse should be specified, as well as the degree of prolapse, i.e., incomplete, complete, or unspecified.

Example: Second degree uterine prolapse, with erosion and cervicitis due to trauma from clothing.

ICD-9-CM diagnosis codes: 618.1, Uterine prolapse without mention of vaginal wall prolapse, and 616.0, Cervicitis and endocervicitis.

Noninflammatory Disorders of the Cervix, Vagina, and Vulva

Category 622 describes noninflammatory disorders of the cervix; code 622.1x, Dysplasia of the uterine cervix, describes specific abnormal pap smear or biopsy findings. Dysplasia is an abnormal condition with disordered growth of cervical cells. Several systems have been developed by pathologists to classify the types of abnormal cells, including the Bethesda system and CIN system. The classification systems are not always equivalent with each other and some laboratories interpret the guidelines for grading pap smears more strictly than others. This causes great confusion among patients—and coders.

Example:

Low-grade squamous intraepithelial dysplasia (LGSIL), 622.11

Cervical intraepithelial neoplasia, CIN II, 622.12

Cervical dysplasia, 622.10

Fourth-digit categories for different anatomical areas of dysplasia (cervix, vagina, vulva) contain similar terms. The terms dysplasia, leukoplakia, laceration, stricture or stenosis, polyp, and hematoma are used in repetitive fashion in categories 622, 623, and 624. Generally speaking, conditions that complicate labor and delivery, carcinoma *in-situ*, infections, and congenital problems are excluded from these three categories. The coder should read the Excludes notes carefully for cross-references to these specific conditions elsewhere.

Pelvic Pain

Category 625 describes different types of pain associated with the female reproductive organs. Generalized pelvic pain, not otherwise specified is coded to 625.9. Other diagnoses included in this rubric include ovulation pain, or **mittleschmerz**, dysmenorrhea, **PMS**, and stress incontinence. Excluded from code 625.6, Stress incontinence, female, are codes for mixed incontinence, 788.33, and stress incontinence, male, 788.32.

Disorders of Menstruation

Category 626 describes disorders of menstruation and abnormal bleeding. These conditions include menstruation that is too frequent, infrequent, absent, irregular, dysfunctional, or associated with puberty and postcoital bleeding. An Excludes note at the beginning of this category eliminates Menopausal and premenopausal bleeding, 627.0; Pain and other symptoms associated with the menstrual cycle, 625.2–625.4; and Postmenopausal bleeding, 627.1.

Menopause and Postmenopausal Disorders

Menopausal disorders are categorized in rubric 627. Excluded from 627 is Asymptomatic age-related or natural postmenopausal status, V49.81. Not all menopausal conditions are associated with bleeding disorders. Besides premenopausal and postmenopausal bleeding, this category includes atrophic vaginitis, hot flashes, insomnia, fatigue, and other symptoms associated with either artificial or natural menopause.

Example:

1. A patient presents who is status post menopause, currently without symptoms, V49.81.
2. A 56-year-old patient presents with hot flashes, fatigue, and mood swings. She is prescribed hormone replacement therapy, 627.2, Symptomatic menopausal or female climacteric states, and V07.4, Postmenopausal hormone replacement therapy.

Infertility

Codes for female infertility are found in category 628. Physicians differentiate types of infertility as primary and secondary. Primary infertility is defined as the inability of a woman to conceive for the first time. Secondary infertility is defined as the inability of a woman to conceive after having at least one child. Codes in this section are divided into the originating site of infertility: tubal, uterine, or cervical. Use code 628.0, Infertility associated with *anovulatory cycle,* when a patient does not ovulate. Code 628.1 should be assigned if a pituitary or hypothalamic origin can be determined. Instructions under 628.1 tell the coder to code the underlying cause first.

Example: Primary infertility due to polycystic ovarian syndrome.

ICD-9-CM diagnosis codes: 628.0, Infertility associated with anovulation and 256.4, Polycystic ovaries.

EXERCISE 15.1

Instructions: Link the correct diagnosis code to the appropriate surgical procedure. Both ICD-9-CM and CPT® code books should be referenced for full descriptions of each code.

1. 58104, Myomectomy, excision of fibroid tumor   _____
2. 56440, Marsupialization of Bartholin's cyst   _____
3. 57454, Colposcopy with biopsy   _____
4. 58120, D&C, nonobstetrical   _____
5. 58240, Pelvic exenteration for gynecological malignancy   _____
6. 58672, Laparoscopic fimbrioplasty   _____
7. 57284, Paravaginal defect repair   _____
8. 58300, Insertion of IUD   _____

ICD-9 Codes:

795.00	V25.1	218.9	626.2
618.3	616.2	628.2	182.0

Neoplasms

There are multiple types of malignant neoplasms of the uterus, vagina, ovaries, and fallopian tubes. Most of those involving the uterus and ovaries are influenced by hormones and/or genetics. Certain genetic markers are now known to predispose women to certain types of ovarian cancer.

Endometrial carcinoma is the fourth most common type of cancer in women. Abnormal bleeding often brings patients in for treatment, which is quite successful when caught in the early stages. Risk factors for endometrial carcinoma include obesity, years of menstruation, irregular ovulation, estrogen replacement therapy, and nulliparity.

Fibromas are benign, connective tissue tumors that are commonly found in the uterus, but also grow in the ovaries. Treatment includes excision of the fibroma, hysterectomy or oophorectomy. Fibromas, also known as *leiomyomas,* are coded to category 218. Figure 15.1 shows uterine fibroid tumors. Fourth digits are assigned based on the location of the tumor:

- Submucous: Located just below the inner lining of the uterus, 218.0
- Intramural: Located within the muscular layer of the uterus, 218.1
- Subserous: Located just below the outer surface of the uterus, 218.2

Ovarian cancer does not produce outward signs of any abnormality and is often diagnosed at a much later stage than uterine cancers. Only about 25 percent of ovarian malignancies are diagnosed at an early stage. Symptoms of ovarian cancer include dull ache and pelvic pain, nausea, vomiting, bloating, and a change in bowel habits. Table 15.1 demonstrates the various types of ovarian tumors, both malignant and benign.

Teratomas are derived from the egg-producing part of the ovary. Both the benign and malignant forms of teratoma include tissue that resembles respiratory cells, bone, hair, teeth, and other irregularly placed tissue. Older women are more at risk of developing a benign, mature form of teratoma, while younger women and girls have a greater chance of developing the malignant form.

Malignant neoplasms of the female reproductive system are classified to categories 179–184 of ICD-9-CM and are arranged by anatomical site. Carcinoma *in-situ* is excluded from these codes, since it is not a true invasive malignancy. As with any neoplasm, the pathology report should be checked to confirm the behavior of the neoplasm before coding.

Unless specified as such, ovarian cysts are not considered neoplasms. These are classified in category 617 or 620 as follows:

- 617.1, Endometriosis of ovary
- 620.0, Follicular cyst of ovary

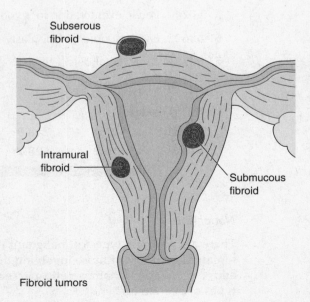

Figure 15–1   Common locations of uterine fibroids.

Table 15–1   Types of Ovarian Tumors

Cell Type	Origin	Characteristics
Stromal	Ovarian connective tissue—produces estrogen and progesterone	Includes fibromas, thecomas and low-grade, slower growing cancers.
Epithelial	Cells found on the outer surface of the ovary	Most common and aggressive type of ovarian cancer; approximately 85 percent of all ovarian cancers are this type.
Germ	Ova-producing cells	Most are benign, although teratomas have both benign and malignant forms.

- 620.1, Corpus luteum cyst or hematoma
- 620.2, Other and unspecified ovarian cyst

Category 620.2 excludes conditions such as cystadenoma and polycystic ovaries, which are cross-referenced to different chapters of ICD-9-CM.

Example:

Chocolate cyst of the ovary, 617.0

Hemorrhagic corpus luteum cyst, 620.1

Benign serous cystadenoma, 220

Polycystic ovarian disease, 256.4

EXERCISE 15.2

Instructions: Assign the correct ICD-9-CM code to the diagnoses listed below.

1. Malignant hydatidiform mole   _____

2. Admit for chemo for uterine cancer with metastasis to bone   _____

3. Benign ovarian teratoma   _____

4. Metastasis to breast, from ovarian primary   _____

5. Carcinoma *in-situ* of the cervix   _____

V Codes

Healthcare services for women encompass a variety of settings and circumstances. A large section of the V codes are devoted to persons encountering health services in circumstances related to reproduction and development. The V codes related to contraceptive management as well as procreative management are discussed below; those related to pregnancy are discussed in Chapter 16.

- Category V25, Encounter for contraceptive management, includes initiation of contraceptive measures, surveillance of previously prescribed contraceptive methods, insertion of implantable subdermal contraceptives, and other types of contraceptive management for both male and female patients. A male patient admitted for a vasectomy and female admitted for tubal ligation are both assigned V25.2 for sterilization. Contraceptive management is typically part of a routine annual "well-woman" exam, which includes a screening pap, pelvic and breast exam. Depending on the patient's age, hormone replacement therapy may be discussed.

■ Category V26, Procreative management, includes genetic counseling and testing, fertility testing, sterilization status, and codes for specific surgical procedures and aftercare. These codes may also be used for either male or female patients, depending on the narrative of the code.

EXERCISE 15.3

Instructions: Assign the correct V code for the scenarios listed below.

1. Annual pap and pelvic exam   _____

2. History of endometriosis   _____

3. Status posthysterectomy ten years ago   _____

4. History of ovarian cancer   _____

5. Screening for venereal disease   _____

6. Fertility testing   _____

7. Negative serum HCG test   _____

8. Refill of birth control pills   _____

9. Admission for tubal ligation   _____

10. Counseling on STDs   _____

11. Promiscuous sexual behavior   _____

12. Follow-up visit, dressing change after Raz procedure _____

13. Norplant® status   _____

14. Postmenopausal status, natural   _____

15. Quarterly administration of Depo Provera shot   _____

CPT® CODING OF THE FEMALE REPRODUCTIVE SYSTEM

Vulva, Perineum, and Introitus

These terms include the entire external female genitalia. This area includes the urethra, Bartholin's and Skene's glands, labia majora and minora, clitoris, and vestibule.

Incision

Incision codes 56405–56420 describe I&D of abcesses of the vulva or Bartholin's glands. An I&D of the Skene's gland is cross-referenced to code 53060, in the Urinary chapter of CPT®. Use code 56440 for the *marsupialization* of a Bartholin's gland or cyst. Marsupialization means that the cyst is evacuated, and the walls of the cyst are sutured to the edges of the skin, creating a small pocket, thus preventing re-formation of the cyst.

Destruction

Lesions of the vulva such as condyloma or plaques can be removed with different methods depending upon the diagnosis. Laser, cryotherapy, chemosurgery, and electrocautery are all used successfully on lesions of the vulva. Use code 56501 for simple destruction and code 56515 for extensive destruction. The physician—not the coder—should make the determination as to complexity of destruction. Do not incorrectly assign dermatology destruction codes on the genitals.

Excision

Single lesion biopsies of the vulva or perineum are described by 56605. Use add-on code 56606 for each additional lesion that is sampled.

> **Example:** A patient had three raised lesions biopsied on the vulva. The pathology report returned showing VIN III.
>
> ICD-9-CM Diagnosis: 233.3
> CPT® Procedure: 56605 × 1 and 56606 × 2

The vulvectomy codes in this section follow similar logic as the prostatectomy codes. They are divided by the complexity of the procedure (simple or radical) and further subdivided by partial or complete procedures and removal of lymph node structures. Coders should carefully read operative reports to determine the extent of lymphadenectomy. These procedures are performed to excise neoplasms.

Code 56740 describes the excision of a Bartholin's cyst, in which the entire cyst is shelled out, and the deep and superficial layers of the cavity are closed with sutures. This is different from a marsupialization because a pocket is not created.

Repair

Codes 56800–56810 describe plastic repairs of the vulva and perineum. These procedures are commonly performed for relaxation of the introitus, prolapse, sex change operations, and repair of congenital defects. Several parenthetical instructions in CPT® cross-reference the coder to other chapters or sections for genital wounds or injuries. Be sure to distinguish this type of repair from obstetrical injuries, which are assigned from the Maternity chapter of CPT®.

> **Example:**
> 1. A patient fell on the balance beam at school, sustaining periurethral and vulvar tears. These were surgically repaired.
>   ICD-9-CM Diagnosis: 878.4
>   CPT® Procedure: 57210
> 2. A 50-year-old female with relaxation of the introitus has a plastic repair performed.
>   ICD-9-CM Diagnosis: 618.82
>   CPT® Procedure: 56800

Colposcopy

A colposcope is a microscope on wheels with special lights that allows the physician to examine the vulva, vagina, and/or cervix under magnification. Colposcopy and colposcopy with biopsy of the vulva are described by codes 56820 and 56821. Read the operative report carefully to determine the correct anatomic site of colposcopy. Separate colposcopy codes are listed under the anatomic headings of vagina and cervix in CPT®.

Vagina

Incision

Use 57020 for a colpocentesis when it is performed as a stand-alone or separate procedure. Use 57000 for an incision of the vagina with exploration and 57010 with drainage of pelvic abscess through a vaginal incision. Since the vagina offers access to structures deep within the pelvis, it is sometimes used as an approach to drain a pelvic abscess, or to aspirate fluid from the cul-de-sac area behind the cervix. A colpocentesis is sometimes called a "culdocentesis" for this reason. The incision codes for the vagina contain two codes for the I&D of vaginal hematomas, which are divided into obstetrical, 57022, and nonobstetrical, 57023.

Destruction

Destruction of vaginal lesions can be accomplished using laser, electrocautery, cyrosurgery, or chemosurgery. Two codes, 57061 and 57065, describe the simple or extensive destruction of vaginal lesions.

Excision

Codes 57100 and 57105 are biopsies of the vaginal mucosa, either simple or extensive. Many of the remaining codes in this section of CPT® involve excision of all or part of the vaginal tissue due to malignancies. These procedures distinguish between partial and complete vaginectomies, each with codes describing radical vaginectomy with or without lymphadenectomy.

Introduction

This section describes the insertion, irrigation, fitting of devices, and packing of the vagina. All of these procedures are easily performed in the office setting. Use code 57180 for vaginal packing of a nonobstetrical hemorrhage from trauma or hormonal imbalance causing heavy uterine bleeding. Diagnosis codes for introduction procedures may include neoplasms, prolapse, contraceptive measures, vaginitis, and nonobstetrical hemorrhage.

Repair

A variety of different types of vaginal repairs are listed here. These include procedures that describe suture of injury; repair of cystocele, rectocele, enterocele, or stress incontinence; closure of fistula; and other plastic repairs. Terminology should be carefully read in this section because many of the words are similar. Watch for different approaches for the same procedure to avoid confusion.

Example:

57268, Repair of enterocele, vaginal approach (separate procedure)

57270, Repair of enterocele, abdominal approach (separate procedure)

Several procedures are commonly known by eponyms, or people's names. Check the CPT® index for procedures such as Marshall-Marchetti-Kranz or Kelley urethral plication. The name is associated with a particular surgical technique that makes the procedure distinct from other procedures on the same anatomy.

Manipulation

The common thread among the codes in this section is that all are performed under anesthesia. Code 57400 describes the dilation of the vagina; 57410 is a pelvic examination; and 57415 is used for removal of an impacted foreign body. Extenuating circumstances such as age, mental, or emotional status of the patient may require the use of anesthesia to perform these procedures, so diagnosis codes should reflect the reason why anesthesia is required.

Example: A 25-year-old mildly mentally retarded female who is suspected of having been sexually abused in her group home is brought into the outpatient surgery department for a pelvic exam under anesthesia. The patient is very uncooperative and frightened.

> ICD-9-CM Diagnosis: V71.5, 318.0
> CPT® Procedure: 57400

Endoscopy

Colposcopy codes were expanded in 2003 to include two new codes describing vaginal colposcopy. Code 57420 describes colposcopy of the entire vagina, with cervix, if present, and code 57421 describes the same colposcopy, including biopsies. Use Modifier 51 when reporting colposcopies of multiple sites, such as vagina, cervix, and vulva.

Cervix

Endoscopy

An endoscopic exam, or colposcopy, of the cervix is a method of viewing the cervix under magnification to determine the presence or absence of disease processes. This procedure is normally performed to diagnose reasons for abnormal pap smears. It is also done to evaluate genital warts, pain, bleeding, and cervicitis. The cervix is stained with acetic acid and/or Lugol's solution, which outlines areas of abnormal tissue. These acetowhite areas are then biopsied. Several methods of biopsy include cold knife (scalpel); endocervical **curettage (ECC),** using a spoon-shaped curette with sharp edges; and loop electrode biopsy **(LEEP),** using a wire with electrical current to slice off thin layers of tissue. A cone biopsy is performed by using a scalpel and/or cutting a cone-shaped piece of tissue off the cervix. Cone biopsies retrieve deeper samples of tissue than a simple biopsy.

Codes 57452–57461 describe colposcopy using various biopsy techniques. When the technique involves the vulva or vagina, the coder is directed to use codes specific to those anatomic sites.

Formula for Success

1. An endocervical curettage (ECC) is not indicated on pregnant women.
2. ECCs do not extend into the uterine cavity, only to the inside of the cervix.

Excision

Some of the excision codes on the cervix are exactly the same as those performed at colposcopy, only they are done under direct visualization rather than magnification.

Cautery of the cervix destroys the top layer of cells. Codes 57510–57513 describe cautery of the cervix performed using heat, freezing, or laser. Use code 57511 for cryotherapy of the cervix, whether it is the initial or repeat procedure.

Code 57520 is a conization of the cervix, performed with or without fulguration, with or without dilation and curettage, with or without repair using a cold knife or laser. Code 57522 is a cone biopsy performed by loop electrode excision, or LEEP.

Use code 57530 for trachelectomy, which is an amputation of the cervix. This is specified as a separate procedure in CPT®, thus should not be assigned when it is performed as an integral part of a larger procedure.

The remaining codes in this section of CPT® are directed at the excision of the entire cervix from the uterus, or the stump of the cervix, which remains after a supracervical hysterectomy. These procedures are done for malignancies, bleeding, or prolapse. The coder should carefully watch for documentation of the approach, as some codes differentiate between abdominal or vaginal approach and may include pelvic floor repair, anterior/posterior, or enterocele repair at the same operative session.

EXERCISE 15.4

Instructions: Assign the correct CPT® codes for the following scenarios.

1. Colposcopy with biopsy and ECC for CIN III found on pap smear   _____

2. Marsupialization of Bartholin's gland cyst   _____

3. Extensive condyloma accuminata lasered from the vulva with two lesions in the vagina   _____

4. Removal of infected synthetic sling with revision   _____

5. Incision and drainage of vaginal hematoma, 1 week postpartum   _____

Uterus

Excision

Endometrial biopsy, excision of uterine fibroids, and different types of hysterectomies fall into this category of CPT®.

Use code 58100 for any method of simple endometrial biopsy or sampling, with or without endocervical biopsy, without cervical dilation. This is noted to be a separate procedure, thus care should be taken not to unbundle this from larger procedures.

Codes 58140–58146 describe the excision of uterine fibroids by number and weight of the myomas, and by approach—either abdominal or vaginal. Look for documentation of this in the operative report and/or the pathology report.

Hysterectomy codes begin with code 58150. Use this code for a total abdominal hysterectomy (TAH). Removal of fallopian tubes and ovaries are optional with this code and do not impact the relative value units. Therefore, when the coder sees the acronyms "TAH/BSO" (total abdominal hysterectomy and bilateral salpingo-oophorectomy), it means that the uterus, ovaries, and tubes have all been removed. Use the same code (58150) if the ovaries and/or fallopian tubes are removed. All abdominal approaches within this section follow the same pattern of optional removal of tubes and ovaries.

Example:

- 58180, Supracervical abdominal hysterectomy, with or without removal of tube(s), with or without removal of ovary(s)
- 58200, Total abdominal hysterectomy, including partial vaginectomy, with para-aortic and pelvic lymph node sampling, with or without removal of tube(s), with or without removal of ovary(s)
- 58210, Radical abdominal hysterectomy, with bilateral total pelvic lymphadenectomy and para-aortic lymph node sampling (biopsy), with or without removal of tube(s), with or without removal of ovary(s)
- 58240, Pelvic exenteration for gynecologic malignancy, with total abdominal hysterectomy, with or without removal of tube(s), with or without removal of ovary(s), with removal of bladder and ureteral transplantations, and/or abdominoperineal resection of rectum and colon and colostomy, or any combination thereof.

Unlike the abdominal approach, the vaginal hysterectomy codes do separate the removal of ovaries and tubes into codes that are distinct from uterine removal. Repairs of enterocele and colpourethrocystopexy with or without endoscopic control are included as separate codes also. Code assignment for most of the vaginal hysterectomy codes is dependent upon the weight of the excised uterus. For a uterus under 250 grams, use codes 58260–58270. A uterus weighing greater than 250 grams should be assigned to codes 58290–58294. In 2003, five new vaginal hysterectomy codes were added to this section for uteri weighing greater than 250 grams.

Introduction

Insertion and removal of **IUDs** are included in this section of CPT®. When IUDs are inserted in the physician office, be sure to also assign a HCPCS code for the IUD itself. Also included are artificial insemination, procedures to check the fallopian tubes for patency, and endometrial ablation. Cross-references to radiology codes are given for hysterosalpingography, which require supervision and interpretation using radiology-specific codes.

Repair

Uterine suspension, repair of ruptured uterus, and plastic repairs of uterine anomalies are described by codes 58400–58540. Code 58400, uterine suspension, is noted to be a separate procedure. This is normally performed in conjunction with a more comprehensive operation, and should not be coded unless it is a stand-alone procedure. Code 58520 is a hysterorrhaphy, or repair of ruptured uterus. CPT® designates this as a nonobstetrical procedure; therefore, this code should only be used for traumatic diagnoses.

Laparoscopy/Hysteroscopy

The difference between a laparoscopy and a hysteroscopy is the approach. Laparoscopy involves the insufflation of the abdomen with air and puncture of the abdominal cavity to look at the surface of the abdominal contents. A hysteroscopy is the insertion of a scope into the uterine cavity through the vagina to look at the inside of the uterus and perform surgical procedures from the inside of that organ.

The uterus, tubes, and ovaries can all be removed laparoscopically. Five new laparoscopic codes were added to CPT® in 2003 to describe the removal of fibroids and different types of hysterectomy, using similar terminology and logic as the open hysterectomy codes. The diagnostic code for laparoscopy is 49320, which is found in the Gastrointestinal chapter of CPT®.

Formula for Success

1. Do not confuse an open hysterectomy with a laparoscopic hysterectomy approach.
2. Codes 58550–58554 are known as "laparoscopically assisted vaginal hysterectomies," or LAVH.

Hysteroscopy codes include the diagnostic, or base code of 58555, and associated surgical hysteroscopies performed on the inside of the uterus. These procedures involve biopsies, lysis of adhesion or resection of intrauterine septum, removal of fibroids or foreign bodies, and endometrial ablation.

Oviducts

Incision

This section of CPT® includes the codes for tubal ligation. These codes do not distinguish between unilateral or bilateral tubal ligations. A woman who has previously had one fallopian tube removed will only have one tube remaining for ligation. Several different types of open procedures are described by codes 58600–58615.

Code 58600 is a ligation of fallopian tube(s), abdominal or vaginal approach, unilateral or bilateral. Code 58605 utilizes the same description as above, but states that the procedure is performed postpartum, during the same hospitalization as delivery. This code is listed as a separate procedure and is commonly performed a day or two after delivery. Code 58611 is a tubal ligation that is performed at the time of a C-section or other intra-abdominal surgery. This code is *NOT* listed as a separate procedure and is designated as an add-on code.

Formula for Success

Assign code 58611 as a secondary procedure without Modifier 51.

Code 58615 is the clipping of a fallopian tube using a device such as a band, Falope ring, or clips that are fired from a stapling device. The method used here is slightly different than the "cut and burn" method of the previously listed codes. Failure rates of this type of tubal ligation are also slightly higher than the codes listed above.

Laparoscopy

All of the codes listed in this section are surgical laparoscopies. For a diagnostic procedure, the coder is cross-referenced to code 49320 in the Gastrointestinal chapter of CPT®. Codes 58660–58679 include tubal ligations performed laparoscopically, lysis of adhesions, removal of ovaries and/or fallopian tubes, and fimbrioplasty, or plastic repair of the tubal fimbria. Codes 58672 and 58673 are designated as unilateral procedures by CPT®. If the fimbrioplasty or salpingostomy is performed bilaterally, the coder is directed to use Modifier 50 on the surgical code. The laparoscopic treatment of an ectopic pregnancy is not included in this section. It is found in the Maternity section of CPT®.

Excision

The removal of fallopian tubes and/or ovaries as stand-alone or separate procedures is described by codes 58700 and 58720. Both codes identify complete or partial, unilateral or bilateral procedures. These codes do *NOT* include open treatment for surgical removal of an ectopic pregnancy. All pregnancy related codes are found in the Maternity chapter of CPT®.

Repair

Plastic repairs are commonly performed on the fallopian tubes to establish patency for an infertile woman, whether the infertility problem is congenital, acquired (from repeated infection), or the reversal of a previous tubal ligation. In addition, adhesions that are bothersome to the patient are assigned to code 58740. This is performed to free the fallopian tubes from adhesions to other structures in the pelvis. The lysis of ahesions is normally bundled into larger procedures when it is used to gain exposure of the operative site. However, some adhesions are very thick and troublesome to clear away. In these cases, a Modifier 22 should be used on the primary procedure to indicate that additional time and effort was expended. Documentation should indicate how complicated the case was due to extensive adhesions and the amount of time spent clearing them away. Simple thin adhesions are normally cleared with blunt dissection using the fingers or instruments. Complicated adhesions may require sharp dissection with scissors or scalpel to take down the adhesions.

Ovary

Incision

Drainage of ovarian cysts and abscesses is described by codes 58800–58823. The coder should carefully watch for documentation of the operative approach, whether vaginal or abdominal. Code 58800 is designated as a separate procedure. This can be performed either bilaterally or unilaterally. Code 58825 describes the transposition of the ovaries, in which the ovaries are pushed behind the uterus and sutured into place prior to pelvic radiation therapy. The uterus acts as a shield to spare the ovaries from radiation and preserve fertility.

Excision

Many of the codes in this section of CPT® deal with removal of the ovaries for malignancy. Codes 58943–58960 are assigned to ovarian excision with various degrees of lymph node removal, hysterectomy, salpingectomy, and omentectomy. Make sure that a diagnosis of malignant neoplasm accompanies these procedural codes.

Codes 58900–58940 describe the excision of all or part of the ovary. These codes are also designated as either unilateral or bilateral codes. When the excision is performed laparoscopically, be sure to refer to the laparoscopic codes rather than the open procedure codes.

In Vitro Fertilization

These codes include the procurement of eggs for in vitro fertilization; injection of the embryo into the uterus; and transfer of egg, sperm, or embryo to the fallopian tube.

EXERCISE 15.5

Instructions: Assign the correct CPT® (and HCPCS codes when indicated) to the following scenarios.

1. Insertion of Mirena IUD for contraception _____
2. Endometrial biopsy performed for dysfunctional uterine bleeding _____
3. Hysteroscopic endometrial thermoablation performed on a patient with menometrorrhagia _____
4. Wedge resection of the left ovary for polycystic ovarian syndrome _____
5. Salpingo-oophorectomy on right side due to endometriosis _____

CHAPTER REVIEW

1. A leiomyoma is located
   a. in the fallopian tubes
   b. in the uterus
   c. in the ovary
   d. on the cervix

2. Procedures that are performed on postpartum patients are only included in the Maternity chapter of CPT®.
   a. True
   b. False

3. CIN II of the cervix is considered to be a
   a. dysplastic lesion
   b. carcinoma *in-situ*
   c. neoplasm of uncertain behavior
   d. benign lesion

4. A teenage patient does not remember removing a tampon and cannot find a string. She comes to the Urgent Care department and the tampon is removed. Give the ICD-9-CM and CPT® codes for this scenario.

   a. 939.2, E871.9

   b. 939.1, E871.9

   c. 939.2, E915

   d. 939.1, E915

5. A patient comes in for a tubal ligation. She previously had one tube and ovary removed several years ago for ectopic pregnancy. A tubal ligation is successfully performed and the patient is sent home the same day. Give the correct CPT® code for this scenario.

   a. 58600-52

   b. 58615-52

   c. 58611

   d. 58600

6. Code for a dilation and curettage performed for premenopausal menometrorrhagia:

   a. 626.2, 58120

   b. 627.0, 57800

   c. 626.6, 57505

   d. 627.1, 57456

7. Of the following procedural codes, which best describes a laparoscopic oophorectomy?

   a. 58720

   b. 58940

   c. 58661

   d. 58554

8. When colposcopies are performed on multiple sites, which modifier is most appropriate?

   a. 52

   b. 50

   c. 51

   d. 53

9. Give the correct diagnosis code for asymptomatic menopause status.

   a. 627.0

   b. 627.4

   c. 256.2

   d. V49.81

10. When a procedural code contains the statement "with or without tube(s), with or without ovary(s)," the coder should code for these separately when they are performed.

   a. True

   b. False

Case Studies

Case Study 15.1

Preoperative Diagnoses

Uterine fibroids, menorrhagia, pelvic pressure.

Postoperative Diagnoses

Uterine fibroids, menorrhagia, pelvic pressure.

Procedure Performed

Total abdominal hysterectomy with bilateral salpingoophorectomy.

Anesthesia

General

Description of Procedure

Once adequate general anesthesia was obtained, the patient was prepped and draped in the usual sterile fashion. A Pfannenstiel skin incision was performed and carried down through the subcutaneous and fascial layers. Peritoneum was entered without difficulty. Exploration of the abdomen and pelvis revealed normal anatomy except for a fibroid uterus. The bowel was packed away. The uterus was elevated. The right round ligament was clamped, cut, and suture-ligated, opening up the right broad ligament. The right ureter was identified. Infundibulopelvic ligament was clamped, cut, and suture-ligated. The same procedure was repeated on the left. The uterine vessels were then doubly clamped, cut, and suture-ligated bilaterally down to the level of the external os. The final ligature incorporated the uterosacral ligaments bilaterally. The vaginal vault was entered and the uterus removed. The vaginal cuff was closed with a running locked 0 Vicryl suture. Hemostasis was noted. The pelvis was irrigated. Again, hemostasis was noted. All instruments were removed. The peritoneum was reapproximated with a 2-0 Vicryl suture. The fascia was closed with a running 0 Vicryl suture. The subcutaneous space was irrigated. Minimal cautery was needed for hemostasis. The skin was then reapproximated with a running 4-0 Monocryl.

The patient was stable upon completion. Urine output was clear and adequate at the end of the procedure. Sponge and needle counts were correct.

ICD-9-CM Diagnosis code: _____

CPT® Procedure code: _____

Case Study 15.2

Preoperative Diagnosis

CIN III of the cervix.

Postoperative Diagnosis

Same.

Procedure Performed

Cone biopsy of the cervix.

Anesthesia

General.

Description of Procedure

After an adequate level of general anesthesia was obtained, the patient was placed in the dorsal lithotomic position. The upper vagina and cervix were stained with Lugol's solution. There was an area of increased uptake of the Lugol's right around the cervical os. The cervix was injected with a dilute solution of pitressin. Two lateral sutures were placed; one at the 2–4 o'clock position, the other at the 8–10 o'clock position. These were tied and tagged. A circumferential incision was made around the ectocervix with the electrocautery unit. The specimen was removed. A stitch was placed at the 12 o'clock position to aid the pathologist in orientation of the specimen. Following this, the cone bed was cauterized. Estimated blood loss was less than 50 cc. She was taken to the recovery room in stable condition.

ICD-9-CM Diagnosis code: _____

CPT® Procedure code: _____

Case Study 15.3

Preoperative Diagnosis

Undesired fertility.

Postoperative Diagnosis

Sterility.

Procedure

Laparoscopic sterilization with bipolar cautery.

Anesthesia

General.

Description of Findings

The uterus was about 18-week size. The ovaries were normal. The fallopian tubes were normal.

Description of Procedure

After an adequate level of general anesthesia was obtained, the patient was placed in the supine position on the operating room table and the abdomen was sterilely prepped and draped. A 1–2 cm transverse supraumbilical skin incision was made with the knife, and the Veress needle was inserted into the peritoneal cavity laparoscopically. The peritoneal cavity was insufflated with about 3–4 liters of CO_2 gas. The 5 mm laparoscopic trocar was inserted into the peritoneal cavity without difficulty. The laparoscope was inserted into the sheath. A 1 cm left transverse incision was made in the patient's left lower quadrant area. Under direct laparoscopic visualization, a 5 mm trocar was inserted into the peritoneal cavity though this lower incision. With the patient in the left lateral tilt position, the right fallopian tube was identified and followed to its fimbriated end, grasped in its mid-portion with Kleppinger cautery forceps and cauterized. The tube was regrasped 1 cm proximal and 1 cm distal to the initial cautery site and cauterized. Good blanching effect was noted. No bleeding was noted.

The patient was then placed in the right lateral tilt position. The left fallopian tube was identified and followed to its fimbriated end. It was grasped in its mid-portion with the Kleppinger cautery forceps and cauterized in a similar fashion as the opposite tube. Following this, the laparoscope and accessory trocar were removed from the peritoneal cavity and the CO_2 gas was allowed to escape from the abdomen. The two incisions were reapproximated using interrupted 3-0 plain suture. Estimated blood loss was about 30 cc. She was taken to the recovery room in stable condition.

ICD-9-CM Diagnosis code: _____

CPT® Procedure code: _____

Case Study 15.4

Preoperative Diagnosis

Recurrent cystocele and rectocele with pelvic pain.

Postoperative Diagnosis

Recurrent cystocele and rectocele with pelvic pain.

Procedure Performed

Anterior and posterior colporrhaphy.

Anesthesia

General.

Description of Procedure

After an adequate level of general anesthesia was obtained, the patient was placed in the dorsal lithotomy position. There was a moderate cystourethrocele. There was a mild rectocele. Cervix and uterus were surgically absent. She had a previous hysterectomy in 2000. The vagina and perineum were prepped with PVP. Allis clamps were used to grasp the apex of the vagina. An anterior colporrhaphy was performed in a routine fashion by making a linear incision from the level of the apex of the vagina, cephalad or superior to the level of the urethra. The pubocervical fascia was dissected off the bladder and anterior vaginal wall mucosa. Following this, Kelly plication sutures were placed in a routine fashion by using interrupted 0 Vicryl suture. There appeared to be good support of the urethrovesical angle and the bladder. Following this, the excess anterior vaginal wall mucosa was excised, and the anterior vaginal wall mucosa was reapproximated using a running stitch of 2-0 Vicryl suture. The posterior colporrhaphy was performed in a routine fashion by making a diamond-shaped incision from the level of the posterior fourchette of the vagina cephalad to the level of the apex of the vagina posteriorly. The endopelvic fascia and rectum were dissected off the posterior vaginal wall mucosa. The levator ani muscles were plicated in the midline using interrupted 0 Vicryl sutures. On two or three occasions, I performed a digital rectal exam and did not palpate any sutures in the rectum. Following this, excess posterior vaginal wall mucosa was incised. The posterior vaginal wall mucosa was reapproximated using a running stitch of 2-0 Vicryl suture. The perineal body was reapproximated with 3-0 Vicryl suture, and a vaginal pack was placed. The urine was clear at all times. Estimated blood loss as about 600 cc. She just had a fair amount of generalized oozing during both the anterior and posterior repair. She was taken to the recovery room in stable condition. The instrument, sponge, and lap counts were correct.

ICD-9-CM Diagnosis code: _____

CPT® Procedure code: _____

Case Study 15.5

Preoperative Diagnosis

Right ovarian cyst with history of polycystic ovarian disease.

Postoperative Diagnosis

Right ovarian cyst with history of polycystic ovarian disease.

Procedure Performed

Laparoscopy with needle aspiration of right ovarian cyst.

Anesthesia

General.

Description of Findings

The left ovary was normal. The fallopian tubes were normal. The uterus was normal. The upper abdomen was normal. There as a 4 5 cm benign-appearing cyst on the right ovary. I aspirated it and with about 15 cc of clear yellow fluid aspirated out of the cyst. The cyst ball collapsed. No bleeding was noted.

Description of Procedure

After an adequate level of general anesthesia was obtained, the patient was placed in the dorsal lithotomy position. The vagina, perineum, cervix, and abdomen were sterilely prepped and draped. An acorn cannula and tenaculum were applied to the cervix. A 2 cm transverse infraumbilical skin incision was made with a knife and a Veress needle was inserted into the peritoneal cavity without difficulty. The peritoneal cavity was insufflated with about 2 liters of carbon dioxide gas. The Veress needle was removed from the peritoneal cavity and a laparoscopic trocar was inserted into the peritoneal cavity without difficulty. The laparoscope was inserted through a sheath. A 1 cm transverse suprapubic skin incision was made with a knife, and under direct laparoscopic visualization, an accessory trocar was inserted into the peritoneal cavity without difficulty. The pelvic organs were more adequately visualized. The abovementioned right ovarian cyst was aspirated. No bleeding was noted. The laparoscope and accessory trocar were removed from the peritoneal cavity and carbon dioxide gas was allowed to escape from the abdomen. The two incisions were reapproximated using interrupted 3-0 plain suture. The acorn cannula was removed from the cervix. EBL was about 30 cc and she was taken to the recovery room in stable condition.

ICD-9-CM Diagnosis code: _____

CPT® Procedure code: _____

Maternity and Delivery

OBJECTIVES

1. Memorize the fifth-digit assignments for episode of care and when to use them—there are only five!
2. Correctly assign ICD-9-CM diagnosis codes for normal and complicated obstetrical care.
3. Recognize what services should be billed for complicated OB care.
4. Correctly assign CPT® codes for physician services.
5. Differentiate between global and component maternity codes.

TERMINOLOGY AND ACRONYMS

AB   Abortion; can be spontaneous, legal, or illegal.

Abruptio placenta   Premature separation of the placenta from uterine wall, causing hemorrhage.

Amniocentesis   The removal of amniotic fluid through a needle in the abdomen.

Antepartum   Prenatal, or before birth.

Cerclage   Suturing the cervix closed with heavy suture to prevent fetal loss with incompetent cervix.

CPD   Cephalopelvic disproportion.

C/S or **CS**   Cesarean section.

D&C   Dilation and curettage.

D&E   Dilation and evacuation.

ECC   Endocervical curettage.

EDC   Estimated date of confinement/delivery.

Ectopic pregnancy   A pregnancy that develops outside the uterus.

Grand multigravida   A woman who has been pregnant six or more times.

HCG   Human chorionic gonadotropin. Levels are measured in either blood (serum) or urine testing for pregnancy.

Intrapartum   During the delivery process.

IUGR   Intrauterine growth retardation.

IUP   Intrauterine pregnancy.

Hyperemesis gravidarum   Varying degrees of morning sickness.

LGA   Large for gestational age.

LMP   Last menstrual period.

Missed AB   Retention of a dead fetus.

Multigravida   A woman carrying second and subsequent pregnancies.

NST   Non-stress test.

NSVD   Normal spontaneous vaginal delivery.

Oligohydramnios   Scant or absent amniotic fluid.

Placenta previa   The placenta covers all or part of the cervical opening, complicating pregnancy and delivery.

Polyhydramnios   Too much amniotic fluid.

Postpartum   Following delivery, up to 6 weeks; also known as the puerperium.

Pre-eclampsia   Hypertension complicating pregnancy; can progress to toxemia.

Primigravida   A woman carrying her first pregnancy.

PROM   Premature rupture of membranes OR prolonged rupture of membranes.

SAB   Spontaneous abortion or miscarriage.

SGA   Small for gestational age.

Toxemia   Severe hypertension during pregnancy with albuminuria, edema, and convulsions.

VBAC   Vaginal birth after cesarean.

◼◼◼ *INTRODUCTION*

Obstetrical codes for both ICD-9-CM and CPT® encompass the entire spectrum of maternity care, covering the antepartum (prenatal), intrapartum (delivery), and puerperium (postpartum) periods. Many conditions that affect pregnant women complicate the pregnancy, or the pregnancy exacerbates pre-existing conditions. Diagnostic conditions must be carefully coded so the condition is appropriately identified, and the correct episode of care is assigned. Procedural coding involves more flexibility due to the longer global period involved with obstetrical care. By keeping the suggestions below in mind, obstetrical coding is enjoyable as well as challenging.

Formula for Success

Tips for Maternity Coding

1. <u>Read</u> ICD-9-CM Chapter 11, Complications of Pregnancy, Childbirth, and Puerperium, codes 630–677.
2. <u>Read</u> V codes V22–V28.
3. <u>Read</u> the CPT® chapter on Maternity Care and Delivery.
4. <u>Know</u> which episode of care the visit occurs in—prenatal, intranatal, or postnatal.
5. <u>Determine</u> what services each physician provided.

While the Maternity sections in both ICD-9-CM and CPT® are short, they hold a wealth of information about normal and complicated obstetrical care. It is crucial that the coder become familiar with the terms and anatomy in these chapters in order to assign the correct codes.

▬▬ *DISEASE PROCESSES AND ICD-9-CM CODING FOR MATERNITY*

Ectopic Pregnancy

Pregnancies can occur outside of the expected implantation sites in the uterus. Implantation usually occurs several days after fertilization. Sometimes the fertilized egg does not make it to the body of the uterus before it implants, or it encounters an obstruction, which prevents it from traveling through the fallopian tube. An **ectopic pregnancy** can be life-threatening to the mother and is often diagnosed because of bleeding following fetal demise. Only on rare occasions has a pregnancy developed to term or near term outside the uterus. These, of course, would have to be delivered by cesarean section (**CS**). Table 16.1 demonstrates various sites of implantation of the fertilized egg and the ICD-9-CM code assignment.

Code 633.9 is used to classify ectopic pregnancies that are unspecified. It is suggested that these be sent back to the dictating physician for clarification.

Abortions

The term *abortion* (**AB**) refers to the interruption of a pregnancy before 22 weeks gestation. In order to correctly assign a diagnosis code, it must be determined if the abortion was a spontaneous miscarriage (category 634) or an induced abortion. Induced abortions fall into two categories:

- ■ Legally induced, category 635
- ■ Illegally induced, category 636

Two additional categories exist in ICD-9-CM:

- ■ Unspecified abortion
- ■ Failed attempted abortion

Fourth-digit subdivisions are used in categories 634–637 to classify various types of complications of abortions. These include:

- ■ .0, Complicated by genital tract and pelvic infection
- ■ .1, Complicated by delayed or excessive hemorrhage
- ■ .2, Complicated by damage to pelvic organs and tissues
- ■ .3, Complicated by renal failure
- ■ .4, Complicated by metabolic disorder
- ■ .5, Complicated by shock

Table 16–1   Sites of Implantation

Site of Ectopic Pregnancy	Description of Implantation Site	ICD-9-CM Code(s)
Abdominal	Within the peritoneal or abdominal cavity	633.00, without concurrent IUP 633.01, with concurrent IUP
Tubal	Anywhere along the fallopian tube	633.10, without concurrent IUP 633.11, with concurrent IUP
Ovarian	On the surface of the ovary	633.20, without concurrent IUP 633.21, with concurrent IUP
Other sites	Cervical, cornual	633.80, without concurrent IUP 633.81, with concurrent IUP

- .6, Complicated by embolism
- .7, With other specified complications
- .8, With unspecified complication
- .9, Without mention of complication

Fifth-digit code assignments are required on categories 634–637. Fifth digits identify whether the abortion was complete, incomplete, or unspecified. For example, a woman with an incomplete spontaneous abortion (**SAB**) is coded as 634.91. An incomplete abortion refers to products of conception that are retained within the uterus, normally requiring surgical intervention such as a **D&C**. A complete abortion is noted to have all of the products of conception expelled at once, including the fetus, amniotic sac, cord, and placenta.

Category 639 is set aside for complications of abortions and ectopic and molar pregnancies for the following conditions:

- When the complication itself was responsible for an episode of medical care, the abortion, ectopic or molar pregnancy itself having been dealt with at a previous episode, OR
- When these conditions are immediate complications of ectopic or molar pregnancies classifiable to 630–633 where they cannot be identified at fourth-digit level.

These complication codes follow the same format as the fourth-digit assignments for categories 634–638.

Formula for Success

Designating the Episode of Care

Fifth-digit codes are required on codes in categories 640–676 (with the exception of code 650) to indicate the current episode of care. Fifth digits are described as follows:

- 0, Unspecified as to episode of care or not applicable
- 1, Delivered, with or without mention of antepartum condition—use when delivery has occurred during this admission and there is mention of a prenatal condition complicating the current episode of care.
- 2, Delivered, with mention of postpartum complication—use when there is mention of a postpartum complication and the patient has delivered this admission.
- 3, Antepartum condition or complication—use for prenatal visits and when the patient is hospitalized and discharged undelivered.
- 4, Postpartum condition or complication—use when the patient has delivered at a previous admission and now has developed a complication.

Hemorrhage in Pregnancy

Bleeding during pregnancy is a warning flag that something is wrong. This can imply complications such as a threatened abortion, **placenta previa** (see Figure 16.1), or **abruptio placenta**. Any bleeding can be a threat to the viability of the pregnancy, and massive hemorrhage can also threaten the life of the mother. Use code categories 640–641 for hemorrhage in early pregnancy, abruptio placenta, or placenta previa.

Hypertension in Pregnancy

Rising blood pressure is another warning flag in pregnancy. Code pre-existing hypertension to 642.0–642.2 with fifth digits assigned for episode of care. Eclampsia is a condition only affecting pregnant or **postpartum** women. It is characterized by coma due to high

PLACENTA PREVIA

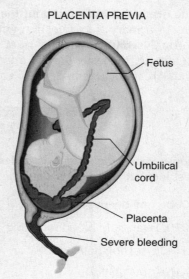

Fetus

Umbilical cord

Placenta

Severe bleeding

Figure 16–1 Example of placenta previa.

blood pressure, proteinuria, and edema. With adequate prenatal care, women who show signs of **pre-eclampsia,** or high blood pressure, proteinuria, and edema are treated before the condition becomes life-threatening to the patient or her fetus. Assign codes from the 642 category for hypertension or pre-eclampsia.

Hyperemesis

The term **emesis** means to vomit. Hyperemesis is a condition common to pregnant women having more than usual morning sickness or vomiting due to the pregnancy. Vomiting is most common in the early stages of pregnancy, when there are large hormonal surges in the bloodstream. Most women experience morning sickness for the first trimester, however, some women persist with vomiting throughout the duration of the pregnancy. When the patient becomes dehydrated and loses weight, her physician must break the cycle through IV fluids, antiemetic drugs, vitamins, and a hyperemesis diet. The hyperemesis codes describe mild hyperemesis and hyperemesis with metabolic disturbance, both occurring before 22 weeks gestation. Use 643.2x, Late vomiting of pregnancy, when the vomiting starts after the 22nd week of gestation. Code 643.9x should be used when the length of gestation is unspecified.

Late Pregnancy

Two codes are currently used to identify postterm or "overdue" pregnancies. Code 645.1x identifies pregnancies over 40 completed weeks to 42 completed weeks gestation. Code 645.2x identifies pregnancies over 42 completed weeks.

Other Complications of Pregnancy

Codes in category 646, Other complications of pregnancy, not elsewhere classified, should be coded with an additional code to specify the complication. These complications include papyraceous fetus, excessive weight gain/edema, habitual aborter, peripheral neuritis, liver disorders, and unspecified renal disease. Use 646.68 for specified complications such as fatigue, insufficient weight gain, and uterine size/date discrepancy.

Two codes in particular deserve further discussion. Code 646.5x is used for asymptomatic bacteruria in pregnancy. Many women have bacteria in their urine, which does not cause any symptoms. This is true for pregnant women as well, but may be diagnosed on routine urine checks throughout the pregnancy. Just as frequently, women may have symptoms of urinary tract infection with back pain, abdominal pain, and positive findings on urinalysis. Code urinary tract infections to 646.6x. An additional code may be added to identify the exact type of infection, such as 599.0 or 595.9, along with the infectious organism, if documented.

EXERCISE 16.1

Instructions: Match the diagnosis codes at the bottom of this exercise to the procedure which best indicates medical necessity.

1. 59000, Amniocentesis   _____

2. 59030, Fetal scalp blood sampling   _____

3. 59514, C-section delivery   _____

4. 59610, VBAC delivery   _____

5. 59820, Treatment of missed AB, 1st trimester   _____

6. 59120, Surgical treatment of ectopic pregnancy   _____

7. 59430, Postpartum care   _____

8. 59160, Curettage, postpartum   _____

654.21	**V24.2**	**666.22**	**V28.0**
660.41	**632**	**656.30**	**633.10**

Other Current Conditions

Category 648 is used to describe other current conditions in the mother classifiable elsewhere, but complicating pregnancy, childbirth, or the puerperium. Included in this category are pre-existing conditions, such as diabetes, anemia, thyroid conditions, drug dependence, mental disorders, cardiovascular conditions, and bone and joint disorders. An abnormal glucose tolerance test and/or gestational diabetes is coded as 648.8x. This condition may arise during pregnancy and complicate care and then disappear following delivery. However, many women who have gestational diabetes are prone to developing adult-onset-type diabetes later in life. The Includes notes for category 648 instruct the coder to use this code when the listed condition complicates the pregnant state, is aggravated by the pregnancy, or is a main reason for obstetric care. Excluded from this category are conditions in the mother that are known or suspected to have affected the fetus.

Normal Delivery

Code 650 is assigned to spontaneous deliveries that require very little or minimal assistance. The patient may require an episiotomy, but does not require fetal rotation or forceps. The infant must be in a cephalic presentation and be a full-term, single, live-born infant via vaginal delivery.

Formula for Success

ICD-9-CM instructs the coder that no other code from 630–676 may be used with 650.

In reality, few deliveries are completely spontaneous, normal vaginal deliveries (**NSVD**) that meet all of the requirements for code 650. The coder should be aware that a complicated pregnancy does not mean that the patient will have a complicated delivery. Likewise, a complicated delivery does not mean that the **antepartum** portion of the pregnancy was complicated.

Multiple Gestation

Use category 651 to identify multiple gestations. When multiple fetuses are developing, it is not uncommon to identify the demise of one fetus. Codes 651.3x–651.6x identify the loss of at least one fetus for twin, triplet, quadruplet, or other multiple pregnancies.

Malposition

A fetus in an abnormal position during the delivery process puts both mother and infant at increased risk. A fetus in an abnormal position may require a cesarean delivery, or a version to turn him or her into a proper position for vaginal delivery. The attending physician will mention any malpresentation of the fetus in the delivery note. Use code 652.1x when a cephalic version successfully turns the fetus into a cephalic presentation for a normal delivery.

Disproportion

The term *disproportion* refers to the following two types of problems that can slow or stop labor:

- Cephalopelvic disproportion: A problem exists with the shape of the mother's pelvis.
- Fetopelvic disproportion: The presenting part of the fetus is too large to pass.

In either case, the fetus may require forceps or vacuum extraction. If the fetus shows signs of distress, a C-section is usually performed. Assign codes from category 653 for disproportion.

Abnormality of Organs and Soft Tissues of the Pelvis

Category 654 includes both congenital and acquired abnormalities that complicate antepartum, **intrapartum,** or postpartum care. Code 654.2x specifically classifies previous C-sections. Use this code on patients who have had a previous cesarean section and are attempting either a **VBAC** or repeat cesarean birth.

Known or Suspected Fetal Abnormality

A number of different types of abnormalities are listed under category 655. The coder is reminded that the diagnoses assigned to this category are not extrapolated from the patient's record by the coder, but are clearly documented by the physician as affecting the management of the mother. Included in this category are chromosomal abnormalities of the fetus, hereditary diseases in the family, suspected damage to fetus due to viral disease in the mother, maternal alcohol addiction, and damage from radiation or drugs. Only fifth digits 0, 1, and 3 are allowed on this category.

Example:
1. Patient's chart notes a history of alcoholism on prenatal visit; no direct correlation to this pregnancy.
   Correct code assignment: V23.89, V11.3
   Incorrect code assignment: 655.43

2. Patient's prenatal visit notes fear of fetal alcohol syndrome due to continued alcohol dependence in the mother, well documented by MD.

Correct code assignment: 655.43

Other Fetal and Placental Problems Affecting Management of Mother

Use category 656 for fetal–maternal hemorrhage, Rh incompatibility, ABO isoimmunization, as well as fetal distress affecting management of mother. Fetal distress is documented by a change in fetal heart rhythm and/or fetal scalp blood samples. This category also classifies intrauterine death after 22 weeks of gestation, abnormal fetal growth, and **meconium in liquor,** which is the staining of amniotic fluid by fetal bowel movement, indicating the fetus is in distress. Only fifth digits of 0, 1, and 3 are allowed on this category.

Polyhydramnios and Other Problems with Amniotic Cavity and Membranes

An excessive amount of amniotic fluid may indicate a problem with the fetus. **Polyhydramnios** is diagnosed when there is greater than 2,000 ml in a single pocket of amniotic fluid. This is diagnosed on ultrasound and may be indicative of congenital deformities of the fetus. Code this condition from category 657. A lack of amniotic fluid, or **oligohydramnios,** is coded to category 658. Also included in this category is premature rupture of membranes (**PROM**), prolonged rupture of membranes, infection of the amniotic cavity, and delayed delivery.

Other Indications for Care

Category 659 includes conditions related to failed mechanical or medical induction of labor, fever and infection during delivery, abnormality in fetal heart rhythm, and complications associated with the mother's age and parity.

Complications of Labor and Delivery

Codes 660–669 include obstructed labor, rapid labor and delivery, uterine inertia, prolonged labor, umbilical cord complications, perineal/vulvar lacerations and trauma, hemorrhage, and anesthesia complications. Additional codes should be assigned if necessary to completely describe the complication. Code 660.6x is used for a failed trial of labor, without mention of condition or suspected condition. Use 660.7x for failed forceps or vacuum extractor, without mention of condition.

Complications of the Puerperium

Codes 671–676 list complications that are common in the postpartum state, but they should also be used if complications occur in the antepartum or intrapartum stages. Watch for valid fifth digits in brackets under each code, as not all fifth digits are allowed. These conditions include major puerperal infections, venous complications such as DVT, varicose veins and hemorrhoids, fever, pulmonary embolism, wound infection, hematoma or dehiscence, and breast/nipple complications or infections.

Late Effect

Code 677, Late effect of complication of pregnancy, childbirth, and the puerperium, is used to indicate conditions in 632–648.9 and 651–676.9 as the cause of late effects. This may include conditions that are specified as late effects, or as sequelae, that may occur at any time after the puerperium. Any sequelae should be coded first, followed by code 677.

EXERCISE 16.2

Instructions: Assign the correct ICD-9-CM code to the scenarios below. Be sure to note episode of care for correct fifth-digit assignment.

1. Pregnancy at 23 weeks with urinary tract infection   _____

2. Dehiscence of cesarean section wound, 10 days postop   _____

3. Prenatal visit, fetus small for dates   _____

4. Gestational diabetes with pre-existing hypothyroidism, delivered   _____

5. Retained placenta with hemorrhage during delivery   _____

6. Pregnancy at 41 weeks gestation, delivered   _____

7. Pregnancy at 38 weeks, size greater than date, undelivered   _____

8. Premature delivery at 34 weeks gestation   _____

9. Mastitis, 3 weeks postpartum   _____

10. Normal spontaneous vaginal delivery (NSVD)   _____

11. Incomplete septic abortion, spontaneous   _____

12. Cephalopelvic disproportion noted at 39 weeks gestation   _____

13. Previous cesarean section, with successful vaginal birth, dismissed today   _____

14. Ruptured tubal pregnancy; ultrasound reveals empty uterus   _____

15. Twin pregnancy, with fetal distress during labor, delivered yesterday by C-section   _____

V Codes

Codes V22–V23 describe the supervision of normal and high-risk pregnancies. Code V22.0 should be used to describe services involving the supervision of a normal first pregnancy. V22.1 is used for a multigravid patient with a normal, uncomplicated pregnancy. V22.0 or V22.1 should be listed as primary when used on routine prenatal visits, and **other codes from the OB chapter may not be listed.** Code V22.2, Pregnant state, incidental, is used when the condition that the patient is being treated for is not related to or complicating her pregnancy. ICD-9-CM coding guidelines specifically state, "Should the physician document that the pregnancy is incidental to the encounter, then code V22.2 should be used in place of any Chapter 11 codes. It is the physician's responsibility to state that the condition being treated is not affecting the pregnancy."

Example:

1. A pregnant patient who has a benign mole removed from her arm, stated by the physician to be unrelated to the pregnancy.

   #### ICD-9-CM Codes:

   216.6, Benign neoplasm of skin of upper limb, including shoulder
   V22.2, Pregnant state, incidental

2. A pregnant patient presents with low back pain. No statement by the physician is made indicating this is NOT related to the pregnancy.

ICD-9-CM Codes:

648.73, Pregnancy complicated by bone and joint disorders of back, pelvis, and lower limb
724.2, Low back pain

Formula for Success

V Codes

1. Coding Guidelines for Obstetrics specify that it is the physician's responsibility to state that the condition being treated is not affecting the pregnancy. V22.2 should be used in place of any other Chapter 11 codes (630–677).
2. Do not use categories V22 and V23 and Chapter 11 codes interchangeably during a pregnancy, unless the problem is self-limiting. Following a diagnosis of high risk or a serious complication, the pregnancy cannot be considered a normal, routine pregnancy again.

V23 category codes describe the supervision of high-risk pregnancies. This includes patients who have had problems with previous pregnancies and are currently pregnant, or patients who are at high risk with the current pregnancy because of stated conditions, such as elderly **primigravida,** or young **multigravida.** Excludes notes in this category should be read carefully. If the stated condition is complicating the pregnancy, rather than simply putting it at high risk, then the appropriate code from Chapter 11 should be selected.

EXERCISE 16.3

Instructions: Assign the correct ICD-9-CM V code to each scenario:

1. Pregnancy with history of gestational diabetes _____
2. Normal first pregnancy, 29 weeks _____
3. Ultrasound to check for intrauterine growth retardation _____
4. Thirteen-year-old primigravida _____
5. Pregnancy, with history of SAB _____
6. Routine postpartum visit _____
7. Pharyngitis, not related to pregnancy _____
8. Gravida 8, para 7 female age 30 with late prenatal care _____
9. Cultures taken for Group B Strep _____
10. History of Down syndrome with previous pregnancy; in for prenatal amniotic screening _____

The outcome of delivery is recorded on the mother's record. Category V27 classifies single and multiple births and indicates stillborn or live births.

CPT® CODING FOR MATERNITY

Uncomplicated maternity care includes routine antepartum, delivery, and postpartum care. Each component of maternity services is described below:

- *Antepartum care* includes the initial and subsequent history, physical examinations, and recording of weight, blood pressure, fetal heart tones, routine dipstick urinalysis, monthly visits up to 28 weeks gestation, biweekly visits to 36 weeks gestation, and weekly visits until delivery. When complications occur and extra office visits or hospital visits are necessary, these may be billed separately according to documentation. Ultrasounds and laboratory studies are also separately billable.
- *Delivery services* include the hospital admission, physical examination, management of uncomplicated labor, and vaginal or cesarean delivery. A normal delivery can include an episiotomy and forceps.
- *Postpartum care* includes hospital visits until discharge in the absence of complications and a six-week postpartum check. Any readmissions for complications are separately billable utilizing codes from the Evaluation and Management Services section.

When complications of pregnancy include surgical procedures such as appendectomy, hernia, and ovarian cyst, codes from the Surgery section should be used.

When a physician provides all or part of the antepartum and/or postpartum care but does not perform the delivery, use codes 59425, 59426 and 59430. This situation can occur when there is a transfer of care or a termination of the pregnancy.

Antepartum Services

These procedures may be reported in addition to the global obstetric care codes and include:

Amniocentesis: The collection of fluid contained in the amniotic sac for analysis or fluid reduction. This is performed with ultrasound guidance and uses a needle inserted through the abdominal wall for collection. This procedure is usually performed between 16–18 weeks gestation; it can be performed as early as 12 weeks and extend to term.
Cordocentesis: The collection of fetal blood from the umbilical vessels under ultrasonic guidance. This procedure is primarily performed in the second and third trimester.
Chorionic villus sampling: A sample of the placenta is aspirated, by any method, and the placental cells are analyzed for chromosomal abnormalities.
Fetal contraction stress test and Fetal **non-stress test:** These tests are both performed through external monitoring of the fetal heart rate and uterine contractions.
Fetal scalp blood sampling: This test assesses fetal distress during labor. It is performed by a scalp incision when the cervix is dilated more than 2 cm and the fetal vertex is low.
Fetal monitoring during labor by consulting physician: An electrode is attached directly to the scalp of the fetus during labor. A written report is included and can include supervision and interpretation or interpretation only.

The ICD-9-CM diagnostic link for these procedures includes any of the complications of pregnancy codes ranging from 641.X3–662.X3 as well as:

- Management of normal pregnancy, V22.0 and V22.1
- Management of high-risk pregnancy, V23.X
- Antenatal screening, V28.8

EXERCISE 16.4

Instructions: Assign the correct CPT® codes to the following scenarios.

1. A pregnant patient with polyhydramnios has a therapeutic amniocentesis. _____

2. A pregnant patient undergoes a chorionic villus sampling to test for suspected trisomy 21 of the fetus. _____

3. A fetal non-stress test is performed, in the office, on a patient with toxemia. _____

Excision

The majority of procedures in this section are used in the treatment of ectopic pregnancies. An ectopic pregnancy is the implantation of a fertilized egg outside of the expected site, the uterus.

EXERCISE 16.5

Instructions: Assign the correct CPT® codes to the following scenarios.

1. An abdominal hysterotomy performed on a patient with a hydatidiform mole. _____

2. A patient is surgically treated for a cervical ectopic pregnancy. _____

3. The on-call physician sees a patient from another practice. She had delivered the previous day. He treats her for a retained placenta, even though she is not hemorrhaging. _____

Introduction

The insertion of a cervical dilator is a separate procedure code that describes the placement of laminaria or prostaglandin into the endocervix to stimulate and dilate the canal. This procedure is used to induce labor or to prime the cervix before induction.

Repair

An episiotomy or vaginal repair is included in the delivery procedure unless a physician other than the attending performs it. Use code 59300 when another physician performs the episiotomy.

A **cerclage** of the cervix is performed for problems with cervical incompetence, or a failure of the cervix to remain closed during pregnancy. Heavy suture material is used to keep the cervix closed until the pregnancy reaches term. Use code 59320 for a vaginal cerclage and 59325 when the cerclage is applied to the cervix through an abdominal incision. Diagnosis code 654.5x is linked to these CPT® codes.

Code 59350 describes the procedure to surgically treat a lacerated or ruptured uterus caused by pregnancy. Use diagnosis codes 665.0x and 665.1x.

EXERCISE 16.6

Instructions: Assign the correct CPT® code for the following scenario.

1. A vaginal cerclage of the cervix is placed in a pregnant patient who is threatening labor at 23 weeks because of cervical incompetence. _____

Vaginal Delivery, Antepartum and Postpartum Care

The codes in this section include the routine obstetric care with vaginal delivery, as well as the codes used when different physicians provide complete care. Figure 16.2 shows the stages of delivery.

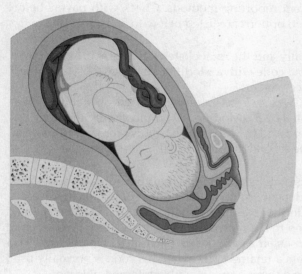

FIRST STAGE:
First uterine contraction to dilation of cervix

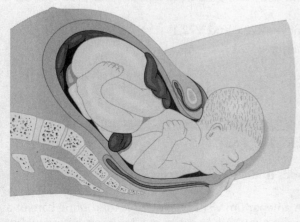

SECOND STAGE:
Birth of baby or expulsion

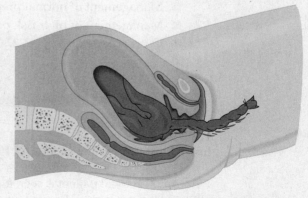

THIRD STAGE:
Delivery of placenta

Figure 16–2 Three stages of labor.

Example

1. A patient moves from one city to another. If the patient begins care with a physician in one city but continues with another physician after moving, the physician in the first city reports only his or her share of the antepartum care. The codes for antepartum care are divided into two groups: 4–6 visits, 59425; or 7 or more visits, 59426.

2. If the same patient has seen Dr. A for three visits or less, the appropriate Evaluation and Management code is reported for each visit based on documentation. The first visit may be coded with 99204, with 99213 for the second and third visits. Dr. B, who performs the delivery, will report the delivery only and postpartum care code, 59410; and only the number of antepartum visits he or she performed once the patient moved to his or her location.

Multiple Births

When reporting the care for a multiple gestation, such as twins, the coder should recognize that different payers may require different reporting methods. Check with payers before submitting claims for multiple births. Two options are listed below to assist in reporting:

Option 1: If both are delivered vaginally and the total obstetrical care is provided by the same physician, report the global code with a Modifier 22; 59400-22. This is the method preferred by most insurance payers.

Option 2: Report the global code for Twin A, 59400, and the delivery only code with a Modifiers 52 and 59 for Twin B; 59409-52,59. Modifier 59 would signify that this is a separate delivery of a different infant and the Modifier 52 allows for the reduced services involved in the delivery of the second infant.

Use diagnostic codes for multiple gestation, 651.xx, and multiple outcome of delivery, V27.2–V27.9. Both ICD-9-CM codes are dependent upon the number of infants involved.

Other codes in this section include the external cephalic version, 59412, a method used to turn a fetus in the breech position to the normal cephalic presenting position; and delivery of the placenta, 59414, which is listed as a separate procedure. Do not use 59414 when the delivering physician encounters a retained placenta. This code is normally used when the delivery is unattended and the patient presents with a retained placenta.

The diagnostic link for these procedures in this section of CPT® can include any of the complications of pregnancy ICD-9-CM codes ranging from 641.X3–662.X3 as well as:

- Management of normal pregnancy—V22.0 and V22.1
- Management of high-risk pregnancy—V23.X
- Outcome of delivery—V27.X

EXERCISE 16.7

Instructions: Assign the correct CPT® codes to the following scenarios.

1. An obstetrical patient is seen for five antepartum visits by Doctor A for routine care of a second pregnancy. The patient moves to New York because of a job promotion and begins care with a new physician, Doctor B. This physician sees the patient through the remaining antepartum care, eight visits, delivers the baby vaginally with no complications, and follows up with a postpartum visit. Assign codes for both doctors. _____

2. An obstetrical patient is rushed to the hospital by taxi. During the trip to the hospital, the patient delivers in the taxi. The cord was cut before arrival to the hospital, leaving the obstetrician the delivery of the placenta in the emergency room. _____

3. An obstetrical patient is found by ultrasound to have a fetus in the breech position. The physician is able to turn the fetus by external version into the correct cephalic position. _____

4. An obstetrical patient delivers while on vacation. Her family physician has provided all of the normal antepartum care for a first pregnancy and her six-week postpartum check. Assign the codes reported by the family physician. _____

5. An obstetrical patient delivers a baby boy after treatment with the same physician throughout the pregnancy and delivery. She experiences a long labor with a third-degree laceration during delivery, and the infant has the umbilical cord wrapped around his neck x 1. _____

6. An obstetrical patient who lives in a rural area is rushed to the hospital with a history of rapid deliveries. Once at the hospital, the patient vaginally delivers live triplets with the help of her regular family physician who has followed her through the pregnancy. _____

Cesarean Delivery

This method of delivery is performed through a vertical or horizontal incision in the abdomen and uterus. Since there are at least two patients, it is common practice to have an assistant surgeon for a cesarean delivery. The services provided by the assistant at surgery are reported as 59514-80. Multiple gestations are more commonly performed with a cesarean delivery. The method of reporting cesarean delivery is similar to the explanation given in the vaginal delivery section. The delivery of twins is most commonly reported using the global code with a Modifier 22; for example, 59510-22, when all care is provided by the same physician. Another method is to report the global code and the delivery only code with the Modifiers 52,59 on all infants after the first delivery; for example, 59510 and 59514-52,59.

Add-on code 59525 is used to report a subtotal or total hysterectomy after a cesarean section. This code cannot stand alone and is intended to be used in conjunction with codes 59510, 59514, 59515, 59618, 59620, or 59622.

EXERCISE 16.8

Instructions: Assign the correct CPT® codes to the following scenarios:

1. An obstetrical patient receives all of her antepartum care from one physician. She has a normal delivery of twin boys by cesarean section. There is also an assistant surgeon present. Code for both physicians. _____ _____

2. An obstetrical patient, pregnant for the second time, is followed by her family physician for all of her normal antepartum care. When she is admitted to the hospital, her physician continues to follow the labor; however, there is a prolonged latent phase. The patient is uncomfortable and the baby is in distress. The physician consults with an obstetrician who agrees to perform a cesarean delivery. This is the only service provided by the obstetrician and the patient is to follow up with her family physician postpartum. Code for both physicians. _____ _____

3. An obstetrical patient begins to have severe pre-eclampsia and is admitted to the hospital in the middle of the antepartum period. Her obstetrician admits her to the hospital
with a level II initial care and is seen for the next two days and receives level I subsequent hospital care. She is then discharged the following day with a routine 15 minute
discharge. She continues her antepartum care and sees her obstetrician every other day
in the office. She is seen for a total of twenty antepartum visits. The last two weeks she
is seen seven times and the obstetrician has documented level II visits. She is admitted
two weeks later and delivers a baby boy by cesarean section. The pre-eclampsia is present throughout the pregnancy and delivery. Code for all billable services.

Delivery after Previous Cesarean Delivery

This method of delivery is referred to as VBAC, vaginal birth after cesarean. The codes in
this section are used to report either a successful or unsuccessful attempt at a vaginal
birth after a previous cesarean delivery. Two codes, 59610 and 59618, are global codes, i.e.,
they contain all three components of maternity care—antepartum, delivery, and postpartum services.

Formula for Success

Make a notation in your CPT® book next to codes 59610 and 59618 indicating that
these are global codes. Note that 59610 is for a successful VBAC and 59618 is for an
unsuccessful VBAC.

EXERCISE 16.9

Instructions: Assign the correct CPT® codes to the following scenarios.

1. An obstetrical patient has been followed for a normal pregnancy of her second child
by her obstetrician. She has previously had a cesarean section and wishes to try a vaginal delivery. Her obstetrician delivers the baby vaginally with little problem and bills
for the entire global care. _____

2. Determine the correct code if the patient in question 1 had a difficult labor and had to
deliver by cesarean section. _____

Abortion

For the purposes of CPT® coding there are two types of abortions, spontaneous and induced. After a spontaneous abortion, treatment includes the dilation of the cervix and extraction of uterine contents, performed by a suction machine, followed by scraping with
a sharp curette to ensure that the uterus is empty. Table 16.2 shows a summary of coding
for abortions.

An induced abortion terminates a pregnancy by several different methods (see
Table 16.3).

The diagnostic link for these procedures includes:

■ Other abnormal products of conception
■ Legally induced abortion

Table 16–2   Abortions

CPT® Code	Unique Description	Trimester	ICD-9-CM Link
59812	Incomplete abortion, completed surgically	Any trimester	634.x1
59820	Missed abortion, completed surgically	First trimester	632; before 22 weeks gestation
59821	Missed abortion, completed surgically	Second trimester	632; before 22 weeks gestation 656.4x; intrauterine death after 22 weeks gestation
59830	Septic abortion, completed surgically		634.xx–637.xx

- Unspecified abortion
- Known or suspected fetal abnormality affecting management of mother
- Other fetal and placental problems affecting the management of mother
- Other indications for care or intervention related to labor and delivery

EXERCISE 16.10

Instructions: Assign the correct CPT® codes.

1. An obstetrical patient is surgically treated for a missed abortion in her eighteenth week. _____

2. A patient has found out through an amniocentesis that the fetus has a chromosomal abnormality. The mother is given the option of a therapeutic abortion. She is treated in an outpatient setting by the dilation and evacuation method for termination of the pregnancy. The procedure is completed without any complications. _____

Table 16–3   Types of Induced Abortions

CPT® Code	Unique Description	Delivery of Fetus Included
59840	Dilation and curettage	No
59841	Dilation and evacuation	No
59850	*Intra-amniotic injections *Hospital admission and visits	Yes
59851	*Intra-amniotic injections *Dilation and Curettage and/or Evacuation *Hospital admission and visits	Yes
59852	*Intra-amniotic injections *Hysterotomy for failed intra-amniotic injections *Hospital admission and visits	Yes
59855	*Vaginal suppositories *Hospital admission and visits	Yes
59856	*Vaginal suppositories *Dilation and curettage and/or evacuation *Hospital admission and visits	Yes
59857	*Vaginal suppositories *Hospital admission and visits	Yes

3. A pregnant patient with a history of drug abuse has found out that her baby has sustained damage from the drug use and will never be normal. She is treated in an inpatient setting with amniotic injections and remains in the hospital until the fetus is aborted. The abortion is complete and there are no complications. _____

Other Procedures

- ■ Code 59866 is used to report the multifetal pregnancy reduction (MPR), which eliminates one or more fetuses in an attempt to save the remaining fetuses.
- ■ Code 59870 describes uterine evacuation and curettage for hydatidiform mole, also known as a molar pregnancy.
- ■ Code 59871 describes the removal of a cerclage suture under anesthesia. This cerclage is used as treatment for an incompetent cervix.

CHAPTER REVIEW

1. List the services included in antepartum care.

2. When complications occur and a patient is admitted during the antepartum global care, additional office or hospital visits are included in the global.   **T or F**

3. When an obstetrical patient is carrying a fetus in the breech position, the external cephalic version is included in the global of the antepartum care.   **T or F**

4. Match the following descriptors with their modifiers:
   a. Discontinued Service
   b. Assistant Surgeon
   c. Staged or Related Procedure During a Postoperative Period
   d. Reduced Services
   e. Distinct Procedural Services

   52   58   80   53   59

5. A pregnant patient is seen in the clinic at 41 weeks gestation by her attending obstetrician. Her cervix is 2 cm dilated; she is at 0 station and 70% effaced. A prostaglandin suppository is inserted and she is sent home to await labor. Give the ICD-9-CM and CPT® codes for this scenario.
   a. 645.13, 59200
   b. 650, 59200
   c. 645.23, 99213
   d. 650, 59400

6. A 40-year-old G4, P3 patient with pre-existing diabetes mellitus is seen for her fourth prenatal visit. She is transferring her care to a specialist for high-risk pregnancies. Give the ICD-9-CM and CPT® codes for the services that will be coded/billed by her primary care physician.
   a. 648.83, 99214 x 4
   b. 648.03, 59400
   c. 648.03, 59425
   d. 648.83, 59400

7. A patient is in labor with a twin gestation. She delivers the first baby vaginally. The second twin is in the breech position and is delivered by C-section. The obstetrician provided all of the antepartum care and delivered the infants. Give the correct ICD-9-CM diagnosis code and correct sequence of CPT® procedure codes with modifiers:

ICD-9-CM: _____

CPT®: _____ _____

8. Give the rationale for reporting the CPT® codes and modifiers in question 7.

Case Studies

Instructions: Assign the correct codes as directed at the end of each scenario to the following operative reports.

Case Study 16.1

Diagnosis

Intrauterine pregnancy at 39-4/7 weeks gestation in a Group B strep positive patient.

Procedure

Vaginal delivery of male infant.

Anesthesia

Stadol.

Estimated Blood Loss

Less than 300 cc.

Summary

At 1833, this 34-year-old, gravida 3, now para 3 at 39-4/7 weeks gestation delivered a viable male infant with Apgar scores of 8 after one and 9 after five. Delivery was via normal spontaneous vaginal delivery. There was no noted nuchal cord. The infant was bulb-suctioned at the perineum. The cord was clamped and the infant was handed off to the awaiting nurse. Cord blood gases were obtained. Placenta was delivered intact with trailing membranes. The vaginal vault was explored. No tears were noted. The infant and the mother tolerated the procedure well. Pitocin, 20 units, were placed in a 1-L bag of normal saline and run open. Code for global obstetrical care.

ICD-9-CM Diagnosis code: _____

CPT® Procedure code: _____

Case Study 16.2

Preoperative Diagnosis

1. Intrauterine pregnancy at 36 weeks gestation with diabetes mellitus requiring insulin.
2. Pregnancy-induced hypertension.
3. Pre-eclampsia.
4. Undesired fertility.
5. Transverse presentation.

Postoperative Diagnosis

1. Delivery of a 5 pound 9 ounce male with Apgars of 8 and 9.
2. Sterility.

Procedure

Primary low transverse cervical cesarean section and tubal sterilization.

Anesthesia

Spinal.

Description of Procedure

After an adequate level of spinal anesthesia was obtained, the patient was placed in the left lateral tilt position on the operating room table and the abdomen was sterilely prepped and draped. A Pfannenstiel skin incision was made to enter the abdomen. This incision was carried down through the subcutaneous tissue to the anterior rectus fascia, which was incised laterally in both directions. The midline was identified. The rectus muscles were separated. The peritoneal cavity was entered bluntly. The vesicouterine peritoneum over the lower uterine segment was incised in a curvilinear fashion. A bladder flap was created. A hysterotomy incision was made in the lower uterine segment with a knife and extended in a curvilinear fashion with the bandage scissors. The abovementioned infant with the abovementioned Apgars, weight, and sex was delivered. The infant was in the transverse presentation with the fetus noted to be breech on ultrasound. The infant's nose and mouth were suctioned with bulb suction. The cord was clamped and cut. Cord blood was obtained. The placenta was delivered manually. A three vessel intact placenta was noted and sent for microscopic analysis. The ovaries and fallopian tubes appeared normal bilaterally. The patient received 20 units of oxytocin in a liter of IV fluids that were already infusing after delivery of the infant and 1g of Ancef IV. The hysterotomy incision was reapproximated and closed.

The right fallopian tube was identified, followed to its fimbriated end, and grasped in its mid position with a Babcock clamp. Two plain sutures were placed around the portion of the tube and then about an inch-size piece of tube was excised. The tubal lumen were identified and cauterized. Hemostasis was noted to be adequate. Attention was directed to the left fallopian tube, which was identified, followed to its fimbriated end, and grasped in its mid position with a clamp. Two interrupted plain sutures placed around the portion of the tube, both proximally and distally. Then about an inch-size piece of tube was removed. Tubal lumen were identified and cauterized. Hemostasis was noted to be adequate. The uterus was placed back in the peritoneal cavity and the gutters were cleansed free of clot and old blood. The anterior abdominal wall and peritoneum were reapproximated using a running stitch suture. The skin was closed with staples. Estimated blood loss was about 500 cc. The Foley catheter was draining clear yellow fluid at the termination of the procedure. Instrument and sponge counts were correct.

Code this as if the physician had not provided antepartum care.

ICD-9-CM Diagnosis codes: _____

CPT® Procedure codes: _____

Case Study 16.3

Preoperative Diagnosis

1. A 32-year-old G7, P4 at 37-0/7 weeks gestation with twins, vertex breech presentation.
2. Group B strep positive.
3. Spontaneous onset of labor with assisted rupture of membranes and arrest of active phase.
4. Desires permanent sterility.

Postoperative Diagnosis

1. Fetus A, male infant in the vertex position with Apgars of 7 and 8, weighing 5 pounds, 15 ounces.

2. Fetus B, female in the breech position with a double nuchal cord, as well as a double knot in the cord, with Apgars of 7 and 9, weighing 5 pounds 3 ounces.

Procedure

1. Primary low transverse cesarean section.
2. Bilateral Pomeroy tubal ligation.

Anesthesia

Epidural.

Estimated Blood Loss

800 cc.

Procedure Summary

The patient is a 32-year-old G7, P4 who presented to labor and delivery with spontaneous labor at 37-0/7 weeks gestation with twins in the vertex breech position. She initially consented to attempt vaginal delivery, however, despite adequate contractions, she had arrest of active phase, and requested proceeding to cesarean section. She also requested permanent sterilization.

Once adequate epidural anesthesia was obtained, the patient was prepped and draped in the usual sterile fashion. A Pfannenstiel skin incision was made and carried down through the subcutaneous and fascial layers. The recti muscles were split in the midline, and the peritoneum was entered without difficulty. A bladder flap was created with a combination of sharp and blunt dissection. A sharp incision was made in the lower uterine segment and extended bilaterally with blunt dissection. The presenting fetus, which was a male, was delivered from the vertex position and had Apgars of 7 and 8. He weighed 5 pounds 15 ounces. The nonpresenting fetus, which was a female, was delivered from the breech presentation; after rupture of the membranes, the fetus was delivered without difficulty using the usual maneuvers, including Mauriceau to deliver the head. A double nuchal cord was noted, as well as a double knot in the cord. She had Apgars of 7 and 9 and weighed 5 pounds 3 ounces. The placenta was delivered with uterine massage. It was intact and revealed two 3-vessel cords. Intravenous Pitocin was used to involute the uterus. The uterus was cleared of all clots and membranes. The uterine incision was inspected, no extensions were noted. The incision was then closed with a running locked suture. Hemostasis was obtained. The right tube was identified out to the fimbria, and a 3 cm segment suture ligated with plain gut suture and removed. Hemostasis was noted. The right ovary was normal in appearance. The left tube was then identified out to the fimbria, and a 3 cm segment suture ligated with plain gut and removed. Telescoping tube was noted, both on the right and left tube on each end of the incised segments. Hemostasis was noted on the left. The left ovary was visibly normal. Hemostasis was again noted. The gutters were cleared of all clots, and debris of the pelvis was irrigated. The fascia was reapproximated with a running suture. The subcutaneous space was irrigated. Minimal cautery used for hemostasis. The skin was reapproximated with staples. Urine output was clear at approximately 400 cc. Sponge and needle counts were correct. The patient was stable upon completion.

Code procedures, eight antepartum visits, no postpartum follow-up for the obstetrician, and the services of an assistant surgeon.

ICD-9-CM Diagnosis codes: _____

CPT® Procedure codes: _____

CHAPTER 17

The Nervous System

OBJECTIVES

1. Recognize nervous system disorders and injuries.
2. Distinguish between the sympathetic and autonomic nervous systems.
3. Correctly code ICD-9-CM diagnoses relating to the nervous system.
4. Correctly code CPT® procedures performed on the nervous system.
5. Assign modifiers appropriate to the given situations.

TERMINOLOGY AND ACRONYMS

Absence seizure   A mild seizure noted by a blank stare. Also known as *petit mal* seizure. May be easily misconstrued as daydreaming.

Aphasia   Language disorder due to brain dysfunction such as stroke or brain injury.

Ataxia   Muscular incoordination.

Cerebrovascular accident   Infarction of the brain; also known as a stroke or CVA. A CVA can be either embolic or hemorrhagic in origin.

Diplegia   Bilateral paralysis, such as both legs.

Epilepsy   Chronic neurological disorder characterized by seizures and/or altered states of consciousness.

Facet joint   Smooth "thumbprint" surface of the vertebral column, which articulates with other vertebrae.

Foramen   An opening in the surface of a bone through which blood vessels and nerves may pass.

Hemiplegia   Unilateral paralysis on one side of the body.

LOC   Loss of consciousness.

Meningocele   Protrusion of the protective layers of spinal cord covering out between the vertebral column.

Meningomyelocele   Also known as *spina bifida:* A protrusion of the meninges, nerve roots, and spinal cord that is not covered by skin.

Monoplegia   Paralysis of only one limb.

Quadriplegia   Paralysis of all four limbs.

Spina bifida   See *Meningomyelocele.*

Status epilepticus   State of continuous epileptic seizures.

TIA   Transient ischemic attack—an episode of insufficient blood supply to the brain, causing brief neurological deficit without permanent damage.

Tonic/clonic   Type of seizure that alternates between sustained muscular contraction and relaxation.

INTRODUCTION

The nervous system can be compared to a computer, which governs multiple aspects of the human body at one time. Nerve impulses continuously give feedback to the brain, and the brain sends out instructions through the nerves, whether we are awake or asleep. An interruption in the flow of information either to or from the brain will change the way the body functions or behaves. Brain death signals the cessation of all spontaneous bodily functions and many of the automatic functions as well. This chapter will focus on disease entities of the nervous system, traumatic injuries, and surgical procedures that are performed to correct these problems.

ANATOMY

The nervous system is composed of two distinct zones within the body. The *central nervous system* includes the brain, meninges, and spinal cord. Three layers of membrane make up the *meninges*, or covering of the brain. The other zone, the *peripheral nervous system*, includes all of the nerves that send signals back to the brain. The peripheral nervous system is broken down into two types of nerve fibers, each with different functions:

■ Somatic nerves: Include deliberate muscle activity such as movements of eyes, tongue, facial expression, locomotion, and dexterity.
■ Autonomic nerves: Control internal organs such as stomach, intestines, lungs.
  ■ Parasympathetic: Controls automatic, unconscious nerve impulses such as those for digestion, respiration, and the "fight-or-flight" response.
  ■ Sympathetic: Reverses the effects of the parasympathetic nervous system; calms the "fight-or-flight" response and returns the body to a normal state.

See Anatomy Plate 18 in Appendix A.

DISEASE PROCESSES AND ICD-9-CM CODING FOR THE NERVOUS SYSTEM

Infections and Inflammatory Diseases

Meningitis is an infection of the meninges. This infectious process may be due to bacteria or caused by nonbacterial infections such as viruses or fungi. Symptoms are generally the same and include confusion and other mental changes, severe headache, fever, and painful neck flexion, which can then progress to seizures, coma, and death if not recognized and treated appropriately. The most common method of diagnosis is a lumbar puncture to obtain a spinal fluid specimen for culture. Treatment is directed toward the organism identified on culture. Use category 320 to identify bacteria responsible for the meningitis infection and category 321 for meningitis due to other organisms. Instructions in both categories tell the coder to first code underlying disease processes. This includes diseases or organisms that are not already listed in category 320 or 321. Unspecified types of meningitis should be coded to category 322.

Myelitis and encephalitis are infections of the spinal cord and brain, respectively. Symptoms are similar to those found in meningitis, but vary a bit more in their causes.

Certain types of encephalitis are more "exotic" in nature, such as malaria, West Nile virus, and other types with insect vectors. Medications, chemical exposure, and parasites are less common causes of encephalitis. Category 323 is assigned to the various types of encephalitis. The coder is instructed to code first the underlying cause of these infections.

Formula for Success

1. Code the underlying disease first when meningitis is the manifestation of another disease process.
2. Use category 047 when the meningitis is due to an enterovirus.

Hereditary and Degenerative Diseases

Alzheimer's disease is one of the leading causes of dementia in the United States. Several causes are thought to be at least partially responsible for this disease. One form of Alzheimer's is familial in nature, with symptoms beginning at a much younger age. Another form is felt to be due to plaque formation in the brain. Symptoms of Alzheimer's include loss of concentration, gradual memory loss, disorientation, and behavior changes. While a few people exhibit these symptoms under age 65, most patients are older. Greater than 50 percent of patients older than age 85 will exhibit some signs of Alzheimer's disease. Currently, there is no cure for this progressive disease, although medications such as cholinesterase inhibitors will help alleviate symptoms.

Parkinson's disease is a motor system disorder. This disease is characterized by a loss of dopamine-producing cells in the brain, which help control movement. Four main symptoms are common to patients with Parkinson's:

- Tremor in extremities, jaw, or face
- Rigidity or stiffness of extremities and trunk
- Slowed movements, called *bradykinesia*
- Impairment of balance and coordination

Some patients may have a genetic predisposition to Parkinson's, plus a possible environmental trigger, which starts the disease process. Like Alzheimer's, Parkinson's disease is progressive and has no cure. Medications such as Levodopa and derivatives of this type help control movements. Surgeons can now destroy specific areas in the brain that cause the abnormal movements. They can also perform deep brain stimulation with electrodes to help alleviate symptoms.

Huntington's disease, or chorea, is an inherited degenerative brain disorder with no known cure or effective treatment of symptoms. HD is commonly diagnosed in midlife. The genetic trait is passed on, with each child in the family having a 50 percent risk of inheriting the genetic mutation. All children with the gene will develop the disease and may pass it on to the next generation. In 1993, the gene was isolated, and now carriers of the mutation can be tested prior to the development of symptoms. Deterioration begins with lack of coordination, clumsiness, twitching, and forgetfulness, which progresses. Within a period of a few years, many patients require total care with the inability to control any bodily functions.

EXERCISE 17.1

Instructions: Assign the correct ICD-9-CM code to the diagnostic statements below. Do not assign E codes.

1. Parkinson's disease   _____

2. Tarsal tunnel syndrome   _____

3. Seizure disorder   _____

4. C1-C2 spinal cord injury, complete   _____

5. Multiple sclerosis   _____

6. Subdural hemorrhage with concussion   _____

7. Diabetic peripheral neuropathy, with good control   _____   _____

8. Concussion with 3-minute loss of consciousness   _____

9. Epilepsy, tonic/clonic type   _____

10. Head contusion   _____

11. Stroke 1 year ago with aphasia   _____   _____

12. Myasthenia gravis without acute exacerbation   _____

13. Bell's palsy   _____

14. Spina bifida   _____

15. Classical migraine   _____

16. Encephalitis due to West Nile virus   _____   _____

Other Disorders of the Central Nervous System

Multiple sclerosis involves the destruction of the insulating portion of nerve fibers, called the myelin sheath, by plaques. The most common initial symptom is a problem with vision. Other symptoms may present with sudden or slow onset, with varying degrees of severity. These symptoms include numbness, paresthesias, muscle weakness, and problems with balance and coordination. MS is commonly diagnosed in young adulthood. Currently, there is no cure; however, steroids are used to alleviate the symptoms during flares. Only in the worst cases are patients totally disabled by MS. Most people live with varying stages of the disease without progression. The cause of MS is still being researched. It is thought to be due to several different causes, such as genetics, autoimmune triggers, and infection. Only one code in ICD-9-CM, 340, is assigned to multiple sclerosis.

Cerebral palsy is the name given to a group of chronic disorders that become evident within the first few years of life. Some cases of cerebral palsy are thought to be due to errors in cell development during the early stages of pregnancy. Other types are due to insults to the brain near or at the time of birth, such as neonatal stroke, brain hemorrhage, or umbilical cord problems causing fetal anoxia. This disorder does not worsen with the passage of time, and each patient will exhibit different symptoms ranging from mild physical impairment without mental impairment to those with severe seizures requiring total care. Braces and drugs are used to help control muscular problems. Physical therapy, occupational therapy, and speech therapy enable the patient to lead a fuller, near normal life. Codes 343.0–343.9 describe different types of cerebral palsy. Excluded from this group of codes are hereditary cerebral paralysis and spastic paralysis that are specified as noncongenital or noninfantile.

Epilepsy is a diagnosis given to a patient who has had two or more seizures. This is a disorder with many potential causes. Diagnosis is made through EEG or brain scans, and treatment is begun as soon as the condition is diagnosed. Usual treatment consists of medication, with the most severe cases requiring surgical intervention. Epilepsy sometimes lessens in severity as a patient ages. A patient with a diagnosis of seizure disorder does not necessarily have epilepsy. The coder should be careful to make this distinction and ask the physician for clarification if epilepsy is used as a blanket term. Epilepsy is divided into two main types:

■ **Generalized,** involving the entire brain.
■ **Partial seizures,** which involves a specific location in the brain.

Each type of epilepsy can have a convulsive or a nonconvulsive component. These specific types are listed in ICD-9-CM. Codes 345.0x and 345.1x describe generalized nonconvulsive epilepsy and generalized convulsive epilepsy, respectively. These codes describe the difference between petit mal (absence) seizures and grand mal (or **tonic-clonic**) seizures.

The term *status*—as in **status epilepticus** or petit mal status—refers to the patient's having 5 minutes or more of continuous seizure activity. Some clinicians require that the patient have at least 30 minutes of continuous seizure activity before assigning this diagnosis. Use codes 345.2 and 345.3 for grand mal and petit mal status.

Partial epilepsy is described by codes 345.4x and 345.5x. Patients with partial epilepsy often report an "aura" of flashing lights, other visual disturbances, or certain smells immediately prior to a seizure. Some patients with partial epilepsy report feelings of "dejà vu" during their seizure and are aware of happenings around them. These codes also distinguish between levels of impairment of consciousness.

Disorders of the Peripheral Nervous System

ICD-9-CM classifies peripheral nervous system disorders from the head to the toes, beginning with the cranial nerves. Specifically excluded from categories 350–359 are diseases of the third, fourth, sixth, and eighth cranial nerves; peripheral autonomic nerves; peripheral neuritis in pregnancy; and neuralgia, neuritis, or radiculitis that are not otherwise specified or are rheumatic in nature. Common conditions such as trigeminal neuralgia, Bell's palsy (see Figure 17.1), phantom limb syndrome, carpal tunnel (see Figure 17.2), and tarsal tunnel are located in categories 350–359.

Muscular dystrophy is a group of approximately nine genetic diseases involving the voluntary muscles. It affects all age groups and is generally slow progressing. No curative treatment exists, but symptoms are treated with braces, physical therapy, and surgery to

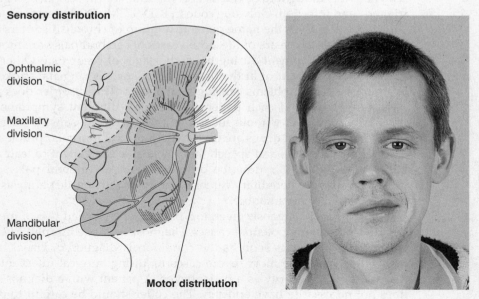

Sensory distribution

Ophthalmic division

Maxillary division

Mandibular division

Motor distribution

Figure 17–1   Example of Bell's Palsy.

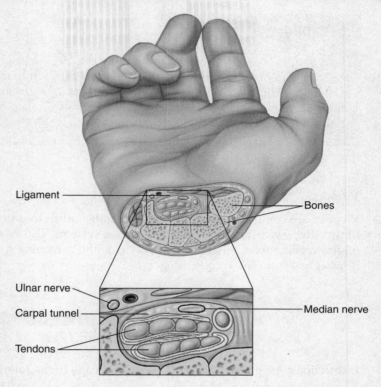

Figure 17–2 Cross-section of wrist where carpal tunnel occurs.

correct severe contractures and abnormally positioned joints. All types of muscular dystrophy are classified under 359.1.

Intracranial Injuries

A concussion is the result of a blow to the head, which causes the brain to strike against the inside of the cranial vault. Minor concussions involve headache and confusion, while severe concussions include loss of consciousness and intracranial bleeding. Category 850 is assigned to cerebral concussions without laceration or hemorrhage of the brain. Fourth-digit subcategories define the time periods for loss of consciousness. Documentation in the medical record should specify whether the patient experienced any loss of consciousness and the duration. Cerebral lacerations, hemorrhages, and other injuries are coded to categories 851–854. Fifth-digit subclassification for these categories specifies the duration of loss of consciousness using the same terminology as in category 850, Concussion. Coders should read documentation carefully, as categories 851–854 divide codes into those with and without open intracranial wounds.

Example:

1. A patient suffered an intracranial hematoma following a fall from a tree. There was no evidence of an open intracranial wound or fracture. The patient was noted to have loss of consciousness of approximately 10 minutes.
   ICD-9-CM codes: 853.02, E884.9

2. A patient was shot in the back of the head with a small caliber handgun during an argument. CT scan showed a cerebellar laceration. The patient was unconscious when brought to the ER and later died of his injury.
   ICD-9-CM codes: 851.75, E965.0

Formula for Success

Use code 920, Contusion of face, scalp, and neck except eye(s), for a diagnosis of head, scalp, or facial contusion when there is no fracture or open wound (laceration). Use code 959.0x for unspecified head injury or injury of the face and neck. Excluded from categories 920 and 959 are specific injuries that are best classified in other sections of ICD-9-CM.

V Codes

V codes are commonly used in the physician's office to describe many of the encounters for health services that involve the nervous system. History of nervous system disease or injury, vaccinations, rehabilitation services, and screening for infectious diseases may all be assigned from the V code category.

EXERCISE 17.2

Instructions: Assign the correct ICD-9-CM V code to the following:

1. Vaccination against Hemophilus influenza   _____

2. History of malignant neoplasm of the facial nerve   _____

3. History of febrile seizure at age 2   _____

4. History of head injury, 5 years ago   _____

5. Family history of Huntington's chorea   _____

6. Pregnant with history of spina bifida in previous pregnancy   _____

7. Observation of newborn for congenital muscular dystrophy,
   ruled out   _____

8. Cerebral shunt present   _____

9. Adjustment of spinal neuropacemaker   _____

10. Speech therapy following stroke   _____

11. Screening for West Nile virus   _____

12. Screening for Alzheimer's disease   _____

CPT® CODING FOR THE NERVOUS SYSTEM

This chapter of CPT® is broken into three primary headings:

- Skull, including meninges, and brain
- Spine and spinal cord
- Extracranial nerves, peripheral nerves, and autonomic nervous system.

In order to select the correct code category, the student should first determine which area of the nervous system is being treated then determine the type of procedure.

Surgery of Skull Base

A medical term that is often misunderstood is *skull base*. Many people interpret this to be the brainstem, or the brain's point of attachment to the spinal column. The skull base is actually the point of contact between the brain and the floor of the cranium. The skull base is divided into three distinct areas:

- Anterior, or the area in front of the ears and behind the eyes and nasal sinuses
- Middle, or the area above the ears
- Posterior, or the area behind the ears and above the spinal column

Procedures that are performed on the skull base are divided into three categories:

1. Surgical approach
2. Definitive procedure
3. Repair or reconstruction

It is common for more than one surgeon to be involved in this type of surgery; therefore, the breakdown of the procedures into different categories makes the reporting easier for each surgeon. Each surgeon reports only the component of the surgery he or she performed. If a surgeon performs the entire operation alone, then he or she would have at least two distinct codes to report, with Modifier 51 added to the secondary procedure.

CPT® describes the approach as the procedure that gains adequate exposure to the lesion in the brain. Surgical approaches are further divided in to these anatomic areas:

- Anterior cranial fossa
- Middle cranial fossa
- Posterior cranial fossa, including brain stem or upper spinal cord

The definitive procedure treats the lesion by biopsy, excision, and resection and includes closure of the dura, mucous membranes, and skin. The definitive procedures are also divided into anatomic areas, the same as for the surgical approach.

Repair/reconstruction procedures are only reported separately if there is extensive grafting of the dura, muscles, or skin. Not all skull base procedures will have repair and/or reconstruction performed.

Example: Dr. A performed a craniofacial infradural approach to the anterior cranial fossa for malignant neoplasm of the frontal lobe.

Codes reported:

ICD-9-CM: 191.1
CPT®: 61580

Dr. B. performed an excision of the lesion, without grafting.

ICD-9-CM: 191.1
CPT®: 61601

If Dr. B performed the entire procedure himself, he would report:

ICD-9-CM: 191.1
CPT®: 61601, 61580-51

If Dr. A assists Dr. B on the definitive portion, then she would report codes in the following manner:

ICD-9-CM: 191.1
CPT®: 61580, 61601-80-51

Modifier 62 is not appropriate to use in this circumstance. Each physician is reporting only the procedure he or she performs, so there is not a split of the fees for a single CPT® code, as would be done with a Modifier 62.

EXERCISE 17.3

Instructions: Link the following CPT® codes and descriptors with the appropriate diagnosis code. Do not assign E codes.

_____ 1. 61140, Burr hole with drainage of brain abscess   **a.** 354.0

_____ 2. 61570, Craniotomy with excision of bullet   **b.** 742.3

_____ 3. 62270, Spinal tap   **c.** 191.2

_____ 4. 63005, Lumbar laminectomy   **d.** 724.2

_____ 5. 64550, Application of TENS unit   **e.** 800.00

_____ 6. 64721, Carpal tunnel decompression   **f.** 851.10

_____ 7. 62273, Injection of blood patch   **g.** 324.0

_____ 8. 62000, Elevation of depressed skull fracture   **h.** 780.31

_____ 9. 61518, Excision of brain tumor, temporal lobe   **i.** 349.0

_____ 10. 62223, Creation of ventriculo-peritoneal shunt   **j.** 724.00

Spine and Spinal Cord

Many of the procedures in this section are similar to procedures that are performed on the skull, meninges, and brain. It is important for the coder to keep the anatomy in mind when choosing a code, to avoid errors.

Injection, Drainage, or Aspiration

This subheading deals with the injection of drugs, dye, or other chemicals for diagnostic or therapeutic purposes. It also includes spinal tap, biopsy, and lysis of adhesions. Code 62263 describes the percutaneous lysis of adhesions in the epidural space using either enzymes or saline, or by using a catheter to mechanically break the adhesions. This code specifies multiple sessions performed on two or more days. If the procedures take place on only one day, use 62264. Codes 62263 and 62264 should not be used together.

Diagnostic lumbar punctures (see Figure 17.3) are reported with code 62270. This procedure is commonly performed in the emergency room, urgent care, or a physician office to help diagnose acute infections such as meningitis, encephalitis, or other problems with cerebrospinal fluid. Remember to code for other associated services and add Modifier 25 to evaluation and management codes performed on the same day.

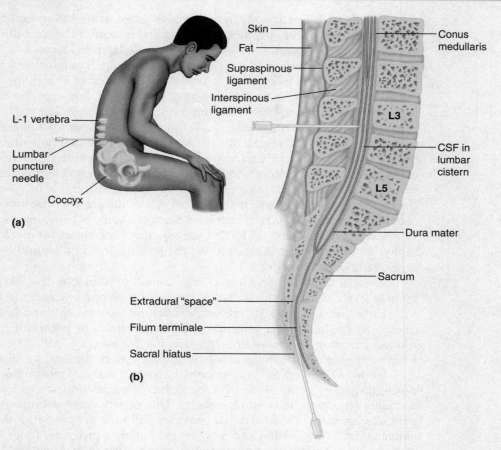

Figure 17–3　Diagnostic lumbar puncture.

　Example:　A patient is seen in urgent care with a severe headache and stiff neck. A detailed HPI, detailed physical exam and moderate level medical decision making are performed to evaluate the symptoms. A lumbar puncture is performed for cerebrospinal fluid studies and complete blood count is drawn. The patient is treated for probable meningitis; definitive diagnosis is pending lab results.

　　ICD-9-CM: 784.0, 719.58
　　CPT®: 99214-25, 62270, 36415-51, 85004

　　　An epidural injection of what is called a "blood patch" or "clot patch" is performed on patients who suffer from a spinal headache. A spinal headache occurs when there is a hole left in the dura that does not close spontaneously following a spinal tap or spinal anesthesia. Cerebrospinal fluid drains out of the hole, and when the patient stands up, gravity pulls more cerebrospinal fluid from around the brain. The traction exerted by this causes an excruciating headache, only relieved by lying down. To treat the spinal headache, a few ccs of the patient's blood is drawn from the arm and injected into the same needle tract left by the spinal needle in the patient's back. The blood clots and forms a patch over the hole in the dura. Small-bore needles are typically used for spinal injections/aspirations to avoid larger holes in the dura.

　Example:　A patient has a spinal headache postoperatively. The anesthesiologist performs a blood patch with quick relief of the headache.

　　ICD-9-CM: 349.0
　　CPT®: 62273

In order to correctly code from this code range, as well as several other subsections in the nervous system chapter, the coder must first recognize the basic difference between an injection and an infusion. An injection is known in layman's terms as a "shot." It is a single dose of medication delivered with a needle and syringe. An infusion is known in layman's terms as an "IV." It is medication delivered over a period of time (hours or days) through a catheter placed in a vein. In the context of this chapter, however, the catheter is placed in the epidural space of the spinal column rather than in a vein. The medication is mixed in a bag with IV fluid and run continuously through the catheter for a period of time.

Codes 62280–62282 describe the injection or infusion of a neurolytic substance into the subarachnoid or epidural spaces of the spine. A neurolytic chemical destroys nerve endings, so this procedure should be considered a permanent destruction, depending upon the chemical used. It is performed for severe, intractable pain and is different than the injections used for pain management when anesthetics or steroids are injected. The coder should carefully note which level along the spine is being injected.

Codes 62284, 62290, and 62291 are injection procedures for myelography or diskography. As with all spinal procedures, the level of injection should be documented and carefully read by the coder.

Code 62287 is the percutaneous aspiration of a lumbar disk. This method does not involve an incision and should not be confused with open excisions of herniated disks.

Codes 62310 and 62311 are single injections into the epidural or arachnoid space of diagnostic or therapeutic substances. CPT® is careful to point out that this is not performed by using an indwelling catheter, but by injection only. The coder should note whether the injection is in the cervical/thoracic area or lumbar/sacral area.

Codes 62318 and 62319 are very similar to the above two codes; however, they are distinguished by being performed through continuous infusion or by intermittent bolus and thus require an indwelling catheter. This is performed commonly for postoperative pain management. The anesthesia provider will visit the patient in the hospital to make adjustments in medication and monitor the patient's progress. These visits should be reported with evaluation and management codes, such as 99231 or 99232.

Reservoir/Pump Implantation

Codes 62360–62368 are used to report implantation, removal, or replacement procedures for various types of pumps, which provide delivery of a medication to the nervous system. These are implanted beneath the skin, similar to a pacemaker with a catheter that is threaded to the area where the drug is deposited. A needle inserted through the skin into the reservoir refills the pump.

Laminotomy/Laminectomy and Decompression Procedures

Patients who have herniated disks, also known as "slipped disks," are often treated by procedures known as laminotomy or laminectomy. These terms refer to the opening or removal of a portion of the vertebra in the spinal column as a surgical approach before treating the displaced intervertebral disk. CPT® describes several different approaches:

■ Posterior approach
■ Transpedicular or costovertebral approach
■ Anterior or anterolateral approach

The posterior approach is made through an incision on the back with the patient prone on the operating table. A transpedicular or costovertebral approach is made from the side of the vertebral column, and an anterior approach is made through the neck, chest, or abdomen with the patient lying supine on the operating table. The anterior approach requires the assistance of a thoracic or general surgeon to move the neck structures, chest, or abdominal contents aside in order for the neurosurgeon or orthopedic surgeon to complete his or her portion of the surgery. Use a Modifier 62 when both surgeons are working together as primary surgeons. The anterior approach is also used for vertebral corpectomies, which is the removal of a crushed vertebrae. A fusion is used to preserve the height of the vertebrae and protect the spinal cord. Arthrodesis (fusion) procedures should be separately coded, using codes from 22548–22812. Diskectomies above or below the injured segment are bundled into the vertebral corpectomy code. Reconstruction of the spine may also be performed following vertebral corpectomy. Use codes 20930–20938 for bone grafting and codes 22840–22855 for spinal instrumentation, if performed.

Formula for Success

Look for the diagnosis code for slipped/herniated disks in the alphabetic index under "Displacement, intervertebral disk." Flag the main term until you become familiar with its location.

Within each type of approach, the codes are divided into anatomic areas—cervical, thoracic, and lumbar, or combinations of those areas. Coders should realize the distinction between the terms *interspace* and *vertebral segments*. An interspace refers to the space between the bones containing the disk material. A vertebral segment is the vertebral bone itself. The phrase "L4–L5 interspace" makes reference to the space between the L4 and L5 vertebral segments. An operative report that discusses L4 *and* L5 is also making reference to the bony vertebral segments, rather than the interspace.

Add-on codes are used within each type of approach to describe additional interspaces or vertebral segments.

Example: Anterior thoracic diskectomies are performed at the T9-10 and T10-11 interspaces. Two surgeons are working together throughout the case.

CPT® codes reported by both surgeons: 63077-62, 63078-62.

Incorrect CPT® codes: 63077-62, 63078-51. The second code is an add-on code, and therefore is Modifier 51 exempt. As long as both surgeons continue to work as primary surgeons throughout the case, a Modifier 62 is appropriate to use on the add-on code.

Other types of lesions on the spinal cord besides herniated disks may be reported using codes 63250–63290. These include neoplasms, arteriovenous malformations, and other lesions. These codes are also segregated by anatomic site: cervical, thoracic, lumbar, and sacral. Codes 63275–63290, which describe the excision of neoplasms, are divided further into extradural, intradural, or combined excisions. The operative report should specify the technique used; if not, then the physician should be queried.

Excision of Intraspinal Lesions

Two surgeons commonly work together when an anterior or anterolateral approach is used to excise a lesion/tumor on the vertebrae or to remove a crushed vertebrae. Similar to the codes described above, codes 63300–63307 describe a vertebral corpectomy that is differentiated by anatomic site (cervical, thoracic, lumbar, or sacral) and further differentiated by approach, such as transthoracic or thoracolumbar. The transthoracic approach involves access through the ribs to the vertebral column, and the thoracolumbar approach involves an incision through the diaphragm.

Neurostimulators

A neurostimulator is used internally for pain control or to control muscle spasms. It has components similar to a pacemaker, with a pulse generator (battery pack) and electrode catheters with varying numbers of contact points on each catheter. The catheter and electrode plates are positioned within the epidural space and lead to a subcutaneous receiver. An external controller is worn by the patient, which allows the patient to control the amount of electrical stimulation. The coder should be careful to look for the method of insertion. Code 63650 describes the percutaneous implantation of electrodes into the epidural space, and code 63655 describes a laminectomy, or open procedure for the implantation of electrodes into the epidural space. The codes in this section of CPT® are differentiated by implantation, revision or removal, as well as the component parts (electrode, pulse generator, or receiver).

Repair

Codes 63700–63710 describe repairs of the spinal column, which may or may not require a laminectomy. Codes 63700–63706 are used for repairs of **meningoceles** and **myelomeningoceles** (spina bifida). The herniation is coded by size—less than 5 cm and larger than 5 cm in diameter. Also included in this section are the repairs of dural or cerebrospinal fluid leaks. These are differentiated by whether a laminectomy is used. Figure 17.4 shows an example of spina bifida.

Extracranial Nerves, Peripheral Nerves, and Autonomic Nervous System

Introduction/Injection of Anesthetic Agent (Nerve Block), Diagnostic or Therapeutic

Codes 64400–64505 are called peripheral nerve blocks. These are typically used for pain management services and are divided into two anatomical groups—somatic nerves and sympathetic nerves. Somatic nerves are those that innervate skeletal muscle for voluntary movement. Sympathetic nerves belong to the autonomic nervous system. They are involuntary and innervate the internal organs. The use of nerve stimulators to locate somatic nerves is not separately reportable.

The nerves in codes 64400–64450 are specified by name. CPT® instructs coders not to report code 01996 (Daily hospital management of epidural or subarachnoid continuous drug administration) along with codes 64416 and 64446–64448, because the code descriptor already includes daily management. Unlike code 01996, the place of service does not specify a hospital setting.

Codes 64470–64484 describe the injection of an anesthetic agent or steroid into a facet joint or facet joint nerve. The level—cervical, thoracic, lumbar, or sacral—should be

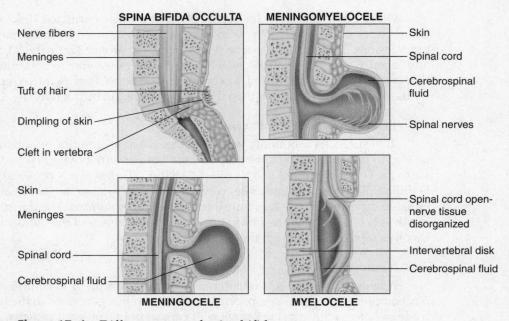

Figure 17–4   Different types of spina bifida.

determined. When multiple injections are performed, each additional level that is injected is described by an add-on code specific to that anatomic level. If fluoroscopy is used for real-time imaging, it should be reported separately in addition to the injection codes.

Example:

1. Mr. Jones arrives at the pain management clinic for an injection of the L5 facet joint. Two levels are injected with a combination of Depo Medrol, 120 mg and 4 cc of Marcaine, .25%. His private insurance will be billed. Evaluation and Management services are not provided at this follow-up visit.

   CPT® codes reported: 64475, 64476
   HCPCS codes reported for drugs: J1030 × 3 and S0020 × 1

2. Mary Smith is brought to the OR for reduction of a fractured humerus due to metastatic disease. She has considerable bone pain. The anesthesiologist places a brachial plexus nerve block by continuous infusion prior to surgery.

   CPT® code reported by the anesthesiologist: 64416
   Incorrect CPT® codes: 64416, 01996.

Codes 64479–64484 are used to describe a transforaminal epidural, which is generally performed on herniated disks. Identify the level being injected and use the add-on codes for each additional level.

Formula for Success

Drugs are included as part of the facility charges for ambulatory surgery centers or hospitals. When the physician is supplying the medications in a physician-owned clinic or pain center, be sure to assign HCPCS codes for injectable or intravenous meds.

Neurostimulators, Peripheral

Neurostimulators on the peripheral nervous system are used for pain control. They are similar to intracranial and spinal neurostimulators. The coder should determine if the procedure is an initial implantation of electrodes, revision/removal of electrodes, or the placement/revision/removal of the pulse generator.

Destruction by Neurolytic Agent

Nerves can be destroyed to give a patient long-term pain relief or to release muscle contractures due to injury or congenital birth defects. Nerves will slowly regenerate over a period of time, so the effect is not permanent when these methods are utilized. Depending on the agent used, results vary from six to eight weeks with Botox and one month to a year with alcohol or phenol. Other techniques include the use of electrical current, radiofrequency, or heat to destroy nerves. Similar to the nerve block codes, the destruction codes are divided into two anatomic sections, somatic and sympathetic nerves. Codes 64622–64627 are used for destruction of nerves in the **facet joints** of the back. These codes are unilateral in nature, so a Modifier 50 must be added when it is performed bilaterally on the same level. Fluoroscopy used to visualize needle placement should be reported separately with 76005.

Formula for Success

The term *rhizotomy* refers to the cutting of a spinal nerve root for pain relief. Use codes 63185–63190 for surgical rhizotomy or 64620–64640 for chemical or radiofrequency rhizotomy.

Neuroplasty for Exploration, Neurolysis, or Decompression

CPT® describes neuroplasty as "the decompression or freeing of intact nerve from scar tissue, including external neurolysis and/or transposition." Nerve groups are identified by anatomic site in this section. Commonly performed procedures found in this section include carpal tunnel decompression and release of ulnar nerve entrapment at the elbow or wrist.

Transection or Avulsion

Codes 64732–64772 are used to report the cutting or removal of a nerve for pain relief. This gives permanent pain relief to patients with incapacitating pain from injury, neoplasms, or other diseases.

Excision

Neuromas are benign tumors that develop on nerves. Codes 64774–64786 describe the excision of neuromas. A Morton's neuroma is located deep within the ball of the foot between the bones of the toes. This should be coded using 28080 from the musculoskeletal chapter of CPT®, rather than a code from the nervous system chapter. The excision codes are divided into somatic and sympathetic nerves. Coders should be careful to watch for procedures on sympathetic nerves that are performed bilaterally and add a Modifier 50 when applicable. The operating microscope is bundled into codes 64820–64823 and should not be separately reported.

Neurorrhaphy

Suturing of nerves is commonly performed utilizing the operating microscope. In this section of CPT®, the operating microscope is NOT bundled into the CPT® code and should be separately reported. Codes are reported for each individual nerve; additional nerves are reported with add-on codes. When nerve grafting is performed, the sural nerve in the ankle is harvested for the graft. Codes 64885–64902 identify the site of repair and the length of graft that is used. A cable nerve graft is one that involves multiple grafts that are sutured onto multiple ends of an injured nerve, creating a cable effect with improved innervation.

Formula for Success

Remember that pain management services can include injection of anesthetic agents or destruction of peripheral nerves. It is extremely important for the coder to distinguish between these two types of procedures.

EXERCISE 17.4

Instructions: Assign the correct modifier and/or CPT® code for the scenario given.

1. A patient has a bilateral intercostal nerve destruction performed due to chronic hiccoughs. _____

2. Drs. A and B together perform an extradural vertebral corpectomy on C3 to remove a lesion on the spine. Dr. B does not help with the corpectomy performed on C4, but she performed the arthrodesis of both segments. Report the codes and modifier(s) for Dr. A. _____ _____

3. Using the same scenario as question 2, report the codes for Dr. B. _____ _____ _____

4. Dr. Jones performed both the approach and definitive procedure for a skull base operation. Modifier _____ is assigned to the procedure that is sequenced second.

5. A lumbar puncture is performed in the Emergency Department. A complete history and physical exam are documented, with moderate medical decision making. _____ _____

CHAPTER REVIEW

Instructions: Choose the correct code combination from the multiple-choice questions below.

1. A patient is admitted to outpatient surgery for a C6-C7 hemilaminectomy. She has been diagnosed with a herniated disk and has had right arm numbness, pain, and tingling of the fingers for approximately eight months. An arthrodesis is also performed.
   a. 722.0, 63015
   b. 722.71, 63015, 22600-51
   c. 722.0, 63020, 22600-51
   d. 722.71, 63020

2. A 3-year-old child was brought to the urgent care clinic with a high fever and elevated white count. While in the clinic, the patient had a febrile seizure. A lumbar puncture was performed.
   a. 780.31, 99214, 62272
   b. 780.6, 780.39, 99214-25, 62270
   c. 780.6, 99214, 62272
   d. 780.31, 99214-25, 62270

3. A 40-year-old male was involved in a motorcycle accident when he failed to negotiate a curve on the road. He was found unconscious; no witnesses were available to document the time of the accident. He was brought to the operating room with a subdural hematoma, which was evacuated through a burr hole.
   a. 852.26, E816.2, 61154
   b. 852.26, 61156
   c. 432.1, E816.2, 61154
   d. 852.06, 61156

4. A 7-year-old patient with congenital spastic cerebral palsy is admitted for an L4–5 rhizotomy.
   a. 343.8, 63185
   b. 344.9, 63190
   c. 344.81, 63185
   d. 437.8, 63190

5. A patient with congenital hydrocephalus requires a ventriculoperitoneal shunt.
   a. 331.4, 62223
   b. 742.3, 62223
   c. 331.4, 62220
   d. 742.3, 62220

6. A patient with two fractured ribs from a fall is referred to the pain management clinic for a regional nerve block. Three nerves are blocked, providing the patient with good relief.

    a. 807.00, E888.9, 64420

    b. 807.02, E888.9, 64620

    c. 807.00, E888.9, 64421

    d. 807.02, 64421, E888.9

7. A 67-year-old patient suffered a severe laceration to his hand from an electric meat slicer at work, severing the digital nerve of the first two fingers on the right hand. The nerves were repaired using the operating microscope.

    a. 883.0, E920.3, 64831-RT, 69990-51

    b. 883.1, E920.2, 64834-RT, 69990

    c. 955.6, E919.8, 64831-F6, 64832-F7, 69990

    d. 955.6, E919.8, 64834-F6, 64837-F7

Case Studies

Case Study 17.1

Preoperative Diagnosis

Chiari I malformation with symptoms of vertical nystagmus, suboccipital headache pain, dizziness, and gait instability.

Postoperative Diagnosis

Chiari I malformation with symptoms of vertical nystagmus, suboccipital headache pain, dizziness, and gait instability.

Name of Operation

Occipital craniectomy with C1-C2 laminectomies and duraplasty for treatment of Chiari I malformation with tonsils extending down the C2 vertebral body.

Anesthesia

General.

Summary

The patient was brought to OR, placed on PAR cart in the supine position where she underwent successful induction of general anesthesia and placement of an endoctracheal tube. Correct placement of the ET tube was checked by anesthesia and when confirmed to be in the correct position, the airway was secured. The patient was then maneuvered into a prone position on a Wilson laminectomy frame and her head was placed in Mayfield head fixation with the neck in a slightly flexed position. Her hair was shaved posteriorly well above inion and then draped on in a sterile manner using double-glove technique. A midline incision was made from approximately 4 cm above the inion down to approximately the C3 spinous process, carried down sharply to the cervical fascia, and hemostasis was accomplished. A periosteal graft was harvested over the posterior portion of the skull and wrapped in a wet sponge for use in the duraplasty later at the end of the procedure. Dissection was carried down sharply in the midline raphe exposing the lamina of C1 and C2 as well as the occipital aspect of the skull. Self-retaining retractors were placed. A C1 and C2 laminectomy was carried out and a posterior fossa craniectomy was performed. Two burr holes were placed in the occipital bone over both cerebellar hemispheres. The dura was elevated away from the inner convexity of the posterior fossa, and then using Midas Rex dissecting tool, a piece of bone was removed to perform the occipital craniectomy. Following this, the dura was opened in a Y-fashion beginning lateral-superior over the cerebellar hemispheres, down to a straight incision over the upper cervical spinal cord, then down to approximately the upper portion of the C3 lamina. The cerebellar tonsils extended to approximately 1 cm above the C3 lamina.

Following this, the operating microscope was brought into the field. The cerebellar tonsils were elevated and the dense adhesions around the medial and anterior portion of the tonsils were dissected away to open up into the fourth ventricle to get good communication of CSF. After this had been accomplished, the piece of periosteum, which had been harvested at the beginning of the procedure, was then sewn into place to enlarge the dura over the tonsillar herniation. A watertight closure was obtained using running dural sutures. Just before the final stitches were placed, the intrathecal area was irrigated with normal saline solution to irrigate as much air out of the exposure as possible before the final stitches were placed.

Following this, the entire exposure was copiously irrigated with Bacitracin and saline solution, and a piece of Gelfoam was placed over the craniectomy and laminectomy sites. The incision was then closed in layers in the usual fashion and the skin was closed with skin staples. The incision was then covered with Bacitracin and sterile 4x4s, which were taped to the back of the patient's neck. The patient was taken out of the Mayfield head fixation, maneuvered back into a supine position where she underwent successful reversal of general anesthesia and extubation. She was moving all extremities well at the end of the procedure and tolerated the surgery without complications. Blood pressure remained stable throughout the procedure with no significant blood pressure lability noted. EBL was 75 cc.

ICD-9-CM Diagnosis Code(s): _____

CPT® Procedure Codes(s): _____

Case Study 17.2

Preoperative Diagnosis

Recurrent L5-S1 disc herniation.

Postoperative Diagnosis

Recurrent L5-S1 disc herniation.

Anesthesia

General.

Procedure

Right posterior hemilaminectomy L5-S1 with decompression of S1 nerve root.

Summary of Procedure

In the operating room in the supine position, the patient was given general endotracheal anesthesia. She was then turned into the prone position and laminectomy rolls and all pressure points were carefully padded. The back was then prepped with betadine scrub followed by an alcohol rinse, followed by draping in the usual manner.

The midline incision at the L5-S1 level was opened and extended 1 cm rostrally and caudally. It was deepened through the subcutaneous tissue and dorsal fascia. A paravertebral muscle dissection was then performed, stripping the muscles off the spinous processes and right lamina of L5 and S1. A Scoville self-retaining laminectomy retractor was placed to keep the wound open.

With 2.5 power loupe magnification and an operating headlight, the medial edge of the residual L5 lamina was identified and a small amount of additional lamina and facet was resected. The epidural fibrosis was bluntly dissected away from the bone. The fibrous tissue and residual ligament were resected and the lateral aspect of the S1 nerve root was identified. Probing within the ventral epidural space identified fibrosis over the disc. This was bluntly opened. This allowed for entrance into the ventral epidural space ventral to the S1 nerve root. There was evidence of free fragment disc herniation. A 12 mm fragment was removed from the ventral epidural space ventral to the S1 nerve root. A more centrally located perforation within the annulus was probed and entered with a micropituitary forceps. Additional fragments of degenerated disc material were removed from the space. A second larger fragment was removed from a central location in the ventral epidural space. This provided excellent decompression of the S1 nerve root, which was now slack to medial retraction. The ventral epidural space was probed with various sized nerve hooks, confirming the absence of any residual fragments.

The wound was irrigated with saline. The bone edges were waxed and Gelfoam was placed in the laminotomy defect for hemostasis. The fascia and skin were closed. The patient was returned to a supine position and extubated and then taken to the recovery room in good condition with stable vital signs.

ICD-9-CM Diagnosis Code(s): _____

CPT® Procedure Codes(s): _____

Eye and Ear

1. Recognize the basic anatomy of the eye and ear.
2. Correctly assign ICD-9-CM codes to diseases and conditions of the eye and ear.
3. Correctly assign CPT® codes to procedures performed on the eye and ear.
4. Identify CPT® and HCPCS modifiers needed for eye and ear procedures.

TERMINOLOGY AND ACRONYMS

AD   Right ear.

AS   Left ear.

AU   Both ears.

Blepharoptosis   Drooping of the upper eyelids due to paralysis or aging.

BOM   Bilateral otitis media.

Canaliculi   Ducts that carry the tears from the glands to the nose, where they are released.

Chalazion   A small mass in the eyelid causing inflammation.

Conjunctivorhinostomy   A communication, surgically created, between the lacrimal sac and the nasal mucosa. A tube may also be inserted into this opening.

Contralateral   On the opposite side.

Dacryocystorhinostomy   An opening in the lacrimal sac causing a communication between the lacrimal sac and underlying bone and nasal mucosa.

Ectropion   The turning outward of the margin of the lower eyelid.

ENT   Ear, nose, and throat.

Entropion   The inversion of the margin of the eyelid.

EOM   Extraocular movement.

Everted punctum   A lacrimal punctum turned outward.

Intraocular lens   IOL—The artificial plastic lens that replaces the natural lens.

Ipsilateral   On the same side.

Iris bombe   A condition where the iris balloons forward, blocking aqueous outflow channels.

Lacrimal punctum   Small openings in the inner canthus of the eye.

OD   Right eye.

OM   Otitis media.

OS   Left eye.

OU   Both eyes.

POAG   Primary open angle glaucoma.

Ptosis   A term used to describe the drooping caused by paralysis or aging.

TM   Tympanic membrane.

Trichiasis   The ingrown or misdirected growth of the eyelashes.

DISEASE PROCESSES AND ICD-9-CM CODING OF THE EYE AND ADNEXA*

ICD-9-CM codes for the eye are arranged by disorders of the globe listed first in category 360, followed by the disorders of the inner structures and layers of the eye from back to front. The eye is an extremely sensitive organ, with multiple layers of delicate tissue. Diseases and disorders can affect each anatomical part of the eye, including systemic diseases such as diabetes. It is important for the coder to understand the various parts of the eye and how to assign codes for the conditions listed in ICD-9-CM. See Anatomy Plate 19 in the Appendix and Figure 18.1 for anatomic illustrations of the eyeball.

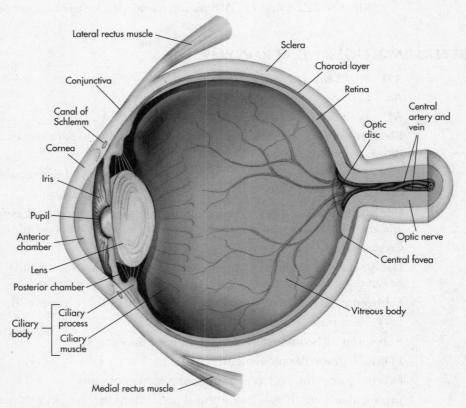

Figure 18–1   Anatomic structures of the eye.

*Diagnostic tests performed on the eye and ocular adnexa are found in Chapter 21 of this text. Refer to that section for additional coding practice.

Inflammations

Inflammations of the globe are assigned to categories 360.0 and 360.1. Fifth digits describe the specific type of ophthalmitis—acute, chronic, parasitic, and so on. The prefix *pan*, as used in *panophthalmitis* and *panuveitis* means "all." Panuveitis is an inflammation of the entire vascular layer of the eye. Inflammations of the eye are quite painful and cause patients to seek medical care within a few days of onset.

Disorders of the Globe

Category 360 describes conditions of the eye associated with low pressure, or hypotony. This condition is the opposite of glaucoma, or high intraocular pressure. Subcategory 360.4x contains degenerative conditions, including code 360.42, Blind hypertensive eye, with loss of vision due to extremely high intraocular pressure. Use code 360.43 to describe blood pooled inside the eyeball not related to a current injury. Traumatic injuries are excluded from this code and cross-referenced to open wounds or contusions of the eyeball.

Categories 360.5 and 360.6 describe retained old foreign bodies. Read documentation carefully to determine if the foreign body is metallic or nonmetallic and assign fifth digits based on location within the eye.

Retinal Disorders

Categories 361 and 362 describe problems with the retina of the eye. The retina is the light-sensitive layer covering the entire posterior chamber of the eye. The retina can become detached and pull away from the wall of the eye. This can cause dramatic light flashes when it occurs and blindness opposite the area of detachment. The detachment can be partial or total in nature and may have single or multiple defects.

When coding for diabetic retinopathy, first assign code 250.5x for the diabetic condition, followed by the retinopathy code, 362.0x. Diabetic retinopathy is classified into two types: proliferative, 362.01; and nonproliferative, 362.00. The proliferative type includes retinal detachment and vitreous hemorrhage caused by an uncontrolled growth of small blood vessels in the retina. These blood vessels can grow into the vitreous gel. Nonproliferative diabetic retinopathy is common among Type II diabetes. It is also known as Preproliferative, or background, diabetic retinopathy and causes deterioration and leakage of the small blood vessels in the eye, leading to macular edema. Both types of retinopathy can progress to eventual blindness, so any hemorrhages or detachments should be treated as quickly as possible.

The macula is located at the center of the back of the eye. It is where all of the central vision occurs in the eye. The remaining retina surrounding it is all used for peripheral vision. Blindness in this area of the eye appears as a dark spot surrounded by normal peripheral vision. Problems with macular degeneration are assigned to 362.5x.

Disorders of the Choroid

The choroid layer of the eye is located beneath the retina. This is a vascular layer with connective tissue between the retina and sclera. Category 363 describes various types of chorioretinitis, pars planitis, scars, detachment, dystrophies, and atrophy of this layer.

EXERCISE 18.1

Instructions: Assign the correct ICD-9-CM code to the following diagnoses.

1. Entropion   _____

2. Papilledema   _____

3. Glaucoma suspect   _____

4. Presbyopia   _____

5. Blindness, both eyes   _____

6. Conjunctivitis, 3-week-old infant   _____

7. Pinguecula   _____

8. Astigmatism   _____

9. Primary open angle glaucoma   _____

10. Subtotal retinal detachment, new onset   _____

Disorders of Iris and Ciliary Body

Use category 364 for disorders of the iris and ciliary body such as inflammation, degeneration, cysts, and adhesions. The iris is the colored portion of the eye that surrounds the pupil. The ciliary body is a ring of vascular tissue that surrounds the lens of the eye. It helps in changing the shape of the lens, known as *accommodation,* and also secretes aqueous humor, the transparent liquid within the eye.

Glaucoma

Glaucoma is a condition of elevated intraocular pressure. The "angles" of the eye constantly drain excess fluid from the internal parts of the eye. When the drain cannot keep up with the production of fluid, the buildup of fluid and pressure is called glaucoma. Category 365 describes multiple forms of glaucoma. Use 365.0x for glaucoma suspect, also known as preglaucoma or borderline glaucoma. Open angle glaucoma is commonly called Primary Open Angle Glaucoma, or **POAG.** This type of glaucoma is often painless, with a gradual loss of peripheral vision. Most patients are controlled with medication, which must be continued for life. Angle closure glaucoma is much more rare than POAG. It is characterized by a blockage of the drainage system. The iris can push into the drainage area, causing a "papillary block." Laser treatments are commonly used for acute angle closure glaucoma. Glaucoma that is associated with systemic conditions, congenital anomalies, and dystrophies is coded with the associated disorder sequenced first and the glaucomatous condition second.

Example: Neurofibromatosis with glaucoma is coded as 237.7 and 365.44.

Cataracts

Category 366 describes various types of cataracts. A cataract is a clouding of the lens of the eye, which obscures visual acuity. Cataracts can occur at any age, but senile cataracts are common in patients over age 60. Infantile, juvenile, and presenile cataracts are coded to 366.0x, with fifth-digit assignment based on the location and type of cataract. Senile cataracts are coded to 366.1x with fifth digits again assigned to type and location. Some systemic diseases and conditions can affect the eyes, leaving patients prone to cataracts. Subcategory 366.4x describes cataracts due to other conditions. Instructional notes here remind the coder to first code the underlying condition before assigning a code for the cataract.

Example: A patient with documented diabetic cataract with diabetes under good control is coded as 250.50 and 366.41.

Disorders of Refraction

Refractive errors include conditions such as farsightedness, nearsightedness, astigmatism, and presbyopia, which is the loss of accommodation due to aging. Assign refractive errors and disorders of accommodation to category 367.

Blindness

Blindness is coded according to the degree of impairment in each eye. Excluded from category 369 is any correctable vision impairment due to refractive errors. Refer to the table in ICD-9-CM that describes levels of visual impairment. The subcategories of 369 are arranged in the following manner:

- 369.0, Profound impairment both eyes
- 369.1, Moderate or severe impairment, better eye, profound impairment lesser eye
- 369.2, Moderate or severe impairment, both eyes
- 369.3, Unqualified visual loss, both eyes
- 369.4, Legal blindness, as defined in the United States
- 369.6, Profound impairment, one eye
- 369.7, Moderate or severe impairment, one eye
- 369.8, Unqualified visual loss, one eye
- 369.9, Unspecified visual loss

Keratitis

Inflammation of the cornea is also known as keratitis. Various types of corneal ulcer, keratitis, neovascularization, and keratoconjunctivitis are coded to category 370. Watch the Excludes notes in this category. Additional codes may be required to fully describe infectious conditions.

Corneal Disorders

Keratoconus, codes 371.60–371.62, is a common condition of the cornea that manifests itself by a cone-shaped bulging of the cornea. Conservative medical treatment of this condition consists of hard contact lenses; otherwise, surgical repair may be performed for acute conditions. Code corneal disorders due to contact lens to code 371.82. This code specifically excludes corneal edema due to contact lens, code 371.24.

EXERCISE 18.2

Instructions: Assign the correct ICD-9-CM code to the following diagnoses.

1. Nuclear cataract   _____

2. Macular degeneration   _____

3. Panophthalmitis   _____

4. Retained steel BB in posterior wall   _____

5. Solar retinopathy   _____

6. Senile cataract   _____

   7. Visual field defect   _____

   8. Retinitis pigmentosa   _____

   9. Dry eye syndrome   _____

10. Strabismus   _____

11. Nystagmus   _____

12. Red eye   _____

13. Ulcerative blepharitis   _____

14. Hordeolum externum   _____

Disorders of the Conjunctiva

Inflammation of the conjunctiva is coded to category 372.0x. More than eighteen types of conjunctivitis are classified here. Read Excludes notes carefully and code underlying disease entities when instructed. Other conditions listed in this category include pinguecula, pterigium, scars, cysts, and hemorrhage.

Inflammations of the Eyelids

Inflammations of the eyelids are coded to category 373. Blepharitis is one type of inflammation. Several types of glands, which are prone to becoming infected, are found in the eyelids. The eyes provide a warm, moist environment, ideal for bacterial growth. Sebaceous glands that become infected in the eyelash follicles are known as styes, code 373.11, or hordeolum externum. The meibomian glands are oil-producing glands found on the inner edge of the eyelid. An infected meibomian gland is called a hordeolum internum, code 373.12. A **chalazion,** code 373.2, is a cyst of the meibomian gland.

Other Disorders of the Eyelids

Entropion and **ectropion** are common disorders of the eye, which cause the eyelashes to turn in or out, causing irritation or dryness of the eyes. Entropion may be treated conservatively at first by taping the inturning eyelid to the cheek and allowing the eyelashes to grow outwards. Ectropion is corrected by resecting a wedge of eyelid and tightening the outward droop of the lid. Code these conditions to 374.0x and 374.1x. Lagophthalmos, an incomplete closure of the eye, is coded to 374.2x, and **blepharoptosis,** a drooping of the upper eyelid, is coded to 374.3x.

EXERCISE 18.3

Instructions: Assign the correct ICD-9-CM diagnosis codes (and E codes where necessary) to the following diagnoses.

   1. Retinoblastoma, primary   _____

   2. Benign neoplasm of the bony orbit   _____

3. Choroidal metastasis from the lung   _____   _____

4. Contusion of eyeball, elbowed in sports, without fall   _____   _____

5. Optic nerve injury from car accident   _____   _____

6. Laceration of globe due to flying glass from explosion   _____   _____

Formula for Success

Blepharoplasty is a plastic repair performed for drooping eyelids. This procedure is considered cosmetic, unless visual field deficits caused by drooping lids are well documented. Check with individual payers regarding guidelines for reimbursement.

Disorders of the Lacrimal System

Code disorders of the lacrimal system to category 375. Conditions listed here include insufficient or excessive tear production, inflammation, obstruction, or stenosis. Treatments for some of these conditions can be performed in the physician office, such as insertion of punctual plugs to keep the eyes moist, probing for obstructions, and insertion of stents to open narrowed lacrimal ducts.

Disorders of the Orbit

Exophthalmos is an abnormal protrusion of the eyeball. This condition has multiple causes including endocrine disorders, bleeding, or fluid behind the eye. Code exophthalmos to subcategories 376.2–376.3. Conditions associated with a thyroid disorder should have the thyroid problem sequenced first.

Disorders of Eye Movement

Strabismus is also known in layman's terms as "crossed eye." It is caused by an imbalance in one or more eye muscles. The condition may affect one or both eyes. It may be congenital or acquired later in life as a result of head injury, neoplasm, or infarction. Code strabismus and related eye movement disorders to category 378. Nystagmus, which is a rapid, involuntary eye movement, is specifically excluded from category 378. Code nystagmus to subcategory 379.5x.

EXERCISE 18.4

Instructions: Link the following procedures to the diagnosis that best describes medical necessity.

_____ 1. Refraction   **a.** V72.0, Routine eye exam

_____ 2. New patient, intermediate exam   **b.** 361.01, Retinal detachment, single defect

_____ 3. Probing of nasolacrimal duct

_____ 4. Postop follow-up visit

_____ 5. Insertion punctual plug

_____ 6. Laser repair of retina

_____ 7. Removal shrapnel, anterior
         chamber

c. 375.15, Dry eye syndrome

d. 360.51, FB, magnetic, in anterior
       chamber

e. 367.0, Hyperopia

f. 375.53, Stenosis of lacrimal canaliculi

g. V43.1, V45.61, Pseudophakia and
       cataract extraction

DISEASE PROCESSES AND ICD-9-CM CODING OF THE EAR*

See Anatomy Plate 20 in the Appendix and Figure 18.2 for illustrations of the anatomy of the ear.

Otitis

The term *otitis* refers to an inflammation of the ear. ICD-9-CM categories 380–382 classify several different types of otitis. These include inflammations of the external and middle ear. Infections of the pinna, or external ear, are coded to category 380. Watch

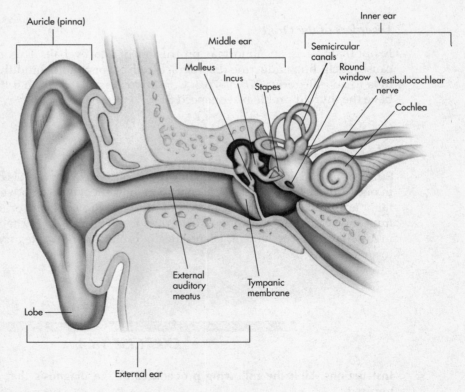

Figure 18–2   Anatomic structures of the ear.

*Diagnostic tests performed on the ear are found in Chapter 21 of this text. Refer to that section for additional coding practice.

for Excludes notes in this category, as well as several instructions to code first the underlying disease. Middle ear infections are divided into two main types—nonsuppurative and purulent. The nonsuppurative types include serous, mucoid, sanguinous, and allergic otitis media (**OM**) that may be either acute or chronic in nature. Code nonsuppurative otitis media to category 381. Acute or chronic otitis of a purulent nature is coded to category 382. Inflammations of the middle ears are often due to upper respiratory infections, while external inflammations are due to skin infections. Children under 4 years of age are at greater risk of developing otitis media due to the immature development of the eustachian tubes. In infancy, the short eustachian tubes are almost horizontal to the ear canal and are easily plugged. As the child ages, the eustachian tube grows to a 45-degree angle, facilitating drainage into the oropharynx. Untreated middle ear infections may lead to speech and language delays due to partial hearing loss.

EXERCISE 18.5

Instructions: Assign the correct ICD-9-CM codes to the following diagnoses.

1. Ménière's disease, in remission   _____
2. Eustachian tube dysfunction   _____
3. Chronic otitis externa   _____
4. Serous otitis media   _____
5. Recurrent cholesteatoma, status post mastoidectomy   _____
6. Tympanosclerosis   _____
7. Acute allergic serous otitis media   _____
8. Tinnitus   _____
9. Otorrhea   _____
10. Bullous myringitis   _____
11. Glue ear   _____
12. Bilateral otitis media   _____
13. Cochlear otosclerosis   _____
14. Acoustic neuritis   _____
15. Sensineural hearing loss   _____

Mastoiditis

Mastoiditis is an inflammation of the mastoid air cells, which are located posteriorly to the ear canal. Category 383 classifies acute mastoiditis with or without complications, chronic mastoiditis, and complications following mastoidectomy.

Vertiginous Syndromes

Ménière's disease or syndrome is characterized by recurrent attacks of sudden vertigo and tinnitus. Prolonged, severe attacks may lead to permanent deafness. It is unknown what causes the disease, but it may be exacerbated by a high salt diet, air travel, swimming in cold water, or ear infections. Diuretics such as hydrochlorothiazide and/or antiemetics such as meclizine are prescribed to help treat the symptoms. There is no known cure for this disease. Labyrinthitis is an infection of the inner ear, also known as otitis interna. This is an infection of the semicircular canals or the cochlea of the inner ear. Assign these inner ear conditions to category 386, with the exclusion of vertigo, which is coded to 780.4.

EXERCISE 18.6

Instructions: Assign the correct ICD-9-CM codes to the following diagnoses.

1. Family history of deafness   _____

2. Laceration of pinna due to dog bite   _____   _____

3. Primary malignancy of the eustachian tube   _____

4. Benign neoplasm, cartilage of the ear   _____

5. Puncture tympanic membrane due to ear swab   _____   _____

6. Metastatic disease of external ear   _____

CPT® CODING OF THE EYE AND OCULAR ADNEXA

Eyeball

Removal of Eye

The procedures in this section describe three different methods of removal of all or part of the eye:

- *Evisceration* is the removal of the contents of the eyeball, including the vitreous, retina, choroids, lens, iris, and ciliary muscles.
- *Enucleation* is the removal of the eyeball, performed by severing the extraorbital muscles and the optic nerve.
- *Exteneration* is the removal of the entire contents of the orbit and the suturing of the eyelids closed.

Each procedure can include extra procedures such as implants, muscle reattachment, bone removal, or muscle flaps. The diagnostic link for these procedures includes neoplasms, trauma, replacement of the eye globe, fitting and adjustment of artificial eye.

Secondary Implant(s) Procedures

Secondary implants are implanted inside the muscular cone. Implants maintain the shape of the orbit following removal of the orbital contents. A prosthesis is an artificial eye that fits inside the implant. The procedures in this section include the insertion of the implant after evisceration or enucleation, reinsertion, modification, and removal of the ocular implant. These procedures are commonly performed for disorders of the globe, conjunctiva, and orbit; fractures; replacement of the globe; fitting and adjustment of artificial eye.

Table 18–1   Removal of Foreign Body of the Eye

Code	Site	Code Specific Method
65205	**Conjunctiva** Superficial	Removal with edge of beveled needle
65210	**Conjunctiva** Embedded	Non-perforating-removal with a V-shaped incision
65220	**Cornea**	Without slit lamp-removal with edge of beveled needle
65222	**Cornea**	With slit lamp-removal with edge of beveled needle
65235	**Intraocular** Anterior chamber	Small incision removal with forceps
65260	**Intraocular** Posterior segment	Magnetic-removal with electromagnetic or magnetic probe
65265	**Intraocular** Posterior segment	Non-magnetic-removal with intraocular forceps

Removal of Foreign Body

Procedures to remove a foreign body from the eye are dependent upon the depth and location of the foreign body. The foreign body may be removed using the beveled edge of a needle or a small incision may be needed for embedded foreign bodies. The methods described in this section are shown in Table 18.1. Figure 18.3 shows the irrigation of the eye for foreign body.

To find these procedures, look in the CPT® index under "Removal foreign body, conjunctiva, cornea, and external eye."

Repair of Laceration

Laceration repairs are dependent upon the depth of the wound and the method of repair. Graft tissue, if needed, is obtained from the conjunctiva or a sliding flap from circumcorneal incision. When the repair is complete, a soft contact lens may be placed as a splint to aid in healing. The diagnostic link for these procedures is open wound to the eyeball, 871.x. The methods described in this section can be divided as shown in Table 18.2.

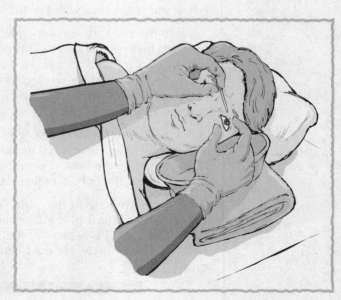

Figure 18–3 Irrigation of the eye.

Table 18–2   Types of Treatment for Eye Lacerations

Code	Site	Code Specific Method
65270	**Conjunctiva**	Direct closure
65272	**Conjunctiva**	Flap or graft mobilization, without hospitalization
65273	**Conjunctiva**	Flap or graft mobilization, with hospitalization
65275	**Cornea,** nonperforating	Suture repair with or without foreign body
65280	**Cornea,** perforating not involving uveal	Suture repair
65285	**Cornea,** perforating involving uveal	Repositioning of the uveal tissue and suture repair
65286	**Cornea**	Tissue glue
65290	**Extraocular muscle, tendon and/or Tenon's capsule**	Layer by layer repair with sutures

EXERCISE 18.7

Instructions: Assign the correct CPT® codes to the following scenarios.

1. A patient is diagnosed with cancer of the eyeball. The patient is surgically treated by enucleation of the eye. The patient is unsure at this time if he wishes to have an ocular implant or what type he should have. _____

2. Two months later, the patient in question 1 decides to have the implant procedure with the muscles attached to the implant. The second procedure is within the global of the first. _____

3. Give the correct CPT® code if the patient in question 1 had elected to have an ocular implant with muscles attached at the time of the original surgery. _____

4. After working outside in the wind, a construction worker has a foreign body sensation in his eye. A foreign body is identified on the patient's cornea at the ophthalmologist's office and is removed with the aid of a slit lamp. _____

5. An auto mechanic is working under a car one day when some debris is dislodged and falls into his eyes. He tries to cleanse the eye and then returns to work. He continues to rub his eyes for several days. He visits his ophthalmologist and it is discovered that a small piece of metal has worked its way into the posterior segment of the eye. With the use of a magnetic device, the physician is able to remove the foreign body through the anterior approach. _____

6. A 5-year-old boy is the passenger in a motor vehicle accident involving a collision with another car. He is taken to the Emergency Room to be treated for several lacerations caused by the broken windshield. One of the wounds is a perforating laceration to the cornea. The ophthalmologist on call performs the repair. _____

7. A farmer is working in the wind when he has a foreign body sensation in his eye. He is able to return to the farmhouse quickly where he flushes his eye with water. Later in the day he is seen by the local ophthalmologist who examines the eye and finds no foreign body. He does find a laceration of the sclera and treats it with tissue glue. _____

Anterior Segment

The procedures for the anterior segment of the eye are divided into the cornea, anterior chamber, anterior sclera, iris, ciliary body, and the lens. The procedures for the anterior segment are listed with the outermost layer of the eye first and continue inward.

Cornea

Excision. The procedures in this section include:

- Biopsy
- Excision of lesion
- Excision or transposition of *ptergium,* which is the fleshy conjunctiva covering the medial cornea.

Removal or Destruction. The methods used for the removal or destruction of a lesion on the cornea include:

- Scraping
- Chemocauterization
- Cryotherapy, photocoagulation, or thermocauterization
- Multiple punctures

Removal and destruction methods may also be used to stimulate new growth in the outer layer of the eye. Cryotherapy, or freezing, is the most common method. These procedures are performed for neoplasms, keratitis, and disorders of the cornea.

Keratoplasty. The procedures in this section mainly pertain to corneal transplants, which include the grafts and the preparation of the donor material. New terminology for this section includes:

- *Lamellar* is the thin outermost layer of the cornea.
- *Penetrating* refers to the full thickness of the donor cornea.
- *Aphakia* refers to patients who have undergone cataract surgery and are without a lens.
- *Pseudophakia* refers to patients who have an artificial lens or are without a natural lens.

Keratoplasties are performed for corneal problems, congenital anomalies, and burns of the eye and adnexa.

Other Procedures. The procedures listed in this section of codes, ranging from 65760 to 65775, describe different types of refractive correction techniques. These are popular methods of vision correction. They are generally considered cosmetic and may not be covered by many insurance carriers. Common diagnoses include disorders of refraction and accommodation, keratitis, corneal and conjunctival problems, and congenital anomalies.

EXERCISE 18.8

Instructions: Assign the correct CPT® codes to the following scenarios.

1. A patient presents to the ophthalmologist with a lesion on the cornea. The physician excises the lesion and receives a report back from pathology that the lesion is benign. _____

2. Give the CPT® code for a patient who is seen for the same type of lesion as in question 1, but the physician performs cryotherapy destruction instead of an excision. _____

3. Due to a decrease in vision, a patient is surgically treated with a full thickness keratoplasty for congenital opacity of the cornea. _____

4. A patient who is near-sighted has vision correction by radial keratotomy. _____

Anterior Chamber

Incision.   A *paracentesis* is the aspiration of aqueous fluid between the iris and cornea. An improper amount of fluid in this chamber can cause permanent damage to the eye. *Vitreous* humor is a gel-like fluid that can become displaced into the space between the iris and cornea. The *hyaloid* membrane, found between the lens and vitreous, may also need to be destroyed. When fluid is removed, the pressure within the eye may be normalized with the injection of air. Varying types of paracentesis are described by codes 65800–65815.

Paracentesis is routinely performed for retinal detachment; other retinal, iris, or ciliary body disorders; and glaucoma.

Goniotomy, code 65820, is an incision made in the scleral-corneal juncture to improve fluid drainage. *Trabeculotomy ab externo*, code 65850, refers to a surgical approach from outside of the eye to open the ring of meshlike tissue known as the trabecular meshwork and improve fluid drainage from the eye. Trabeculoplasty may require several sessions where a selective burning of the trabecular meshwork is performed to improve the drainage of fluid. Use code 65855 for one or more sessions of laser trabeculoplasty.

These procedures are often performed for complications of diabetes mellitus, glaucoma, and congenital anomalies of the eye.

Other Procedures.   The procedures listed in code range 65865–66030 describe removal and repair of adhesions or scar tissue of the eye. The diagnostic link for these procedures includes:

■ Retinal, iris, or ciliary body disorders
■ Corneal opacity and other disorders of the cornea
■ Congenital anomalies of the eye

EXERCISE 18.9

Instructions: Assign the correct CPT® codes to the following scenarios.

1. A glaucoma patient is diagnosed with acute angle closure and has had the first of a series of trabeculoplasty laser treatments. _____

2. A patient with goniosynechiae is surgically treated with an incisional technique. _____

Anterior Sclera

Excision.   Lesions of the sclera can be excised with scleral scissors through a simple conjunctival incision. Use code 66130 for an excision of a lesion on the sclera. Excisions are performed for neoplastic lesions of the eye and other disorders. A majority of codes in this section are performed to create a new pathway for drainage of fluids in the eye. These treatments include fistulization and shunting and commonly treat glaucoma, cataracts, congenital eye anomalies, and birth trauma.

Repair or Revision. *Staphyloma* is a bulging protrusion of the vascular coating of the eye into a thin, stretched portion of the sclera. Repair of this type of defect may be performed either with or without grafting. Use codes 66220–66225 for repair of staphylomas. A revision of an operative wound of the anterior segment is described by code 66250.

EXERCISE 18.10

Instructions: Assign the correct CPT® codes to the following scenarios.

1. A patient with chronic simple glaucoma who has not responded to drug therapy is treated surgically with a trabeculectomy with the *ab externo* approach. _____

2. A patient with scleral staphyloma is surgically treated with a repair using a graft. _____

Iris, Ciliary Body

Several codes throughout this section are noted to be separate procedures. Do not assign a code for a separate procedure when it is part of a related procedure.

Formula for Success

Highlight the statement (separate procedure) in the code descriptors to help visually distinguish these codes.

Incision. An *iridotomy*, or the incision of the iris, may be performed by stab incision and is another method used to control pressure in the eye. Use code 66500–66505 to describe iridotomies made by an incision. A cross-reference is made in CPT® to use code 66761 when the iridotomy is performed by photocoagulation.

Conditions requiring iridotomies include disorders of iris, ciliary body or conjunctiva, glaucoma, after cataract blurring, and congenital anomalies of the eye.

Excision. An *iridectomy* is the excision of a full-thickness piece of the iris to provide a passageway for the aqueous fluid. Do not confuse this term with *iridotomy*, described above. Use codes 66600–66635 for iridectomies. A *cylectomy*, code 66605, refers to a deeper burn or cut into the iris, which goes through the ciliary body. These procedures may be performed for neoplasms, retinal, iris and ciliary body disorders, glaucoma, corneal problems, and congenital anomalies of the eye.

Repair. The repair of trauma to the iris, code 66680, may be performed through an incision. Repair of the ciliary body, code 66682, describes the retrieval of sutures if dissolving sutures are not used. Link these procedures to disorders of the iris and ciliary body, cataracts, and open wound of the eyeball.

Destruction. Destruction of the ciliary body is performed when high intraocular pressure cannot be controlled in any other way. These methods reduce the production of aqueous fluid. The destruction procedure can be performed by several different methods:

■ *Diathermy:* Use of a heat probe.
■ *Cyclophotocoagulation:* Use of a laser to burn holes in the ciliary body.
■ *Cryotherapy:* Use of a freezing probe.
■ *Cyclodialysis:* Method where a spatula is passed through an incision in the eye and the ciliary body and the scleral spur are separated.

Release of intraocular pressure can also be accomplished by other procedures, such as iridotomy/iridectomy performed with a laser and iridoplasty.

EXERCISE 18.11

Instructions: Assign the correct CPT® codes to the following scenarios.

1. A patient is seen in the ophthalmologist office for decreased vision. The physician finds that the patient has iris bombe. The patient is treated later in the day at an ambulatory surgery center by an iridotomy with transfixion. _____

2. A patient is seen for an annual eye exam. He is found to have increased intraocular pressure in the left eye. He has no history of glaucoma. During the exam, the patient is found to have a lesion of the iris that could be blocking the drainage of fluid and causing the glaucoma. The lesion is surgically removed by peripherial iridectomy. Upon return to the physician's office, the pathology report has returned with a benign result and the patient's eye pressure has returned to normal. _____

3. An ophthalmologist evaluates a glaucoma patient who has been on long-term corticosteroid therapy. Because of the medication history, the normal treatments have failed. The physician schedules treatment of the patient's steroid induced glaucoma by performing a surgical destruction of the ciliary body using cryotherapy. _____

Lens

Incision.   An after cataract occurs when the capsule or its attached membrane, the anterior hyaloid, have become opaque, causing blurry vision, and must be destroyed. This can be performed by either a stab incision technique or by laser surgery. The method used is called a *discission* of a secondary cataract, described by code 66820.

The repositioning of **intraocular lens** prosthesis, code 66825, can be performed through an incision in the junction of the cornea and sclera. The physician is able to adjust the artificial lens so that the haptics or attachments of the implant are secure.

Removal of Cataract.   Codes 66830–66986 describe different types of cataract removals. Depending upon the method used, cataract removals may include a number of the following procedures: lateral canthotomy, iridectomy, iridotomy, anterior capsulotomy, posterior capsulotomy, viscoelastic agents, enzymatic zonulysis, pharmacological agents, and subconjunctival or subtenon injections.

When the capsule and/or the membrane attached to it become opaque after extracapsular cataract surgery, the capsule is removed by an *irrigating cystotome*. The irrigating cystotome is an instrument that cuts and suctions the posterior lens capsule. Watch for documentation of specific types of cataracts for diagnostic code linkage.

The removal of lens material for the treatment of cataracts can be performed by a number of different methods including:

■ *Aspiration:* An irrigating/aspirating probe is inserted into the lens, and the lens is destroyed and aspirated.

■ *Phacofragmentation:* Similar to the aspiration method except that the probe vibrates approximately 40,000 times per second, using sound waves to break up the lens. This is also known as *phacoemulsification.*

■ *Pars plana approach:* A method whereby the physician enters the lens capsule from behind. A small suction device is used to remove the lens.

■ *Intracapsular cataract extraction,* also referred to as ICCE: The lens is removed intact.

■ *Extracapsular cataract extraction,* also referred to as ECCE: The anterior shell and the lens capsule are removed, leaving the posterior shell intact.

The codes listed below differentiate the various techniques used in lens extractions and replacement procedures:

■ Codes 66830–66940 do not include the placement of an intraocular lens.

■ Codes 66982–66984 include the intraocular lens placement.

■ Code 66985 is used to report the intraocular lens placement when performed in separate surgical setting from the cataract removal.

■ Code 66986 describes the exchange of intraocular lens.

■ Code 66825 describes the repositioning of an intraocular lens requiring an incision.

EXERCISE 18.12

Instructions: Assign the correct CPT® codes to the following scenarios.

1. A patient diagnosed with nuclear sclerosis cataract of the right eye is surgically treated using the extracapsular extraction method with insertion of intraocular lens. _____

2. The patient in question 1 is treated one month following the first procedure in the left eye for the same condition. Assign the proper codes and modifiers for a cataract extraction on the left eye with a 90-day global period. _____

3. A patient presents to the ophthalmologist with decreased vision in the left eye two months after a cataract extraction. The patient is diagnosed with after-cataract blurring of vision. The patient is surgically treated by discission of secondary membranous cataract with the YAG laser. _____

4. A patient who had cataract extraction with intraocular lens placement two years previously has decreased vision in the right eye. After examination by an ophthalmologist, it is discovered that the intraocular lens has become dislodged. The physician repositions the lens prosthesis and clear vision is regained. _____

5. An ophthalmologist examines a 3-year-old after the patients' parents suspect a vision problem. The patient is diagnosed with bilateral juvenile anterior subcapsular polar cataract. The physician begins treatment by performing an extracapsular cataract removal with insertion of intraocular lens on the right eye only. _____

Posterior Segment

Vitreous

Vitreous is the clear gel-like fluid filling the posterior cavity of the eye. Removal of vitreous can be performed by methods shown in Table 18.3.

Table 18–3   Removal of Vitreous

Code	Approach	Vitrectomy Method	Includes
67005	Anterior	Aspiration	Partial removal
67010	Anterior	Mechanical	Subtotal removal
67015	*Pars plana*	Aspiration or release	Vitreous, subretinal or choroidal fluid
67036	*Pars plana*	Mechanical	Vitrectomy only
67038	*Pars plana*	Mechanical	With epiretinal membrane stripping
67039	*Pars plana*	Mechanical	With focal endolaser photocoagulation
67040	*Pars plana*	Mechanical	With endolaser panretinal photocoagulation

The difference in the performance of these methods is as follows:

- *Anterior approach* is performed by inserting the aspirating needle into the limbus or cornea.
- *Aspiration by pars plan approach* is performed by inserting the aspirating needle by posterior approach and may involve instruments such as a rotoextractor or vitreous infusion suction cutter (VICS).
- *Mechanical vitrectomy* is performed with three small incisions into the eyeball using a *pars plan* approach. The incisions are used for the light, infusion cannula, and cutting or suction instrument.

Other procedures described in this section are:

- Injection of vitreous substitute replaces the removed vitreous fluid and restores normal pressure to the eye.
- Implantation of intravitreal drug delivery system to deliver a controlled amount of medication over a period of months.
- Intravitreal injection of pharmacologic agent to introduce medication to the posterior segment of the eye.
- Dissection and severing of the vitreous strands cut away membranous strands, adhesions, and opacities that obstruct vision.

Some common diagnoses for these procedures include diabetes, disorders of the globe, retinal detachment, inflammation of the choroids, glaucoma, cataract, disorders of the cornea, trauma, congenital eye problems, and complications of procedures.

Retina or Choroid

Repair. The detachment of the retina is a serious condition and can result in the loss of vision. When the retina detaches, the blood supply is lost and the retina falls into the posterior cavity of the eye. There are several different methods of correcting this condition, including:

- *Cryotherapy or diathermy:* Reattachment of the retina to the back of the eye by freezing and sealing the retina to the back of the eye.
- *Photocoagulation:* A method using a laser light or xenon arc that goes through a dilated pupil. A spot is burned at the site of the detachment, and this seals the retina back into place.
- *Scleral buckle:* A Silastic band placed circumferentially around the external eye. The band places pressure on the eye and allows the retina to reattach.

These methods may be performed with a vitrectomy or the injection of air or other gas. Code 67112 is used specifically for patients having a previous ipsilateral retinal detachment. The codes for reporting the removal of the scleral buckle and any implanted material are also included in this section.

Repairs on the retina or choroid are performed for disorders such as:

■ Disorders of the globe
■ Eye disorders, including the sclera, vitreous, lens, and nystagmus
■ Glaucoma
■ Vision disturbances
■ Strabismus and other disorders of binocular eye movements
■ Complications of procedures

Prophylaxis. The procedures in this section can be performed in multiple sessions. Because of this, the methods of reporting these services may vary. Descriptors in this section are used to report *all* sessions in a treatment period only once. The two methods listed in this section include:

■ Cryotherapy or diathermy, code 67141
■ Photocoagulation by laser or xenon arc, code 67145

Prophylactic procedures are commonly performed for diabetes mellitus, retinal detachment and other retinal disorders, and choroidal inflammation and scars.

Destruction. The destruction of a localized lesion of the retina in one or more sessions can be performed by:

■ Cryotherapy or diathermy
■ Photocoagulation
■ Radiation by implantation of source

The destruction of a localized lesion of the choroid can be performed by:

■ Photocoagulation
■ Photodynamic therapy

Report photodynamic therapy for one eye using code 67221. Report therapy on the second eye during one session with code 67225 add-on code to 67221.

Cryotherapy, diathermy, and photocoagulation are used for destruction of progressive retinopathy, during one or more sessions. Use codes 67227–67228 to describe these services.

Sclera

Repair. Two codes are currently assigned to this section of CPT®. Codes 67250 and 67255 describe a scleral reinforcement for a thin or weakened sclera, performed with or without a graft. The sclera can be reinforced by overlapping or a patch can be grafted over the area.

EXERCISE 18.13

Instructions: Assign the correct CPT® codes to the following scenarios.

1. A patient is seen by an ophthalmologist for decreased vision. Upon examination, the patient is found to have a vitreous hemorrhage in the left eye. The patient is treated with a subtotal removal of vitreous with mechanical vitrectomy. _____

2. An ophthalmologist treats a patient with vitreous strands in both eyes with bilateral laser severing. _____

3. A patient is seen by an ophthalmologist after seeing flashes of light intermittently for two days. He diagnoses the patient with a retinal detachment in the right eye and treats the patient with scleral buckling and vitrectomy. _____

4. A patient is surgically treated for choroidal neovascularization of the left eye by photo-coagulation. _____

Ocular Adnexa

Extraocular Muscles.   Strabismus surgery is performed to correct an imbalance in the muscles of the eyeball that control movement. Codes in this section are listed by the orientation of the muscle—horizontal or vertical—and the number of muscles strengthened or weakened. One code, 67318, is used to report the strabismus surgery performed on the superior oblique muscle by any method.

Several add-on codes are found in this section to report conditions, which add difficulty to strabismus surgeries. Conditions reported by these add-on codes include:

- Transposition of any extraocular muscle
- Previous eye surgery or injury not involving extraocular muscles
- Scarring of extraocular muscles
- Posterior fixation suture technique
- Adjustable sutures
- Exploration and/or repair of detached extraocular muscle(s)

Watch for diagnostic code linkage to include procedures such as:

- Muscular dystrophies and other myopathies
- Visual disturbances
- Strabismus and other disorders of binocular eye movements
- Eye disorders, other including the sclera, vitreous, lens, and nystagmus

A less invasive procedure to correct muscular imbalance is the chemodenervation of extraocular muscles, described by code 67345. This describes the use of an electromyographic needle to inject a specific quantity of botulin toxin. This medication causes paralysis of the muscle, with effects lasting from four to eight weeks.

Orbit

Exploration, Excision, Decompression.   An orbitotomy is a surgical incision into the orbit of the eye. Patients who have neoplasms of the eye; retinal, lacrimal, or optic nerve disorders; visual disturbances or trauma may require exploration, decompression, or excisional procedures on the orbit. Codes in this section describe the fine needle aspiration of the orbital contents and several methods for orbitotomy.

Formula for Success

Watch CPT® descriptors carefully to assure the correct approach is chosen for codes 67400–67450.

Other Procedures.   The procedures described in this section include:

- *Retrobulbar injection:* An injection through the lower eyelid or transconjunctival method. An injection is used to deposit medication or alcohol behind the eye.
- *Tenon's capsule injection:* An injection along the surface of the globe beneath the conjunctiva and between the sclera and Tenon's capsule.

CPT® contains a reminder to code separately for the supply of medication when using code 67500. Use 67505 for a retrobulbar injection of alcohol or 67500 for a retrobulbar injection of medication. A subconjunctival injection is described in a different heading of the eye chapter under code 68200.

- *Optic nerve decompression,* described by code 67570, is performed to relieve pressure on the optic nerve by *fenestration* or the creation of openings in tissue.

These procedures are commonly performed for neoplasms, trauma, eye, retinal orbital and optic nerve disorders, glaucoma, visual disturbances, congenital anomalies, late effects of injuries, and complications of procedures.

EXERCISE 18.14

Instructions: Assign the correct CPT® codes to the following scenarios.

1. A patient is diagnosed with monocular esotropia of the left eye and is surgically treated with strabismus surgery of two horizontal muscles. _____

2. Using the patient in question 1, give the correct CPT® code if the patient had scarring of extraocular muscles. _____

3. A patient receives a Botox injection of the right extraocular muscle for multiple sclerosis. _____

4. An orbitotomy with bone flap and lesion removal is performed on a patient with a malignant neoplasm of the cartilage of the right eyelid. _____

Eyelids
Incision.   Types of incisional eyelid procedures include:

- *Blepharotomy,* code 67700: An incision into the eyelid for the drainage of an abscess.
- Severing of *tarsorrhaphy,* code 67710: Severing of sutures that close the eyelid. A tarsorrhaphy is sometimes performed to protect the cornea after a surgical procedure.
- *Canthotomy,* code 67715: Slitting of the canthus to enlarge the opening between the upper and lower eyelids. This code is also noted to be a separate procedure and is often performed as part of a larger procedure.

Excision.   The codes in this section are used to report lesion removal of more than skin. When lesion removal involves mainly the skin of the eyelids, codes from the Integumentary section should be used. Several codes in this section identify specific diagnoses, such as chalazion and **trichiasis,** within the descriptor. Care should be taken to ensure correct diagnosis linkage to these procedures.

Removal of a chalazion can be reported by codes 67800–67808, which describe single or multiple-same lid, multiple-different lid, or the use of general anesthesia and/or hospitalization for single or multiple chalazions.

Correction of trichiasis may include epilation by forceps, cryotherapy, laser, or electrosurgery. Trichiasis can also be corrected by incision of the lid margin, which can include a free mucous membrane graft. Report trichiasis procedures using codes 67820–67835.

Other procedures described in this section are biopsy, excision, and destruction of lesions of the eyelid. Link these diagnoses to neoplasms, eyelid inflammations, disorders of the lacrimal system and eyelids, and congenital anomalies of the eye.

Tarsorrhaphy.   *Tarsorrhaphy* is the temporary closure of the eyelid by suture. The construction of intermarginal adhesions is included in this section and can include a transposition of tissue from the upper or lower lid. The diagnostic link for these procedures includes:

- Neoplasms
- Facial nerve and eyelid disorders
- Keratitis
- Corneal opacity and other disorders of cornea
- Open wound of ocular adnexa
- Burns confined to eye and adnexa

Repair (Brow Ptosis, Blepharoptosis, Lid Retraction, Ectropion, Entropion). Problems with drooping eyelids or eyebrows are not always cosmetic procedures. Patients may have documented problems with visual acuity due to obstruction, or dry eyes from eyelids that turn outwards. Correction of these problems is described by codes 67901–67908.

Codes 67914–67924 describe specific procedures for the treatment of ectropion and entropion. The methods of repair of these conditions are shown in Table 18.4.

Reconstruction.   Procedures for blepharoplasty can include the lid margin, tarsus, and/or palpebral conjunctiva in addition to the skin of the eyelid. Procedures described in this section include:

- Suture of recent wound, partial and full thickness
- Removal of embedded foreign body of the eyelid
- *Canthoplasty*, or reconstruction of the canthus
- Extensive excision and repair of the eyelid, up to one-fourth of the lid margin and over one-fourth of the lid margin.
- Reconstruction of the eyelid, full thickness transfer of tarsoconjunctival flap:
  - One stage or first stage
  - Total lower eyelid, one stage or first stage

Table 18–4   Coding Methods of Repair for Ectropion and Entropion

Repair	Suture	Thermocauterization	Blephroplasty Excision Tarsal Wedge	Blephroplasty Extensive
Ectropion	67914	67915	67916	67917
Entropion	67921	67922	67923	67924

■ Total upper eyelid, one stage or first stage
■ Second stage

EXERCISE 18.15

Instructions: Assign the correct CPT® codes to the following scenarios.

1. A patient with a chalazion of the left upper eyelid is treated by excision. _____

2. An ophthalmologist treats a patient with trichiasis of the right eye by electrosurgical epilation. _____

3. A patient is surgically treated for bilateral senile entropion with excisional blepharoplasty. _____

4. A patient is brought into the Emergency Room after he was assaulted and beaten in an alleyway. Most of the wounds were superficial, but his left eyelid required a full thickness repair including the lid margin and conjunctiva. _____

5. Using the same patient in question 4, assign the CPT® code if the patient sustained an injury that required a single stage reconstruction with a full thickness transfer of a tarsoconjunctival flap. _____

Conjunctiva

Incision and Drainage. These procedures include the incision and drainage of a conjunctival cyst, code 68020, and expression (or drainage) of conjunctival follicles, code 68040. Diagnostic links for these procedures include trachoma, conjunctival diseases and disorders, and late effects of other infectious and parasitic diseases.

Excision and/or Destruction. The procedures in this section include biopsy, excision of lesions, and destruction of lesions of the conjunctiva. Excision codes specify the size of the lesion up to or over one centimeter and if adjacent sclera was excised.

Injection. A subconjunctival injection is used to deliver a steroid or antibiotic with a small gauge needle into the subconjunctival space. This procedure is used to treat a variety of conjunctival disorders.

Lacrimal System

Incision

Incision of the lacrimal gland, lacrimal sac, or **lacrimal punctum** is performed to ensure that the conjunctiva and cornea remain moist. The lacrimal system is responsible for the production, distribution, and elimination of tears (see Figure 18.4). Conditions associated with these procedures include disorders of the lacrimal system, category 375, and congenital eye anomalies in category 743 of ICD-9-CM.

Excision

The procedures in this section include:

■ Excision of lacrimal gland, partial or total (dacryoadenectomy)
■ Biopsy of lacrimal gland or lacrimal sac

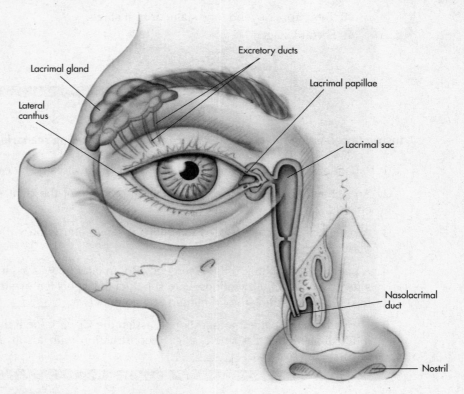

Lacrimal gland

Excretory ducts

Lacrimal papillae

Lateral
canthus

Lacrimal sac

Nasolacrimal
duct

Nostril

Figure 18–4   The lacrimal system.

- Excision of lacrimal sac (dacryocystectomy)
- Removal of foreign body of dacyrolith of the lacrimal passages
- Excision of lacrimal gland, frontal approach or including osteotomy

These procedures are performed for neoplasms, lacrimal system disorders, and for-eign bodies on external eye.

Repair

The procedures described in this section are performed to enable proper tear flow. A common procedure performed as treatment of dry eye, 375.15, is the closure of the lacrimal punctum using a punctual plug. These tiny plugs can be made of a temporary or permanent material and are placed within the opening or punctum. The procedure is performed in the physician office. Temporary plugs are often placed before permanent plugs to see if the condition improves. Temporary plugs are made of collagen and are gradually absorbed.

Probing and/or Related Procedures

The lacrimal system can become obstructed in the punctum or the duct. Procedures to relieve obstruction include:

- Dilation of the lacrimal punctum using a probe, catheter, or suture.
- Probing of the nasolacrimal duct with a probe inserted into the canaliculus, through the lacrimal sac, and into the nasolacrimal duct. Stent placement and general anesthesia can also be included.

- Probing of the canaliculi.
- Injection of contrast media for dacryocystography involving the injection of a radiopaque dye and the use of radiography for visualization.

EXERCISE 18.16

Instructions: Assign the correct CPT® codes to the following scenarios.

1. A physician drains a conjunctival cyst of the right eye by incision. _____

2. A patient has an excision of a 2.5 cm lesion of the left conjunctiva that pathology reports as malignant. _____

3. A physician performs conjunctivoplasty with a free graft of buccal mucosa membrane on a patient with symblepharon of the right eye. _____

4. A patient is seen for chronically red left eye. He is found to have a dacryolith in the lacrimal passage. The physician performs an excisional removal of the dacryolith. _____

5. A patient is diagnosed with dry eye syndrome of both eyes. The optometrist places punctual plugs in both lower lids. _____

6. A patient is treated for stenosis of the right lacrimal punctum with probing of the nasolacrimal duct and the placement of a stent. _____

Modifiers

Modifier usage is important to indicate which eye is being surgically treated, and also for reimbursement purposes. Some of the CPT® codes in the Eye and Ocular Adnexa chapters have parenthetical reminders to use Modifier 50 for bilateral procedures. Use this modifier when the code indicates a unilateral procedure, and both eyes are operated on.

Right and left eyes are indicated by HCPCS modifiers RT and LT. Use HCPCS modifiers on Medicare claims and other payers who require their use. Other HCPCS modifiers identify specific eyelids:

- E1, Upper left eyelid
- E2, Lower left eyelid
- E3, Upper right eyelid
- E4, Lower right eyelid

CPT® CODING OF THE AUDITORY SYSTEM

The auditory system is broken down into three sections in CPT®: external, middle, and inner ear procedures. Diagnostic tests performed on the auditory system are found in Chapter 21 of this text. Refer to that section for additional coding practice.

External Ear

Incision

The incision procedure codes in this section consist of the drainage of abscess or hematoma for the external ear (simple or complicated) and the external auditory canal. Ear piercing is also listed in this section, although it is rarely performed. The diagnostic linkage for incisional procedures includes the following.

Excision

The excision procedures for the external ear are shown in Table 18.5.

Formula for Success

Tips for Coding External Ear Excisions

1. When resection of the temporal bone is performed, use 69535.
2. When skin grafting is performed, see codes 15000–15261.

Removal of Foreign Body

The removal of a foreign body from the external auditory canal can be performed using forceps, a cerumen spoon, or suction. Codes allow for removal with or without general anesthesia and the removal of impacted cerumen for one or both ears. Look for documented diagnoses specific to these procedures—foreign body in ear, 931, and impacted cerumen, 380.4.

The *mastoid cavity* is located posterior to the ear canal. Once a patient has undergone a mastoidectomy, the cavity requires debridement every three to six months. The debris can be removed using suction, cerumen spoon, and forceps. The debridement can be simple or complex (requiring anesthesia). The diagnostic link for these procedures can include:

- Tuberculosis of the mastoid
- Disorders of the external ear, eustachian tube, tympanic membrane, middle ear, and mastoid
- Infections, such as otitis media or mastoiditis

Formula for Success

Keep the mastoid cleaning procedure codes 69220–69222 distinct from the surgical excision of the cavity, codes 69501–69511.

Repair

The repair procedures listed in this section include reconstructive procedures and *otoplasty*, which is the surgical correction for protruding ears. Reconstruction and plastic repairs are often performed for trauma and deformities of the external ear. Note that code

Table 18–5   Excision Procedures for the Ear

Code	Procedure	Site	Specific Method
69100	Biopsy	External ear	Scalpel or punch
69105	Biopsy	External auditory canal	Scalpel, curette, forceps
69110	Excision	External ear	Partial, simple repair
69120	Excision	External ear	Complete amputation
69140	Excision	External auditory canal	Exostosis
69145	Excision	External auditory canal	Soft tissue lesion
69150	Radical Excision	External auditory canal lesion	Without neck dissection
69155	Radical Excision	External auditory canal lesion	With neck dissection

69310 is listed as a separate procedure and should not be unbundled when part of a larger procedure.

Formula for Success

Tips for Coding External Ear Repair

1. When the reconstruction is performed with middle ear reconstruction, see codes 69631 and 69641.
2. When the reconstruction includes grafts of skin, cartilage, or bone, see codes 13150–15760 and 21230–21235.

EXERCISE 18.17

Instructions: Assign the correct CPT® codes to the following scenarios.

1. A patient with a large malignant lesion of the left external auditory canal is surgically treated with a radical excision, including a neck dissection. _____

2. A 5-year-old boy is seen by his family practice physician, in his office, to remove a bead placed in the left ear. _____

3. An elderly gentleman is seen by his physician for hearing loss. Upon examination, it is found that the man has cerumen impaction of both ears. The ears are both cleaned by irrigation and the hearing check after the procedure is normal. _____

4. A patient with congenital atresia of both external auditory canals is surgically treated with a single stage reconstruction. _____

Middle Ear

Introduction

The *eustachian tube* leads from the middle ear to the pharynx and aids in draining fluid from the ear. The procedures listed in this section aid in treating a blocked or collapsed eustachian tube and include:

- *Transnasal* eustachian tube inflation using a nasopharyngoscope to place a small catheter through the nose. When performed without catheterization, air is used as resistance to inflate the tube.
- *Transtympanic* eustachian tube catheterization is performed through the middle ear.
- *Baffle technique* is a method that provides an assessment of middle ear disease using sound waves.

These procedures are used as treatment for diagnoses such as nonsuppurative otitis media and eustachian tube disorders, found in category 381, and hearing loss in category 389 of ICD-9-CM.

Incision

The procedures in this section include:

- *Myringotomy,* which is an incision into the tympanic membrane (**TM**).
- *Tympanostomy,* which is an incision into the tympanic membrane and the placement of a ventilation tube for drainage.
- *Tympanolysis,* which is the removal of adhesions or scars from the tympanic membrane.

Aspiration of fluid and the insertion of a tube is performed with these methods to drain fluid from the middle ear. These procedures can be performed under local or general anesthesia. Removal of the ventilation tubes can be billed separately using code 69424 if general anesthesia is required. Myringotomies are performed primarily for infections, but can also be performed for disorders of the vestibular system, and other ear problems.

Excision

A mastoidectomy is a removal of diseased mastoid mucosa. This procedure may be performed by different methods including:

- *Transmastoid antrotomy*, where the mastoid cortex is removed. This is performed when the diseased tissue is limited to the antrum region to facilitate drainage.
- Complete mastoidectomy.
- Modified radical mastoidectomy, where the posterior bony canal is taken down to the level of the facial nerve and is repaired using skin flaps.
- Radical mastoidectomy, where the posterior and superior bony canals walls are removed down to the facial nerve.
- Radical mastoidectomy, including *petrous apicectomy*.

Mastoidectomies are performed for neoplasms; eustachian tube, middle ear, and mastoid disorders and infections; otitis media; otosclerosis; certain types of deafness; and congenital anomalies of the ear.

Codes 69540–69554 describe excisions of ear polyps and vascular tumors called *aural glomus tumors*. The excision of aural polyps is performed through the external canal using a snare or forceps. Aural glomus tumors are removed through several different approaches:

- *Transcanal:* Through the auditory canal.
- *Transmastoid:* Through an incision into the mastoid cavity exposing the mastoid sinus.
- *Extended* or *extratemporal:* Through an incision in front of the ear. This method also includes a complete mastoidectomy.

These procedures are performed for neoplasms, infection, and disorders of the middle ear, mastoid, and vestibular system.

Repair

Occasionally, a revision of a mastoidectomy is performed to convert a simple mastoidectomy into the following outcomes:

- Complete mastoidectomy, 69601
- Modified radical mastoidectomy, 69602
- Radical mastoidectomy, 69603
- Mastoidectomy with apicectomy, which opens the petrous apex for drainage, 69605

Keep in mind that each consecutive code indicates a more complex procedure than the previous code.

Tympanic membrane perforations can happen spontaneously, as a result of infection that progresses to rupture or from trauma. Be sure to link diagnoses specific to the cause of perforation.

Tympanoplasty is the repair of the tympanic membrane. The procedures in this section include many related procedures with a separate code for each combination. The three main types of tympanoplasty include:

- Tympanoplasty without mastoidectomy, 69631
- Tympanoplasty with antrotomy *or* mastoidotomy, 69635
- Tympanoplasty with mastoidectomy, 69641

Highlight key words in the descriptors that specify "with," "or," and "without" to help distinguish these codes from each other. Beneath each code are additional procedures that identify the magnitude of the surgery, along with any ossicular chain reconstruction. These procedures are performed for infections, deafness, trauma, and congenital anomalies.

Procedures performed on the stapes include the following:

- Stapes mobilization: Corrects stapes fixation.
- Stapedectomy or stapedotomy: Includes replacement of the stapes with prosthesis.
- Revision of stapedectomy or stapedotomy: A repositioning, revision, or replacement of the prosthesis.

These procedures are performed for disorders of the middle ear and mastoid, otosclerosis, deafness, and trauma.

Other Procedures

The implantation, removal, repair, and replacement for hearing devices are described in codes 69710–69718. Such devices include electromagnetic bone conduction and osseointegrated implants. Some codes specify "with" or "without" mastoidectomy in the descriptor.

Several procedures on the facial nerves are also listed in this section. The coder should determine if the procedure is being performed medial or lateral to the geniculate ganglion. Decompression and suture of the facial nerve is performed for neoplasms, infection, deafness, trauma, and disorders of the middle ear, mastoid, and vestibular system.

EXERCISE 18.18

Instructions: Assign the correct CPT® codes to the following scenarios.

1. A 10-year-old patient diagnosed with eustachian tube dysfunction of the right ear is treated by the insertion of eustachian tubes with a transtympanic approach. _____

2. A 3-year-old patient suffering from chronic otitis media is treated by tympanostomy and the placement of bilateral ventilation tubes in the operating room setting. _____

3. A patient is surgically treated for recurrent mastoiditis with a bilateral modified radical mastoidectomy. _____

4. The patient in question 3 returns after six months for a simple debridement of the mastoid cavities for granular tissue formation. _____

5. A patient with conductive hearing loss of combined types in the left ear is surgically treated with a tympanoplasty, mastoidectomy, reconstruction of the canal wall, and ossicular chain reconstruction. _____

Inner Ear

Incision and/or Destruction

Labrinthotomy includes several other procedures and is performed either by transcanal approach or through the mastoid cavity after a mastoidectomy. The endolymphatic sac operation is performed through the mastoid cavity and includes a shunt if placed. These procedures are performed for diagnoses such as meningitis, disorders of the vestibular system, trauma, and late effects of injury to the nervous system.

Fenestration and revision of fenestration of the semicircular canal is an opening created in the horizontal canal. The eardrum and canal skin are then repositioned to cover this opening. These procedures are treatment for:

- Otosclerosis
- Deafness
- Congenital anomalies of the ear

Excision

Labrinthectomy is the removal of the horizontal, posterior, and superior semicircular canals and the lining. The approach can be either transcanal with the use of a right angle hook or through the mastoid cavity including a mastoidectomy. The vestibular nerve sectioning is performed through the mastoid cavity. This procedure includes a labrinthectomy and cuts the vestibular nerve while preserving the facial nerve. Labyrinthectomy is commonly performed for mastoiditis and disorders of the middle ear, mastoid, and vestibular system.

Introduction

A cochlear device is used for treatment of hearing loss. The implantation procedure, code 69930, includes an internal coil that is secured inside the temporal bone with an electrode threaded into the cochlea. The Medicine chapter of CPT® supplies additional codes for the evaluative and therapeutic services required for programming and postoperative analysis, as well as aural rehabilitation of these patients.

EXERCISE 18.19

Instructions: Assign the correct CPT® codes to the following scenario.

1. A patient is surgically treated for cholesterin granuloma with a transcanal labyrinthectomy of the right ear. _____

Temporal Bone, Middle Fossa Approach

Codes 69950–69970 describe various approaches by craniotomy to expose the temporal lobe of the brain. This requires the dura to be elevated off the floor of the middle fossa. From there, the vestibular nerves can be cut or decompressed, or tumors of the nerve can be removed. Decompression of the internal auditory canal can be performed using a muscle graft for replacement. The removal of a temporal bone can also be performed using this approach. These procedures are surgical treatment for conditions including neoplasms; meningitis; disorders of the facial nerve, middle ear, mastoid, and vestibular system; and trauma.

Operating Microscope

The use of the operating microscope can be a separately reportable component of a procedure. The use of microsurgery techniques can be reported using the add-on code 69990. The use of the operating microscope gives the physician improved visualization of fine structures. The use of magnifying loupes or corrected vision does not qualify for the use of this code. The microscope may be operated by hand or foot controls. Code 69990 may not be reported in addition to codes 15756–15758, 15842, 19364, 19368, 20955–20962, 20969–20973, 26551–26554, 26556, 31526, 31531, 31536, 31541, 31561, 31571, 43116, 43496, 49906, 61548, 63075–63078, 64727, 64820–64823, and 65091–68850. This list of code exclusions can be found in the code descriptor in the CPT® book.

Formula for Success

Certain procedures include the operating microscope as an inherent part of the procedure. Check the list of excluded codes before reporting 69990.

CHAPTER REVIEW

1. The removal of the eyeball only is referred to as:
   a. Evisceration
   b. Enucleation
   c. Exenteration
   d. a and b

2. An example of a secondary ocular implant is an intraocular lens.   **T or F**

3. The cornea is a part of the:
   a. Posterior segment
   b. Anterior sclera
   c. Anterior segment
   d. Iris, ciliary body

4. Phacoemulsification is a technique used in:
   a. Repair of a retinal detachment
   b. Treatment of glaucoma
   c. Destruction of a retinal lesion
   d. Cataract extraction

5. The correction of extraocular muscles is referred to a strabismus surgery.   **T or F**

6. Ectropion and entropion are disorders of the:
   a. Eyelids
   b. Brow ptosis
   c. Conjunctiva
   d. Lacrimal system

7. Otoplasty is a surgical correction of the:
   a. Middle ear
   b. Inner ear
   c. Mastoid
   d. External ear

8. Myringotomy, mastoidectomy, and tympanoplasty are all examples of procedures for the:
   a. Inner ear
   b. Middle ear
   c. External ear
   d. Temporal bone, middle fossa approach

9. Give the Evaluation and Management modifier used when a minor procedure is performed the same day as a separately identifiable Evaluation and Management service:
   a. 21
   b. 22
   c. 24
   d. 25

10. Which modifier would be appended to a related procedure performed by the same physician in the global period of the original procedure?
    a. 76
    b. 77
    c. 78
    d. 79

11. Which modifier would be appended to a staged procedure?
    a. 53
    b. 54
    c. 57
    d. 58

12. A procedure that cannot be described by any existing code is referred to as:
    a. A separate procedure
    b. An unlisted procedure
    c. An add-on code
    d. A Modifier 51 exempt code

13. A code that cannot stand alone, is Modifier 51 exempt, and never has a fee reduction is referred to as:
    a. Modifier 51 exempt code
    b. Separate procedure code
    c. Add-on code
    d. Unlisted procedure code

14. When a procedure is unusual, difficult, or involves more time than usual, Modifier _____ should be used.
    a. 21
    b. 22
    c. 23
    d. 24

15. The modifier used for and Evaluation and Management service in a postoperative global period that is unrelated to the original surgery is:
    a. 22
    b. 23
    c. 24
    d. 25

Case Studies

Instructions: Assign the correct ICD-9-CM and CPT® codes for each case study.

Case Study 18.1

Preoperative Diagnosis

Nuclear and cortical cataract right eye.

Postoperative Diagnosis

Nuclear and cortical cataract right eye.

Procedure

Phacoemulsification cataract extraction with intraocular lens implantation.

Anesthesia

Local infiltrative and Retrobulbar 2% Xylocaine with Epinephrine and Wydase mixed ½ and ½ with 0.5% Marcaine, with monitored anesthesia care.

Description of Procedure

After the above anesthetic was applied to the eye, the Honan balloon was placed in the eye until the eye was soft. The eye was prepped and draped in a sterile manner. The lids and lashes were isolated on a 3M drape. A self-retaining lid speculum was placed in the eye. Using a temporal approach, a limbal stab incision was made at 4:30. A temporal clear corneal single hinge incision was made with a diamond knife after Healon was used to fill the anterior chamber. An anterior capsulotomy was performed with a bent #25 gauge needle. 0.3 ccs of 1:1,000 aqueous Epinephrine and 4 mg of Garamycin was added to a 500 cc bottle of BSS and used for irrigation throughout the case. The lens nucleus was removed using 0.36 minutes of phacoemulsification. Cortical material was aspirated and the Kratz scratcher was used to polish the posterior capsule. Healon was placed in the capsular bag and anterior chamber, then a +20.00 diopter CLRFLXB lens was placed in the capsular bag.

Amvisc was aspirated and the eye reformed with BSS solution. The wounds were inspected and found to be self-sealing. The eye was dressed with Pilopine gel, soft patch, and shield. The patient tolerated the procedure well and was transferred to the recovery area in stable condition.

ICD-9-CM Codes: _____

CPT® Codes: _____

Case Study 18.2

Preoperative Diagnosis

Macular hole of the right eye.

Postoperative Diagnosis

Macular hole of the right eye.

Procedure Performed

Pars plana vitrectomy with epiretinal membrane peeling.

Anesthesia

Local infiltrative and retrobulbar.

Description of Procedure

After the above anesthetic was applied to the right eye, the eye was prepped and draped in a sterile manner. The lids and lashes were isolated on a 3M drape. A self-retaining lid speculum was placed in the eye. Curvilinear conjunctival incisions were made 2 mm posterior to the limbus, extending from 1:00 to 3:00 and from 7:00

to 11:00. Sclerotomy sites were prepared 3 mm posterior to the limbus at 2:00, 8:30, and 9:30. Through the 8:30 sclerotomy created with a V-lance blade a 3.5 mm incision canula was sutured to the globe with a horizontal mattress suture of 8-0 Vicryl. Through this, BSS+ was used for intraocular irrigation throughout the case. Superior sclerotomies were made to accommodate the ocutome handpiece and fiberoptic light pipe.

Through the operating microscope, an irrigation handheld contact lens, and a widely dilated pupil, posterior vitrectomy proceeded. A central core vitrectomy was performed. The vitreous was dissected quite far peripherally.

Attention was turned to the macular area where there was noted to be a full thickness macular hole. There was no posterior vitreous separation. There was preretinal tissue noted in the temporal macula. There was also a small punctuate hemorrhage along the superior temporal arcade. Using the Q-20 pick, the posterior vitreous cortex was elevated, and then bluntly dissected from the surface of the retina with a Michels #1 pick with some effort. It was removed from the eye with the ocutome handpiece. Then, using the membrane forceps, preretinal tissue from the temporal macula was gently peeled from the surface of the retina with fair difficulty. There was a small punctuate hemorrhage in the temporal macula. The extrusion needle was used to remove free blood from the surface of the retina. The hemorrhage did not enlarge. With scleral plugs in place, the retina was examined with the indirect ophthalmoscope and scleral depression. No peripheral defects were noted.

Then using autologous serum, a drop was placed over the central macula. Using 16% per fluoropropane, a gas fluid exchange was performed, filling approximately 80% of the vitreous cavity.

After prolapsing vitreous was excised, sclerotomy sites were closed with modified figure-of-eight sutures of 8-0 Vicryl. The conjunctiva was closed with modified interrupted sutures of 7-0 chromic collagen. 20 mg of Garamycin and 0.5 cc of Celestone Soluspan were injected subconjunctivally under direct visualization. The eye was dressed with 1% atropine ointment, a soft patch, and shield. The patient tolerated the procedure well and was transferred to the recovery area in stable condition. The patient was given specific postoperative positioning instructions and asked to return on the following day for postoperative check.

ICD-9-CM Codes: _____

CPT® Codes: _____

Case Study 18.3

Preoperative Diagnosis

1. Proliferative diabetic retinopathy of the right eye.
2. Vitreous hemorrhage of the right eye.

Postoperative Diagnosis

1. Proliferative diabetic retinopathy of the right eye.
2. Vitreous hemorrhage of the right eye.

Procedure Performed

1. Pars plana vitrectomy with epiretinal membrane peeling.
2. Pars plana vitrectomy with panretinal endolaser photocoagulation.

Anesthesia

Local infiltrative and retrobulbar.

Description of Procedure

After the above anesthetic was applied to the right eye, the eye was prepped and draped in a sterile manner. The lids and lashes were isolated on a 3M drape. A self-retaining lid speculum was placed in the eye. Curvilinear conjunctival incisions were made 2 mm posterior of the limbus, extending from 1:00 to 3:00 and from 7:00 to 11:00. Sclerotomy sites were prepared 3 mm posterior to the limbus at 2:00, 8:30, and 9:30. Through the 8:30 sclerotomy created with a V-lance blade a 3.5 mm infusion cannula was sutured to the globe with a horizontal mattress suture of 8-0 Vicryl. Through this, BSS+ was used for intraocular irrigation throughout the case. Superior sclerotomies were made to accommodate the ocutome handpiece and fiberoptic light pipe.

Through the operating microscope, an irrigation handheld contact lens, and a widely dilated pupil, a posterior vitrectomy proceeded. A central core vitrectomy was performed. There was a moderate amount of mid vitreous blood encountered. With the aid of scleral depression by the surgical assistant, inferior vitreous blood and the posterior vitreous cortex were dissected as far peripherally as possible without damage to the vitreous base or intraocular lens implant.

Attention was turned to the macular area. The optic nerve looked good, as well as the macula. There was preretinal blood along the inferior temporal arcade, but the traction that had appeared on the ultrasound had been released. There was retinal edema in the temporal macula and some questionable neovascularization.

Using the passive extrusion needle, free blood was removed from the surface of the eye. Then the endolaser probe was introduced into the eye and 581 spots at 0.1 seconds and 0.4 watts were applied to the mid periphery in all quadrants.

With scleral plugs in place, the retina was examined with the indirect ophthalmoscope and scleral depression. There was a defect at 12:00 that had previously been surrounded with laser scars. No further peripheral defects were noted.

After prolapsing vitreous was excised, sclerotomy sites were closed with modified figure-of-eight sutures of 8-0 Vicryl. The conjunctiva was closed with multiple interrupted sutures of 7-0 chromic collagen. 20 mg of Garamycin and 20 mg of Kenalog were injected subconjunctivally under direct visualization. The eye was dressed with 1% Atropine ointment and a soft patch. The patient tolerated the procedure well and was transferred to the recovery area in stable condition. He was asked to return on the following day for a postoperative check.

ICD-9-CM Codes: _____

CPT® Codes: _____

Case Study 18.4

Preoperative Diagnosis

Bilateral protruding ears.

Postoperative Diagnosis

Bilateral protruding ears.

Procedure

Otoplasty.

Anesthesia

General endotracheal.

Technique

The patient was brought into the operating room and placed supine on the operating table. General anesthesia was induced. The patient was intubated with an endotracheal tube. The left ear was addressed first. One percent lidocaine with 1:100,000 parts epinephrine was injected. An elliptical incision was made in the postauricular area. Using a 25-gauge needle placed through the anterior portion of the ear, folding the antehelix into place, horizontal mattress sutures were then placed of 4-0 Mersilene to hold the antehelix in place. A small amount of conchal bowl was then resected using a 15-blade scalpel. The tissue over the mastoid cavity was elevated and a horizontal Mersilene stitch was used to set the conchal back, setting the conchal bowl posteriorly, keeping the external auditory canal open. The wound was then closed with 5-0 nylon suture. The right ear was then addressed in a similar fashion. Again, 1% lidocaine with 1:100,000 parts epinephrine was injected into the posterior auricular area. An elliptical incision was made through the skin. Twenty-five-gauge needles were then used to form the antehelix anteriorly and then 4-0 Mersilene sutures were then used to develop the antehelix. These were placed in a horizontal mattress suture fashion. A small portion of the conchal bowl was then resected posteriorly and again the tissue over the mastoid was opened and a horizontal mattress suture was used to set the conchal bowl posteriorly. The postauricular wound was then closed with 5-0 nylon suture. Bilateral mastoid dressings were then placed. The patient tolerated the procedure well and was transferred to the recovery room in stable condition.

ICD-9-CM Codes: _____

CPT® Codes: _____

Radiology Services

OBJECTIVES

1. State the rationale for coding oral contrast as "without contrast."
2. Recognize the differences between diagnostic testing and interventional procedures.
3. Define technical component and professional component.
4. Assign modifiers appropriately when required.
5. Describe what conditions are necessary in order for a global radiology code to be used.

TERMINOLOGY AND ACRONYMS

Antegrade   Performed in the usual direction of flow or movement (ex: blood or urine).

AP   Anteroposterior.

Ba   Barium.

BE   Barium enema.

Contrast   Radio-opaque dye that is swallowed or injected, such as barium.

C-spine   Cervical spine film.

DSA   Digital subtraction angiography.

IVP   Intravenous pyelogram.

KUB   Kidney, ureter, and bladder.

LOA   Left anterior oblique.

LPO   Left posterior oblique.

LS   Lumbosacral.

Oblique   A slanted or inclined plane between horizontal and vertical.

Odontoid view   A view of the cervical spine to visualize C1, usually taken through an open mouth.

Opacification   An organ or tissue visualized through contrast material.

PA   Posteroanterior.

PET   Positron emission tomography, a subspecialty of radiology.

Retrograde   Performed against the direction of flow or movement.

ROA   Right anterior oblique.

RPO   Right posterior oblique.

SBFT   Small bowel follow-through.

Stereotactic view   Three-dimensional view.

S&I   Supervision and interpretation.

Swimmer's view   A lateral thoracic view with the patient's arm raised over the head.

UGI   Upper gastrointestinal series.

US   Ultrasound.

DISEASE PROCESSES AND ICD-9-CM CODING OF RADIOLOGY PROCEDURES

ICD-9-CM Diagnostic Coding and Reporting Guidelines for Outpatient Services state that patients who receive diagnostic services only during an encounter or visit should have the reason for the encounter, the diagnosis, condition, or problem sequenced first. Other diagnoses may be sequenced as secondary. If a physician has interpreted the diagnostic tests and the final report is available at the time of coding, code any confirmed or definitive diagnosis(es) documented in the interpretation. Do not code related signs and symptoms as additional diagnoses.

Formula for Success

Code V72.5, Radiological examination, not elsewhere classified, is not recognized as a diagnosis that meets medical necessity for many payers, and results in claim denial. Use this code with caution.

Medicare has published specific guidelines regarding the assignment of ICD-9-CM codes for diagnostic testing. Read Medicare Transmittal AB-01-144, dated September 26, 2001, for additional information regarding ICD-9-CM codes for Medicare beneficiaries. This transmittal pertains to laboratory diagnoses also.

Examples:

1. Dr. Smith sees a patient in the Urgent Care Clinic with wrist pain following a fall off his skateboard. An x-ray is taken, and Dr. Smith determines that the wrist is fractured, and documents this in the patient's record.

   Correct ICD-9-CM codes: 814.00, wrist fracture, and E885.2, fall from skateboard
   Incorrect ICD-9-CM code: 719.43, wrist pain

2. A patient with chronic low back pain has a lumbar spine series and myelography performed. The results of these studies are not expected back for several days. The claim is sent out the day after the encounter with the diagnosis code of 724.2, low back pain.

CPT® CODING OF RADIOLOGY PROCEDURES

The guidelines for the radiology chapter can be found on the colored pages in the beginning of the chapter. Some of the guidelines are similar to those of the surgery chapters, while others are unique to this section alone.

A written interpretation of radiological procedures is an integral part of a radiologic service, whether provided by a radiologist or the ordering physician. A report of this nature should include the symptoms, final diagnosis, pertinent physical findings, procedure performed including the number and type of views, concurrent problems, and follow-up care.

A phrase that is unique to this section is *Supervision and Interpretation* (**S&I**). Supervision and Interpretation is when two physicians are involved in the radiological portion of the procedure. Radiological procedures may occasionally involve the work of two physicians. This part of the service is reported using a radiology code with Modifier 26 appended. The Modifier 26 is used for the *professional component*, or the interpretation and report portion of the service. When an ordering physician owns the radiologic equipment and his or her staff is performing the procedure, but he or she requests the interpretation of another physician (usually a radiologist), the ordering physician reports the radiology code with the HCPC modifier TC. Modifier TC is used for the *technical component* portion of the radiological procedure. When a physician owns the equipment, his or her staff is performing the procedure, and he or she is interpreting the outcome of the test, the *global* code is used. That is, the physician would report the radiological procedure code without the use of Modifier 26 or Modifier TC.

Example: Dr. Smith sends her patient with a wrist injury to the radiology department of her multi-specialty clinic. A two-view x-ray is taken by staff employed by the clinic. Dr. Jones, a radiologist, reads the x-ray. The radiology code may be reported as:

Dr. Smith: 73100-TC

Dr. Jones: 73100–26

If the same patient is sent across town to a free-standing radiology practice, code 73100 is reported as a global code without modifiers because the physician who reads the x-ray also owns the equipment and pays the staff.

The reimbursement varies when using Modifier 26 or TC. The fee is reduced because only part of the total service is provided; however, the actual percentage of reduction varies due to the complexity of equipment involved, the qualifications of the staff, and the complexity of the interpretation of results.

Modifiers

The modifiers used for this section include:

- 22, Unusual procedural services
- 26, Professional component
- 50, Bilateral procedure
- 51, Multiple procedure
- 52, Reduced services
- 53, Discontinued services
- 58, Staged procedure
- 59, Distinct procedural services
- 76, Repeat procedure by the same physician
- 77, Repeat procedure by another physician
- RT, Right side
- LT, Left side
- TC, Technical component

When using most of these modifiers, the standard rules and descriptions apply. However, when multiple radiological procedures are performed, the fees are not reduced. When Modifier 51 or Modifier 50 is used, care should be taken that the full allowable amount for each service is received from the payer. Typically, Modifier 51 signifies a fee reduction of 50%, and since multiple radiology procedures are not reduced, 100% of the allowable amount should be received for all procedures performed. A similar problem exists when using Modifier 50. Procedure codes submitted with the Modifier 50 are usually reimbursed at 150% instead of the full 200%. Because of this problem, it may be more appropriate to report each procedure on a separate line with the modifier LT or RT appended instead of using Modifier 50. Another option is to use Modifier 59 on one procedure to signify that it is distinctly separate from the other procedure.

Formula for Success

Make sure that EOBs are monitored closely for reimbursement and that modifiers have not been dropped/added by the payer or a global fee applied inappropriately.

Administration of Contrast Materials

Several types of radiological procedures use **contrast,** or dye, to enhance the imaging. Coding choices will be made based on procedures performed with or without contrast. When the phrase *"with contrast"* is used, contrast must be administered either intravascularly, intra-articularly, or intrathecally. When intra-articular injections are made, the appropriate joint injection code should be reported separately. Oral and/or rectal contrast administration alone does not meet requirements for a study *"with contrast."*

Low osmolar contrast material, LOCM, is a contrast material suitable for patients with allergies to iodine or a history of previous reaction to routine contrast material. There are medical necessity criteria with the use of LOCM, including:

- History of adverse reaction to contrast media
- History of asthma or allergy
- Cardiac dysfunction
- Generalized severe debilitation
- Sickle cell disease

Guidelines Common to All Sections

- *Subsection information* can be found in the guidelines section of this chapter. As with all sections, similar procedures or body areas are grouped and listed by code ranges.
- *Unlisted service or procedure* code may be used when there is no other code in a section that adequately describes a service.

Types of Radiological Imaging Procedures

- *X-ray* is the most common radiological technique performed and involves a beam of ionizing radiation that travels through the body and creates an image on a film placed under the body. Because of the variation of density in body structures, the x-ray passes through the body in different degrees and makes different shades of gray on the x-ray film.
- *Fluoroscopy* is a series of pictures taken by sending an x-ray beam through the body and creating a moving series of pictures for viewing the motion of internal structures as they function.

■ *Myelography* is the use of fluoroscopy to view the central nervous system. With the use of contrast material injected into the subarachnoid space, an enhanced structure can be viewed on a television screen.

■ *Cisternography* uses high-speed x-ray films to take a series of images in motion.

■ *Xeroradiography* uses the x-ray technique and an electrically charged photosensitive plate to create an image on paper instead of on a film.

■ *Dual energy x-ray absorptiometry (DEXA)* uses two x-ray beams with different levels of energy to create a two-dimensional projection used to determine bone density.

■ *Mammography* is the use of a special type of low dose x-ray that does not penetrate tissue as easily and can be used to diagnose breast masses or cysts too small to palpate.

■ *Magnetic resonance imaging (MRI)* is a radiation-free, noninvasive technique that produces high quality sectional images of inside of the body in multiple planes. In this method, the natural magnetic properties of our bodies emit radiofrequency signals when exposed to radio waves within a strong electromagnetic field. These signals are processed and converted into detailed, three-dimensional images with the use of a computer.

■ *Magnetic resonance angiography (MRA)* is a type of MRI that visualizes blood vessels and blood flow to evaluate vascular disorders.

■ *Nuclear medicine* is a subspecialty of radiology that uses radioisotopes for internal imaging.

■ *Computerized tomography (CT or CAT scan)* uses multiple narrow beams of x-rays around the body area being studied and uses computer imaging to produce thin cross-sectional views of various layers of the body. These images appear like cross-sectional slices of the body part being studied.

■ *Computerized tomography angiography* is a specialized type of CT scan of vessels to detect aneurysms, blood clots, and other vascular irregularities.

■ *Diagnostic ultrasound* is a technique that uses sound waves far above the level of human hearing (ultra). These sound waves pass through different densities of interior body tissue and are reflected back to the receiving unit at varying speeds. The unit then converts the wave to electrical pulses that are displayed in picture form on a screen.

Figures 19.1 and 19.2 illustrate several of these radiological procedures.

Formula for Success

The most important thing to determine in radiology coding is the type of imaging study that is being performed, i.e., ultrasound, diagnostic x-ray, CT scan, MRI, etc.

Diagnostic Radiology (Diagnostic Imaging)

The first part of the Radiology section is diagnostic radiology. The diagnostic radiology section begins with the musculoskeletal portion, starting with the head and neck and continuing down to the feet. The codes are then listed for the soft tissue procedures, beginning with the abdomen and continuing through the vascular procedures.

Each body area section is covered beginning with the most cephalic (toward the head) position and continuing downward to the feet and toes. Each section is further broken down by type of procedure:

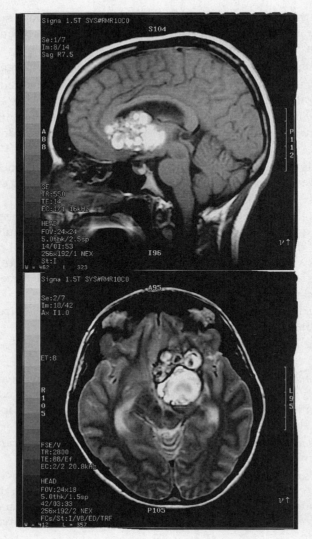

Figure 19–1 MRI of the head showing hemorrhagic lesion.

■ *Radiological examination,* including myelography, cisternography and x-ray procedures.
■ *Magnetic Resonance Imaging (MRI)*
  –without contrast material
  –with contrast material
  –without contrast material, followed by contrast material
■ *Computed Tomography (CT)*
  –without contrast material
  –with contrast material
  –without contrast material, followed by contrast material

Head and Neck

Communication is very important in coding of any radiology procedures. The head, in particular, contains many small, intricate bones, and a specific description is required to assign the correct code. Technologists are trained to obtain the best film by coning down, or focusing the beam on the smallest area possible, to obtain a high quality image. Because of this, a "set of skull films" may actually be for facial bones, which would change the code selection.

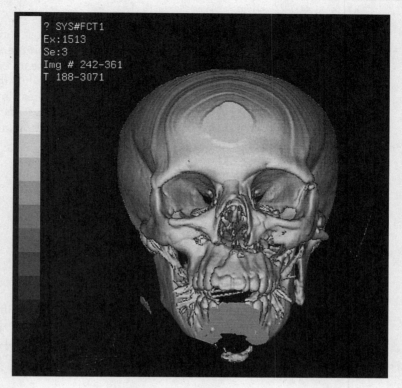

```
? SYS#FCT1
Ex:1513
Se:3
Img # 242-361
T 188-3071
```

Figure 19–2   3-D CT Scan of the head.

Formula for Success

Tips for Coding Head and Neck Procedures

1. Understand the specific area of interest: skull vs. facial bones or facial bones vs. nose.
2. Know how many views were taken.
3. Watch for unilateral or bilateral procedures.

EXERCISE 19.1

Instructions: Assign the correct radiology CPT® and ICD-9-CM codes.

1. A patient is seen by his family practice physician for chronic sinusitis. The patient has been suffering with this condition for over a month and a decision between changing antibiotics and referring for sinus surgery must be made. The physician orders a two-view sinus x-ray. _____

2. The patient in question 1 is referred to an ear, nose, and throat specialist who orders a CT scan of the head with contrast. _____

3. A patient is seen in an urgent care facility after being in a fistfight. The patient took a blow to the nose and a fracture of nasal bones is confirmed with a two-view x-ray of the nose. _____

Chest

When coding for chest x-rays, be aware that the most common views performed are **PA** and lateral. PA stands for Posterior to Anterior. When the x-ray beam travels through the body, the description for the view begins where the beam enters the body to where the beam exits the body. In this case, the beam enters through the patient's back and exits through the front or chest. The body part of most interest is placed closest to the film. X-rays travel like light rays and diverge from the source. If the chest x-ray is taken **AP** instead of PA, the size of the heart is greatly distorted and appears abnormally large.

Formula for Success

Tips for Coding Chest Procedures

1. Be aware of any "special views."
2. Watch for rib films that include a PA chest film as well.
3. Rib x-rays may be unilateral or bilateral.

Another technique used for chest x-rays is taking the film on inspiration. When we breathe in, the diaphragm moves downward and the lungs expand. This creates the optimum image of the lung field. Some physicians like to compare the lung fields on inspiration and expiration. This would be reported with the addition of a Special view, 71035.

EXERCISE 19.2

Instructions: Assign the correct radiology CPT® and ICD-9-CM codes.

1. A patient presents to the clinic for a pre-employment asbestos physical. As part of the physical, a PA chest x-ray is performed. _____

2. A patient presents to the clinic with a chronic cough. The patient has a long history of smoking and a two-view chest x-ray is performed. Upon review of the films, the physician sees a suspicious shadow near the clavicle. The physician orders a lordotic view and confirms the presence of a lung mass. _____

3. A rancher is brought into an urgent care facility after being kicked in the ribs by a cow. The physician orders unilateral rib x-ray of the right side to include the chest. The films confirm the fracture of three ribs and a pneumothorax, and the patient is transported to the emergency room for further treatment. _____

4. A patient is referred to a surgeon after a suspicious-looking mass is found on a routine chest x-ray. The surgeon orders a MRI of the chest with contrast and identifies mediastinal lymphadenopathy. _____

Spine and Pelvis

The spine radiology codes are listed according to the level of the spine being examined. The exceptions are:

- 72010, Entire spine survey, AP and lateral
- 72020, Single view of the spine, specify level

Formula for Success

Tips for Coding Spine and Pelvis Procedures

1. Watch for scoliosis specific studies; there are two different x-ray codes.
2. When coding a specific section of the spine, watch the number of views as well as the type of view taken, such as oblique, flexion, bending.

Obtaining images of the spine leads to some unique challenges. The shape of the vertebra itself, as well as the delicate opening for the spinal cord and the projections off of the vertebra that protect the spinal cord and the intervertebral spaces, require special views not usually taken of other body areas. For example, the cervical spine has the following coding choices:

- Two or three views
- Minimum of four views
- Complete, including oblique and flexion and/or extension studies

Codes 72170 and 72190 describe x-rays of the pelvis. Care should be taken when hip x-rays are performed as well. Code 73520 is a bilateral hip examination including an AP of the pelvis. In this case, the pelvis codes are bundled into the hip x-ray code.

Other procedures unique to this section include:

- *Myelography,* which is a study of the spinal cord and nerve roots with the use of fluoroscopy. This procedure can be performed on any level or the entire spine.
- *Epidurography* is a study of the veins lining the spinal canal using fluoroscopy.
- *Diskography,* or neucleography, uses fluoroscopy and ionated contrast to study the intervertebral discs.

EXERCISE 19.3

Instructions: Assign the correct radiology CPT® and ICD-9-CM codes.

1. A patient is seen in her physician's office for neck pain after the car she was driving collided with another vehicle at a stop light. The physician orders a complete x-ray of the cervical spine. At the level of C-5 there is a shadow that appears to be a bone chip. The physician refers the patient for further evaluation from an orthopedic surgeon. _____

2. The patient in question 1 is seen by an orthopedic surgeon who orders a CT scan of the cervical spine, without contrast and then followed by contrast, at his office. The films are sent to a radiologist in private practice for interpretation. The radiologist confirms a fracture at the C-5 vertebra. Code for the orthopedic surgeon and the radiologist. _____

3. A patient comes into his physician's office after falling on the ice. The patient complains of lower back and buttock pain. The physician orders two-view x-rays of the sacrum/coccyx and is able to diagnose a dislocation of the coccyx. _____

Upper Extremities

X-ray procedures for the upper extremities include examination of joints as well as long bones. In general, fewer views are needed of the long bones than of the joints. For example, there is one code for an adult forearm x-ray, and this is for two views. The other forearm code is for an infant. In contrast, the wrist and elbow codes have the choice of two or three views. X-rays provide a two-dimensional image, and long bones can usually be visualized adequately with two views. Because of their shape and the involvement of more bones, joints require more views to visualize the joint from every angle. This section and the lower extremity section add procedure codes for arthrography. *Arthrography* is the injection of air or contrast media into a joint with the use of fluoroscopy. This procedure helps in the diagnosis of cartilage abnormalities, arthritis, and bursitis.

Imaging studies unique to this section include:

- Acromioclavicular joint, which can be performed with or without weights. The extra weight is added to help show a dislocation when present.
- Upper extremity of an infant. Note that the infant views are not divided into joints and long bones as they are for adults.
- Magnetic resonance procedures for any joint of the upper extremity; there is only one code, no differentiation between joints.

EXERCISE 19.4

Instructions: Assign the correct radiology CPT® and ICD-9-CM codes.

1. A patient comes into the physician's office after falling while rollerblading. She complains of right elbow and wrist pain. The physician orders x-rays of both joints and three views of each were performed. No fracture of either joint can be found and a diagnosis of elbow and wrist contusion is made. _____

2. A patient who suffers chronic pain from an old sprain and tendon injury to the left shoulder is scheduled for an MRI with contrast to determine if surgery is necessary. _____

Lower Extremities

This section, as with the upper extremity section, contains procedure codes for joints and long bones. The codes in this section begin with the hip and are listed in order downward. The hip codes can be unilateral or bilateral. The bilateral hip code also includes a view of the pelvis. When using this code, it would be incorrect to use the pelvic x-ray code as well. The radiological examination codes unique to this section include:

- Examination of the hip during an operative procedure
- Arthroscopy procedures for the hip, sacroiliac, knee, and ankle
- Bilateral standing knee views
- Hip and lower extremity for an infant
- Magnetic resonance imaging for any lower extremity joint

EXERCISE 19.5

Instructions: Assign correct radiology CPT® and ICD-9-CM codes.

1. An elderly patient fell at home in the night and is found on the floor by her daughter in the morning. The patient is experiencing extreme left hip pain. The physician orders a complete unilateral hip x-ray along with a single view pelvic x-ray for comparison and screening purposes. The x-rays confirm that the patient has a fractured femur neck. _____

2. A podiatrist orders a right calcaneus x-ray for a new patient with foot pain. _____

3. A patient who still has left knee pain after sustaining an old fracture in college has an MRI without contrast followed by contrast. The surgery options depend on the results of the MRI. _____

Abdomen

The radiological examination of the abdomen differs from the previous procedures discussed because it is a soft tissue exam. Unlike the chest x-rays, the abdominal x-rays are performed AP, or anterior to posterior view. Films can include an upright (erect), flat (supine), decubitus, and a single view chest. *Decubitus* is when the patient is lying down in any position and the x-ray beam is horizontal. *Lateral decubitus* is a view of a patient lying on one side with the x-ray beam passing AP through the patient.

New terminology in this section includes:

- ■ *KUB* or kidneys, ureter, and bladder. Although KUB isn't referred to as such in this section, KUB refers to code 74000, single AP abdomen x-ray. This view acts as a scout film or a before-treatment film for many abdominal radiologic procedures.
- ■ *Peritoneogram* is a radiological exam done on the peritoneal cavity to define the pattern of air in the cavity after injection of air or contrast.

EXERCISE 19.6

Instructions: Assign correct radiology CPT® and ICD-9-CM codes.

1. A patient is seen in the physician office for abdominal pain. A complete series of abdominal x-rays is taken, and the patient is found to have an obstructed colon. _____

2. The patient in question 1 is sent to the hospital for an abdominal CT without contrast followed with contrast. The surgeon on call, who is not an employee of the hospital, reads the CT scan and proceeds with surgery. _____

Gastrointestinal Tract

This section is unique because the procedures performed are not just stationary films. To understand if there is a functional problem with the gastrointestinal tract, studies are performed to analyze the movement occurring within the GI tract. There are also procedures in this section that act as visualization for the placement of tubes, catheters, and the completion of surgical procedures. Terminology unique to this section includes:

■ *Swallowing function with cineradiography/videoradiography* studies the pressure and duration of the esophagus with the use of a catheter. While the catheter is being swallowed, the pressure of the contraction waves is being recorded.

■ *High density barium* is a contrast medium that is swallowed while different views are taken using fluoroscopy. The barium (**Ba**) can be followed as it continues down through the GI tract into the small intestines.

■ *Enteroclysis tube* is a tube passed through the patient's mouth and through to the small intestine. A pump sends barium through the tube for visualization.

■ *Duodenography* is similar to the enteroclysis with the tube being passed into the duodenum.

■ *Barium enema* (**BE**) is the use of barium contrast to study the large intestine, colon.

■ *Therapeutic enema for reduction of intussusception* is the use of an enema of air or barium contrast to reduce a section of bowel that has slipped into another loop of bowel. Left untreated, intussusception can cause necrosis of tissue and death.

■ *Cholecystography* is the study of the gallbladder after oral ingestion of a radiopaque pill.

■ *Cholangiography* is an intraoperative study of the common bile duct injected with radiopaque material. This procedure is performed during a cholecystectomy.

■ *Endoscopic catheterization* is a radiological procedure to study the completeness of an ERCP, or endoscopic retrograde cholangiopancreatography.

Figure 19.3 shows an upper GI series x-ray.

Formula for Success

Tips for Coding Gastrointestinal Radiology

1. Note whether a KUB or scout film has been performed.
2. When coding for radiological visualization of procedures, be aware of who is interpreting the films and the setting for the procedure.
3. The code for the surgical portion of the procedure is listed parenthetically under the radiology code descriptor.

EXERCISE 19.7

Instructions: Assign the correct radiology CPT® and ICD-9-CM codes.

1. A patient with a complaint of dysphagia is seen by her family practice physician. The physician orders a barium swallow study to be performed and interpreted in the radiologist clinic. The study shows normal esophageal function. Code for the radiologist. _____

2. A 50-year-old male patient is seen for an annual physical exam. As part of the preventive medicine exam, the physician orders a barium enema as a colon cancer screen. The study is performed and interpreted in the radiologist clinic. Code for the radiologist. _____

3. A surgeon performing a cholecystectomy for cholelithiasis with acute cholecystitis orders two sets of intraoperative cholangiograms to be read by a radiologist not employed by the hospital. Code for the radiologist. _____

4. A gastroenterologist is performing the placement of a percutaneous gastrostomy tube because of malnutrition and dysphagia. Radiologic films show satisfactory placement.

Figure 19–3 Upper GI series showing stomach and portions of small intestine with barium contrast.

Code for the gastroenterologist who interprets the films but is not employed at the hospital where the procedure is performed. _____

Urinary Tract

The procedures in this section are typically performed to study the function and movement of the urinary tract. *In the urinary section, the KUB or scout film is included in the study, as opposed to the gastrointestinal section where there are separate codes for with or without the KUB.* Terminology unique to this section includes:

- *Urography* or *pyelography* is radiological imaging of the kidneys and ureters performed before and after the administration of an intravenous contrast.
- *Retrograde* is against the normal flow of urine, from the bladder up to the kidneys.
- *Antegrade* is following the normal flow of urine, beginning with the kidneys.
- *Cystography* is a radiologic study of the bladder.
- *Vasography* is the radiologic study looking for an obstruction in the epididymis, seminal vesicles, or vas deferens.
- *Corpora cavernosography* is a study for venous leakage in the penis.
- *Urethrocystography* is a radiological exam of the urethra and bladder to diagnose strictures, obstructions, and abnormalities.

Formula for Success

Tips for Coding Urinary Tract Procedures

1. When coding for radiological visualization of procedures, be aware of who is interpreting the films and the setting for the procedure.
2. The code for the surgical portion of the procedure is listed parenthetically under the radiology code descriptor.

EXERCISE 19.8

Instructions: Assign the correct radiology CPT® and ICD-9-CM codes.

1. A physician who has been treating a patient suffering chronic E. coli urinary tract infections orders a urography to be performed and interpreted at the radiology clinic. No abnormalities are found. Code for the radiologist. _____

2. A couple has unsuccessfully tried to conceive for several years. After performing a seminal analysis, it is found that the sperm count is extremely low. He is referred to a urology clinic. A vasography is performed and it is found that there is a stricture in the vas deferens. The urologist is able to perform the procedure in his facility. _____

Gynecological and Obstetrical

Terminology unique to this section includes:

- *Pelvimetry* is an x-ray study for abnormalities of the pelvis and adequacy for delivery.
- *Hysterosalpingography* is a radiographic visualization of the cervix, uterus, and fallopian tubes after the injection of contrast.
- *Perineogram* is an examination of the area between the vulva and anus performed when an infant is born with ambiguous genitalia.

EXERCISE 19.9

Instructions: Assign the correct radiology CPT® and ICD-9-CM codes.

1. A couple has unsuccessfully tried to conceive for several years. The male has a normal seminal analysis. The physician orders a hysterosalpingography of the female to try to identify the problem. The patient has this procedure performed at the radiologist's office. The results are then interpreted by her gynecologist, who finds an obstruction of the right fallopian tube. Code for each physician. _____

Heart

The radiology Supervision and Interpretation codes for cardiac catheterizations have been moved to the cardiac catheter section in the Medicine chapter. The radiology procedures in this section describe MRI procedures for the morphology, function, and velocity flow of the heart. This technique uses a radiation-free, noninvasive method to produce three-dimensional imaging of the heart.

Aorta and Arteries

The main trunk of the systemic arteries is the aorta. The aorta is comprised of the ascending aorta, descending aorta, and the arch. A catheter is a flexible tube inserted into an area of the body and used for the introduction or withdrawing of fluid. There are two types of catheter placement procedures: nonselective and selective. Catheter placement is considered nonselective when a catheter is placed directly in an artery and either not advanced further or placed only into the aorta. Selective catheter placement indicates that the catheter has been guided into an arterial position other than the aorta or the artery where the catheter entered.

Vascular catheterizations are coded using *component coding*. This means that there is a code for the surgical portion (the vascular catheterization) and another code for the radiological S&I procedure. Sometimes these procedures are performed by two physicians, or by one physician who performs both the surgical and S&I components.

Selective vascular catheterizations are coded to include the introduction and all lesser order catheterizations used for the approach. Any second- and third-order arterial catheterizations within the same family of arteries should be expressed as 36218 or 36248. When additional first-order or higher catheterizations in a vascular family are supplied by a first-order vessel that is different from a previously coded vessel, they should be coded separately.

The radiology supervision and interpretation services are reported for each visualization technique performed. This is in contrast to the catheter codes where the lower orders are bundled into the higher orders, and only the highest order studied in any vascular family is reported.

Formula for Success

Tips for Coding Selective Vascular Catheterization Procedures

1. When coding the radiology supervision and interpretation portion, report all angiography procedures performed.
2. When coding the vascular catheterization portion, only the highest order within a vascular family is reported.
3. The method used to report the S&I portion and the method used to report the vascular catheterization portion is different, therefore the number of codes reported from each section will not necessarily be equal. For example, one catheter code reported with two radiology codes.
4. The corresponding vascular catheterization code is listed parenthetically under the radiology S&I codes.
5. Watch for descriptors that differentiate between unilateral and bilateral procedures.

The codes in this section begin with the aortography procedures. This is important because these are nonselective catheterizations and are the starting point for many of the selective catheterizations to follow.

■ *Thoracic aortography without serialography* is performed through a puncture in the femoral artery, threading the catheter into the thoracic aorta, removing the guidewire, and injecting contrast and taking the films or *angiograms*.
■ *Thoracic aortography with serialography* is performed using a series of individual x-ray films.
■ *Abdominal aortography by serialography* is performed through a puncture in the femoral artery, threading the catheter into the abdominal aorta, and producing a series of individual x-ray films.
■ *Abdominal aortography plus bilateral iliofemoral lower extremity* studies the abdominal aorta but lets the contrast flow through the aorta and into the arteries of both legs.

With these descriptions in mind, the procedures in this section continue the arterial pathway through the body. These codes all have a surgical counterpart in the cardiovascular section for the placement of the catheters.

Example: An aortogram with runoff was performed on a patient with peripheral vascular disease. Access was gained through the right common femoral artery. An abdominal serial aortogram was performed to the level of the renal arteries and bilateral runoff was performed. An extremity angiography showing above-knee and below-knee popliteal artery into the bifurcation and into the anterior tibial artery was performed from the runoff. Findings included occlusion of the femoral and tibioperoneal within the calf.

    ICD-9-CM codes assigned: 444.22 for the diagnosis of peripheral vascular
                                         disease

    CPT® codes assigned: 36200 for the catheterization of the aorta
                                         75625 for the aortography with serialography
                                       75716 for the angiography of bilateral extremity

Veins and Lymphatics

New terms in this section include the following.

- *Lymphangiography* procedures are performed by injecting vital blue dye into the subcutaneous tissues for outlining of skin lymphatics. After the blue can be visualized, access can be gained into the lymph vessel. A small amount of dye is injected, and the x-rays are made.

- *Shuntogram* procedures are performed by injecting contrast material into the shunt reservoir and into the tubing. The shunt tubing is a drain placed in hydrocephalus patients to drain excess cerebral spinal fluid. Peritoneal-venous shunts are placed in patients with abdominal ascites to drain fluid into a major vein.

- *Splenoportography* is the visualization of the splenic vein with the placement of a catheter and radiopaque dye placement.

- *Venography* is the visualization of veins with the injection of dye through the use of catheterization of the vein in question.

- *Percutaneous transhepatic portography* is the placement of a needle through the abdomen, using fluoroscopic guidance, into the portal vein and injecting contrast and study the hemodynamic pressures of the portal vein.

- *Hepatic venography* is performed through the common femoral vein and into the hepatic vein. Blood movement and pressure through the liver can be monitored.

- *Wedged hepatic venography* is when the catheter is wedged into a small hepatic vein branch.

- *Free hepatic venography* is when the catheter tip lies free in the hepatic vein.

Formula for Success

Tips for Coding Vein and Lymphatic Procedures

1. Component coding for vein procedures includes the injection procedure, codes 36000–36015 and 36400–36510, in addition to the radiology supervision and interpretation codes.

2. Component coding for lymphatic procedures includes the injection procedure, code 38790, in addition to the radiology supervision and interpretation codes.

Transcatheter Procedures

These procedures are the visualization techniques used for transcatheter procedures in the cardiovascular section and include:

■ Transcatheter therapy, follow-up, and exchange
■ Mechanical removal, pericatheter and intraluminal obstruction material
■ Percutaneous placement of an inferior vena cava filter
■ Intravascular ultrasound
■ Endovascular repair and prosthesis placement
■ Transcatheter stent placement and retrieval
■ Transluminal balloon angioplasty
■ Transcatheter biopsy
■ Percutaneous drainage placement and tube change

Formula for Success

Tips for Coding Transcatheter Supervision and Interpretation

1. Component coding for transcatheter procedures includes the radiology S&I code and the transcatheter placement procedure found in the cardiovascular section.

2. The corresponding surgical procedures are listed parenthetically under the radiology procedure code descriptor.

Transluminal Atherectomy

The transluminal atherectomy codes, like the transcatheter codes, have the corresponding cardiovascular procedure listed parenthetically under the radiology supervision and interpretation codes. The procedures listed in this section include the transluminal atherectomy of:

■ Peripheral artery
■ Renal
■ Visceral artery

Other Procedures

When the radiologist provides fluoroscopy services that are not included as an integral part of a procedure, the service is measured and reported in time increments. Other radiologic services listed in this section include:

■ Fluoroscopic guidance for needle placement
■ Fluoroscopic guidance of needle or catheter for spinal or paraspinous procedures
■ Manual application of physician-applied stress
■ Single view of child for foreign body
■ Fluoroscopic or CT for percutaneous vertebroplasty
■ Bone and osseous studies
■ Bone density studies using CT and DEXA
■ Radiographic absorptiometry
■ Radiologic exam of abscess, fistula, or sinus tract
■ Computer aided mammography
■ Mammography and mammary ductogram or galactogram
■ Breast imaging with magnetic resonance imaging
■ Stereotactic localization and mammographic guidance of needle/wire placement

- Radiological exam of surgical specimen and body section
- Cineradiography/videoradiography when not included in procedure
- Consultation, written report, on x-ray made elsewhere
- Xeroradiography
- Subtraction with contrast studies
- CT guidance for needle placement, tissue ablation, radiation therapy, and follow-up
- Reconstruction of CT or MRI into three-dimensional image
- Magnetic resonance spectroscopy
- Magnetic resonance guidance for needle placement, tissue ablation, and bone marrow blood supply

Figure 19.4 shows an example of a mammogram.

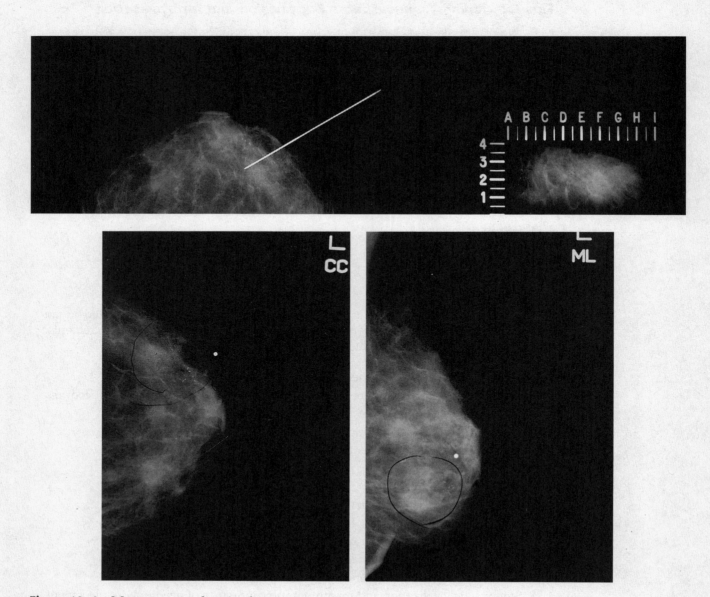

Figure 19–4   Mammogram showing breast cancer.

EXERCISE 19.10

Instructions: Assign the correct cardiovascular and radiology CPT® and ICD-9-CM codes.

1. An angiogram of the right cerebral carotid was performed on a patient with right carotid stenosis and complete occlusion of the left carotid. The common femoral artery was punctured and an arch aortogram was performed. The catheter was selectively placed in the right common carotid artery and multiple projections of the right cervical and intracranial right circulation were performed. The catheter was withdrawn to the level of the right common femoral artery, and a selective right common femoral artery arteriogram was performed. Angiogram included the right cervicovertebral arteries, the right cerebral carotid, right cervical carotid, and the right vertebral cervical arteries. _____

2. A 66-year-old patient with end-stage renal disease is seen for a nonfunctioning dialysis catheter. Access to the right common femoral vein is accomplished and a guidewire is passed centrally. A gooseneck snare is then passed to grasp the intravascular portion of the catheter. The catheter is stripped multiple times and a thrombus is removed. Contrast dye is injected and both ports are functioning with no evidence of residual fibrin. The catheter is then removed. _____

3. A patient with right renal artery stenosis presents for a bilateral renal angiogram and intravascular stent placement. The radiologist performs this procedure at a hospital where he is not an employee. Access into the right common femoral artery is achieved. The catheter was placed through the right groin and selectively placed into the right renal artery. Following the right renal artery angiogram, a wire was placed into the upper-pole right renal artery and a balloon-expandable stent was placed at the right proximal renal artery extending to the renal artery ostium. The distal stent was dilated to 4.0 mm and the proximal stent was in the region of the ostium and dilated. A selective right external iliac artery angiogram was then performed following withdrawal of the sheath to evaluate stent placement. _____

4. A patient with effusion of the left hip is seen in the emergency room by the on-call internal medicine physician. The physician is not an employee of the hospital and performs a hip joint aspiration under fluoroscopic guidance. _____

5. A 46-year-old patient with chronic hepatitis C requires a liver biopsy. A transjugular liver biopsy is performed at the radiologist office. Using ultrasound guidance, an 18-gauge needle is used to access the right internal jugular vein. A guidewire and cannula are advanced over the guidewire into the right hepatic vein. Contrast injection was performed. An 18-gauge transjugular biopsy needle is inserted through the inducer and several core samples are obtained. _____

Diagnostic Ultrasound

Diagnostic ultrasound (**US**) is a technique that uses sound waves far above the level of human hearing to pass through different densities of tissue and be reflected back to the receiving unit at varying speeds. The unit then converts the wave to electrical pulses that are displayed in picture form on a screen. Terminology that is unique to this type of imaging includes:

- *A-scan* is a type of ultrasound that creates a one-dimensional image.
- *M-mode* is a type of one-dimensional ultrasound that can record the movement of the trace by amplitude and velocity of echo-producing structures.

■ *B-scan* is a type of ultrasound that utilizes sound waves to display a two-dimensional image.

■ *Real-time scan* displays a two-dimensional structure in motion.

■ *Echoencephalography* is a type of imaging that determines the ventricular size and can confirm fluid masses or other intracranial abnormalities, and cerebral contents.

Figure 19.5 shows an example of an ultrasound.

Head and Neck

The procedures in this section include imaging of the cerebral contents, eyes, and the soft tissue of the head and neck.

Chest

The two procedures described in this section are for B-scan or real-time images of the chest and breast. The breast ultrasound can be either unilateral or bilateral.

Abdomen and Retroperitoneum

The ultrasound procedures described in this section use B-scan or real-time images. The ultrasound of a transplanted kidney can be performed with or without *duplex Doppler. Doppler* uses the shifts in frequency of the emitted waves against their echoes to measure velocity. Doppler can be used to study moving fluids such as blood flow.

Spinal Canal

There is one code for this section: ultrasound of spinal canal and contents.

EXERCISE 19.11

Instructions: Assign the correct radiology CPT® and ICD-9-CM codes.

1. An ophthalmologist performs a biometry A-scan ultrasound for the evaluation of a patient's nuclear cataract of the left eye. The physician owns the equipment and interprets the results. _____

2. If the physician in question 1 performs the same exam, does not own the equipment, but still interprets the results, what codes would be used? _____

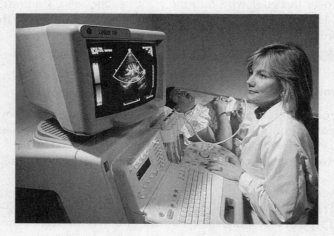

Figure 19–5   Ultrasound being performed on a patient.

3. A patient with a palpable breast lump presents for a mammogram. Because the location of the lump is almost axillary, the lump does not show on the film. An ultrasound is performed and interpreted at the radiologist's office. The breast mass is measured to have a 2 cm diameter and appears benign but will be biopsied at a later date. _____

4. A patient who received a kidney transplant one month ago is in for a recheck. Part of the examination for possible rejection includes an ultrasound with Doppler. This procedure is performed and interpreted at the nephrologist's office. _____

Obstetrical

The first trimester ultrasound procedures include:

- Determination of the number of gestational sacs and fetuses, their measurements, and study of visible structures.
- Qualitative assessment of the amniotic fluid volume and gestational sac shape.
- Examination of the uterus and surrounding structures.

The ultrasound performed after the first trimester includes:

- Determination of the number of fetuses; gestational age measurement; study of intracranial, spinal, abdominal, and four-chambered heart of the fetus.
- Location and evaluation of the umbilical cord insertion and placenta.
- Amniotic fluid assessment.
- Examination of visible maternal anatomy.

Pregnant uterus ultrasound codes 76811 and 76812 include the same studies as codes 76805 and 7806 plus additional evaluation of:

- Fetal brain and ventricles and face.
- Heart, chest, and abdomen anatomy.
- Limbs for number, length, and structure.
- Evaluation of umbilical cord and placenta.
- Other fetal anatomy clinically indicated.
- *Limited* ultrasounds of a pregnant uterus act as a "quick look" exam.
- *Follow-up* ultrasounds are performed to reassess the fetus size, growth, or abnormalities. This code should be reported for each fetus studied and Modifier 59 appended to all fetuses after the first.
- *Transvaginal* obstetrical ultrasounds may be performed alone or in addition to a transabdominal ultrasound.
- *Fetal biophysical profile* uses ultrasound to assess a near-term fetus with fetal movements, tone, breathing, heart rate, and amniotic fluid volume.
- *Fetal nonstress test* can be performed as a part of the biophysical profile or alone. It monitors the fetal heart rate over a period of twenty minutes or longer watching for accelerations with movement from the fetus.
- *Echocardiography* uses ultrasound to bounce sound waves off of the fetal cardiovascular system for study.
- *Doppler,* when added to echocardiography, is used to study fluid velocity such as blood flow.

EXERCISE 19.12

Instructions: Assign the correct radiology CPT® and ICD-9-CM codes.

1. A pregnant patient is seen for the first time by her obstetrician. She is twelve weeks pregnant and has a routine transabdominal ultrasound, which reveals twins. This ultrasound was performed and interpreted in the physician's office. _____

2. The patient in question 1 returns on a regular basis, and at 28 weeks, the physician performs and interprets an ultrasound including a detailed fetal anatomic examination due to a family history of birth defects. _____

3. The patient in questions 1 and 2 continues her care, and at 32 weeks, the physician performs and interprets a limited ultrasound. _____

4. At 41 weeks, the patient in the above questions is overdue and her physician sends her to the hospital for a biophysical profile with a nonstress test, which he then interprets. _____

Nonobstetrical

The procedures described in this section include:

- Transvaginal ultrasound.
- *Sonohysterography* is an ultrasonic study of the uterus.
- Pelvic ultrasound.

Genitalia

The procedures described in this section include:

- Ultrasound of scrotum and contents.
- Transrectal ultrasound.
- Transrectal of prostate volume for brachytherapy planning. *Brachytherapy* is the application of radioelements to a cancer treatment area.

Extremities

The procedures described in this section include:

- Nonvascular extremity ultrasound.
- Ultrasound of infant hips, *dynamic,* which requires physician manipulation.
- Ultrasound of infant hips, limited or *static,* which does not require manipulation.

Ultrasonic Guidance Procedures

When a procedure is performed that requires precision, ultrasonic guidance may be used to visualize the affected area. The procedures for which these ultrasounds act as guidance are listed parenthetically under each code descriptor. The procedures using ultrasonic guidance include:

- Pericardiocentesis.
- Endomyocardial biopsy.
- Arterial pseudoaneurysm or arteriovenous fistula compression repair.
- Potential vascular access site patency.

■ Visceral tissue ablation.

■ Intrauterine fetal transfusion or cordocentesis.

■ Needle placement for biopsy, aspiration, injection, or localization.

■ Chorionic villus sampling.

■ Amniocentesis.

■ Aspiration of ova.

■ Placement of radiation therapy fields.

■ Interstitial radioelement application.

Other Procedures

The codes listed in this section include:

■ Follow-up studies.

■ Gastrointestinal endoscopic ultrasound.

■ Bone density measurement of peripheral sites.

■ Intraoperative ultrasound.

■ Unlisted procedures.

EXERCISE 19.13

Instructions: Assign the correct radiology CPT® and ICD-9-CM codes.

1. A woman visits her gynecologist for an annual exam. During the exam, the gynecologist detects a pelvic mass. She performs a complete pelvic ultrasound and identifies a large ovarian cyst. _____

2. A man presents to his urologist for urinary frequency, incomplete emptying of bladder, and dysuria. Upon rectal examination, the physician feels an enlarged prostate. The physician performs a transrectal ultrasound and is able to diagnose benign prostatic hypertrophy. He will also order laboratory tests to confirm the diagnosis. _____

3. A patient evaluated for a lump in the right breast and scheduled for a biopsy needs a preoperative placement of a needle location wire. The radiologist places the needle under ultrasonic guidance. Code for radiology and needle placement. _____

4. A 37-year-old patient who is pregnant for the first time is seen by her obstetrician for her routine antenatal care for an uncomplicated pregnancy. The physician performs an amniocentesis because of the patient's advanced age. _____

Radiation Oncology

The procedures in this section are for teletherapy and brachytherapy and include:

■ Initial consultation.

■ Clinical treatment planning.

■ Simulation.

■ Medical radiation physics.

■ Dosimetry.

■ Treatment devices.

■ Special services.

■ Clinical treatment management.

■ Normal follow-up care during treatment and three months after completion.

Consultation: Clinical Management

Please see the appropriate procedure codes from the Evaluation and Management, Medicine, or Surgery sections when evaluation of the patient is prior to decision to treat.

Clinical Treatment Planning (External and Internal Sources)

The complex process of treatment planning includes:

■ Interpretation of special testing.

■ Tumor localization.

■ Determination of treatment volume, time/dosage, choice of modality, and number and size of treatment ports.

■ Selection of appropriate treatment devices.

There are three levels for *treatment planning:*

■ *Simple* requires a single treatment area, single port or simple parallel ports, with simple or no blocking.

■ *Intermediate* requires three or more converging ports, two treatment areas, multiple blocks, or special time constraints.

■ *Complex* requires highly complex blocking, custom shielding blocks, tangential ports, special wedges or compensators, three or more treatment areas, rotational or special beam considerations, and a combination of modalities.

Simulation must be performed on a dedicated simulator, radiation therapy treatment unit, or diagnostic x-ray machine. There are four levels and an unlisted procedure code for *radiology simulation-aided field setting:*

■ *Simple* requires a single treatment area, single port or parallel opposed ports, and no blocking.

■ *Intermediate* requires three or more converging ports, two treatment areas, and multiple blocks.

■ *Complex* requires tangential ports, three or more treatment areas, rotation or arc therapy, complex blocking, custom shielding blocks, brachytherapy source verification, hyperthermia probe verification, and any use of contrast materials.

■ *Three-dimensional* requires a computer-generated three-dimensional reconstruction of the tumor volume and surrounding critical normal tissue structures from CT and/or MRI data for non-coplanar therapy. This simulation uses a three-dimensional beam's eye view volume-dose displays of multiple or moving beams. Documentation must include the three-dimensional volume reconstruction and dose distribution.

Medical Radiation Physics, Dosimetry, Treatment Devices, and Special Services

These procedures are unique to this section and are an integral part of the complex radiation therapy treatment. New terminology found in this section includes:

■ *Dosimetry* is the calculation of the radiation dose that is delivered to the tumor. These calculations include the energy level and the modality of the beams to be used for each port. This procedure is performed even if one treatment is given.

■ *Intensity modulated radiotherapy (IMRT)* is the variance of the intensity of radiation exposure in a portion of the field. This is important when the tumor or other body structures are present in the beam pathway.

■ *Teletherapy isodose plan* is a computerized plotting of the lines of the same dosage levels to be delivered within the treatment field. One plan may be reported per therapy course. Different levels of teletherapy are determined by the number of ports and the complexity of devices and beams used.

■ *Brachytherapy* is the application of radioactive isotopes for internal radiation treatment. The codes in this section describe the planning of therapy and levels are based on the number of radioactive sources or ribbons that are placed.

■ *Special dosimetry* uses special measuring and monitoring devices to calculate the total amount of radiation delivered to a patient at a given point.

■ *Treatment devices* are customized blocks that protect the healthy tissue surrounding the treatment area. The professional (Modifier 26) portion of this service comes from physician participation in the design of the block. The technical (Modifier TC) portion comes from the construction and materials. The levels of service are determined by the complexity of the devices.

Consultation services in this section include the ongoing reports of medical physics, quality assurance, assessment of treatment parameters, and review of treatment documentation. Special consultations are a detailed written analysis of the treatment, performed at the request of the radiation oncologist.

Radiation Treatment Delivery

Radiation treatment delivery is the actual delivery of the radioactive electromagnetic beam to a treatment area. The codes in this section are listed according to the number of ports and the energy level measured in megavolts (MeV).

Radiation Treatment Management

When reporting radiation treatment management, each unit is five fractions or treatment sessions and is reported regardless of the time period. The dates of service need not be consecutive. Multiple sessions per day may be reported separately, as long as there has been a break between therapy sessions. Code 77427, five treatments, may be used if there are three or four fractions beyond the multiple of five at the end of treatment. One or two treatments beyond a multiple of five would not be reported separately. Code 77431 is to be used to report the treatment of one or two fractions when that is the entire treatment, not to fill in the last treatments of a longer session. These services consist of:

■ Review of port films.
■ Review of dosimetry, dose delivery, and treatment parameters.
■ Review of patient treatment setup.
■ Examination of the patient for response and coordination of care.

Proton Beam Treatment Delivery

Proton beams are positively charged particles used in the treatment of malignancies of the optic nerve and spinal cord. The treatments in this section are listed according to the level of complexity:

■ *Simple* proton treatment delivery is for a single treatment area with a single non-tangential port. The custom block, which is a device that is made to attach to the treatment unit to manipulate radiation, can be with or without compensation.

- *Intermediate* proton treatment delivery is for one or more treatment areas with two or more ports or one or more tangential ports; it uses custom blocks and compensators.
- *Complex* proton treatment delivery uses one or more treatment areas, two or more ports per area with matching fields and/or multiple isocenters, and custom blocks and compensators.

Hyperthermia and Clinical Intracavitary Hyperthermia

Hyperthermia is used in addition to radiation therapy or chemotherapy and uses heat in an attempt to speed up cell metabolism. With the use of microwaves, ultrasound, or a low-energy radiofrequency, this treatment can increase potential cell destruction and make tumor cells more susceptible to therapy.

Hyperthermia treatments include external, interstitial, and intracavitary. Interstitial treatments are placed within an organ or tissues. Intracavitary treatments are placed within a body cavity, such as the thoracic or abdominal cavity. Physics planning, interstitial insertion of temperature sensors, and the use of external or interstitial heat-generating sources are included. They also include management during the course of therapy and three months of follow-up care. The preliminary consultation is reported using codes 99241–99263.

Clinical Brachytherapy

This method of treatment uses either natural or man-made radioelements applied into or around the affected area. A therapeutic radiologist performs the supervision of radioelements and dose interpretation. These services include admission to the hospital and subsequent care. For the insertion of ovoids and tandems, use code 57155; for the insertion of Heyman capsules, use code 58346.

New terminology for this section includes:

- *Source placement* the intracavitary placement or permanent interstitial placement.
- *Ribbons* are temporary interstitial placement.

The codes are listed according to complexity of placement and include the descriptions:

- *Simple* is an application with one to four sources.
- *Intermediate* is an application with five to ten sources or ribbons.
- *Complex* is an application with greater than ten sources or ribbons.

EXERCISE 19.14

Instructions: Assign the correct CPT® codes only.

1. A patient receives intermediate radiology treatment planning and intermediate simulation. _____

2. The patient in question 1 then receives an intermediate brachytherapy plan and placement of intermediate interstitial radiation sources. _____

3. A patient receives eight radiation treatment management services. _____

4. A patient receives complex teletherapy planning and radiation delivery treatment of three separate treatment areas at 8 MeV. _____

Nuclear Medicine

The procedures listed in this section may be performed independently or as a part of total medical care. If the physician providing these services is responsible for diagnostic work-up and follow-up care, these services may be reported separately. Figure 19.6 illustrates a bone scan using nuclear medicine.

Radioimmunoassay tests, codes 82000–84999, can be found in the Clinical Pathology section and can be used by any specialist performing the tests in a laboratory that is certified for radioimmunoassay.

The use of physician-supplied radium or other radioelements may be reported separately using the code 78990 for diagnostic radiopharmaceutical and code 79900 for therapeutic radiopharmaceutical.

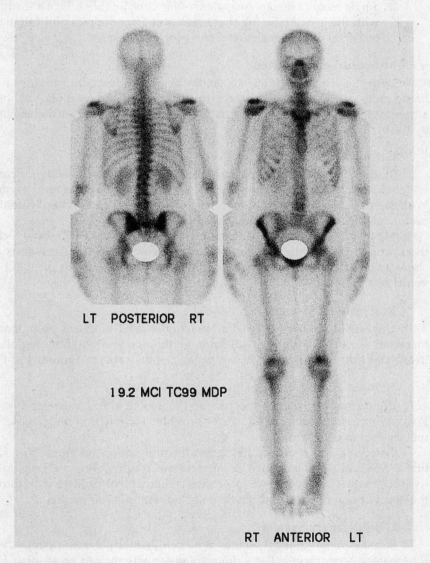

LT   POSTERIOR   RT

19.2 MCI TC99 MDP

RT   ANTERIOR   LT

Figure 19–6 Nuclear medicine bone scan with typical grainy appearance.

Diagnostic

Endocrine System

The study of thyroid function is measured by the amount or radioactive iodine taken up by the thyroid. The other purpose of these procedures is to determine the location and spread of tumors. The thyroid, parathyroid, and adrenal glands are studied in this section.

Hematopoietic, Reticuloendothelial, and Lymphatic Systems

Studies performed in this section help diagnose problems with the production, function, and survival rate of the various blood components. With the injection of radioactive elements such as sulfur colloid, iodinated serum albumin, radioactive chromium, or radiolabeled patient's blood, these procedures can trace and visualize the component of study.

Gastrointestinal System

The function or presence of a tumor can be determined for the liver, stomach, or intestines using gamma-emitting radioactive materials. New terminology in this section:

- *Single photon emission computerized tomography (SPECT)* is a study of liver function with the use of imaging that uses a rotating single or multiple-head camera and provides three-dimensional cross-sectional views.

Musculoskeletal System

With the use of gallium, a calcium analogue, imaging provides a study of the inflammatory processes, such as osteomyelitis. Single and dual photon absorptiometry use a noninvasive technique to measure absorption of a mono- or dichromatic photon beam by the bone.

Cardiovascular System

Studies for the cardiovascular system are performed using a scintillation camera, which detects radioactivity after the injection of a radiolabeled macroaggregated albumin. With these studies, the blood flow can be observed for narrowing, widening, obstructions, occlusions, and extraluminal accumulations.

Myocardial exams or *positron emission tomography (PET)* show ischemic or fibrotic tissue and the metabolic function of cardiac tissue. Thallium stress tests are performed to show areas of infarction. Perfusion studies show the amount of blood ejected from the ventricle during a cardiac cycle.

Respiratory System

Nuclear pulmonary perfusion imaging is used to detect pulmonary embolism and measures the ventilation for each lung. Ventilation studies show regional distribution of inspired air through the lung tissue, uptake, and clearance dynamics of the lungs.

Nervous System

Brain imaging studies the function, chemistry, and vascular flow of brain tissue. Positron emission tomography (PET) provides information on glucose, oxygen, or drug metabolism in the brain.

Cerebrospinal fluid studies provide information on fluid flow in or around the brain. Medical problems such as intracranial trauma, surgery, infection, malformation, hydrocephalus, or neoplasms can cause cerebrospinal fluid to leak into and drain from the nasal or oral cavities and can be detected with nuclear medicine.

Genitourinary System

Kidney imaging and vascular flow can be studied using gamma-emitting radioactive materials or tracers. The urinary bladder activity can be studied for residual urine volume and reflux with the use of an injected radiopharmaceutical.

Other Procedures

These studies are used for tumor localization and inflammatory processes in limited areas, whole body, and SPECT. The provision of diagnostic radiopharmaceuticals is also described in this section. The code is reported separately from the nuclear medicine procedure.

Therapeutic

These procedures use radiopharmaceutical therapy to treat thyroid cancers and hormone overproduction. Thyroid cells readily take up radioactive iodine, making this an effective treatment.

Radiopharmaceutical therapy is also used to treat polycythemia vera and chronic leukemia. This treatment acts to slow the rate at which the bone marrow produces cells and induces a remission state.

Colloid radioactive therapy works because it is relatively impermeable to the vascular membrane. It is used for intracavitary or interstitial placement because it allows only a lower dose of radiation to surrounding tissues. Radiopharmaceuticals are also used in treatments because they inhibit lesion growth and membrane swelling.

The provision of radiopharmaceuticals can be reported separately in addition to the procedure code.

▬ CHAPTER REVIEW ▬

1. The modifier to identify the professional component of radiology services is:
   a. 22
   b. 24
   c. 25
   d. 26

2. In radiology, the term "with contrast" refers to contrast administered:
   a. intravascularly
   b. intra-articularly
   c. intrathecally
   d. all of the above

3. The most common method of diagnostic imaging is:
   a. ultrasound
   b. fluoroscopy
   c. x-ray
   d. magnetic resonance

4. The x-ray beam travels in a similar manner to:
   a. light particles
   b. radiation
   c. sound waves
   d. magnetic fields

5. A form of imaging that does not use x-rays is:
   a. fluoroscopy
   b. myelography
   c. DEXA
   d. MRI

6. A patient is seen for shortness of breath and a cough. The physician orders a PA and lateral chest x-ray. The patient is diagnosed with pneumonia. The correct codes are:

   a. 786.05, 786.2, 71010

   b. 486, 786.05, 786.2, 71020

   c. 486, 71020

   d. 486, 71010

7. A patient is seen for evaluation of back pain. Upon x-ray, the patient seems to have decreased joint space between L-5 and S-1. The patient is referred for an MRI of the spine without contrast, followed by contrast. The patient is diagnosed with a displaced disc between L-5 and S-1. The codes for the MRI and diagnosis are:

   a. 722.10, 72148

   b. 722.10, 72148, 72149

   c. 722.11, 72157

   d. 722.10, 72158

8. An elderly patient fell in her home. She has experienced right shoulder pain since the fall. The physician orders a complete set of shoulder x-rays and diagnoses the patient with a fractured proximal humerus. The correct codes are:

   a. 812.00, E888.9, E849.0, 73060-RT

   b. 812.00, E888.9, E849.0, 73030-RT

   c. 821.20, E888.9, E849.0, 73030-RT

   d. 812.00, E888.9, E849.4, 73020-RT

9. A standard scout, or KUB, film is included on radiology studies of the:

   a. abdomen

   b. gastrointestinal tract

   c. urinary tract

   d. gynecological and obstetrical

10. An intraoperative cholangiogram can be performed as a part of a:

    a. gall bladder removal

    b. appendectomy

    c. inguinal hernia repair

    d. fundoplasty

11. A 78-year-old patient is in need of central venous access for chemotherapy and medication administration. The patient has a post-surgery wound infection. The placement of a double lumen PICC line is requested. Access to the left basilic vein was obtained with ultrasound guidance using a 21-gauge needle. Using fluoroscopic guidance, the guidewire catheter length was measured. The tip of the catheter was positioned at the cavoatrial junction. The correct codes are:

    a. 998.59, 36555, 76942

    b. 998.59, 36556, 76936

    c. 998.59, 36556, 76942

    d. 998.51, 36556, 76936

12. A 50-year-old patient who is in need of PICC line placement for lower extremity cellulitis presents to the radiologist office. Contrast material was injected through the patient's indwelling IV site on the back of the right hand and the cephalic vein was selected for the puncture site. The skin was punctured with a micropuncture needle. A guidewire was superior vena cava and a 5-French dual lumen PICC catheter was placed at the junction of the superior vena cava and the right atrium. The correct codes are:

    a. 682.6, 36556, 76003

    b. 682.6, 36555, 76003

    c. 682.6, 36556, 76003-26

    d. 682.6, 36556, 76003-26, 76003-TC

13. Diagnostic ultrasounds include all of the following except:

    a. A-mode

    b. M-mode

    c. B-scan

    d. C-scan

14. Pelvic ultrasounds are located in the following subsections:

    a. Obstetrical and Non-Obstetrical

    b. Abdominal, Obstetrical, and Non-Obstetrical

    c. Obstetrical, Non-Obstetrical, Genitalia

    d. Transabdominal and Transvaginal

15. All of the following are a part of Radiation Oncology except:

    a. Clinical Treatment Planning

    b. Nuclear Medicine

    c. Radiation Treatment Delivery

    d. Hyperthermia

Case Studies

Instructions: Code for all procedures and diagnoses as if this were a radiologist performing the procedures in his or her privately owned facility.

Case Study 19.1

Indication

Central venous access required for treatment of fever.

Impression

1. Right subclavian vein occlusion
2. Fever

Procedure

Right upper extremity venogram, angioplasty of the right subclavian vein, and placement of double-lumen PICC line via right upper extremity.

Discussion

The patient is a 74-year-old male with an indwelling right subclavian central venous catheter being used for therapy. He currently has a fever and requires central venous access for treatment. We are requested to place a double-lumen PICC line. Consent for the procedure is obtained from the patient.

    The right upper arm is prepped and draped in the usual fashion. Lidocaine is used for local anesthesia. Using ultrasound guidance, the right basilica vein is punctured with a 21-gauge needle, and the guide wire is passed more centrally. Peel-away sheath is placed. The catheter does not pass the subclavian vein, which shows central occlusion of the right subclavian vein, which may be related to the existing subclavian vein or other previous stenosis.

    Subsequently, a 5-French Bernstein catheter is advanced through the peel-away sheath and, utilizing a guidewire, the area of occlusion is crossed without tunneling. A 6 mm balloon is then used to dilate the area of occlusion. This is performed to facilitate passage of the PICC line via this access. Subsequently, a 6-French double-lumen PICC line is trimmed to 45 cm and inserted through the peel-away sheath. The tip of the catheter is positioned at the cava atrial junction. The catheter is then secured to the skin surface with suture and a dressing is applied. The catheter is fully functional and ready for use.

    ICD-9-CM Code(s): _____

    CPT® Code(s): _____

Case Study 19.2

Report

Arch aortogram and bilateral carotid angiogram.

Preoperative Diagnosis

Carotid stenosis.

Procedure

The patient was interviewed prior to the procedure with discussion of the procedure and its risks and possible complications with apparent good understanding. Written consent was obtained. The skin over the right groin was prepped and draped in the usual sterile fashion. The skin was anesthetized locally with 1% xylocaine. A small dermatotomy incision is made. The right common femoral artery was punctured with an Inrad needle and a guidewire was placed. A 5-French configuration catheter was reformed in the ascending aorta and selective catheterization of the right and left common carotid arteries was performed. The catheter was then advanced into the ascending aorta for arch aortography. Contrast material was injected. The patient seemed to tolerate the procedure well, and no immediate complications were identified. Hemostasis was obtained in the groin with manual compression.

Findings

Arch Aortogram

The origin of the brachiocephalic vessels is well demonstrated and appears normal. There is considerable tortuousity in the right innominate artery. The vertebral flow is forward bilaterally.

Right Carotid, Cervical Portion

There is a 50% to 70% ulcerated stenosis in the origin of the right internal carotid artery. There are actually two areas of apparent ulceration: one just above the bulb and the second one slightly higher up in the proximal internal carotid artery.

Intracranial Portion:

Normal.

Left Carotid, Cervical Portion

There is mild ulcerated stenosis in the proximal left internal carotid artery, no greater than 20% to 40% overall luminal compromise. There is ulceration in the distal end of the stenosis.

Intracranial Portion:

Normal.

    ICD-9-CM Code(s): _____

    CPT® Code(s): _____

Case Study 19.3

Procedure

Dialysis graft declot and venous angioplasty.

Indication

1. Thrombosed dialysis graft.
2. End-stage renal disease.

Contraindications

1. Allergies to IV contrast and lidocaine.
2. Patient requests sedation.

Discussion

The patient is a 47-year-old female with end-stage renal disease. She has a dialysis graft in the left forearm, which recently became thrombosed. We are requested to restore patency.

The area of the graft was prepped and draped in the usual fashion. Nesacaine was used for local anesthesia. Access to the graft pointing toward the venous anastomosis was made with a 21-gauge needle. Of note, the venous anastomosis is positioned medially. A guidewire was passed into the graft and a 6-French sheath was placed. A 5-French catheter was then advanced up the basilic vein. When adequate blood return was obtained, the patient was administered 125 mg Solu-Medrol, as well as 50 mg Benadryl, to aid in premedication for her IV contrast allergy. This has been used in the past with good results. Additionally, the patient was administered 25 mcg Fentanyl and 1 mg Versed for sedation.

Subsequently, a Trerotola device was then used to macerate thrombus throughout the graft with administration of 2,500 units of heparin. A second access to the graft pointing toward the arterial anastomosis was then made with the placement of a 5-French sheath. A 3-French Fogarty catheter was then advanced across the arterial anastomosis, the balloon was inflated and pulled back through the graft to restore inflow into the graft. Contrast injection at this point was performed. These show fairly tight narrowing at the venous anastomosis. There was also a tight segment of narrowing within the venous limb of the graft at the site of the multiple needle punctures from dialysis. There was also narrowing at the arterial anastomosis.

Subsequently, a 7-mm balloon was used to dilate all three areas. The venous anastomosis, as well as the venous side of the graft, expanded fairly well. The arterial anastomosis was somewhat refractory to complete dilation.

After completion of the dilations, there was excellent flow through the graft. Further contrast injections are performed to evaluate the outflow centrally. There was no central stenosis present. Subsequently, the 6-French sheath was replaced with a Dialese catheter for dialysis. A 5-French sheath was removed and hemostasis achieved with direct compression. The patient tolerated the procedure well and was taken to dialysis.

ICD-9-CM Code(s): _____

CPT® Code(s): _____

Case Study 19.4

Report

Right upper extremity arteriogram, fistulogram, and venous angioplasty.

Indications

1. Poor arterial pressures.
2. End-stage renal disease.

Discussion

The patient is a 59-year-old male with end-stage renal disease on dialysis. He has a right upper arm AV fistula for dialysis. At dialysis, there was an adequate arterial flow. We are requested to perform fistulogram to further evaluate the fistula. Additionally, we were requested to perform right upper extremity arteriogram to evaluate the in-flow to the fistula. Consent for the procedure was obtained from the patient.

The area of the fistula was prepped and draped in the usual fashion. Lidocaine was used for local anesthesia. Access to the fistula pointing toward the arteriovenous anastomosis was made with a 21-gauge needle. A guidewire was passed centrally and a 5-French sheath placed. A 5-French catheter was then advanced into the arterial end of the right brachial artery utilizing a guidewire. The catheter was then advanced into the central right innominate artery. Contrast injection was performed at each location to evaluate the arterial inflow to the fistula. The level of the arteriovenous anastomosis was also evaluated. Subsequently, further contrast injections were performed via the sheath to evaluate the venous outflow centrally.

These images show a patent arterial system flowing into the arteriovenous fistula. The fistula arterial inflow is from a branch from the profunda branch of the upper arm. The arteriovenous anastomosis itself was widely patent. There was focal evaluation of the fistulas at the level of the anastomosis. Subsequently, the venous outflow shows mild-to-moderate narrowing at the level of the valve in the right axillary vein. Otherwise, central runoff was patent.

Subsequently, it was elected to perform angioplasty of the narrowed segment to see if that would improve flow through the fistula because the arterial inflow was otherwise normal. A new access to the graft pointing centrally is then obtained with a 21-gauge needle and a 6-French sheath placed. The area of narrowing was dilated with an 8 mm balloon. There was mild improvement through this area postangioplasty. Subsequently, sheaths were removed and hemostasis achieved with direct compression. The patient tolerated the procedure well.

ICD-9-CM Code(s): _____

CPT® Code(s): _____

Case Study 19.5

Report

Shuntogram, venous angioplasty, left upper extremity arteriogram.

Indication

1. Poor graft function.
2. End-stage renal disease.

Discussion

A 65-year-old patient with end-stage renal disease has a dialysis graft in the left forearm. At dialysis, there was poor flow. We were requested to perform a shuntogram. Additionally, we were requested to catheterize the central arterial system of the left upper extremity to evaluate arterial inflow. Consent for the procedure was obtained from the patient.

The area of the graft was prepped and draped in the usual fashion. Lidocaine was used for local anesthesia. Access to the graft at the apex is obtained with a 21-gauge needle. The guidewire was passed centrally. A 5-French sheath was then placed into the graft, pointing toward the arterial anastomosis. Subsequently, utilizing a LT guidewire and a 5-French catheter, the catheter was advanced into the proximal left subclavian artery adjacent to the aortic arch. Contrast injections were performed with imaging of the left upper extremity arterial inflow to the graft. The catheter was then withdrawn back into the shunt and further imaging was performed of the shunt as well as of the venous outflow.

These images show the arterial inflow to be widely patent. There was moderate narrowing of the arterial anastomosis with the graft. Within the graft itself, there were two high-grade stenoses on the venous side, one of which was at the venous anastomosis. The venous runoff centrally in the upper arm was all patent. Subsequently, a 7 mm diameter balloon was used to dilate both the arterial anastomosis and the areas on the venous side of the graft. After multiple inflations, especially on the venous side of the graft, patency was restored with fairly good luminal diameter.

Flow at this point through the graft was excellent. The sheath was removed. The patient tolerated the procedure well.

    ICD-9-CM Code(s): _____

    CPT® Code(s): _____

Case Study 19.6

Report

Abdominal aortogram, bilateral lower extremity runoff, bilateral renal arteriogram, and left renal artery stent placement.

Preoperative Diagnosis

1. Progressive hypertension with multiple medications.
2. Abnormal renal artery duplex examination.
3. Leg pain with walking.

Postoperative Diagnosis

1. Significant left renal artery stenosis.
2. Minimal narrowing of right renal artery.
3. Runoff to lower extremities bilaterally is essentially normal.

Discussion

The patient is a 70-year-old female with difficult-to-control hypertension. Additionally, she has difficulty with walking due to leg pain. We were requested to perform an abdominal aortogram and lower extremity runoff as well as evaluation of renal arteries and possible intervention as indicated. Consent for the procedure was obtained from the patient.

    The right groin was prepped and draped in the usual fashion. Lidocaine was used for local anesthesia. Access to the right common femoral artery was obtained with an 18-gauge needle. The guide wire was passed centrally and a 4-French pigtail catheter was advanced into the abdominal aorta to the level of the renal arteries. Contrast injection was performed with imaging of the abdominal aorta. The catheter was then repositioned to a level just above the aortic bifurcation. Further contrast injections were performed with imaging of the lower extremity with runoff to the feet bilaterally, with an additional oblique view of the pelvic vasculature.

    These images show single renal arteries bilaterally. There was mild narrowing at the origin of the right renal artery and significant 70 percent narrowing of the original of the left renal artery. The abdominal aorta is fairly smooth. The iliac arteries bilaterally are normal.

    Runoff in both lower extremities showed patent femoral and popliteal system and three-vessel runoff to the feet bilaterally. There was no significant narrowing of either of the lower extremities and the runoff was fairly normal.

    Subsequently, the pigtail catheter was replaced with a 5-French catheter. This was used to select first the left renal artery. Contrast injections were performed with imaging of the left renal artery. Subsequently, a long 6-French sheath is placed and a .018 guidewire advanced into the left renal arterial system. The left renal artery was primarily stented with placement of a 6 × 12 mm stent. This was inflated to 6 mm in diameter. Follow-up contrast injection after stent placement shows excellent result with no residual narrowing present. The catheter was then placed in the right renal artery. Contrast injection shows minimal narrowing near the origin of the right renal artery. Pressure gradients across this show no evidence of gradient. Catheters and sheaths were removed and hemostasis achieved. The patient tolerated the procedure well.

    ICD-9-CM Codes: _____

    CPT® Codes: _____

Pathology and Laboratory Services

OBJECTIVES

1. Recognize the difference between the Pathology and Laboratory chapter and other chapters of CPT®.
2. Relate the differences between laboratory, cytology, and histology procedures.
3. Locate procedure codes correctly within the Pathology and Laboratory chapter.
4. Recognize the importance of linking ICD-9-CM diagnoses for medical necessity to Pathology and Laboratory procedural codes.

TERMINOLOGY AND ACRONYMS

Analyte   The substance or component in a sample for which an analysis is being conducted or that is being measured.

Anti kickback statute   A federal regulation to prevent anyone from knowingly soliciting or receiving offers or cash payments of any kind for referrals to an entity receiving payments from Medicare or Medicaid. Violations are enforced by audits and penalties and can include giving anything of value and payments not of market value.

Assay   An analysis or testing of a substance or mixture to determine its constituents and relative proportions.

Certificate of waiver   Based on CLIA registration as a low complexity laboratory and requires that only tests approved for waived status will be performed. These labs do not meet the stringent requirements of the higher complexity labs and are usually found in physician clinics.

CLIA (Clinical Laboratory Improvement Act)   Legislation that requires all laboratories to be registered and graded as to the complexity of the lab. It requires labs to meet standards based on quality control and quarterly surveys.

Peak   The highest concentration of a drug reached in the blood after a medication dosage.

Plasma   The fluid portion of blood when an anticoagulant is present.

PPM (provider-performed microscopy)   Microscopic examinations performed in the office setting by providers carrying a special certificate to perform moderately complex microscopic procedures.

Qualitative testing   Considered sensitive and can also be referred to as a screening method. Qualitative results are provided in positive or negative form.

Quality assurance   A program of activities designed to achieve a desired level of care.

Quality control   A procedure comprised of performing every test on a laboratory menu using specimens of known values. The quality control specimens each have a range of tolerance for accuracy. Quality control specimens consist of either two or three samples of normal and abnormal values and are used to determine a procedure's accuracy. When the values fall out of range, a test should not be run on patient specimens because the accuracy of results cannot be guaranteed.

Quantitative testing   Considered specific for the analyte being tested. Because of the specificity, the instrumentation is able to provide an exact quantity, measured amount, or numerical value for the analyte being tested.

Reagents   Substances added to a patient sample to cause a measurable chemical reaction to occur.

Sensitivity   The degree of a response to a change in the ligand or molecule being measured by a test or assay. It is also referred to as a *detection limit.*

Serum   The fluid portion of blood after coagulation has taken place.

Seventy-two-hour rule   Reference to any radiology or laboratory diagnostic test performed on an outpatient basis within seventy-two hours of a Medicare hospital admission. These services are bundled into the DRG payment and are not to be billed separately. This is enforced by the Office of the Inspector General (OIG) and billing separately is considered double billing.

Specificity   The degree to which a protein binds to a particular ligand and not to a structurally similar compound.

Stark I and II   Federal legislation that prohibits a physician from referring his or her patients to a facility, such as a reference laboratory, in which the physician has financial interest. This prevents the physician from receiving a monetary gain or kickback from such referrals. These regulations carry penalties of up to $15,000 per service, up to $100,000 for any scheme to circumvent Stark law, $10,000 per day for reported violations, and sanctions from Medicare/Medicaid participation.

Survey specimen   A preserved test sample similar to a human specimen that is prepared by an independent agency as an "unknown" to participating laboratories. This is one part of CLIA compliance, and in addition to being required quarterly, it must be accurate on a regular basis or the individual test failing the survey may not be performed to report patient values.

Trough   The lowest concentration in the blood of a medication reached, usually before the next dose is given.

Waived testing   Low complexity laboratory testing that requires a limited number of steps that can be performed in an office setting. It is designated with the Modifier QW for Medicare claims.

WB (whole blood)   A substance made up of blood cells and plasma. When laboratory tests are performed on whole blood, an anticoagulant is present and the collection tube is not spun in a centrifuge to separate the cells from the fluid portion. Instead, the sample is gently rocked so that the specimen stays well mixed.

DISEASE PROCESSES AND ICD-9-CM CODING OF PATHOLOGY AND LABORATORY PROCEDURES

See page 406 for ICD-9-CM and Medicare guidelines regarding diagnostic testing.

Formula for Success

Code V72.6, Laboratory examination, not elsewhere classified, is not recognized as a diagnosis that meets medical necessity for many payers and may result in claim denial. Use this code with caution.

CPT® CODING OF PATHOLOGY AND LABORATORY PROCEDURES

Guidelines for the Pathology and Laboratory chapter of CPT® can be found on the colored pages in the beginning of the chapter. Some of the guidelines for this chapter are similar to those of the surgery chapters, while others are unique to this section alone.

A physician provides services in pathology and laboratory. Technologists or technicians under the supervision of the physician perform most procedures in this section.

Subsection information can be found in the guidelines as well. Here the subsections are listed by title and code ranges. Unlisted procedure codes are included and represent procedures that are not adequately described by any other code.

Special reports in this section may be provided when a service is rarely provided, unusual, variable, or new. Information included in a special report should include the nature, extent, need for the procedure, time, effort, and equipment necessary to provide the service. Other factors to consider including in a special report are the complexity of symptoms and the final diagnosis, pertinent physical findings, diagnostic and therapeutic procedures, concurrent problems, and follow-up care.

Modifiers

Modifiers used in this section:

- *Modifier 90* is used when a party other than the treating or reporting physician performs a laboratory procedure. Medicare has specific instructions on the use of this modifier. Payer preferences should be researched before claim submission.

- *Modifier 91* is used when it is necessary to repeat the same laboratory test on the same day to obtain multiple test results. This modifier is not to be used when a test is rerun for confirmation, if there are testing problems with the specimen or equipment, or any reason when one reportable result is all that is required. This modifier may not be used when code descriptors allow for multiple series testing, such as glucose tolerance testing.

- *Modifiers 26 and TC* are not typically used in this section. Laboratory services are all-inclusive and include the reading and interpretation in the basic global code. Pathology and laboratory services have separately reportable consultation codes for circumstances where a pathologist is consulted for interpretation. These modifiers may be used in an instance where a specimen is sent to an outside laboratory for preparation and is then read by the original physician—for example, with dermatology slides that are prepared by the lab and then sent back to the dermatologist for reading.

- *Modifier QW* is a HCPC modifier used on Medicare claims to signify that a test is a low complexity test that is classified as waived according to **CLIA.**

Other modifiers may be used for laboratory codes when they are appropriate; however, when multiple pathology and laboratory procedures are performed, the fees are not reduced. Modifier 51 is not routinely used or needed in this section.

EXERCISE 20.1

Instructions: Give the correct answer for the questions below.

1. Name the pathology and laboratory specific modifier for repeat laboratory tests.

2. Name the legislation that states that laboratories must register according to complexity.

3. Name the legislation aimed at stopping physician conflict of interest.

4. Quarterly survey specimens are required to be run by what legislation?

Organ or Disease-Oriented Panels

A *panel* is a group of tests that are performed together. The laboratory panels listed in CPT® were developed for coding purposes. These panels are not intended to limit the physician in ordering specific tests or test combinations. Therefore, if extra tests are run in addition to those listed in the panels, these tests are reported separately from the panel codes. Likewise, when reporting a panel, *all tests listed in the panel must be run* and must meet the criteria set in the descriptors for each individual test. In certain instances, insurance companies or Medicare may not recognize panels, and the only way to report a panel is by coding the individual tests. This should not be an automatic practice for all insurers, because it may be construed as unbundling to receive increased payment.

Formula for Success

Tips for Coding Organ or Disease-Oriented Panels

1. Tests included in panels frequently change; always refer to an updated CPT® for accurate information.
2. Have good communication with your laboratory and keep updated on equipment changes that may change the codes used.
3. Always make sure that *all* of the tests listed in a panel are being run.
4. Watch for duplicate tests on more than one panel; this is considered unbundling.

Example   When reporting a basic metabolic panel, calcium, carbon dioxide, chloride, creatinine, glucose, potassium, sodium, and urea nitrogen tests must all be performed, and the tests must match the code descriptors for each individual test. The individual test codes are listed next to each test in the panel code descriptor.

Example   When reporting a general health panel, a blood count (CBC) fitting the description of 85025, 85027 and 85004, 86027 and 85007, or 85009, must be conducted.

Drug Testing

Coding for drug testing can be confusing. The drugs tested for in this section can be prescription medications and their metabolites; however, these tests are mainly used as screening for illicit drug use or overdose of drugs physicians are not expecting to find or are trying to confirm for treatment.

■ Code 80100 is described as a *qualitative* method. This means that it is a test for the presence of a drug. *Qualitative tests provide a positive or negative result.* The *chromatographic* method uses a mobile phase to promote separation between this and a stationary phase. This separation is then graphically plotted to display a series of bands. Using this method, several drugs or drug classes can be screened for at the same time. It is possible to perform this procedure in a combination *mobile* and *stationary phase,* which is counted as one procedure or unit of 80100.

■ Code 80101 is also a qualitative test; however, the method is an *immunoassay* or *enzyme **assay,*** which is a competitive binding of a protein to an antibody. This also gives a positive or negative answer but can only be performed for one drug at a time. These methods often involve a color change reaction and are simple to run and to read.

Example

■ Five drugs were tested for with a chromatographic method; one procedure = one unit of 80100.

■ Five drugs were tested for with a chromatographic method; one in a stationary phase and five in a mobile phase = five units of 80100.

■ Five drugs were tested for by immunoassay = five units of 80101.

When a drug is detected in serum or urine by one of the screening methods, it is then tested by a confirmatory method. Screening tests are *sensitive,* which means they can detect a small amount or presence of a substance but may also detect substances other than that being tested for, an interfering substance. Confirmatory methods are *specific* for the drug they are testing for and allow for optimal conditions to detect the drug and report an accurate level of the drug.

Occasionally, tissues may be used for drug testing. This requires the sample to be processed and turned into a form that can be tested. Use 80103 to report this service.

Therapeutic Drug Assays

Therapeutic drug testing is used to monitor medications that a physician has prescribed for a patient. These drugs are tested for using a *quantitative* method. **Quantitative testing** is specific for the drug or other analyte being tested. Because it is specific, the equipment or method used is able to assign a numerical value, not just a positive or negative result, to the presence of the substance. Some of the medications in this section can have *toxic levels,* which is a poisonous and sometimes-fatal condition caused by a level of a therapeutic agent that is too high. These medications are tested with a **peak,** the highest concentration reached after a dosage, and a **trough,** the lowest concentration reached, usually before the next dose is given. When two identical tests are performed on the same day at different times, Modifier 91 can be used for multiple tests and/or Modifier 59 for separate procedure at a separate time. Depending on the insurance carrier, both modifiers may be needed to clarify this situation. The medications tested in this section include:

■ Antibiotics
■ Antidepressants
■ Sedatives
■ Anticonvulsant
■ Immunosupressants
■ Tranquilizers
■ Antiarrhythmic

Evocative/Suppression Testing

The panels in this section involve the administration of evocative or suppressive agents. Baseline and subsequent measurements are used to determine the effects of the chemical constituents. These codes report the laboratory component of the testing portion. Other reportable services that may be billed separately include:

- Physician administration of the evocative or suppressive agents, codes 90780–90784.
- Supplies and drugs are reported with a generic 99070 or specific HCPC code.
- Physician attendance and monitoring during the test, Evaluation and Management codes.
- Prolonged infusions, codes 90780 and 90781 are used instead of prolonged physician care codes.

These tests are made up of panels with specific components and the number of times they are tested. These descriptions must be obtained to report the specific codes.

Consultations (Clinical Pathology)

Clinical pathology consultation services are performed by a pathologist in response to a request from an attending physician for interpretation of test results. This interpretation is given in written form. Test results reported without the interpretation of a pathologist do not qualify as a clinical pathology consultation.

These services differ from the consultations in the Evaluation and Management section because they involve no patient contact or exam. The services in this section consist of an interpretation of test results with or without the patient's history and medical records.

Urinalysis

One of the most common laboratory tests performed is the urinalysis. It is an inexpensive way for physicians to obtain information about a patient's health using the most readily available source.

The urinalysis begins with a *colormetric* testing of the urine with a dipstick. The dipstick is a plastic strip with pads containing chemicals that react with the urine and turn different colors (Figure 20.1). These colors are matched to a chart to give semiquantitative results for the chemical and cellular components of urine. These dipsticks can either be read manually or with an automated instrument that reads and reports the results (see Figure 20.2).

When the dipstick shows positive results for cellular components present in urine, a microscopic examination is performed. The sedimentation from the urine is concentrated in a centrifuge, the liquid portion is discarded and the sediment is examined with the microscope. A technologist or technician performs this portion of the testing, so it is not considered a waived urinalysis. A non-automated or automated urinalysis without microscopy is considered a waived procedure and is reported with the Modifier QW for Medicare.

Other tests in this section include:

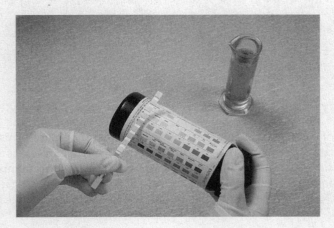

Figure 20–1 Colormetric testing of urine with a dipstick.

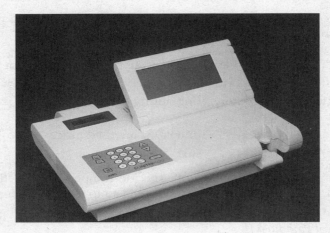

Figure 20–2   Clintec 100 for automated urinalysis.

- Qualitative or semiquantitative urinalysis, except immunoassay.
- Bacterial screen, except culture or dipstick.
- Microscopy only.
- Two- or three-glass tests, which involve a bacterial culture of the urine.
- Urine pregnancy by visual color comparison, which is a waived test.
- Volume measurement for timed collection used for the calculation of 24-hour tests such as creatinine clearance.

Chemistry

The material examined for chemical components may be from any source unless specified in the code descriptor. Whenever it is necessary to test the same analyte using multiple or different sources, the code for the analyte tested may be reported separately for *each source* and *each specimen*. The examination is considered quantitative unless otherwise specified.

Clinical information, which is derived or calculated from the results of laboratory data, is considered part of the test procedure and not separately reportable.

Formula for Success

Tips for Coding Diagnostic Chemistry Procedures

1. Read all of the code choices for each test. Some tests have more than one source, such as urine, whole blood, plasma, serum, joint fluid, and cerebral spinal fluid. Watch for tests that have a choice between a quantitative, semiquantitative, and qualitative methods.
2. Some tests include wording to separate single and multiple testing or testing per specimen.
3. Watch for tests that are further divided by methodology.
4. There are a number of laboratory specific abbreviations; always clarify when there is any uncertainty of the full name.

Most laboratory tests are listed alphabetically according to the **analyte** being tested. However, some tests are listed according to the methodology used without listing the analyte. An example of this is the chromatography, qualitative, column. This procedure is found under chromatography, and the descriptor states that the analyte is not elsewhere specified and lists the codes of this method according to the type of membranes used in testing. Another unique characteristic about reporting quantitative chromatographic procedures is that they are separated into single analyte or multiple analytes. When more than one analyte is tested by different stationary and mobile phases, two units of 82491 are reported. However, if two analytes are tested using a single stationary phase, one unit of 82492 would be reported.

Occult blood by peroxidase activity is a test commonly performed in the clinic setting. This procedure is considered a waived test and is a one-step color change reaction. This test is referred to as a *guiac test*. Use CPT® code 82270 or HCPC code G0107 (for Medicare screening occult blood tests) to report one to three simultaneous tests. Occult blood cards are routinely sent home with a patient to obtain three separate specimens. When these cards are tested, only one unit of 82270 is reported. The pH on the fecal occult cards is specific for feces, not other body fluids. Do not use 82270 to report this service on body fluids other than feces. Use code 82273 for other sources of occult blood. Code 82273 reports testing gastric secretions or nipple discharge for occult blood.

Glucose testing has several different methods:

- *Body fluid*, other than blood, refers to joint fluid and cerebral spinal fluid.
- *Quantitative, blood, except reagent strip*, is the "routine" glucose, usually performed when the patient has been fasting for eight hours.
- *Quantitative, blood using a reagent strip* is performed with a finger stick. Using a **reagent** strip, the reaction is timed, blood drop blotted, and color reaction manually compared to a chart.
- *Post glucose dose*, including glucose "glucola," may also be referred to as a postprandial test. The sample may be obtained two hours after a meal or glucose solution consumption. A one-hour postprandial screen may be performed on pregnant women for gestational diabetes.
- *Glucose tolerance testing (GTT)*, includes the glucose dose. A blood specimen is obtained for serum testing before the administration of the glucose, then every hour after the dose for three hours. There is an additional code for each additional specimen beyond the first three. Keep in mind that these specimens each involve a venipuncture, using code 36415. Multiple collections will need to be reported with Modifier 59. Modifier use is payer specific, so check before reporting.
- *Glucose monitoring device for blood, for home use* is commonly referred to as "glucometer" testing and may be performed in any setting. This is a waived test and would be reported with Modifier QW.

Codes 83890–83912 are used to report molecular diagnostic techniques for nucleic acids. These codes describe the procedure instead of the analyte and each is coded separately for each procedure used in an analysis.

Near the end of the chemistry section are two codes for Gonadotropin, chorionic (HCG). These are out of alphabetic order and are serum pregnancy tests. Code 84702 is quantitative and may also be used as a tumor marker as well as for the detection of pregnancy. Code 84703 is a qualitative pregnancy test and is also a waived procedure.

EXERCISE 20.2

Instructions: Give the short answer or correct Pathology and Laboratory CPT®/ICD-9-CM code(s) as indicated below.

1. A patient is seen for hypertension by his physician. As part of the monitoring process, the physician orders sodium, potassium, chloride, and carbon dioxide levels. _____

2. A patient is seen for an annual exam. Part of the exam includes the laboratory tests for calcium, chloride, creatinine, glucose, potassium, sodium, and blood urea nitrogen. _____

3. A patient is seen for urine drug testing for her employer. She is tested for five drugs using an enzyme method. _____

4. If the patient in question 3 is found to be positive for one of the drugs and has a drug confirmation procedure performed, what CPT® code would be used? _____

5. Determine the CPT® codes used for a patient who has a peak and trough of tobramycin performed. _____

6. A pediatrics patient with short stature is tested with a growth hormone stimulation panel. _____

7. A patient presents to her family physician with dysuria and hematuria. An automated urinalysis with microscopy is performed and the patient is diagnosed with a urinary tract infection. _____

Hematology and Coagulation

Hematology is the study of blood cells and blood-forming tissues. Many different types of instruments are available for the analysis of blood cells, and this is part of the reason so many different types of procedure codes exist for blood counts. Complete blood counts are also referred to as a CBC. This procedure is usually performed by an automated method using an instrument that is able to measure:

- *Erythrocytes*, red cells, in a given volume of blood.
- *Hematocrit (HCT)*, the ratio of red cells to fluid.
- *Hemoglobin (HGB)*, the red-colored protein that carries oxygen to the body's cells.
- *Indices MCV, MCH, and MCHC*, calculated values that determine if the morphology of the red blood cells is normal. These values are derived from the hemoglobin, hematocrit, and the number of red cells present. Indices cannot be coded separately from the rest of the CBC.
- *Leukocytes*, white blood cells, that fight infection in the body.
- *Platelets*, small sticky cells that help begin the clotting process in the body.

Figure 20.3 shows the elements of blood.
There are separate codes for components of a CBC such as:

- Hemoglobin
- Hematocrit
- Leukocytes
- Red blood cell
- Platelet
- Manual cell count

In addition to a white cell count there is also what is referred to as a differential WBC count. This can be performed by some hematology instruments or by a manual method. There are five basic types of white blood cells:

- *Neutrophils*, either in band or segmented form
- *Lymphocytes*

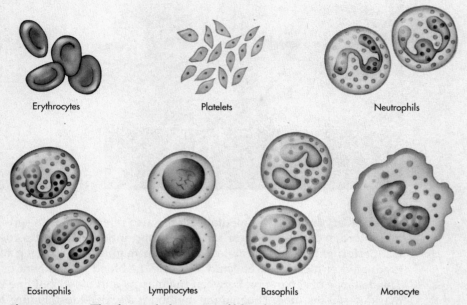

Figure 20–3   The formed elements of blood.

- Monocytes
- Eosinophils
- Basophils

When a manual differential is performed, the technologist or technician counts the different types of white blood cells present on a stained hematology slide under the microscope. One hundred cells are counted, and a percentage of each white blood cell type present is determined. The number and morphology of the white cells, red cells, and platelets are also observed when a manual differential is performed. An automated differential is performed by the hematology instrument and provides the same basic numerical information. When abnormal cell morphology is detected, a manual differential is usually performed for confirmation. When the percentage of a specific white blood cell type is abnormal, physicians are able to determine if the patient has a bacterial, viral, or fungal infection or if there is reason for further testing for leukemia. The observed red cell morphology along with the calculations for the indices helps the physician recognize different types of anemias and other red cell production abnormalities. When abnormal or immature cells of any cell line are observed, a pathologist or oncologist may review the slide and provide a written interpretation, code 85060.

Figure 20.4 shows a blood smear.

When immature red cells, *reticulocytes,* are present on a peripheral smear, differential, another series of stains and slides are used to detect and quantitate them. This is mainly seen in infants when the mother's blood type is different from the baby's, and the mother's antibodies are destroying the newborn's red blood cells. It can also be seen in cases of extreme anemia when the body is attempting to replace lost red cells so quickly that immature red cells are released too soon from the bone marrow and are circulating in the blood stream.

When anemias or leukemias are suspected, a number of other tests are performed to quantify the chemical components. Another study that is performed is a study of the bone marrow because this is where the blood cells originate. The bone marrow interpretation codes are found in the laboratory section; however, the obtaining or procurement of specimens is reported with codes 38220 or 38221.

Figure 20–4   Blood smear.

The erythrocyte sedimentation rate, also referred to as a sed rate or ESR, is a commonly ordered screening test for protein and inflammation disorders. It is a nonspecific test performed by an automated method or manually by placing whole blood (**WB**) in a graduated or measured tube and allowing the blood to sediment or settle for 60 minutes. The distance of separation between the plasma and blood cell line is measured using the markings on the tube. The manual method is a waived test. Figure 20.5 shows a Withrobe tube and Westergren test.

Coagulation tests are the study of the body's ability to clot, or stop bleeding. The first stage in the body's clotting process is the functioning of platelets. The platelets are the smallest cellular form in blood. When functioning properly, they are sticky and will stick together to cover an injury or cut. Platelets are also present in occlusions formed in the blood vessels of coronary artery disease patients. The use of aspirin decreases the functioning ability of the platelets. This is why small doses of aspirin are recommended for people with heart disease and why patients are instructed not to take aspirin in the days

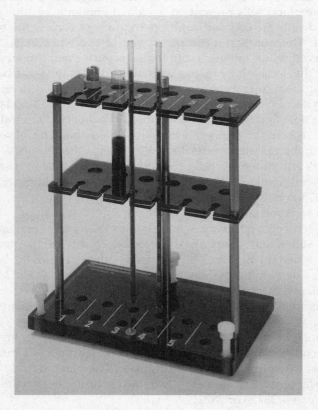

Figure **20–5** Withrobe tube and Westergren test.

leading up to a surgery. Aspirin does not decrease the number of platelets; therefore, obtaining a CBC including a platelet count does not offer any information about platelet function. Platelet function tests include:

- ■ *Bleeding time,* a time measurement for the clotting of a cut.
- ■ *Clot retraction,* the time it takes blood to clot in a tube kept at body temperature.
- ■ *Platelet aggregation,* the study of platelet clumping with the addition of certain chemicals.
- ■ *Platelet neutralization,* a test for the lupus anticoagulant.

The next stage in the clotting process is the formation of the clot itself. The clotting process is very complex; however, in a clinic or physician coding setting, the most common tests encountered are the prothrombin time, also referred to as protime or PT, and partial thromboplastin time, PTT. A patient diagnosed with a clot, embolism, thrombosis, phlebitis, etc., is treated in the hospital setting with the anticoagulant heparin. This is administered intravenously and monitored with the PTT. When the patient is ready to be discharged and it is determined that he or she would benefit from anticoagulation therapy, oral coumadin is prescribed and the patient is monitored on an outpatient basis with protime testing. Other conditions, such as atrial fibrillation and congestive heart failure, are also treated with coumadin. These conditions cause a pooling of blood, which can also lead to clotting.

EXERCISE 20.3

Instructions: Assign the correct Pathology and Laboratory CPT® codes (and ICD-9-CM diagnosis codes when specified) for the scenarios below.

1. Which complete blood count codes are included in a General Health Panel, 80050? _____

2. Determine what codes are used when a physician orders an automated H & H, hemoglobin and hematocrit. _____

3. An Rh-positive baby is born to an Rh-negative mother. The fetomaternal hemorrhage appears to be worse than expected, and it is felt that the mother will need extra doses of RhoGam to counteract the formation of a D antibody by the mother. A Kleinhauer-Betke and a rosette test are performed on the mother and confirm a fetal-maternal hemorrhage during delivery. Give the diagnosis code and CPT® codes. _____

4. A physician orders a facility specific coagulation panel consisting of a bleeding time, platelet count, protime, and partial thromboplastin time. What code(s) are reported? _____

5. A patient has been treated in the hospital for a pulmonary embolism, has been placed on coumadin therapy, and will be monitored with protimes at the physician's office. What diagnosis code is linked to the protime code 85610? _____

6. A patient with rheumatoid arthritis presents to the clinic laboratory to have an automated sed rate performed. What CPT® and ICD-9-CM codes are used? _____

Immunology

Immunology is the study of the components of the immune system and their function. A majority of the tests in the first section of immunology are listed in alphabetical order according to the type of test or methodology. For example, "Agglutinins, febrile" is an *agglutination* test, which tests antigen–antibody reactions. If an antibody is present in a patient serum specimen, it will bind with the antigen present on solid particles used for identification. When there is a binding of antigen and antibody clumping takes place, the test is considered positive. This procedure can be used to identify many different antibodies present in blood.

Formula for Success

Tips for Coding Immunology Procedures

1. A good understanding of procedures is needed because they can be used in the detection of many different conditions.
2. When reporting the same technique to detect different components, Modifier 59 should be used on second and subsequent codes to avoid the appearance of duplication.

Procedures are also listed that are used for the identification of specific agents. Many of these methods are listed by screening and titer. When a screen is positive, a titer or dilution may be performed to determine the actual strength of the antibody; when both procedures are performed, both codes may be reported.

Three codes are found in this section that are actually blood bank services not listed in the Transfusion Medicine section. These are blood bank physician services and each requires a written report:

- Difficult crossmatch and/or evaluation of irregular antibodies.
- Investigation of transfusion reaction.
- Authorization for deviation from standard blood banking procedures.

Qualitative or semiquantitative immunoassays, which are performed by multiple step methods and detect antibodies to infectious agents, are listed in the second half of this section. Code 86318 is used for a single step immunoassay. When using these codes, the identification of the antibody should be coded as accurately as possible. When multiple tests are performed for the detection of antibodies to organisms more precisely than the available codes allow, separate codes for each service may be reported. Multiple assays performed for antibodies of different immunoglobulin classes should be reported separately.

Tissue Typing

The tests in this subsection are performed primarily for the matching of potential donor tissues to transplant patients. Be aware of the wording *visual crossmatch* and understand that this refers to tissue and not a blood banking procedure. Human lymphocyte antigens (HLA) can cause rejection in allotransplantation and require compatibility testing also described in this section.

EXERCISE 20.4

Instructions: Assign the correct Pathology and Laboratory CPT® and ICD-9-CM codes for the scenarios below.

1. A patient with joint pain is suspected of having rheumatoid arthritis. The physician orders an ANA. _____

2. A physician sees a patient with hyperlipidemia and wants to screen for coronary heart disease using a C-reactive protein. _____

3. A patient is having preoperative lab work performed. During the blood bank screening, the serum is reacting with all of the reagent cells at room temperature. The technologist performs a test for a cold agglutinin, which is positive. She then performs a titer and confirms a cold agglutinin. _____

4. A male patient presents complaining of dysuria. He states that he has had sexual contact with a person with Chlamydia. The physician orders a Chlamydia antibody test and confirms the presence of *Chlamydia trachomatis*. _____

5. A physician calls a patient back to be seen after a unit of blood he has donated has tested positive for HIV. The physician begins by ordering an antibody test for HIV-1 and HIV-2. These tests have returned with positive results; however, they are considered inconclusive until confirmatory tests are performed. _____

Transfusion Medicine

Transfusion medicine may also be referred to as blood banking. These procedures are a specialized type of immunology testing. Some procedures in this section use red cells from a clotted specimen and test for the presence of antigens on the cell surface. Other tests are for the detection of antibodies in a serum specimen. Procedures found in this section include:

- *Antibody screen*, routinely performed in addition to patient blood typing to detect unexpected antibodies that may cause transfusion reactions or hemolytic disease of the newborn.
- *Antibody identification*, performed on a specimen with a positive antibody screen to confirm a specific antibody and its strength. Procedures in this process include:
  –Elution
  –Pretreatment of RBCs
  –Hemolysins and agglutinins
- *Antihuman globulin or Coombs test*, routinely performed on newborns to detect mother's antibodies bound to the antigens on baby's cells. This test is also used to detect a transfusion reaction.
- *Blood typing for ABO and Rh*, routine blood typing procedures.
- *Antigen screening*, performed on blood units and the patient when an unexpected antibody is detected and identified to help screen for compatible units for the patient.
- *Blood typing for paternity testing.*
- *Compatibility testing for each unit*, also referred to as the crossmatch.
- *Leukocyte transfusion*, for chemotherapy patients with leukemia or severe infection.
- *Blood product processing*, the handling of the blood and its components to be transfused:
  –Autologous blood processing is reported for the special handling of the blood components donated by and used by the same patient.
  –Autologous intra- or postoperative salvage is also referred to as cell saver.
  –Fresh frozen plasma thawing, used for the clotting factors.
  –Frozen blood preparation per unit—freezing, thawing, or freezing and thawing. Used in the case of rare antibodies either for a rare donor or autologous blood.

–Irradiation of blood product; used for immunosuppressed patients.

–Pooling of platelets or other blood products, the combining of several units of blood products for ease of transfusion or fluid reduction.

–Splitting of blood or blood products from a unit of whole blood into its component parts.

Figure 20.6 illustrates a cytotoxic allergy.

EXERCISE 20.5

Instructions: Assign the correct Pathology and Laboratory CPT® and ICD-9-CM codes for the scenarios below.

1. A patient is blood typed for ABO and Rh and has an antibody screen performed for a pre-operative evaluation. _____

2. A patient is to receive two units of blood in his physician's clinic because of his chronic blood loss anemia during renal dialysis for end-stage renal disease. The cross-match consist of an ABO and Rh typing of the patient, antibody screen, and the cross-match of the two units using the immediate spin, incubation, and antiglobulin technique. _____

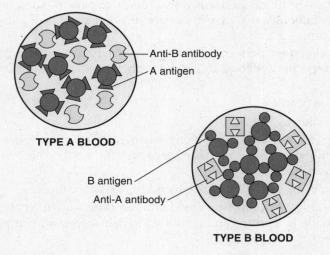

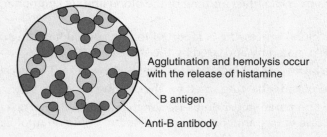

Figure 20–6 Cytotoxic allergy.

Microbiology

Microbiology is the study of microorganisms including bacteria, fungus, parasites, and viruses. *Presumptive identification* is the identification of a microorganism based on the colony morphology, growth on selective media, and Gram stains or other biochemical tests. *Definitive identification* of microorganisms is the identification of genus or species level, which is accomplished through additional tests and biochemical panels.

Formula for Success

Tips for Coding Microbiology Procedures

1. When additional tests are performed using molecular probes, chromatography, or immunologic techniques, these should be coded in addition to the definitive identification procedures.
2. Testing on multiple specimens or sites should be reported with Modifier 59.
3. Repeat laboratory testing performed on the same day should be reported with Modifier 59.

Many procedures found in the first subsection of microbiology are specific for the type of culture performed. For example:

- *Aerobic* refers to an organism living in the presence of oxygen. Specimen specific codes include:
  - Blood
  - Stool
  - Any source other than urine, blood, or stool
  - Quantitative, any source other than urine, blood, or stool
- *Anaerobic* refers to an organism living without the presence of oxygen. Specimen-specific codes include:
  - Quantitative, any source other than urine, blood, or stool
  - Isolation, the separation of one organism from any others present
- *Bacterial for urine*
- *Fungi; yeast or mold*
- *Mycoplasma*
- *Chlamydia*
- *Tubercle or acid-fast bacilli*
- *Mycobacterial*
- *Culture typing by method*

Figure 20.7 illustrates a blood agar plate and equipment.

Procedures listed by methodology follow the culture procedures. Some of these procedures are specific for a particular organism, and others can be performed based on the type of source. When an organism is identified, it then must undergo *susceptibility* testing. This is a method used to find an antibiotic that can be used to treat the infection.

The remaining codes in this subsection describe different types of staining techniques used to identify organisms with specific characteristics. Some of these procedures require specialized equipment, and others are fast and easily performed in the physician office setting.

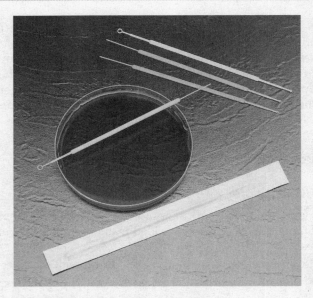

Figure 20–7 Blood agar plate and equipment.

Formula for Success

Tips for Coding Infectious Agent Procedures

1. Primary source codes are to be used for infectious agents identified by antigen detection, immunofluorescence microscopy, or nucleic acid probe techniques.
2. Techniques should be reported as precisely as possible.
3. If there is no specific agent code, general methodology codes should be used.
4. Antibody identification for infectious agents should be reported using codes 86602–86804.
5. Separate assays performed for different species or strain should be reported separately.

EXERCISE 20.6

Instructions: Assign the correct Pathology and Laboratory CPT® and ICD-9-CM codes for the scenarios below.

1. A urine specimen is submitted to the laboratory for a presumptive culture. The culture results are positive after twenty-four hours. The culture appears to be >100,000 colonies of a pure Gram-negative organism. A presumptive identification is performed. The organism is present on blood agar or the Gram-negative specific agar; therefore, susceptibility studies are set up with a disk method with ten different antibiotics. The identification of the organism is *Escherichia coli,* or *E. coli,* and a suitable antibiotic is identified. _____

2. A patient is seen in the clinic and is suspected of having pulmonary tuberculosis. A sputum culture for tuberculosis is set up. The culture is positive for growth after three days and the organism is the identified as pulmonary tuberculosis. _____

3. A patient travels to Mexico and returns with diarrhea. The physician orders an aerobic and anaerobic stool culture and an ova and parasite study. The organism identified is *Giardia lamblia.* _____

4. A 6-month-old is brought into the pediatrician with a respiratory infection. The symptoms are classic for respiratory syncytial virus. The laboratory assistant collects a nasopharyngeal specimen and a multistep immunoassay technique specific for respiratory syncytial virus is performed. The results are positive and the patient is admitted to the local hospital. _____

5. A male patient is seen for dysuria and admits to having unprotected sex. The physician orders a DNA direct probe for *Chlamydia trachomatis* and *Neisseria gonorrhoeae*. The results are positive for Gonococcal urethritis. _____

Anatomic Pathology

Postmortem Examination

The procedures in this section represent physician services only. When using an outside laboratory for these procedures, use the Modifier 90 appended to the CPT® code. New terminology for this section includes:

- *Necropsy* is synonymous with autopsy.
- *Gross examination* is performed without the use of a microscope.
- *CNS* refers to the central nervous system.
- *Limited necropsy* is the examination of only certain organs or tissues.
- *Forensic examination* is performed for providing evidence in a court of law.
- *Coroner's call* is for a public official investigating a death from unnatural causes.

Cytopathology

Cytopathology or *cytology* is the study of cells. The procedures in this section are performed on a number of different sources; however, a majority of codes in this section pertain to what is commonly called the "pap" smear. The specimens used in this section are considered live or potentially infectious because they are not processed using formalin. This makes a difference in the laboratory handling of the specimen as well as the type of slides and/or stains used. Thin prep pap smears are collected differently and involve mixing the specimen with fluid so the slide contains only one layer of cells, rather than clumps that are difficult to interpret.

Formula for Success

Tips for Coding Cytopathology

1. Determine the source of the specimen to be processed.
2. Codes 88150–88154 report pap smears using the non-Bethesda method.
3. Codes 88164–88167 report pap smears using the Bethesda system.
4. Codes 88142–88143 report specimens collected in a fluid medium and use the automated thin layer preparation.
5. Codes 88174–88175 report automated screening of specimens prepared with automated thin layer preparation and use any system of reporting.
6. When coding for pap smears, one code should be chosen from within the three families of screening methods.
7. Codes 88141 and 88155 are add-on codes used in addition to the primary code.

New terminology for this section includes:

- *Bethesda system* reports the results of a pap smear according to any epithelial cell abnormalities.
- *Non-Bethesda system* reports the level of dysplasia. Example: cervical intraepithelial neoplasia, CIN.
- *Manual screening* under physician supervision means that a technologist has screened the slide.
- *Manual screening and re-screening* under physician supervision means that two technologists have screened a slide.
- *Manual screening and computer-assisted rescreening* means that rescreening is performed using computer-assisted cell selection.
- *Automated screening* under physician supervision indicates that sophisticated instrumentation has screened the slide.
- *Flow cytometry* is an automated method used to identify different types of lymphocytes.

EXERCISE 20.7

Instructions: Assign the correct Pathology and Laboratory CPT® and ICD-9-CM codes to the scenarios below.

1. A cervical specimen is sent to the pathology laboratory for a thin prep pap smear. The specimen is screened with an automated method. The instrument flags some abnormal cells and the specimen is then rescreened by the cytotechnologist. She confirms the abnormal cells and refers the specimen to the pathologist on duty, who reviews the slide and diagnoses CIN II. _____

2. A cervical specimen is sent to the pathology laboratory for a routine pap smear. The manual screening is negative for abnormal cells. _____

Cytogenetic Studies

Cytogenetics is the study of cellular structure and function relative to genetics or heredity. The procedures in this section include:

- *Tissue cultures,* cytogenetic studies for non-neoplastic, benign, or neoplastic, malignant, disorders. The cells can be stimulated and grown in a culture medium.
- *Cryopreservation,* the specialized freezing technique performed for maintaining cells for subsequent culture and analysis.
- *Chromosome analysis,* a highly specialized study of human chromosomes for hereditary abnormalities.

Surgical Pathology

Surgical pathology or *histology* is the study of tissues. The procedures performed in this section include accession or preparation, examination, and reporting of results. Services reported by codes 88311–88365 are coded additionally when provided.

Coding of units for pathology services is based on the number of specimens of tissue or tissues that are submitted for individual and separate examination and diagnosis.

When two or more specimens from the same patient are each examined separately, they are reported individually. The codes in this section are listed by level and signify the amount of complexity required for the examination. Examination of a specimen not listed under any of the assigned levels should be assigned the code that most closely reflects the physician's work involved.

■ *Level I—gross examination only* is reported when a pathologist can accurately diagnose without microscopic examination. This may include the identification of teeth that are extracted or foreign bodies, such as bullets or coins.

■ *Level II—gross and microscopic examination* is performed on a specimen to confirm identification and the absence of disease.

■ *Levels III–VI—gross and microscopic examination* are used based on the type of specimen.

Other procedures described in this section and reported in addition to other services provided include:

■ Special staining and specimen preparation techniques

■ Consultation and report

■ Pathology consultation during surgery and frozen section specimens

■ Immunohistochemistry and immunofluorescent studies

■ Morphometric analysis, which is the study of structure, composition, and function of muscle, nerve, and tumor.

■ Nerve teasing for a nerve function study.

■ Protein analysis by Western Blot, which is a confirmatory test for certain viral antibodies.

■ Microdissection, which is a method of obtaining cells from specific microscopic regions of tissue sections for the study of disease.

EXERCISE 20.8

Instructions: Assign the appropriate CPT® and ICD-9-CM codes for the scenarios below:

1. A family practice physician performs an excision of skin tags and sends one specimen to the pathology laboratory for interpretation. The results confirm skin tags. Code for the pathologist. _____

2. A dermatologist performs a biopsy of a suspicious skin lesion on the arm. The specimen is sent to the pathology laboratory for preparation, and the slide is returned to the dermatologist for interpretation. The lesion returns with a malignant result. Code for the dermatologist and pathologist. _____

3. The pathologist on call is consulted for a single frozen section on a breast lesion. The specimen requires histochemical staining and the specimen is positive for malignancy with clear surgical margins. _____

4. The pathology laboratory receives a prostate needle biopsy specimen. The result confirms prostate cancer. _____

5. If the specimen in question 4 were obtained by excision and not radical resection, what CPT® code would the pathologist report? _____

Transcutaneous Procedures

Transcutaneous bilirubinometry measures the bilirubin concentration in subcutaneous tissue and is performed mainly in newborns.

Other Procedures

Procedures found in this section include:

- Body fluid cell counts and differential, except in blood.
- Fecal leukocyte, fat, meat fibers, and starch granule assessment.
- Crystal identification of body fluids.
- Duodenal intubation and aspiration specimen analysis.
- Gastric intubation and aspiration analysis.
- Nasal smear for eosinophils.
- Sputum collection by aerosol induction.
- Sweat collection by iotophoresis.
- Water load test.

Reproductive Medicine Procedures

This is an area of laboratory that has and will continue to increase and diversify by leaps and bounds. As methods become more and more sophisticated, the code selection will also increase and change. The procedures in this section include:

Procedures for the handling of human sperm include:
- Analysis of sperm for vitality.
- Sperm storage, cryopreservation.
- Sperm thawing.

Procedures for the handling of oocytes/embryos include:
- Identification.
- Preparation.
- Culture.
- Fertilization.
- Insemination.
- Storage.
- Thawing.

EXERCISE 20.9

Instructions: Assign the correct Pathology and Laboratory CPT® codes.

1. A joint fluid specimen is submitted to the laboratory for cell count, differential, and crystal identification. _____

CHAPTER REVIEW

1. Which modifier is not used in the Pathology and Laboratory chapter?
   a. 91
   b. 90

   c. 59

   d. 50

2. What code(s) would be used to report a serum Sodium, Potassium, Chloride, and Carbon dioxide?

   a. 82374, 82435, 84132, and 84295

   b. 80051

   c. 80048

   d. b and c

3. The code reported for a hepatic panel would be:

   a. 80074

   b. 80076

   c. 80069

   d. 80053

4. A patient with seizure disorder has a phenobarbital level drawn to monitor his medication. The codes reported are:

   a. 345.90, 80185

   b. 345.90, 80184

   c. 780.39, 80185

   d. 780.39, 80184

5. An obstetrical patient is tested and confirmed to have gestational diabetes with a four-hour glucose tolerance test. The codes reported are:

   a. 648.83, 82951, 82952

   b. 648.83, 82951

   c. 648.03, 250.00, 82951, 82952

   d. 648.83, 82947 $\times$ 4

6. A 50-year-old male patient is due for his yearly prostate screening. The physician orders a total PSA. The codes reported are:

   a. V76.44, 84154

   b. 600.00, 84153

   c. 600.00, 84154

   d. V76.44, 84153

7. A patient with anemia is monitored on a regular basis with a CBC without a differential. The codes reported are:

   a. 295.9, 85025

   b. 281.0, 85025

   c. 285.9, 85027

   d. 285.9, 85004

8. A rheumatologist orders a CBC with an automated differential and an automated sedimentation rate on a patient with rheumatoid arthritis. The codes reported are:

   a. 714.0, 85025, 85652

   b. 714.0, 85025, 85651

   c. 714.0, 85027, 84652

   d. 715.90, 85027, 84651

9. A patient presents to his family practice physician with joint pain. The physician orders a uric acid to rule out gout and an automated sedimentation rate and antinuclear antibody to rule out arthritis. The codes reported are:

    a. 274.9, 716.90, 84550, 85652, 86038

    b. 274.9, 716.90, 719.40, 84550, 85652, 86038

    c. 719.40, 84550, 85652, 86038

    d. 719.40, 84550, 85651, 86939

10. An ABO and Rh blood type and antibody screen are ordered on a patient as part of a preoperative workup. The codes reported are:

    a. V72.83, 86870, 86900, 86901

    b. V72.83, 86850, 86900, 86901

    c. V72.83, 86850, 86900, 86905

    d. V70.0, 86850, 86900, 86905

11. A patient has had a rash for one week and is seen at her doctor's office where they perform a KOH tissue exam and find *Tinea manuum.* The codes reported are:

    a. 110.2, 87210

    b. 110.9, 87210

    c. 110.4, 87220

    d. 110.2, 87220

12. A fine needle aspiration of a breast lump is taken to the laboratory where it is evaluated for adequacy and interpreted by a pathologist. A written report is then sent to the referring physician. The codes reported by the pathology laboratory are:

    a. 217, 88173

    b. 217, 88172, 88173

    c. 611.72, 88172, 88173

    d. 610.0, 88173

13. A cervical specimen submitted for a thin layer pap smear is performed by automated method as part of a yearly pap and pelvic exam. The codes reported by the pathology laboratory are:

    a. V76.2, 88174

    b. V72.31, 88174

    c. V76.2, 88142

    d. V72.31, 88142

14. A patient undergoes a vasectomy. A pathologist examines the specimen. The codes reported by the pathology laboratory are:

    a. V25.2, 88304

    b. V25.2, 88302

    c. V25.2, 88304

    d. V26.52, 88302

15. A pathologist examines a breast biopsy specimen. It is determined after careful examination that the diagnosis is carcinoma *in-situ* of the breast. The codes reported by the pathology laboratory are:

    a. 233.0, 88305

    b. 174.9, 88307

    c. 233.0, 88309

    d. 233.0, 88307

Medicine

OBJECTIVES

1. Correctly assign injection codes for vaccination/globulins and link to diagnosis.
2. Identify and code diagnostic tests.
3. Determine the appropriate modifier for repeat services and diagnostic tests.
4. State what the "8-minute rule" means.

INTRODUCTION

Physician offices perform a variety of nonsurgical services and diagnostic tests. It is important for the coder to realize that individual payers may require different reporting guidelines for these services. Only selections of subheadings from the Medicine chapter are detailed in this chapter. The attached CD-ROM contains advanced coding scenarios and case studies that will interest coders who desire more challenging work.

VACCINATIONS, INJECTIONS, AND INFUSIONS

TERMINOLOGY AND ACRONYMS

dc'd or DC   Discontinued; as in stopping an IV infusion, or taking out the IV line.

D5/LR   5% Dextrose in Lactated Ringer's.

HL   Heparin lock.

IV   Intravenous.

IVP   Intravenous "push" technique.

IVPB   IV piggyback.

NS   Normal saline (.9% saline).

1/2 NS   Normal saline at 1/2 dilution (.45% saline).

RL   Ringer's lactate (or LR, Lactated Ringer's solution).

SIVP   Slow IV "push" technique.

SL   Saline lock.

TKO   To keep open.

WO   Running the IV rate at "wide open."

ICD-9-CM CODING OF VACCINATIONS AND DRUG RESISTANCE

Each type of single vaccine or combination vaccine is assigned to categories V03 through V06 in ICD-9-CM. Look in the alphabetic index under "Immunization" or "Admission for . . ."

EXERCISE 21.1

Instructions: Assign the correct ICD-9-CM codes for the immune globulins/vaccines listed below.

1. Flu vaccine, intranasal route   _____

2. RSV immunoglobulin   _____

3. Varicella   _____

4. Polio (IPV) given subcutaneously   _____

5. MMR (measles, mumps, and rubella)   _____

6. Cholera vaccine   _____

7. Hepatitis B, pediatric three-dose schedule   _____

8. Anthrax vaccine   _____

9. Human (Ig) globulin, IM   _____

10. Pneumovax (pneumococcal, adult) given subcutaneously   _____

Category V09

Increased and indiscriminate use of antibiotics has resulted in infections that have evolved to become resistant to the very antibiotics that previously cured the infection. ICD-9-CM contains a code category that describes the drug resistance by individual classes of antibiotics. Most well known of the resistant infections is Methicillin Resistant Staph Aureus, or MRSA. Methicillin is a form of penicillin. Assign code V09.0, Infection with microorganisms resistant to penicillins, for MRSA. These codes are classified based on the type of drug resistance, not the microorganism (see Table 21.1).

Table 21–1   V09 Codes

ICD-9 Code	Class of Antibiotic	Common Drug Names
V09.0	Penicillins	Ampicillin, Pen G
V09.1	Cephalosporins	Keflex, cephalexin
V09.2	Macrolides	Erythromycin, Azith
V09.3	Tetracyclines	Doxycycline
V09.4	Aminoglycosides	Streptomycin, gentamicin, Amikacin
V09.5	Quinolones	Ciprofloxin
V09.6	Sulfonamides	Septra, Septra DS

Formula for Success

Be sure to watch for ICD-9-CM codes that indicate "with" or "without" resistance to multiple drugs.

CPT® CODING OF INJECTIONS AND INFUSIONS

Several different types of injections are described in this chapter. Two types of injections are described in this section. Immune globulins are not vaccines. When a patient has been exposed to a disease, immune globulins are given to prevent infection and boost the patient's immune system. Several types of immune globulins include broad-spectrum anti-infective globulins, antitoxins, and isoantibodies. An example of how globulins differ from vaccines can be demonstrated by examining codes 90375 and 90675. The globulin code (90375) is given when there has been an exposure to rabies. The vaccine (90675) is given prophylactically to prevent rabies in animal handlers and veterinarians. A similar prophylactic animal vaccine is used for dogs, cats, horses, and other pets. Look in the CPT® index under "Immune globulins" to locate these codes.

The vaccine/toxoid codes in CPT® identify the vaccine product only. These codes include the usual childhood vaccinations and other prophylactic vaccines given to adults and adolescents. The route of administration (IM, subcutaneous) must be determined prior to code selection. The dosage schedule must also be considered—either two- or three-dose schedule. Most states supply different vaccines for children's health programs at either a reduced rate or free of charge. Check with your state for specific coding/billing requirements. Look in the CPT® index under "Vaccine" to code these correctly.

Figure 21.1 shows angles of needle insertion for four types of injections.

Formula for Success

If your state regulations specify that patients may not be charged for state-supplied vaccine, make sure that the code drops on the claim form with a "zero charge." Check with your state to see if separate injection administration codes may be charged.

Injection Administration

Two codes are typically used for vaccine injections: one for the vaccine or medication being injected and a second code for administration. *Administration* describes the services provided by the nurse to give the injection. In the clinic setting, a patient may be seen for an office visit and have a vaccination during the same visit. The vaccine administration codes describe the route of administration and single or multiple vaccinations. The diagnosis code(s) associated with the vaccine is linked to the administration code.

Example:

1. A patient comes into the clinic requesting a hepatitis shot.

   CPT® codes reported: 90477, Hepatitis A vaccine and 90471, Vaccine administration
   ICD-9-CM diagnosis: V05.3, Need for hepatitis vaccination. Link this diagnosis code to both CPT® codes to demonstrate medical necessity

2. A patient came into the Community Health Center where it was noted that he was lacking several important vaccinations. Link the codes in this manner:

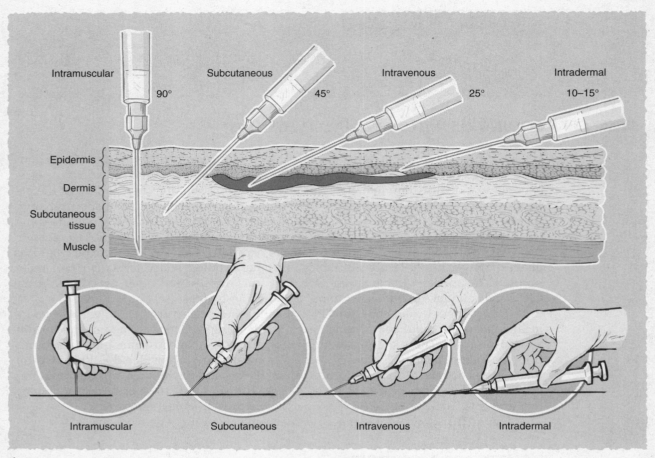

Figure 21–1   Angle of needle insertion for four types of injections.

Codes reported:

> 90477, Hepatitis A vaccine with V05.3
>
> 90713, IPV (polio) with V04.0
>
> 90471, Vaccine administration with V05.3
>
> 90472, Each additional vaccine administration with V04.0

Formula for Success

The total number of units for codes 90471 and 90472 should total the number of vaccinations given. Code 90742 is reported in units after the first vaccination (90471.)

Use administration codes 90782 to 90784 for administration of immune globulins, depending on the method of injection.

Diagnostic/Therapeutic Infusions

These codes require physician presence and involve the use of an IV drip. Codes 90780 and 90781 should not be used to report routine IV injections, subcu, intradermal, or intramuscular injections. Clues that the coder should watch for include the terms "IV drip" or "infusion" and nursing start/stop times documented for the IV. A physician's order is written for the IV with the type of IV solution and flow rate. At least one IV bag is hung for an infusion, and one or more smaller bags may be hung "piggyback" onto the larger bag to help dilute a strong medication. Nursing start and stop times indicate the length of time an IV solution is infused. Use 90780 for the first hour and 90781 for each additional hour of infusion. These codes may never be used in addition to prolonged service E/M codes. Figure 21.2 illustrates IV therapy.

Note: Physicians typically do not bill infusions in the hospital setting unless they start the IV and stay for the duration. These are normally billed by the facility. Example: A physician sees a patient in Labor and Delivery and orders a Pitocin drip to augment her labor. The nurses start the IV and manage the infusion according to protocol. The physician does not code or bill for this service when performed by facility staff.

Formula for Success

When coding in the clinic or urgent care setting, do not forget to charge for the bags of IV solution and any associated drugs that are injected into the IV line or hung piggyback. Flag the "J" code section of your HCPCS book to help you look up drugs. Considerable reimbursement can be lost by a practice because drugs are not billed correctly.

Example: The Urgent Care physician order documents: 1 liter NS/IV WO, 50 mg Demerol IVP. Nurses notes document: 1 liter NS - start @ 1700, 50 mg Demerol IVP @ 1710. IV dc'd at 1803.

Codes reported by urgent care physician for these services: 90780, 90784, J7300 x 1, J2175 x 1.

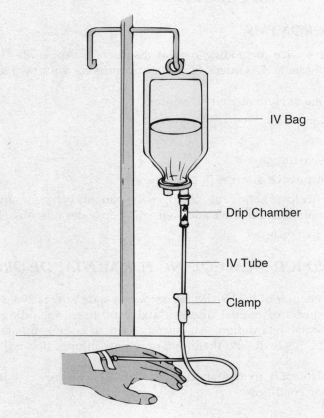

Figure 21–2   IV therapy.

EXERCISE 21.2

Instructions: Give the CPT® infusion/injection codes and HCPCS codes for the scenarios below. Note the number of units for each CPT® and HCPCS code.

1. A 50-year-old patient came into the urgent care clinic complaining of abdominal pain. Flat plate and upright x-rays of the abdomen were ordered, along with CBC and urinalysis. The physical exam and laboratory results indicated a possible acute appendicitis. The physician ordered an IV of 1 liter normal saline with 75 mg of Demerol and 25 mg of Phenergan IV push. The IV injections were given at 7:05 and 7:10 P.M. The IV infused for a total of 2 hours while arranging for out-of-town hospital transfer and waiting for the ambulance to arrive. The second liter of IV solution was hung just prior to ambulance transfer. _____ _____ _____ _____ _____ _____

2. Two grams of Rocephin was given to a patient with pneumonia. _____, _____

3. A patient came into the Urgent Care clinic with an allergic reaction. He was given 125 mg Solu-Medrol in the left gluteus and 50 mg of Benadryl IM in the right gluteus. _____ _____ _____

4. A patient with severe low back pain was given an injection of 100 mg of Demerol and 50 mg of Phenergan in the clinic. This was drawn up in the same syringe and injected into the left gluteus. _____ _____ _____

PSYCHIATRY

TERMINOLOGY AND ACRONYMS

An often-neglected resource for coding mental disorders is Appendix B in the ICD-9 codebook, Glossary of Mental Disorders. Flag this appendix for your own reference.

ADHD   Attention Deficit Hyperactivity Disorder.

BPD   Bipolar disorder.

DT   Delerium tremens.

ECT   Electroconvulsive therapy.

OCD   Obsessive-compulsive disorder.

Psychotropic drug   Antipsychotic drug. Changes the patients behavior and mental functioning by reducing agitation and panic and shortening episodes of schizophrenia.

SAD   Seasonal affective disorder.

DISEASE PROCESSES AND ICD-9-CM CODING FOR MENTAL DISORDERS

The mental disorder chapter of ICD-9-CM encompasses code ranges 290–319. This chapter categorizes all aspects of mental diseases and conditions, including alcohol/substance abuse and mental retardation. An introduction to coding mental disorders is found in Chapter 2 of this textbook; therefore, only new information will be presented here.

Some V codes also apply to mental disorders. The V11 category classifies a personal history of the following conditions:

- V11.0, Schizophrenia.
- V11.1, Affective disorders.
- V11.2, Neurosis.
- V11.3, Alcoholism.
- V11.8, Other mental disorders.
- V11.9, Unspecified mental disorder.

V17.0 describes a family history of psychiatric condition, and V18.4 describes a family history of mental retardation.

Category V40 should be used when the conditions listed are specified as diagnoses or problems. These codes include:

- V40.0, Problems with learning.
- V40.1, Problems with communication (including speech).
- V40.2, Other mental problems.
- V40.3, Other behavioral problems.
- V40.9, Unspecified mental or behavioral problem.

In the psychiatric office, there are a multitude of nonmedical diagnoses that affect the mental well-being of a patient. Categories V60–V68 classify circumstances relating to housing, marital/family counseling, psychosocial situations, psychological or physical stressors, and other types of counseling.

Category V71.0 describes observation for suspected mental conditions that after examination and observation are found not to exist. Use these observation codes for suspected adult antisocial behavior, childhood or adolescent antisocial behavior, or other suspected mental conditions.

Use category V79 when the patient is being screened for mental disorders or developmental handicaps:

- V79.0, Depression.
- V79.1, Alcoholism.
- V79.2, Mental retardation.
- V79.3, Developmental handicaps in early childhood.
- V79.8, Other specified mental disorders and developmental handicaps.
- V79.9, Unspecified mental disorder and developmental handicap.

EXERCISE 21.3

Instructions: Assign the ICD-9-CM diagnosis code for the scenarios below.

1. Casey is a 2-year-old child who seems to be lagging behind developmentally. He has only been walking for two months and points rather than speaks. He seems content and happy otherwise. He is in the office for developmental testing today. _____

2. Mr. Brown comes into the office for treatment of depression. He has been unemployed for six months and is unable to find anything other than minimum wage jobs. _____ _____

3. Patients over age 12 who come into the Community Health Center during Mental Health Month are screened for depression. _____

4. Mary has a history of anorexia nervosa, which now appears to be under good control. _____

5. A 12-year-old patient with ADHD comes into the office for counseling regarding his behavior and learning difficulties due to the ADHD. Today's session is focused on learning techniques for school and how to improve his relationship with his siblings. _____ _____

6. Kathy is a 50-year-old patient who lives in a home for the mentally handicapped. She is mildly retarded. Her caregiver is concerned that another resident may be sexually abusing her. The family practitioner questions her and, after a physical exam, finds no clinical evidence of sexual assault. A rape kit was sent into the state for processing. _____ _____

CPT® CODING FOR PSYCHIATRIC SERVICES

The psychiatric subheading of the Medicine chapter deals with nonhospital services. When a psychiatric patient is admitted to an inpatient or partial hospitalization setting, the attending physician should use Evaluation and Management codes 99221–99233 to describe his or her services. Codes from the Medicine chapter that indicate medical E/M services are included (i.e., 90807, 90809, 90811, 90813, etc.) should be reported alone, not in addition to E/M service codes from 99201–99499.

Any type of psychotherapy or electroconvulsive therapy that is provided in addition to hospital evaluation and management services may be reported separately. Use Modifier 22 to indicate more extensive services when appropriate or Modifier 52 when the service is reduced or less extensive than the usual service.

Other E/M services that may be coded include consultations in addition to psychotherapy only or other psychiatric services. Consultation services do not involve psychiatric treatment and are limited to initial or follow-up services.

Use code 90801 for an intake examination that includes a history, mental status exam, and disposition. This may include communication with family or other sources and ordering and medical interpretation of laboratory or other diagnostic studies.

Interactive psychiatric services are typically furnished to children. These services may include a diagnostic interview exam (90802), office or outpatient facility setting (90810–90815), or inpatient hospital/partial hospital/residential care setting (90823–90829).

Formula for Success

Only a physician can render a medical evaluation and management service. Highlight the following CPT® codes as a reminder: 90805, 90807, 90809, 90811, 90813, 90815, 90817, 90819, 90822, 90824, 90827, and 90829. Do not use codes from the Evaluation and Management chapter of CPT® with these codes.

EXERCISE 21.4

Instructions: Give the appropriate CPT® code(s) for the scenarios below.

1. A 45-year-old patient is provided with 45 minutes of individual psychotherapy by a psychologist. Hypnotherapy is also provided as a separate service. _____ _____

2. A 4-year-old child who was molested by a stranger is given an interactive initial diagnostic interview exam with a court-appointed psychiatrist. _____

3. On the second day of inpatient hospitalization, the attending psychiatrist receives old records on her patient. She evaluates these records and documents a formal diagnosis based on her clinical findings. In addition, she documents a problem-focused interval history and straightforward medical decision making on her subsequent hospital care visit. _____ _____

4. A patient is seen for a change in psychotropic medication dosage. The attending physician documents only minimal medical psychotherapy. _____

DIALYSIS

TERMINOLOGY AND ACRONYMS

Bruit   A sound heard when venous blood mixes with arterial blood in an arteriovenous shunt.

CRF   Chronic Renal Failure.

Epo or Epogen   Medication used to build red blood cells in ESRD patients.

ESRD   End-stage renal disease.

ICD-9-CM CODING FOR DIALYSIS

Patients who are undergoing dialysis treatments are typically in end-stage renal disease, although some patients may have other reasons for requiring dialysis. End-stage renal disease indicates irreversible kidney failure. This condition requires regular dialysis to cleanse toxins from the patient's bloodstream in place of the kidneys. ICD-9-CM category V56 is used to describe encounters for dialysis and dialysis catheter care. An additional code should be assigned to identify the associated condition, such as chronic renal failure. Any preparation for dialysis should be coded to the medical condition, rather than using a V code.

> **Example:**   Mr. Lewis is admitted for creation of a Cimino AV shunt for dialysis because of chronic renal insufficiency. It is anticipated he will need hemodialysis within two months.
>
> ICD-9-CM Code: 593.9, Renal insufficiency

Six weeks later, the Cimino shunt has matured and he is brought to the Dialysis Center for his first hemodialysis session.

> ICD-9 Codes: V56.0, Encounter for extracorporeal dialysis (renal dialysis, NOS)
>   593.9, Renal insufficiency

Use code V56.1 for fitting and adjustment of extracorporeal dialysis catheter, or V56.2 for fitting and adjustment of a peritoneal dialysis catheter. Any concurrent dialysis procedures should be coded with V56.0, Extracorporeal dialysis, or V56.8, Peritoneal dialysis

Code V45.1, Renal dialysis status, is used to identify dialysis patients or the presence of an AV shunt.

> **Example:**   A patient is brought into the Emergency Department unconscious with an acute myocardial infarction. It is noted that she has an AV shunt in her left arm. The patient is admitted and family members are contacted. They provide additional medical history regarding her dialysis status.

ICD-9-CM Codes: 410.91, Acute myocardial infarction
V45.1, Renal dialysis status

EXERCISE 21.5

Instructions: Assign the correct diagnosis code for the scenarios and diagnostic statements below.

1. A 43-year-old patient is brought to the Dialysis Center for a peritoneal equilibration test. _____

2. A dialysis patient comes to the outpatient surgery department for replacement of her temporary dialysis catheter. A new Groshong catheter is placed. _____

3. Mrs. Jones is scheduled for placement of a peritoneal dialysis catheter for chronic renal failure. _____

4. A dialysis patient is admitted for declotting of his AV graft. _____

5. A patient came in with an embolism of her new AV graft. _____

6. Mr. White had blockage of his insulin pump with failure of insulin delivery. _____

CPT® CODING FOR DIALYSIS

Two main types of dialysis procedures are described in CPT®—hemodialysis and peritoneal dialysis. Other types of dialysis are categorized under peritoneal dialysis. Hemodialysis involves cleansing the blood through a dialysis machine several times per week in a facility setting. The patient must have venous access established through a fistula, arteriovenous shunt, graft, or temporary catheter placement. Peritoneal dialysis is most often performed in the home setting. Patients using peritoneal dialysis must instill sterile dialysate fluid into the abdominal cavity through a peritoneal dialysis catheter and drain out the waste fluid after a period of time.

All of the hemodialysis procedures are grouped in codes 90935–90940. Codes 90935 and 90937 include hemodialysis procedures plus any evaluation and management services related to the patient's renal disease on the same day. These codes are used for inpatient and outpatient ESRD or non-ESRD procedures and services. Modifier 25 should be appended to unrelated, separately identifiable evaluation and management services on the same date of service.

> **Example:** Dr. B. visits Mr. Jones shortly before his scheduled dialysis service for chronic renal failure. He reviews medications and lab results and signs the record. After his dialysis session, Mr. Jones requests to see Dr. B again regarding a lump in his neck. Dr. B documents a problem-focused HPI and problem-focused exam. The patient is scheduled to see a general surgeon for biopsy of the lump.
>
> CPT® Codes: 585, Chronic renal failure, and 90935, Dialysis procedure with single physician evaluation
> 784.2, Mass in neck, and 99212-25, Established outpatient visit

Peritoneal dialysis, hemofiltration, or continuous renal replacement therapies are described by codes 90945–90947. These codes include evaluation and management services related to the patient's renal disease when performed on the same day of the procedure. Use a Modifier 25 for E/M services unrelated to the renal failure when they are rendered at a separate session. Other codes in the Miscellaneous Dialysis Procedures subheading include dialysis training for the patient and/or helper for an entire course or per training session.

End-Stage Renal Disease Services

Patients who are in end-stage renal disease require regular dialysis, evaluation, and management visits pertaining to the dialysis; other dialysis management; and occasional phone calls to their physicians. Coding and billing for all of these services are done on a monthly (30-day) basis when the patient remains an outpatient. If the patient is hospitalized, service days are reported on a per diem basis only for the days out of the hospital. Inpatient codes are used during the hospitalization. ESRD codes are divided into two sections—full month and daily services. Each section is subdivided further by patient age. Use the following guidelines to help determine code assignment:

1. If a patient is hospitalized during any given month, report the per diem codes (90922-90925) for each day the patient is NOT in the hospital.
2. Report the inpatient hospital codes for each day of hospitalization, as appropriate.
3. Report any dialysis procedures separately, whether the patient is an inpatient or outpatient.

   Example: Mrs. Smith, age 68, has a dialysis calendar that appears like this for the month of September:

Sunday	Monday	Tuesday	Wednesday	Thursday	Friday	Saturday
	1 Daily Service 90925	2 Daily Service 90925	3 Daily Service 90925	4 Daily Service 90925	5 Daily Service 90925	6 Daily Service 90925
7 Daily Service 90925	8 Daily Service 90925	9 Daily Service 90925	10 Daily Service 90925	11 Daily Service 90925	12 Hemodialysis Repeat Evaluation/ Daily Service 90937/90925	13 Initial Hospital Care 99222
14 Hemodialysis visit 90935	15 Hemodialysis Visit 90935	16 Inpatient Subsequent Care 99232	17 Hospital Discharge Hemodialysis Visit 90935	18 Daily Service 90925	19 Daily Service 90925	20 Daily Service 90925
21 Daily Service 90925	22 Daily Service 90925	23 Daily Service 90925	24 Daily Service 90925	25 Daily Service 90925	26 Daily Service 90925	27 Daily Service 90925
28 Daily Service 90925	29 Daily Service 90925	30 Daily Service 90925				

Codes for the services listed above are reported like this:

ESRD 90925 × 25—use this code for each day of dialysis service.
Hemodialysis 90935 × 3—ESRD services; use only during inpatient dialysis runs.
Initial Hospital Care 99222 × 1

Subsequent Hospital Care 99232 × 1—use only on days when there is no dialysis service.

Hospital Discharge Services are normally not billed by the same physician when a dialysis run is performed on the same day as discharge.

Formula for Success

1. Do not bill Evaluation and Management services the same day as dialysis unless the physician is managing a problem that is distinct and unrelated to ESRD, such as pneumonia.
2. Each dialysis facility keeps a log of dialysis runs for each patient. Before billing, request a HIPAA-compliant copy of the dialysis runs for your physician's patients to ensure the exact number and types of services for the month.

At the time of this printing, CMS has recommended changes to the way physicians are reimbursed for dialysis services. Be sure to check the most recent updates to billing for Medicare patients.

OPHTHALMOLOGY

TERMINOLOGY AND ACRONYMS

Accommodation   Change in shape of the lens to focus on objects nearby or at a distance.

Aphakia   Without a lens.

Cycloplegia   Paralysis of the ciliary muscle of the eye with associated loss of accommodation.

EOM   Extraocular movement.

Gonioscope   Mirrored contact lens on a stick; allows viewing of anterior chamber of the eye.

gt or gtt   Abbreviation for "drops."

IOL   Intraocular lens.

Low vision   Refers to corrected vision ranging from 20/70 to 20/400. Severe low vision of 20/200 is considered "legal" blindness.

Mydriasis   Dilation of the pupil with drops.

OD   Right eye.

OS   Left eye.

OU   Both eyes.

Pseudophakia   Artificial lens in the eye.

Tonometry   Measures pressure in the eye.

ICD-9-CM CODING FOR OPHTHALMOLOGY

Refer to Chapter 18 for information regarding specific eye diagnoses.

EXERCISE 21.6

Instructions: For additional coding practice, assign the correct ICD-9-CM diagnosis code to the diagnostic statements below.

1. Admission for routine eye exam   _____

2. Astigmatism   _____

3. Diabetic cataract, diabetes in good control   _____   _____

4. Fitting of artificial eye   _____

5. Patient is status-post cataract and IOL, no further care _____   _____

6. Myopia and dry eyes   _____   _____

7. Contact lens fitting   _____

8. Patient is status-post corneal transplant   _____

9. Visual field deficit with blind spot   _____

10. Glaucoma suspect; preglaucoma   _____

CPT® CODING FOR OPHTHALMOLOGY

General ophthalmology services are similar to the Evaluation and Management codes in the first chapter of CPT®. The difference between the two types of codes is that specific ophthalmology services are included in codes 92002–92014. These codes are divided into New Patient or Established Patient and Intermediate or Comprehensive visit under each category. It is up to the provider to decide which type of code to assign—either Evaluation and Management or Ophthalmology. Usually, routine eye exams are assigned to the Medicine chapter, with medical problems or trauma assigned to the Evaluation and Management chapter.

Formula for Success

Visits that are coded from the Medicine chapter are often documented using an ophthalmology template or check sheet. Providers who choose to use the Evaluation and Management codes must meet documentation guidelines to determine the level of service for Medicare beneficiaries.

Intermediate level services include the evaluation of a new or existing problem, complicated with a new diagnostic or management problem that may be related to the primary diagnosis. These services include:

- History.
- General medical observation.
- External ocular and adnexal exam.

■ Any other indicated diagnostic procedures.

■ Mydriasis, if necessary.

Comprehensive services include a general exam of the complete visual system (see Figure 21.3), which is not required to be completed at one session. Initiation of diagnostic and treatment programs is always included. These services include:

■ History.

■ General medical observation.

■ Gross visual field exam.

■ Basic sensorimotor examination.

Additional services that are often included with comprehensive services are:

■ Biomicroscopy.

■ Exam with cygloplegia or mydriasis.

■ Tonometry.

These codes are distinct from Evaluation and Management codes because the medical decision-making component cannot be separated from the examination techniques. Services that are bundled into the ophthalmology codes include:

■ Slit lamp.

■ Keratometry.

■ Routine ophthalmoscopy.

■ Retinoscopy.

■ Tonometry.

■ Motor evaluation.

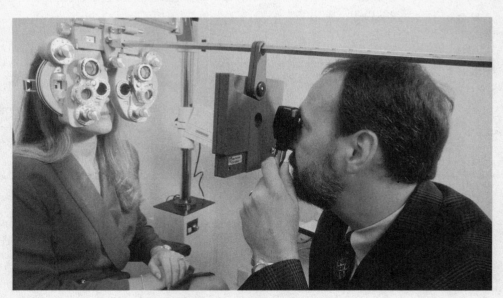

Figure 21–3   Ophthalmologist examining a patient.

EXERCISE 21.7

Instructions: Assign only CPT® codes to the scenarios below.

1. A new patient is referred to Dr. A, an ophthalmologist, for evaluation of possible diabetic retinopathy. A comprehensive new patient visit is performed, including ophthalmoscopy, tonometry, and slit lamp exam. _____

2. A teenager is scheduled for a routine annual eye exam with his optometrist. An intermediate exam is performed, including a dilated exam. _____

3. Dr. A is called by the Emergency Department physician to evaluate a patient with a laceration to the orbit. She performs a comprehensive history, comprehensive eye exam, and high complexity medical decision making. She determines that the patient should have surgery immediately to salvage the eye. _____

4. Mr. Smith visits his regular ophthalmologist for a routine comprehensive eye exam. A dilated exam is refused by the patient because of an important business meeting immediately following the appointment. He returns the following afternoon for the dilated portion of the exam.

    Day 1: _____
    Day 2: _____

Special Services

These are services or special treatments that are provided in addition to the general ophthalmology services and may be billed separately.

Code 92015, Determination of refractive state, is known as refraction. This is performed to determine the degree of correction required for refractive errors of the eye, such as near-sightedness, far-sightedness, and astigmatism. It involves a subjective response by the patient to multiple lens trials on each eye until satisfactorily corrected vision is achieved.

Other codes in this section include gonioscopy, when performed as a stand-alone service; exams under anesthesia; sensorimotor exam; and fitting of contact lenses for treatment of disease. When a visual field exam is done, look for documentation specifying a limited, intermediate, or extended exam.

Additional tests for glaucoma include serial tonometry and tonography, described in codes 92100–92130. These tests measure changes in eye pressure throughout the day or describe glaucoma testing by gently pressing on the eye with a weighted plunger.

Routine ophthalmoscopy is normally included as part of general and special ophthalmologic services. Codes 92225 and 92226 describe extended initial and subsequent ophthalmoscopy, which requires a retinal drawing with interpretation and report.

Fluorescein angioscopy, code 92230, is performed to evaluate the vasculature of the posterior chamber of the eye. Fluorescein dye is injected into an IV in the arm, and the retina is examined. Use code 92235 when photographs are taken in timed succession to document the circulation of the eye.

Code 92250 is used for fundus photography with interpretation and report. Fundus photography is an excellent tool to help diagnose many different types of eye disease, such as macular degeneration, neoplasms, and diabetic retinopathy. Fundus photography (see Figure 21.4) is performed through a dilated eye and does not require the injection of dye.

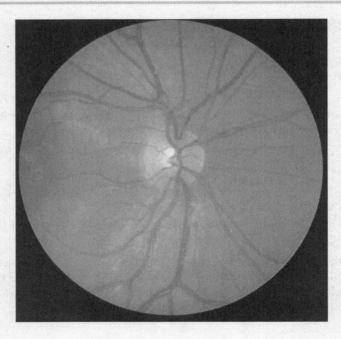

Figure 21–4   Photograph of retinal blood vessels/fundus.

Other specialized services include codes 92265–92287, which describe a variety of additional tests. Color vision testing, code 92283, is included in a routine eye exam and in code 99172, which is a test of visual acuity. Do not unbundle color vision testing from these codes.

Formula for Success

Under Medicare LCD guidelines, use of some of these codes may have restrictions. Be sure to check with your local Medicare carriers for specific coding and billing instructions.

Contact Lens, Ocular Prosthetics, and Spectacle Services

Contact lens prescription is not bundled into general ophthalmologic services. Use codes 92310–92313 to describe the prescription and fitting of contact lens with medical supervision. Codes 92314–92317 describe the prescription of contact lens with medical supervision of fitting by an independent technician. Codes 92310 and 92314 specify prescription and fitting for both eyes. When only one eye is attended to, use Modifier 52 to identify the reduced services.

The term "fitting" of contact lens includes instruction, training, and any revision of the lens during the training period. Code follow-up exams of successfully fitted extended-wear contact lens with established patient visits 92012 or 92014 as appropriate. Add Modifier 26 to the fitting code when the contact lens supply is coded separately with 92391 or 92396. If the lens supply is included with the fitting, do not use Modifier 26 or code for the supply separately.

Codes for fitting of ocular prosthetics are set up similar to contact lens fitting. Use 92330 for the fitting and supply of prosthetic eyes under medical supervision. Code 92335 describes the prescription, direction of fitting, and supply by independent technician under medical supervision.

Fitting of glasses is distinct from refraction and prescription of lens services. The presence of a physician is not required to fit glasses. Fitting services include measuring anatomical facial landmarks and writing measurements and special instructions to the lab, with final adjustments to fit the patient. Code the supply of materials (lenses/frames or both) separately.

EXERCISE 21.8

Instructions: Assign the correct CPT® code to the following scenarios.

1. A patient who is aphakic in the right eye comes into the office for an appointment to determine the corrective lens prescription. Her ophthalmologist orders the prescription, and a technician gives the patient initial instruction on how to insert, remove, and care for the lens. The patient practices with a trial lens and schedules a follow-up visit in one week, when the order arrives. _____

2. Mr. Brown had continued problems with his new hard contact lens for the left eye. Another lens was ordered from the lab with beveled edges to increase his comfort level. _____

3. A large magnifying lens on a floor stand for reading purposes is supplied to a patient whose corrected vision is 20/160. _____

4. A patient arrives at her ophthalmologist's office for fitting of a prosthetic eye prescribed and ordered by the physician. The patient is billed separately by the lab for the prosthesis. List the codes for each provider's services:

   Physician: _____
   Prosthetic lab: _____

OTORHINOLARYNGOLOGY (ENT)

TERMINOLOGY AND ACRONYMS

AC Auditory canal.

AD Right ear.

AS Left ear.

AU Both ears.

EAC External auditory canal.

ENT Ear, nose, and throat.

PE tube Ventilating tube inserted in the eardrum.

ICD-9-CM CODING FOR OTORHINOLARYNGOLOGY SERVICES

Refer to Chapters 8 and 18 for information regarding specific ENT diagnoses.

EXERCISE 21.9

Instructions: For additional coding practice, assign the correct ICD-9-CM code to the following diagnostic statements.

1. Serous otitis media   _____

2. Vertigo, due to Ménière's disease   _____

3. Routine preschool hearing exam   _____

4. Recurrent cholesteatoma in mastoid cavity   _____

5. Three-year-old with Eustachian tube dysfunction   _____

6. Sensorineural hearing loss   _____

7. Presbycusis   _____

8. Chronic otitis externa   _____

9. Family history of deafness in brother   _____

10. Screening for inner ear dysfunction   _____

11. Puncture of eardrum from pencil   _____   _____

12. Chronic tonsillitis and adenoiditis   _____

CPT® CODING FOR OTORHINOLARYNGOLOGY SERVICES

These services are supplied in addition to, or independent of, evaluation and management services. All of these services include medical diagnostic evaluation. Audiologists perform many of these services under the supervision of a physician, or the physician may personally perform the service. Figure 21.5 is an illustration of a hearing test.

Use code 92502 for an otolaryngologic exam under general anesthesia. Code range 92502–92526 includes two codes listed as separate procedures. They are binocular mi-

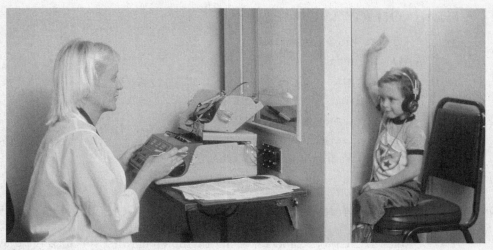

Figure 21–5   A hearing test.

croscopy and nasopharyngoscopy. Do not code these procedures separately when they are performed as part of another comprehensive service or procedure.

Vestibular Function Studies

Codes 92531–92548 describe methods used to induce nystagmus, which is a rapid, uncontrolled eye movement. Nystagmus may indicate problems or disease of the vestibule of the inner ear. These tests are used to determine if the problem involves either the right or left ear. Services are divided into two groups—those performed with electrical recording and those without recording. Code 92547 is an add-on code to be used with codes 92541–92546. Many of these codes require irrigation of each ear with warm and cold water to induce the nystagmus.

Audiology Tests

Codes 92551–92597 imply the use of special electronic equipment to test both ears. Use Modifier 52 if a test is performed only on one ear. Code 92559 describes audiometry testing of groups. The specific test that is being performed should be identified.

Formula for Success

Medicare does not reimburse hearing aid services. Patients should be informed that hearing aid services are an out-of-pocket expense.

Evaluative and Therapeutic Services

Cochlear implants allow deaf patients to hear through impulses sent through an electrode in the inner ear. This is connected to an internal receiver and external transmitter. The transmitter and headset are worn on the implanted side of the head. Cochlear implant codes in this section describe only diagnostic and programming services for the implant. The surgical portion of the implant is described by code 69930 in the auditory surgical procedures. Codes 92601 and 92602 are used for diagnostic analysis on patients under 7 years of age. Use 92601 for programming and 92602 for subsequent reprogramming. Codes 92603 and 92604 should be used on patients older than 7 years of age in the same manner.

Codes 92605–92609 describe evaluation or therapeutic services for speech-generating devices and other communication mechanisms. Some of these codes are time-based, so the coder should look for documentation in the chart to support these services.

Other services provided in this section include swallowing studies. Use codes 92615 or 92617 for physician interpretation and report when fiberoptic endoscopic evaluation is done of the larynx using cine or video recording. It is important to distinguish between flexible fiberoptic diagnostic laryngoscopy (31575) from the flexible fiberoptic endoscopic studies for swallowing function or for laryngeal sensory testing.

EXERCISE 21.10

Instructions: Assign the correct CPT® code for the services described below.

1. Pure tone audiometry including both air and bone, is performed on a patient. _____

2. A patient with a cochlear implant comes to the clinic for aural rehabilitation by the audiologist. _____

3. A caloric vestibular test without electrical recording was completed only on one ear. The patient had positive findings and began vomiting due to severe nystagmus and dizziness. _____

4. Tympanometry and acoustic reflex testing is performed on a preschooler with chronic otitis media. _____

5. A patient with laryngeal carcinoma is evaluated for an artificial larynx. He spent approximately an hour and thirty-five minutes with the audiologist. _____

6. Evaluation of swallowing function, with real-time fluoroscopy and a video recording. _____

7. A patient comes in for a check of both hearing aids. _____

CARDIOVASCULAR

TERMINOLOGY AND ACRONYMS

See Chapter 10 of this text for additional terms and abbreviations.

AMI   Acute MI.
CABG   Coronary artery bypass graft.
CAD   Coronary artery disease.
CHF   Congestive heart failure.
CP   Chest pain.
CPR   Cardiopulmonary resuscitation.
CV   Cardiovascular.
DVT   Deep vein thrombosis.
ECG/EKG   Electrocardiogram.
NSR   Normal sinus rhythm.
PTCA   Percutaneous transluminal coronary angioplasty.
S1, S2, S3, S4   S1 and S2 are first and second heart sounds; S3 and S4 are abnormal heart sounds.
tPA   Tissue plasminogen activator.

ICD-9-CM CODING FOR CARDIOVASCULAR SERVICES

Refer to Chapter 10 for information regarding specific cardiac diagnoses.

EXERCISE 21.11

Instructions: For additional coding practice, assign the correct ICD-9-CM code to the following diagnostic statements.

1. Dissecting abdominal aortic aneurysm   _____

2. Subclavian steal syndrome   _____

3. Hyperkinetic heart disease   _____

4. Acute viral pericarditis   _____

5. Mitral stenosis with regurgitation   _____

6. Left ventricular failure   _____

7. Hypertensive cardiomegaly without heart failure   _____

8. Failure of prosthetic valve to close properly with valve leakage   _____

9. Infected pacemaker pocket   _____

10. Pain at the site automatic defibrillator implant   _____

CPT® CODING FOR CARDIOVASCULAR SERVICES

The cardiovascular section of the Medicine chapter is composed of a combination of diagnostic and therapeutic services. Some are invasive procedures, such as heart catheterizations; others, such as cardiography, involve external hookups for EKG, Holter monitor, and event recorders. This text will focus on the simpler aspects of the cardiology section. For more challenging advanced exercises, including echocardiography, electrophysiology, and cardiac catheterizations, refer to the attached CD-ROM.

Therapeutic Services

Services listed in this section include CPR, cardioversion, "clot-busting" procedures, and angioplasty/stenting procedures. It is common for some of these services to be missed during the coding/billing sequence. Consequently, it is important for coders and physicians alike to understand which services are bundled into critical care.

Code 92950, cardiopulmonary resuscitation, is not bundled into critical care and may be separately reported. Temporary transcutaneous pacing, code 92953, is a temporary pacemaker that is inserted into the heart through a peripheral vessel. This service *is* bundled into critical care. Electrodes are placed externally on the chest, rather than in a skin pocket, to regulate the heartbeat. Use code 92960 and 92961 for an electively scheduled defibrillation. Documentation should specify whether the cardioversion attempt is internal or external.

Code 92971 is a method of external circulatory assistance. Military anti-shock trousers (MAST) are applied to trauma patients or those requiring circulatory assistance. The trousers inflate and deflate in rapid succession, simulating a heartbeat, thus relieving the heart somewhat of its circulatory burden.

Thrombolysis is also known as "clot-busting." Drugs such as urokinase, streptokinase, and tPA are injected into a blood vessel or directly into the clot to dissolve it. Imaging studies are often taken during the procedure to document the process and determine if additional drugs or procedures are required. Thrombolytic procedures described by codes 92975–92977 are performed on coronary vessels only.

Stenting is another method used to open coronary vessels. A catheter is placed percutaneously and threaded into the area of stricture. If necessary, obstructed areas are cut away or a small balloon is inflated to open the vessel. The stent is deployed to keep the vessel open. Patients who have stents commonly take anticoagulation drugs to prevent occlusion of the stent by clot formation. Use code 92980 for the transcatheter placement of a single intracoronary stent. Code 92981 should be used for each additional vessel stented using the same method.

Balloon angioplasties are reported with code 92982. Add-on code 92984 may be used to report each additional vessel for balloon angioplasty or for other procedures where an additional vessel was treated.

PTCA is a method used to clean atheromatous plaques out of blood vessels. Typically, small blades are used on a catheter tip to clean plaque out of a vessel. Code 92995 is a PTCA using mechanical or other methods and may include balloon angioplasty. Imaging studies are performed at the same time to point the physician toward the area of occlusion.

EXERCISE 21.12

Instructions: Assign the correct CPT® codes or narrative to the procedures described.

1. A patient in the office waiting room collapses. A code is called, and the ambulance arrives within minutes. In the interim, CPR is begun, and an IV is established. Attempts at stabilizing the patient are unsuccessful. Endotracheal intubation is performed by the paramedics upon arrival. The patient is immediately taken to the nearest emergency room with CPR in progress. Determine which services should be coded and reported by the physician office.

   a. Office visit, CPR, critical care, and intubation

   b. CPR, critical care, IV start with IV fluids

   c. CPR, IV start, and IV fluids

   d. Intubation, CPR, IV start, and office visit

2. A stent is placed in the LAD coronary artery following PTCA of the same vessel. A PTCA is also performed on the circumflex artery.

   a. 92980, 92981, 92995

   b. 92995, 92996, 92980

   c. 92980, 92997, 92998

   d. 92982, 92984, 92980

3. A patient arrives in the ER complaining of increasing chest pain. EKG, cardiac enzymes, and troponin levels indicate acute MI. Urokinase is added to the IV already infusing. The patient is taken directly to the cardiac cath lab for further treatment. Code for the ER physician's services.

   a. 92977

   b. 92975

   c. 92973

   d. 92975, 92973

Cardiography encompasses diagnostic recordings of the heart. These codes are commonly split into the professional component and a technical component following the "global" code. This component coding allows the facility to code and bill only for the portion of the service that was performed in the facility, using the facility's equipment and staff. The professional component includes only those services provided by the physician. An example of how to report the components is demonstrated in Table 21.2 for a 12-lead EKG. Figure 21.6 shows the sensors used for the 12-lead EKG.

A rhythm EKG, also known as rhythm strip, is not the same as a 12-lead EKG. It involves only one to three leads applied to the patient and typically prints out a tracing on paper similar to a cash-register tape. It is used for a quick analysis or monitor of heart

Table 21–2   Reporting 12-Lead EKG Components

CPT® Code	CPT® Descriptor	When to Report
93000	Electrocardiogram, routine EKG with at least 12 leads; interpretation and report	Use this code when the physician owns the equipment, pays the staff, and interprets the report, *OR* when the facility employs the physician.
93005	Tracing only	Used by the facility.
93010	Interpretation and report only	Used by the physician who does not own the equipment or pay the staff, but provides an independent interpretation.

rhythm to determine if additional testing may be required. Use 93040 if the physician owns the equipment, pays the staff, and interprets the results. Use codes 93041–93042 if the global code must be split into professional and facility (technical) components. A rhythm strip is bundled into an EKG, and likewise, an EKG is bundled into stress testing.

Formula for Success

Codes that are already split into professional and technical components do not need Modifiers 26 or TC appended. The code is predetermined to be either professional or technical in nature.

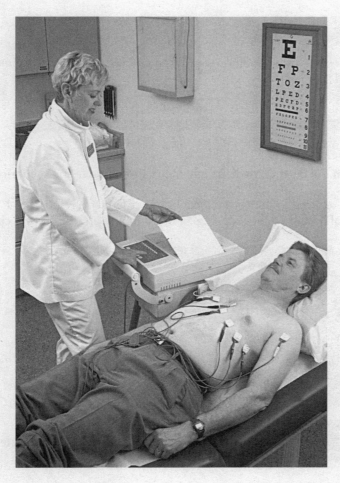

Figure 21–6 The sensors used for the 12-lead EKG.

Be sure to use a Modifier 59 if stress testing and EKGs are used at different times during the same day. An EKG with Modifier 59 is important to assign, especially when Critical Care services are provided at a separate time.

Example: A patient comes into the hospital complaining of sharp substernal chest pain that radiates to his jaw that has now subsided. An EKG is ordered and demonstrates some minor abnormalities. He is sent home with nitroglycerin. Later that evening the patient experiences an acute MI with cardiac arrest. In this case, the first EKG is distinct from others that may be ordered during the episode of critical care.

Holter monitors (see Figure 21.7) are used to provide cardiac recordings for prolonged periods. A Holter may be placed anywhere from 24 hours to 30 days. CPT® codes are assigned depending upon the technology of the equipment. Look to see if the monitoring service includes:

- Continuous vs. noncontinuous EKG recording.
- Storage with or without visual superimposition scanning.
- Miniaturized printout.
- Full-sized waveform tracings.
- Real-time data analysis.

External event recorders also capture abnormal heart rhythms or disturbances. These are coded once per 30-day time period. An internally implanted cardiac event monitor is reported using codes from the Cardiac chapter of CPT®.

Formula for Success

Watch monitor codes for an additional component of recording that includes hookup, recording, and disconnection.

EXERCISE 21.13

Instructions: Assign the correct Medicine chapter CPT® code to the scenarios listed below.

1. Mrs. Jones is referred to the cardiologist from her family physician. She has symptoms of shortness of breath and feeling like "a fish flopping around" in her chest. Coughing

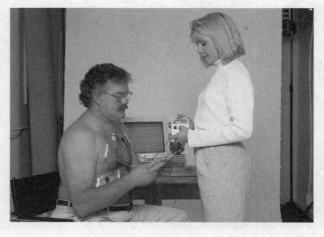

Figure 21–7   A patient hooked up to a Holter monitor.

used to make the sensation stop, but that is no longer effective. Previous EKGs have all been negative. An event recorder is placed on the patient by the office staff, and she is instructed to press a button on the device when she feels strange sensations in her chest. She is to return in one month for the disconnect.

   a. 93235

   b. 93268

   c. 93236

   d. 93270

2. Dr. A is a cardiologist who is contracted to read EKGs for the local hospital. Today she reads a 12-lead EKG for John Doe. Report the correct code for this service.

   a. 93000

   b. 93005

   c. 93010

   d. 93010 and 93042

PULMONARY

TERMINOLOGY AND ACRONYMS

CPAP   Continuous positive airway pressure.

FRC (functional residual capacity)   The amount of air left in the lungs after a normal expiration.

FVC (forced vital capacity)   The volume of air that can be exhaled with maximum force.

IPPB   Intermittent positive pressure breathing.

PFT   Pulmonary function test.

RV (residual volume)   The amount of air left in the lungs after a maximum expiration.

Spirometry   The most basic pulmonary function test, from which multiple other studies can be performed, depending upon technology used.

TLC (total lung capacity)   The total volume of air in the lungs after maximum inhalation effort.

VC (vital capacity)   The maximum volume of air that can be slowly exhaled.

ICD-9-CM CODING FOR PULMONARY SERVICES

Refer to Chapter 9 for information regarding specific respiratory diagnoses.

EXERCISE 21.14

Instructions: For additional coding practice, assign the correct ICD-9-CM code to the following diagnostic statements.

1. Exercise-induced bronchospasm   _____

2. Stab wound to chest with lacerated lung   _____   _____

3. Screening for chronic lung disease in pre-employment physical   _____   _____

4. Pneumonia due to SARS-associated coronavirus   _____

5. Adult respiratory distress syndrome   _____

6. Smoke inhalation from house fire   _____   _____

7. Acute laryngitis   _____

8. Asthma with acute exacerbation   _____

9. Aspiration pneumonia   _____

10. Upper respiratory infection due to influenza   _____

CPT® CODING FOR PULMONARY SERVICES

Physicians and respiratory therapy departments use codes from the pulmonary subsection of the Medicine chapter. These codes include any associated laboratory procedures and interpretation of results. Evaluation and Management services that are separately identifiable should be reported separately. Confusion often arises when assigning pulmonary codes because of the term "pulmonary function study." PFTs may vary from clinic to clinic and hospital to hospital, depending upon the equipment in the pulmonary lab. The most basic pulmonary function study is spirometry. Look at codes 94010–94621. Many of these codes reflect different tests that have spirometry as a basic component of a more complex study.

Spirometry measures the air going in and out of the lungs (see Figure 21.8, a spirometer). Two main problems can be diagnosed with spirometry:

- ■ Obstructed airflow: Found in diseases such as asthma, bronchitis, neoplasms, and trauma.
- ■ Restricted airflow: Found in tuberculosis, obesity, pregnancy, musculoskeletal deformities, and neurological diseases.

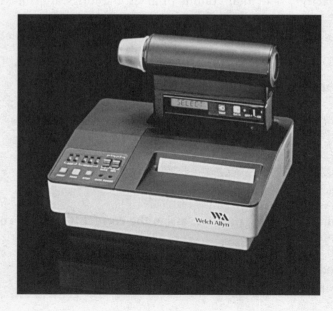

Figure 21–8 One type of spirometer.

Pulmonary function studies are done to manage or treat patients with pulmonary disease, determine the status of a patient's pulmonary disability, or to give preoperative clearance for abdominal and chest procedures, especially if the patient is a smoker over age 40.

Patients who have problems with obstructed airflow are often treated with nebulizers. Use code 94640 to report nebulizer treatments. If multiple treatments are performed on the same date of service by the same physician, append a Modifier 76 and/or 59 on second and subsequent nebulizer codes to indicate a repeat procedure.

Formula for Success

Remember to assign HCPCS codes for nebulizer medications such as Albuterol, Atrovent, or Budesonide.

Codes 94656 and 94657 are used for ventilator management. Use 94656 for initial ventilator setup and 94657 for each subsequent day of ventilator management. These codes are bundled into critical care and may not be used by the same physician who is providing critical care services.

Example: A patient was admitted to the hospital in acute respiratory failure. Dr. A, who is a pulmonologist, provided critical care for two hours, including intubation and initial ventilator management services. The next day Dr. B, an internal medicine specialist, provided critical care services for 45 minutes, and Dr. A provided only ventilator management services.

Day 1—Dr. A:

99291, Critical Care, first hour

99292 × 2, Critical Care, each additional half-hour

31500, Endotracheal intubation

Check with individual payers regarding use of Modifier 25 with Critical Care services.

Day 2—Dr. A:

94657, Ventilator management, subsequent day

Dr. B: 99291, Critical care, first hour

Pulse oximetry is a simple measurement of the percent of oxygen in the bloodstream. The monitor clips onto an earlobe or finger and is often used as an additional vital sign. When pulse oximetry is used as a routine vital sign, or when medical necessity is not present, it should not be reported for reimbursement. Use code 94760 for a single determination or 94761 for multiple determinations. Medicare and many private insurers will no longer reimburse for pulse oximetry unless it is a stand-alone service.

EXERCISE 21.15

Instructions: Assign the correct CPT® code for the scenarios below.

1. A patient was scheduled in the office for a bronchospasm evaluation, pre- and post-bronchodilator. An Albuterol nebulizer was given for the second portion of the test.
   a. 94060, J7619
   b. 94620, J7619
   c. 94060, 94060-76, J7619
   d. 94620, 94620-76, J7619

2. A 72-year-old male comes into the clinic for routine treatment of his COPD and brief visit with his physician. A single pulse oximeter is taken along with vital signs to check his oxygen status.

   a. 99212, 94761

   b. 99212-25, 94760

   c. 99212, 94760

   d. 99212, pulse oximeter is not reported.

ALLERGY

TERMINOLOGY AND ACRONYMS

Anaphylaxis   Severe reaction to an allergen; can be life-threatening.

Antigen   External substance; when introduced into the body stimulates mast cells.

Desensitization   Series of treatments with gradual increasing doses of antigen to boost immunity.

Mast cells   Cells that release histamine to begin an allergic reaction.

ICD-9-CM CODING FOR ALLERGY SERVICES

When coding for allergy tests, the diagnosis code linkage must indicate the reason why the test is being performed; i.e., airway obstruction, seasonal allergies, animal allergies, etc.

Code category 995 should be used with caution. Code 995.0, Other anaphylactic shock, is used when the cause of the reaction is not specified or when it is due to an adverse effect of the correct medicinal substance that was properly administered. Use an E code to identify the drug if known. Specific types of anaphylactic reaction are excluded from this category. Use 999.4 to code for an anaphylactic reaction due to serum or 995.60–995.69 for anaphylaxis due to an adverse food reaction.

If the adverse effect of a medicine that is properly administered is not specified, use code 995.2. Pathological drug intoxication (292.2) is excluded from this category.

Do not code specific types of allergic reactions such as hay fever, dermatitis, or allergic diarrhea to category 995.3. These conditions are excluded, and only unspecified types of allergic reactions should be coded to 995.3.

Code V07.1, Desensitization to allergens, should be used when the patient comes into the office for routine allergy injections. Check with individual payers; some insurance companies may prefer a medical diagnosis, such as 477.9, Hayfever, or 995.6x, Food allergy, as the primary diagnosis.

Categories V14 and V15 identify a personal history of allergies to medicinal agents, foods, insects, and other substances.

EXERCISE 21.16

Instructions: Assign the correct ICD-9-CM code for the scenario below. The CPT® code is already assigned.

1. Mary, age 25, comes into the office to receive her weekly injection of weed, tree, and grass allergen extract. The nurse takes her vial from the refrigerator and draws up a maintenance dose.

    a. V07.1, 477.9, 95120

    b. 995.3, 95120

    c. 477.9, 95120

    d. a or c, depending on documented payer requirements

CPT® CODING FOR ALLERGY SERVICES

The allergy section of CPT® is split into two subsections—allergy testing and allergy immunotherapy. When a patient undergoes allergy testing, the protocol is adjusted to the individual patient. In the physician office setting, most patients are tested with sequential and incremental doses of allergenic extract. Codes are assigned based on the method of testing. The tests listed in CPT® fall into two categories:

- Intracutaneous, meaning intradermal.
- Percutaneous, meaning scratch, puncture, or prick.

When allergy tests are administered by the intradermal method, a "wheal" is created by injecting the allergen into the subcutaneous tissue of the upper arm or back. The same allergen is diluted and injected multiple times until an end point with no immediate reaction is noted. Treatment for allergies is directed by the end-point dosage, with a gradual build-up in allergenic extract over a period of time until the patient reaches a "maintenance" dose. This allows the patient greater tolerance of the offending allergen and inhibits mast cell release, which triggers an allergic reaction. Codes in the immunotherapy section are divided into several groups:

- Injection only, without provision of allergen extract.
- Injection in physician office or facility including allergen extract.
- Injection and preparation of allergen extract, single dose per vial.
- Injection and preparation of allergen extract per multiple doses of stinging insect venom.
- Injection and preparation of single or multiple allergens, per dose.

Formula for Success

Watch Medicare LCDs for guidelines on coding for allergy testing and immunotherapy.

EXERCISE 21.17

Instructions: Assign the correct CPT® code to the scenario below.

1. John brings two vials of allergen extract to college with him. On a weekly basis, the Student Health staff nurses give him an injection from each vial.

    a. 95125

    b. 95117

    c. 95144 × 2

    d. 95165 × 2

PHYSICAL REHABILITATION AND MEDICINE

Physical therapy services are often provided by sports medicine and orthopedic specialists. Keep in mind that acute care hospitals and rehabilitation hospitals are governed by different reimbursement rules than clinics.

TERMINOLOGY AND ACRONYMS

Acupuncture   The use of fine needles to treat disorders or provide anesthesia.

ADL   Activities of daily living.

AROM   Active range of motion.

Cryotherapy   Therapeutic use of cold.

DTR   Deep tendon reflex.

e-stim   Electrical stimulation.

OT   Occupational therapy.

Phonophoresis   The use of ultrasound to transmit medication through the skin and into deeper tissues.

PT   Physical therapy.

ROM   Range of motion.

TE   Therapeutic exercise.

TENS   Transcutaneous electrical stimulation.

US   Ultrasound.

WP   Whirlpool.

ICD-9-CM CODING FOR PHYSICAL REHABILITATION

Refer to Chapters 8 and 17 for information regarding specific musculoskeletal and nervous system diagnoses.

EXERCISE 21.18

Instructions: For additional coding practice, assign the correct ICD-9-CM code to the following diagnostic statements.

1. A 15-year-old patient comes in for fitting and adjustment of an artificial leg status post below the knee amputation. _____ _____

2. Mr. Smith is sent to PT for therapeutic exercise following his knee replacement surgery. _____ _____ _____

3. A patient with continued problems from an old traumatic brain injury comes in for occupational therapy. _____ _____

CPT® CODING FOR PHYSICAL REHABILITATION

Modalities

The first grouping of codes under this section describes initial or subsequent evaluations by physical therapists, occupational therapists, or sports medicine specialists. After the patient has been evaluated, he or she may be treated using therapeutic procedures or modalities. According to CPT®, a modality is "any physical agent applied to produce therapeutic changes to biologic tissue; includes but is not limited to thermal, acoustic, light, mechanical or electrical energy." Modalities can include hot or cold packs, whirlpool, electrical stimulation, traction, etc. CPT® has split the application of modalities into two parts:

- Supervised: Not requiring one-on-one patient contact.
- Constant attendance: Requires one-on-one patient contact.

Providers may be supervising several patients who are undergoing various treatments at the same time. Providers may not attend to more than one patient when using a treatment requiring constant attendance. Modalities requiring constant attendance should have time well documented. These services may be coded and billed in increments of 15 minutes. Medicare guidelines regarding the *"8-minute rule"* are detailed below:

In AB-00-14, CMS states that when billing units of therapy, one unit is equal to or greater than 8 minutes but less than 23 minutes of care. Two units are equal to or greater than 23 minutes but less than 38 minutes, and so on. Providers are instructed not to bill for anything less than 8 minutes of care.

CMS also states that "pre- and post-delivery services are not to be counted in determining the treatment service time. In other words, the time counted as intraservice begins when the therapist or physician or an assistant under the supervision of a physician or therapist is delivering treatment services. The patient should already be in the treatment area (e.g., on the treatment table or mat or in the gym) and prepared to begin treatment."
Check with individual payers for their guidelines on billing physical therapy time.

Example: Mary had contrast baths provided by her physical therapist. She requested that the treatment be stopped after 24 minutes due to discomfort.

CPT® code reported: 97034 × 2 units (15 minutes plus 9 minutes)

Therapeutic Procedures

Therapeutic procedures are required to have one-on-one patient contact (see Figure 21.9). Some procedures are reported in 15-minute increments; others are reported only once per day. Therapeutic procedures include therapeutic exercise, gait training, massage, myofascial release, prosthetic training, self-care training, work reintegration, and wheelchair training. Work hardening is a conditioning program designed to prepare injured workers for eventual return to duty. Use 97545 for an initial two hours of work hardening per day with 97546 for each additional hour of conditioning.

Active Wound Care Management

Wound debridements may be performed in a variety of healthcare settings. Codes 97601 and 97602 distinguish between selective and nonselective types of debridement. Anesthesia is not used in either code. Both codes also require topical application of dressings, wound assessment, and instructions for ongoing care. Code 97601 describes sharp

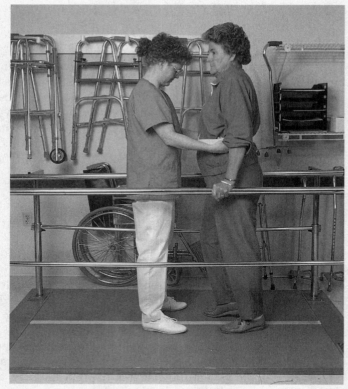

Figure 21–9   Physical therapist assisting a patient on parallel bars.

selective debridement, meaning that a scissors, scalpel, or tweezers is used to remove dead or sloughed tissue and the wound is redressed. Code 97602 describes a nonselective debridement, meaning that the wound is cleaned with enzymes, gentle abrasion, and redressed.

Formula for Success

Do not use these codes in addition to 11040-11044, which are used for surgical debridement.

Modifier Usage

Note the following HCPCS modifiers that pertain to physical medicine:

A1, Dressing for one wound
A2, Dressing for two wounds
A3, Dressing for three wounds
A4, Dressing for four wounds
A5, Dressing for five wounds
A6, Dressing for six wounds
A7, Dressing for seven wounds
A8, Dressing for eight wounds
A9, Dressing for nine wounds
GP, Services delivered under an outpatient physical therapy plan of care.

Use Modifiers K0, K1, K2, K3, and K4 to describe lower extremity prosthesis functional levels. The therapist should assign these modifiers dependent upon the patient's level of ambulation.

Check with individual private payers to see if these modifiers are recognized.

Supplies

Code for supplies that are provided by the physician for the patient's home use, such as orthotics, canes, crutches, stump socks, braces, ADL accessories, dressings, and so on.

EXERCISE 21.19

Instructions: Assign the correct CPT® code and corresponding time units (if applicable) to the scenarios below.

1. A patient was seen for the first time in the physical therapy department for treatment following a car accident. She was evaluated and a plan of care was instituted. The plan of care consisted of 30 minutes of therapeutic exercise to improve range of motion and 15 minutes of myofascial release. _____ _____ _____

2. A stroke patient spends 60 minutes with the physical therapist working on cognitive skill development. _____

3. A patient with cerebral palsy spends 30 minutes in the pool with the aquatic therapist and an assistant. Therapeutic exercises are done to relieve muscle spasms. _____

CHAPTER REVIEW

Instructions: Assign the correct ICD-9-CM and CPT® codes to the scenarios below.

1. A patient with bilateral keratoconus is treated with a special contact lens.
   a. 371.61, 92070
   b. 371.60, 92310
   c. 371.60, 92070
   d. 371.62, 92310

2. A patient arrives in the office with exacerbation of her asthma. The patient is given an Albuterol/Atrovent nebulizer with good resolution of the symptoms. The physician documents an expanded problem-focused history, detailed physical exam, and moderate medical decision making.
   a. 99214-25, 94640, J7644, J7619
   b. 99213-25, 94640, J7644, J7619
   c. 99214-25, 94664, J3535
   d. 99213-25, 94664, J3535

3. A 60-year-old ESRD patient with chronic renal failure travels to a family reunion and requires hemodialysis while on vacation. His nephrologist, Dr. A, has sent the plan of care to the dialysis center near his hotel. The patient was evaluated by the nephrologist, Dr. B, at the dialysis center and undergoes two treatments without problem before returning home.

    a. 585, 90925 × 2

    b. 586, 90925 × 2

    c. 585, 90935, 90925 × 2

    d. 586, 90935, 90925 × 2

4. A patient with acute paranoid schizophrenia is given 60 minutes of individual psychotherapy while hospitalized. His physician also documents psychotropic medication management and treatment of a mild upper respiratory infection.

    a. 295.33, 90818

    b. 295.30, 465.9, 90819

    c. 295.31, 90821

    d. 295.30, 465.9, 90822

5. A patient is seen at the clinic by the ENT physician in consultation for a persistent, nagging cough caused by a foreign body sensation in the back of his throat. A detailed history, expanded problem-focused exam, and moderate-complexity medical decision making were documented by the physician. She decides to perform a nasopharyngoscopy in the office. This was done with negative findings. A swallowing study is scheduled to work up the problem.

    a. 786.2, 92511

    b. 786.2, 933.0, 99242

    c. 933.0, 99242-25, 92511

    d. 786.2, 99242-25, 92511

6. The acronym "ESRD" stands for:

    a. End-stage respiratory distress

    b. End-stage renal distress

    c. End-stage renal dialysis

    d. End-stage renal disease

7. Ophthalmologists and optometrists have the option of using one of the following types of codes to report their office services:

    a. Ophthalmology or Evaluation and Managment

    b. Ophthalmology or Eye Surgical codes

    c. Evaluation and Management or Eye Surgical codes

    d. Eye Surgical codes or Nervous System codes

8. Otorhinolaryngology services may be performed:

    a. Independent of Evaluation and Management services

    b. In addition to Evaluation and Management services

    c. Only by a physician

    d. Both a and b

9. The following service is not bundled into critical care:

    a. EKG

    b. Temporary pacemaker

    c. CPR

    d. Insertion of IV lines

10. Medications are bundled into the code for nebulizer treatments.   **True/False**

CHAPTER

22

Billing and Reimbursement

OBJECTIVES

1. Recognize the importance of team effort in the billing functions.
2. Identify methods to help streamline billing efficiency in the medical office.
3. Distinguish the characteristics of a well-developed superbill.
4. State the difference between an appeal and a corrected claim.

TERMINOLOGY AND ACRONYMS:

ANSI   American National Standards Institute.

Appeal   Request for reconsideration of a denied or partially denied claim.

Assignment of benefits   Allows the payer to reimburse the provider directly, rather than the patient.

Birthday rule   When dependents are covered by both parents' policies, the birthday rule states that the primary policy is the one belonging to the parent with earliest birthday in the year, regardless of year of birth of either parent.

Clean claim   A claim that contains all the information to pass payer edits.

Clearinghouse   A company that receives electronic claims transmissions from providers and distributes them to insurance companies, often performing editing or claim scrubbing functions.

Contractual obligation   The discount taken by the payer for participating providers that is written off and not billed to the patient.

EOB (explanation of benefits)   A summary of benefits paid to a provider.

HIPAA   Health Insurance Portability and Accountability Act of 1996.

Non-par provider   A provider who has not contracted with the payers to accept the allowed amount and may bill the patient for the unpaid balance.

Par provider   One who has contracted to accept the payers allowed amount as payment in full after the patient has paid deductible and co-pay amounts.

PCP   Primary care provider.

RA   Remittance advice.

Timely filing deadline   The period of time predetermined by payers in which they will consider claims for payment; typically up to one year from the date of service. Medicare allows claims up to eighteen months old to be filed. Some third-party payers contract for short periods of time, such as six months or less.

INTRODUCTION

Similar to the art of coding, the act of obtaining timely and appropriate reimbursement for services in today's atmosphere of shrinking healthcare dollars has also become an art form, if not a science. All physician practice business office managers can relate their reimbursement woes with the increasing regulatory burdens and potential fines. It is imperative for coders to understand that just because an encounter can be coded and billed, there is no guarantee of payment. A multitude of things can happen to forestall payment, and if the practice is not organized and educated about the process, it can easily see 50% or more of its revenue lost.

A claim is well on its way to being generated from the moment a patient walks in the door. Successful reimbursement depends on how well the office staff understands the individual roles they play and how each employee is an important link in the reimbursement chain. In this chapter, the flow of paperwork is examined from the encounter to the posting of payment. Keep in mind that depending upon the size of the medical practice, the following functions may all be performed by one person or by people in several different departments.

THE REIMBURSEMENT CHAIN

Reception

The reception staff makes the first contact and the first impression with the patient. The receptionist must be a true multitasker and make sure that all of the patient's demographics and insurance information are updated with *each visit*. Competition and ever-increasing premiums among insurance companies cause employers to switch healthcare coverage for their employees frequently. Changes in insurance companies must be kept current. Many insurance plans are shortening their timely filing deadlines, so a claim that is erroneously sent to a lapsed insurance plan eats up valuable time.

Front desk duties before the patient sees the physician include:

- Scheduling the appointment.
- Sending registration papers to the patient.
- Verifying insurance benefits.
- Entering demographics/insurance information into the computer.
- Inactivating old insurance.
- Signing **HIPAA** paperwork.
- Signing authorization to release medical information.
- Generating charge ticket.
- Creating patient chart.

The receptionist enters the patient information from the registration form into the computer and copies the patient's insurance card front and back. It is important for the medical practice to set up its insurance files in the computer in a consistent manner, so the same insurance company is not listed multiple times with slight variations. These insurance files should be audited periodically to look for inconsistencies.

Example: Blue Cross of Nebraska may be spelled out, or entered as BC/BS of NE, or BC of Nebr.

Patients who have new insurance should have the old company inactivated in the computer system to prevent a claim from going to the wrong company. Most billing/accounts receivable software will prevent the deletion of old insurance files, which may be necessary to refile old claims.

It is important to note whether the patient needs preauthorization when scheduling a procedure and how much co-pay is required by the plan. Although most plans place the responsibility for preauthorization with the patient, it is a good idea for the practice to double check and perform that duty rather than risk nonpayment. The patient's insurance card will contain a phone number so the staff can call and verify insurance benefits and/or preauthorize services. Many practices will send paperwork to the patient prior to the appointment.

The reception staff should know what plans the practice participates in, because this will directly affect the patient's out-of-pocket expenses. A certain percentage of the physician's fee is written off as a **contractual obligation** and is not billed to the patient. Patients who see an out-of-network physician do not get a discounted rate and may be billed the difference between the amount allowed by the insurance company and the amount charged by the physician.

Charge Tickets

The form that is used by the practice to record the services that are provided is known by several names—encounter form, charge ticket, superbill, and charge slip. This form is generated by the front desk and contains basic patient demographics that may be printed or handwritten, the name of the physician, date of service, and insurance information. Some practices print stickers and put these on when the patient arrives. The charge ticket contains a listing of the most common CPT codes for that practice and, in some cases, will also list common ICD-9-CM codes. The charge ticket should be reviewed annually at a minimum. The codes should be updated to reflect any changes in the current year's CPT books. If ICD-9-CM codes are included, then the ticket should be reviewed for those updates as well. Claims that are denied due to new codes may be resubmitted later when the payer is ready to accept them. Likewise, claims that are denied due to outdated codes may be corrected and resubmitted. Well-designed charge tickets contain the most common codes that are assigned by the practice with succinct descriptors that are not ambiguous or misleading.

Formula for Success

When printing Evaluation and Management codes on superbills, be sure that *all* levels of the type of service are listed, so the physician is not "pigeon-holed" into using only high-level or low-level codes.

Post Appointment

Immediately following the patient–physician encounter, the physician should circle on the charge ticket the services that were provided. The charge ticket is then brought to the checkout area with the patient. The checkout process should include totaling the fees for the services and collecting the patient's co-pay, or payment in full (when possible) if the patient does not carry insurance coverage. Post appointment activities include:

- Checking copy of charge ticket.
- Checking to see if patient has an outstanding balance due.

■ Determining co-pay, coinsurance, and deductible.
■ Scheduling follow-up appointment.
■ Referring patient to account manager if necessary to set up payment schedule.

The reception staff is often responsible for keeping the charge tickets in a folder or box for the coding staff. When charge tickets are given to the coding staff, they may be sorted by provider, by payer (Medicare, Medicaid, third party), or alphabetically, depending on how coding assignments are handled by the individual facility. If possible, dictation should be reviewed to ensure that the level of service is correctly assigned and all ancillary department charges are captured.

BUSINESS OFFICE PROCEDURES

Charge Posting

Once the charge ticket has been coded and reviewed for accuracy, the codes, date of service, and other pertinent information are entered into the patient's account. This process is known as *charge posting.* The accounts receivable software links each CPT code to a specific fee and drops the ICD-9-CM, CPT, and HCPCS codes onto the claim along with the patient's insurance information, date of service, provider numbers, and facility address. All of the accounts from that day are batched and sent electronically to a **clearinghouse** or to individual payers. Paper claims may be generated, manually sorted, and reviewed before mailing.

Electronic Filing

HIPAA transactions involve the electronic transfer of healthcare information. Payers, software vendors, third-party billing services, and claims clearinghouses all rely on implementation guides to stay in compliance with HIPAA's electronic transactions and code set requirements. HIPAA does not require solo providers or small practices to conduct the standard transactions electronically, but those that are sent electronically must meet the requirements specified in HIPAA regulations. Eventually, the goal is to have all insurance claims processed electronically. Paper claims, such as the CMS 1500 claim form, are considered nonstandard transactions and do not meet the same requirements as electronic claims.

Physician claims are submitted electronically on an 837 Professional Claim form. Only certain medical code sets have been approved for use by HIPAA:

■ ICD-9-CM for diagnosis
■ NCD, National Drug Codes
■ CDT, Current Dental Terminology
■ HCPCS
■ CPT-4

Local codes, such as those created by state Medicaid programs, are no longer allowed under HIPAA.

Nonmedical code sets include zip codes, telephone area codes, remittance advice remark codes, claim status category codes, or other administrative types of codes that are used in the claim adjudication process.

Claims that are sent electronically will generate a report back to the practice that shows which claims were received and if there were any edits that caused a claim rejection. The unprocessable claims must be investigated, corrected, and resubmitted. The medical practice should check its own report against the report from the clearinghouse to make sure that all claims sent were actually received. Occasionally, batches may not download properly and must be resubmitted.

Paper Claim Filing

The CMS 1500 paper claim form (see Figure 22.1) is used to report physician and allied health professional services. The claim form is printed in OCR red and contains 33 boxes, or data fields. All payers require the patient name, date of birth, insured's name, relationship to patient, policy number, date of service, provider name, address, provider number, and diagnosis code with procedure code as basic requirements. Each payer also has unique information required that may or may not be required by other payers. It is therefore in the best interest of the practice for the reception staff to gather as much information as possible at the time of service so that valuable time is not wasted calling the patient back for additional billing information.

It is important when printing paper claims that the information is lined up squarely within each box and does not run outside the borders.

Day Files

The business office should have a good filing mechanism in place to ensure that the charge tickets for each day can be easily found in a day file and are not filed into medical records or otherwise split up after charges are posted. OBRA regulations require providers to maintain copies of government claim forms and any attachments for six years. Some offices keep the original charge ticket; others print out plain paper copies of each claim and keep these in the day file also. Likewise, a tracking methodology should be in place to locate missing charge tickets to ensure that charges have been posted for each patient visit. Some practices number their charge tickets for the day; others track them by a printing out a schedule for each physician and checking them off. Nothing is more frustrating to business office staff than to be handed a charge ticket that has been lost for over a year, that has resurfaced once the **timely filing deadline** has passed.

Likewise, the reports generated from the electronic claims submission should be filed where they are easily accessed. Depending on the size of the medical practice and the amount of storage available, these may be filed along with the charge tickets or kept separately. Large offices may elect to scan their day files and keep those in electronic format, allowing the paper files to be stored off-site.

Copies of individual checks, bulk checks, **EOB**s, and deposit slips may also be kept in the same day file.

Payment Posting

At the same time charge posting is performed, the account may be credited for any payments that were made at the time of service. Checks that arrive in the mail from patients and insurance companies are sorted, stamped for deposit, and the payments posted to individual patient accounts. Checks may come with an individual EOB or as a bulk check with multiple patients listed on it. A legend is found on each EOB or remittance that explains the allowed charges, patient deductible, any co-payment owed by the patient, and the amount paid by the insurer. After the checks are posted, they are entered on a deposit slip and taken to the bank. The amount that is deposited in the bank should balance to the amount that is posted to the patient accounts for that day. Some Medicare carriers and a few third-party payers have automatic remittance, which posts the payment electronically to the correct charges in the individual patient account. Any discrepancies are found on an error report and can be applied manually. By using electronic filing in combination

PLEASE
DO NOT
STAPLE
IN THIS
AREA

APPROVED OMB-0938-0008

CARRIER

HEALTH INSURANCE CLAIM FORM

PICA ⊤⊤⊤

| | | PICA |

1. MEDICARE (Medicare #) MEDICAID (Medicaid #) CHAMPUS (Sponsor's SSN) CHAMPVA (VA File #) GROUP HEALTH PLAN (SSN or ID) FECA BLK LUNG (SSN) OTHER (ID)

1a. INSURED'S I.D. NUMBER   (FOR PROGRAM IN ITEM 1)

2. PATIENT'S NAME (Last Name, First Name, Middle Initial)

3. PATIENT'S BIRTH DATE MM DD YY   SEX M F

4. INSURED'S NAME (Last Name, First Name, Middle Initial)

5. PATIENT'S ADDRESS (No., Street)

6. PATIENT RELATIONSHIP TO INSURED   Self Spouse Child Other

7. INSURED'S ADDRESS (No., Street)

CITY   STATE

8. PATIENT STATUS   Single Married Other

CITY   STATE

ZIP CODE   TELEPHONE (Include Area Code) ( )

Employed   Full-Time Student   Part-Time Student

ZIP CODE   TELEPHONE (INCLUDE AREA CODE) ( )

9. OTHER INSURED'S NAME (Last Name, First Name, Middle Initial)

10. IS PATIENT'S CONDITION RELATED TO:

11. INSURED'S POLICY GROUP OR FECA NUMBER

a. OTHER INSURED'S POLICY OR GROUP NUMBER

a. EMPLOYMENT? (CURRENT OR PREVIOUS) YES NO

a. INSURED'S DATE OF BIRTH MM DD YY   SEX M F

b. OTHER INSURED'S DATE OF BIRTH MM DD YY   SEX M F

b. AUTO ACCIDENT?   PLACE (State) YES NO

b. EMPLOYER'S NAME OR SCHOOL NAME

c. EMPLOYER'S NAME OR SCHOOL NAME

c. OTHER ACCIDENT? YES NO

c. INSURANCE PLAN NAME OR PROGRAM NAME

d. INSURANCE PLAN NAME OR PROGRAM NAME

10d. RESERVED FOR LOCAL USE

d. IS THERE ANOTHER HEALTH BENEFIT PLAN? YES NO *If yes*, return to and complete item 9 a-d.

READ BACK OF FORM BEFORE COMPLETING & SIGNING THIS FORM.

12. PATIENT'S OR AUTHORIZED PERSON'S SIGNATURE I authorize the release of any medical or other information necessary to process this claim. I also request payment of government benefits either to myself or to the party who accepts assignment below.

SIGNED _____   DATE _____

13. INSURED'S OR AUTHORIZED PERSON'S SIGNATURE I authorize payment of medical benefits to the undersigned physician or supplier for services described below.

SIGNED _____

PATIENT AND INSURED INFORMATION

14. DATE OF CURRENT: MM DD YY   ◄ ILLNESS (First symptom) OR INJURY (Accident) OR PREGNANCY(LMP)

15. IF PATIENT HAS HAD SAME OR SIMILAR ILLNESS. GIVE FIRST DATE MM DD YY

16. DATES PATIENT UNABLE TO WORK IN CURRENT OCCUPATION MM DD YY   MM DD YY FROM   TO

17. NAME OF REFERRING PHYSICIAN OR OTHER SOURCE

17a. I.D. NUMBER OF REFERRING PHYSICIAN

18. HOSPITALIZATION DATES RELATED TO CURRENT SERVICES MM DD YY   MM DD YY FROM   TO

19. RESERVED FOR LOCAL USE

20. OUTSIDE LAB? $ CHARGES YES NO

21. DIAGNOSIS OR NATURE OF ILLNESS OR INJURY. (RELATE ITEMS 1,2,3 OR 4 TO ITEM 24E BY LINE)

1. ____ . ____   3. ____ . ____

2. ____ . ____   4. ____ . ____

22. MEDICAID RESUBMISSION CODE   ORIGINAL REF. NO.

23. PRIOR AUTHORIZATION NUMBER

24.	A					B	C	D		E	F	G	H	I	J	K
	DATE(S) OF SERVICE					Place of Service	Type of Service	PROCEDURES, SERVICES, OR SUPPLIES (Explain Unusual Circumstances)		DIAGNOSIS CODE	$ CHARGES	DAYS OR UNITS	EPSDT Family Plan	EMG	COB	RESERVED FOR LOCAL USE
	From MM DD YY			To MM DD YY				CPT/HCPCS	MODIFIER							
1																
2																
3																
4																
5																
6																

25. FEDERAL TAX I.D. NUMBER   SSN EIN

26. PATIENT'S ACCOUNT NO.

27. ACCEPT ASSIGNMENT? (For govt. claims, see back) YES NO

28. TOTAL CHARGE $

29. AMOUNT PAID $

30. BALANCE DUE $

31. SIGNATURE OF PHYSICIAN OR SUPPLIER INCLUDING DEGREES OR CREDENTIALS (I certify that the statements on the reverse apply to this bill and are made a part thereof.)

SIGNED _____   DATE _____

32. NAME AND ADDRESS OF FACILITY WHERE SERVICES WERE RENDERED (If other than home or office)

33. PHYSICIAN'S, SUPPLIER'S BILLING NAME, ADDRESS, ZIP CODE & PHONE #

PIN#   GRP#

PHYSICIAN OR SUPPLIER INFORMATION

(APPROVED BY AMA COUNCIL ON MEDICAL SERVICE 8/88)   **PLEASE PRINT OR TYPE**   FORM HCFA-1500 (12-90) FORM OWCP-1500   FORM RRB-1500

Figure 22–1   The CMS 1500 claim form.

with electronic remittance, the turnaround time from claim submission to reimbursement can be as little as two weeks when clean claims are submitted.

The person who is posting payments should also note if a claim has been denied or if only partial payment is allowed on a claim. These should be investigated to see if there was an error made that can be corrected. The EOB that accompanies an insurance check will have reason codes on it that explain the different actions taken by the payer. It is important for the provider to follow up on all denials or partial payments. In many cases, a simple technical error will cause a denial of payment, such as a missing digit from a diagnosis code.

Appeal vs. Corrected Claim

Payers will reject a claim that is missing information and mark it as unprocessable. Errors of this type should be corrected and the claim resubmitted. When resubmitting paper claims, make sure that the claim is clearly marked as a corrected claim, or it will be rejected once again as a duplicate claim for that date of service. Attach supporting documentation and a copy of the EOB. Make sure that a copy of all the documents is made and kept in a tickler file until the claim is resolved.

A formal **appeal** letter should be sent when the claim was rejected for other than technical reasons. When sending a formal appeal, send a letter requesting reconsideration and cite any research that supports the appeal, such as Coding Clinic, Official ICD-9-CM Coding Guidelines, CCI edits, or CPT Assistant. Some payers require their own special forms for appeals and corrected claims, so check with the payer before using a standard appeal letter. Some physician associations or societies can also assist with appeals and may have standardized appeal letters.

Fee Schedules

Physicians who participate with an insurance company are contracting for a certain dollar amount that is allowed for each CPT code. The amount that is allowed will vary from company to company and from region to region within the United States. Insurance actuaries determine fee schedules based on health and reimbursement statistics from geographic regions, often by zip code. Physician fee schedules are determined by individual practices and will vary considerably from those developed by payers. The medical office should review its fee schedule at least annually to ensure that it is not overcharging or undercharging for services in its area. The American Medical Association (AMA) at www.ama-assn.org and Medical Group Management Association (MGMA) at www .mgma.com have specialty-based information available to help in the development of a good fee schedule.

▰▰▰ CHAPTER REVIEW ▰▰▰

1. If a patient does not assign his or her insurance benefits to the provider, an insurance check will be mailed to:
   a. The provider
   b. The patient
   c. The insurance company will not pay
   d. Both a and b

2. All of the following information is true about charge tickets except:
   a. They should be updated at least annually.
   b. They should contain each level of the E/M services listed.

    c. They can be sent to the insurance company in lieu of a claim form.

    d. They should be tracked to prevent missed charges.

3. Electronic format claims for physicians are sent on a:
   a. 837 Professional claim
   b. 855 Institutional claim
   c. 827 Professional claim
   d. 837 Institutional claim

4. The timely filing deadline for insurance plans begins:
   a. At the date of service.
   b. When the claim is received by any insurance company.
   c. When the claim is received by the correct insurance company.
   d. On the date the provider sends it to the payer.

5. A contractual obligation is the amount that is:
   a. Billed to the patient as part of the provider contract.
   b. Allowed by the insurance company.
   c. Reimbursed back to the insurance company.
   d. Written off by the provider and not billed to the patient.

6. An EOB does not need to be reviewed. It is only good to show the amount paid by the insurer.
   a. True
   b. False

7. Physician fee schedules should be updated at least every three years.
   a. True
   b. False

8. Information in the business office day files should be kept a minimum of six years.
   a. True
   b. False

9. An ICD-9-CM code that has been submitted with a missing digit will still get paid, but more slowly than clean claims.
   a. True
   b. False

10. Reception staff is important for its role in claim submission.
    a. True
    b. False

11. Physicians should update their fee schedules at least annually.
    a. True
    b. False

Appendix A

Anatomy Plates

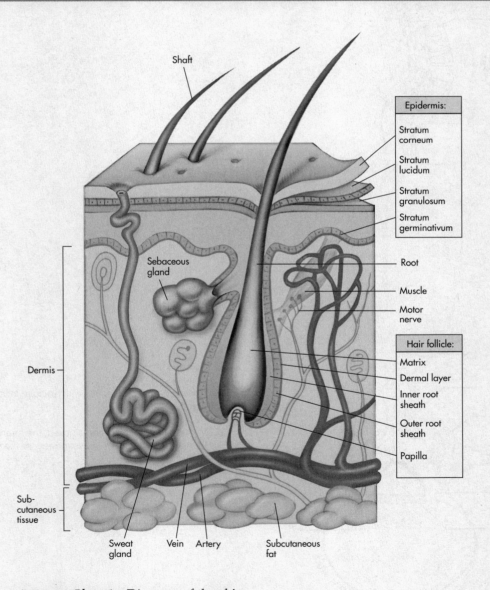

Shaft

Epidermis:

Stratum corneum

Stratum lucidum

Stratum granulosum

Stratum germinativum

Sebaceous gland

Root

Muscle

Motor nerve

Hair follicle:

Matrix

Dermal layer

Inner root sheath

Outer root sheath

Papilla

Dermis

Subcutaneous tissue

Sweat gland

Vein

Artery

Subcutaneous fat

Anatomy Plate 1   Diagram of the skin.

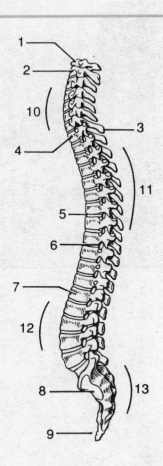

1. First cervical vertebra or atlas
2. Second cervical vertebra or axis
3. Seventh cervical vertebra (vertebra prominens) spinous process
4. First thoracic vertebra—body
5. Intervertebral disc—fibrocartilaginous disc found between bodies; compresses to absorb shock.
6. Intervertebral foramen—opening between vertebrae through which spinal nerves emerge.
7. First lumbar vertebra—body
8. Sacrum—a label line is on articular surface for ilium
9. Coccyx
10. Cervical curve—secondary
11. Thoracic curve—primary
12. Lumbar curve—secondary
13. Sacrococcygeal curve—primary curve

Anatomy Plate 2   Musculoskeletal system.

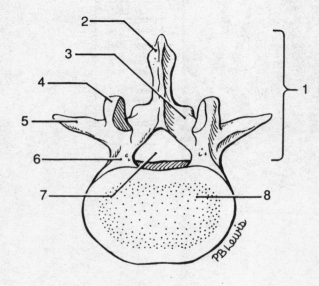

1. Vertebral (neural) arch
2. Spinous process
3. Lamina
4. Superior articular process with articular facet
5. Transverse process
6. Pedicle
7. Vertebral foramen—when stacked, the foramina form the vertebral canal, the passageway for the spinal cord
8. Body

Anatomy Plate 3   Musculoskeletal system.

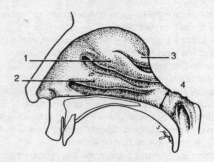

A. THE LATERAL WALL OF THE RIGHT SIDE OF THE NASAL CAVITY

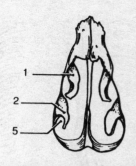

B. ANTERIOR VIEW OF THE BONES OF THE NOSE

1. Middle nasal concha
2. Inferior nasal concha
3. Superior nasal concha
4. Internal nares or choanae are the openings from the nasal cavity into the pharynx. The arrow indicates its position at the posterior limit of the nasal septum, not shown here.
5. Inferior meatus. The opening for the nasolacrimal duct is found here.

Anatomy Plate 4   The respiratory system.

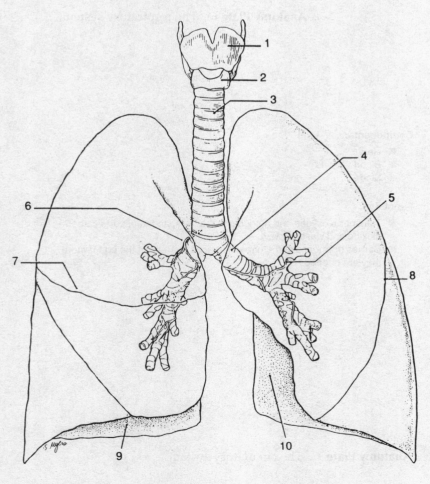

1. Thyroid cartilage. This is commonly called the "Adam's apple." In the male it is more prominent because it is formed from two plates that fuse anteriorly at a 90° angle. In the female the angle is 120°.
2. Cricoid cartilage. This is the only complete ring cartilage of the larynx. On its posterior extremity the two triangular-shaped *arytenoid cartilages* are located.
3. Trachea
4. Left primary bronchus—smaller and less direct than the right primary bronchus. The primary bronchi result when the trachea bifurcates. They enter the root of the lung.
5. Secondary bronchus—three of these are on the right, one for each lobe. Only two are on the left. Each branches to form several numbered and predictable tertiary bronchi.
6. Bronchial arteries—provide blood to the bronchial tree.
7. Horizontal fissure to separate lobes; the oblique fissure is inferior. The fissures divide the right lung into three lobes.
8. Oblique fissure—the only fissure on the left because the left lung has only two lobes.
9. Diaphragmatic surface—the lungs are just superior to the diaphragm.
10. Cardiac impression—the heart indents the medial inferior surface of the left lung.

Anatomy Plate 5   The respiratory system.

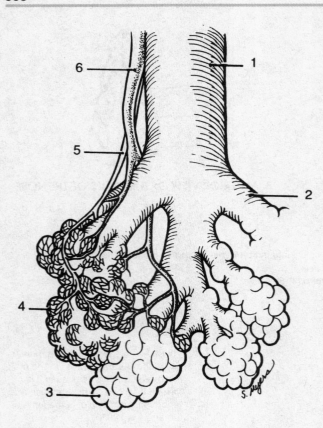

1. Terminal bronchiole—the last segment of the bronchial tree to contain cartilage.
2. Respiratory bronchiole—when the air reaches this portion of the tube there can be some exchange of gasses. The tubes contain no cartilage and have alveolar ducts and sacs.
3. Alveoli—the thin epithelium sacs that are the termination of the bronchial tree. They receive the air.
4. Capillaries—between the pulmonary arteries and pulmonary veins. Carbon dioxide in the blood is exchanged for oxygen from the alveoli.
5. Pulmonary arteriole bring poorly oxygenated blood from the right ventricle.
6. Pulmonary venule takes well-oxygenated blood back to the left atrium.

Anatomy Plate 6   The respiratory system.

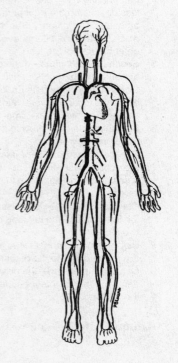

Components:

- Heart
- Blood vessels
- Blood

Functions:

- Transports oxygen and nutrients to the cells, and transports carbon dioxide and wastes away.
- Carries hormones and other substances to areas of the body where they are needed.

Anatomy Plate 7   The circulatory system.

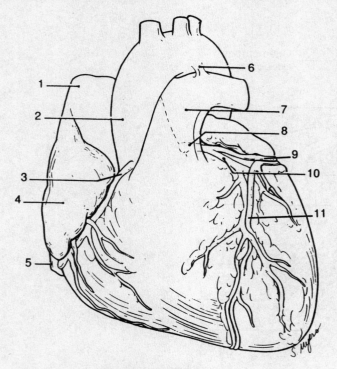

A. ANTERIOR VIEW

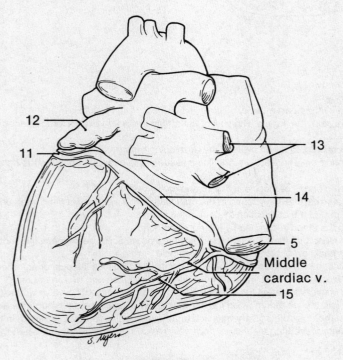

Middle
cardiac v.

B. POSTERIOR VIEW

1. Superior vena cava (SVC) brings venous blood to the right atrium from the upper body.
2. Ascending aorta contains blood being pumped by the left ventricle to all the systems of the body.
3. Right coronary a. leaves the base of the aorta to the right of the pulmonary trunk and lies in the fat-filled coronary sulcus as it passes to the posterior heart.
4. Right auricle—ear-like flap of atrium.
5. Inferior vena cava (IVC) enters the heart just after passing through the diaphragm.
6. Ligamentum arteriosum remnant of an embryonic vessel.
7. Pulmonary trunk, for blood being pumped by the right ventricle to the lungs for a fresh supply of oxygen.
8. Left coronary a. This vessel leaves the base of the aorta and turns to lie in the coronary sulcus, the depression between atria and ventricles.
9. Circumflex a.—the continuation of the left coronary a. to the posterior heart. It lies in the coronary sulcus.
10. Anterior interventricular a. (referred to as the left anterior descending (LAD) in clinical literature). This branch of the left coronary a. lies in the fat-filled anterior interventricular sulcus, the depression over the interventricular septum. It supplies blood to both ventricles.
11. Great cardiac vein lies in the anterior interventricular sulcus beside the artery. It continues by turning to lie in the coronary sulcus with the circumflex a. and then terminates on the posterior heart.
12. Left auricle—ear-like flap of left atrium.
13. Pulmonary veins take oxygenated blood into the left atrium.
14. Coronary sinus—termination of the great cardiac vein. It lies in the coronary sulcus and serves as a reservoir for the venous blood.
15. Posterior interventricular artery (direct continuation of the right coronary a.)—lies in the posterior interventricular sulcus.

Anatomy Plate 8   The heart.

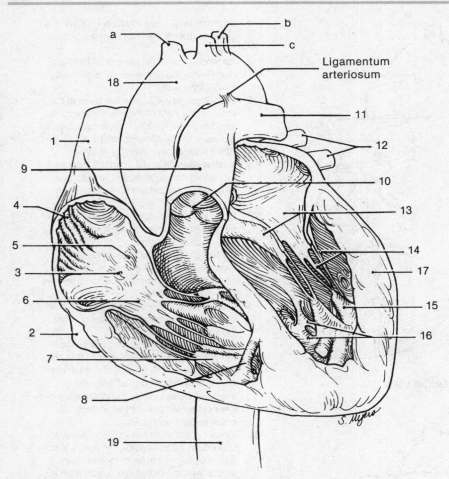

1. Superior vena cava—brings blood from the upper body.
2. Inferior vena cava—brings blood from the lower body.
3. Opening of the coronary sinus—brings blood used by the heart muscle.
4. Right atrium—pectinate muscles in its flaplike extension, the auricle. The wall of the atrium is smooth except for the ridges of muscle in the auricle.
5. Fossa ovalis—thin region of interatrial septum. Location of foramen ovale in the developing embryo.
6. Tricuspid valve. Three thin membranous flaps formed from endocardium, the lining tissue of the heart. It separates the right atrium from the right ventricle.
7. Papillary muscle—specialized trabeculae carnae, the ridges of muscle in the ventricles.
8. Moderator band—another specialization of trabeculae carnae. Only found in the right ventricle, it extends from the interventricular septum to the right ventricular wall and carries part of the conduction system of the heart.
9. Pulmonary trunk—the elastic artery through which the blood is pumped by the right ventricle.
10. Pulmonary semilunar valve—prevents backflow of blood into the right ventricle. There is also an aortic semilunar valve (not seen here) at the entrance to the aorta; it prevents backflow of blood into the left ventricle.
11. Left pulmonary artery. The pulmonary trunk bifurcates to take blood to both the right and the left lungs via the pulmonary arteries.
12. Left pulmonary veins bring the highly oxygenated blood back to the atrium. There are two on the left and two on the right.
13. Bicuspid, mitral, or left atrioventricular valve. Only two flaps separate the left atrium from the left ventricle. This valve works just like the right AV valve to prevent backflow of blood into the left atrium when the left ventricle is pumping blood through the aorta.
14. Chordae tendinae—fibrous cords that attach from the apex of papillary muscles to atrioventricular valves. (See them in the right ventricle also.) The cords are passive restraints preventing the valves from being forced back into the atria when the ventricles contract.
15. Papillary muscle
16. Trabeculae carnae—general term for ridges of muscle in both ventricles.
17. Myocardium, muscle of the heart. Note that the muscle here is three times as thick as that of the right ventricle because the blood must be pumped over such a great area and distance.
18. Arch of the aorta—branches a, b, and c.
19. Descending (thoracic) aorta. The arch takes the aorta to the posterior heart, where it descends through the thorax.

Anatomy Plate 9   The heart.

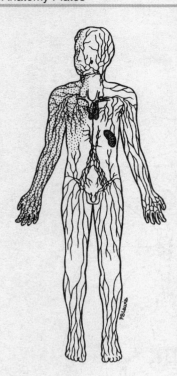

Components:

- Lymph vessels and nodes
- Spleen
- Thymus gland
- Tonsils
  (With red bone marrow, these are structures of immune system, a functional system.)

Functions:

- Returns lymph (formerly interstitial fluid) to the cardiovascular system.
- Filters blood and lymph.
- Produces white blood cells to protect the body from disease.

Anatomy Plate 10   The lymphatic system.

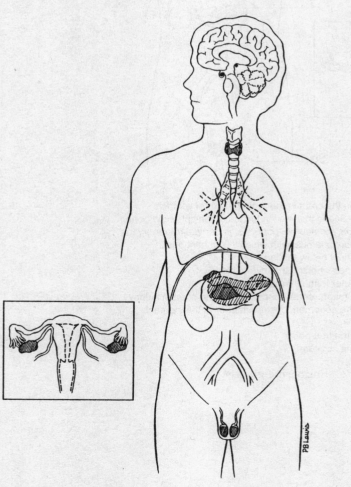

Components:

- Hormone-producing structures:
  - Pituitary, pineal, thyroid, parathyroid, and adrenal glands
  - Ovaries, testes, and pancreas

Functions:

- Communications system that uses hormones as chemical messengers.
- Helps maintain homeostasis by regulating body activities.

Anatomy Plate 11   Endocrine anatomy.

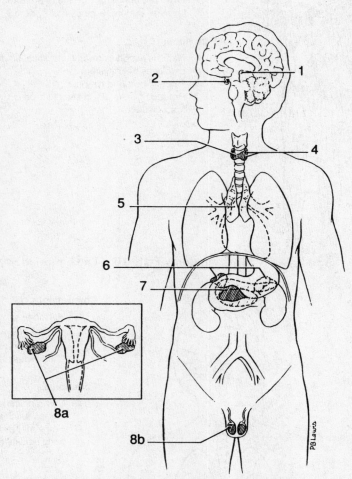

1. Pineal gland—in the brain in the roof of the third ventricle
2. Pituitary gland—found in the sella turcica of the sphenoid bone. It's posterior lobe, the neurohypophysis, is derived from nervous tissue of the hypothalamus, with which it is continuous.
3. Thyroid gland—just below the larynx.
4. Parathyroid glands—behind the thyroid gland.
5. Thymus—posterior to the sternum
6. Adrenal glands (suprarenal)—cap superior end of each kidney
7. Pancreas—in the abdomen, postero-inferior to the stomach
8. Gonads
    a. ovaries—in the true pelvis
    b. testes—in the scrotum

Anatomy Plate 12   Endocrine glands.

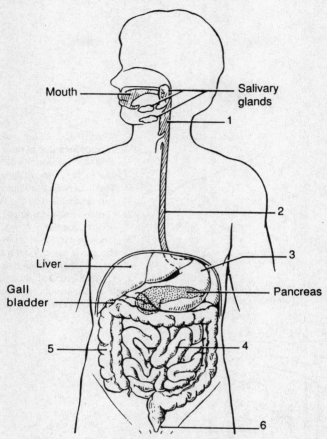

1. Pharynx—shared passageway of respiratory and digestive system.
2. Esophagus—the direct continuation of the pharynx. This muscular tube collapses unless a bolus of food is being squeezed through by peristalsis, the action of the longitudinal and circular muscles located in the wall. The esophagus passes through the thorax and pierces the diaphragm.
3. Stomach—located largely in the upper left quadrant of the abdomen. Important in storage of food (holds about 1 liter). Some chemical change occurs here. Protein digestion begins.
4. Small intestine—approx. 16 feet of convoluted tube. This is the site of most of the chemical change as well as absorption of nutrients and liquid by capillaries.

   The duodenum, about 10 in. long, is the shortest and most fixed segment. The accessory organs empty their digestive juices into this segment of the tube.

   Next is the jejunum, approximately 2/5 of the tube. The ileum, the remaining 3/5, terminates at the ileocecal junction.
5. Large intestine, or colon. Although some absorption of fluid occurs here, mostly solid waste remains in this portion of the tube.
6. Anal canal, passage for the elimination of solid waste.

   Note: The three accessory digestive organs within the abdomen, *liver, gall bladder,* and *pancreas,* can also be seen in this figure.

Anatomy Plate 13   The gastrointestinal system.

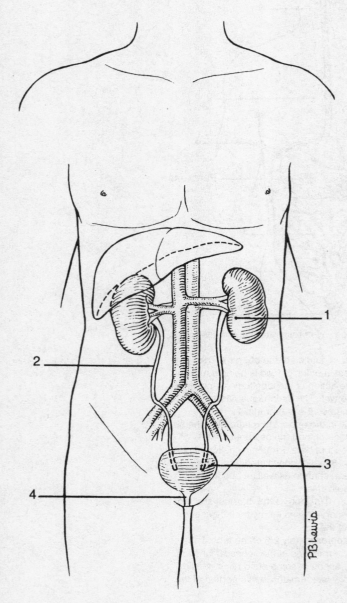

1. Kidney—paired, bean-shaped structures, reddish brown in color because of their vascularity. Located retroperitoneally between the 12th thoracic and third lumbar vertebrae, they are partially protected by ribs 11 and 12. The kidney on the right is slightly lower because of the space occupied by the liver.
2. Ureter—muscular tube (10–12 in.); propels urine to the urinary bladder.
3. Urinary bladder—a hollow muscular organ situated in the pelvis just behind the symphysis pubis. It is the storage vessel for urine before it is expelled from the body.
4. Urethra—tubular structure for the passage of urine from the bladder out of the body. Much shorter in the female than the male.

Anatomy Plate 14 The organs of the urinary system.

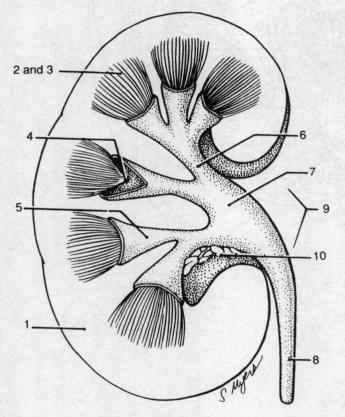

1. Renal cortex—the outer layer
2. Renal medulla—inner layer. It contains the cone-shaped renal pyramids. In this type of section they appear to be pyramids.
3. Renal pyramid—made up of many microscopic collecting ducts.
4. Renal papilla—the tip of a pyramid. Urine passes out from this site.
5. Minor calyx—funnel-shaped connective tissue structure that slips over the tip of the pyramid to receive the urine from the papilla.
6. Major calyx—2 or 3 of these are formed when minor calyces join.
7. Renal pelvis is formed when the major calyces join. Urine collects here and then passes into the ureter.
8. Ureter
9. Hilus—the entrance into the medial, concave area. The tubes carrying urine, the nerves, lymph, and blood vessels enter and leave this site.
10. Renal sinus—fat-filled space between the tissue of the kidney and the renal pelvis.

Anatomy Plate 15   Coronal section of a kidney.

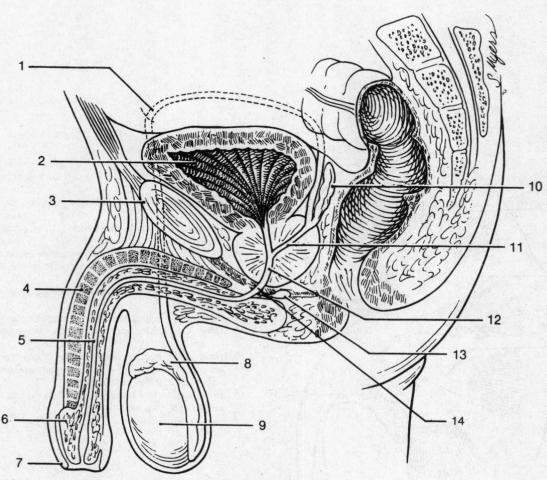

1. Ductus deferens emerging from the deep inguinal ring.
2. Urinary bladder
3. Symphysis pubis
4. Corpus cavernosum penis.
5. Penile urethra seen within corpus spongiosum penis.
6. Glans penis, expanded end of corpus spongiosum.
7. Prepuce, skin that covers glans; removed in circumcision.
8. Epididymis
9. Testis
10. Seminal vesicle
11. Ejaculatory duct
12. Prostatic urethra
13. Bulbourethral gland
14. Membranous urethra

Anatomy Plate 16   The male reproductive system.

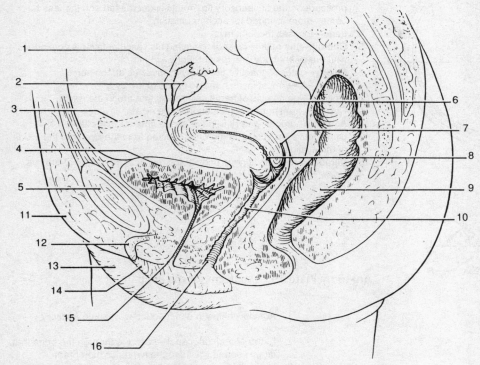

1. Ampulla of uterine tube
2. Ovary
3. Round ligament of the uterus
4. Urinary bladder
5. Symphysis pubis
6. Myometrium of body of uterus
7. Fornix
8. Cervical canal, passageway through cervix
9. Rectum
10. Vaginal canal
11. Mons pubis—mound of fat over the symphysis pubis
12. Clitoris—erectile tissue, homologue of male penis
13. Labia majora—outer, larger fold or lip. This is the direct continuation of tissue from the mons pubis and is the homologue of the scrotum in the male. In female development, the tissue separates to provide openings for both the genital and urinary structures.
14. Labia minora—smaller, inner lip. The two folds come together ventrally at the clitoris.
15. Urethral orifice—anterior opening between lips of labia minora.
16. Vaginal orifice—posterior to the urethral opening.

Anatomy Plate 17   The female reproductive system.

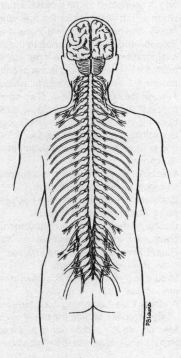

Components:

- Brain
- Spinal cord
- Nerves
- Sense organs: eyes, ears, tongue, and sensory receptors in the skin

Function:

- Communication system that detects changes in internal and external body environment and, by way of a nerve impulse, responds by producing some effect in muscle or gland.

Anatomy Plate 18   The nervous system.

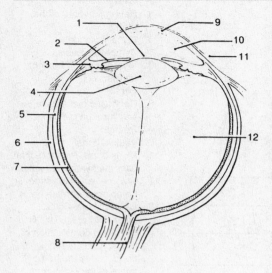

1. Pupil—opening through which light enters
2. Iris—circular, pigmented structure containing smooth muscles. It controls the size of the pupil and, therefore, the amount of light which passes through the lens.
3. Ciliary body—muscle that surrounds the lens. When it contracts, the pressure on the suspensory ligaments is decreased and the lens becomes more rounded for accommodation.
4. Lens—focuses the light rays.
5. Choroid—the middle layer of the eye. This vascular layer is continuous with the ciliary body and iris anteriorly.
6. Sclera—outer connective tissue layer; muscles attach here.
7. Retina—innermost layer, nervous tissue of the eye.
8. Optic n.—processes of nerve cell bodies that are in the retina.
9. Cornea—transparent continuation of the sclera.
10. Aqueous humor—watery filling of space anterior to the lens.
11. Conjunctiva—mucous membrane reflected from the eye onto the inside of the eyelids.
12. Vitreous body—gelatinous body helps maintain the shape of the eye.

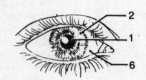

Anatomy Plate 19   Anatomy of the eyeball.

1. Auricle—helps to direct sound waves into auditory canal.
2. External auditory canal—passage through the bone that directs sound waves to the tympanic membrane.
3. Lobe
4. Tympanic membrane (ear drum)—vibrates when sound waves enter the canal. Separates external ear from middle ear.
5. Malleus—one of three small bones called *ossicles*. This one is connected to the tympanic membrane and moves when sound waves strike the membrane.
6. Incus—the ossicle attached to the malleus.
7. Stapes—the ossicle attached to the incus. It fits into the oval window leading to the inner ear. When it is set into motion it causes the fluid in the cochlea to move. The movement stimulates hair cells, which send impulses through the cochlear nerve. (Two small muscles, tensor tympani and stapedius, decrease movement of the bones to prevent damage by loud sound.)
8. Semicircular canals—a fluid-filled inner ear structure that is arranged to detect movement of the head in all directions.
9. Vestibular n.—originates in the semicircular canals and conducts stimuli for equilibrium.
10. Cochlear n.—originates in the cochlea and conducts impulses for the sense of sound.
11. Cochlea—the fluid-filled compartment housing the apparatus for sound. It is an inner ear structure.
12. Round window—membrane covered, allows fluid to move in the closed system.
13. Middle ear—an air-filled chamber in which the ossicles are located.
14. Auditory tube—a cartilaginous tube leading from the pharynx (space behind the nose) to the middle ear. It allows air into the middle ear to equalize internal and external pressure across the tympanic membrane.

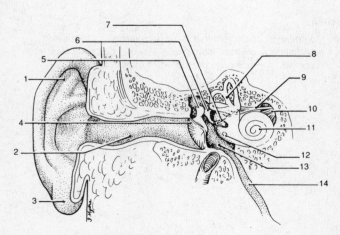

Anatomy Plate 20   Anatomy of the ear.

Exercise Answer Key

Chapter 1   Introduction to Coding

Exercise 1.1

1. Bundling: Individual procedures that are considered part of a larger operation, and are grouped together, or "bundled."
2. False claim: knowingly presenting a false or fraudulent claim to the federal government for payment, or presenting false records or statements in order to get a claim paid.
3. CCI edit: Series of code sets in which one code is excluded from use because of its direct correlation to the other.
4. Medical necessity: Medical necessity is analogous with ICD-9-CM diagnostic coding.
5. Clean claim: A complete, correct health insurance claim that passes through age, sex, diagnosis to procedure and other edits set up by third party payers, Medicare and Medicaid.

Exercise 1.2

1. Abuse
2. Fraud
3. Fraud
4. Abuse
5. Fraud

Chapter 2   Introduction to ICD-9-CM Coding

Exercise 2.1

1. False
2. False
3. True
4. False
5. True
6. True
7. False
8. True
9. True
10. True

Exercise 2.2
1. Benign
2. Unspecified
3. Primary
4. Poisoning
5. Accident
6. Benign
7. Assault

Exercise 2.3
1. Pericarditis
2. Sprain
3. Disorder
4. Varicose
5. Ulcer
6. Cellulitis
7. Disease
8. Pain
9. Cholecystitis
10. Headache
11. Paget's disease
12. Meningitis infection
13. Hodgkin's lymphosarcoma
14. Incarcerated hernia

Exercise 2.4
Part I
1. V72.31
2. V05.4, V05.3
3. V54.13
4. V25.41
5. V14.0
6. V30.01
7. V58.1
8. V67.00
9. V76.12
10. V64.1
11. V72.41
12. V20.2
13. V10.3
14. V71.5
15. V77.1, V81.1

Part II
1. E880.9
2. E898.1
3. E905.3
4. E918
5. E920.8, E917.4
6. E923.0
7. E911
8. E930.0
9. E960.0, E968.7
10. E952.0
11. E828.2

12. E820.0
13. E816.1
14. E831.1
15. E849.6

Exercise 2.5

1. 782.5, 786.05
2. 786.52
3. 789.07
4. 791.6, 791.0
5. 796.2
6. 793.80
7. 787.01
8. 788.33
9. 780.2
10. 783.41

Exercise 2.6

1. 438.11
2. 906.7
3. 751.3
4. 907.4
5. 749.03
6. 745.10
7. 753.13
8. 138

Exercise 2.7

1. 303.00
2. 300.00
3. 296.80
4. 295.35
5. 305.22
6. 309.0
7. 314.01
8. 315.02
9. 305.01
10. 313.81
11. 290.21
12. 300.3
13. 291.0
14. 333.4, 294.10
15. 301.50

Exercise 2.8

1. 008.8
2. 041.86
3. 003.9
4. 038.11
5. V08
6. 599.0, 041.7
7. 022.1
8. 042, 782.1
9. 482.0
10. 078.19

11. 079.6
12. 099.41
13. 110.4
14. 133.0
15. 112.0

Exercise 2.9

1. 813.05
2. 873.52
3. 883.0
4. 864.01
5. 845.00
6. 959.01
7. 913.5
8. 850.11
9. 836.0
10. 806.15
11. 927.20, 955.6
12. 891.0

Exercise 2.10

Part I
1. Poisoning
2. Adverse effect
3. Poisoning
4. Adverse effect
5. Poisoning

Part II
1. 988.1, 787.01, E865.5
2. 276.8, E944.2
3. 785.1, E858.1
4. 984.1, E861.5
5. 983.2, 947.2, E980.6

Exercise 2.11

1. 239.4
2. 185
3. 162.5
4. 216.4
5. 174.8
6. 233.1
7. 170.7
8. 172.2
9. 204.00
10. 199.0
11. 201.90
12. 202.80, 198.81
13. 198.5, 199.0
14. 236.0
15. 197.7, 162.9

Chapter 3   Introduction to CPT® and HCPCS Coding

Exercise 3.1

1. ICD-9-CM
2. CPT®

3. CPT®
4. CPT®
5. ICD-9-CM
6. ICD-9-CM
7. CPT®
8. ICD-9-CM
9. ICD-9-CM
10. CPT®

Exercise 3.2

Part I

1. Add-on code for mesh, used for ventral/incisional hernia repairs
2. Modifier-51 exempt

Part II

1. True
2. True
3. False
4. False

Exercise 3.3

1. 44140
2. 73000
3. 00851
4. 27524
5. 17110-17111
6. 45387
7. 47480
8. 46083
9. 43243
10. 24160
11. 65410
12. 46706
13. 49250
14. 28292
15. 44316
16. 30210
17. 54650
18. 83615-83625
19. 57460
20. 15829

Exercise 3.4

Part I

1. HCPCS
2. HCPCS
3. CPT®
4. HCPCS
5. HCPCS
6. CPT®
7. CPT®
8. HCPCS

Part II

1. QZ
2. FA
3. QB

4. SL
5. QW
6. GA
7. H9
8. GE

Exercise 3.5

1. G0101, Q0091
2. J1642
3. A4245 x 2
4. S9441
5. D1120
6. E0110
7. G0168
8. J1030
9. L0210
10. L8030
11. P9019 x 10
12. Q0136 x 8
13. Q4055
14. S4995
15. T1021

Chapter 4   Evaluation and Management Services

Exercise 4.1

1. Outpatient Consult
2. Office/Other Outpatient Visit, New Patient
3. Follow-up Inpatient Consult
4. Critical Care
5. Newborn Care—Other Than Hospital
6. Domiciliary, Rest Home, or Custodial Care
7. Basic Life/Disability Evaluation
8. Office/Other Outpatient Visit

Exercise 4.2

1. 99242
2. 99232
3. 99344

Exercise 4.3

1. Established Patient Office Visit
2. Observation Services
3. Established Patient Office Visit
4. New Patient Office Visit

Exercise 4.4

1. Subsequent Hospital Care
2. Outpatient Consultation
3. Initial Inpatient/Hospital Discharge Services
4. Observation or Inpatient Care Services (Including Admission and Discharge Services)
5. Observation Services
6. Initial Observation (day 1); Unlisted E/M Service **OR** Outpatient visit (day 2); Observation Discharge (day 3) **Note:** Day 2 is dependent upon payer preference.
7. Outpatient Consultation

8. Confirmatory Consultation
9. Initial Inpatient Consultation (day 1); Follow-up Inpatient Consultation (day 2)
10. Outpatient Consultation (first visit); Established Office Visit (second visit)

Exercise 4.5

1. V77.1
2. V72.31
3. V77.0
4. V20.2 and V78.0
5. V76.51
6. V76.12
7. V82.5
8. V70.0, V74.1
9. V70.0, 380.4
10. V72.31, 401.9

Exercise 4.6

1. V72.31, 99396; 462, 780.6, 99212-25
2. V70.5, 99385
3. 486, V64.0, 99213
4. V70.0, V77.91, V76.44, 99387
5. V65.42, V25.09, 99402
6. V62.82, 99213
7. V76.2, G0101, Q0091

Exercise 4.7

1. 99201
2. 99213
3. 99244
4. 99231
5. 99285
6. 99301

Chapter 5   Anesthesia

Exercise 5.1

1. Regional—epidural
2. Regional—IV
3. Local
4. Regional—IV
5. Regional Spinal
6. General

Exercise 5.2

1. 0730-0847
2. Laparoscopic cholecystectomy
3. 0747-0833
4. General—IV

Exercise 5.3

1. QX, P6
2. P1
3. 23, P1
4. P2

5. QZ, 99140
6. QS
7. AA
8. QZ, 99116

Chapter 6   Overview: The Surgery Section of CPT®

Exercise 6.1

1. a. 25
   b. 21
   c. 24
   d. 57
2. a. 51
   b. 54
   c. 50
   d. 52
   e. 32
   f. 59
   g. 63
   h. 56
   i. 91
   j. 22
   k. 53
   l. 55
   m. 23
3. a. 76
   b. 58
   c. 78
   d. 77
   e. 79
4. a. 80
   b. 47
   c. 81
   d. 62
   e. 82
   f. 26
   g. 90
   h. 66

Chapter 7   The Integumentary System

Exercise 7.1

1. Tinea pedis
2. Alopecia
3. Decubitus ulcer
4. Carbuncle
5. Ecchymosis
6. Urticaria
7. Nevus
8. Abscess
9. Cicatrix
10. Verruca

11. Sebaceous cyst
12. Acrochordon

Exercise 7.2

1. 172.2
2. 198.2, 199.1
3. 702.0
4. 176.0
5. 216.4
6. 214.1
7. 692.75
8. 702.19
9. 701.9
10. 228.01

Exercise 7.3

1. 703.8, 110.1
2. 256.4, 704.1
3. 873.52, E816.1
4. 882.0, 881.00, E920.8, E917.4
5. 920, 922.31, 923.09, E968.2
6. 881.02, E956
7. 692.76, E926.2
8. 916.1, 692.6, E920.8
9. 991.0, E901.0
10. 912.5, E906.4
11. 782.3

Exercise 7.4

1. 692.71, E926.2
2. 692.9
3. 682.9
4. 695.1
5. 690.11
6. 708.4
7. 707.14
8. 706.1
9. 172.2
10. 698.9, 704.8
11. 945.22, 948.00, E924.0

Exercise 7.5

1. Rosacea
2. Keloid
3. Bulla
4. Impetigo
5. Paronychia
6. Pemphigus
7. Actinic keratoses

Exercise 7.6

1. 10121
2. 11000
3. 11100

 4. 11056
 5. 10061

Exercise 7.7

 1. 11310
 2. 11200
 3. 11621

Exercise 7.8

 1. f
 2. c
 3. j
 4. h
 5. a
 6. e
 7. i
 8. d
 9. b
 10. g

Chapter 8   The Musculoskeletal System

Exercise 8.1

 1. Kyphosis
 2. Genu valgum
 3. Lordosis
 4. Hallux malleus
 5. Pes planus
 6. Scoliosis
 7. Fracture

Exercise 8.2

 1. 717.7
 2. 714.9
 3. 719.46
 4. 841.2
 5. 719.7
 6. 723.5
 7. 724.1
 8. 727.1
 9. 728.85
 10. 733.42
 11. 781.5
 12. 781.3
 13. 755.01
 14. 754.0
 15. 756.2

Exercise 8.3

 1. 850.11, E885.2
 2. 848.41, E927
 3. 800.01, E828.9
 4. 836.0, E917.5, E849.4
 5. 802.7, E960.0

6. 832.00, E884.0, E849.6
7. 808.49, E828.2
8. 821.01, E814.7

Exercise 8.4

Part I
1. Arthritis
2. Osteomyelitis
3. Tear
4. Degeneration
5. None—see Admission for aftercare, or Aftercare
6. Dislocation
7. Follow-up
8. Disease
9. Pain or Follow-up
10. Lupus

Part II
1. 714.0
2. 730.07
3. 840.4, E927, E849.4
4. V54.16
5. 715.96
6. 837.0, E880.9
7. V54.27
8. 732.4
9. 719.45, V54.81, V43.64
10. 710.0

Exercise 8.5

1. 214.8
2. 170.7
3. 198.5, 199.1
4. 171.2, 198.5
5. 172.9, 198.89

Exercise 8.6

1. b
2. e
3. g
4. a
5. f
6. h
7. d
8. j
9. i
10. c

Exercise 8.7

1. 29240; Supply: figure-8 strap
2. 29515-RT, Supply: plaster cast material
3. 25600-LT
4. 26608-RT, 26608-51-59-RT
5. 27758

Exercise 8.8

1. 29827
2. 29888
3. 29821, 23105
4. 29880
5. 29830

Exercise 8.9

1. a. 99244-57
   b. 27507-LT
2. a. 99214-25
   b. 20610-50
   c. 29540-51, RT

Chapter 9   The Respiratory System

Exercise 9.1

1. Pharyngitis
2. Nasopharyngitis or rhinitis
3. Allergic rhinitis
4. Tuberculosis
5. Coal worker's pneumoconiosis
6. Influenza (respiratory type)

Exercise 9.2

1. 780.51
2. 769
3. 987.9
4. 786.05
5. 861.22, 807.00
6. 786.2
7. 934.0
8. 466.19
9. 495.0
10. 487.1
11. 478.74
12. 519.02

Exercise 9.3

1. 462
2. V74.1
3. 034.0
4. 474.02, 474.11
5. 491.9
6. 491.21
7. 512.8
8. 507.0
9. 470
10. 518.82
11. 477.0
12. 465.9
13. 482.1
14. 011.90
15. 112.4

16. 493.20
17. 496
18. 508.0
19. 795.5
20. 277.02

Exercise 9.4

1. 197.0
2. 162.3
3. 160.3, 196.1
4. 212.1
5. 162.3, 198.3
6. 508.0, E879.2
7. V58.0, 198.5
8. 160.2

Exercise 9.5

1. 30905
2. 30124
3. 30110
4. 30300
5. 30465
6. 30120
7. 30000

Exercise 9.6

1. 31205
2. 31254
3. 31239

Exercise 9.7

1. 31400
2. 31515
3. Day 1—31528; Day 2—31529
   Critical Thinking Skills—No modifiers are needed because there are no global days associated with endoscopy.

Exercise 9.8

1. 31601
2. 31631
3. 31603
4. 31612

Exercise 9.9

1. 32201
2. 32484
3. 32420

Exercise 9.10

1. 32654
2. 32659

Exercise 9.11

1. 31000-50
2. 31625-LT, 31623-51-59-LT

Chapter 10   The Cardiovascular System

Exercise 10.1

1. Chest pain with EKG
2. Cardiac arrest with cardiopulmonary resuscitation
3. Atrial fibrillation with elective cardioversion
4. Hypoxia with arterial blood draw
5. Bleeding esophageal varices with blood transfusion

Exercise 10.2

1. 403.00
2. 401.1
3. 401.9, 429.9
4. 403.90
5. 404.91, 428.0
6. True

Exercise 10.3

1. 412
2. 410.01
3. 410.92
4. 411.89
5. 411.1

Exercise 10.4

1. V58.83, V58.61
2. V45.81
3. V45.01
4. V53.31
5. V58.73, V43.3
6. V81.1
7. V45.82
8. V42.1
9. V12.52
10. V17.3

Exercise 10.5

1. 33020
2. 33208
3. 33224

Exercise 10.6

1. 33403 and 33530
2. 33420 and 33471-51

Exercise 10.7

1. 33512
2. 33533 and 33521

Exercise 10.8

1. 33877

Exercise 10.9

1. 34111
2. 34421

Exercise 10.10

1. 34800, 34820-51 and 75952-26
2. 35082
3. 35141

Exercise 10.11

1. 35236
2. 35456-RT

Exercise 10.12

1. 36557
2. 36600
3. 36821
4. 36831

Chapter 11   Hemic and Lymphatic Systems, Mediastinum and Diaphragm, and Endocrine System

Exercise 11.1

1. 282.5
2. 285.1
3. 281.0
4. 289.7
5. 288.3
6. V18.2
7. 287.3
8. V78.0
9. 286.0
10. 284.9
11. V70.8
12. 285.22
13. 289.0
14. 283.2
15. 289.1

Exercise 11.2

1. 229.0
2. 206.10
3. 201.95
4. V10.62
5. 196.0
6. 204.01
7. 238.4
8. 203.00
9. 996.85
10. V83.02

Exercise 11.3

1. 241.9
2. 250.40, 581.81
3. 245.2
4. 278.01
5. 251.2
6. 276.8
7. 255.0

  8. 274.9
  9. 276.6
 10. 272.4
 11. 251.0
 12. 252.0
 13. 250.30
 14. 250.01
 15. 250.82

Exercise 11.4

  1. 227.3
  2. 211.7
  3. 194.0, 199.1
  4. V58.1, 183.0
  5. 193
  6. 874.2, E966
  7. 164.8
  8. V77.3
  9. 157.9, 186.1
 10. V77.91
 11. V42.83
 12. V45.85

Exercise 11.5

  1. 38525

Exercise 11.6

  1. 39503
  2. 39530

Exercise 11.7

  1. Procedure 1: 60100
     Procedure 2: 60252-58
     Modifier 58 signifies a staged or planned procedure. When the biopsy result was positive for malignancy, the thyroidectomy was performed based on these results.

Exercise 11.8

  1. 60500, 60512
  2. 60521
  3. 60640
  4. 60650
  5. 60600

Chapter 12   The Digestive System

Exercise 12.1

  1. 564.2
  2. 558.1
  3. 550.01
  4. 531.20
  5. 003.0
  6. 070.44
  7. 574.00, 574.10
  8. 121.3
  9. 577.2
 10. 571.1

Exercise 12.2

1. 153.8
2. 197.7 and 199.1
3. 211.4
4. 230.0
5. 235.3

Exercise 12.3

1. V01.7, V15.85, E920.5
2. V16.0, V76.51
3. V55.1

Exercise 12.4

1. 40654
2. T
3. 40702 and 40720-58
4. 40814

Exercise 12.5

1. 41008
2. 41100
3. 41850

Exercise 12.6

1. 42140
2. 42200

Exercise 12.7

1. 42330

Exercise 12.8

1. 42700
2. 42825
3. 1—42821, 2—42962-78

Exercise 12.9

1. 43100
2. 43112

Exercise 12.10

1. 43330
2. 43415
3. 43453

Exercise 12.11

1. 43610
2. 43621
3. 43750

Exercise 12.12

1. 43830
2. 43846

Exercise 12.13

1. 44050
2. 44130
3. 44160

Exercise 12.14

1. 44346-78
2. 44605
3. 44620
4. 44660

Exercise 12.15

1. 44950
2. 45005
3. 45110
4. 45116
5. 45120
6. 45130

Exercise 12.16

1. 43262
2. 43265
3. 44378
4. 45330
5. 45340
6. 45378-52
7. 45382
8. 46612 and 46604-51, 59

Exercise 12.17

1. 49322
2. 49650-50
3. 44204
4. 44970

Chapter 13   The Urinary System

Exercise 13.1

1. V10.51, V44.6
2. V13.01
3. V42.0
4. V53.6
5. V10.47
6. V55.5
7. V45.73
8. V58.76, V10.46
9. V59.4
10. V18.61

Exercise 13.2

1. 189.0, 196.2
2. 188.0
3. 198.0, 199.1
4. 198.5, 188.9
5. 223.0
6. 236.7

Exercise 13.3

1. 788.37
2. 867.0
3. 592.1

4. 598.9
5. 593.9
6. 185
7. 592.0
8. 593.2
9. 599.2
10. 600.00

Exercise 13.4

1. 52281-53
2. 99212-25, 51705
3. 52290 (no modifier—states already bilateral)
4. 50780-50
5. 92255-57

Chapter 14   The Male Reproductive System

Exercise 14.1

1. 198.5, 199.1, V10.47
2. 187.4
3. 186.9, 197.0
4. 222.3
5. 236.6

Exercise 14.2

1. 607.1
2. 112.2
3. 099.41
4. 110.3
5. 098.12
6. 131.02
7. 054.13
8. V01.6
9. 132.2
10. 608.4
11. 998.59

Exercise 14.3

1. 959.14, E960.0
2. 926.0, 928.01, E919.7
3. 878.1, 878.3, E922.1
4. 922.4, E844.0

Exercise 14.4

1. V10.47
2. V13.61
3. V25.2
4. V26.22
5. V26.52
6. V41.7
7. V47.5
8. V50.2
9. V58.76
10. V65.45
11. V69.2
12. V76.44

Exercise 14.5

1. 54056
2. 54150
3. 54250
4. 54336
5. 54340-78

Exercise 14.6

1. 54520

   Since the biopsy is taken in the same session as the full removal of the testicle, it is not reported in addition to the definitive surgery.
2. 54670

Exercise 14.7

1. 54901, 69990
2. 55000
3. 55150
4. 55250
5. 49520 and 55520-51

   At the time of this printing, these procedures are not bundled according to CCI edits.
6. 55680

Chapter 15   The Female Reproductive System

Exercise 15.1

1. 218.9
2. 616.2
3. 795.00
4. 626.2
5. 182.0
6. 628.2
7. 618.3
8. V25.1

Exercise 15.2

1. 236.1
2. V58.1, 179, 198.5
3. 220
4. 198.81, 183.0
5. 233.1

Exercise 15.3

1. V72.31
2. V13.29
3. V45.77
4. V10.41
5. V74.5
6. V26.21
7. V72.41
8. V25.41
9. V25.2
10. V65.45
11. V69.2
12. V58.76, V58.3
13. V45.52

14. V49.81
15. V25.49

Exercise 15.4

1. 57454
2. 56440
3. 56515, 57061-51
4. 57287
5. 57022

Exercise 15.5

1. 58300, J7302
2. 58100
3. 58563
4. 58920
5. 58720

Chapter 16   Maternity and Delivery

Exercise 16.1

1. V28.0
2. 656.30
3. 660.41
4. 654.21
5. 632
6. 633.10
7. V24.2
8. 666.22

Exercise 16.2

1. 646.63, 599.0
2. 674.14
3. 656.53
4. 648.81, 648.11, 244.9
5. 666.02
6. 645.11
7. 646.83
8. 644.21
9. 675.24
10. 650
11. 634.01
12. 653.43
13. 654.21
14. 633.10
15. 651.01, 656.31

Exercise 16.3

1. V23.49
2. V22.0
3. V28.4
4. V23.83
5. V23.2
6. V24.2
7. 462, V22.2
8. V23.3, V23.7

9. V28.6
10. V23.5, V28.0

Exercise 16.4

1. 59001
2. 59015
3. 59025

Exercise 16.5

1. 59100
2. 59140
3. 59160

Exercise 16.6

1. 59320

Exercise 16.7

1. 59425 for Doctor A
   59426 for Doctor B
   59410 for Doctor B
2. 59414
3. 59412
4. 59426, 59430
5. 59400
6. 59400-22 **OR** 59400 and 59409-52,59, 59409-52,59.

Exercise 16.8

1. For the primary care physician:
   59510-22 or 59510, 59514-52,59
   For the assistant at surgery:
   59514-22,80 or 59514-80, 59514-80,52,59
2. For the family care physician:
   59426
   59514-80
   59430
   For the obstetrician:
   59514
3. For the OB care:
   59510
   For the hospital stay during the pregnancy:
   99222
   99231 x 2
   99238
   For the extra office visits above and beyond the average antepartum with
   supporting documentation:
   99212 x 7

Exercise 16.9

1. 59610
2. 59618

Exercise 16.10

1. 59820
2. 59841
3. 59855

Chapter 17   The Nervous System

Exercise 17.1

1. 332.0
2. 355.5
3. 780.39
4. 952.01
5. 340
6. 852.29
7. 250.60, 337.1
8. 850.11
9. 345.10
10. 920
11. 438.11
12. 358.00
13. 351.0
14. 741.90
15. 346.00
16. 066.41

Exercise 17.2

1. V03.81
2. V10.86
3. V12.49
4. V15.5
5. V17.2
6. V23.89
7. V29.1
8. V45.2
9. V53.02
10. V57.3
11. V73.5
12. V80.0

Exercise 17.3

1. 324.0
2. 851.10
3. 780.31
4. 724.00
5. 724.2
6. 354.0
7. 349.0
8. 800.00
9. 191.2
10. 742.3

Exercise 17.4

1. 64620-50
2. 63300-62, 63308
3. 63300-62, 22554-51, 22585
4. Modifier 51
5. 99284-25, 62270

Chapter 18   Eye and Ear

Exercise 18.1

1. 374.0
2. 377.00
3. 365.00
4. 367.4
5. 369.3
6. 771.6
7. 372.51
8. 367.20
9. 365.11
10. 361.05

Exercise 18.2

1. 366.16
2. 362.50
3. 360.02
4. 360.65
5. 363.31
6. 366.10
7. 368.40
8. 362.74
9. 375.15
10. 378.9
11. 379.50
12. 379.93
13. 373.01
14. 373.11

Exercise 18.3

1. 190.5
2. 224.1
3. 198.4, 162.9
4. 921.3, E917.0
5. 950.0, E819.9
6. 871.4, E923.9

Exercise 18.4

1. e
2. a
3. f
4. g
5. c
6. b
7. d

Exercise 18.5

1. 386.04
2. 381.81
3. 380.16
4. 381.10
5. 383.33
6. 385.00
7. 381.04

8. 388.30
9. 388.60
10. 384.01
11. 381.20
12. 382.9
13. 387.2
14. 388.5
15. 389.10

Exercise 18.6

1. V19.2
2. 872.01, E906.0
3. 160.1
4. 215.0
5. 872.61, E920.8
6. 198.2

Exercise 18.7

1. 65101
2. 65130-58. Modifier 58 is used because the second procedure is in the global of the first and it has been planned or staged. Modifier 78 is also acceptable.
3. 65105
4. 65222
5. 65260
6. 65280
7. 65286

Exercise 18.8

1. 65400
2. 65450
3. 65730
4. 65771

Exercise 18.9

1. 65855
2. 65865

Exercise 18.10

1. 66170
2. 66225

Exercise 18.11

1. 66505
2. 66625-LT
3. 66720

Exercise 18.12

1. 66984-RT
2. 66984-LT,79
3. 66821-LT,78
4. 66825-RT
5. 66982-RT

Exercise 18.13

1. 67010-LT
2. 67031-50

3. 67108-RT
4. 67220-LT

Exercise 18.14

1. 67312-LT
2. 67312-LT and 67332
3. 67345-RT
4. 67420-RT

Exercise 18.15

1. 67800-E1
2. 67825-RT
3. 67923-50
4. 67935-LT
5. 67971-LT

Exercise 18.16

1. 68020-RT
2. 68115-LT
3. 68335-RT
4. 68530-LT
5. 68761-E2
   68761-E3-51, 59. Modifier 59 may not be needed in addition to Modifier E3 for all insurance companies. These procedures may also be reported as:
   68761 and 68661-51,59 for insurance companies who do not recognize HCPCS modifiers. However, this method of reporting does not specify which eyelids are being treated.
6. 68815-RT

Exercise 18.17

1. 69155-LT
2. 69200-LT
3. 69210
4. 69320-50

Exercise 18.18

1. 69405-RT
2. 69436-50
3. 69505-50
4. 69220-50
5. 69644-LT

Exercise 18.19

1. 69905-RT

Chapter 19   Radiology Services

Exercise 19.1

1. 473.9, 70210
2. 473.9, 70460
3. 802.0, E960.0, 70160-52. Because only two views were taken and the nasal bone x-ray codes specifies a minimum of three views, Modifier 52 is used to signify that fewer than three views were taken.

Exercise 19.2

1. V70.5, 71010
2. 786.6, 71021

3. 807.03, 860.0, E906.8, 71101-RT
4. 785.6, 71551

Exercise 19.3

1. 793.7, E813.0, 72052
2. **Orthopedic surgeon:**
   805.05, E813.0, 72130-TC
   Radiologist:
   805.05, E813.0, 72130-26
3. 839.41, E885.9, 72220

Exercise 19.4

1. 923.11, E885.1, 73080-RT
   923.21, E885.1, 73110-RT
2. 905.8, 73222-LT

Exercise 19.5

1. 820.8, E888.9, E849.0, 73510-LT, 72170
   The pelvis x-ray can be billed for as well as the unilateral hip code because there is no code specifying both.
2. 729.5, 73650-RT
3. 719.46, 905.4, 73723-LT

Exercise 19.6

1. 560.9, 74020
2. 560.9, 74175

Exercise 19.7

1. 787.2, 74230. Since nothing new was revealed with the study, the signs and/or symptoms would be reported.
2. V76.51, 74270
3. 574.00, 74300-26, 74301-26
4. 263.9, 787.2, 74350-26

Exercise 19.8

1. 599.0, 041.4, 74400
2. 608.85, 74440

Exercise 19.9

1. Radiologist: 628.2, 74740-TC
   OB/GYN: 628.2, 74740-26

Exercise 19.10

1. 433.10 and 36216-RT, Initial second order thoracic catheterization
   75650-RT, Angiography, cervicocerebral
   75676-RT, Angiography, unilateral cervical carotid
   75665-RT, Angiography, unilateral cerebral carotid
   75685-RT, Angiography, vertebral, cervical and/or intracranial
2. 996.73, 36595, 75901
3. 440.1, 37205, 36245-51, 75960-26, 75722-26
4. 719.05, 20610-LT, 76003-26
5. 070.54, 37200, 36011-51, 75970, 76942

Exercise 19.11

1. 366.16, 76516-LT
2. 366.16, 76516-LT, 26

   3. 611.72, 76645
   4. V42.0, 76778

Exercise 19.12

   1. 651.03, 76801, 76802
   2. 651.03, V28.3, 76811, 76812
   3. 651.03, 76815
   4. 645.13, 651.03, 76818-26

Exercise 19.13

   1. 620.2, 76856
   2. 600.00, 76872
   3. 611.72, 19290, 76942
   4. V23.81, V28.2, 59000, 76946

Exercise 19.14

   1. 77262 and 77285
   2. 77327 and 77777
   3. 77427-2 units or x2
   4. 77315 and 77413

Chapter 20   Pathology and Laboratory Services

Exercise 20.1

   1. Modifier 91
   2. CLIA or Clinical Laboratory Improvement Act
   3. Stark I and II
   4. CLIA or Clinical Laboratory Improvement Act

Exercise 20.2

   1. 401.9, 36415 and 80051
   2. V70.x, 36415, 82310, 82435, 82565, 82947, 84132, 84295, and 84520
   3. V72.6, 80101-32x5. Modifier 32 may be used since this is requested by the patient's employer.
   4. 80102
   5. 36415, 36415-59, 80200 and 80200-59 and/or 91
   6. 783.43, 80428
   7. 599.0, 81001

Exercise 20.3

   1. 85025 or 85027 and 85004, 85007, or 85009
   2. 85014 and 85018
   3. 656.02, 85460, 85461
   4. 85002, 85049, 85610, and 85730
   5. V58.61
   6. 714.0, 85652

Exercise 20.4

   1. 719.40, 86038
   2. 272.4, 86140
   3. 283.0, 86156, 86157
   4. 099.41, 86631
   5. 795.71, 86703

Exercise 20.5

   1. V72.83, 86850, 86900 and 86901
   2. 280.0, 585, 86850, 86900, 86901, 86920 x2, 86921x2, and 86922x2

Exercise 20.6

1. 599.0, 041.4, 87086, 87088, and 87181
2. 011.94, 87116
3. 007.1, 87045, 87075, 87207, and 87177
4. 079.6, 87420
5. 098.0, 87490, and 87590

Exercise 20.7

1. 622.1, 88175 and 88141
2. V76.2, 88150

Exercise 20.8

1. 701.9, 88304
2. Dermatologist: 173.6, 11100 and 88305-26
   Pathologist: 173.6, 88305-TC
3. 174.9, 88307, 88331, and 88314
4. 185, 88305
5. 88307

Exercise 20.9

1. 89050, 89051, and 89060

Chapter 21   Medicine

Exercise 21.1

1. V04.81, 90660
2. V04.82, 90378
3. V06.4, 90716
4. V04.0, 90713
5. V06.5, 90707
6. V03.0, 90725
7. V05.3, 90744
8. V03.89, 90581
9. V05.9, 90281
10. V03.82, 90732

Exercise 21.2

1. 789.00, 90780, 90781, 90784 x 2, J2550 x 1, J2175 x 1, J7030 x 2
2. 486, 90788, J0696 x 8
3. 995.3, 90782 x 2, J2930, J1200
4. 724.2, 90782, J2175 x 1, J2550 x 2

Exercise 21.3

1. V79.3
2. 311, V62.0
3. V79.0
4. V11.8
5. 314.01, V65.49. Codes V40.3, V40.0 may be assigned also.
6. V71.5, 317

Exercise 21.4

1. 90806, 90880
2. 90802
3. 99231, 90885
4. 90862

Exercise 21.5

1. V56.32
2. V56.1
3. 585
4. V56.0
5. 996.73
6. 996.57

Exercise 21.6

1. V72.0
2. 367.20
3. 250.50, 366.41
4. V52.2
5. V45.61, V43.1
6. 367.1, 375.15
7. V53.1
8. V42.5
9. 368.42
10. 365.00

Exercise 21.7

1. 92004
2. 92012
3. 99245-57
4. Day 1—92014; Day 2—No charge

Exercise 21.8

1. 92315-RT
2. 92325
3. 92392
4. Physician—92330-26; Lab—92393

Exercise 21.9

1. 381.4
2. 386.00
3. V72.1
4. 383.32
5. 381.81
6. 389.10
7. 388.01
8. 380.23
9. V19.2
10. V80.3
11. 872.61, E920.8
12. 474.02

Exercise 21.10

1. 92553
2. 92510
3. 92533-52
4. 92567, 92568
5. 92607, 92608 x 1
6. 92611
7. 92593

Exercise 21.11

1. 441.02
2. 435.2
3. 429.82
4. 420.91
5. 394.2
6. 428.1
7. 402.90
8. 996.02
9. 996.61
10. 996.72

Exercise 21.12

1. C
2. D
3. A

Exercise 21.13

1. B
2. C

Exercise 21.14

1. 493.81
2. 861.32, E966
3. V70.5, V81.4
4. 480.3
5. 518.82
6. 987.9, E890.2
7. 464.00
8. 493.92
9. 507.0
10. 487.1

Exercise 21.15

1. A. Descriptor states before AND after bronchodilator.
2. D

Exercise 21.16

1. D

Exercise 21.17

1. B

Exercise 21.18

1. V52.1, V49.75
2. V57.1, V43.65, V58.78
3. V57.21, 907.0

Exercise 21.19

1. 97001, 97110 x 2, 97140 x 1
2. 97532 x 4
3. 97113 x 2

Chapter Review Answer Key

Chapter 1: Introduction to Coding

1. c
2. e
3. b
4. c
5. b
6. d
7. b
8. d

Chapter 2: Introduction to ICD-9-CM Coding

1. a
2. a
3. e
4. c
5. d

Critical Thinking Skills

  b

Chapter 3: Introduction to CPT® and HCPCS Coding

1. d
2. a
3. b
4. a
5. c

Chapter 4: Evaluation and Management Services

1. Office Visit—New Patient
   Expanded Problem Focused History
   Problem Focused Physical Exam
   Low Complexity Medical Decision Making
   CPT® Code 99201
2. Office Visit—Established Patient
   Expanded Problem Focused History
   Expanded Problem Focused Physical Exam
   Moderate Complexity Medical Decision Making
   CPT® Code 99213

3. Emergency Department Visit
   Detailed History
   Detailed Physical Exam
   Low Complexity Medical Decision Making
   CPT® Code 99283
4. Critical Care
   History—N/A
   Physical Exam—N/A
   Medical Decision Making—N/A
   CPT® Code 99291
5. Office/Outpatient Consult
   Detailed History
   Detailed Physical Exam
   Low Complexity Medical Decision Making
   CPT® Code 99243
6. 3
7. G codes
8. c
9. c
10. Place of Service
11. False

Chapter 5: Anesthesia

Part I
   a. 47562, laparoscopic cholecystectomy
   b. 00790
   c. 7 units base
   d. time—77 minutes
   e. 5 units time
   f. P2-0 units
   g. None
   h. None
   i. QZ

Part II
   1. $240.00
   2. 574.10

True/False
   1. False
   2. True
   3. False

Multiple Choice
   1. b
   2. d

Chapter 6: Overview: The Surgery Section of CPT®

1. False
2. Diagnostic
3. The process of including smaller components of a surgical procedure under one code.
4. True (with Modifier 59)
5. True
6. Add-on and Modifier 51 exempt
7. Add-on
8. True

Chapter 7: The Integumentary System

1. c
2. a
3. a
4. c
5. False
6. c
7. True
8. True
9. c
10. d
11. b
12. False
13. b

Case Study

1. 702.0, 17000, 17003 x 3

Chapter 8: The Musculoskeletal System

1. c
2. d
3. b
4. a
5. b
6. d
7. d
8. a
9. c
10. b
11. b

Case Studies

1. 215.2, 26115
2. 821.01, 27502
3. 836.0, 836.1, 29881

Chapter 9: The Respiratory System

1. warm, humidify, and filter the air
2. carbon dioxide
3. gas exchange
4. 3,2
5. chronic airway
6. collapsed lung
7. T
8. T
9. a mirror is used with the indirect method
10. brushing
11. planned and emergency
12. open and thoroscopic

Case Studies

1. 510.9, 511.0, 32602-51,LT, 32320-LT
2. 197.0, 32484-LT
3. V71.89, 31622
4. 473.8, 31255-50, 31256-50,51
5. 473.8, 471.0, 31255, 31267-51, and 30110-51
6. 518.81, 934.8, 31500, 31622

Chapter 10: The Cardiovascular System

1. d. recording device
2. T
3. F. Repositioning is a part of the original placement only when it is performed within the first fourteen days of placement. Any repositioning after that time frame, but still in the 90-day global period, would need a Modifier 78, but would be billed out.
4. c. Code 33512 is a venous graft code from the Venous Grafting Only section and is meant to be used only when venous grafts are the only type of graft used. When reporting a combination arterial-venous grafting, the venous graft code must come from the 33517–33523 code range.
5. a. Angioplasty of the aneurysm to be repaired would be considered in the "target treatment zone" and not separately billable. Angioplasty of other areas outside of the area where the endoprosthesis is to be placed can be reported separately.
6. T. Procedures from this section include the preparation or the artery and endarterectomy.
7. b. The saphenous vein graft harvesting is included in the code description for 35501–35587
8. T
9. c. Only the highest order within a vascular family is reported.
10. F. When a catheter of any kind is placed into the area of interest and is not advanced farther into other branches, it is referred to as nonselective. When a catheter is advanced through bifurcations or areas of branching off, the physician determines and selects the route. Therefore, it is a selective catheterization.
11. d. 36415, Collection of venous blood by venipuncture
12. c. 36600, Arterial puncture, withdrawal of blood for diagnosis. On a routine basis catheterizations are not performed for blood gasses. 36415 is a venous code.
13. T. This type of anastomosis is performed to facilitate regular hemodialysis on a patient with end-stage renal failure.
14. b. 37730, Ligation and division and complete stripping of the long and short saphenous vein is treatment for varicose veins. If the procedure is performed on both legs, Modifier 50 would be appended to the code.
15. a. 22
    b. 50
    c. 78
    d. 58
    e. 79
    f. 51
    g. 59
16. a. Separate Procedure
    b. Add-on
    c. Unlisted Procedure
    d. Modifier-51 Exempt

Case Studies
1. 427.89, 33208
2. V53.31, 33213
3. 433.10, 35301-LT

Chapter 11: Hemic and Lymphatic Systems, Mediastinum and Diaphragm, and Endocrine System

1. False
2. False
3. True
4. b
5. d

6. a
7. c
8. c
9. 203.00, 38221
10. 135, 39400
11. c
12. a
13. c
14. d

Case Studies
1. 785.6, 38500
2. 193, 60240

Chapter 12: The Digestive System

1. F. Integumentary codes are used for the repair around the lip area and the lip repair codes in the digestive chapter are for the vermilion or pink portion of the lip itself.
2. b. Resection.
3. F. Tonsils and adenoids can be removed at the same time or each one at separate times.
4. c.
5. d. Esophagogastroduodenoscopy.
6. c. Gastrorrhaphy.
7. F. 44015 is an add-on code that must be used with another primary procedure.
8. a.
9. c
10. T
11. c
12. a
13. b
14. d. The add-on code for the use of mesh is used only for incisional/ventral hernias.
15. a. There are no age-related ventral hernia repair codes.
16. a. 51
    b. 52
    c. 80
    d. 78
    e. 58
    f. 59
    g. 79
    h. 53

Case Studies
1. 553.3, 530.19, 478.5, 43239
2. 202.83, 38570 and 571.8, 47000-51
3. 574.10, 47562

Chapter 13: The Urinary System

1. a
2. b
3. d
4. b
5. d
6. a
7. c
8. b
9. a
10. d

11. c
12. False
13. True

Case Studies

1. 617.3, 52310
2. 996.65, 50398
3. 601.2, 599.1; 55725, 53400-51
4. 598.9, 53020
5. 596.0, 52601

Chapter 14: The Male Reproductive System

1. d
2. b
3. F
4. T
5. c

Case Study

1. 456.4, 55530

Chapter 15: The Female Reproductive System

1. b
2. b
3. a
4. c
5. d
6. a
7. c
8. c
9. d
10. b

Case Studies

1. 218.9, 626.2; 58150
2. 233.1, 57520
3. V25.2, 58670
4. 618.01, 618.04, 625.9, 57260
5. 620.2, 256.4, 49322

Chapter 16: Maternity and Delivery

1. Initial and subsequent history, physical examinations, recording of weight, blood pressures, fetal heart tones, routine chemical urinalysis, monthly visits up to 28 weeks, biweekly visits to 36 weeks, and weekly visits until delivery.
2. False
3. False
4. a. 53
   b. 80
   c. 58
   d. 52
   e. 59
5. a
6. c
7. ICD-9-CM: 652.61; CPT® 59510 and 59409-51, 59
8. The C-section is the most expensive/highest-valued procedure, so it is listed first even though the vaginal delivery was first chronologically. The vaginal delivery is coded as a "delivery only."

Case Studies
1. 646.61, 041.02 and V27.0, 59400
2. 648.01, 642.41, 644.21, 652.31 and V27.0, 59514
   V25.2, 58611
3. 651.03, 652.23, 646.63, and 041.02, 59426
   651.01, 652.21, 663.21, 646.61, 041.02, and V27.2, 59618-22
   V25.2, 58611
   For the assistant surgeon:
   59618-22,80   651.01, 652,21, 663.21, and 041.02
   58611-80   V25.2

Chapter 17: The Nervous System

1. c
2. d
3. a
4. a
5. b
6. d
7. c

Case Studies
1. 348.4, 61343
2. 722.10, 63042. This is a recurrent herniation, so the CPT® code reflects re-exploration.

Chapter 18: Eye and Ear

1. b
2. False
3. c
4. d
5. True
6. a
7. d
8. b
9. d
10. c
11. d
12. b
13. c
14. b
15. c

Case Studies
1. 366.15, 66984
2. 362.54, 67038-RT
3. 379.23, 67040-RT; 250.50, 362.02, 67038-RT, 51, 59. Don't worry about which procedure would have Modifiers 51,59. Since the RVUs and fees have not been given, there is no way to know which would be the more highly valued of the two. It is more important to know that the modifiers are needed in this situation.
4. 744.29, 69300-50

Chapter 19: Radiology Services

1. d
2. d
3. c
4. a
5. d

6. c
7. d
8. b
9. a
10. a
11. c
12. a
13. d
14. a
15. b

Case Studies

1. 459.2, 35476, 75978, 76942
   780.6, V58.62, 36556-51, 36005-51, 75820
2. 433.30, 36216-RT, 36215-51,59,LT; 75650, 75680, 75671
3. 996.73, 35476, 36870-51, 36145-51, 36145-51,59, 75978, 75790
4. 996.73, 35476, 36120-51, 36145-51,59, 75790, 75978, 75710
5. 996.73, 36870, 35476-51, 36120-51, 75978, 75790, 75710
6. 440.1, 37205, 36245-51,LT, 36245-51,59,RT, 75960, 75724, 75716

Chapter 20: Pathology and Laboratory Services

1. d
2. b
3. b
4. d
5. a
6. d
7. c
8. a
9. c
10. b
11. d
12. c
13. a
14. b
15. d

Chapter 21: Medicine

1. c
2. a
3. c
4. b
5. d
6. d
7. a
8. d
9. c
10. False

Chapter 22: Billing and Reimbursement

1. b
2. c
3. a
4. a
5. d

6. False
7. False
8. True
9. False
10. True
11. True

Index

Page numbers followed by a *t* indicate tables; page numbers followed by an *f* indicate figures.

Cerebral palsy, 353
Cerebrovascular accident, 350
Cerlage, 329
Certificate of waiver, 440
Certified Registered Nurse Anesthetists (CRNAs), 73
Cervix, 319–20
  noninflammatory disorders, 312
Cesarean delivery, 343–44
Cesarean section (CS), 329
Chalazion, 369
Charge posting, 500
Charge tickets, 499
Chemistry, 446–48
Chest, radiology procedures, 412–13, 424
CHF (congestive heart failure), 188
Chief complaint (CC), 44, 62
Chlamydia, 295
Cholecystitis, 240–41
Cholelithiasis, 240–41
Choroid, 386–87
  disorders, 371
Chronic disease, ICD-9-CM coding guidelines, 14
Chronic Obstructive Lung Disease (COLD), 153–54
Chronic renal failure (CRF), 272–73, 471
  diabetes and, 271–72
CIA. see Corporate Integrity Agreement
Ciliary body, 383–84
  disorders of, 372
Circumstances other than disease or injury, ICD-9-CM coding guidelines, 14
Cirrhosis, 239–40
Clean claim, 1, 3, 497
Clearinghouse, 497
Clear to auscultation (CTA), 150
Cleft lip, 245
Clinical Laboratory Improvement Act (CLIA), 440
Closed treatment, 136
Clustering, 1
CMS. see Center for Medicare and Medicaid Services
Coagulation, 448–51
Coagulopathy, 217
Coding
  conventions, 12–13, 39
    HCPCS, 39
    ICD-9-CM, 12–13
  documentation and medical necessity, 3–4
  federal regulations and compliance, 4–7

guidelines, 13–15
  ICD-9-CM, 13–15
history of, 2–3
Co-existing conditions, ICD-9-CM coding of, 14
COLD. see Chronic Obstructive Lung Disease
Colon, 243
Colposcopy of the vulva or perineum, 317
Compliance plans, 1, 5–6
Composite grafts, 209
Comprehensive physical examination, 65
Concurrent care, 44
Condyloma acuminatum, 290
Confirmatory consultation codes, 52–53
Congenital anomalies, 22
Conjunctiva, 391
  disorders, 374
Conjunctivorhinostomy, 369
Consultations, 51–53
  clinical pathology, 445
  confirmatory, 52–53
  follow-up inpatient, 52
  initial inpatient, 52
  office or other outpatient, 51–53
Contact dermatitis, 99
Contractual obligation, 497, 499
Contralateral, 369
Contrast, 405
Contusion, 123
Cooperating parties, 2–3
Cornea, 381
Corneal disorders, 373
Coronary artery bypass graft (CABG), 198–200
  arterial, 200
  combined arterial-venous, 199
  venous only, 198–99
Coronary artery disease (CAD), 189
Coronary endarterectomy, 200
Corpora cavernosa, 298
Corporate Integrity Agreement (CIA), 6
Cor pulmonale, 154
Correct Coding Initiative, 87
Counseling, 44, 47
CPD (cephalopelvic disproportion), 329
CPT, 3, 34–38
  definitions of musculoskeletal system, 136
  guidelines, 36
  instructions, 36–37
  navigating, 34–36
  punctuation/symbols, 36

CPT-4, 2
  history of, 3
CPT coding
  for allergy services, 491
  of the auditory system, 393–99
  for cardiovascular services, 483–87
  of the cardiovascular system, 193–211
  for dialysis, 472–74
  of the digestive system, 245–63
  of the endocrine system, 230–32
  of the eye and ocular adnexa, 378–93
  of the female reproductive system, 316–23
  of the hemic and lymphatic systems, 228–29
  of injections and infusions, 465–68
  of the male reproductive system, 297–307
  maternity and delivery, 339–46
  of the mediastinum and diaphragm, 229
  of musculoskeletal procedures, 136–44
  of the nervous system, 356–65
  for ophthalmology, 475–79
  for otorhinolaryngology (ENT), 480–82
  for physical rehabilitation, 493–95
  for psychiatric services, 470–71
  of radiology services, 406–33
  of the respiratory system, 158–81
  of the urinary system, 274–85
CPT modifiers, 88–96; see also Modifiers
  21, 89
  22, 89
  23, 89
  24, 89
  25, 90
  26, 90
  32, 90
  47, 90
  50, 91
  51, 91
  52, 91
  53, 91
  54, 91–92
  55, 92
  56, 92
  57, 92
  58, 92
  59, 92–93
  62, 93
  63, 93